Writing TODAY

WRIT3002

2nd Custom Edition for
Fanshawe College

Mc Graw Hill Education | Custom Publishing

McGraw-Hill Education

Selected Materials From:
Writing Today, Second Edition, by Donald Pharr, Santi Buscemi, Erin MacDonald and Robert Muhlbock.
ISBN 0-07-105118-X
Writing Today, First Edition, by Donald Pharr, Santi Buscemi, Erin MacDonald and Robert Muhlbock.
ISBN 0-07-072611-6
The Act of Writing, Eighth Edition, by Ronald Conrad.
ISBN 0-07-096929-9
Experiencing Race, Class, and Gender in the United States, Sixth Edition, by Roberta Fiske-Rusciano.
ISBN 0-07-811161-7

Group Product Engineer: Jason Giles
Learning Solutions Manager: Rick Palmerio

Cover Design: Jason Giles

Printed and bound in Canada

CONTENTS

CONTENTS

READINGS

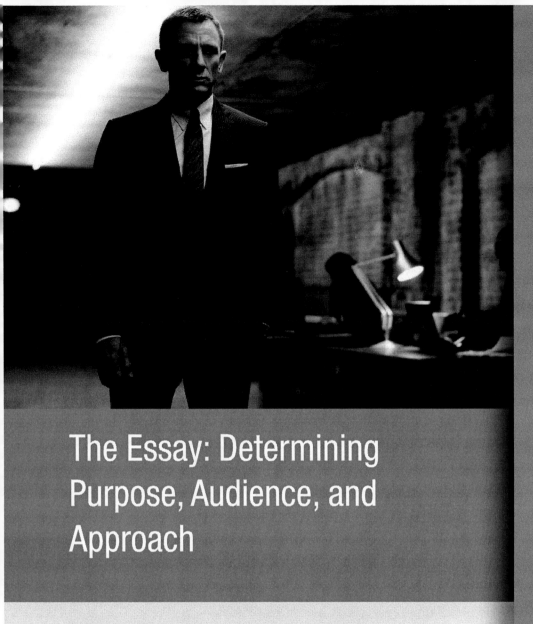

The Essay: Determining Purpose, Audience, and Approach

Determining PURPOSE, AUDIENCE, AND APPROACH in the Real World

To achieve any goal successfully requires a strong understanding of purpose, audience, and approach. For example, consider the most recent James Bond films. The studio's **purpose** was to reboot the James Bond franchise. Their ideal **audience** would be made up of both older fans who have followed the character since its creation and younger fans who might have only a passing knowledge of Bond. Their **approach** was to portray him as a straight-up, serious action hero as opposed to a campy spy. In the end, considering the monumental success of the reboot, this strategy paid off.

In regards to writing, effective business letters, newspaper editorials or opinion columns, short technical proposals, and sets of instructions all demonstrate the importance of beginning with a clear purpose. Once you know your purpose for writing (to inform or explain, to persuade, or to entertain), you can begin to focus on your audience. Are you writing a report or letter for your boss or for a client? Are you writing an amusing newspaper

LEARNING OUTCOMES:

▶ Apply analysis of purpose, audience, and context to essay writing

▶ List the expectations of the academic audience

▶ Define rhetoric and rhetorical options

▶ Apply active reading strategies to essay writing and critical responses

▶ Name the steps of the writing process

column for a general readership? Or are you writing a formal essay for your university or college writing class? Finally, knowing your readers will enable you to tailor your approach to their expectations. Your professor or boss may expect you to use objective language and to follow a standard rhetorical structure such as compare/contrast, whereas a newspaper or magazine editor will likely want you to inject more of your own creativity and personality into your writing, in order to fulfill the primary purpose of entertaining.

THE ESSAY: A MEANS TO AN END

Many students dread the thought of having to write an essay. They say that they will never write essays in their "real jobs." They may be right. However, let's explore this idea using the analogy of working out. Many students belong to gyms and spend hours every week doing repetitive exercise routines. Will these students ever be faced in their working lives with the demand of doing daily reps of arm curls or of climbing flights of stairs? Probably not (unless the elevator is broken). Exercise is a means to an end: you'll probably never have to do bench-presses outside of the gym; but the strength and endurance you acquired there will make you better able to keep up during a busy day, to run for a bus, or to stay alert throughout the afternoon.

The Essay Is Your Stairmaster

Consider essay writing in this same way: writing essays teaches skills necessary for the increasingly complex writing assignments found later in your education and for applications in the world of work. Many types of writing, from formal letters to magazine articles, use a variation of the basic essay structure. In fact, there are three very good reasons that your instructors hold the ability to write essays in such high regard:

1. Someone who can write solid essays proves that he or she can communicate effectively with educated adult readers.

2. Essays provide an unparalleled opportunity for readers to judge someone's critical thinking, organization, and language skills.

3. The writer of a successful essay has thought through a topic, taken ownership of the developed thesis, and worked through the stages of the writing process, thereby creating an essay that can be a source of pride.

In short, essay writing teaches you critical thinking, research skills, and language development—all valuable tools for success in today's job market, whether this includes winning over clients, impressing the boss, or preparing an important report.

UNDERSTANDING PURPOSE, AUDIENCE, AND CONTEXT

As you plan an essay, consider the following:

Purpose: What will the essay be about and what do you hope to accomplish by writing it? Often the topic itself will suggest the essay's purpose; for example, not many people would write an essay about gun laws without arguing either for or against them.

Audience: For whom are you writing? What does the reader know or need to know? What will impress this audience? Your classmates may not know much about firearm regulations in Canada, but readers of a hunting magazine will. The latter audience will probably expect much more persuasion in the way of facts and statistics than a group of young college students, who may be more prepared to consider appeals to emotion.

Context: Where will your message appear or be delivered? Will one person read your writing, or will many? Will your writing be read aloud or only made available in print? Will it be a 4-page academic essay delivered to your professor, or will it appear as a short article in the local newspaper? The context of your writing will greatly inform your decisions about word choice, content, and formality.

Defining Your Purpose

Every piece of writing begins with a **purpose.** Will the writing help people order food, or will it help them set up the text-messaging feature on their cellphones? When an instructor gives you an essay assignment, you must determine both the instructor's purpose and your own purpose or goal.

Narrowing Your Purpose Traditionally, purposes for writing can be divided into four categories: (1) to **explain,** (2) to **inform,** (3) to **entertain,** and (4) to **persuade.** Thinking about these four very general purposes can help you shape your conceptual process as well as the document that you produce. However, these four are just a starting point; they lead you into a world of options that will enable you to decide on a much more specific purpose for the document that you intend to write.

Defining Your Audience

Just as your purpose defines every document that you write, so will your **audience.** Before you begin an essay, consider these three questions:

- **Where** will your writing appear or be delivered?
- **Who** will read the document that you write?
- **What** are the needs and expectations of your audience?

These questions are part of an activity known as **audience analysis.** Engaging your readers at a level that will heighten their experience and allow you to show your level of skill will help you achieve your purpose.

Audience analysis will determine how you approach the following choices when writing:

- the content or type of information given
- the amount of information given
- the tone
- the level of formality
- the amount of proofreading and revision done

For many assignments in college or university, the audience is one person: the professor. While newspapers are usually written for an audience with a minimum grade eight education, your professor expects your work to be better than the work of an eighth-grader. Your professor is part of an **academic audience** that has specific expectations regarding academic work. Obviously, reading and understanding your professor's assignment expectations are your first concerns. Once you fully understand the specific assignment requirements, you can turn your attention to the general expectations of the academic audience.

Originality: Whether you are preparing an essay or a business report, the academic audience expects insight and intellectual rigor on the part of the writer. A simple, obvious argument will impress no one. No matter what you write, try to find a unique angle— something to discuss and analyze that very few people have done before (see Chapter 2 and Chapter 8 for help on constructing theses and sophisticated research topics).

Flawless language: An original idea is great, but if your language is muddled, wordy, or just grammatically incorrect, your credibility as a professional will suffer. The academic audience expects your language to have a formal tone and to use a variety of sentence types and words. Finally, your language should be free of all grammatical and spelling errors. (See Part 4 for a discussion of these topics.)

Documented research: Using research in your writing (where applicable) shows the academic audience that you are a serious scholar who has searched your topic thoroughly—you know what has been said before (so you don't repeat it), and what theories are questionable or accepted; and you have used this material when preparing your document to support and advance new ideas. Not only does the academic audience expect you to have thoroughly explored all available research on your topic, but this audience also expects any information you have summarized, paraphrased, or quoted to be documented properly to avoid plagiarism. (See Chapters 3, 16, and 17 for discussion on these topics.)

Peer review: Professional writing—whether essays, articles, or reports—is often peer reviewed. Many students understand peer review as a type of exercise where fellow classmates critique each other's work and provide feedback on issues of language and argumentation (see Chapter 7); however, peer review as it applies in the academic world and for the academic audience is slightly different. In your classroom, your peers are not necessarily experts or authorities on your topic; they may point out writing errors or confusing spots in your language, but they might not have the knowledge to critique your originality, research, or conclusions at a significant level. For professional academics, however, the stakes are much higher. Work submitted to a professional academic journal for publication needs to meet the approval of a board of peers who must feel the work is significant enough to warrant publication; otherwise, the work is rejected.

In short, the *gold standard* of academic writing is original, beautifully written, and thoughtfully researched. Furthermore, it must meet the approval of other professionals before it is considered acceptable.

Defining Your Context

Context refers to the place where your message will appear or the form in which it will be delivered. In most college and university settings, that context takes the shape of five major written assignment forms, each with its own expectations for word choice, content, and formality. Each form is discussed in detail throughout this text; however, let's review these forms briefly here, regarding audience expectations:

1. **Email:** Communications must be short, clear, and to the point. They must have a clear subject line. Attachments are included for messages that contain extra details.

2. **Memo:** Communications must follow appropriate memo format, including a specific subject line. Memos are usually no longer than a page and, like emails, must be short and clear. They also contain graphical highlights.

3. **Letter:** Communications must follow appropriate letter format. Letters can be longer than a page depending on their purpose. Their language must be clear, but may be less concise than a memo, depending on the topic.

4. **Essay:** Communications can be anywhere from two to twenty pages, depending on the topic. Format depends on your discipline's documentation style.

5. **Report:** Communications can be anywhere from one to twenty pages, depending on the topic. Often, graphics and lists of figures are included, as well as extra front and back material such as a table of contents, list of figures, and appendix.

Understanding the audience's expectations associated with your writing's context is integral to the success of your message.

EXERCISE 1.1

Develop a short piece of writing (one or two paragraphs, 200 words) for one of the following combinations of purpose, audience, and context.

1. Purpose: To inform your audience about bicycle safety

   Audience: Young children

   Context: Pamphlet

2. Purpose: To inform your audience about bicycle safety

   Audience: Adults

   Context: Pamphlet

3. Purpose: To inform your audience about your failing grade

   Audience: Parents

   Context: Email

4. Purpose: To inform your audience about your failing grade

   Audience: Friend

   Context: Email

5. Purpose: To persuade your audience against the creation of a new parking lot

   Audience: City council

   Context: Letter

6. Purpose: To persuade your audience to support opposition to a new parking lot

   Audience: General public

   Context: Flyer

7. Purpose: To persuade and inform your audience regarding the dangers of fatty foods

   Audience: Your professor

   Context: Research essay

8. Purpose: To entertain your audience

   Audience: Various friends and family members at your sibling's wedding

   Context: A speech

STRUCTURES OF WRITING

Unfortunately, the word **essay** has developed negative associations for many students; they see this form of writing as divorced from other forms of real-world writing. The truth is quite different. Almost all writing follows what is sometimes called the classical pattern. Although it has variations, this pattern always includes an introduction, a body, and a conclusion. Your sense of this rhetorical structure will help you to determine the best way to approach any writing situation—in other words, any **context.**

The Classical Pattern of Organization

In the classical pattern, the **introduction** welcomes the reader into the chosen topic, then indicates the specific direction that the essay will take while developing the topic. The thesis (or main argument) often appears in the essay's introduction. The **body** paragraphs develop the focus, which is the essay's central idea as expressed formally in a thesis statement. The **conclusion** comments on the implications raised by the body paragraphs and then brings the essay to an appropriate end.

What Is Rhetoric?

Rhetoric is the art of persuasion. Rhetoric may be present in speech, writing, or visual imagery. Sometimes all three combine to produce highly persuasive messages. For example, imagine Tiger Woods hitting a perfect drive, wearing Nike gear while the slogan "Just Do It" appears below him. Whether you know it or not, you are exposed to rhetoric daily. Advertisements use both visual and verbal rhetoric to persuade buyers that their products contain value.

Some people believe that all writing is rhetorical. Memos, letters, slogans, speeches, and essays all try to convince their readers to act in some way, even if it's just to believe the honesty of the writer. Rhetoric is a very powerful tool and may be accomplished through a number of rhetorical options. The art of rhetoric and its three popular appeals of logos, ethos, and pathos are discussed and defined further in Chapter 7 on Argumentation.

What Are Rhetorical Options?

Part 2 of this text discusses **rhetorical options.** These are the basic patterns that writers use to structure essays. If asked to tell how a machine works, a writer would not proceed to describe the appearance of the machine but would instead explain the process of its operation. If asked to describe a mountain valley, a writer would tell how it looks, sounds, and smells, not narrate the history of events that have taken place there. The standard rhetorical options help writers not only to make sense of the world but also to transmit this understanding to their audience.

The chapters in Part 2 contain student-written essays that illustrate these options. Part 2 also contains essays written by professional writers, and these writers sometimes break from established essay form. Frequently, their essays aren't so much models as they are examples of how far a pattern of development can be taken.

Part 2 discusses nine rhetorical options and illustrates ways that these options can be blended. The nine chapters of Part 2 examine the following patterns of development:

- **Description** (essays that describe a significant person, animal, place, or thing)
- **Narration** (essays that tell a story)
- **Exemplification** (essays that use examples to prove a point or illustrate an idea)
- **Process analysis** (essays that explain how a process unfolds or that tell the reader how to work through a process)
- **Causal analysis** (essays that explain why an event happens or that explain the effects of an event)
- **Definition** (essays that define, explain, and/or illustrate a key idea or term)
- **Classification** (essays that analyze a large group of entities by placing them in distinct categories)
- **Comparison and contrast** (essays that examine two or more ideas, people, events, places, or things to show their differences and possible similarities)
- **Argument** (essays that support a position on a disputed issue)

Academic Writing

Literature theme courses and composition classes often include assignments asking students to respond critically to others' writing. Instead of only assigning journals or first-person opinion papers, most instructors will ask you to respond in an objective tone, usually in the form of an essay. Often this essay needs no outside research, but requires you to analyze, interpret, and critique the arguments and claims of the writer while using your own opinions and insights to form the perfect counter-argument.

ACTIVE READING

Academic writing begins with **active reading.** Whatever type of work you are reading, you need to approach it in a systematic and careful manner. Reading a novel or a book of short stories for the sheer pleasure of it is certainly worthwhile. However,

<aside>
Consider Your Options

Students sometimes say, "I really love to write and would like to make it a career, but how?" If this statement describes you, consider the growing field of technical writing. What do technical writers do? As an example, think of the user's guide that you receive with virtually every product that you purchase. Someone was paid to write, design, and edit that guide.
</aside>

reading literature or critical essays assigned in a college or university course is often a far more demanding and time-consuming task. The very purpose of reading a novel or a scientific essay in a class is to prompt analytical, interpretive, and evaluative responses from students, thereby improving their ability to think critically and to discuss sophisticated ideas intelligently.

Reading with a Purpose

Skilled readers have reasons—purposes—that guide their approach to their reading. For example, they may be reading for entertainment, or they may be studying or doing research. To get the most value from this activity, active, analytical readers use the following strategies, which can be divided into pre-reading, reading, and post-reading activities.

As this list illustrates, reading is not a passive process. You, the reader, interact with the text—questioning, agreeing, disagreeing, and wondering. At some point, you will find yourself evaluating the writer's output in the following ways:

Pre-Reading

- Ask yourself, What do I already know about this topic? What would I like to know?
- Interpret the **title**. Is it straightforward or perhaps ironic?
- Look for any prefatory information. Is there an editor's preface or **introduction** or a biographical section about the author? Can you anticipate a particular bias on the part of the author or determine the author's credibility?
- Look for any stylistic clues—**subheadings**, for example—that highlight the essay's organization.
- Has the author used any references to other people's work? If so, are they documented and is a list of sources provided? (Multiple, well-documented references usually suggest that the writing is academic.)

General GUIDELINES for Writing about Writing

Use last names: Refer to authors by their last names.

Provide citations: If you quote directly, summarize, or paraphrase from a primary or secondary source, provide citations for those sources. The essay you are reading and analyzing is one type of **primary** source. A book, journal article, or other scholarly commentary about that piece of literature is a type of **secondary** source. Two of the main systems normally used to cite such sources are the one recommended by the Modern Language Association and found in the *MLA Handbook for Writers of Research Papers, Seventh Edition* (2009) and the style specified by the American Psychological Association, or APA. MLA and APA style are also discussed in Chapters 3 and 17 of this textbook.

Be accurate: Double-check to make sure that you are quoting, summarizing, or paraphrasing accurately. You can find out more about using direct quotations, summaries, and paraphrases in Chapter 3.

Use the present tense: Whether you are analyzing a story, novel, poem, play, film, or critical essay, use the present tense (sometimes called the **literary present**). For example, at the beginning of Katrina Onstad's essay "The Dark Side of Celebrity," she **discusses** the impact tabloids **have** on females. We don't say that she **discussed** this impact, because her article still exists in the present tense—it is not a historical event that has passed.

Reading

- Is there a clear **thesis?** What is it?
- **Annotate** the text. If you own the text, you can write your responses in the margins or between lines. If a passage is confusing, mark it with an asterisk or question mark. If you don't know a word or phrase, circle it. Come back to these areas later.
- Look for logical proof for the author's thesis. Does he or she use persuasive facts or examples?
- Take **notes** on a separate piece of paper. List the most important points.
- **Reread** the passages that caused you trouble. Use a dictionary to look up words that you didn't know.

Post-Reading

- **Evaluate** what you have read.
- **Summarize** the essay in one paragraph. Do you understand the author's argument?
- Are the examples sufficient to prove the author's point?
- Is the analysis logical? Has the author used any logical fallacies? (See Chapter 7.)
- Has any information been left out—deliberately or inadvertently—that would have changed the writer's approach had the information been present?
- Is the writer's conclusion warranted? In other words, was the work effective in persuading you of its point?
- Do you like what you have read? Does it make you want to learn more about this subject or other related subjects? Would you recommend this author to people?

THE DARK SIDE OF CELEBRITY
Katrina Onstad

Katrina Onstad is a Canadian writer whose work has appeared in The Globe and Mail, Salon, *and the* Guardian. *Formerly, she wrote the column "Modern Times" for* Chatelaine. *Her essay "The Dark Side of Celebrity" appeared in that column in December 2007. Onstad's recent book,* Everybody Has Everything, *was published in 2012 and was long-listed for the 2012 Scotiabank Giller Prize.*

1   I remember flipping through *People* in the 1980s, when it was equal parts adoring Lady Diana profiles and stories about regular joes who grew root vegetables in funny shapes. Today, Canadians can choose their diversion from more than 60 magazines documenting the famous and the near-famous, hundreds of online stalkerazzi sites and a maw of celebrity TV shows. Yet is this stuff actually fun anymore? The morning-after delivery of disturbing images of Lindsay, Nicole and Paris—bedroom transgressions and head shaving and car crashing and jail-door weeping—has become a ritual humiliation. As the feminist critic Katha Pollitt put it, these women "are being made into these icons of female ruin."

2   In fact, they hardly qualify as women. Just a few years ago, Britney was a girl in knee socks begging, "Hit me baby, one more time," while teen Lindsay Lohan grinned on the red carpet, a giant freckle in a slit-up-to-here designer gown. That unnerving girl–woman hybrid, the sexualized innocent, is an unstoppable marketing tool, an age-old psycho-sexual brand.

3   But when Britney and Lindsay began to live the image off the page, in nightclubs and bad relationships with sub-literate layabouts, they earned a collective tsk tsk from their audience. They're popular, yes, but loathed. It may have been borderline okay for Britney to splay and preen as a teenager, but not as a mom showing her postpartum belly in a jewel-studded bikini. The fallout of the MTV awards told this 25-year-old what we think of a woman who dares parade the soft curves of motherhood: You are old. You are undesirable. You are disposable.

4   There've always been celebrity scandals. Married Ingrid Bergman had an affair with Roberto Rossellini that led to a child out of wedlock; Marilyn Monroe posed nude; Ava Gardner was rumoured to have slept with Lana Turner. But these were women in their late twenties and thirties, not girls celebrating their twenty-first birthdays on leave from institutions with names like Promises.

5   In the past, most celebrities were not famous for being famous, like Nicole Richie and Paris Hilton, or the reality-TV stars of the gossip-and-tan smash *The Hills*. When these women fall—another DUI; another sex tape—the public doesn't mourn, because we never really liked them. Were they ever anything more than a collective joke? Did they ever matter to us?

6   Britney and Lindsay now exist almost entirely as tabloid food, but they started as, respectively, a singer and an actor. Like others in their sad circle, they became singers-actors-models-designers. Perhaps they've attained some twisted version of have-it-all feminism—women with professionally flourishing lives who seem to take no joy in their

success, nor have any say in it, corralled from the shadows by stage parents and sleazy managers.

7   And yet these girls aren't exactly victims. They seem eager to participate in their own exploitation. Just hours after Britney's MTV disaster, she was photographed panty-free. A few days later, she grinned for the cameras, toting her son Jayden, eager for a flattering "family" shot to temper the bad press; her every move is orchestrated for public consumption. It's doubly hard to feel sorry for these girls when the thriving careers of other actresses prove that it's possible to live a private life in Hollywood. But Claire Danes, Natalie Portman and Anna Paquin share a common history that the celebutantes don't: They went to college. There's nothing like a good education to teach a starlet that her worth might extend beyond her body. What's sad is that the Britneys don't seem to want to live privately. There's no value or profit in the invisible, worked-out brain.

8   So maybe it's time to disarm these girls by not looking. When we read celeb magazines and click on Perez Hilton, we're voyeurs turned on by a person's illness, the way gawkers toured mental hospitals in the Victorian age. Consider what researchers wrote in a study by the American Psychiatric Association confirming that girls who are sexualized too soon are at risk of serious damage: "Girls who had a more objectified relationship with their bodies were more likely to experience depression and had lower self-esteem."

9   The celebutantes are too young to remember a time before the technological scrutiny of the internet. Being measured and talked about is all they know. In fact, they seem to lack any subjectivity, any awareness of themselves that isn't refracted by someone else's eyes.

10   Why do we want to see our young women this way? Almost the only time we hear of women in their twenties in the media is when they're disgraced or staging a comeback that usually involves a glossy magazine spread torn from the porn world. (Lohan played a stripper in her most recent film, *I Know Who Killed Me;* Britney's first major TV performance in three years had her writhing, mouth open, in front of 7 million.) Their brand of fame doesn't support the dubious post-feminist idea that there's empowerment in hypersexuality. These women are lethargic, powerless, silly. They don't matter, and women need to matter.

Essay Analysis

There are two ways to read an essay actively and analytically. One way is to look at the **context**—the writer's purpose and audience, and where the article is published. The second way is to look at the essay's **effectiveness**—its logic, its evidence, and the impact that it makes upon the reader (in this case, you). Let's go through Onstad's essay with these ideas in mind.

The Essay's Context

"The Dark Side of Celebrity" combines many of the different purposes for writing that we mentioned above. It is meant to **inform,** to **entertain,** and to **express** the writer's own sardonic style. However, its primary goal is rhetorical—to **persuade.** The author uses strong language, shocking contemporary examples, and comparisons to past celebrity scandals to convince readers that certain young female stars are being degraded more than they are being empowered by their no-holds-barred exposure in media. Knowing that her **audience** of women's magazine readers is probably a generation or two older than the women she writes about enables Onstad to appeal to their greater wisdom, through her carefully chosen language; for example, consider such phrases as "orchestrated for public consumption" (paragraph 7) and her examples of past celebrity scandals as well as her reference to Victorian-era mental hospitals. She knows she is writing for a medium- to well-educated audience, so she can fit her vocabulary and wit to that readership.

The Essay's Effectiveness

Onstad states her central idea or **thesis** in the first paragraph: "The morning-after delivery of disturbing images of Lindsay, Nicole and Paris—bedroom transgressions and head shaving and car crashing and jail-door weeping—has become a ritual humiliation. As the feminist critic Katha Pollitt put it, these women 'are being made into these icons of female ruin.' " By invoking a credible source right away (albeit, one that needs a proper MLA or APA citation), Onstad lets readers know from the beginning that the essay is more than just entertainment; and referring to a feminist critic also signals her personal stance. We can be clear from the start that one of her goals in writing is to elevate the status of women in society.

Like any good essay that follows the rhetorical structure of **argumentation**, the body of Onstad's piece uses plenty of **examples** to support her position and cites reliable **research** such as "a study by the American Psychiatric Association" (paragraph 8). She also brings up the opposing side to her argument and shows why it doesn't hold up. For example, in paragraph four, she admits that "there've always been celebrity scandals," but goes on to explain how those past situations differ from those of today. However, Onstad also uses quite a bit of emotion (also known as an **emotional appeal**—see Chapter 7) and is not afraid to let her anger come through in her **diction** (word choices). She calls the fallen women of the gossip columns "a collective joke" and refers to their managers as "sleazy" (paragraphs 5 and 6). Made-up words such as "stalkerazzi" and "celebutantes" also add to the emotional appeal of her writing style. Because she is writing for a magazine, this type of subjective language is acceptable, whereas it would likely not be formal or objective enough for an academic essay.

To make smooth transitions between each of her points, the author uses **transitional phrases** such as "in fact," "but when," "and yet," and "so maybe." These short phrases are enough to connect the examples to each other, and to Onstad's main point.

At the end of the essay, Onstad concludes by returning to the same idea of humiliation with which she opened her piece and reinforces her thesis argument by reminding readers, "These women are lethargic, powerless, silly. They don't matter, and women need to matter."

 EXERCISE 1.2

Using Onstad's rhetorical approach, write a short essay persuading readers that young male celebrities are also humiliating themselves with their public behaviour.

A WRITER'S EYE

Being aware of your **purpose** and **audience** doesn't mean considering these two issues at the start of the writing process and then forgetting them once you begin to draft. Each sentence that you write and then revise must be a conscious, deliberate gesture toward your audience, reflecting your general purpose and the specific purpose of this particular part of your essay. Your reader depends upon his or her reading skills to interpret your meaning but also upon *you* to provide the clearest possible communication.

Student Lewisa Clark was asked to write a timed critical response to Onstad's "The Dark Side of Celebrity," to discuss whether she agreed or disagreed with Onstad's argument. Below is a portion of her annotated copy of Onstad's essay, followed by her critical analysis paper. (For more on drafting in-class assignments, see Chapter 2.)

 AN EXCERPT OF LEWISA'S ANNOTATED ONSTAD ESSAY

Today, Canadians can choose their diversion from more than 60 magazines documenting the famous and the near-famous, hundreds of online stalkerazzi sites and a maw of celebrity TV shows. Yet is this stuff actually fun anymore? The morning-after delivery of disturbing images of Lindsay, Nicole and Paris—bedroom transgressions and head shaving and car crashing and jail-door weeping—has become a ritual humiliation. As the feminist critic Katha Pollitt put it, these women "are being made into these icons of female ruin."

In fact, they hardly qualify as women. Just a few years ago, Britney was a girl in knee socks begging, "Hit me baby, one more time," while teen Lindsay Lohan grinned on the red carpet, a giant freckle in a slit-up-to-here designer gown. That unnerving girl-woman hybrid, the sexualized innocent, is an unstoppable marketing tool, an age-old psychosexual brand.

But when Britney and Lindsay began to live the image off the page, in nightclubs and bad relationships with sub-literate layabouts, they earned a collective tsk tsk from their audience. They're popular, yes, but loathed. It may have been borderline okay for Britney to splay and preen as a teenager, but not as a mom showing her postpartum belly in a jewel-studded bikini. The fallout of the MTV awards told this 25-year-old what we think of a woman who dares parade the soft curves of motherhood: You are old. You are undesirable. You are disposable.

There've always been celebrity scandals. Married Ingrid Bergman had an affair with Roberto Rossellini that led to a child out of wedlock; Marilyn Monroe posed nude; Ava Gardner was rumoured to have slept with Lana Turner. But these were women in their late twenties and thirties, not girls celebrating their twenty-first birthdays on leave from institutions with names like Promises.

Margin annotations:

Is this a real word?

True! This must be her thesis. Being an icon of ruin is a sad state indeed!

Plenty of examples.

Educated language.

Does the same standard exist for men? Are all males tainted when one sleeps around or poses nude?

Uses contractions; must be casual tone.

In the past, most celebrities were not famous for being famous, like Nicole Richie and Paris Hilton, or the reality-TV stars of the gossip-and-tan smash *The Hills.* When these women fall—another DUI; another sex tape—the public doesn't mourn, because we never really liked them. Were they ever anything more than a collective joke? Did they ever matter to us?

Yes, but why? Is the audience jealous? Spiteful? Why do they not receive compassion?

Lewisa's In-Class Critical Response

What follows is Lewisa's in-class critical response to the Onstad article. She was asked to respond to the subject matter of Onstad's article, not to critique her writing style. Please note that if this was a formal academic assignment, she would have to document all direct quotations in whatever citation style her instructor requested, and she would have to provide a Works Cited or References page. (For more on documenting sources and citation styles, please see Chapters 3 and 17.)

Fallen Angels: Female Celebrities and Public Scorn

Lewisa begins by naming the author and essay, and by summarizing the essay's main claims.

In "The Dark Side of Celebrity," Katrina Onstad argues that the public enjoys watching (via tabloids and entertainment news) female celebrities engaged in "ritual humiliation." She states that these humiliated females are often "loathed" by the public to begin with and "hardly qualify as women" since most are in their late teens. Onstad believes that celebrity scandals are particularly damaging to females as they reinforce the stereotype that women should only be valued for their looks, and that once these fade, the victim is "disposable." **This argument is sound for many reasons: people are less likely to feel sympathy for someone with whom they share no personal connection, and the public is more likely to judge harshly the sexual indiscretions of a female celebrity than it is a male's.**

Ideally Lewisa's thesis would be 3 points; however, even at two points it's still very good. Her thesis appears at the end of her first paragraph and provides an outline of her essay's organization.

Onstad mentions that many current celebrities, such as Paris Hilton, are "famous for being famous" and that the public delights when these people get into trouble. Although Paris Hilton has tried to establish careers as both a singer and an actress, she hasn't managed to produce art with substance. Most people regard her as the one thing she truly is: the offspring of a very rich corporate CEO. Her constant appearance at local parties and fashion shows—a life that very few people will ever know—makes her an object of both jealousy and scorn. The public can forgive a famous person for being wealthy and gaudy as long as they feel the person has enough character to overshadow this tackiness. **Before her death, Amy Winehouse was a punchline in the tabloids as well; however, the public treated her with a little more sympathy because, unlike Hilton, Winehouse had proven musical talent (having won five Grammies in 2008). Winehouse's**

death is still regarded a major loss for music fans. Conversely, Paris Hilton's only major contribution to the arts was the sex tape in which she starred.

This example underscores another point in Onstad's argument: when one female behaves indecently, the whole sex seems to suffer. However, consider this argument from the opposite side: when Russell Crowe punches a photographer or Hugh Grant is caught with a prostitute, people regard these as isolated instances as opposed to examples of how violent or sexually promiscuous all males are. Yet, each female celebrity sex scandal works on a larger scale. Every leaked sex tape or nude candid is just one more piece of propaganda that devalues women. Rather than showing women to be intelligent, charismatic, hard-working people, these types of pornography reaffirm the old stereotype that women are most valued when they are naked—a message that men absorb with lust and women disown with disgust. **Fortunately, some female celebrities rise above this type of exploitation. While Kim Kardashian continues to plaster her bikini-clad body on every magazine that will have her, celebrities like Taylor Swift, Rachel McAdams, and Emma Stone prove that females can be respected for their talents as opposed to how much skin they expose.**

Katrina Onstad's essay "The Dark Side of Celebrity" reminds us that no matter how much someone succeeds, the slightest indiscretion or scandal can ruin an image—and the public can be just as unforgiving. In a world of reality television where viewers enjoy watching bad singing, horrible acting, and broken love relationships, it should come as no surprise that **there is little sympathy for celebrities who fall from riches to rags. However, famous women seem to bear more of the public's scorn than celebrity men. Sadly, these starlets drag the rest of the female population down with them.**

Lewisa frequently uses signal phrases naming the author when referring to the original essay's arguments. She also uses transitional words and phrases to connect her points.

Even though Lewisa agrees with Onstad's essay, she does not merely repeat it. She adds to it by providing many new examples.

Lewisa makes excellent use of current examples.

Added to include restatement of Lewisa's two thesis points.

Lewisa's conclusion not only sums up her essay's thesis, but it reflects on its content as well.

(EXERCISE **1.3**

Answer the following questions to evaluate Lewisa's essay "Fallen Angels: Female Celebrities and Public Scorn."

1. What is Lewisa's purpose? Who is her audience? Has she successfully addressed the audience and fulfilled her purpose? Explain.

2. The thesis of this essay is stated in the last sentence of the first paragraph: "people are less likely to feel sympathy for someone with whom they share no personal connection, and the public is more likely to harshly judge the sexual indiscretions of a female celebrity than they are a male's." Is this thesis significant enough and specific enough to build an essay around? What might an alternative thesis have been?

3. Lewisa strengthens her argument by giving specific examples to prove her points. Can you find three instances where she does this?

4. Lewisa does not address instances where females can be overtly sexual, but still have substance that extends beyond their sexuality. Make a counter-argument for female celebrities who seem to pull off this balance. For example, does Lady Gaga's image help females more than it exploits them?

EXERCISE 1.4

1. Take the opposite approach of Lewisa: write a critical response disagreeing with Onstad's article.
2. Write an essay analyzing Onstad's writing style (tone, diction, and rhetorical strategies) instead of her content.

THE WRITING PROCESS

Writers do not produce effective or successful essays in one step. Instead, they employ a series of steps, collectively known as the **writing process.** Here is a brief summary of what this process entails:

- **Planning.** At this stage, you consider the assignment and its requirements. You consider your purpose and your audience, then start to generate ideas. (See Chapter 2)
- **Prewriting.** Some students skip this step in their rush to complete an assignment; after the planning stage, they proceed to the drafting stage, producing essays with weak, unfocused structures and poorly developed ideas. As you cluster, outline, research, or freewrite (or use some other method of prewriting, as discussed in Chapter 2), you generate more ideas and start to see the logical "shape" of your essay.
- **Focusing, analyzing, and drafting.** If your planning and prewriting have pointed you in the right direction, you will be able to focus your ideas into a thesis, create an outline, and write your first draft. It may be very rough, but even a very rough draft gives you an opportunity to develop your ideas. (See Chapters 2 and 4 for more about drafting your writing.) Be prepared to write multiple drafts if you want to do your best work.
- **Revising for structure.** After your first draft, you should put the essay aside for a day, if at all possible, before you attempt to revise. Then consider these issues: Does your essay produce what its introduction promises? Are all of your paragraphs fully developed around clearly stated topic sentences? Are your paragraphs sequenced in the way that is most appropriate and creates the most impact? (See Chapter 5.)
- **Revising for content.** As you revise, read your essay, focusing on its content and its message.

    Have you written all that you intended, and is what you have written sufficient to meet the assignment's expectations? Do all of the points, quotations, and examples in your essay work towards proving your overall point or thesis?

Although structure and content are two separate considerations for a writer, revision for both structure and content frequently takes place simultaneously. Revision may involve **peer review,** during which one or more of your classmates read your essay and offer you helpful feedback. (Chapter 5 discusses these issues.)

- **Editing and proofreading.** Many students tend to produce as their final draft an essay that sounds very good when read aloud. However, your reading audience will more likely be looking at your paper, not listening to a recitation of it. The editing and proofreading stage, in which you edit specifically for grammar and mechanics, helps you to catch serious errors that can undercut your credibility with your readers, and also helps you to polish your essay by making final word choices and fine-tuning your sentences. (Chapter 6 concentrates on editing and proofreading.)

Chapters 2–6 will take you through these steps of the writing process. Throughout these chapters, we will concentrate on the various options that each stage of the writing process offers you.

Using the Internet

Go to these websites to find more tips, techniques, and insights on approaches to the essay:

The Purdue University Writing Lab
Students can access useful handouts from this online writing lab (OWL). Included are materials on planning a writing project and writing various types of papers.
http://owl.english.purdue.edu/

The UVic Writer's Guide
This website, sponsored by the University of Victoria's English Department, provides ample support for writing several types of essays, as well as successful student models. The site also provides good advice on outlining, organizing, and writing introductions and conclusions.
http://web.uvic.ca/wguide/

The University of Richmond Writing Center's Writer's Web
This site offers useful suggestions for getting started on a paper and writing thesis statements.
http://writing2.richmond.edu/writing/wweb.html

CHAPTER
2

Shaping Your Essay: Planning, Prewriting, Focusing, Organizing, and Drafting

PLANNING AND DRAFTING in the Real World

Most major projects require planning to be successful. Before a building or bridge is built, plans and drafts must be drawn up. Before a product is manufactured, a prototype is created. Before a film is shot, a storyboard artist will illustrate each shot.

Consider planning and drafting your writing as you would think of training or practising. Athletes and musicians (such as Arcade Fire, pictured above) don't just practise their techniques once; they practise continuously before the big game or concert. They do this for their audience as much as for themselves.

Your writing should follow the same path. Very few pieces of writing are perfect the first time they are written. Most excellent writing requires initial planning and drafting so that the final result is as flawless as it can be.

The Writing Process

Essays are not produced in one step. Instead, good writers employ a series of steps, collectively known as the writing process, to help them. This process involves six steps that were already mentioned at the end of Chapter 1. Let's review the first three, outlined in brief below:

- **Planning.** In this stage, you consider the assignment and its requirements. You consider your purpose and your audience, and then you start to generate ideas.
- **Prewriting.** As you cluster, outline, research, or freewrite (or use any other method of prewriting), you generate more ideas and start to see the logical "shape" of your essay.
- **Focusing, analyzing, and drafting.** If your planning and prewriting have pointed you in the right direction, you will be able to focus your ideas into a thesis, create an outline, and write your first draft. It may be very rough, but even a very rough draft gives you an opportunity to develop your ideas. Be prepared to write multiple drafts if you want to do your best work.

PLANNING

Too often, students begin their essays by immediately writing their introductory paragraphs without first planning their work. They they find themselves in trouble midway through their drafts. They realize that their topic focus, which seemed fine early on, is now inappropriate. As a result, they struggle to finish; they find it impossible to provide evidence that somehow supports the topic sentences and ideas of those last few paragraphs.

Before you start to write, you need to spend some time generating and organizing ideas and putting together a road map of your essay—a plan that says where you want to begin and where you hope to end up. This plan will help you to envision the overall structure of your essay before writing even one word. But before you build your road map, you must choose your topic.

Choosing Your Topic

Instructors may limit your range of topic, but you are in control of how you wish to pursue your topic. Always try to choose a topic in which you have an interest. Not only will this stipulation make the writing process more enjoyable, but the end result will likely be of higher quality because of your emotional investment. You have a world of experience, so be sure to explore your own areas of knowledge and expertise to find the best possibilities for your assignment. Remember, though, that opinion and personal experience should only appear in the final paper if your instructor has requested a personal essay.

Often students will pick topics that are too large to discuss properly in a short paper. Although four or five pages may seem long to you, keep in mind that entire books have been written on many of these topics. Here are a few examples of topic choices that are too broad, along with suggestions for narrowing them to make them more manageable:

Course: Pop culture
Professor's topic: Consumerism
What you do: Many ideas rush to your head: smartphones, fast food, and cars—we all buy too many of these things!
What you could do: Writing a short essay about consumerism covering these three areas is too much to explore. Each of these topics could be written on separately. Pick only one. You might discuss three negative effects of fast food culture, for example.

Course: Writing and rhetoric
Professor's topic: A current public debate
What you do: Fighting in hockey
What you could do: Fighting in hockey is a worthy topic that lends itself nicely to debate in a short essay. Just make sure that you have strong examples to support whatever side you argue, and don't fall back on your own personal taste or opinion. Depending on your professor's requirements, you may need to make sure you include evidence gathered from research studies, rather than just quotations from NHL players and their coaches.

Course: Canadian history
Professor's topic: Natural resources and their history of supply and demand both inside and outside of Canada.
What you do: You feel that focusing on the resources of timber, fish, and petroleum would be more than adequate.
What you could do: Organizing your paper based on resources is a good way to structure your paper; but, if a province offers more than one major resource you wish to cover, you might find yourself repeating information. We suggest organizing this essay by province (but no more than three provinces for a short essay!). However, it might be even better to pick one major resource (fish, for example) and discuss its exportation/international demand from the perspective of only one province (local consumption, national consumption, and international consumption).

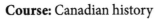

EXERCISE **2.1**

For the following topics, consider a narrower topic that you could do justice to in an essay of 3–4 typed pages.

1. Travel: Vacationing inside of Canada instead of going to another country
2. Nutrition: Sports energy drinks
3. Citizenship: Public protest
4. Environment: Earth Day

Establishing Purpose, Audience, and Context: A Review

As mentioned in Chapter 1, planning also helps you address three essential features of your approach: purpose, audience, and context.

1. **What is my purpose?** Your purpose for most assignments is to inform, to entertain, or to persuade your audience. You may want to explain something so that your reader understands it (to inform), or make the reader laugh (to entertain), or convince the reader to change an opinion or a behaviour (to persuade).

2. **Who is my audience?** If your instructor asks you to write a process document showing the reader how to perform a specific computer function, your logical next question will be, "For whom?" Is your audience hostile? Accepting? Indifferent? Knowledgeable? Analyzing your audience is an important consideration when producing an appropriate piece of writing.

3. **What is my context?** Context refers to the form or venue by which your message will be received. Is your piece of writing a short email to a co-worker or an email to a friend? Is it a speech given on stage during a student council election? An editorial published in a local newspaper? An academic essay assigned in one of your classes? Each of these contexts will determine various features of your writing such as length, tone, and formality.

EXERCISE 2.2

Create a small piece of writing for one of the following purposes, audiences, and contexts (this exercise is very similar to Exercise 1.1, but the importance of establishing purpose, audience, and context makes this type of exercise well worth repeating):

1. Purpose: To inform about the dangers of pesticides

   Audience: Adults

   Context: Brief newspaper article

2. Purpose: To encourage people to recycle

   Audience: Children

   Context: Pamphlet

3. Purpose: To entertain and to show that you love your sibling(s)

   Audience: Mixed ages

   Context: Wedding speech

4. Purpose: To receive an extension on an assignment

   Audience: Your instructor

   Context: Email

An Essay with No Purpose

Establishing purpose, audience, and context in the early stages is extremely important. Notice what happens in the following essay, in which the writer never figured out what he wanted to accomplish.

Computers: A Modern Marvel

The greatest invention of the 20th Century must be computers. The earliest computers were huge, filling up a big room. Now barcode scanners and bank machines cover the world. Imagining a world without computers is difficult at best. One sees computers everywhere: stores, doctors' offices, etc. They're there to suit your needs. Students write essays on them and then revise them as needed. Current word-processing programs allow the writer to choose any font you want and make the type bigger so that it fills up the page.

Unfortunately computers can also be a problem. Many of them crash without warning. Some will not allow you to reboot after a crash. Others become infected with viruses and spyware. When the infection becomes too severe, you might have to take your tower into a repair depot or call the Geek Squad to your door. Computers can also be used for accounting.

Everyone should have a computer. In fact, why doesn't the Federal Government start a program to give computers to the less fortunate? Many believe they should. Everyone should have access to the hilarious videos on YouTube.

Analyzing the "essay with no purpose" One of the factors contributing to this essay's lack of purpose is the sheer scope of the topic; the author hasn't narrowed the topic sufficiently. In addition, the essay attempts at times to inform and at times to persuade, but it rarely succeeds in either of these missions because of unfocused writing and inappropriate details. Besides a great number of stylistic lapses and errors, the essay also lacks a cohesive structure. It wanders and it contradicts itself. The writer barely scratches the surface, piling one random thought upon the next without giving any thought to the essay's overall goal.

This essay can't be revised; it must be rewritten. However, with careful prewriting and drafting, you will be able to produce a *serviceable* first draft, one you can deal with and improve upon. This chapter works through the steps of the prewriting and drafting process, starting from the beginning.

Establishing Your Voice: "I," "You," and Other Pronouns

Whether you are writing in class or at home, in longhand or on a computer, for yourself or for your professor, you must determine the voice you will use throughout your essay. Are you planning to write an objective essay, without any references to your feelings and personal impressions? Or are you planning to write about an experience or a person close to you? The answers to these questions will help determine the "voice," or persona, that you create in your essay and will help you resolve a sometimes sticky issue: which pronouns are acceptable in a college- or university-level essay. The points below should help you in your decision:

1. **Avoid using the pronoun "I" to refer to yourself in your essay:** Academic writing is often supposed to be objective—that is, free from bias and personal opinion. Openly using the pronoun "I" subverts such an attempt. "I" gives your writing a tone more akin to a casual conversation or a blog.

AWKWARD:	**I feel** advertising often manipulates the insecurities of its intended audience.
IMPROVED:	Advertising often manipulates the insecurities of its intended audience.

There are other areas of writing where the word "I" is perfectly acceptable, such as in business or legal writing; however, formal argumentative essays are a different matter. Finally, "I" language creates wordy, redundant expressions. *You* know you're writing the essay; *your instructor* knows you've written the essay. So why repeat this information to tell him/her at the beginning of every sentence?

2. **Avoid using the pronouns "you" or "one" in your essay:** *You* is acceptable under only one condition: if the writer is speaking directly to the reader, such as in a letter, a process analysis, or a textbook. However, students frequently use "you" (or its more formal cousin "one") when they give their reader examples.

AWKWARD:	While watching television, **you** might feel that advertisers are directly speaking to **you.**
AWKWARD:	While watching television, **one** might feel that advertisers are directly speaking to **one.**

Once again, such writing is wordy and can confuse the reader. Whenever possible, rewrite your sentences to omit the use of "you." The best way, outlined below, is to use third-person plural.

3. **Use the third person plural:** Using plural pronouns based on the context of your writing (such as "clients," "customers," "victims," players," or "protesters") is a clearer way to convey your meaning than using "one" or "you."

AWKWARD:	While watching television, **one** might feel that advertisers are directly speaking to **one.**
IMPROVED:	While watching television, **viewers** might feel that advertisers are directly speaking to **them.**

4. **Use "he or she" when necessary:** Unless you're specifically writing about an all-male or all-female audience, using some variation of "he or she" is standard today. It can, however, cause rhythm problems or general awkwardness. Thus, if you need an indefinite pronoun to refer to a person of either gender, try to rephrase the sentence so that it has a plural context:

AWKWARD:	Every student took **his or her** seat.
IMPROVED:	All the students took **their** seats.

However, sometimes the plural won't work, as in the following:

The scholarship winner must complete **his or her** high school education at least four months prior to registering at Parker College.

In this situation, there will be only one winner.

PREWRITING

Prewriting is the act of generating and organizing your ideas before you write your draft. Prewriting can help you test out your topic to see how well it holds up under development. It also helps you establish connections among your ideas. Many different options for prewriting are discussed below. You might find some of them

Consider Your Options

What is your current writing process? Does it work for you? What parts of it could you change?

unhelpful, or even silly; but please know that they are all valuable to someone. Everyone learns in different ways.

Considering Your Learning Style

Most of us prefer one of the three basic approaches to learning: aural (sound), verbal (writing), or visual (sight). Your preferred learning style will influence your choice of prewriting option(s), although you should always try several prewriting techniques. Even those that aren't really compatible with your learning style can yield results. Many methods of prewriting are at your disposal, but you must find the one that works best for you (and maybe for this particular assignment). Very few students would want to use all of these prewriting approaches for one essay.

Brainstorming with Questions (All Learners)

No matter what learning style you prefer, asking questions about your chosen or assigned topic is always a great way to generate ideas for prewriting. Since all argumentative essays require their writers to take a position on a topic, some of the most effective questions for prewriting are those which help the writer choose a side or decide on which points to argue. This method is helpful for a variety of disciplines:

Culinary students may be asked to write on the best method of preparation for a specific dish. In this example, questions about restaurant patrons, ingredients, and time of preparation are all applicable.

Police Foundations students may be asked to write about the most effective method of diffusing a hostile situation. In this example, questions about the number of people involved, the location, and the time of day would be important.

Business students may be asked to write about the best way to handle an awkward customer service situation. In this example, questions about types of customers, compensation, and competition should be addressed.

Engineering students may be asked to write a report on the best way to provide energy for a building. In this example, questions about budget, location, and environmental concerns are all applicable.

EXERCISE 2.3

For each essay topic, brainstorm two to three questions that you would generate through prewriting to help form an essay thesis.

1. Allowing all high schools across the country to have wi-fi access
2. Raising the legal drinking age
3. Adding an extra tax to unhealthy foods
4. Adding fluoride to drinking water

Brainstorming with Peers (Aural Learners)

Take the opportunity to talk about your topic with your classmates. You may get some valuable insights and feedback by running your ideas past other people and hearing their responses. (Don't forget to take notes.) You can also do the same for them.

One of the interesting features of the brainstorming process is that even if you sit and listen without saying a word, you will still learn a great deal about the general topic from your peers' approaches to it. In other words, the "shape" of the assignment will become clearer to you.

Note that you don't have to be restricted to your classmates; you can brainstorm with a friend or family member or anyone else who is willing to listen and respond.

Brainstorming with a Recorder (Aural Learners)

A digital recorder allows you to brainstorm aloud, then play back or read your spoken thoughts. This method is convenient, but it has drawbacks as well as advantages. A digital recorder can be used in a variety of situations, but eventually you will need to transcribe your thoughts. Moreover, this type of brainstorming is solitary; you won't get the benefit of a peer's feedback. Nonetheless, some writers prefer such an approach.

Brainstorming on Paper (Verbal Learners)

During brainstorming, no idea is too large or too small. You can use the six questions favoured by journalists—*who, what, when, where, why,* and *how*—to generate ideas and details; or you can just jot down thoughts as they occur to you. Remember that you will eventually need specific details in your writing.

Brainstorming is *not* the time to worry about the mechanics of writing. You are compiling a list of ideas, facts, and details. Work quickly; this is no time to let your "internal editor" take over.

Freewriting (Verbal Learners)

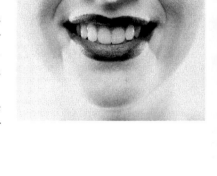

Freewriting is another version of brainstorming, but instead of writing a list of ideas and details in point form, you concentrate on writing out your thoughts as they occur to you—spontaneously. There is no reason to worry about paragraph unity or coherence; just let go and write. Each sentence doesn't necessarily need to "follow" its predecessor.

Some people would argue that the "Essay with No Purpose" is an excellent piece of freewriting. Although it reads like a random collection of sentences, it has actually generated a few major topics that this writer could focus on and develop further:

- Life before computers (How did we get by?)
- The many uses of the computer (Are they best for work or play?)
- Our dependence on computers (How do we cope when they freeze up?)
- The price of computers (Will they come down in price so everyone can afford them?)

Clustering and Chart Making (Visual Learners)

Clustering and chart making are two graphically oriented methods, ideal for visual learners. Students who use these methods prefer to "see" the developing essay. In **clustering,** you write the topic in the centre of a piece of paper, then write ideas suggested by that topic around it, connecting these to the topics with lines. Follow the same procedure with your subtopics. Figure 2.1 illustrates how the clustering approach could be used as prewriting for the essay "Computers: A Modern Marvel."

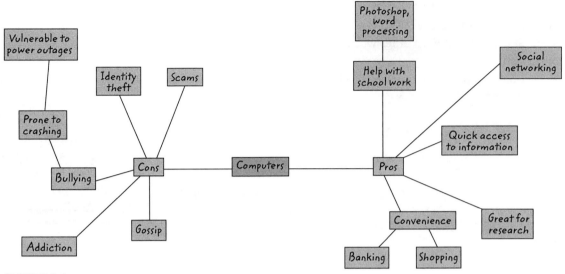

FIGURE 2.1
A clustering diagram based on the topic "Computers: A Modern Marvel."

Prewriting for the essay about computers is presented in **chart** form in Figure 2.2. This approach allows the writer to arrange information uniformly, left to right, centred on a common theme. It works particularly well for the comparison/contrast option.

OCCUPY CANADA ESSAY CASE STUDY:
PREWRITING

Leslie's English professor assigned the class essay topics based on current issues in the news. Leslie selected the Occupy Wall Street movement. She is supposed to come up with an original thesis for her essay; however, she's not sure where to begin.

Leslie considers herself a verbal learner and has decided that a combination of freewriting, brainstorming, and asking questions is her most successful way to generate ideas. Below are samples of her work. Later in this chapter, you will find out how Leslie generated a thesis out of this prewriting:

What does Wall Street do? Bank regulations. CEO salaries.

Why are people angry? Housing bubble. Mortgage foreclosures. Gap between rich and poor.

Who are the angriest? What does the average CEO make compared to his or her workers?

What is the current rate of unemployment? Compare Canada to the US.

What does the occupy movement want to accomplish?

Computers		FIGURE 2.2

Computers

Pros of Computers	Cons of Computers
Keep us connected with friends and relatives	Vulnerable to scams and identity theft
Make writing and editing easy	When the power goes out or they break, we're in trouble!
Help with research	Websites can be faked or give out the wrong info
Make life activities such as banking and shopping more convenient	Some people become addicted to the Internet or chatrooms

FIGURE 2.2
Essay prewriting
in chart form.

FOCUSING

Prewriting helps you think about your ideas and put a range of information and details on paper for future use. After prewriting, you should have a solid idea of how you will approach your topic. This approach works well for professor-assigned common knowledge, opinion-focused, or text-analysis essays. If your assignment requires research, however, now is the time to go to the library to start collecting sources for additional support before you create your thesis. (For more information on the entire research essay process, please see chapter 8.) If your essay doesn't require research, however, go ahead and determine your **thesis statement,** the guiding idea of your essay.

What Is a Thesis?

A **thesis** is a sentence or group of sentences that states the main idea of your paper. A good thesis does any or all of the following:

- Summarizes the essay's key insight
- Makes a claim
- Takes a position
- Shares a discovery
- Puts forth an insight about a topic based on a student's reading and research of this topic
- Informs the reader about what will follow
- Interests the reader in the possibilities that lie ahead

A **working thesis** can be defined as "my thesis right now." It may well change, but it's a good starting point.

The Specific Thesis vs. the General Thesis

The thesis statement appears in the introduction of your essay, normally toward the end of the introduction, and provides the point that your essay argues. Some essays use a general thesis while others use a specific one. For example, consider the two types of theses presented for an essay arguing the importance of social workers:

A **general thesis** does not exhaustively list the individual contents of the essay, but instead provides the essay's guiding argument.

Social workers help the disadvantaged of society by offering a variety of services.

A **specific thesis** lists the main points that the essay will argue and works as a type of road map or preview of the essay's contents.

> Social workers help the unemployed find work, the abused find security, and the impoverished find necessities.

Your instructors may prefer one thesis type over the other; however, both may be valid, depending on the type of writing you are asked to produce. Less formal writing, such as a newspaper column, would likely not require a specific thesis, whereas an academic essay would. Your topic and its length, scope, audience, and purpose usually dictate which thesis type you use. An essay that contains many points will not list them all in a specific thesis; such a thesis statement would be simply too long and awkward. An essay that discusses two to four main examples of one topic should probably name them. Doing so makes the essay easier to follow and to understand.

An Effective Thesis

A Thesis Should Generate Interest You should always aim to make your reader *want* to read your essay. A carefully written thesis statement can confirm and intensify this desire. Note the following thesis:

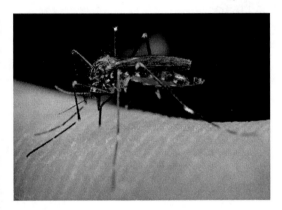

> Mosquitoes are generally bothersome and can have many negative effects on people and the environment.

This thesis does no more than impart information—information that seems obvious when stated in this way. However, notice how the following revision engages the reader:

> **If uncontrolled, mosquitoes can produce two negative effects: discomfort and disease.**

This version is more concise and has a sense of urgency. We can visualize the clouds of pests, hear their buzz, feel their bites, and cringe at the possibility of catching a deadly disease.

A Thesis Should Not Be Too Complicated A thesis statement generally should *not* be a complicated, self-referential device. The following thesis for an essay on tax policy that is intended for general readers is an example of what *not* to do:

> In the following essay, I will prove that granting the proposed tax increase will allow the city to pry from overtaxed residents more dollars that they would have otherwise spent in the private sector, where spending belongs.

A structured approach is more suitable to the writer's audience and purpose. Note this revision:

> **The tax increase proposed by the city of Calgary will have negative consequences: reduced growth, an overburdened citizenry, and unspecified use of revenues.**

The revised thesis avoids the heavy-handed and subjective use of "I" found in the original. In your thesis, as elsewhere, don't refer to your essay as if it were some science fair project. Avoid starting out with "In this essay, I will discuss . . ." or "In my paper, I will show . . ." Address your reader in natural, mature, clear language, avoiding a didactic and self-referential tone.

Let's look at some more examples of weak vs. effective thesis statements:

WEAK	I believe a 15% tuition rise will anger students.
EFFECTIVE	**Returning students forced to pay an additional 15% for tuition may find themselves having to cut expenses in other areas of life such as leisure or travel.**
WEAK	I think Lady Gaga is an amazing entertainer because she sings about the things that matter.
EFFECTIVE	**While some criticize her eccentricities, Lady Gaga has brought excitement to the music industry through her spectacular live shows and her message of individuality and self-acceptance.**
WEAK	The CEO of Maple Bank learned a valuable lesson last autumn.
EFFECTIVE	**To avoid further public outcry at the mismanagement of funds, Maple Bank should change its image by allowing fewer service charges, lower interest rates, and more customer appreciation days.**
WEAK	In Arthur Miller's Death of a Salesman, Willy Loman creates his own problems.
EFFECTIVE	**In Arthur Miller's Death of a Salesman, Willy Loman creates his own problems through his excessive temper, naive idealism, and foolish pride.**

EXERCISE 2.4

The following thesis statements are too wordy, self-referential, flat, and/or boring. Working alone or in pairs, rewrite them. Be creative and add details as necessary.

1. The food in the residence cafeteria is awful.
2. In this essay, I hope to prove that stress, one of the university student's worst enemies, can be successfully combatted.
3. The following essay will explain how Canadian media is very affected by American politics.
4. It is impossible to imagine the effects of open admissions across the community college system.
5. Downey Highway, the city's main thoroughfare, needs to be widened.

A Thesis Should Be Obvious A specific and focused thesis will naturally stand out in your introductory paragraph much more than a weak or vague one. Let's use one of the previous examples to illustrate this point.

AWKWARD:	Lady Gaga is a pop culture force. Her albums have sold millions of copies, and her videos and fashion sense have both confounded and intrigued viewers. Lady Gaga is an amazing entertainer because she sings about the things that matter.
REVISED:	**Lady Gaga is a pop culture force. Her albums have sold millions of copies, and her videos and fashion sense have both confounded and intrigued viewers. While some criticize her eccentricities, Lady Gaga has brought excitement to the music industry through her spectacular live shows and her message of individuality and self-acceptance.**

Since an essay introduction usually begins with general statements, the thesis statement in the awkward example hardly stands out—it's just one more vague declarative statement thrown on the pile; conversely, the thesis in the revised example not only blends seamlessly with the content before it, but also stands out as a true thesis. For more on thesis placement and paragraph construction, please see Chapter 4.

A Thesis Should Not Contain Examples Sometimes students will put examples within their thesis, examples that would be better left to the essay's body paragraphs. Consider the following two choices:

AWKWARD:	Lady Gaga has brought excitement to the music industry through her spectacular live shows. For example, she has outrageous outfits and even uses fake blood on stage. Lady Gaga has also brought excitement to the music industry through her message of individuality and self-acceptance. For example, her song "Born This Way" encourages people to be proud of themselves no matter what race, religion, or sexual orientation they are.
REVISED:	**Lady Gaga has brought excitement to the music industry through her spectacular live shows and through her message of individuality and self-acceptance.**

While the examples contained in the first thesis are certainly valid, they would be better placed in the essay's individual body paragraphs rather than being clumsily shoved in between its thesis points.

Focusing Your Thesis

To be successful, a thesis needs to be neither too narrow nor too broad. A thesis that is too narrow will leave you no freedom, and your essay will likely be of little interest to most audiences.

Mononucleosis makes a person tired.

Mono makes a person tired? Okay. But where do you go from there? How do you write 3 to 4 pages on how mono makes a person tired? How about expanding the thesis to include other symptoms of mono or, even better, how having mono can affect a person's life?

People who suffer from mononucleosis, an often overlooked but debilitating illness, experience extreme mental fatigue, dizziness, and a lack of energy.

This thesis is not only more specific and detailed, but it also attempts to interest the reader by appealing to his or her empathy for others.

The opposite problem occurs when the thesis is too broad:

The treatment of the homeless in Canada is shameful.

This thesis statement works for a long sociological study of homelessness—seven or eight hundred pages might cover the varying approaches and policies used by the many provinces and cities to deal with the question of how to help the homeless. However, in an assignment requiring a maximum of 1000 words, you would be reduced to writing a series of generalizations if you used this thesis.

Note how the revised thesis statement allows the writer enough "room" yet restricts the discussion to a manageable range:

Our city's new vagrancy law has one purpose: to drive the homeless to the next city in order to increase the property value of downtown businesses.

This thesis provides the basis for a lively argument that can be handled in 1000 words or less.

Key Elements of an Effective Thesis

An effective thesis accomplishes three things:

- It indicates your purpose and your main argument.
- It provides a general "road map" for your essay.
- It engages your reader.

Here are some ways to ensure that your thesis works:

1. Phrase your thesis as a complete sentence and not as a title or topic.

NOT   The dangers of fighting in hockey.

BUT   **Fighting in hockey should be banned because it endangers players, cheapens the game, and promotes violence to young Canadians.**

2. State your point outright; do not announce intentions of opinions.

NOT   I am going to argue that in my opinion fighting should be banned in hockey because it is dangerous.

NOT   This paper will argue that fighting should be banned in hockey.

BUT   **Fighting in hockey should be banned because it endangers players, cheapens the game, and promotes violence to young Canadians.**

3. Make your thesis as specific and pointed as you can.

NOT   Fighting in hockey is dangerous and should be banned.

BUT   **Fighting in hockey should be banned because it endangers players, cheapens the game, and promotes violence to young Canadians.**

OCCUPY CANADA ESSAY CASE STUDY:
CREATING A THESIS

After prewriting on the topic of the Occupy movement in Canada, Leslie took her notes and tried to form a thesis from them. Below are some of her attempts, from her weakest to her most successful. Later in this chapter, you will see how she places this thesis into a formal outline to flesh out her essay's organization.

> Protesters in the Occupy Canada movement are disgruntled with the rich.

WEAK: This thesis is too vague and simplifies this complex issue.

> Protesters in the Occupy Canada movement are dissatisfied with wealth distribution and wealth management in Canada.

GENERAL: This thesis is better. It could be more specific; however, wealth distribution and wealth management are certainly concrete issues that one can explore in an essay.

> Protestors in the Occupy Canada movement are dissatisfied with dwindling job opportunities, the gap between wages for workers and management, and an ineffective government that allowed the financial crisis to occur in the first place.

SPECIFIC: This thesis will work best for a short research paper since it names three manageable areas that can be explored about this topic.

EXERCISE 2.5

Read the following scenarios. Decide if each thesis is effective, too narrow, or too broad for an essay of 750–1000 words. Explain your reasoning.

1. Your college has undergone many renovations over the past year. When you return in September, you are surprised with the results.

   Topic: Are the facilities offered at the college better than those offered last year?

   Audience: Your instructor/fellow students

   Essay type: Comparison/contrast

   Thesis statement: The new facilities available at our college are superior to those offered last year.

2. You work as a math tutor in a computer lab. Your job is to help students by using the tutorial software. On Wednesday, your supervisor announces that the long-awaited replacement for the aging software has arrived and will be loaded on Friday. She hands you the user's manual and the technical support documentation, then asks you to write a simplified document to hand out to the students who use the lab.

Topic: How to use the new math tutorial software

Audience: Math students in need of academic support

Essay type: Process analysis

Thesis statement: The new tutorial software has many features and requirements that differ from those of the old software.

3. Your professor has lectured and led discussions on controversial issues for the past two weeks.

   Topic: Argue one side of an issue about which many Canadians have strong feelings.

   Audience: Your instructor

   Essay Type: Argument

   Thesis statement: Poverty can be eliminated if we all work together to improve education in our nation.

4. You drive a great deal: to work, at work, to school. Your city is becoming increasingly congested, with more cars each year. Your local newspaper asks readers to write in with their opinions.

   Topic: What is a cause or set of causes for local traffic congestion?

   Audience: The newspaper's readership

   Essay type: Causal analysis

   Thesis statement: The real reason for local traffic problems is not congestion but the lack of proper lane-changing procedures by area drivers, leading to unnecessary accidents.

5. You are an outgoing, gregarious person with many, many friends.

   Topic: What is the difference between a friend and an acquaintance?

   Audience: Your instructor

   Essay type: Classification

   Thesis statement: A friend is someone you like, while an acquaintance is someone you know only somewhat.

ORGANIZING

At this point, you have moved further in the writing process than you might have guessed. After choosing a topic, establishing audience and purpose, generating ideas, and developing a working thesis, you are now ready for the last step prior to drafting: **structuring** your prewriting so that it can guide you through the rest of the writing process.

Basic Essay Structure and the Five-Paragraph Model

Basic essay structure follows this pattern: an introductory paragraph (ending with a thesis), body paragraphs directly relating to the thesis points, and a concluding paragraph. Most high school classes (and a few university and college ones) insist on

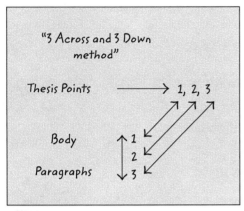

FIGURE 2.3
Suggested thesis/body paragraph organization.

Essay Outline

Introduction
- Hook (interest the reader without being gimmicky)
- Background info
- Thesis

Body Paragraph One
- Topic sentence (relating to thesis point 1)
- Proof and examples
- Proof and examples
- Concluding and/or transitional statement

Body Paragraph Two
- Topic sentence (relating to thesis point 2)
- Proof and examples
- Proof and examples
- Concluding and/or transitional statement

Body Paragraph Three
- Topic sentence (relating to thesis point 3)
- Proof and examples
- Proof and examples

Concluding and/or transitional statement

Conclusion
- Summary of thesis points
- Evaluation of topic and summative comments

FIGURE 2.4
A template for a formal essay outline.

three body paragraphs, thus bringing the total number of paragraphs in your paper to five. For a standard 1000-word essay (3–4 typed pages), this method works quite well; however, please note that every essay and every essay topic may require you to adapt this method. In short, not every essay is five paragraphs long! Some college and university assignments are 20 pages long; and even in a short essay, one paragraph should never take up an entire page. How paragraphs are organized matters much more than their exact number. Accordingly, constructing an **outline** of what you intend to do will help you "see" your essay before you begin. An outline can also reveal gaps—places where you need to do more thinking and prewriting.

Basic Essay Structure: The 3 Across and 3 Down Model

One of the key elements to organizing an essay is to make sure that your thesis points match your body paragraphs. We suggest the "3 across and 3 down model" (see Figure 2.3). Your thesis sets up expectations for your reader, and your organization should reward your reader's expectations. Sometimes students will have a really strong thesis, and then completely ignore it! Instead they put completely separate (yet sometimes still valid) points in their body paragraphs—a type of "1, 2, 3 across and 4, 5, 6, down" model. However, be careful: your thesis points should directly correspond to your essay's body paragraphs.

Essay Outlines

Outlines function as guides, giving writers a path to follow and something to fall back on if the essay takes a wrong turn. Most follow the same general structure, but some are more detailed than others. Some writers may choose to list only the major topic of each body paragraph (an **informal outline**), while others will try to include as much detail as possible, such as topic sentences and proofs (a **formal outline**). The template in Figure 2.4 provides a detailed framework for a formal essay outline.

DRAFTING

At this point, you have organized your ideas and are ready to begin a first draft—but don't expect it to be your final draft. No one is able to write a perfect first draft; even people who tend to write very strong first-draft essays realize the need for revision and redrafting.

Essays tend to be written in two distinct circumstances: in supervised classrooms with relatively stringent time requirements or out of the classroom at the writer's discretion, with a time limit (a due date) but no restrictions on when or where the essay will be written. For the most part, similar drafting strategies work for both situations, with a few minor variations.

OCCUPY CANADA ESSAY CASE STUDY: CREATING A FORMAL OUTLINE

After prewriting on her topic to develop a thesis, Leslie is now ready to begin crafting the shape of her essay via a point-form outline. The more detail you place in your outline, the easier it will be to craft your essay's rough draft. Leslie has broken her point form outline down by paragraph and has included as many examples as she can. Later in this chapter, you will see how she shapes these points into a rough draft.

INTRODUCTION:

Hook: how it started. . ..adbusters. . .civil rights. . ..revolution!

Background Info: begins on Wall Street. Spreads across the world and into Canada and its major cities (Toronto, Vancouver, Halifax, etc). calling it rich vs poor is too simple—they have specific concerns.

Thesis: protesters are concerned with unemployment, severe wage gaps, lack of government response

PARAGRAPH 1:

Topic Sentence: unemployment and job opportunity is a central issue.

Example: Unemployment rate in Canada 7.6%; Oct 2011 Canada loses 71 700 jobs

Example: Electro-Motive plant closes—540 skilled employees out of work.

Concluding/transition statement: Plant closes because workers wouldn't take a 50% pay reduction.

The income gap between workers and management is another issue.

PARAGRAPH 2:

Topic Sentence: the slogan "we are the 99%"; top 1% of wage earners in Canada control 32% of the country's wealth

Example: Electro-Motive had a record profit of 5 billion dollars last year; its CEO made $10.5 million annually.

Example: larger trend. highest paid CEOs in Canada now make nearly 200 times more money than the national average: a 27% raise from 2009. Average Canadian worker earns $44 366

Concluding/transitional Statement: the 99% are not merely jealous. . .how the 1% get and maintain wealth is usually aided by the government. Low regulation, low taxation.

PARAGRAPH 3:

Topic Sentence: mortgage crisis of 2008; US government responded with bank bailouts

Example: No bailouts in Canada, but taxes on rich have decreased from 43% to 29% despite report that taxation needed to bridge gap between rich and poor.

Example: Government still doesn't help; the provincial government is attacking teachers instead of raising corporate taxes; Harper attacking Air Canada workers instead of doing the same

Concluding/transitional Statement: no wonder people are angry!

CONCLUSION:

Topic Sentence: movement is not made up of lazy, greedy, or jealous people
Restate Thesis: people just want a living wage, job security, and a gov't to look out for them.
Concluding statement: Occupy protestor's sign—people have a right/duty to revolt
Resources: Global and CTV articles

Drafting In-Class Essays

Writing an essay in class under time constraints is a situation that many students fear. You might not have enough time to do a great deal of planning and prewriting; but as we pointed out earlier, skipping the prewriting stage and moving directly into a draft is a serious mistake. Instead try the following steps:

- Do as much planning as time will allow, as even the simplest essay outline can help organize your thoughts. We suggest approximately 10% of the time allotted for the in-class essay.
- Try to produce the best first draft you can—slowly and conscientiously.
- Read your work over again, fixing spelling and grammar where needed.

Drafting Out-of-Class Essays

Luckily, out-of-class assignments offer extra time to complete them. However, sometimes all the time in the world isn't enough to get your assignment done. Life events and personal motivation often play a strong role. The single most important ingredient to good writing is time: time to plan, time to draft, time to revise and edit.

Always avoid using a single day to go through all the writing-process steps discussed in this chapter. Your work will be improved if you can split the total amount of time spent over a few weeks, returning to your writing with a fresh eye (and brain) on each new day.

Starting the Drafting Process

Here are some suggestions for getting ready to work (and to keep you working once you've started!):

1. **Avoid constant editing:** Don't obsess over the mechanical spelling, grammar, and word choice issues in the first draft of an essay; instead, concentrate on completing a serviceable, well-structured text, and revise later.
2. **Avoid writer's block:** Evidence suggests that people who don't prewrite have more trouble with writer's block than people who have planned and prepared.

When you prewrite, thoughts arise and percolate in your brain, generating more mental activity. However, sometimes the only cure for writer's block is a *short* diversion.

3. **Avoid panic:** Give yourself TIME to write. Concentrate on the steps of your writing, not the outcome. To write an essay properly, you will need to achieve a series of objectives. Work on each step; the outcome should take care of itself.

4. **Avoid the stalled introduction:** If you simply can't put your introduction into words, write the balance of your essay first, then come back and write the introduction. Many writers follow this pattern: prewrite, write the body, write the introduction, write the conclusion.

5. **Avoid a bad writing environment:** Try to make yourself as comfortable as possible, and try to ignore distractions. A distracting environment affects some students more than others; many students are quite comfortable working in their rooms, whereas others get claustrophobic and work better while riding on a city bus or sitting in a room full of people watching television.

The first draft of Leslie's Occupy essay follows. The call-out boxes highlight specific areas that need attention. In Chapter 5, you will see a peer review of this essay, as well as a comparison between this draft and the final revision.

LESLIE'S FIRST DRAFT
Leslie Buckley
Prof. R. Muhlbock
COMM 1011
February 13, 2013

Occupy Canada

Vague title.

What first began as a march on Wall Street, quickly spread around the world due to the fact that people wanted to protest issues about corporate greed among other things, etc. In Canada, occupy movements sprung up in all major cities. For some, the movement was vaguely defined as a poor vs. rich dispute. But I think such comments trivialize what the movement is about and why its participants are really mad.

Wordy.

Avoid I.

Protestors in the Occupy Canada movement are dissatisfied with dwindling job opportunities, the gap between wages for workers and for management, and an ineffectual government that allowed these injustices to occur in the first place.

Great thesis—result of prewriting and drafting.

Currently the unemployment rate in Canada is not that bad compared to the US, but the youth unemployment rate is 14.5%.

Source needed.

In October of 2011, Canada lost 71 700 full-time jobs, many of them in "manufacturing and construction." One such example is the Electro-Motive plant (owned by Caterpillar Inc.) in London, Ontario, which recently closed its doors, forcing some 54 skilled employees out of work because they wouldn't take a 50% pay cut. Another key aspect in the Ocupy Canada movement is the income gap between workers and management. The Occupy movement's slogan is we are the 99%. The top 1% of wage earners in Canada control 32% of the country's wealth, while the other 99% of citizens have to divide up what's left amid surging unemployment.

Typo! The actual number is 540.

spelling errors: "Ocupy", "Catarpillar".

Catarpillar closed its Electro-Motive plant after workers refused to take a 500% pay reduction, but the same company not only posted a record profit of

Source needed.

5 billion dollars last year, but allowed its CEO to make $10.5-million annually (Size). Caterpillar is just one example. According to the CBC, the highest paid CEOs in Canada now make nearly 200 times more money than the national average.

Source needed.

The average Canadian worker earns $44 366. The ways that the top 1% acquire and maintain their wealth is through low government regulation and taxation. In 2008, after the mortgage crisis, the government bailed out US banks and financial institutions and enraged the public. However, taxation for Canada's rich has steadily declined from 43% in 1981 to 29% in 2010 ("OECD report"). At the provincial level, to curb Ontario's massive debt, the McGuinty liberals are instead requesting a wage freeze for high school teachers, while at the Federal level the government is threatening to legislate Air Canada workers back to their jobs ("Federal labour").

Source needed.

Occupy Canada is not made up jealous or lazy people. Equality in wealth may not be possible. Simple fairness is. I believe the public wants a livable wage and job security. Elected officials must protect the public they serve. When they fail, people have a right to be angry.

Overall, conclusion is rather short and choppy.

Works Cited

http://www.ctvnews.ca/oecd-report-finds-income-inequality-rising-in-canada-1.735650

http://globalnews.ca/news/219851/federal-labour-minister-watching-threat-of-strike-by-air-canada-workers/

http://www.ctv.ca/CTVNews/TopStories /20120203/caterpillar-closing-electromotive-plant-120203/

Works Cited page is not only incomplete, but also incorrectly formatted.

EXERCISE 2.6

Choose one of the general topics below. Then develop the topic by using the following steps:

1. Identify your purpose and audience.
2. Use one of these prewriting methods to narrow your topic and generate ideas: brainstorming, freewriting, clustering, or making a chart.
3. Decide on a working thesis.
4. Structure your essay by using an informal outline or a formal outline.
5. Compose your first draft.

Topics:

1. In what ways is your life easier than your parents' or grandparents' lives were when they were about your age? In what ways is it more difficult? Try interviewing a parent, grandparent, or older relative to gather information for this assignment.

2. "Good first impressions are essential to good relationships." Agree or disagree.

3. How do gender stereotypes affect students' lives?

4. What are the reasons that students are tempted to cheat on exams or plagiarize papers?

5. Individual Canadians can make a difference in the fight against global warming. Agree or disagree.

6. Most popular music today is overly commercial and shallow. Agree or disagree.

7. You stand to inherit a restaurant provided that you do not change the nature of the restaurant or sell it to someone else. You must make the restaurant profitable. Unfortunately, the restaurant has been shut down because of health and safety issues. How will you achieve success?

Using the Internet

Go to these websites to find more tips, techniques, and insights on prewriting and drafting:

Mindomo
This free mind-mapping software allows anyone to create effective and engaging mind maps to begin the essay drafting process.
http://www.mindomo.com/

The University of Richmond Writing Center's Writer's Web
This site offers excellent advice on writing first drafts in various academic disciplines. The section on "focusing and connecting ideas" is also helpful. A topic index and search engine make finding useful material easy, especially in regard to addressing your audience, determining your voice, and deciding on your purpose in various contexts. This website also discusses freewriting, brainstorming, clustering, and other prewriting techniques.
http://writing2.richmond.edu/writing/wweb.html

University of Buffalo Composition Website
This multi-layered site contains numerous pages on the writing process and describes valuable strategies for planning and drafting an academic paper. It also contains a link to a Dartmouth University site that explains the differences between academic writing and other types of writing.
http://libweb.lib.buffalo.edu/infotree/resourcesbysubject.asp?subject=English+ Composition

Garbl's Writing Process Links
This site provides an annotated list of several other valuable websites (with links) that provide information on the writing process—from overcoming writer's block to planning and drafting to proofreading.
http://garbl.home.comcast.net/~ garbl/writing/

Using Sources: Summarizing, Paraphrasing, and Integrating Quotations

PLAGIARISM in the Real World

Plagiarism is theft of intellectual property. Those who partake in plagiarism are, legally speaking, frauds. Plagiarism can occur at all income levels and in all careers. For example, musician Joe Satriani sued the band Coldplay for copyright infringement in 2008. Satriani claimed that Coldplay's song "Viva La Vida" borrowed heavily from his song "If I Could Fly." In the same year, Owen Lippert, a speech writer for the Conservative Party resigned after admitting to copying large portions of a speech written for Stephen Harper in 2003 from a speech delivered by then–prime minister of Australia, John Howard. Lippert later apologized, claiming he was "pressed for time." More recently, in 2013, Chris Spence, Director of Education for the Toronto District School Board, admitted to plagiarizing portions of an article he wrote that appeared in the Toronto *Star,* while Germany's Education Minister, Annette Schavan, admitted to plagiarizing portions of her doctoral thesis. Considering that both of these individuals were in education, they certainly should have known better. The consequences of their actions were quite similar: both lost their jobs, with Schavan losing her Doctorate as well. Plagiarism has serious consequences.

LEARNING OUTCOMES:

▶ Recognize and avoid plagiarism

▶ Paraphrase and summarize source material for inclusion in student writing

▶ Integrate direct quotations of source material into student writing using signal phrases

▶ Properly cite borrowed material using MLA or APA methods

> **Note**
>
> Chapter 3 provides students with the fundamentals of summary, paraphrase, and quotation integration. A basic discussion of APA and MLA citation methods and examples is also included.
>
> This material is often saved for research and citation styles chapters tucked at the end of a text; however, many students in composition classes need an explanation of these skills to complete early term assignments as well as to write end-of-term research papers.
>
> For a more in-depth discussion of the research process and citation styles, see Chapters 16 and 17.

SECONDARY SOURCES IN THE ACADEMIC WORLD

Researching, evaluating, and applying the work of others are integral to academic writing. As students advance in their studies, their own opinions and life experiences have increasingly limited value. Conversely, research exposes students to the thoughts, theories, and debates occurring in the wider academic world—information that enriches assignments and gives them greater scope and objectivity.

Students can incorporate the work of others into their own writing in three distinct ways: summary, paraphrase, and direct quotation—each of which is explained in detail in this chapter. A fourth "method," plagiarism, involves stealing someone else's work and presenting it as your own. Plagiarism is a serious academic offence and should be completely avoided.

PLAGIARISM

Plagiarism is using someone else's words or ideas without giving the original source appropriate credit. A serious offence, plagiarism violates the very purpose of education, which is, essentially, the search for truth; it is usually punished severely. Indeed, penalties for plagiarism can range from failure of the assignment to dismissal from the college or university. Most offences are recorded on a student's permanent academic record.

Why Do Students Plagiarize?

Owen Lippert's reason for plagiarizing the speech of another world leader sounds familiar: he was "pressed for time." There are many reasons why students pass off the work of others as their own; however, none are acceptable. Below are a few of the more common causes of plagiarism:

Panic: Just as Lippert was "pressed for time," so might you be, in your studies. As deadlines approach, students get desperate, and plagiarism seems like an easy solution. When your dishonesty is discovered, however, as it most often is, the consequences will not save you time, especially if you end up retaking a course as a result.

Low self-confidence: Sometimes students feel they can never write as well as a professional, so they cut and paste pieces of someone else's writing into their own writing to give it more intellectual credibility. However, stealing from someone else's work is not the solution—this will cause greater damage to your grade than less spectacular ideas which are, at least, your own.

Ignorance: We live in a world where every time someone burns a CD or downloads a video illegally, copyright laws are being broken. This type of behaviour has become a way of life for many. Students are so used to the free flow of information available from the Internet, not to mention cutting and pasting it from various sources whenever they feel like it, that the concept of individual ownership sometimes doesn't exist for them. Think to yourself, how would I feel if someone took my work without permission and claimed it was his or her own?

Why Documentation Matters

Ethics: Students have an ethical obligation to their readers to show where their ideas stop and another's ideas begin. Not acknowledging this difference is taking credit for someone else's intellectual property.

Legality: Taking someone else's work without permission and/or without properly giving credit to the original author can sometimes become a legal issue. You can be sued or fined for doing so, and if you use someone's work illegally in a professional setting, you may lose your job.

Courtesy: Letting your readers know where you got some of your ideas is also a matter of courtesy. What if your reader really enjoyed your essay or article and wanted to do further reading or research on the subject? Your works cited or references page would provide a good starting point for someone looking to increase his or her knowledge of your essay's topic.

Consequences of Plagiarism

Intellectual theft has many consequences. Below are a few examples:

Failure of assignment or course credit: If you're caught plagiarizing, your instructor might let you off with a warning or require you to rewrite the questionable content, depending on the severity of the incident; however, instructors often have little tolerance for this fraud (since most course syllabi make specific mention of its consequences); they may very well give your offending assignment a zero, thus putting your credit in jeopardy.

Tarnished academic record and/or expulsion from college or university: Academic institutions hold intellectual honesty in high regard; all institutions have specific rules and regulations outlining the consequences of plagiarism. Most begin by recording the incident on some sort of official documentation (i.e., an Academic Offence form). From there (as outlined above), discretion is up to the instructor regarding the consequences; however, in cases of repeated plagiarism, offenders may be expelled from the university or college after as few as three occurrences.

Loss of job: Many places of employment depend on their honesty to stay in business. News organizations in particular must have credible sources, and they must also attribute their information to these sources, whenever possible. Failure to do so can result in embarrassment to the news organization as well as consequences for employees. In 2007, for example, CBS news anchor Katie Couric read material in an online video essay that was directly plagiarized from *The Wall Street Journal*. The material was "prepared" by a producer who was immediately fired for the indiscretion.

Tarnished reputation: Plagiarism is similar to lying. As in the story "The Boy Who Cried Wolf," a frequent liar has no credibility even when telling the truth. Once you plagiarize, re-establishing a sense of trust with your colleagues or employers may be incredibly difficult.

Legal fees or damages: Since plagiarism is theft, it is punishable by law—victims of plagiarism have a legal right to sue their plagiarizers for damages and lost income. Whether these legal cases are settled in or out of court, the results are often costly for the plagiarizer.

How to Avoid Plagiarism

Intentional plagiarism involves deliberately copying something from a source, usually word for word, and using it without quotation marks. However, students who are just learning to write research papers sometimes commit **unintentional plagiarism,** which can result from any of the following actions:

1. Forgetting to put quotation marks around quoted material when taking notes, or forgetting to include quotation marks when placing those notes in the text of the paper.
2. Using material that has been summarized or paraphrased and forgetting to tell readers the source of that material.
3. Paraphrasing or summarizing incorrectly, including accidentally adopting the sentence and/or paragraph structure of the original or including many of the words from the original (other than proper nouns, which cannot really be changed).

Note that even if these actions are not done intentionally, they still constitute a serious problem and may result in a zero or a substantially lower grade than the paper could have earned.

Contrast a direct quotation from Frank Ancona's book *Myth* with a partially plagiarized paraphrase. Then look at a legitimate paraphrase and summary of the same material.

Original

In *The Interpretation of Dreams,* Freud recognized the difficulty inherent in trying to communicate with the unconscious. He attributed the problem to what he called a "censor." He believed that some elements of consciousness did not want the messages from the unconscious to surface (23).

Plagiarized Paraphrase

In *The Interpretation of Dreams,* Freud recognized how difficult it was to communicate with the unconscious. He theorized that the problem was caused by something he called a "censor." He believed that some parts of consciousness did not want messages from the unconscious to come out (Ancona 23).

Legitimate Paraphrase

According to Freud, a "censor" within the conscious mind kept the unconscious mind from communicating with it. In his book *The Interpretation of Dreams,* he theorized that an aspect of the conscious mind prevented troublesome ideas from emerging (Ancona 23).

> Freud theorized in *The Interpretation of Dreams* that something within the conscious mind attempts to keep out information buried within the unconscious (Ancona 23).

The plagiarized paraphrase contains words taken directly from the original. In this case, the student needs to rephrase the lines or simply put the author's original wording in quotation marks. Note, however, that when using either a legitimate paraphrase or a legitimate summary, proper citation information needs to be given. Because you are taking the idea or ideas about Freud's work from the work of another author, you need to give that person credit.

We will discuss proper APA and MLA citation styles later in this chapter.

Citing Sources: Parenthetical Citations and the References Page

You are allowed to "use" the work of another writer, within reason, as long as you acknowledge and credit this source. You must do so in two ways, both of which are inextricably linked to each other:

A parenthetical citation: No matter how you use another author's material—whether through summary, paraphrase, or direct quotation—a parenthetical citation **must** appear after the source material. What you place in the bracketed citation, however, depends on which method of documentation your instructor has recommended (i.e., MLA or APA). The rest of this example gives some preliminary examples of formatting parenthetical citations. See Chapter 9 for a more detailed set of examples.

The references page: A references page collects all of the sources you've used to write your paper. Each entry on this page must directly correspond to a parenthetical citation that appears somewhere in your essay. Again, the format (and even the name) of your references page and its entries will depend on which documentation method you are using. See Chapters 16 and 17 for a detailed list of reference page entries as well as sample essays.

A research paper shouldn't be just an unbroken string of direct quotations, paraphrases, and summaries from other sources. Your instructors want to read *your* analysis of the material, not just the words of published authors. When you support your own thoughts with an idea or quotation taken from someone else, however, you must cite your source.

What Kind of Information Needs to be Cited?

1. A direct quotation of another person's writing or speech, even if only a few words.
2. A paraphrase or summary of another person's writing or speech.
3. An opinion expressed by another person.
4. Statistical data produced by another person.
5. Graphic or audiovisual material produced by another person.

What Kind of Information does not Need to be Cited?

1. Common knowledge: Canadian citizens must pay taxes on their income; water freezes at 0 C; all mammals are warm blooded.

2. "Background" knowledge generated from your research that appears in numerous sources. (Be careful not to interpret this category too broadly.) If you are researching an essay on global warming, for example, and twelve sources in a row indicate that the problem is serious, you have no need to cite a source for this opinion. On the other hand, if one of these sources claims that global warming is the *most* serious problem afflicting the world, and you express this opinion in any way, you must credit its source.

When in doubt, cite all sources. The consequences for being too careful are minimal compared to the damage that plagiarism can wreak.

Plagiarism Prevention Programs

Students, with their iPhones and video games and YouTube, seem to forget that their professors also know how to use technology. The world is completely dependent on computers, and assuming that your professor doesn't have access to the same electronic resources that you do is extremely naive.

Students intentionally plagiarize in one of two ways: they purchase essays online, or they cut and paste large chunks of text from websites or online periodicals. Either method, if discovered, may result in a failed assignment and sometimes a failed course credit. Some students will also submit essays that they have previously submitted to a different instructor. This trick of double-submitting qualifies as plagiarism.

Most academic institutions subscribe to plagiarism prevention programs that check students' work electronically against information available online (and please note that many books and magazine articles are available online, so copying text from print sources also carries a huge risk). Professors often will not accept assignments unless they have been submitted to one of these databases.

Turnitin.com One of the most popular plagiarism prevention programs is Turnitin.com. This website compares uploaded student essays against billions of web pages, looking for matching text. The site then issues an "originality report" that alerts instructors to areas of a paper that are plagiarized (whether intentionally or unintentionally) from other sources. If you look at the column on the right-hand side of the screenshot in Figure 3.1, you will see percentages highlighted in different colours. These percentages correspond with website addresses where the coloured portions of text on the left are found. The third comment on the right means that the system has found that 8% of the student's essay matches exactly with information found on Wikipedia.org. In other words, this student has copied all of the portions of his or her essay that are highlighted in blue from Wikipedia, or from another source that has taken its wording from Wikipedia.

Originality Checking

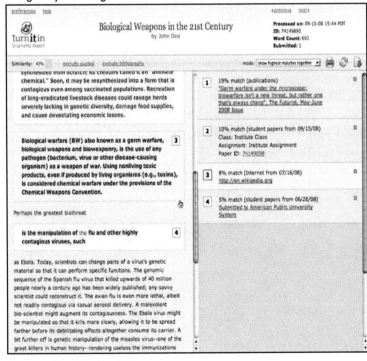

FIGURE 3.1
An "originality report" produced by Turnitin.com.

When a teacher or professor sees such a high-percentage match, he or she will check to see if the source has been correctly cited within the student's essay. If it has not, the student will be considered to be guilty of plagiarism. Some instructors allow students to upload and re-upload work before the final due date so that students can locate areas of their paper that need to be cited or rewritten, and you should take this opportunity seriously. However, most of the time you will not have a second chance, and it is *your* responsibility to make sure that your writing is free from plagiarism.

SUMMARIZING

Summarizing is one way to borrow material from an outside source. Summaries condense information into a shorter form than the original while expressing the same main idea. Using summaries rather than quoting directly in your paper will help you avoid the common problem of losing your own voice in a sea of quotations.

Preparing to Summarize

To summarize effectively, simply try to focus on the main point or idea the author is expressing in a passage or paragraph, and state that idea in one or two sentences in your own words. For example, let's say you need to summarize the following paragraph from the online essay "Scar Sands," by Curtis Gillespie:

> The beauty of the boreal forest that surrounds Fort McMurray and covers most of northern Alberta lies in its magnitude, but once you arrive at oil-sands central, what you see is a landscape erased, a terrain stretching in a radius of many hundreds of square kilometres that is not so much negatively impacted as forcibly stripped bare and excavated. Dominating this landscape are half a dozen giant extraction and refining plants with their stacks and smoke and fire, disorientingly wide and deep mines, and tailings ponds held in check by some of the world's largest dams. As a panoramic vision, it's all rather heartbreaking but, if one is forced to be honest, also awe-inspiring, [*sic*] such is the energy and the damage produced by human ambition.

First, you need to engage in two basic steps: *reading* the paragraph and *understanding* the paragraph. If you cannot (or do not) do either of these tasks, your summary will be unsuccessful. Okay, let's assume that you *have* read it and you *do* understand it—now what? A summary is short—much shorter than the original. A summary gives all of the main information in the paragraph and is stated in the writer's own words. Finally, any summary **MUST** cite the original source at some point, whether at the beginning in a signal phrase or at the end in a **parenthetical citation** (and sometimes in both places).

How to Summarize

Some people can read a small paragraph (or even a large one) and immediately repeat or write down in their own words the main idea of it. Some people, however, must work at a summary in steps.

Here are the basic steps to creating a proper summary:

1. **Highlight key words,** expressions, and main points of the paragraph. Do not highlight any repeated information or examples that prove the main points.
2. Go back and **cross out** any words or **smaller points** that describe ideas mentioned under the larger, overarching point.
3. Write your own paragraph, using only the highlighted points that you have not crossed out, **expressing those ideas *in your own words.***
4. **Cite** the original source at the end of the summary, using a parenthetical citation.

In the Gillespie example, some highlighted words might be "magnitude," "stripped bare," and "heartbreaking." Substituting synonyms for these words right away will help you to avoid plagiarism. Remember that writing appropriate summaries is hard work and requires some creativity.

> The **beauty of the boreal forest** of northern Alberta lies in its **magnitude,** ~~but once you arrive at~~ **oil-sands central,** ~~what you see is a~~ **landscape erased, forcibly stripped bare** and **excavated.** Dominating this landscape are **half a dozen giant extraction and refining plants** with their stacks and **smoke and fire,** ~~disorientingly~~ **wide and deep mines,** and ~~tailings ponds held in check by~~ some of the **world's largest dams.** ~~As a panoramic vision,~~ it's all rather **heartbreaking** but, **also awe-inspiring,** [*sic*] ~~such is the energy and the damage produced by~~ **human ambition.**

After you have worked through the paragraph, you might write a summary of Gillespie's paragraph in the following way:

> Gillespie describes the oil sands of northern Alberta as being ravaged by industry. However, his description is emotionally conflicted: while expressing sadness for the barren landscape, Gillespie can't help acknowledging with a sense of wonder the human ingenuity that is capable of such destruction.

This summary begins with a **signal phrase** indicating the original author. Moreover, this summary identifies the main point of Gillespie's paragraph—that, in his opinion, the land in northern Alberta is suffering because of industrial exploration. The summary does not include a parenthetical citation at its end since the source is online with no specific page numbers. Finally, notice that the summary doesn't recount specific details or examples in the paragraph. If it did, it would be considered a paraphrase.

PARAPHRASING

A paraphrase, like a summary, is stated in the writer's own words; however, unlike a summary, it contains most of the main ideas and examples contained in the original. You might want to use a paraphrase in your essay when the information is central to your argument and a bare-bones summary will not suffice, but the details are too long or complicated to be given in a direct quotation. Paraphrases are usually a bit shorter than the original paragraph, but they are sometimes the same length.

How to Paraphrase

The beginning steps to paraphrasing are identical to those mentioned for summarizing: you need to *read* and *understand* the paragraph. Since a paraphrase is more detailed than a summary, the process of paraphrasing is a bit more engaged.

Here are the basic steps to paraphrasing a section of text:

1. **Highlight key words,** expressions, and main points. You'll probably have more highlighting than when summarizing.
2. Write down the main points and terms, **putting them in your own words.** Use a thesaurus to find synonyms if you need to (but overusing the thesaurus will make your language sound awkward).
3. Rewrite the same points you just wrote down, but in a **different order.**
4. **Cite** the original source at the end of the paraphrase using a parenthetical citation.

Let's look at the original paragraph again with key words in bold.

> The **beauty of the boreal forest** that surrounds Fort McMurray and covers most of **northern Alberta** lies in its **magnitude,** but once you arrive at **oil-sands central,** what you see is a **landscape erased,** a terrain stretching in a radius of many hundreds of square kilometres that is not so much negatively impacted as **forcibly** stripped bare and **excavated.** Dominating this landscape are **half a dozen giant extraction and refining plants** with their stacks and **smoke and fire,** disorientingly **wide and deep mines,** and tailings ponds held in check by some of the **world's largest dams.** As a panoramic vision, it's all rather **heartbreaking** but, if one is forced to be honest, also **awe-inspiring,** [*sic*] such is the **energy and the damage produced by human ambition.**

Now, take your highlighted key words and expressions and put them in your own words. Then rearrange the order of the points so that your paragraph does not follow the same structure as the original. Once you have completed these steps, you might arrive at the following suitable paraphrase:

> In his description of the northern Alberta landscape, Gillespie highlights the irony of a magnificent boreal forest dwarfed by the competing industry of the oil sands. Gigantic barren expanses, menacing dams, and polluting mines evoke both horror and awe in the viewer. This once-beautiful land has been raped by the power and ingenuity of corporate greed.

This successful paraphrase begins with a **signal phrase** indicating the original author; and it captures the main idea found in the original paragraph, as well as specific examples. The information is in the new writer's own words and appears in a different order than in the original. Again, it does not conclude with a parenthetical citation since the online source has no page numbers.

INTEGRATING QUOTATIONS

What happens when the original paragraph is written so well that you feel you cannot summarize it any better? Then you must use a direct quotation.

Being able to choose and include a proper quotation is essential in a number of different contexts. In addition to writers of research papers, attorneys preparing written arguments ("briefs") and journalists writing news articles know that including a key quotation—and doing so properly—can dramatically improve the impact of a document.

Direct quotations use the exact words of the source. Sometimes you will read a passage with insights that are so precise, clear, or moving that you will want to repeat them exactly. A direct quotation is a word-for-word copy of the original. As with summary and paraphrase, direct quotations need to be properly cited according to whichever citation style you are using.

General Principles for Quoting Text

1. **Quote accurately.** Too often, original sentences such as "Leonard Cohen recorded *Songs of Love and Hate* in 1971" become "Lenard Coen recorded Songs of Love and hat in 1791." Check your transcription to avoid introducing errors. In the real world, you can be sued for misquoting someone.

2. **Preserve the integrity of your sources.** Never omit text in a way that changes the meaning of a quotation; if a quotation doesn't support your point, don't try to "reshape" it so that it does. (Later in the chapter, we indicate how to remove unnecessary text from a quotation.)

3. **Give full credit to your sources.** This example explains how to avoid plagiarism. Reread this example if you are still unclear about what constitutes plagiarism.

4. **Don't try to merge text from different parts of a source into one quotation.** For example, connecting a sentence from page 5 with one from page 16 by using an ellipsis (. . .) is intellectually dishonest. Instead, introduce and quote the first sentence, followed by its citation; then introduce and quote the second one, followed by its citation, as in the following example (which follows MLA guidelines):

   > Cohen points out that the winters in his boyhood were difficult. "I grew up in some of the worst weather in the twentieth century," he writes (Smith 29). Later, he reiterates his point: "My grandmother told me that she had never seen winters so cold" (Smith 55).

5. **Don't over-quote.** Use paraphrase and summary when appropriate, rather than overusing direct quotations.

6. **When you are writing an essay using quotations, don't refer to them as "quotes."** *Quote* is a verb, not a noun. If you need to refer to text that you have quoted, call it a *statement*, a *passage*, or a *quotation*, not a *quote*.

7. **Use signal phrases where possible.** Signal phrases use the author's name or some contextual details to introduce quoted material and provide an excellent blending tool. For example, *Jones states that* "signal phrases make for smoother writing" (77).

8. **Find out which style your professor expects** to see you use for quoting and citing your sources—MLA or APA—and follow it to the letter. The rest of this chapter will be devoted to a summary of these rules as they pertain to integrating direct quotations.

OCCUPY CANADA ESSAY CASE STUDY: CITATION ERRORS

In Chapter 2, we saw Leslie create a rough draft for her essay on the Occupy Canada movement. While it's understandable that her draft would have many errors in it, the number of times she borrows material from another source without proper citation is particularly alarming. Below is a small paragraph from this draft:

> Currently the unemployment rate in Canada is not that bad compared to the US, but the youth unemployment rate is 14.5%. In October of 2011, Canada lost 71 700 full-time jobs, many of them in "manufacturing and construction." One such example is the Electro-Motive plant (owned by Caterpillar Inc.) in London, Ontario, which recently closed its doors, forcing some 54 skilled employees out of work because they wouldn't take a 50% paycut. Another key aspect in the Occupy Canada movement is the income gap between workers and management.

source needed

source needed

source needed

Remember that any time you borrow material from another source—whether through summary, paraphrase, or direct quotation—you must properly document this material or you risk an academic offence.

See the end of Chapter 6 for a side-by-side comparison of Leslie's draft and the final revision where her citation errors are corrected.

MLA AND APA CITATION STYLES

The Modern Language Association (MLA) and the American Psychological Association (APA) have decided what methods of citation and essay formatting work best for their disciplines and have published these guidelines in their own handbooks, the *MLA Handbook for Writers of Research Papers,* seventh edition (2009), and the *Publication Manual of the American Psychological Association,* sixth edition (2009). Although there are other citation methods, such as Chicago style (used primarily in History departments), MLA and APA are the two most widely used citation styles. English and some of the other humanities use MLA, while social sciences such as psychology and sociology use APA. (If you were to try to use APA style in a paper analyzing a poem, you would run into an insurmountable problem: the APA *Publication Manual* offers no guidelines for citing poetry.) Your professor will tell you which style he or she expects you to follow.

Chapter 9 explains how to list source materials on a references page—using a Works Cited section in MLA format or a References page in APA format. In this chapter, however, we concentrate on how to quote text, along with how to handle basic citations of page numbers. We'll start with the MLA guidelines and then show how the same sample text would be treated in the APA system.

The examples in this section are taken from a paragraph that comes from George Orwell's essay "Shooting an Elephant." This paragraph is found on page 165 in Orwell's book *Shooting an Elephant and Other Essays*:

> The orderly came back in a few minutes with a rifle and five cartridges, and meanwhile some Burmans had arrived and told us that the elephant was in the paddy fields below, only a few hundred yards away. As I started forward practically the whole population of the quarter flocked out of the houses and followed me. They had seen the rifle and were all shouting excitedly that I was going to shoot the elephant. They had not shown much interest in the elephant when he was merely ravaging their homes, but it was different now that he was going to be shot. It was a bit of fun to them, as it would be to an English crowd; besides they wanted the meat. It made me vaguely uneasy. I had no intention of shooting the elephant—I had merely sent for the rifle to defend myself if necessary—and it is always unnerving to have a crowd following you. I marched down the hill, looking and feeling a fool, with the rifle over my shoulder and an ever-growing army of people jostling at my heels.

MLA Guidelines for Citations

MLA uses a **parenthetical documentation** system, also known as an **in-text citation** system. It involves citing sources in parentheses in the text of the paper. A parenthetical (in-text) documentation system such as the one used by MLA style identifies quickly and unobtrusively the source of any quotation, paraphrase, or summary used in the research paper. MLA discourages the use of notes, except for further explanations of concepts or citations included in the text.

Every MLA citation contains two pieces of information: the author of the work you are quoting from and the page number of the passage from which you are quoting.

Use Signal Phrases Correctly Quotations must be *connected* to your text, not detached from it. **Signal phrases,** such as "Orwell writes" in the example below, give the reader a connection—a context in which to understand the quotation you are citing.

> Orwell writes, "They had seen the rifle and were all shouting excitedly that I was going to shoot the elephant" (165).

The author cited is Orwell; the page from which the quotation has been taken is 165. The period follows the citation.

Alternatively, if you are not using the author's name in your signal phrase, the author's name must appear with the page number in parentheses.

> The narrator states that the natives "wanted the meat" (Orwell 165).

Citing summaries and paraphrases in MLA style requires the same approach, with the exception that no quotation marks are used.

> In his essay "Shooting an Elephant," Orwell discusses his uneasiness with his assigned task and the excitement of the natives, which drives him on (165).

When using a paraphrase or a summary, you should introduce the author's name first and finish with the page reference. Otherwise, the reader will not be able to tell when the paraphrase or summary begins and ends.

Integrate Direct Quotations Carefully Often students will simply drop a quotation next to their original sentence. The result is choppy writing that leaves too much for the reader to figure out. Your job as a writer is to make your points easily readable. Thus, combining, or **integrating,** your observation with the quotation by using an introductory or signal phrase provides a smoother experience.

INEFFECTIVE: DROPPED QUOTATION	The tension builds as Orwell receives the gun. "They had seen the rifle and were all shouting excitedly that I was going to shoot the elephant" (165).
EFFECTIVE: QUOTATION PRECEDED BY INTRODUCTORY PHRASE OR CLAUSE	**According to Orwell, "They had seen the rifle and were all shouting excitedly that [he] was going to shoot the elephant" (165).**

OR

Orwell notes with annoyance, "They had seen the rifle and were all shouting excitedly that I was going to shoot the elephant" (165).

Note the use of the **literary present tense** ("Orwell notes"), since unlike a historical event, literature is not something that happens once and is then over.

Vary Your Signal Words and Phrases Signal words and phrases connect quoted material to your own writing for a smoother experience. You are encouraged at all times to integrate your source material with your own writing. However, don't get caught using the same method over and over, which would be too repetitive. Previously we showed you the following sentence:

Orwell writes, "They had seen the rifle and were all shouting excitedly that I was going to shoot the elephant" (165).

Although the signal phrase "Orwell writes" is not incorrect, your writing would certainly get dull fast if you repeated this combination for every signal phrase. There are many verbs in the English language that can be used to introduce your points. Consult the chart below for a small sampling, but don't forget to use the thesaurus:

argues	disputes	presents	responds
asserts	documents	proposes	states
claims	explains	remarks	suggests
comments	notes	replies	supports
compares	observes	reports	writes

Colon vs. Comma vs. No Introductory Punctuation Most of the previous examples used a short signal phrase and a **comma** to introduce the quotation. Another effective way to introduce a quotation is with a introductory sentence followed by a **colon.**

The tension builds as Orwell receives the gun: "They had seen the rifle and were all shouting excitedly that I was going to shoot the elephant" (165).

The colon at the end of the first sentence indicates that the sentence is introducing the quotation. The words before the colon must make up a complete sentence.

Some students use a comma when they should use a colon and they end up making the error known as a **comma splice.**

> The tension builds as Orwell receives the gun, "They had seen the rifle and were all shouting excitedly that I was going to shoot the elephant" (165).

This writer has tried to join the quoted sentence with the preceding introductory sentence but has created a comma splice. (For more on commas and comma splices, see Chapter 12 in the Grammar Handbook)

Sometimes, you don't need to use either a comma or a colon to introduce a quotation. As long as the quotation fits with your own words to form a grammatically correct sentence, you may not need to add any introductory punctuation, although you will, of course, put the quoted words in quotation marks.

> According to Orwell, the locals "had seen the rifle and were all shouting excitedly that [he] was going to shoot the elephant" (165).

The square brackets around the word "he" in this example indicate that the writer made a change to the original quotation in order to fit the quotation grammatically into the text of his or her essay.

These methods of quoting from sources will help you integrate most source material successfully and add variety to your writing. In addition to these methods, the following guidelines for integrating more complicated material will help you use all quoted source material accurately and effectively.

Advanced Quoting Guidelines

1. **Quoting text containing dialogue.** On page 164 of "Shooting an Elephant," this sentence appears:

> There was a loud, scandalized cry of "Go away, child! Go away this instant!" and an old woman with a switch in her hand came round the corner of a hut, violently shooing away a crowd of naked children.

To indicate the quotation within this sentence, you need to change Orwell's double quotation marks to single quotation marks:

> According to Orwell, "there was a loud, scandalized cry of 'Go away, child! Go away this instant!' and an old woman with a switch in her hand came round the corner of a hut, violently shooing away a crowd of naked children" (164).

However, if you are quoting only the woman's speech, you can use double quotation marks:

> The woman seemed both angry and scared: "Go away, child! Go away this instant!" (164).

2. **Using quotation marks with exclamation points and question marks.** In the example above, the quoted sentence ends with an exclamation point. Note that the exclamation point precedes the closing quotation marks, the page citation, and the added period:

"Go away, child! Go away this instant!" (164).

A quotation that ends with a question mark is treated similarly: "Go away this instant?" (164).

If the exclamation point or question mark is not part of the quotation but ends your sentence that contains the quotation, it follows the closing quotation mark and page reference:

Ironically, Orwell notes that he "had no intention of shooting the elephant" (165)!

The essay writer, not Orwell, is exclaiming here.

3. **Omitting text with ellipses.** Well-chosen quotations can add authority and interest to your writing, but you do not need to quote text that is irrelevant to your point. Omitting extraneous text allows you to quote economically. Note this sentence:

Orwell writes, "They had seen the rifle and were all shouting excitedly that I was going to shoot the elephant" (165).

You might want to remove the end of the sentence:

Orwell writes, "They had seen the rifle and were all shouting excitedly. . . " (165).

The three dots, called an **ellipsis,** indicate that you have removed the end of the sentence. If you don't use these dots, you will be misrepresenting the quotation without letting readers know that you have altered it. To show readers that *you* (as opposed to the author of the quotation) have introduced an ellipsis, leave one space between each dot. If an ellipsis occurs in the original text that you are quoting, do not leave spaces.

If you are eliding (removing) text *within* the sentence, the ellipsis takes the place of the missing words:

The villagers' reaction was immediate: "They. . . were all shouting excitedly that I was going to shoot the elephant" (165).

However, *do not* use the ellipsis if you are removing the beginning of a single quoted sentence:

The villagers "were all shouting excitedly that I was going to shoot the elephant" (165).

In some situations, you may want to quote two adjacent sentences and elide part of one of them. Note how this procedure is done:

ORIGINAL PASSAGE	As I started forward practically the whole population of the quarter flocked out of the houses and followed me. They had seen the rifle and were all shouting excitedly that I was going to shoot the elephant.
QUOTED WITH AN ELLIPSIS	"As I started forward practically the whole population of the quarter flocked out of the houses and followed me. . . . shouting excitedly that I was going to shoot the elephant" (165).

Please note that an ellipsis used at the end of a sentence within a quotation (as in this example) needs four dots instead of just three (one for the period at the end of the sentence and three for the ellipsis).

Finally, you may start a quotation at any logical point in a sentence, but don't omit words in a way that will change the meaning of the sentence you are quoting.

4. **Quoting only a few words.** If you want to quote only a few words from a sentence, don't use the ellipsis; instead, embed the quotation within your sentence:

The concept of an elephant "merely ravaging" (165) a home is a terrifying understatement.

Note that the page reference here appears after the quotation, not at the end of the sentence.

5. **Using square brackets to add your own text.** The next-to-the last sentence in Orwell's paragraph is "He took not the slightest notice of the crowd's approach." Sentences that begin with pronouns can be difficult. (Who is "he"?) Note the following solution:

According to Orwell, "[The elephant] took not the slightest notice of the crowd's approach" (165).

The square brackets indicate that you are adding clarifying information.

Square brackets are also used to indicate an error—either a misspelling or an obvious factual problem—in text that you are quoting. Note the following example:

Smith writes that "George Owel [*sic*] was a great activist" (37).

The use of [*sic*], meaning "thus" (that's the way I found it), tells your reader that you know the source is incorrect.

6. **Using block quotations.** According to MLA guidelines, any passage that (a) consists of more than one paragraph or (b) takes up more than four lines in *your* text must be set off as a block quotation, or extract. Here are guidelines for displaying a block quotation:

- Don't add quotation marks before or after the quotation or alter any quotation marks that appear within the quotation.
- Start the extract on a new line with a block indent of about 3 centimetres from the left margin. With most word-processing programs, use a double-left indent. If you are quoting more than one paragraph, indent the first line of each paragraph an additional three spaces.
- Don't indent the right side of the quotation or attempt to centre the extract.
- Double-space the extract, and leave only a double space above and below it.
- A block quotation should be introduced (integrated) in any of the same ways that a regular quotation can be correctly introduced.
- Place the page reference at the very end of the extract, after the terminal punctuation.

Note the following example:

Orwell writes of the building excitement:

> The orderly came back in a few minutes with a rifle and five cartridges, and meanwhile some Burmans had arrived and told us that the elephant was in the paddy fields below, only a few hundred yards away. As I started forward practically the whole population of the quarter flocked out of the houses and followed me. They had seen the rifle and were all shouting excitedly that I was going to shoot the elephant. (165)

Use block quotations sparingly. Never use them as a way to lengthen your paper—your instructor will not be fooled.

7. **Citing page numbers.** In all of the examples above, note that only a number appears in the parentheses to indicate the page in the source on which the quoted text appears. Do *not* add *page, pg., p.,* or *pp.* If a passage begins on one page and continues to another, then you should indicate the page break this way:

. . . last word" (41–42).

. . . last word" (161–62).

Note that the second hundreds digit is dropped if it is the same as the first one (161–162 becomes 161–62).

EXERCISE 3.1

1. The following passage is excerpted from an article written by Jason Fletcher and published in a regional magazine. The full article appears on pages 22–23 of the magazine. A student wrote an analysis of Fletcher's article; part of this analysis appears after the excerpt.

First, read the excerpt. Then read the student's response, which contains ten errors in quoting from Fletcher's article. Don't try to edit the response, but look for instances in which the student did not follow proper MLA quoting procedure, and correct the student's errors.

The debate over Internet content rages on. The defenders of "freedom of choice" make up one side, and those who would protect young people and traditional standards of morality make up the other.

In the early days of widespread Internet access, several lessons were learned. For example, Wynton's, an upscale grocery chain, offered free Internet access at each of its stores. The practice was stopped when several instances of shoppers' children accessing porn sites brought objections from both the parents and other concerned shoppers. In another instance, the Maple County Library system chose to radically restrict the range of Internet access it provided after complaints of hard-core porn images beaming into the face of every patron who walked past the terminals. According to an assistant librarian, "It was like walking through an adult bookstore."

Do we want to let adults make adult decisions? Certainly.

Do we want to protect children from clearly inappropriate subject matter? Certainly.

The Internet offers a whole new world of information and communication, but it offers serious problems as well. How will we reconcile these two issues?

Student's Analysis of Fletcher's Article

Fletcher's writing is on the debate between the free speech crowd and the morality groups. He states "How will we reconcile these two issues." (23) Parents want to protect their children, and adults want to protect their own personal rights to access adult material.

It's true that Internet content can pose problems in public places; libraries, for instance. Before a local library changed its policy, Fletcher quotes the assistant librarian as describing the situation this way, "It was like walking through an adult bookstore" (23). However, the rights of adults need to be considered as well. The main downfall of Fletcher's writing is he refuses to take a stand. "Do we want to let adults make decisions? Certainly. Do we want to keep children from clearly inappropriate subject matter? Certainly" (23)

Fletcher seems to back the morality groups, and to discount the needs of, "defenders of 'freedom of choice'"(22). However, he needs to state his case more forcefully and not be afraid to take a stand.

2. After correcting the quotation errors in the student's response, revise it so that it is a more effective, coherent, and unified analysis of the passage.

NOTE

At the end of this chapter, you will find another exercise that allows students to apply MLA documentation and the concepts of summary, paraphrase, and quotation integration. Students will write a response to the article "Quebec: From Quiet Revolution to not-so-quiet student riot."

APA Guidelines for Citations

APA also uses a **parenthetical documentation** system for citing outside sources, but the APA format differs from MLA primarily in its inclusion of the date of publication as part of the parenthetical citation. Like MLA, APA relies on parenthetical citing and discourages the uses of notes, except for further explanations of concepts or citations included in the text.

Every APA citation must contain three pieces of information: the author of the work you are quoting from, the year of publication of the source material, and the page number of the passage from which you quoting.

The examples below are the same as those used in the MLA section, reworked to follow the APA guidelines for citations.

Use Signal Words and Phrases Correctly Quotations must be *connected* to your text; use signal phrases to connect quotations to your own ideas.

Orwell (1950) writes, "They had seen the rifle and were all shouting excitedly that I was going to shoot the elephant" (p. 165).

The author cited is Orwell, the essay was published in 1950, the page from which the quotation has been taken is 165, and the number is preceded by *p*. (Use *pp*. for a quotation that spans more than one page in the source text.) The period follows the citation.

Alternatively, if not using the author's name as a signal word, the full APA citation must appear in parentheses at the end of the quotation, as in the following example:

> The narrator states that the natives "wanted the meat" (Orwell, 1950, p. 165).

Parenthetically citing summaries and paraphrases requires almost the same approach, with the exception that page numbers are recommended, but not required.

> In his essay "Shooting an Elephant," Orwell (1950) discusses his uneasiness with his assigned task and the excitement of the natives which drives him on (p. 165).

Integrate Direct Quotations Carefully Students will sometimes simply drop a quotation next to their original sentence. The result is choppy writing that leaves too much for the reader to figure out. Your job as a writer is to make your points easy to follow and understand. Thus, combining, or **integrating,** your observation with the quotation by using an introductory or signal phrase provides a smoother experience.

INEFFECTIVE: DROPPED QUOTATION	The tension builds as Orwell (1950) receives the gun. "They had seen the rifle and were all shouting excitedly that I was going to shoot the elephant" (p. 165).
EFFECTIVE: QUOTATION PRECEDED BY INTRODUCTORY PHRASE OR CLAUSE	**According to Orwell (1950), "They had seen the rifle and were all shouting excitedly that I was going to shoot the elephant" (p. 165).**
	OR
	As Orwell (1950) notes with annoyance, "They had seen the rifle and were all shouting excitedly that I was going to shoot the elephant" (p. 165).

Vary Your Signal Words and Phrases Signal words and phrases connect quoted material to your own writing for a smoother experience. You are encouraged at all times to integrate your source material with your own writing. However, don't get caught using the same method over and over, which would be repetitive. Previously we showed you the following sentence:

> Orwell (1950) writes, "They had seen the rifle and were all shouting excitedly that I was going to shoot the elephant" (p. 165).

Although the signal phrase "Orwell writes" is not incorrect, your writing would certainly get dull fast if you repeated this combination for every signal phrase. Remember, there are many verbs in the English language that can be used to introduce your points. Consult the chart below for a small sampling, but don't forget to use the thesaurus:

argues	disputes	presents	responds
asserts	documents	proposes	states
claims	explains	remarks	suggests
comments	notes	replies	supports
compares	observes	reports	writes

Colon vs. Comma vs. No Introductory Punctuation Most of the previous examples used a short signal phrase and a **comma** to introduce the quotation. Another effective way to introduce a quotation is with a **colon.**

> The tension builds as Orwell (1950) receives the gun: "They had seen the rifle and were all shouting excitedly that I was going to shoot the elephant" (p. 165).

The colon at the end of the first sentence indicates that the sentence is introducing the quotation. The sentence before the colon must be complete before the quoted text begins.

Some students use a comma instead of a colon and end up making the error known as a **comma splice.**

> The tension builds as Orwell (1950) receives the gun, "They had seen the rifle and were all shouting excitedly that I was going to shoot the elephant" (p. 165).

This writer has tried to join the quoted sentence with the preceding, introductory sentence but has created a comma splice. (For more on commas, see Chapter 16. For more on comma splices, see Chapter 12 in the Grammar Handbook.)

Advanced Quoting Guidelines

1. **Quoting text containing dialogue.** On page 164 of "Shooting an Elephant," this sentence appears:

> There was a loud, scandalized cry of "Go away, child! Go away this instant!" and an old woman with a switch in her hand came round the corner of a hut, violently shooing away a crowd of naked children.

To indicate the quotation within this sentence, you need to change Orwell's double quotation marks to single quotation marks:

> According to Orwell (1950), "There was a loud, scandalized cry of 'Go away, child! Go away this instant!' and an old woman with a switch in her hand came round the corner of a hut, violently shooing away a crowd of naked children" (p. 164).

However, if you are quoting only the woman's speech, you can use double quotation marks:

> The woman seemed both angry and scared: "Go away, child! Go away this instant!" (Orwell, 1950, p. 164).

2. **Using quotation marks with exclamation points and question marks.** In the example above, the quoted sentence ends with an exclamation point. Note that the exclamation point precedes the closing quotation marks, the page citation, and the added period:

> The woman seemed both angry and scared: "Go away, child! Go away this instant!" (Orwell, 1950, p. 164).

A quotation that ends with a question mark is treated similarly:

> "Go away this instant?" (Orwell, 1950, p. 164).

If the exclamation point or question mark is not part of the quotation but ends the sentence you wrote to contain the quotation, it follows the closing quotation mark and page reference:

Ironically, Orwell (1950) notes that he "had no intention of shooting the elephant" (p. 165)!

The writer, not Orwell, is exclaiming here.

3. **Omitting text with ellipses.** Well-chosen quotations can add authority and interest to your writing, but you do not need to quote text that is irrelevant to your point. Omitting extraneous text allows you to quote economically.

Note this sentence:

They had seen the rifle and were all shouting excitedly that I was going to shoot the elephant.

You might want to remove the end of the sentence:

Orwell (1950) writes that "they had seen the rifle and were all shouting excitedly" (p. 165).

You might want to remove the beginning of the sentence:

The villagers "were all shouting excitedly that I was going to shoot the elephant." (Orwell, 1950, p. 165).

Note that if you are using APA style, you may omit the beginning of a single quoted sentence and/or the end without indicating that you have done so, unless, perhaps to avoid misinterpretation, you need to let readers know that you are not using the whole sentence. In that case, you will need to indicate an omission; you will need to use an **ellipsis**—three dots in a row to show that you have removed text in a sentence. To show readers that *you* (as opposed to the author of the quotation) have introduced an ellipsis, leave one space between each dot. If an ellipsis occurs in the original text that you are quoting, do not leave spaces.

If you are omitting text *within* the sentence, the ellipsis must be used to take the place of the missing words:

The villagers' reaction was immediate: "They . . . were all shouting excitedly that I was going to shoot the elephant" (Orwell, 1950, p. 165).

In some situations, you may want to quote two adjacent sentences and elide part of one of them. Note how this procedure is done:

ORIGINAL PASSAGE	As I started forward practically the whole population of the quarter flocked out of the houses and followed me. They had seen the rifle and were all shouting excitedly that I was going to shoot the elephant.
QUOTED WITH AN ELLIPSIS	"As I started forward practically the whole population of the quarter flocked out of the houses and followed me. . . . shouting excitedly that I was going to shoot the elephant" (Orwell, 1950, p. 165)

Please note that an ellipsis used at the end of a sentence (as in this example) needs four dots instead of just three.

Finally, you may start a quotation at any logical point in a sentence, but don't omit words in a way that will change the meaning of the sentence you are quoting!

4. **Quoting only a few words.** If you want to quote only a few words from a sentence, don't use the ellipsis; instead, embed the quotation within your sentence:

The concept of an elephant "merely ravaging" (Orwell, 1950, p. 165) a home is a terrifying understatement.

5. **Using square brackets to add your own text.** The next-to-last sentence in Orwell's paragraph is "He took not the slightest notice of the crowd's approach." Sentences that begin with pronouns can be difficult. (Who is "he"?) Note the following solution:

According to Orwell (1950), "[the elephant] took not the slightest notice of the crowd's approach" (p. 165).

The square brackets indicate that you are adding clarifying information.

Square brackets are also used to indicate an error—either a misspelling or an obvious factual problem—in text that you are quoting. Note the following examples:

Smith (2007) writes that "George Owel [*sic*] was a great activist" (37).

The use of [*sic*], meaning "thus" (that's the way I found it), tells your reader that you know the source is incorrect.

6. **Using block quotations.** According to APA guidelines, any passage that consists of more than one paragraph or contains more than forty words must be set off as a block quotation, or extract. Here are guidelines for displaying a block quotation:

- Don't add quotation marks before or after the quotation or alter any quotation marks that appear within the quotation.
- Start the extract on a new line with a block indent of one centimetre from the left margin, which is the default tab indent of most word processing programs. If you are quoting more than one paragraph, indent subsequent paragraphs one centimetre.
- Don't indent the right side of the quotation or attempt to centre the extract.
- Double-space the extract, and leave only a double space above and below it.
- Place the page reference at the very end of the extract, after the terminal punctuation.

Note the following example:

Orwell (1950) writes of the building excitement:

The orderly came back in a few minutes with a rifle and five cartridges, and meanwhile some Burmans had arrived and told us that the elephant was in the paddy fields below, only a few hundred yards away. As I started forward practically the whole population of the quarter flocked out of the houses and followed me. They had seen the rifle and were all shouting excitedly that I was going to shoot the elephant. (p. 165)

Use block quotations sparingly. Never use them as a way to lengthen your paper.

7. *Citing multiple page numbers.* Note that if a passage begins on one page and continues to another, then you should indicate the page break this way:

. . . last word" (pp. 161–162).

. . . last word" (pp. 41–42).

EXERCISE 3.2

1. The following passage is excerpted from an article written by Jason Fletcher and published in a regional magazine. The full article appears on pages 22–23 of the magazine. A student wrote an analysis of Fletcher's article; part of this analysis appears after the excerpt.

   First, read the excerpt. Then read the student's response, which contains ten errors in quoting from Fletcher's article. Don't try to edit or "smooth out" the response, but look for instances in which the student did not follow proper APA quoting procedure, and correct the student's errors.

   The debate over Internet content rages on. The defenders of "freedom of choice" make up one side, and those who would protect young people and traditional standards of morality make up the other.

   In the early days of widespread Internet access, several lessons were learned. For example, Wynton's, an upscale grocery chain, offered free Internet access at each of its stores. The practice was stopped when several instances of shoppers' children accessing porn sites brought objections from both the parents and other concerned shoppers. In another instance, the Maple County Library system chose to radically restrict the range of Internet access it provided after complaints of hard-core porn images beaming into the face of every patron who walked past the terminals. According to an assistant librarian, "It was like walking through an adult bookstore."

   Do we want to let adults make adult decisions? Certainly.

   Do we want to protect children from clearly inappropriate subject matter? Certainly.

   The Internet offers a whole new world of information and communication, but it offers serious problems as well. How will we reconcile these two issues?

Student's Analysis of Fletcher's Article

Fletcher's writing (1998) is on the debate between the free speech crowd and the morality groups. He states, "How will we reconcile these two issues" (p. 23). Parents want to protect their children, and adults want to protect their own personal rights to access adult material.

It's true that Internet content can pose problems in public places; libraries, for instance. Before a local library changed its policy, Fletcher quotes the assistant librarian as describing the situation this way, "It was like walking through an adult bookstore" (p. 23). However, the rights of adults need to be considered as well. The main downfall of Fletcher's writing is he refuses to take a stand. "Do we want to let adults make decisions? Certainly. Do we want to keep children from clearly inappropriate subject matter? Certainly" (p. 23).

Fletcher seems to back the morality groups, and to discount the needs of, "defenders of 'freedom of choice'" (p. 22). However, he needs to state his case more forcefully, and not be afraid to take a stand.

2. After correcting the quoting errors in the student's response, revise it so that it is a more effective, coherent, and unified analysis of the passage.

A READER'S EYE

QUEBEC: FROM QUIET REVOLUTION TO NOT-SO-QUIET STUDENT RIOT
Alex Ballingall

Alex Ballingall is currently a reporter with the Toronto Star. *He writes about "music, politics and all things quirky and interesting." This article appeared on* Macleans.ca *on May 11, 2012.*

1   For more than 12 weeks, tens of thousands of Quebec students have taken to the streets in anger and frustration. They've hurled slogans from worn-out vocal cords, sung and danced and taken their clothes off. Protesters threw stones, smashed windows and clashed with riot police, all in an effort to halt the government's proposal to increase tuition $1,625 over the next five to seven years.

2   Students began walking out on their classes in February. More than three months later, the dispute has become the longest student strike in Quebec history. The stubborn persistence of the strike has left many in the rest of Canada scratching their heads over why there's been such uproar. Even in Quebec, the intensity of the protests has puzzled observers. "The whole political and media class has been taken by surprise," says Eric Pineault, a sociologist at the Université de Quebec à Montréal (UQAM). Quebecers currently enjoy the lowest tuition in the country. And never mind that with Premier Jean Charest's proposed hike, the average tuition in Quebec would then be the second-lowest in Canada. Yet more than 165,000 students are on strike indefinitely. Many of them will lose their semester if they don't head back to class soon. How did the movement attain such strength and longevity?

3   The answer lies largely with a particular thrust in Quebec society that links ideals of social democracy—such as widely affordable university education—to a sense of national identity. These ties date back to the Quiet Revolution of the 1960s, a time when Quebecers became *maîtres,* or masters, of their own province, instituting changes that gave Quebec a more left-leaning bent than elsewhere in North America. "The Quiet Revolution is a very important moment in Quebec history," says André Pratte, editor of Montreal's *La Presse* newspaper. "Every time someone questions the decisions that were made at the time, it's almost as if you are trying to destroy a very important part of that moment."

4   The era spawned the Parent report, a document that created the province's tuition-free colleges (called CEGEPs) and founded its network of universities. At the core of the report lay a dedication to make post-secondary education free for all Quebecers.

5   In the years since, as tuition fees gradually climbed in English Canada and the United States, Quebec students have repeatedly taken to the streets to defend the spirit of the Parent report. "Our parents and our grandparents fought for it," says Fédération étudiante universitaire du Québec (FEUQ) president Martine Desjardins. "We are very proud of this."

6   Even so, as the strike drags on, many might wonder why the parents of protesting Quebecers haven't been more vocal about the conflict. Shouldn't they be upset that their kids might lose a semester, especially if they're footing the bill? It might be because the amount of money on the line is so insignificant; indeed, many Quebec students are completely self-sufficient. But parental tolerance for the lengthy strike also reflects a culture of student protests that spans generations. Just as they took to the streets to protest in decades past, now many of them see it as the duty of their children to do the same.

7   On May 3, protesters incorporated a new theme to their nightly march, eschewing most of their clothes. "We needed to find new methods to shock and bother people without the use of violence," explains Eric Chalut, 23, wearing nothing but a thong. Many marching with him had the protest movement's symbolic red squares—representing antipathy to student debt—painted over their nipples and butt cheeks. Others covered themselves with little else than underwear, a jock strap or a single sock. They carried beer cans and draped their arms over each other's shoulders, while the odd skunky cloud of smoke indicated another joint of marijuana had been lit. "The students have shown a determination that's rare in the history of social movements," says Antoine Bouchard, 20, a history student at UQÀM. "We have nothing left to lose. We will keep going until the very end."

8   That end could be on the horizon. The student movement is showing cracks. Several CEGEPs voted to go back to class last week, while a poll published in *La Presse* found that 68 per cent of Quebecers support the government's plan to raise tuition.

EXERCISE 3.3

After reading "Quebec: From Quiet Revolution to not-so-quiet student riot," write a response paper agreeing or disagreeing with the students' reasons for the strike and their tactics used in the strike. Use either MLA or APA documentation (depending on your professor's instructions) and include all of the following techniques as discussed in this chapter:

1) Summarize a portion of the article.
2) Paraphrase a portion of the article.
3) Integrate a quotation from the article using a colon.
4) Integrate a quotation from the article using at least two different signal phrases.
5) Integrate a quotation from the article using an ellipsis.
6) Integrate a very small quotation that uses only a few words from the original article.

Using the Internet

Go to these websites to find more tips, techniques, and insights on MLA and APA citation styles, as well as information on preventing plagiarism:

Plagiarism.org

This website's mission is to "prevent plagiarism and restore integrity to written work." It does this by giving students a thorough definition of plagiarism (complete with examples) along with tips and strategies on how to avoid it. Also, be sure to click on the link to the WriteCheck website—a Turnitin.com-type website for students that allows you to submit your essay to an online database to check for plagiarism.
http://www.plagiarism.org/

California State University of Long Beach

The library webpage for the California State University of Long Beach has a wealth of articles detailing why students plagiarize as well as commentary from various academics on other aspects of this notorious issue.
http://csulb.libguides.com/infoethics

College and University Policy Sites

Academic institutions usually place their policies regarding plagiarism (and its consequences) on their websites. The following links explain these policies and the disciplinary actions taken for selected institutions:

Kwantlen Polytechnic University: **http://www.kwantlen.ca/policies/C-LearnerSupport/c08.pdf**

University of BC: **http://www.arts1.arts.ubc.ca/arts-one-program/ubc-plagiarism-policy.html**

University of Manitoba: **http://www.umanitoba.ca/student/resource/student_advocacy/cheating_plagiarism_fraud.html**

George Brown College: **http://www.georgebrown.ca/Current_Students/Registrars_Office/Academic_Policies_(PDF)/Student_Code_of_Conduct_and_Discipline_Policy.aspx**

Western University: **http://www.uwo.ca/ombuds/student/cheating.html**

Fanshawe College: **http://www.fanshawec.ca/admissions/registrars-office/policies/cheating-policy**

Citation Machine and Refworks

If you just can't remember if the period goes before or after the bracket, Citation Machine can help. Students choose their desired citation style, fill in all publication information into blank template fields, and submit; Citation Machine then spits out your Works Cited or References entries in the proper order. Citation Machine, however, is not perfect and can sometimes make errors. Thus, always consult a writing guide when checking over your citations. For a more precise program—albeit one that isn't free—check out Refworks.
http://citationmachine.net/
http://www.refworks.com

Online Writing Lab from Purdue University

MLA and APA are discussed everywhere online; however, the first (and best) hit that Google supplies is the Purdue Online Writing Lab (OWL). This website provides proper, up-to-date MLA or APA formatting for every type of source material available, whether electronic or printed. The site also gives numerous writing tips, including information on how to properly paraphrase and summarize work.
http://owl.english.purdue.edu/

Developing Strong Paragraphs: Exploring Your Options

DEVELOPING PARAGRAPHS
in the Real World

Paragraphs rarely stand alone. Maybe you'll read the paragraph on the back of a DVD to know what the film is about or you'll browse a paragraph that describes the functions of a particular product. Most paragraphs, however, are components of larger works of writing that have their own purposes. In short written documents, you'll usually see an introductory paragraph followed by body paragraphs and ending with a concluding paragraph. You'll see this format repeatedly used in memo, article, and essay writing. A paragraph is not merely a collection of random sentences; rather, a paragraph builds on an idea to accomplish a specific purpose.

LEARNING OUTCOMES:

- ▶ Apply organization, coherence, and unity within paragraphs
- ▶ Use effective transitional words when creating paragraphs
- ▶ Write effective paragraphs for specific purposes, such as introductions, conclusions, and various rhetorical options
- ▶ Create effective topic sentences

WHAT IS A PARAGRAPH?

Rather than viewing writing and words as abstract concepts, let's use the analogy of bricklaying to discuss the importance of paragraphing. Words can be compared to bricks. Each row of freshly laid bricks can be compared to lines of sentences. Rows of bricks upon one another form a wall—this is your paragraph. Paragraphs are the walls holding up your essay.

Carefully developed paragraphs are the essential components of effective writing. Without them, the logic and persuasiveness of your essay will collapse; and even Mike Holmes will not be able to make your essay "right."

THE ACADEMIC PARAGRAPH

Length

Paragraphs in academic essays are often longer and more developed than paragraphs in other types of writing. Paragraphs in works of fiction can be very short—sometimes just one or two sentences. Similarly, paragraphs in journalism—whether in magazines or newspapers—or paragraphs in business—such as in memos and emails—are often just as short. Because of their length, these pieces of writing can contain *several* paragraphs *on a single page.*

However, one- and two-sentence "paragraphs" are inappropriate for academic writing. In academic writing, paragraphs are longer: they introduce and develop one specific idea, and they contain numerous examples to achieve their purpose. As you write, keep in mind that if you're hitting the <Enter> key every two sentences or so, chances are that you are not writing academic paragraphs.

Style

Paragraphs in fiction, journalism, and business are often written in a style that is unsuitable for academic writing. As discussed in Chapter 1, determining your purpose and identifying your audience are essential when determining the style of your writing. Certain strategies for engaging a reader when introducing a topic may not be appropriate for all kinds of writing; for example, anecdotes, questions, and provocative statements may not suit the reader of your academic essay.

ANATOMY OF A PARAGRAPH

Students sometimes wonder how many sentences make up a paragraph (since we've already established that two are not enough). There is no official rule that says "a paragraph is X sentences long—no more, and no less." However, as a general guideline, a single paragraph should not take up an entire page. There are also certain component parts that must be included in each and every academic paragraph. They are as follows:

Topic sentence: A topic sentence, quite simply, introduces the topic of your paragraph. It launches the paragraph and sets the tone for its purpose. It should be specific and direct. It should also be strong enough that it invites supporting points.

Supporting sentences: The supporting sentences in a paragraph must naturally build on the topic sentence. If the paragraph's supporting sentences have nothing to do with the topic sentence or if they go off on another topic, the purpose of the paragraph is lost. Thus, supporting sentences should be *specific examples relating to the topic sentence*—whether facts or quotations from secondary sources. More support—or more proof—in the body of your paragraph is always better than less.

Concluding/transitional sentence: Paragraphs should not end abruptly. Just as the conclusion of an essay should sum up the ideas contained within that essay, so too should the final sentence in a paragraph try to provide a summation of the ideas contained within that paragraph. Even better, a more effective concluding sentence will hint at ideas contained in the next paragraph, for a smoother transition.

OCCUPY CANADA ESSAY CASE STUDY: PARAGRAPHING

In Chapter 2, we saw Leslie create a rough draft for her essay on the Occupy Canada movement. Her final revision appears at the end of Chapter 5; however, let's take a look at one of the revised paragraphs right now and examine its component parts. As mentioned, while there is no rule on how many sentences make up an academic paragraph, please note that the following example is six sentences long.

> Unemployment and job opportunities are central issues in the Occupy Canada movement. Currently the unemployment rate in Canada is 7.3% ("Labour Force Survey, April 2012") and "while youth unemployment here is not as bad as in Europe or the U.S . . . people in Canada are still facing a future of McJobs and declining social services". Currently, the youth unemployment rate is 14.5% ("Government scraps"); however, one need not be young to feel the effects of a dwindling job market. In October of 2011, Canada lost 71 700 full-time jobs, many of them in "manufacturing and construction" ("Canada suffers"). One such example is the Electro-Motive plant (owned by Caterpillar Inc.) in London, Ontario, which recently closed its doors, forcing some 540 skilled employees out of work (Size). Previous to the plant closing, workers had been locked out because they refused to take a 50% pay reduction (Size)—a situation which highlights another key issue in the Occupy Canada movement: the income gap between workers and management.

Clear topic sentence, directly related to thesis point.

Background information and supporting point.

Transition: "however"

Supporting point.

Specific example relating to supporting point.

Concluding/transitional sentence.

ACHIEVING UNITY IN PARAGRAPHS

A paragraph needs to develop one idea. When a paragraph has done this successfully, it is said to be unified. Lack of **unity** hinders many student writers because paragraphs with unity problems are frequently the result of poor planning and no sense of purpose.

The Directionless Paragraph

Part of the preparation/prewriting step is determining your purpose for writing. If you want to produce a unified result, you must first know the effect that you intend to produce with a paragraph or an essay.

The following paragraph is a good example of what happens when someone starts writing on a subject without prewriting and without determining a specific purpose:

> Food is important. People need food to live. Many people live without food. The best kind of food is green leafy vegetables. These foods help fight cancer. Cancer is a very problematic disease. Many Canadians will die of cancer. High blood pressure is also a concern. Foods high in saturated fats and salt increase blood pressure. French fries, although popular, are some of the worst foods one can eat.

This paragraph staggers around like a child just learning to walk. What is the writer's purpose? If it is to point out which foods are healthiest, it fails. If it is to list the major diseases caused by poor eating habits, it fails as well. There is no sense of order here.

Let's assume that the purpose of this paragraph is the first one: to list which foods are healthiest. Using a classification strategy for development, the writer can revise the paragraph so that it is unified:

> To eat healthily, one needs to pay attention to Canada's Food Guide. The most important category is fruits and vegetables. Adult males and females are recommended to have 7–10 servings of fruits and vegetables a day. The best types of vegetables to eat are those that are dark green, as they possess the highest amount of antioxidants and other cancer-fighting nutrients.

This paragraph needs to be further developed, but you can see the difference. The paragraph begins with a solid **topic sentence** and builds upon its main ideas from there.

Avoiding Digressions

Another problem with unity occurs when a writer has a clear purpose for a paragraph but includes irrelevant statements within it, leading the reader off the track of the paragraph's central idea. Called **digressions,** these wanderings distract and confuse a reader who is expecting the paragraph to illustrate the development of a single idea. Let's look at another version of the above paragraph:

> To eat healthily, one needs to pay attention to Canada's Food Guide. **Most students learn about Canada's Food Guide in health class. Students receive the handout and are sent home with a new outlook on life.** The most important category is fruits and vegetables. **Some people like fruits more than vegetables because they are sweeter.** Adult males and females are recommended to have 7–10 servings of fruits and vegetables a day. **This seems like a lot, but it's the rule!** The best types of vegetables to eat are those that are dark green, as they possess the highest amount of antioxidants and other cancer-fighting nutrients.

The sentences highlighted in bold are unnecessary because they distract the reader from the paragraph's main point, instead of supporting it.

EXERCISE 4.1

The following paragraphs lack unity. Read each and underline the sentences that lead the text in the wrong direction. Then revise the paragraph to correct the problem.

1. The dog is the most useful creature humanity has ever known. Farmers and ranchers, in particular, have made great use of dogs. Dogs can be used to herd sheep and to help in the herding of horses. Horses themselves are quite useful agrarian animals. So is the mule, which is the offspring of a male donkey and a female horse, and the hinny, which is the offspring of a male horse and a female donkey. Oxen have also been used on farms and ranches. Dogs in rural areas can be used to guard property against trespassers and to help control vermin. Cats can also be used to control vermin, but not to repel intruders.

2. My roommate had his semester fall apart on him this weekend. However, he has only himself to blame. Mike is taking three classes and working thirty hours a week. On Friday afternoon, he got his latest calculus test back and found that he got a 51. Now he probably can't pass the course. Calculus is one of the hardest courses for many students at this school. Of course, it's not as boring as statistics, but that's its only saving grace. Mike tried to cheer himself up, so he went out to a local club that night and didn't get back until 4:00 a.m. A good band was playing at the Emerald, which is one of my favourite night spots. They have great specials and attract the best crowds in town. Mike stayed much too long and then came home and slept until 2:30 p.m. When he awoke, he found a message on the answering machine from his boss, letting Mike know that he had been fired for missing work. On both Saturday night and Sunday night, Mike also hit the club scene. On Monday, he managed to sleep through both his biology exam and the deadline for his research paper in Comp 2. Someone should have a talk with him about getting some help over at the counselling centre.

ACHIEVING COHERENCE

When someone is trying to talk and is babbling or cannot form words, the person is said to be incoherent. In terms of paragraph development, however, **coherence** has a more technical meaning. A paragraph is coherent when the writer has succeeded in guiding the reader through the text. The most common technique that will help you achieve coherence in your paragraphs is using effective transitions.

Transitions within Paragraphs

Transitions are text markers—words and phrases that guide the reader through the text. Think of them as signs indicating where the logic of your argument is going next. When a paragraph does not include transitions, the reader faces a string of

unconnected sentences and is forced to impose order on and make connections among the various thoughts without the writer's help.

Your reader shouldn't have to go back and reread your sentences—in other words, your writing should contain clearly marked transitions that allow the reader to make the right connections the first time that he or she approaches your text. Transitions make these connections for readers.

TRANSITIONAL EXPRESSIONS	
Relationship	Expression
Addition	also, in addition, too, moreover, and, besides, furthermore, equally important, then, finally
Example	for example, for instance, thus, as an illustration, namely, specifically
Contrast	but, yet, however, on the other hand, while, nevertheless, nonetheless, conversely, in contrast, still, at the same time
Comparison	similarly, likewise, in the same way
Concession	of course, to be sure, certainly, granted
Time	first, second, third, next, then, finally, afterwards, before, soon, later, meanwhile, subsequently, immediately, eventually, currently
Location	in the front, in the foreground, in the back, in the background, at the side, adjacent, nearby, next to, in the distance, here, there, to the left, to the right, inside, outside
Result	therefore, thus, as a result, so, accordingly
Summary	hence, in short, in brief, in summary, in conclusion, finally

Effective transitions are one of the true marks of good writing—and this technique is one of the most painless to master. Note the following paragraph, which uses no transitions at all:

Changing a tire is a useful skill to learn. It can save your life. Picture yourself on a deserted road. Your tire blows apart and you bring your vehicle to the side of the road. The person who knows how to change the tire gets to work and is home before the wolves attack. The person who does not know how to change the tire will likely sit in his or her car waiting for help—help that may never come. Be sure to learn how to change a tire.

This paragraph is written in a choppy style: Sentence. Stop. Sentence. Stop. Now see how adding transitional words and phrases improves the paragraph's coherence:

Changing a tire is a useful skill to learn. **Moreover,** it can save your life. **For example,** picture yourself on a deserted road. **Suddenly,** your tire blows apart and you bring your vehicle to the side of the road. **At this point,** the person who knows how to change the tire gets to work and is home before the wolves attack; **however,** the person who does not know how to change the tire will likely sit in his or her car waiting for help—help that may never come. **In short,** be sure to learn how to change a tire.

Transitions between Paragraphs

Using transition words to help make transitions between two separate paragraphs also helps provide coherence in your writing. Even students who have mastered the art of creating effective topic sentences often neglect to write these topic sentences in such a way that two adjacent paragraphs flow logically and inevitably from one another. Consider the following example and how the use of a transition word at the beginning of the second paragraph's topic sentence (in bold) creates a strong, more natural transition between the two paragraphs:

> Changing a tire is a useful skill to learn. Moreover, it can save your life. For example, picture yourself on a deserted road. Suddenly, your tire blows apart and you bring your vehicle to the side of the road. At this point, the person who knows how to change the tire gets to work and is home before the wolves attack; on the other hand, the person who does not know how to change the tire will likely sit in his or her car waiting for help—help that may never come. In short, be sure to learn how to change a tire.
>
> **However,** knowing how to change a tire is not the only survival skill necessary for the average traveller. Basic knowledge of proper oil and radiator gauge levels will also help you avoid unnecessary trouble on the road . . .

The transition word you choose will depend on what the next paragraph intends to accomplish. Will it add information (*in addition*), contrast information (*however*), or acknowledge a counter-argument (*to be sure*)? Its purpose will inform the transitional word you choose to begin it.

EXERCISE 4.2

The following paragraphs have very few transitions and, as a result, very little coherence. Revise each paragraph, adding transitional words and phrases from the Transitional Expressions chart to improve the paragraph's coherence.

1. Today, war is fought differently than it was in the past. Traditional combat depended on information gained from scouts and spies. These brave souls placed their lives in danger by infiltrating enemy lines or attacking exposed areas such as beaches or hills. Modern combat uses satellites and computers to get the job done. In the past, soldiers fought hand to hand and face to face. Soldiers today are frequently miles apart and never see their opponents up close. They are able to kill much more efficiently due to the technology at their command.

2. Colleges sometimes spend money like water. One need leads to another. I work as a student assistant for the Student Activities (SA) office, which recently launched a new and revamped intramural program. SA hired a new coordinator. She needed someone to answer the phone and handle written communication. She hired a secretary. The coordinator found that she could not trust the secretary to make decisions while she was away. She then hired a man to be her assistant. He is an organizational type who likes delegating authority. He hired two student assistants. First, we had one person hired to perform a function. Now we have five, all in the space of a month.

INTRODUCTORY PARAGRAPHS

An essay's introduction might consist of only one paragraph or, in the case of a very long or complex essay (which you will likely not write unless you attend graduate school), of more than one. In either case, the introduction serves three functions: to generate reader interest, to provide the background or context of the essay, and to indicate the **thesis statement,** the essay's controlling idea. (For a refresher on constructing thesis statements, see Chapter 2.)

Getting Your Reader's Attention

Students often forget that reading an essay should be enjoyable. Nobody likes to read boring writing, so your primary goal when writing your essay introduction should be to get your reader's attention. How can you do this? Writers use many different techniques. Notice the devices used by the writers of the following introductory paragraphs. Please note that depending on your **purpose** and **audience,** not all of these examples may be appropriate for an academic essay.

Using an Engaging Anecdote An anecdote is a short amusing story. However, be careful: if you choose to begin your introductory paragraph with an anecdote, be sure that it is still formal enough for an academic essay.

> David's birthday was last week. He turned nine. At his birthday party, he played board games and played baseball with his friends. Next week, he will take his birthday money and buy a copy of *Grand Theft Auto IV.* Very soon, he will be shooting police officers and dealing drugs, all in the comfort of his bedroom.

Here, the writer opens with an anecdote that is alarming in its use of contrast. The reader is instantly engaged.

Using a Provocative Statement A provocative statement is nothing more than a shocking claim posed by the writer. You may argue in defence of a claim, or you may use the claim as a launch pad to discuss reasons why the claim is false. For example, consider the following introduction:

> iPods have killed the music industry. Previous to the invention of the MP3 player, the music industry was thriving; however, once the iPod began to dominate the market, CD sales plummeted and record companies had to engage in mass layoffs.

This writer opens with an intentionally provocative statement to which the reader instantly reacts.

Questioning an Assumption In the next example, Bill Cosby opens his essay "The Baffling Question" by questioning the assumption that children are necessary for personal fulfillment:

> So you've decided to have a child. You've decided to give up quiet evenings with good books and lazy weekends with good music, intimate meals during which you finish whole sentences, sweet private times when you've savoured the

thought that just the two of you and your love are all you will ever need. You've decided to turn your sofas into trampolines and to abandon the joys of leisurely contemplating reproductions of great art for the joys of frantically coping with reproductions of yourselves. Why?

—from Bill Cosby, *Parenthood*

Cosby's essay then goes on to illustrate some of the joys of parenthood.

Using a Quotation Using an appropriate, possibly provocative quotation can lend a poetic or persuasive element to your introduction, if you do it correctly. Opening your essay with a quotation can be effective as long as you avoid too-general or over-used statements. Also, be sure to integrate the quotation properly into your text (as discussed in Chapter 3); don't just drop it in. The following example shows an awkward and very clichéd introduction:

"When it rains, it pours." Whoever first said that was right on track.

Instead, make sure you use a signal word or phrase to introduce your speaker, as in the example below:

In 1973, Pierre Trudeau looked into the hearts and minds of the nation when he declared, "Canada will be a strong country when Canadians of all provinces feel at home in all parts of the country, and when they feel that all Canada belongs to them" (*source required*).

Using a Compelling Statistic Beginning with an interesting statistic is a useful way to bring realism and urgency to your introduction.

About 70% of murders in the U.S. are committed with firearms, while in Canada firearms account for only 30% of murders (*source required*).

Remember that you are trying to engage your reader's attention, to make that person *want* to continue reading your essay. For this reason, you should *never* use a self-referential, heavy-handed approach ("This essay will attempt to prove . . ."). The guideline is simple: don't refer to your essay as an essay while you are writing it.

Note

Many of the statistics in this chapter's examples are fictitious and have been created for the purposes of this discussion. The notation "*source required*" indicates that you would need to provide a source if you were to use such a statistic in an essay. You would then follow the guidelines for whatever documentation system your professor or instructor requires. (See Chapters 3 and 17 for more details about documenting your sources.) The same is true of any place in this chapter where you see the words "*source required*."

Positioning the Thesis

The thesis statement often appears at or toward the end of the introduction. Placing the thesis at the end of the first paragraph gives your reader a clear road map of where your essay is going, as in the following example:

> Medical issues or lack of exercise are causes for obesity; however, one of the main causes of obesity in almost every culture is fast food. One only needs to drive downtown to see various logos dotting the landscape. On television, the situation is even more dire—fast food ads are plentiful, preying on a public that has put convenience above health. The fast food industry is a powerful empire that is largely responsible for the obesity epidemic the public now faces. **This food's popularity is a result of its marketing campaigns, convenience, and affordability.**

The writer provides us with some background by discussing the origins of obesity and identifying fast food as a primary contributor. From here, the thesis statement then lets us know how the essay's body paragraphs will be organized.

Although combining your overall argument and its supporting points in one clear, concise sentence is usually preferable, an essay's thesis does not always have to be confined to one sentence.

> Often people do not consider the effect air pollution can have on our health and our economy. The negative effects of air pollution on the public are outstanding and continuously increasing, mainly in large cities and developing countries where education and money are also a major concern. Throughout the world, though, air pollution has a direct effect on society, resulting in a depletion of vegetation and food supply, an increase in respiratory illnesses among both children and adults, and an increase in health care costs, which consequently results in a negative impact on the economy. **If society had a greater understanding of the connection between air pollution and its negative effects on humans and the environment, prevention or at least reduction of air pollution would be put into action by city officials. Curbing pollution would reduce poor health and rising health care costs, and improve vegetation.**

Notice that the thesis statement for this essay (in bold) spans two sentences. The thesis should be as clear and concise as possible. A one-sentence thesis is preferable, but trying to fit a complicated thesis into one sentence can produce an awkward and/or overly long statement. In some cases, you may need two or more sentences to express your thesis.

The Delayed or Implied Thesis

While most academic essays have a concise thesis placed at the end of the introductory paragraph, a less formal essay's thesis might be delayed until later in the paper, or the thesis may simply be implied. This technique has the advantage of making the author appear more objective as well as giving the reader time to weigh the full argument before coming to a conclusion; however, you risk losing your reader's attention if the direction of your argument is unfocused.

WRITING BODY PARAGRAPHS
Effective Topic Sentences

Just as the thesis statement represents the controlling idea of an essay, the **topic sentence** indicates the controlling idea of a paragraph. Ideally, your topic sentence should directly relate to one of your thesis points. Readers of essays expect a clear topic sentence and a unified paragraph that deals with **one idea.** Moving from one main idea to another within a paragraph, or digressing from the main idea and then returning to it, will result in a lack of unity. The topic sentence may be handled in a variety of ways, normally depending on its placement in the paragraph. Starting a paragraph with a topic sentence is the most common approach; however, the topic sentence may also be implied—in other words, not stated but evident from the development of the paragraph—or it may be carried over from the preceding paragraph.

Topic Sentence at the Paragraph's Beginning

Starting a paragraph with a topic sentence is the most common approach, as in the following example:

> **Recent technological advancements have caused a decline in television viewership.** In the past, the three major networks had a stranglehold on the airwaves, and viewers were forced to pick from a handful of shows; however, with the advancement of the Internet and Netflix, as well as the introduction of DVD boxed sets, an audience now has more choice regarding where to watch its favourite programs. Satellite and cable networks are victims of their own success—more choice means more to ignore. Thus, the evolution of a more sophisticated and discerning television audience may also be blamed for the decline in network television ratings.

Notice the flow of this paragraph. A strong, clear topic sentence is used to catch the reader's attention: "Recent technological advancements have caused a decline in television viewership." From here, the paragraph delivers its primary examples across two sentences: "the advancement of the Internet as well as the introduction of DVD boxed sets" and "the evolution of a more sophisticated and discerning television audience" are the reasons why network television has lost a large portion of its audience.

Topic Sentence as Hook Writing topic sentences intended to "hook" the reader is largely a matter of judgment and degree; the formality of the topic sentence depends upon the formality of the essay. Students might be tempted to begin their paragraphs with topic sentences sounding like something pulled directly out of a comic book, but such beginnings tend to make an essay look unprofessional. Let's examine an informal topic sentence:

> Buzz. Click. SHHHHHH. Don't touch that dial! In the past, the three major networks had a stranglehold on the airwaves, and viewers were forced to pick from a handful of shows.

This example depends on some confusing sounds and a worn out cliché to get started. Topic sentences like this one may create interest, but provide your reader with no clear direction.

Topic Sentence within the Paragraph

The strategy of placing the topic sentence within the paragraph can be very useful, especially when you need to give your reader background information. A few sentences introduce the main idea, which is then presented in the mid-paragraph topic sentence; the rest of the paragraph develops and supports the main idea, as in the following rewritten paragraph from our earlier example:

> In the past, the three major networks had a stranglehold on the airwaves, and viewers were forced to pick from a handful of shows. If you wanted comedy, NBC provided must-see TV; if you wanted sports, ABC *Monday Night Football* was the way to go; and if you craved drama, nobody could beat CBS. **However, recent technological advancements have caused a decline in television viewership.** With the advancement of the Internet and Netflix, as well as the introduction of DVD boxed sets, an audience now has even more choice regarding where to watch its favourite programs. From black and white, to colour, to flatscreen, television is no stranger to superficial redesign; clearly, the evolution of a more sophisticated and discerning television audience may be blamed for the drop in network television ratings. Satellite and cable networks are victims of their own success—more choice means more to ignore.

Topic Sentence Implied

When a writer implies the main idea rather than stating it, he or she is gambling that the development and support within the paragraph will make the main idea obvious, as in the following example:

> Susan is a citizen of Canada. She has not been convicted of a felony and she has not been treated or confined for drug addiction, drunkenness, or mental illness. She is only 14. According to the Firearms Act, however, she is qualified to borrow shotguns and rifles for hunting or target shooting purposes. A few months ago, she decided to exercise this option.

What is the topic of this paragraph? It could be stated this way: "Allowing people under 18 years old to use guns is irresponsible." Would the paragraph be better if it had included this sentence? No. The author's narration is self-evident, and reinforcing this point so obviously would detract from the paragraph's effectiveness.

However, think about the danger that lurks in the word *implied*. As a writer, you can attempt to imply your point, but your attempt will be fruitless if your reader does not grasp your implication. In other words, you are assuming that your reader will *infer* your meaning, a risky proposition. Be careful.

The following paragraph is missing its topic sentence. Read the paragraph carefully, then add the topic sentence where it will be most effective.

According to a story in yesterday's newspaper, this city has spent $11 million on hockey promotion over the last four years. During this time, the team's record has been a combined 12 wins, 32 losses. Seven hockey players have been arrested for violent crimes, and 15 more have been arrested for theft, drug possession, or alcohol-related offenses. The city also plans to spend $15 million to renovate its hockey arena.

Developing Body Paragraphs: Rhetorical Options

Your choice of body paragraphs will largely be determined by which type of essay you choose to write (description, narration, comparison, etc.). However, since you will often use more than one rhetorical strategy within an essay, you may need to use several of the following types of paragraphs in one piece of writing. Topic sentences for each of these example paragraphs appear in bold type.

Description In description, the emphasis is on sensory detail—engaging the reader's ability to see, hear, feel, smell, and so on. Note how the following paragraph focuses on these elements:

Physically, the Wii is quite different from the Xbox 360. The Wii is much smaller and lighter. Its colour is white. The console design is almost futuristic with a green, glowing light that indicates when the power has been turned on. A blue light flashes once around the mouth of the CD slot when the console is turned on but quickly disappears, leaving the player with nothing but the images on the screen. Only game sounds are heard, as the Wii's cooling fan makes no noise.

Narration The narrative essay, or the narrative paragraph within an essay, tells a story in order to entertain the reader or point out a significant effect caused by the story's events. Narrative paragraphs use time order, with the writer employing transitions to ensure that the reader can follow the events without losing the thread of the story. (For a list of transitions, see the Transitional Expressions chart earlier in this chapter.)

The game was close, from start to finish. With ten seconds left to go, Lupul got a penalty for tripping. This left the Leafs with only one of two options: to pull their goalie, or hope that the Penguins would encounter a similar penalty. As luck would have it, as soon as the whistle was blown, Crosby was called for charging. For the next seven seconds, the two teams were evenly matched with both star players off the ice.

In the above example, the writer is trying to accomplish two tasks. The first task is to recount the events of the hockey game without using too much jargon. After all, even though hockey is a popular sport, not everyone has an intimate knowledge of its structure and language. The writer's second task is to tell the story of the climactic, exciting final moments of an important game.

Exemplification When writers use the exemplification option, they are trying to prove a general assertion by providing specific evidence to back the assertion up. Notice how the following paragraph depends on its examples to further explain the main point:

Police officers continually remind drivers to obey the posted speed limits. "Speed kills," they tell us. Actually, speeding doesn't cause accidents; failure to yield the right-of-way and inability to control a vehicle account for almost all accidents. But excessive speeding can lead to both of these errors. Driving ten kilometres an hour over the speed limit is the norm for most Canadians; however, some choose to go 30 or even 50 kilometres over the posted limit. In instances like this, the speeder is going so much faster than the surrounding cars that he or she can get in trouble merely due to the other drivers' expectations. Unless a "normal" driver in the traffic is explicitly aware of the high speed of the fastest car, he or she may well make a lane change without realizing that the fast car is now trapped with nowhere to go and not enough time to stop.

Process Analysis The process analysis strategy has two possible purposes. One is to explain to the reader how to do something: perform a task, repair machinery, and so on. The second purpose is to explain how an activity happened in the past or happens routinely. The first of the following two examples uses the "how to" approach to lead the reader through the "process" of falling asleep:

The first step takes place in the two or three hours before bedtime. This period is not a good time to eat the evening meal, unless you want to run the risk of being awakened by indigestion. Similarly, anything containing alcohol or caffeine can disrupt your ability to fall asleep. Some people may drink a glass of heated milk before bed, while others may indulge in a warm bath. The main objectives are to avoid anything that will disrupt sleep and to take measures conducive to sleep.

The next chapter shows how otherwise promising sales presentations can fail:

Technical skills and social skills need to complement each other. Too often, technical people are adept at showing off the functions of hardware and software, but lack the social skills needed in a sales environment. Asking them a question relating to real-world application usually results in awkward eye contact and stuttered communication. All in all, the solitude that draws many very smart but very shy people into computer software design does not lend itself to interaction with the lay public.

The process that the writer is analyzing has happened in the past; presumably, it will happen in the future as well. Note that this paragraph comes from a definition essay that uses process analysis as an internal strategy. (See the Definition paragraph below.)

Causal Analysis Paragraphs developed using causal analysis normally concentrate on cause and effect. In this example, Naomi Wolf considers possible causes for a perceived change in attitude towards feminism, and then lists the effect (in italics) that this change in attitude created:

> **Thus, feminism stopped being seen as guaranteeing every woman's choice—whatever that may be—and fell captive to social attitudes held only by a minority that often could not even reach agreement among its own members.** To be sure, this development might have been inescapable, a result of the abortion wars that demanded an us-and-them world view. *But, the ideological overloading closed the word "feminism" off to enormous numbers of people: women who are not sure about, or who actively oppose, abortion; women who are terrified of being tarred with the brush of homophobia; women who strongly resist identifying themselves as victims; women who are uneasy with what they see as man bashing and blaming; conservative women; and men themselves.*
> —from Naomi Wolf, *Fire with Fire*

Definition Writers use definition to clear up possible confusion about a troublesome term or to bring new meaning to a commonplace word or idea. Note how the following paragraph defines the idea of "community" in a new way:

> **Most people think of a community as a group of people engaged in a common goal or in a common geography.** We tend to think of communities as tangible things—a small town, or a group of people all cheering for the same sports team. However, such definitions are limiting; some communities have never met face to face. Online communities consist of sometimes hundreds of people all communicating with each other and sharing hopes, dreams, and fears, but never meeting in the physical world. To deprive such a group of the term community seems to go against its very definition.

In this paragraph, the writer begins by giving the popular definition of community, only to challenge it by discussing online communities. The reader must decide if the popular definition is adequate or if it needs to be changed to accommodate this new group.

Classification Writers classify when they take large subjects and divide them into smaller subjects. Classification is a way of making a subject clear by discussing its parts or categories, as in the following example:

> **In this country, we waste an enormous amount of time and energy disapproving of one another in three categories where only personal taste**

matters: hair, sports, and music. We need not review the family trauma, high dudgeon, tsk tsks, and lawsuits caused over the years by hair and how people wear it. Consider the equally futile expenditure of energy in condemning other people's sports. And in music, good Lord, the zeal put into denouncing rock, sneering at opera, finding classical a bore, jazz passé, bluegrass fit only for snuff-dippers—why, it's stupefying. It's incomprehensible.

—from Molly Ivins, "Honky Tonking"

Comparison/Contrast When you compare and contrast two subjects, you have two options for structuring your paragraph or essay. If you use the subject-by-subject approach, you discuss one of the subjects first, then the other. In an essay, you can use various paragraph strategies, including most of the ones in this section. If you use the point-by-point approach, however, you compare and contrast the subjects in relation to one point of comparison per sentence or group of sentences.   The point-by-point approach requires a careful use of transitions, as in the following example:

> **In terms of gas mileage, foreign vehicles are often superior to domestic ones.** For example, the Honda Accord averages 22 kilometres per litre. In contrast, the Ford Explorer averages 15 k.p.l. However, replacing the muffler on your Ford may cost you only $80 with parts and labour; on a Honda, the same part with labour will cost you $120. Of course, one needs to consider which purchase one will make most often: fuel or mufflers.

Argumentation Although you can use any type of paragraph when developing an argument, most paragraphs used in an argument make and support assertions. (For more on argument, see Chapter 7.) In the following example, the writer is arguing against a proposal to offer free tuition to community college students in her province, using exemplification:

> **Free tuition would undermine students as revenue generators for the economy.** It may be a cliché to say the government cannot afford to provide free tuition for all students, but this is still a reality. Tuition is needed for professor salaries as well as part of university and college operating budgets. The government provides bursaries and rebates as it is. Additionally, students should have a personal financial stake in their education: high schools provide a general education on a variety of topics; however, universities and colleges provide a specialized education taught by experts using the latest high tech resources—all of which requires funding and attendance. It's a sad reality, but students seem to take their education more seriously when they know they are paying for it.

Conceding the Point In an argument essay, you are, obviously, trying to prove your point. However, any subject worth arguing has very good arguments on each side. **Conceding the point** is a type of strategy that acknowledges the other side's assertions only to refute them with stronger evidence. This strategy does not appear in all argumentation essays, but it is a useful device. The following paragraph uses this strategy regarding the above argument about tuition:

> **However, opposing the idea of free tuition is difficult.** There are a great many people who find one obstacle standing between them and a college diploma: money. These folk will be relegated to minimum wage and forfeit their considerable skills, whether this be for a nursing, business, or trade-oriented career. Others who can pay for their education spend years paying it back. Yet, the idea of free tuition still needs to be resisted because . . .

In this paragraph, the writer acknowledges that her position may seem harsh and that those who oppose her may well have sound reasons for doing so. The writer is—temporarily—yielding to the other side before resuming her argument.

EXERCISE 4.4

Each example in Part 2 contains an exercise near the end of the chapter called Responding to a Photograph, which uses an exemplary photo to illustrate the rhetorical option that the chapter discusses. For example, the narration chapter has a photograph reflecting a story, the comparison/contrast chapter has a photograph showing a sharp contrast among cast members of a TV sitcom, and so on. Turn to Part 2, and select a photograph that interests you from one of these exercises. Note the title of the chapter, and write a paragraph in response to the photograph, using the rhetorical option covered in the chapter to develop your idea.

CONCLUDING PARAGRAPHS

Along with the introduction, the conclusion of an essay often gives students trouble. Many students make the error of bringing up new topics in the conclusion, topics that beg to be explored, but not at the end of an essay! If you find yourself in this situation, re-examine the structure of your introduction and your body paragraphs. Perhaps these new topics would be better placed within the body of the essay.

Restate but Don't Repeat

In your conclusion, you need to restate your position clearly and confidently, reminding readers of the proof you have offered in the body of the essay. Readers are frequently put off by a word-for-word recap of what they have just read, so try to summarize your main arguments very briefly rather than recounting each point in detail. Finally, use your conclusion to comment about your findings and their implications, but without introducing new information.

The conclusion is the last part of your essay; it should logically derive from the paragraphs that precede it. Therefore, avoid using "In conclusion" or similar phrasing. Your reader can see that this is the end of your essay, so there is no need to announce it. Also avoid stilted sentences such as "As this essay has shown, . . ." Such language can lower the reader's evaluation of an otherwise effective essay.

Consider Your Options

The rhetorical options discussed in this section and in Part 2 are not merely essay patterns; they are ways of thinking. Try this: listen to your favourite music for a day, and list the rhetorical options that you hear used by your favourite artists. Do some songs compare and contrast? Do some songs list a process or classify things or people?

Here are some proven approaches to writing effective conclusions:

Reinforce Your Thesis Don't *repeat* your thesis; *reinforce* it. Let's look again at a portion of the introductory paragraph discussed earlier, along with its thesis:

> The fast food industry is a powerful empire that is largely responsible for the obesity epidemic the public now faces. **This food's popularity is a result of its marketing campaigns, convenience, and affordability.**

Too often students will directly cut and paste portions of their introduction into the concluding paragraph. This method makes for a poor reading experience. Instead, create a strong final impression using the basic points of your thesis and introduction:

> People enjoy convenience and affordability, but let's consider the consequences of these easy actions in relation to fast food. Carrying around an extra 20 pounds is not convenient. Paying for exercise equipment, diet pills, or high blood pressure medication is not convenient. The next time the television tickles your stomach through one of its ads offering a high-calorie temptation, try to do the sensible thing—turn it off.

Comment on Your Essay's Implications If, in your essay, you have analyzed a work, an event, or a situation, now is the time to comment on the implications of your analysis. The following paragraph concludes an essay that examines the problem of boredom in modern life. The writer believes that the modern world's noisy and intrusive entertainment and advertising culture is one of the main causes of boredom.

> In the future, two things are likely to happen. One is that the barrage of media entertainment and advertising will turn to even more violence, noise, and intrusion. These techniques have worked for a long time, and they are not likely to disappear. Correspondingly, the ability to appreciate anything that requires patience—such as a garden, an art museum, or an algebra textbook—will certainly dwindle even more. Our culture is about to become the slave of its entertainment industry.

Use a Call to Action An essay that analyzes a problem can make a recommendation on how to solve the problem or at least improve the situation. The following paragraph concludes an essay about waste caused by consumer pollution and litter, by offering a remedy for this ongoing problem:

> The idea of convenience is what urged consumers to purchase the bottled drink or bagged snack to begin with; convenience in the location of the waste bin is the only thing that will persuade consumers to put trash in the proper place as opposed to on the square of lawn directly in front of them. If venues offered more clearly labelled recycling receptacles, the number of cans and paper cups in our parks would diminish. One cannot depend on the average person

to do the right thing: humans are too self-centred to go out of their way to put waste in the proper place. Increasing the availability of waste bins is the most logical way to reduce consumer pollution.

Refer to an Earlier Anecdote or Example This example contains a paragraph giving the definition of anecdote and offers one that would make a suitable introduction to an essay. The essay introduction discusses a nine-year-old boy, David, who purchased *Grand Theft Auto IV* and then went home to play the game. Hypothetically, this essay is about video game violence. Moreover, we would assume that the essay makes some sort of conclusion about this phenomenon. Once this essay reaches its conclusion, its author may strategically revisit his or her opening anecdote to expand upon the conclusion and give it even more resonance:

> Another year older, David enjoyed his birthday last week. He turned ten. Rather than playing board games or baseball, all twelve of David's friends brought their controllers to David's house and proceeded to engage in co-operative play. Yes, they took turns shooting alien enemies, but they also took turns dancing, playing trivia, and racing. Perhaps there is more to the one-dimensional argument of video games as purveyors of social immorality than we might at first think.

Use an Authoritative Quotation As mentioned in the section on introductory paragraphs, taking advantage of someone else's words can produce a powerful effect. However, be careful: an essay's conclusion should not introduce any new information. Now is not the time to produce that amazing statistic you were saving; this should have already been used in one of your body paragraph. Additionally, a conclusion is supposed to reinforce *your* authority, so quoting from someone else can sometimes undermine your intentions. That said, consider the use of a stylish authoritative quotation in the following concluding paragraph:

> Reality television has always been popular because of our need to feel better than others. We watch *Canadian Idol* to see the bad singers, not the great ones; we watch *Dragon's Den* to see the goofy inventions and not the remarkable ones; and we watch *Jersey Shore* to berate its cast, not to support it. Nell, a character in Samuel Beckett's play *Endgame* said that "nothing is funnier than unhappiness." This may be true, but what it says about our society and its constant need to prey on others' misfortunes should not be ignored.

EXERCISE 4.5

Write a fully developed paragraph on one of the following topics. Remember to use specific, concrete examples and details.

1. **Description.** Choose an object that you are planning to buy or want to buy in the future.

2. **Narration.** Explain the circumstances that led up to a special event in your life or the life of someone you know.

3. **Exemplification.** State a general "rule of thumb." Then give an example of what happens if someone violates this rule.

4. **Process analysis.** Show the reader how to get up and get ready in the morning without wasting time, or write about another task that you complete regularly.

5. **Causal analysis.** What is one cause of student failure? What is one effect experienced by spending too much time surfing the Internet? Choose one of these questions.

6. **Definition.** What defines the ideal roommate? What defines the ideal neighbour? What defines the ideal boss? Choose one of these questions. Rely on definition, but also use examples as necessary.

7. **Comparison and contrast.** Contrast two friends, sports teams, or recording artists.

8. **Argumentation.** Argue against one policy of your college or university.

Using the Internet

Go to these websites to find more tips, techniques, and insights on developing paragraphs:

Guide to Grammar and Writing
This website, maintained by Capital Community College, provides a discussion of several topics relating to paragraph unity, coherence, development, and variety.
http://grammar.ccc.commnet.edu/grammar/

The UVic Writer's Guide
The University of Victoria's English Department website includes helpful information on the rhetorical functions of paragraphs, the topic sentence, unity and coherence, paragraph development, and paragraph patterns.
http://web.uvic.ca/wguide/Pages/MasterToc.html

Reshaping Your Essay: Revising Structure and Content

PEER REVISION in the Real World

Film producers and directors of major releases like the 2012 movie *The Avengers* screen early versions of their work for test audiences to get feedback, business and salespeople bring in focus groups to test new products or ideas, and trades routinely have inspectors who come in to look at individual jobs to make sure they meet all building codes. Most major processes in life incorporate some method of peer review—an exchange which often produces valuable constructive criticism.

Exposing your written work to others for feedback is essential to discovering if it connects with its intended audience and achieves its purpose. Often students will resist letting a peer look over their work out of either vanity ("Of course, my work is excellent!") or fear ("What if my friend thinks I'm a bad writer?"). An extra pair of eyes to look over work gives its creator a new perspective. Peer review is always your opportunity to make your writing (or someone else's writing) better. Unless otherwise instructed, however, peers must never be allowed to actually make changes to the original. They may point out problems only, while it is up to the original author to make any desired revisions.

LEARNING OUTCOMES:

- ▶ Revise essays for structure, content, appropriate thesis, and title
- ▶ Revise essay paragraphs for topic sentences and coherence
- ▶ Edit your own essays effectively and apply this knowledge to peer editing
- ▶ Use the Review toolbar in MS Word 2010 to edit work easily

The Writing Process Revisited

In Chapters 1 and 2, we discussed the necessity of establishing a clear purpose, prewriting extensively, and writing a rough draft based on a well-organized outline. Now we move forward in the writing process to discuss revision. Chapter 4 gave a detailed look at constructing paragraphs, and Chapter 5 will build upon that knowledge while expanding on the next two steps of the writing process: revising for structure and revising for content.

WHY IS REVISION IMPORTANT?

Lack of revision is the main cause of weak writing at the college and university level. **All good writers revise.** Quite simply, it is very difficult for writers to catch errors in their own work. Our brains simply fill in missing content or correct errors during rereading. Thus, before any serious revision can take place, writers must distance themselves from their work. Often students allow themselves too little time to revise (or skip the revision process altogether). They assume the draft is good enough—maybe they've even read it a few times and are sure they've deleted the major errors. However, consider the following sentences, which have circulated as a popular Internet meme:

Unisg the pewor of the hmuan mnid, it dseno't mttaer in waht oderr the lrettes in a wrod aeppar. The olny irpoamtnt tihng is taht the frsit and lsat ltteer be in the rhgit palce.

Chances are you could still read these sentences—fairly easily, too. Quite simply, our brains work faster than our hands and eyes, filling in gaps for us. Proofreading something after it has just been written is often ineffective. Going away from your writing for a few days or even a few hours and coming back later to read it with fresh eyes allows you to gain perspective on the material and to see more clearly whether your essay has gaps in logic or coherence. Even more effective is to read your work aloud, a process which slows you down enough to perceive errors that your mind might have corrected for you.

Revising for Structure

In Chapter 2 we discussed the shape of an essay (see our discussion of the "3 Across and 3 Down Method"). However, now is the time to review the parts of your essay—its entire structure—to see if it achieves its purpose. Consider the following questions about structure:

Introduction:

- Does your introduction begin with a hook that is connected to the essay's main topic?
- Does your essay produce what its introduction promises?
- If your introduction promises to compare two texts, does the essay compare both texts substantially?
- If it argues a position, is this argument clearly identifiable?
- Does the introduction contain a thesis?
- Does this thesis appear at the end of the introductory paragraph?
- Is this thesis specific and manageable enough for the length of your paper?

Paragraphs:

- Are all of your paragraphs fully developed around clearly stated topic sentences?
- Do these topic sentences directly relate to your thesis points?
- Do your paragraphs directly correspond to your thesis points?
- Can a reader follow your ideas within the paragraph without having to double back?
- Have you deleted any sentences that do not support your topic sentence?
- Are your paragraphs sequenced in the way that is most appropriate and creates the most impact?
- Do your first and last paragraphs sound as if they belong in the same essay?

Conclusion:

- Does your conclusion refer back to your thesis and sum up the points you have just argued?
- Does your conclusion avoid adding new material or examples?
- Does your conclusion end with a memorable closing thought?

Revising for Content

Most students believe that revising for content means correcting a few (often superficial) grammar and spelling errors and then handing the assignment in; however, this type of revision comes last in the writing process. Correcting a few errors will not mean much to your professor if your essay is only half a page long and contains no examples whatsoever. Consider the following questions about content:

Length:

- Does your essay meet the assignment expectations for length? (This question may seem obvious; however, length quite literally means content, at least quantity-wise.)

Examples:

- Does your essay contain a satisfactory number of examples?
- Are these examples on topic and do they help argue your thesis?
- Are these examples suitably academic and/or current?
- If you're writing a research essay, do you have the required minimum number of sources?

Quotations:

- If required, does your essay contain the proper number of quotations?
- Are your quotations appropriately detailed or just the odd arbitrary word here and there?
- Do your quotations build on your thesis argument?
- Are your quotations from current and reliable academic sources?

STRATEGIES FOR UNDERDEVELOPED ESSAYS

As previously mentioned, one of the greatest handicaps to even well-written essays is length. A well-written paper that is only two out of four assigned pages is still not meeting the assignment expectations. In reality, it's only delivering half of what is required and therefore should be penalized accordingly. If you find yourself in this position, you will have to go back to earlier steps in the writing process and rework your material. Consider the following steps to help develop essays that might be too thin.

Revising Your Introductory Paragraph

Remember that your introduction should do the following:

1. generate interest,
2. provide the background or context for your essay, and
3. indicate a thesis statement that both informs your reader of the essay's direction and expresses the essay's controlling idea.

Read your draft's introduction to make sure that it provides the proper context. Students frequently do too much or too little here, either writing a huge explanation for their essay that threatens to dwarf the essay itself (e.g., the entire history of firearms) or writing a tiny introduction that does not establish context at all (e.g., just two sentences on gun control). (See Chapter 4 for a list of ways to introduce an essay.)

Revising Your Thesis (Again)

Your thesis is the engine of your essay. If your essay runs out of gas (so to speak) maybe it just needs a bigger engine. If you have only two thesis points, try for three. Also try for thesis points broad enough so that they can be broken down into sub-points. Remember, there is no rule saying your essay must be only five paragraphs.

Two-point thesis: Canada has significantly contributed to the world both culturally and militarily.

Three-point thesis: Canada has significantly contributed to the world culturally, militarily, and scientifically.

Three-point thesis with subpoints: Canada has significantly contributed to the world culturally, militarily, and scientifically. (In this essay, the thesis point "culturally" could be divided into the categories of arts and sports.)

Whichever method you choose, avoid putting specific examples into the thesis; save these for your body paragraphs. Below is a three-point thesis cluttered by unnecessary sentences:

Canada has significantly contributed to the world culturally. For example, musicians like Drake and Justin Bieber are known worldwide. Canada has contributed to the world militarily. Canadian soldiers are known for their efforts in both Afghanistan and Rwanda. Canada has also contributed to the world scientifically. Frederick Banting discovered insulin.

Not only is this thesis choppy, but the writer is spoiling his or her essay. Consider the thesis as a preview of what is to come. Save your thesis examples for your essay's body paragraphs.

Check your thesis statement against the body of your draft. Read your thesis, then each topic sentence. Does your thesis accurately reflect your essay's content, or did your essay take a new direction during the writing process?

If the essay did take a new direction, many students are tempted to go back to the introduction and modify the thesis. After all, it's easier to rewrite the thesis than to rewrite whole paragraphs. However, revising the thesis isn't always the best approach. If the body of your essay has lost its direction or doesn't seem to fulfil the promise of your thesis, then patching the thesis statement won't fix the problem. You will need to revise the body so that it corresponds to the purpose you established during prewriting.

Revising Your Body Paragraphs

If a thesis is the engine powering your essay, then paragraphs function as both your essay's wheels (purpose) and body (examples and proofs). Without a proper purpose, your essay's logic can go clear off the road. Additionally, if your essay looks more like a rusted-out frame than a fully loaded interior, then you need to add material in the form of examples and/or quotations depending on the type of writing you're doing.

Unfortunately, it is possible to write a paragraph or essay full of strong sentences that don't relate to one another and therefore don't work together to develop the paragraph's or essay's controlling idea. Consider this example:

> Our entertainment options today are vastly different from the opportunities for entertainment before World War II. In the 1930s, the standard picture was of families sitting in the living room listening to the huge radios or record players of the time. Yet, how could people enjoy themselves when so much of the public was out of work? Bread and milk were also hard to come by. Modern families have a wealth of entertainment options. They can watch pay-per-view films or surf the Internet. However, surfing the Internet can be dangerous as many people have their identities stolen and their credit cards abused.

Reviewing Your Purpose

This paragraph does a fairly good job sentence by sentence, but what is its purpose? Its first sentence indicates that the paragraph is about how entertainment options have changed from the 1930s until now, but then the writer shifts to discuss life in the 1930s; then the writer comes back to the idea of entertainment, only to end with an example that, although well written, is ineffective and completely off topic.

This paragraph needs major revision; the direction that the revision will take depends upon the writer's true purpose, and we can't be sure of that purpose from reading this paragraph. (Read Chapter 1 on establishing purpose. See Chapter 4 for more on paragraph unity.)

Revising for Effective Topic Sentences

Pay close attention to the topic sentences of your body paragraphs. Does each topic sentence support your thesis, or does one or more of them wander off in a different direction? If a topic sentence heads away from your thesis, ask yourself if you can revise it to fix the problem or if you need to delete and replace the paragraph.

Even if the topic sentences support the thesis, you also need to make sure that each topic sentence is strong and works with the rest of its paragraph. Just as a thesis statement controls an essay, **a topic sentence controls a paragraph.** Sometimes, a topic sentence is too general, providing a weak focus. Other times, a topic sentence can be misleading, promising one type of development while the paragraph actually develops in new, unexplained directions.

EXERCISE 5.1

Each of the following paragraphs has a faulty topic sentence. Working alone or in pairs, read the paragraph and then replace the topic sentence with a more effective one.

1. TV weather forecasters are no good. These "specialists" are upbeat in any situation except for the truly catastrophic. For example, last July, our city went the entire month without rain. Both the days and nights were extremely hot. But each morning and evening, the local forecasters would chirp on about the beautiful day the city was about to have, when a more mature judgment would have been to concentrate on the need for rain. However, Mr. or Ms. Weatherperson is just giving the public what it wants: happy weather. After all, commercial television is a business.

2. A 16-year-old boy wanders through Landon Department Store. He finally comes to the music department and spends almost an hour looking through the compact discs. Eventually, he goes to a cash register and pays $12 for a CD, takes his purchase, and leaves the store. Although he has paid for one CD, he has shoplifted three more, hidden in his backpack.

Revising for Coherence

A document that is **coherent** will (1) follow the direction implied by its thesis statement and (2) use effective transitions to help make connections between paragraphs. When you revise, you need to ask yourself if you have made all the relationships clear for your readers. Will they be able to read your essay straight through without having to reread some of the sections?

Coherence is closely related to the issue of audience. As a writer, you should be trying to write an essay that accommodates the needs of an adult reader. This is not a matter of keeping your text simple (by using common words, simple sentences, and easy transitions, for example). It is more an issue of being able to perceive a possible interpretation problem and taking steps to avoid confusion.

Transitional Sentences Chapter 4 provides strategies for achieving coherence at the paragraph level with emphasis on the use of **transitional expressions.** This strategy is useful at the essay level as well: **transitional sentences** can help you clearly link a paragraph to the one that precedes or follows it. For example, the following transitional sentence links back to the previous paragraph, which is about the advantages of the Internet:

Although the Internet has created a free way for the viewer to catch up on missed television episodes, some people cannot deprive themselves of collecting the boxed sets of their favourite TV shows.

The sentence refers back to the preceding paragraph, while preparing readers for the topic of the current paragraph: television series DVD boxed sets.

EXERCISE 5.2

Read the following paragraphs and make any changes that will improve unity and coherence. Remove sentences that have strayed from the main point of the paragraph.

1. Students who disrupt college classes should be removed from those classes. Often, there is one attention seeker who detracts from the lecture or discussion by calling attention to himself or herself. In fact, these people are often insecure. Perhaps their parents didn't show them enough love as children. However, raising kids isn't easy—it takes a lot of money and a lot of patience. Patience, however, is a virtue. One needs plenty of patience when doing small tasks like building model airplanes or gardening. Gardening is relaxing and at the end of the day you have a basket full of healthy food! Anyway, attention seekers should just be quiet and let those who have paid to hear the professor talk learn what they need to learn. Who wants to hear some blabbermouth go on and on about nothing . . . although some professors are like that too! Maybe professors are insecure and needed parents who loved them more too.

2. Doug Farthington is an example of someone who has turned his life around. Up until the time that he was about 25 years old, Doug was very adventurous. He was also a champion bowler, once winning five tournaments in six weeks. That day, he also drank twelve milkshakes and bought a snail collection. Two things happened to Doug in his twenty-sixth year. One was that he nearly died while riding in a car driven by a drunk driver. The car hit a bridge abutment, and Doug, who was also drunk, was the only survivor. The second event was that Doug met his wife Linda, a divorcee with a child. Linda was a champion boxer and also loved to make crafts out of toothpicks. Once she won the blue ribbon at the local county fair. Linda told Doug that his wild days were over, that she'd already run off one husband for drinking and didn't intend to do so again. Doug married Linda and became a family man. He is devoted to his adopted daughter, Laura. Laura was born hearing-impaired and hears only with very strong hearing aids and by lip-reading. She attends a regular school, though, and is very well-adjusted. She also loves dancing and jumping rope. Jumping rope is good for your blood pressure. At the urging of Linda, Doug went to college part-time for several years. Today he is an accountant for a major law firm, a change that must come as a shock to his old friends.

Revising Your Concluding Paragraph

To improve the content of your conclusion, ask yourself these questions:

- Does this paragraph appear very short when compared to the other paragraphs in my essay?
- Is the conclusion a too-simple summary of my essay?
- Have I repeated the thesis statement in exactly the same words as it appears in my introduction?
- Have I introduced any new topics here that will divert my reader from the main idea of the essay that he or she has just read?
- Have I included any direct references to my essay ("In this essay, I have shown . . .")?
- Have I depended on a clichéd quotation, generalization, or question to end my essay?

If your answer to any of these questions is yes, then you need to revise your conclusion. (For ways to conclude an essay, see Chapter 4.)

Make a Good Final Impression Students sometimes forget a very basic fact: normally, the conclusion is the last part of the essay that an instructor reads before determining a grade. An otherwise strong essay with a weak or confusing conclusion has made its mistake in the wrong place. It's as if you met a new person, made a satisfactory first impression, had a positive conversation, and then muttered a ridiculous or offensive comment just before you parted ways!

Writing and Revising Your Title

While it is tempting to create a title before you write the essay (sometimes called a "working title"), often creating the title after the essay is done makes more sense, since by this point you've firmly established the exact content of the essay and can accurately summarize it in a stylish sentence or two. Here are five guidelines for creating a proper title:

1. **Avoid using a vague or overly general title:**

   Jellyfish and You

   Such titles sound juvenile and tell your reader very little.

2. **Avoid a strained and overly specific title:**

   The Problem Caused by Jellyfish and What the Current Proposal (AR-1789) before City Council Can Do to Solve It

3. **Use a title suitable to your purpose.** Narratives and descriptions frequently have fairly short titles primarily designed to entice the reader:

The Dangers of Jellyfish *or* The Healing Power of Jellyfish

In the case of more analytical essays, however, titles need to be more informative. Consider using a colon to separate the main part of a title from its descriptive second part. "How to Wax a Car" is a factual (and probably accurate) but boring title. How about "Waxing a Car: Preserving the Beauty of Your Automobile"? Remember the title of Leslie's essay: "Occupy Canada: Civil Disobedience and Corporate Greed." It is accurate, meaning that it reflects the essay as a whole, and it is interesting.

4. If you are writing an analysis of one or more works, **the authors and titles of those works should also appear in your title:**

Swine before Pearls: Comparing Pig Imagery in George Orwell's *Animal Farm* and E.B. White's *Charlotte's Web*

5. **Do not add extra formatting** to your title (extra quotation marks, bold type, italic type, underlining, or all-capital letters). Centre it, and capitalize its main words. (For more on capitalization, consult a grammar handbook or Chapter 18 of this text.)

REVISING WITH PEER SUPPORT

Peer review is valuable because reading others' work exposes you to new ideas, new sentence types, new vocabulary, and new ways of approaching a thesis. In short, reading is the best way to improve your own writing.

"Peers" is just a fancy word to describe the people around you. Although they may look ordinary, each person around you is a valuable critic. Everyone has an opinion, whether professional or not, and peer review is a great way to find out how your classmates view your writing. If they can't follow your argument or if they find your sentence structures confusing, chances are good that your other readers, and even your instructor, will also have a problem understanding what you have written. Finally, please note, peers must never be allowed to actually make changes to student work by rewriting. They can point out problems only, while it is up to the original author to make any desired revisions.

The following are some guidelines to help you avoid wasting your peer review time or, even worse, incorporating changes into your writing that will actually damage it:

1. **Treat peer review seriously:** Meeting with your peers to review a paper is not a time for getting together with friends, finding someone to date, or discussing the new film opening this weekend. If your peer review time degenerates into socializing, you will have lost a valuable opportunity (and annoyed both your instructor and the more serious members of your group).

2. **Take part:** Some students are shy, and some come from cultures in which group interaction is much more formal than the atmosphere typically found in a peer review session. If you are uncomfortable with the peer review process, remember that its rewards will outweigh its problems. Try to embrace this process, not shrink from it.

3. **Be receptive to feedback:** It is hard for writers to read their own work with an objective eye, but it is also hard to accept the help of others. Group review was not invented for the purpose of challenging your ego; therefore, listen to what your classmates tell you without reacting defensively. If, for example, you are working with a partner who marks 24 places that need improvement, do not take offence. Perhaps only 12 of the responses are actually valid; even so, your partner has done you a huge favour by pointing them out. And, as careful and particular as your partner might be, your instructor will be a harsher judge of your work.

4. **Use a checklist:** To make sure that you have covered all the important revision issues, use a checklist of standard questions (see Figure 5.1).

5. **Be tactful:** When in doubt of any issue identified by your peer reviewer, discreetly ask your professor or consult a grammar and writing handbook for clarification. If by chance your peer editor was wrong, do not go back and insult him or her. Everyone makes mistakes, and everyone has differing opinions on what constitutes good writing. Similarly, make sure you use tact when commenting on someone else's paper. Knowing how sensitive you are to criticism, you should realize that others may feel the same way. Remember, your job is to help, not to hurt.

6. **Go deeper than spelling errors:** Too often students feel that "peer review" means simply looking for spelling errors; however, this is one of the least valuable aspects of peer review since most computers can do this for you. When you are peer-reviewing someone's work, look beyond spelling errors and evaluate the level of writing at the thesis and paragraph level. Let the writer know if his or her writing has coherence and unity, or if the essay jumps around from topic to topic.

7. **Never rewrite sentences:** When participating in any peer review (whether instructor sanctioned or outside of class), be careful. As a peer reviewer, you may point out sentences that are awkward or word choices that are imperfect in another's work; however, your job is not to rewrite the work you are reviewing. It is academic fraud to write someone else's paper. In addition, passing off entire sentences that your peer reviewer wrote as your own is plagiarism. (See Chapter 3 for an in-depth discussion of plagiarism.)

    A note on the terminology used in this text: Someone who **edits** is actually making changes to the paper. Someone who **reviews** is reading the paper and making suggestions about how it might be improved. You will *edit* your own paper, but you might be asked to *review* someone else's.

8. **Follow instructions:** When your instructor runs a peer review session, he or she will most likely provide all students with a checklist as well as specific guidelines for the session. Follow these exactly.

EXERCISE 5.3

At the end of Chapter 2, you were asked to write the rough draft of a short essay on one of the topics in Exercise 2.6. (If you haven't completed this assignment yet, do so now.) Find and revise this draft, using the techniques discussed in this section. Then exchange drafts with a partner and review (1) your partner's first draft, and (2) your partner's suggested changes to your essay. Use the checklist questions on the next page to guide your review. What else can you suggest that will improve your partner's revision?

FIGURE 5.1
Peer review checklist.

| PEER REVIEW CHECKLIST: 11 STEPS TO A BETTER ESSAY |

Peer review sessions are not solely intended to be error-hunting sessions. Larger issues, such as organization and level of detail, should also be dealt with. Finding specific grammatical or mechanical errors is usually an ongoing process that will take more than one peer review session to fix.

Answer the following questions as you review your partner's draft:

☐ Does the title provide a clear idea of what the essay is about?

☐ Does the introduction provide sufficient and appropriate background and context, without being too general or too detailed?

☐ Does the introduction include a clear thesis statement that provides both an argument/controlling idea and an outline of the major points of the essay?

☐ After you have read the rest of the essay, reread the thesis statement. Is it supported by the rest of the essay? If not, should it be revised, or should one or more body paragraphs be revised?

☐ Is the topic sentence of each body paragraph effective? If not, should it be revised, or should the rest of the paragraph be revised? Are the topic sentences in the body paragraphs supported by specific and concrete evidence?

☐ If other works are quoted from or referred to within the essay, are they properly integrated and cited?

☐ Are there appropriate transitional words or phrases that link sentences and paragraphs smoothly together?

☐ Is the conclusion an effective commentary on the essay, or does it merely repeat the thesis? Does it introduce new information or questions that veer too far from the original topic? Does it end with a clichéd quotation or generalization?

☐ Overall, does the essay suffer from problems in any of the following areas?
  • Unity (in terms of the essay as a whole and each paragraph)
  • Coherence (in terms of the essay as a whole and each paragraph)
  • Language level (formal or informal)

☐ Does the essay contain repeated instances of the same types of grammar, spelling, or punctuation errors? If so, make a list of them so the writer can be sure to check for them in each subsequent draft.

☐ If applicable, is the essay written in the proper format and style required by the assignment guidelines?

Responding to Suggestions for Revision

When another person—a peer, a tutor, or your instructor—has reviewed your draft and suggested changes, you are faced with a new series of choices. You will see specific suggestions that you will want to act on without delay; but you will also note suggestions, queries, and overview comments, all of which you will need to consider carefully before choosing which revisions to make.

After Leslie wrote the first draft of her essay, which appears at the end of Chapter 2, she exchanged drafts with her revision partner, Emma, and each reviewed the other's work. What follows are Leslie's draft peer edited by her classmate, and the final revision of Leslie's essay. For her peer review, Emma marked up Leslie's draft using the *MS Word* Review function (detailed instructions for using this application are found after the peer review), and she included some general thoughts at the bottom of the paper. Please notice how Emma goes beyond merely pointing out an incorrect word here and there; instead, she comments on the entire essay's structure. Finally, notice how Emma gives compliments as well as criticisms.

LESLIE BUCKLEY
Prof. R. Muhlbock
COMM 1011
February 13, 2013

Occupy Canada

What first began as a march on Wall Street, quickly spread around the world due to the fact that people wanted to protest issues about corporate greed among other things, etc. In Canada, occupy movements sprung up in all major cities. For some, the movement was vaguely defined as a poor vs. rich dispute. But I think such comments trivialize what the movement is about and why its participants are really mad. Protestors in the Occupy Canada movement are dissatisfied with dwindling job opportunities, the gap between wages for workers and management, and an ineffectual government that allowed these injustices to occur in the first place.

Currently the unemployment rate in Canada is not that bad compared to the US, but the youth unemployment rate is 14.5%. In October of 2011, Canada lost 71 700 full-time jobs, many of them in "manufacturing and construction." One such example is the Electro-Motive plant (owned by Caterpillar Inc.) in London, Ontario, which recently closed its doors, forcing some

Why not give a brief history of the movement? How did it start originally?

Why not name them?

Kind of sounds conversational—maybe reword?

Awesome thesis!

You should probably give the exact statistic.

Good quotation! But what is the source?

54? Wasn't it higher than that? I remember reading something about this . . .

54 skilled employees out of work because they wouldn't take a 50% pay cut. Another key aspect in the Ocupy Canada movement is the income gap between workers and management.

You should cite where you got these numbers.

The Occupy movement's slogan is we are the 99%. The top 1% of wage earners in Canada control 32% of the country's wealth, while the other 99% of citizens have to divide up what's left amid surging unemployment.

I think Catarpillar is spelled wrong. Also Ocupy.

Catarpillar closed its Electro-Motive plant after workers refused to take a 500% pay reduction, but the same company not only posted a record profit of 5 billion dollars last year, but allowed its CEO to make $10.5-million annually (Size). Caterpillar is just one example. According to the CBC, the highest paid CEOs in Canada now make nearly 200 times more money than the national average. The average Canadian worker earns $44,366. The ways that the top 1% acquire and maintain their wealth is through low government regulation and taxation.

500%! Wouldn't this mean they'd make negative money? Is this right?

Source needed.

In 2008, after the mortgage crisis, the government bailed out U.S. banks and financial institutions and enraged the public. However, taxation for Canada's rich has steadily declined from 43% in 1981 to 29% in 2010 ("OECD report") At the provincial level, to curb Ontario's massive debt, the McGuinty liberals are instead requesting a wage freeze for high school teachers, while at the Federal level the government is threatening to legislate Air Canada workers back to their jobs ("Federal labour").

The topic seems to jump here . . . I didn't follow your argument.

Choppy transition.

Source needed for comment about McGuinty Liberals.

Occupy Canada is not made up jealous or lazy people. Equality in wealth may not be possible, but simple fairness is. I believe the public wants a livable wage and job security. Elected officials must protect the public they serve. When they fail, people have a right to be angry.

I like these examples, but I don't quite follow your line of argument.

"of" needed : "made up of".

1) *You tend to use "I" sometimes and the instructor said to avoid making the essay sound like a journal.*

2) *You have a great thesis—I can clearly see the three points you want to argue!*

3) *Be careful! Many times you give information that is not common knowledge and don't provide a source. And you forgot to include your works cited page!*

4) *Organization seems good, but paragraphing needs work. Your conclusion seems short, too.*

LESLIE BUCKLEY
Prof. R. Muhlbock
COMM 1011
February 13, 2013

Occupy Canada: Civil Disobedience and Corporate Greed

Conceived in September of 2011 through a notice posted in *Adbusters* magazine, the Occupy Wall Street movement has become this generation's attempt at a civil rights revolution (Schwartz). What first began as a march on Wall Street quickly spread around the world as people peacefully gathered to protest issues related to corporate greed, unemployment, and a lack of government regulation. In Canada, occupy movements sprung up in all major cities: Toronto, Vancouver, Ottawa, Montreal, and Halifax are just a few examples. For some, the movement was vaguely defined as a poor vs. rich dispute; however, such summaries trivialize what the movement is about and why its participants are so enraged. Protestors in the Occupy Canada movement are dissatisfied with dwindling job opportunities, the gap between wages for workers and management, and an ineffective government that allowed these injustices to occur in the first place.

Unemployment and job opportunities are a central issue in the Occupy Canada movement. Currently the unemployment rate in Canada is 7.3% ("Labour Force Survey, April 2012") and "while youth unemployment here is not as bad as in Europe or the U.S . . . people in Canada are still facing a future of McJobs and declining social services" ("Will occupy"). Currently, the youth unemployment rate is 14.5% ("Government scraps"); however, one need not be young to feel the effects of a dwindling job market. In October of 2011, Canada lost 71 700 full-time jobs, many of them in "manufacturing and construction" ("Canada suffers"). One such example is the Electro-Motive plant (owned by Caterpillar Inc.) in London, Ontario, which recently closed its doors, forcing some 540 skilled employees out of work (Size). Previous to the plant closing, workers had been locked out because they refused to take a 50% pay reduction (Size)—a situation which highlights another key aspect in the Occupy Canada movement: the income gap between workers and management.

The Occupy movement's slogan is "we are the 99%" (Hedler), a reference to how the top 1% of wage earners in Canada control 32% of the country's wealth, while the other 99% of citizens have to divide up what's left amid surging unemployment ("Richest 1%"). That said, a company concerned with profits

Excellent title.

Nice opening sentence.

Excellent examples.

Clear 3-point thesis.

Clear topic sentence, directly related to the thesis.

Paragraph makes excellent use of sources, all properly formatted.

Nice transitional concluding sentence.

Author concedes a point, only to provide a counter-argument.

is neither surprising nor unjustified, but one hopes that at some point simple ethics will intervene in business decisions.

As mentioned, Caterpillar closed its Electro-Motive plant after workers refused to take a 50% pay reduction; however, the same company not only posted a record profit of 5 billion dollars last year, but allowed its CEO to make $10.5-million annually (Size). This hardly sounds like a company struggling to stay in business and illustrates why the 99% are so upset. Caterpillar is just one specific example of the widening gap between rich and poor. The larger trend is just as disturbing. According to the CBC, the highest paid CEOs in Canada now make nearly 200 times more money than the national average—a 27% raise from 2009 ("Richest CEOs"). So while the average Canadian worker earns $44,366, the average top executive will have made this amount by noon ("Richest CEOs"). Yet, while some could accuse the 99% of simple jealousy, the ways that the top 1% acquire and maintain their wealth are usually highly suspect: low government regulation and taxation.

When the mortgage crisis occurred in 2008, government bailouts for U.S. banks and financial institutions enraged the public, and while it's true that a large majority of corporate scandals occur in the U.S. (Enron, to name one example) Canada is not without its faults (Keoun). Laforet claims that "none of Canada's banks were bailed out and . . . Canada's banking system has been praised as a model of stability for the world," a somewhat comforting thought; however, taxation for Canada's rich has steadily declined from 43% in 1981 to 29% in 2010 ("OECD report"). In this same report, the OECD also says that "reforming tax and benefit policies" is the best way to remedy this division, and yet the government has failed to respond (Kilian). At the provincial level, to curb Ontario's massive debt, the McGuinty Liberals are instead requesting a wage freeze for high school teachers ("Dalton McGuinty"), while at the federal level, the Harper Conservatives prefer not to interfere with the business sector—except when they are threatening to legislate Air Canada workers (who have a legal right to strike) back to their jobs ("Federal labour"). No wonder the public is jaded.

Occupy Canada, and the Occupy Wall Street movement in general, is not made up of disgruntled people too lazy to get a job or people merely jealous of those who have more spending money. Equality in wealth may not be possible, but simple fairness is. At the heart of the movement is the public quest for a livable wage and job security. However, one cannot always trust corporations to do the right thing; that is when elected officials must protect the public they serve. When they fail—to paraphrase a sign held by one Occupy protestor—revolution is not a necessity, but a public duty.

Nice transition: "however".

Excellent use of sources. Nicely developped paragraph.

Nice signal phrase: "Laforet claims...".

Transition: "however".

Excellent use of specific examples.

Stylish concluding statement.

Very well researched and formatted Works Cited page.

Works Cited

"Canada suffers worst monthly job loss since 2009." *The Star.* Toronto Star, 4 Nov. 2011. Web. 12 Mar. 2012.

"Dalton McGuinty pitches wage freeze to teachers on YouTube." *CBC,* 2 Mar. 2012. Web. 9 Mar. 2012.

"Federal labour minister watching threat of strike by Air Canada workers." Globaltoronto. Shaw Media Inc., 7 Mar. 2012. Web. 1 Apr. 2012.

"Government scraps student job centres as youth unemployment climbs." The Star. Toronto Star, 4 Mar. 2012. Web. 12 Mar. 2012.

Hedler, Ken. "Occupy Prescott protesters call for more infrastructure investment." The Daily Courier. Continental Newspapers Canada Ltd., 17 Nov. 2011. Web. 2 Apr. 2012.

Keoun, Bradley. "Citigroup Gets U.S. Rescue From Losses, Cash Infusion." Bloomberg, 28 Nov. 2008. Web. 12 Mar. 2012.

Kilian, Crawford. "Income gap widening in Canada: OECD." The Tyee. N.p., 5 Dec. 2011. Web. 3 Mar. 2012.

"Labour Force Survey, April 2012." StatsCan. N.p., Apr. 2012. Web. 5 May 2012.

Laforet, John. "Hey Protesters: Our Top 1% Differs From U.S." The Huffington Post. The Huffington Post.com, Inc. 18 Oct. 2011. Web. 2 Mar. 2012.

"OECD report finds income inequality rising in Canada." CTV. Bell Media, 5 Dec. 2011. Web. 19 Mar 2012.

"Richest 1% income shares at historic high." Canadian Centre For Policy Alternatives. N.p., 1 Dec. 2010. Web. 4 Mar. 2012.

"Richest CEOs earn 189 times average Canadian." CBC, 3 Jan. 2012. Web. 17 Mar. 2012.

Schwartz, Mattathias. "Pre-Occupied: The origins and future of Occupy Wall Street." The New Yorker. Conde Nast, 28 Nov. 2011. Web. 24 Mar. 2012.

Size, John. "Caterpillar shutting locked-out Electro-Motive plant." CTV News. Bell Media, 3 Feb. 2012. Web. 2 Mar. 2012.

"Will Occupy Wall Street catch on in Canada?" Globalnews. Shaw Media, Inc. 17 Oct. 2001. Web. 2 Mar. 2012.

USING THE COMPUTER TO REVISE

Since most college and university assignments are required to be typed, most students begin the drafting process on the computer. The following guidelines will help you as you revise your essay electronically:

1. **Save multiple versions of your drafts at various stages:** Some students choose to edit the same file over and over. While we are in complete support of revision, we do advise that students save various versions of their drafts at certain stages. You may be surprised to find that writing that you thought was good today, you might not feel is good tomorrow. Or maybe a chunk of text that you deleted as useless today could have been incorporated into a different paragraph of your essay. Just be careful to name each draft separately so you don't get confused!

2. **Use simple graphical highlights:** While rereading your essay, you may want to highlight a portion of the text that you need to rework at a later date. Since you're working from a computer, don't be afraid to totally cover your text with whatever graphical highlights you feel will help you remember to revise. Some people use one of the three traditional tools of **bolding,** underlining, or *italicizing* words or paragraphs they wish to revisit. Others may use the highlighting icon in Word to colour-code certain errors.

3. **Make frequent backup copies:** We know this was already mentioned, but it bears repeating. Print out your work at important moments, such as when you are finished working for the day or have completed a revision stage. Alternatively, you may choose to simply save your work to a flash drive or portable hard drive in addition to saving it to your main computer hard drive. Emailing your work to another address or saving it to an online storage system such as a "locker" are other options.

4. **Use the Review toolbar:** The Review toolbar in *MS Word 2010* has a multitude of functions for revising and editing your work. The benefit of using the Review toolbar is your ability to see all editorial changes to your work as well as to insert comments to remind yourself of text that needs to be fixed or ideas that need to be expanded upon. The Review toolbar is also particularly useful when a peer is reviewing your work, because you are able to see all of the suggestions and comments that your peer reviewer has and accept or reject them individually.

Using the Review Toolbar in *MS Word 2010*

The following steps will give you a brief tutorial on using the Review toolbar in *MS Word 2010* to get the most out of your computer's editing power.

1. **Select the toolbar:** First, you'll need to make sure the toolbar is visible on your screen. To make it appear, select the Review tab located on the top taskbar.

2. **Enable Track Changes:** Track Changes is *MS Word*'s way of showing edits to your text. This function is extremely important to the reviewing process as it allows you to make your changes to the text either hidden or visible. When the Review tab is selected, simply click the Track Changes icon in the toolbar to turn this feature on.

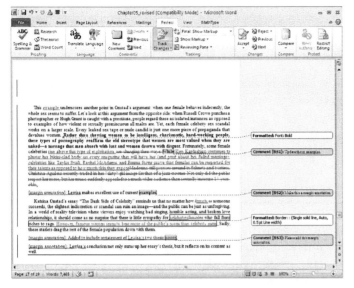

3. **Enabling Colours and Balloons:** For fewer options, click on the icon called Show Markup to see a drop-down menu that lists options for viewing your changes. Selecting the one called "balloons" allows you to see your revisions in balloons located in the right-hand margin or simply within the text itself.

   For detailed control, click on the Track Changes word icon below the picture icon to see a dropdown menu containing "Track Changing Options." From here you can decide how you wish your changes to appear regarding their colour and display format. The choice is up to the editor.

4. **Main Display Options:** The Review toolbar in *MS Word* allows you to rigorously edit your text by highlighting every detail of the editing process, including all insertions and deletions. Some people enjoy seeing these changes so they get a better grasp of how their document is progressing; others find all the colours and lines confusing. The display options on the Review toolbar—located to the upper right of the Track Changes icon as a dropdown menu—allow different writers to see as much of the editing process as they wish. Let's look at the various display options for a sample document edited with the Review toolbar.

   - **Original view.** Shows the document as it appeared originally, errors included, with no editing.
   - **Final view.** Shows the document with all editing changes included.
   - **Final showing markup.** Makes all changes to the document visible. Deleted items are displayed on the right margin in balloons, while insertions show up as red font.
   - **Original showing markup.** Makes all changes to the document visible. Inserted items are displayed in balloons in the right margin, while deleted text is struck through with a line.

5. **Accepting or rejecting changes:** The Review toolbar also contains a feature that allows you to skip through each change that you have (or someone else has) made to your paper and to decide whether to "accept" the change (in which case, it becomes part of your revised essay) or to "reject" it (in which case, your text reverts to its pre-edited state).

6. **Inserting comments:** Sometimes something as simple as adding or deleting a word is all the editing your document may require. However, at other times you might wish there was some way to tell yourself (or the person you are editing for) that certain parts of the document are unclear or confusing. Thankfully, the New Comment function in the Review toolbar allows just that. Clicking on this icon causes a comment balloon to appear in the right margin, directly attached to where the cursor is or to whatever portion of text the cursor highlighted.

Using the Internet

Go to these websites to find more tips, techniques, and insights on revising essays:

Microsoft Office
If you're having trouble getting the most out of the Review toolbar in *Microsoft Office 2010,* don't forget that Microsoft offers online support and help guides for all of their products. Their instructions are clear and detailed with graphics.
http://office.microsoft.com/en-us/word-help

The UVic Writer's Guide
The section titled "Writing Your Essay: Getting It Down" offers suggestions on writing and revising first drafts and for creating effective introductions and conclusions. Other advice covers writing well-developed, coherent body paragraphs that relate to the essay's thesis.
http://web.uvic.ca/wguide/Pages/MasterToc.html

The Write Place Catalogue
Maintained by St. Cloud University, this site provides advice on organization and coherence in paragraphs and essays. Transitions and thesis statements receive special coverage. You can also find information on writing essay introductions and conclusions. All of this information will help you as you edit your own paper and the papers of your peers.
http://leo.stcloudstate.edu/catalogue.html

CHAPTER 6

Refining Your Essay: Editing for Conciseness, Style, and Errors

LEARNING OUTCOMES:

▶ Eliminate wordiness, clichés, and passive voice in essay writing

▶ Establish appropriate tone and correct use of figurative language

▶ Revise choppy writing by using coordinating conjunctions and conjunctive adverbs

▶ Eliminate common grammar errors such as sentence fragments, comma splices, and fused sentences

▶ Vary sentence types in essay writing

EDITING in the Real World

In 2006, Rogers Communications and Aliant Inc. went to court over the placement of a comma in a contractual agreement. The placement of the comma potentially changed the meaning of the contract and could have cost Rogers $2.13 million depending on how the sentence was interpreted. This is one example of how a lack of proofreading and editing for proper spelling, punctuation, and grammar could have disastrous effects financially. Other times, editing mistakes affect credibility: in 2009, a press release by the Harper government repeatedly spelled the Nunavut capital Iqaluit (which means "many fish") as Iqualuit—a derogatory word in the Inuktitut language meaning "people with unwiped bums." In the context of job applications, a misspelled word can be the difference between getting a call to start a new career and having your resumé tossed into the recycling bin with all the other careless applicants. Editing is a mechanical procedure, but it should never be taken lightly. Carefully proofread work gives you professionalism and credibility. At the very least, it also ensures that you say what you mean to say.

The Writing Process: Revisited and Concluded

In Chapters 1 and 2, we discussed the necessity of prewriting and drafting. Chapters 3 and 4 discussed the need to cite sources and to make paragraphs clear, while Chapter 5 gave a detailed look at revision relating to structure and content. We are now ready to look at one last step:

Editing and proofreading. Many students tend to produce as their final draft an essay that sounds very good when read aloud. However, your reading audience will more likely be looking at paper, not listening to a transcript. The editing and proof-reading stage, in which you edit specifically for grammar and mechanics, helps you to catch serious errors that can undercut your credibility with your readers. It also helps you to polish your essay through final word choices and the fine tuning of your sentences.

Chapter 6 presents ways to make your writing clear through examination of its two smallest units: words and sentences. This chapter highlights some common writing challenges and offers ways to deal with these challenges.

Note
If you need additional help with the topics covered in this chapter, consult the Grammar Handbook at the back of this text. This handbook contains extensive treatment of these and other grammatical issues.

REVISING WORDS FOR CONCISENESS

When revising, you might feel that your first draft contains phrases and sentences that are overly complicated or awkward. In addition, you may find phrases or sentences that do not say what you intended them to, or you may find that weak phrasing has caused your writing to lose its punch. This section discusses these wording problems and ways to correct them.

Avoiding Wordiness

Sometimes long ideas call for long sentences and paragraphs; however, stuffing your writing with needless words in an attempt to sound important or just to fill space will annoy your reader much as a listener grows edgy when a speaker takes five minutes to tell a thirty-second story.

Take a look at the list of wordy phrases and their simpler equivalents in Figure 6.1. Don't think that you must always avoid using a phrase from the left-hand column; at times, one of these phrases may be useful and appropriate. However, if you *consistently* use these terms in place of their simpler equivalents, your writing will seem bloated. Note that phrases beginning with "it is" and "there are" in particular should be avoided.

Avoiding Fillers

Fillers are well known but essentially empty expressions that writers use when a more basic expression—or none at all—would work better. A list of fillers includes *all in all, needless to say,* and *first and foremost.*

WORDY EXPRESSIONS	
Wordy Phrase	**Simpler Equivalent**
during the time that	while
due to the fact that	because
in excess of	more than
in all probability	probably
in many instances	often
in a similar manner	similarly
in the event that	if
whether or not	whether
on the part of	by
a large number of	many
a large amount of	much
a small number of	few
a small amount of	little
it is clear that	clearly
it is obvious that	obviously
speaking with the truth	speaking truthfully
walking with care	walking carefully
shouting with excitement	shouting excitedly

Note the following paragraph and its revision:

WORDY   It can be clearly seen that our division's profits may or may not increase next year, with this issue based on the question of whether or not a large number of our current clients adopt the offer on the part of our main competition to sign package deals. Needless to say, in the event that our competitor succeeds, our business's profits, in all probability, will falter.

CONCISE   **Clearly, our division's profits next year depend on whether many of our current clients adopt our rival's package-deal offer. If our competitor succeeds, our business's profits will fall.**

The reader is forced to process 66 words in the original version to get the same meaning contained in the approximately 30 words of the edited version. Unrevised first drafts are frequently as wordy as the original paragraph above. Proper revision and editing should make your writing clear in as few words as possible.

EXERCISE 6.1

Edit the following sentences to be more concise.

1. When all is said and done, I believe that the art gallery's new show is a hit.

2. If and when the new stadium is completed, I doubt that it will meet the financial estimates of the planning committee.

3. The attempt on the part of the art gallery's management to restrict audience numbers in excess of 75 will be seen to be futile.

4. In all probability, the planning committee's estimates will be exceeded by 50 percent or more.

5. Shouting with happiness, Robert approached Anne, who shivered with nervousness.

6. Not a few of the art gallery patrons complained about the number of restrictions; however, the vast majority of those who got in were made happy by the experience.

7. Needless to say, the company's profit margin is my main concern.

8. A small number of the new stadium's supporters are speaking with care about the rash optimism that prevailed during the time that the initial budget planning took place.

EXERCISE 6.2

Edit the following paragraphs to eliminate wordiness.

1. During the time that music was available only on record, people could only hear roughly 40 minutes of new music due to the fact that this is all the time that records could hold. At the present time, artists can record up to 80 minutes of music on CD because CDs have a greater capacity for storage. It is clear that technology has improved for the average lover of music. Speaking the truth, some people prefer to download a large amount of music; however, others complain that in many instances the quality of the music is lower than on CD.

2. "Dahlia, if you'll join me in matrimony, I think you'll find in all probability that in many measures I will surprise you as a husband. I am not ungifted in the arts of love, despite any preconceptions on that issue you might have formed, and in a similar way you will grow to love my home bequeathed to me by my ancestors. Ignore those attempts on the part of your friends to persuade you; it is obvious that they do not know the interests that are best for you."

Avoiding Redundancy

Redundancy—the use of two or more words together that mean the same thing—is another common word-choice problem.

A list of frequently used redundancies appears on the next page, in Figure 6.2. A writer who uses any of the terms from the left-hand column in a final draft is not paying enough attention to what he or she is actually communicating.

EXERCISE 6.3

Edit the following sentences to eliminate redundant constructions.

1. Prior experience tells us that the end result of this initiative will be failure.

2. I think that Jared deliberately planned to ruin my shoes.

3. Your motives are totally obvious, Laura.

4. After failing to break the enemy lines, the patrol returned back to headquarters.

5. The mall was closed, and so we had to postpone our holiday shopping.

6. Eddie left the car, but yet he forgot to give me his key.

7. The mysterious guest vanished from view when approached by Dr. Herzel.

8. It's a small device, grey in colour, oval in shape, and light in weight—it's absolutely unique.

9. My own personal opinion is that modern physics has become too specialized for anyone except people with doctorates in the subject.

10. Unless you have the surgery, Mr. Walker, these symptoms will recur again.

FIGURE 6.2
When editing your work, eliminate redundant phrases.

COMMON REDUNDANCIES	
Redundant Phrase	**Simpler Equivalent**
small in size	small
brown in colour	brown
and therefore	therefore
so therefore	so *or* therefore
but yet	but *or* yet
outside of	outside
future plans	plans
advance reservations	reservations
prior planning	planning
visible to the naked eye	visible
square in shape	square
quite precise	precise
vanish from view	vanish
recur again	recur
advance ahead	advance
can possibly	can
very unique	unique
plan ahead	plan
retreat backward	retreat
completely clear	clear
totally obvious	obvious
in this day and age	now
over and over	continually or regularly
each and every	each or every
deliberately plan	plan
review again	review
past/prior experience	experience
personal friend	friend
final/end result	result
final total	total
my own personal	my
my own	my

Avoiding Textspeak

Thanks to the Internet (email, Twitter, Facebook) and smartphones (text messaging), many people have adopted shorthand methods of typing. While such shorthand may be acceptable when communicating informally with friends and family, such methods are NEVER acceptable for formal academic writing.

| INCORRECT | canada has been **thru** much during its 140 years as a nation. **o**ur universal healthcare helps people who **cant** help themselves. **t**he countr**ys** reputation in the world is very positive. |

| CORRECT | **C**anada has been **through** much during its 140 years as a nation. **O**ur universal healthcare helps people who **cannot** help themselves. **T**he countr**y's** reputation in the world is very positive. |

Can you imagine the first example appearing in a formal college or university essay (let alone an email to a client, customer, or business colleague)? Textspeak that creeps into formal writing erodes your credibility and makes you sound ridiculous. It also demeans your subject. When editing your assignments, always edit out such intrusions and write out words in full. The following list outlines some of the most common textspeak errors:

1. **Capitalization:** All sentences **must** begin with a capital letter. Proper names and the pronoun "I" (despite the use of "I" being discouraged in formal writing) must be capitalized as well.

2. **Apostrophes:** In formal essay writing, you are encouraged to write out all contractions; however, in instances where you do use contractions, be sure that your contractions (as well as all possessives) contain their required apostrophes.

3. **Numbers:** Numbers under two digits (under 10) should always be written out in full. Words containing parts that sound like numbers (such as "forever," "someone," and "together") should be written out in full and not as a combination of words and numbers (e.g., "4ever").

4. **Shorthand:** Write out all words in full, no matter how small. Do not shorten whole words or parts of words into letters or a combination of words and letters (e.g., "u" vs. "you" or "r" instead of "are").

REVISING WORDS FOR STYLE AND PRECISION

Style in writing is one of the harder concepts to define and it is even harder to achieve. A writer's style sets his or her work apart and makes an audience engaged. While there is no magic formula for creating the perfect style, paying attention to your tone, use of figurative language, and number of clichés is vital to establishing your own unique voice and writing style.

Using Appropriate Tone

As discussed in Chapter 1, establishing **purpose** and **audience** are two of the most important steps you can take when beginning to write. These will inform your tone and level of language. There are many ways to categorize language levels, but for our purposes let us concentrate on three types: informal, standard, and formal.

Informal English Informal English is conversational and reflects the spoken English of good friends talking to one another without worrying about being overheard. Because informal English is casual in tone and tends to include slang, it is usually not appropriate for higher education writing, although it may be suitable for a personal narrative such as a journal assignment. Developing and using a personal voice is important, but at the same time you must consider your audience; in the case of slang, which changes very quickly, your audience may not even know what your words mean.

Here is an example of a paragraph written in informal English (in bold type):

I just love the *Trailer Park Boys*. That show is **sick,** it's so **freakin' hilarious. I** can't believe the **crap** they get away with and the crazy **stuff** they do. **Me and my friends** love to get together and put in a DVD and just **laugh our butts off** for most of the night. Then maybe we'll **catch a flick and get some eats.** Then we'll **book it** back to my house to watch another DVD. **Sweet.**

Standard English Standard English avoids the casual tone and slang of informal English, and it also avoids the complex vocabulary and syntax of formal English. This paragraph is a good example of standard English:

Swearing is the salt and pepper of *Trailer Park Boys,* sprinkled liberally into the dialogue of Canada's new favourite rednecks, who, after four seasons on Showcase, have swiftly moved from cult favourite to mass appeal. Since BBC America picked up the show last spring, it's begun to take hold in the U.S. Shot mockumentary-style with a lo-fi, off-the-cuff design, *Trailer Park Boys* follows the lives of Ricky and Julian, loveable residents of Sunnyvale Trailer Park, who, when not in jail, spend their time drinking, smoking weed, smoking hash and trying to get rich, surrounded by pal Bubbles and a colourful cast of characters.

Matthew Woodley, "A walk in the @#$%! Park," Montreal *Mirror,* Dec. 9–15, 2004

The source of this paragraph is the Montreal *Mirror*—a newspaper. The author's use of standard English makes sense since this language is easily understandable by a general audience.

Formal English Formal English is the language of scholarly writing. It avoids the personal voice and uses complex sentence structure and diction to achieve a tone of objective discussion and analysis. Here is an example of a paragraph written in formal English (in bold type):

The Trailer Park Boys phenomenon is encouraging in several ways. First, it represents a truly Canadian **popcultural experience that has resonated** with audiences across the country. It is a successful TV show that will translate—and Telefilm is banking on this—into a successful feature film, *Trailer Park Boys: The Big Dirty.* It involves **serious expatriate talent** in the form of director and producer Ivan Reitman—he of *Ghostbusters* fame—who provided what Holt describes as "significant partnership, contacts and guidance." It also, and perhaps most important, represents the fact that Telefilm has finally **identified a niche** that may just provide the golden key to the audiences long missing from the English-Canadian equation.

Richard Poplak, "Two Cultures: One Cheque," *This Magazine,* Nov/Dec 2005

The source of this paragraph is *This Magazine*, a well-respected Canadian news journal.

As you start revising a first draft, consider your language level. You should have addressed this issue at the prewriting stage when you focused on the audience of the piece. Now that you are looking at a draft, have the language decisions you made in prewriting proved to be appropriate for your purpose? If the language level seems generally adequate, then think about this possible problem: Are there some places where you've used language that clashes with the rest of your text? Have you inadvertently used a slang expression or some off-putting jargon? If so, then this oversight may lodge in the reader's memory and take away from the overall persuasiveness of your paper.

EXERCISE 6.4

The following passage is written in informal English. Revise the paragraph so that it is more suitable for college- or university-level work. In particular, remove the "I" pronoun to make the paragraph sound more objective and universal.

My local computer/music/video store often gives me a load of problems. Lack of great merchandise, scuzzy store, and weird salesguys are the norm. I went there last Saturday to look at some new speakers. Walking past a pack of geeks arguing about the latest monitor, I tripped over a gizmo that even I, good with computers, couldn't put a name to. In the stereo section I ran into the guy who would help my quest. He had obviously been hiding when the Dork Patrol made its last sweep. But he knew a lot about sound systems. He found me the speakers I wanted. He dug up a rebate coupon from somewhere. He gave me enough info so that I wouldn't fry myself when I got home. And the price was right. So, what's to cry about?

Avoiding Passive Voice

Verbs can have two voices: active or passive. In sentences written in the active voice, subjects act; in sentences written in the passive voice, subjects are acted upon. Passive voice also tends to use a form of the verb "to be" such as "was," "is," or "are." Overusing the passive voice causes weak, flabby writing. Examine these two sentences:

PASSIVE   The bonus money was given to us by Ms. Thompson.

ACTIVE   **Ms. Thompson gave us the bonus money.**

The sentence using the passive voice fades away like the dying note of a song, whereas the sentence in the active voice gives the reader the information directly. Keep in mind these simple guidelines: use the passive voice only (1) when you can't—or really don't want to—reveal who did the action or (2) when you want to emphasize the receiver of the action.

Consider the following situation. Police officers checking the back door of a restaurant find a male corpse. It has four visible bullet wounds. No other human beings are in the area. How will the local newspaper "lead" with this story? Probably this way:

A man was murdered last night. . . .

The active voice won't work here because the writer doesn't know the identity of the actor.

Also, you may want to choose the passive voice when you know the responsible party but don't want to mention the name—perhaps the guilty party is your boss, for example.

TACTFUL   **Mistakes were found in the billing of the Andrews project.**

The alternative might be dangerous:

BLUNT   Mr. Waddell committed errors when billing the Andrews project.

Finally, sometimes you will want to emphasize the receiver, not the actor:

The murder weapon was found behind a shed.

The person who found the weapon is not important; the actual discovery is.

Preferring Verbs over Nouns

Examine the following sentence:

There was an immediate burst of applause from the crowd when the popular premier started her speech.

It communicates well enough, but it lacks a certain punch. Note the revision:

The crowd applauded immediately when the popular premier started speaking.

The revised sentence depends on verbs (*applauded, started speaking*), not nouns, to convey what happened, and it gets directly to the point. In the next two examples, the original sentences have a similar problem:

ORIGINAL	The baking of cakes is a source of much pleasure for my retired uncle.
REVISED	**My retired uncle really enjoys baking cakes.**
ORIGINAL	It was in the supervision of trainees that Stephanie found her niche.
REVISED	**Stephanie excelled at supervising trainees.**

The goal is not to write each sentence with the fewest possible words, but to remember that each sentence tells the story of an actor and an action. Concentrate on showing this relationship with active verbs and clear, direct expression.

Revise the following sentences from passive voice to active voice:

1. Doug is frightened by spiders.

2. The goods are produced in Montreal.

3. The meal was prepared by our leading chef.

4. The grassy plains have been burned by the wildfires.

5. Many votes are required to pass the new law.

EXERCISE 6.6

Revise the following noun-based wordy sentences using strong verbs to indicate actions:

1. The new plan created a reduction in waste.

2. The computer performed an analysis of the transit system.

3. The teacher gave consideration to the suggestion.

4. Rob is of the opinion that seafood is delicious.

5. The child engaged in the preparation of a sand castle.

Avoiding Euphemisms and Jargon

Euphemisms are words and phrases used to cover up the literal truth. We sometimes use euphemisms to avoid making a troubling situation worse:

> Uncle Mike **passed on** last night.
> Uncle Mike **died** last night.

Sometimes we use euphemisms to avoid saying what we actually mean.

> Jenkins, we're going to have to **let you go.**
> Jenkins, we're going to have to **fire you.**

In some situations, a euphemism can be appropriate; for example, saying "going to the bathroom" is preferable to saying . . . well . . . what you are literally going to do. However, euphemisms can also be dangerous. Consider the following example:

> The U.S. uses **enhanced interrogation techniques.**
> The U.S. uses **torture.**

In this real-life example based on the U.S. war on terrorism, a euphemism was used to allow the United States to escape accusations of human rights violations (yet all evidence points to their involvement in these violations). In short, if you want to write directly and clearly, avoid using euphemisms.

Jargon is language that is overly or needlessly technical. Sometimes jargon pertains to a specific profession or field, such as law or medicine, and is appropriate in a paper targeted toward that profession; however, jargon can appear anywhere. For example, in their attempt to sound "formal," students sometimes write jargon-filled sentences that they would not dream of saying in real life.

Consider the following:

> Formulated in the early morning hours, the proposal was designed as a primary action item to facilitate interaction between the two sides in the labour dispute.

First, is it necessary to *formulate* a proposal? Second, what is a *primary action item*? Third, what does *facilitate* really mean, anyway? Only certain audiences will understand this term. Here is a plainer version of this sentence:

> **In early morning, the committee finished the proposal that would bring both sides to the bargaining table.**

In other words, write what you mean. Don't cloak your meaning in jargon.

 **EXERCISE 6.7**

Working alone or in pairs, read the following sentences, each of which contains a highlighted term or terms. Decide if each highlighted term is either a euphemism or jargon. If it is one or the other, replace it with a more direct or appropriate expression.

1. Wanda's in **hot water** with the boss; it looks like she **fudged** her travel account.

2. Our former baker **expired** this morning, but I think his family will be okay as I heard he had a lot of **dough.**

3. During our journey, we frequently had to stop so that my young son could go **make water.**

4. **Law enforcement officials** arrested 17 people after last night's **civil unrest** in which cars were smashed and businesses were looted.

5. The new repairs on the Schooner Expressway will **enhance revenues** for the city because of increased tourism.

6. Henry never gives to any charities; he keeps **a tight leash** on his finances.

7. Seventy-four employees were **downsized** in the company's latest cost-cutting efforts.

8. Aunt Linda's **frugality** kept her family going after the death of Uncle Carter.

 **EXERCISE 6.8**

Rewrite the following sentences to avoid jargon and wordiness.

1. Hi, I'm here to facilitate this meeting.

2. According to our statistics, utilization of coffee by our secretaries has undergone an increase of 20 percent.

3. The bad news was communicated by Inspector Laurence.

4. Let's engage in a positive dialogue concerning the implementation of these geographically dispersed enterprises.

5. The termination process of an employee found to be ineffective has been estimated by our personnel department to cost over $5000.

6. I'm trying to conceptualize the scene that you're describing.

7. The ball was hit by the bat and began the process of arcing through the air in the general proximity of the shortstop.

8. My comprehension of your meaning is faulty.

9. Ben is such a ripper—he just did a gnarly flip with his deck over a funbox.

Using Figurative Language Appropriately

Figurative language does not represent a subject directly or literally; instead, it uses expressions and imagery to help explain, define, or add information about the subject. Let's look at the following example:

> Harrison's wrongful-termination lawsuit is the wheel upon which our company may be broken.

The lawsuit is not literally a wheel or any other medieval torture device; it's a legal filing. But claiming that the lawsuit is "the wheel upon which our company may be broken" evokes a startling image in the reader's mind and underscores the severity of the issue.

Simile and Metaphor A **simile** is a comparison using the words "like" or "as." Note how the following passage uses a simile to help make a point:

> Student debt is like a load of bricks on a student's back. If the student is lucky enough to get a good job after he or she graduates, this debt will still need to be repaid. Considering the average yearly interest on a student loan and considering the average yearly wage a new graduate is likely to earn, most graduates will be carrying their load of bricks for a long time, with some loads getting heavier each year.

In this passage, the author uses a simile to compare a student's debt to a load of bricks using the word *like*. The author's use of this simile gives the paragraph a vivid urgency.

Like a simile, a **metaphor** tries to amplify meaning by linking one idea to another, but a metaphor does so without using "like" or similar words to signal comparison. With a metaphor, the writer says that the item being described is (figuratively) the other. Here is an example of the effective use of metaphor:

> If this country is, indeed, headed towards a recession, then it is up to our prime minister, the beloved captain of this great country, to steer us through the rough waters of job loss until we safely reach the port of prosperity.

This paragraph takes the idea of the country as a ship and the prime minister as "captain," leading us through the "rough waters" of a recession.

The following examples show clearly that the metaphor is more forceful than the simile. Unfortunately, however, the metaphor is also somewhat harder to use properly.

SIMILE	After Mike's gruelling day at the office, Laura's welcoming smile was like a rainbow of sanctuary.
METAPHOR	**After Mike's gruelling day at the office, Laura's welcoming smile provided a rainbow of sanctuary.**

Personification A third type of figurative language is **personification,** in which human characteristics are given to nonhuman entities:

The moon smiled at us as we travelled by night.
The night wind whispered its secrets.

As the second sentence indicates, writers who use personification in essays must keep control of their imaginations. A sentence that personifies the night wind is striking, but if the wind whispers through an entire paragraph, readers will soon tire of the idea.

Avoiding Clichés

Using vivid figures of speech will improve your writing, but using **clichés** will hurt it. How can you tell the difference? If an expression is very common, a phrase that you've known most of your life, an "old standard," it's probably a cliché. Note the cliché in the following sentence:

My sister is blind as a bat without her glasses.

This worn-out phrase is not going to make your reader admire your language skills. The expression is not only a cliché; it is an *ancient* cliché. However, note how the writer of the following passage makes good use of a cliché:

Peter McMichaels was hired at the same time as four other people. His work has been no better or worse than theirs. He has no outstanding characteristics other than his willingness to complain when he doesn't get his way. Yet Peter got a raise this month whereas the other four people didn't. It's clearly an instance of the squeaky wheel getting the grease.

The writer has taken a cliché ("The squeaky wheel gets the grease") and used it to good effect. The reader can be expected to know the cliché and not need to see it spelled out, which would belabour the obvious. Remember, though: only rarely can you put a cliché to good use. Most of the time, using one makes your writing sound silly or stale. Consider the following paragraph:

The bottom line is that Rita would be in the lap of luxury if she had nipped that drinking problem in the bud. When push came to shove, the world was her oyster last year; now, she'll be lucky if her company doesn't kick the bucket before the cows come home. Hopefully she can kick it up a notch and take it to the next level to save her skin.

Whew! What a mess. In short, you should avoid clichés like the plague.

Read the following sentences. If a sentence can be made more lively, revise it. Be creative. If a sentence contains a cliché or awkward metaphor, revise the sentence to eliminate the problem.

1. Mrs. Parker hit the nail on the head when she suggested that we pull out all the stops and call everyone in the neighbourhood.

2. My brother-in-law isn't the sharpest knife in the drawer, but he's a good family man.

3. Find him—leave no stone unturned!

4. Myra went up the corporate ladder quickly until her career ran aground after her company was taken over.

5. The recent campaign to "beautify" Parkersville is like putting makeup on a hog.

6. The salmon swam very hard against the current.

7. After her oral presentation bit the dust, Laurel considered dropping her business communications class.

8. This cake batter is as light as a feather.

9. Doug's petition got a shot in the arm when the committee steamrolled the only objection.

10. In a nutshell, here's the straight dope.

Making Language Specific

Specific language usually communicates your ideas and details more effectively than abstract language. Specific language appeals to the senses: sight, hearing, taste, smell, and touch. In Figure 6.3 below, notice the strength of impact, interest, and precision that the sentences on the right have when compared to those on the left:

USING SPECIFIC LANGUAGE	
Abstract	**Specific**
The head of Nidix Co. often became envious of the business success of others.	The head of Nidix Co. often sneered at and cursed others who were successful.
Dogs can be nice.	Dogs are affectionate and will often jump onto your lap and lick your face.
The two candidates hated each other.	The two candidates scowled at each other and often resorted to snide remarks about the other's policies.
Patients hate overcrowded waiting rooms.	Patients can become uncomfortable in overcrowded waiting rooms. Overcrowding can lead to excessive sweating and trouble breathing.
The old man's fingers were sore.	The old man's fingers were arthritic. The fingers of his right hand were swollen, and they curled into a useless claw.

FIGURE 6.3
Use specific, concrete language to communicate effectively.

Specific language gives your readers a **verbal portrait** of what you are communicating and allows them to experience it in their imaginations. This technique is sometimes called "showing, not telling." When you want to transmit your experience of a person, object, place, or problem, abstract language often leaves your readers with only a vague sense of what you mean. As you revise your essay, look for places where specific, concrete details would make your ideas clearer for your audience. (See Figure 6.4 below.)

FIGURE 6.4
The specific items on the right are much more effective and clear than the general terms on the left.

ACHIEVING SPECIFICITY

General	More Specific	Very Specific
book	novel	*Fifth Business*
artwork	oil painting	Tom Thomson's "The Jack Pine"
residence	house	three-bedroom ranch
exercise	aerobic exercise	jogging
motor vehicle	sports utility vehicle	Rav4
restaurant	fast-food restaurant	Jim's Fry Station
tree	maple	red maple
municipality	city	Yellowknife
boat	sailboat	schooner

REVISING SENTENCES FOR STYLE AND PRECISION

Grammar: A Necessary Evil

It's hard to discuss how to correctly write and punctuate language without referring to parts of speech by their correct names. Vague language helps no one. Imagine a mechanic saying, "We're going to stop the thumping in your engine by rearranging some stuff inside your car. Then you'll pay us!" Or imagine a doctor, before surgery, saying, "I'll cut you open and fix whatever I find in there."

While complex and sometimes intimidating to hear, grammatical terms help instructors specifically pinpoint where writing goes wrong. Below are definitions of a few terms used in this chapter:

Complete sentence: A sentence consists of a subject (usually a noun or pronoun that says what the sentence is about) and a verb (an action word that says what the subject is or is doing), and expresses a complete thought.

Independent clause: A clause is a group of related words containing a subject and verb. An independent clause can stand its own as a complete sentence.

Dependent clause: A dependent clause contains a noun and a verb, but it cannot stand on its own as a complete sentence.

Sentence fragment: A sentence fragment is—quite literally—a fragment of a sentence. It is an incomplete thought and tells the reader to expect more. Sentence fragments are sentences without subjects or verbs or both. For example, "In the hallway" would be a sentence fragment.

Comma splice: A comma splice joins two complete sentences together with a comma. Instead of a comma, the writer should be using a period, conjunction (like "and" or "but"), or semicolon.

For examples of the above terms, please see the Grammar Handbook located at the end of this book.

Revising Choppy Sentences

One way to write prose is in **simple sentences,** with each sentence expressing a single idea. For example, consider the following paragraph:

> The Internet is a new world. This world contains many possibilities. One possibility is research. Another possibility is shopping. Another possibility is investing. Students can research topics from home. They don't have to go to a library. Shoppers can buy products from home. They don't have to go to a store. Investors can buy mutual funds directly from home. They don't have to call a broker. The Internet is a major convenience.

Although grammatically correct, this paragraph is choppy and immature, and it reads more like the work of a child than the work of a student in higher education.

Sentence combining allows writers to create persuasive, concise text by merging ideas that are connected to each other in content and by showing their relationships to one another. Popular ways to connect ideas include using **coordinating conjunctions and conjunctive adverbs,** or making one sentence **subordinate** to (or less important than) another. These techniques are not used for economy but, instead, to show the connection between two related sentences.

Types of Sentences

Not all sentences are equal. In fact, writers have identified four specific sentence types that can give your writing variety and impact. They are as follows:

The simple sentence: A simple sentence is a single-clause sentence, which contains a subject and a verb and expresses a single idea.

- The sun is shining.

The compound sentence: A compound sentence is made up of two or more independent clauses joined by coordinating conjunctions or conjunctive adverbs.

- The sun is shining, and the birds are singing.
- The sun is shining; however, it is very cold.

The complex sentence: A complex sentence is made up of one independent clause and one dependent clause.

- Because the sun is shining for the first time this summer, we are going for a picnic.

The compound-complex sentence: A compound-complex sentence contains both compound and complex clauses.

- Because the sun is shining, we are going for a swim, and then we're having a barbeque at Blake's place.

For more examples relating to the four sentence types, please see Chapter 11 in the Grammar Handbook located at the back of this text.

Using Coordinating Conjunctions

When you use coordination as your sentence combining technique, you take two independent clauses and create a **compound sentence** by using coordinating conjunctions or transitional expressions to connect them. Each clause maintains an approximately equal weight.

The **coordinating conjunctions** *for, and, nor, but, or, yet,* and *so* are small words used to join two independent clauses together. (Teachers tell students to remember them by using the acronym FANBOYS.)

Let's look at one of them used in an example:

ORIGINAL	Adulis enjoyed spending time in online chat rooms. His mom had never even been on the Internet.
REVISED	**Adulis enjoyed spending time in online chat rooms, but his mom had never even been on the Internet.**

Here the two sentences are joined with the coordinating conjunction "but," preceded by a comma, to form a **compound sentence.** Using coordinating conjunctions is a great way to combine sentences for smoother writing; however, be aware of the following issue when using them as connectors:

Comma usage: Don't place a comma in front of every *and* or *but* that you write. Besides being used with a comma to form compound sentences, the seven coordinating conjunctions can also be used as simple conjunctions, joining two nouns, verbs, or phrases. In both of the following sentences, the conjunction is not used as a sentence connector but as a simple conjunction—hence, no preceding comma is needed:

Frederick and Angelica are here.
We travelled to Yellowknife but did not see the northern lights.

(For a complete discussion of comma usage, see Chapter 16 in the Grammar Handbook at the back of this text.)

Using Conjunctive Adverbs

Another group of sentence connectors that you can use to combine sentences is **conjunctive adverbs.** You will find a list of the most common conjunctive adverbs as well as a few other transitional expressions in Figure 6.5.

Let's look at our previous example using a conjunctive adverb in place of a coordinating conjunction.

ORIGINAL	Adulis enjoyed spending time in online chat rooms. His mom had never even been on the Internet.
REVISED	**Adulis enjoyed spending time in online chat rooms; however, his mom had never even been on the Internet.**

Note that this sentence has a more formal tone than the compound sentence formed by using *but.*

Conjunctive adverbs and other transitional expressions		
accordingly	in addition	next
additionally	in brief	nonetheless
also	in conclusion	of course
as an illustration	in contrast	on the other hand
at the same time	in short	otherwise
besides	in summary	similarly
certainly	in the same way	specifically
consequently	indeed	still
conversely	instead	subsequently
finally	likewise	then
for example	meanwhile	therefore
for instance	moreover	thus
furthermore	namely	to be sure
hence	nevertheless	

FIGURE 6.5
Conjunctive adverbs and transitional expressions are used to create compound sentences.

Conjunctive adverbs and phrases are extremely useful, provided that you choose carefully and keep the following issues in mind.

Semicolon and colon usage: Unlike coordinating conjunctions, conjunctive adverbs/transitional expressions can appear in different positions within a clause:

Maria was ready to travel to New Brunswick; however, Terrance was not.

Maria was ready to travel to New Brunswick; Terrance, however, was not.

Maria was ready to travel to New Brunswick; Terrance was not, however.

The semicolon is the boundary point between the two independent clauses, but the conjunctive adverb "however" can be placed at the beginning, in the middle, or at the end of the second independent clause. For the purposes of clarity, placing the connector at the beginning of the second clause is recommended; however, you might want to use one of the other patterns for **sentence variety.** (For more on semicolons, please see Chapter 17 in the Grammar Handbook at the back of this text.)

GRAMMAR ALERT: Avoiding Comma Splices and Fused Sentences If you are careless when punctuating sentences that use conjunctive adverbs or transitional expressions, you can end up with **comma splices or fused sentences.**

Simply defined, a comma splice is a comma that joins two complete sentences (also referred to as independent clauses). See the example below:

COMMA SPLICE   The Tragically Hip are from Kingston, Ontario, in addition, all the members went to high school together.

In this example, the comma between "Ontario" and "in" is the problem—this is where the two sentences meet. A comma splice can be corrected in a number of ways; however the easiest method is with a period or semicolon.

CORRECT   **The Tragically Hip are from Kingston, Ontario; in addition, all the members went to high school together.**

A fused sentence occurs when two complete sentences (or independent clauses) are joined without any punctuation separating the sentences at all. See the example below:

FUSED SENTENCE   Most people in the United States have not heard of the band nevertheless their following in Canada is huge.

In this example, the first sentence ends at the word "band" and the second begins at "nevertheless"—this is where the two sentences meet. The easiest way to correct a fused sentence is with a period or semicolon.

CORRECT   **Most people in the United States have not heard of the band; nevertheless, their following in Canada is huge.**

For more detailed explanations of these issues, see Chapter 12 in the Grammar Handbook at the end of this text.

Using Subordinating Conjunctions

To subordinate something is to make it less important than something else. Where matters of grammar are concerned, when you join two sentences by adding a **subordinating conjunction,** one of the two sentences loses its status as an independent clause. Please review the list of some common subordinating conjunctions in Figure 6.6.

Then look at our previous sentences about Adulis and his mother, now using a subordinating conjunction instead of a conjunctive adverb or coordinating conjunction:

ORIGINAL   Adulis enjoyed spending time in online chat rooms. His mom had never even been on the Internet.

REVISED   **Although Adulis enjoyed spending time in online chat rooms, his mom had never even been on the Internet.**

The addition of the subordinating conjunction "although" makes the first clause dependent—lower in rank, so to speak. Since it has become a **dependent clause,** one that cannot stand alone as a sentence, the comma after "rooms" is correct.

Using complex sentences: Most of the time, a writer will use a complex sentence like the one above to show that the independent clause contains information that is

Subordinating conjunctions		
after	once	unless
although	provided that	until
as	rather than	when
because	since	whenever
before	so that	where
even if	so (that)	whereas
even though	than	wherever
if	that	whether
in order that	though	while

FIGURE 6.6
Subordinating conjunctions establish that one clause of a complex sentence is more important that the other.

more important than the information contained in the dependent clause, as in this construction:

Although she stumbled at the start, Angela won the race easily.

The outcome of the race is more important than an event that happened during the race, so the incident (stumbling) is subordinated to the outcome (winning).

Writers sometimes use complex sentences simply to provide variety. The two sentences are equal in importance; and the writer subordinates one to the other only to vary the sentence pattern for his or her reader, who might otherwise become tired of sentences joined by *and, but,* and *however.*

The Wallace family loved cleaning the house, whereas the Jacksons saw it as a chore.

Which fact is more important, that the Wallaces love housework or that the Jacksons hate housework? Neither is. The writer is using the subordinating conjunction *whereas* to provide stylistic variety.

Note

If any of the above grammatical terminology is unfamiliar to you, you can find elaborations on these strategies in the Grammar Handbook at the end of this text.

GRAMMAR ALERT: Avoiding Sentence Fragments If you are careless when punctuating sentences with subordinating conjunctions, you can end up with **sentence fragments.**

A **sentence fragment** is a group of words that is treated like a sentence but is missing a subject and/or a verb and does not represent a complete thought; it is a dependent clause trying to stand alone. A fragment is as severe an error as a comma splice or a fused sentence.

Often students will confuse conjunctive adverbs with subordinating conjunctions and end up with sentence fragments. In the following example, the first sentence is correct; the second, however, is a fragment:

FRAGMENT   I couldn't get to work on time. Because my car wouldn't start.

The sentence "my car wouldn't start" is complete (or independent), but putting the word "because" in front of it makes it dependent and tells your reader to expect more. However, revision in this example is easy; simply form a complete sentence by combining them together:

CORRECT   **I couldn't get to work on time because my car wouldn't start.**

The next example is a little more troubling:

FRAGMENT   I couldn't get to work. Although, I could have asked my neighbour for a ride.

In this case, the writer believes that *although* is a conjunctive adverb, not a subordinating conjunction. To fix this fragment, simply replace *although* with the appropriate conjunctive adverb:

CORRECT   **I couldn't get to work; however, I could have asked my neighbour for a ride.**

(For more help with recognizing and correcting sentence fragments, consult Chapter 12 in the Grammar Handbook at the back of this text.)

EXERCISE 6.10

Each sentence in the following paragraphs consists of a single independent clause. Use coordination and subordination to combine sentences and make the paragraphs read more smoothly. If necessary, add the appropriate sentence connectors to show logical relations between ideas. Make sure that you punctuate your newly combined sentences correctly.

1. Last summer, three of my friends and I were driving through the prairies. In particular, I loved Alberta. It contained lovely natural features and interesting small towns. The cities were bustling with activity. The winters are very cold. We didn't have enough time to drive to the northern part of the province. We concentrated on thoroughly exploring Alberta's middle and southern sections.

2. Someone needs to establish a janitorial service for the Internet—not to clean up the raunchy parts but to get rid of the abandoned, ancient websites. There are an alarming number of outmoded, useless sites. New websites tend to have all the bells and whistles. Old websites have a reek of early technology. New websites tend to rely on graphics and animation. Old websites are dependent on text. Old websites also tend to contain information current in the year they were last updated— say, 2001. This information is no longer needed. Perhaps someday an agency will be allowed to do a search-and-destroy mission on these ancient outposts.

EXERCISE 6.11

Many of the following sentences are incorrectly punctuated, causing comma splices and fused sentences. Correct any faulty punctuation.

1. I'm at war with a blue jay that lives in a tree near my apartment's parking lot. I like the looks of jays in general, nevertheless, we're locked in battle. The jay is guarding a nest, so anyone who walks by is a threat the bird will fly 50 feet to swoop down at me. This is not to say I disapprove of the bird's protective instinct, I just wonder why jays are the only birds that act this way. You walk past a nesting robin nothing happens. Jays, however; treat humans as enemies.

2. I frequently hear people complain about the high salaries paid to professional athletes. People feel that they make too much money, or that no one should get that much for playing a game, this is the way that the argument normally goes. People complain all the time about athletes, however you rarely hear them complain about movie actors. I believe the reason is twofold. One is that most of us have played sports at some time in our lives therefore we have a familiarity with what athletes are doing, the second is the opposite, most of us have never tried to act, so we give actors more credit than they might deserve.

EXERCISE 6.12

The following paragraph contains fragments caused by treating dependent clauses as sentences. Find the fragments and fix them in one of two ways: (1) by revising the fragment so that it becomes part of an adjacent sentence, or (2) by changing the subordinating conjunction into a conjunctive adverb. Make sure that you punctuate your revised sentences correctly.

The allure of the box-office idol seems just as strong today as in the past. People normally go to movies based on who is starring. Or who is not. In some cases, these stars have drawing power that lasts for decades. Some stars can even carry a film single-handedly. Angelina Jolie, Julia Roberts, Brad Pitt, and Robert Downey Jr. All are big names who can do this. Despite each of these actors having been in at least one box office failure. Only in rare cases is the director's name just as popular as the lead actor or actress's. People will usually turn out in droves to see anything directed by Steven Spielberg or Peter Jackson. Because these directors have created some of the most popular movies ever.

Varying Your Sentence Types

Sentences joined by coordination and subordination form recognizable patterns with formal names, some of which we have already encountered:

COMPOUND SENTENCE

My computer is three years old, but it still suits my needs.
My computer is three years old; however, it still suits my needs.

COMPLEX SENTENCE

Although my computer is three years old, it still suits my needs.

My computer still suits my needs although it is three years old.

COMPOUND-COMPLEX SENTENCE

Although my computer is three years old, it still suits my needs, so I probably won't buy a new one for a few more years.

In fact, you can generate a limitless number of new sentences by changing the subject, changing the verb, changing the connector, and so on. You can also generate sentences that contain many clauses—collections of independent clauses and dependent clauses that represent increasingly complex thoughts. Consider the following examples:

1. Although my MP3 player is three years old, it still suits my needs; therefore, I probably won't buy a new one for a few more years.

2. My MP3 player still suits my needs although it is three years old, so I probably won't buy a new one for a few more years.

3. My MP3 player still suits my needs although it is three years old; therefore, I probably won't buy a new one for a few more years.

4. I probably won't buy a new MP3 player for a few more years; my current MP3 player still suits my needs although it is three years old.

5. I probably won't buy a new MP3 player for a few more years; although my current MP3 player is three years old, it still suits my needs.

Be careful, however: long sentences are not necessarily wrong, but think of your reader. Do you want to subject your audience to 85-word sentences? Of course not. The patterns that we have explored will allow you to generate sentences of any length, long or short. It is up to you to vary your sentence structures and to use these options wisely.

EXERCISE 6.13

Examine each set of word groups below, and construct a sentence for each, using an appropriate sentence type. Use at least three of the different sentence types discussed in this chapter.

1. My friend Jason. 2006. Graduated. Got engaged. Moved to British Columbia.

2. Dark clouds. High winds. Heavy rains. Ruined picnic.

3. Bad relief pitching. Slow base runners. Strange managerial decisions. Won 11–3.

4. Flat tire. Crashed hard drive. Monthly sales award. Nice bonus. Strange day at the office.

5. Torn ear. Blind eye. Arthritic hip. Horrible excuse for an iguana.

PROOFREADING

Proofreading is the final rereading of your essay to check for those nagging typographical and format errors—the gremlins—that always seem to sneak into your paper no matter how many times you look it over. If you are using a computer to write your essay, at this point you should have your latest draft on some type of portable medium and also on the hard drive, if possible. You should have a paper copy of the draft with handwritten revision comments on it. Now you are ready to finish your essay by reviewing your existing file. The following guidelines will help (see also Figure 6.7 for a specific checklist):

1. Check your existing electronic draft for any areas that are still highlighted or marked in boldface. Also check for any annotations or comments that you may have inserted and be sure to delete these; and if you have used MS revision tools, be sure to send the *final* version of your essay, without showing your changes.

2. Use a standard font style and size, and double space your printout. One of the great advantages of the computer is that it allows you to determine font, point size, and line spacing, but is it any wonder that composition instructors get angry when they receive a paper in ten-point type, single-spaced font? Use a non-display font—the older, conservative fonts such as Times New Roman, Courier, Garamond, Goudy, and Palatino will work well. Use 12-point type unless your instructor specifies something different. Don't use a cursive font, all-capital letters, coloured ink, or any other formatting that will distract your reader. Use one-inch margins, and don't crowd your page.

3. Make your revisions from paper to screen. Once you are satisfied that you have finished this step, save and print out the corrected version. Now check this printout against the paper source; it's easy to miss corrections when revising on computer.

4. After you have made your last correction, print out a paper copy and read it again.

5. Run the spell-checker. If your computer has a grammar-checking program, you might use this as well. You should not *rely* on either one, however. Such software programs aren't perfect and often—in the case of spell-checkers—replace incorrectly spelled words with words that seem similar, but have a different meaning ("definitely" vs. "defiantly," for example). Additionally, a spell-checker can't distinguish among *their, there,* and *they're;* and spell-checkers often use American, not Canadian, spellings. A grammar-checker, on the other hand, might highlight sentences that have no errors but seem too long, according to the software's programming. Remember that the quality of the essay is *your* responsibility.

6. Read your essay aloud. *Listen* for problems that you might not *see* when reading silently. At this stage, you can catch awkward phrasings and typographical errors.

7. When preparing your essay for its final printing, check your assignment one last time. Is there any requirement that you missed or forgot? Does the instructor

FIGURE 6.7
Final proofreading checklist.

FINAL CHECKLIST

While the following checklist includes issues discussed in previous chapters, it also works as a good final proofreading checklist.

☐ Does your essay have **a specific title** (and not something vague like "Essay 1" or "Research Paper"?

☐ Does your essay **avoid** starting with a generic, uncontextualized quotation or—even worse—a basic definition from dictionary.com?

☐ Does your essay **use clear and concise language** (as opposed to giant words just to make the author sound "smart")?

☐ Does your essay's introduction **avoid extremely general statements** that are not specifically relevant to your thesis argument (e.g., "Marriage has been a theme in literature since the beginning of time," or "When one is a teenager, one has to figure out one's identity," or "Women have struggled for equal rights for centuries.")?

☐ Does your essay **avoid using wordy and self-referential phrases** like "as previously stated/mentioned," "in this essay," "as we can see," "it could be said that," or "it is clear that"?

☐ Does your essay **avoid** having paragraphs that are more than a page long, that are three or fewer sentences short, that discuss more than one point, or that discuss points that do not prove your thesis argument?

☐ Is your essay **properly formatted** (i.e., double-spaced, correct font type and size, correct MLA or APA documentation, correct professor name and course code)?

☐ Have you **proofread your essay at least twice** and eliminated all spelling and grammar errors, passive voice (a reliance on "is," "was," "are," and "were"), and vague pronoun references (i.e., "this" and "it")?

☐ Have you **avoided placing quotations randomly** in your essay? Have you introduced all quotations and integrated them into your own sentences? Have you properly documented them?

☐ Have you **cited all information** that did not come from your own mind?

include information about how he or she wants your typed essay to be formatted? Now is the time to confirm that your response meets the physical demands of the assignment.

8. After you have printed out the final draft of your essay, save your work once again to two different places, in case disaster strikes.

9. Spell your professor's name correctly!

NOTE

Sometimes the best defence is a good offence. What does this common expression mean in the context of essay writing? It means that essay writers need to think ahead and anticipate issues before they arise. Three of the most important "rules" relating to essay writing are as follows:

- Do not leave your essay until the night before it's due.
- Remember that a clear thesis statement and a carefully prepared outline usually result in a clear, well-organized essay.
- Do not forget that your professor can help you (as long as the assignment isn't already late).

Following the above rules may not guarantee you an A paper, but they will certainly make your essay-writing experience more productive and less stressful.

What? There's More?

This chapter discussed some of the most important aspects of sentence and word editing; however, many other writing issues are covered in the Grammar Handbook at the back of this book:

- Parallelism (Chapter 12)
- Subject–verb and pronoun agreement (Chapters 23 and 24)
- Restrictive and non-restrictive clauses (Chapter 16)
- Participle, prepositional, and absolute phrases (Chapter 11)

Please note that all of these grammatical issues are important to good writing; however, discussing all of them here would be redundant. For more information on the above topics as well as many more, please consult the Grammar Handbook.

Using the Internet

Go to these websites to find more tips, techniques, and insights on editing words and sentences:

The Elements of Style
This is an online edition of the classic work of American usage, written by William Strunk, Jr., for his students at Cornell University. It was later revised by E.B. White, who had been one of those students.
http://www.bartleby.com/141

Guide to Grammar and Style
Created by Professor Jack Lynch of Rutgers University, this website contains a search engine that allows you to access information on English usage. The list of additional readings on grammar and usage is also useful.
http://andromeda.rutgers.edu/~jlynch/

Guide to Grammar and Writing

Among the most useful pages on this site are "Confusable Words," which lists words we often get mixed up, and "Plague Words and Phrases," which we should avoid.
http://grammar.ccc.commnet.edu/grammar/

The Write Place Catalogue

Maintained by St. Cloud University, this site contains abundant resources on sentence structure and style, including advice on how to combine sentences for variety and clarity, techniques to avoid and correct wordiness, and coverage of matters pertaining to word choice.
http://leo.stcloudstate.edu/catalogue.html

The Writer's Web

The website of the University of Richmond's Writing Center, the Writer's Web, contains advice on editing for clarity and style, with emphasis on avoiding sexist language, distinguishing between commonly confused words, and avoiding clichés.
http://writing2.richmond.edu/writing/wweb.html

Argumentation:
Facts and Fallacies

Using ARGUMENTATION in the Real World

Arguments take place all the time. You might argue in an informal way with your parents, siblings, instructors, or spouse. You might argue over who is to blame for something, over what movie to see, or against a major purchase, such as a car. Finally, you might argue in support of your opinions or beliefs, not unlike the judges of *American Idol*.

Formal argumentation is different from the arguments you might have in your daily life, and it takes place in all spheres of life. Argumentation takes place on many levels in the legal system: lawyers on both sides argue for their clients' innocence, and then the judge makes a ruling, which is sometimes influenced by a jury's decision—which they, in their turn, have argued, or deliberated, over. In the political arena, politicians argue over (or debate) issues, while citizens use argumentation to lobby or persuade government officials of their views, such as preserving wetlands from urban development. In sales, advertisers and retailers commonly use argumentation

LEARNING OUTCOMES:

▶ Support the claims of an argument with proper evidence

▶ Identify and avoid various logical fallacies

▶ Apply persuasion and appeals to essay writing

▶ Prewrite, draft, and revise an argumentative essay

in the form of comparison and contrast between one product and another to promote the superiority of a particular consumer good. In industry, a worker might use argumentation to persuade a boss that he or she deserves a raise, or unions may use argumentation to negotiate differing viewpoints with management, while a supplier might argue to convince a company to switch to its equipment. Even a resumé proposes an argument: that you are the right person for the job. Wherever a desire for change and the need to persuade is expressed in civilized society, you can be sure that argumentation will be used as a strategy to implement that change.

HOW DOES ARGUMENTATION WORK?

Academics use the term **argument** differently than students do. If you and a friend have a screaming match, calling each other names and shouting insults, this is not an argument, academically speaking. It is a **quarrel.** Similarly, merely disagreeing over an issue by disparaging the other side's beliefs, opinions, or choices is not an argument in the academic sense.

An **argument** is a communication in which the writer takes a stand on an issue, while providing proof and evidence of that stand's validity and importance, with the goal of persuasion. The writer is aware that the "other side" has value as well (commonly called "conceding the point"; see later in this chapter). Arguing for causes of problems, overturning long-standing assumptions, and proposing solutions to problems are all explicit purposes for using argument as a rhetorical option—known as **argumentation.** A writer who argues an issue fairly, acknowledging the valid points of the opposing side, will always have **persuasion** as his or her underlying purpose.

Avoiding Faulty Arguments: Fact, Inference, and Opinion

For an argument to be considered sound, it must have at its base a verifiable truth—something that can be proven or supported through research. A **sound argument** has at its root a series of provable assertions and facts as evidence; conversely, a **faulty argument** will rely heavily (or solely) on inference and opinion.

Fact A fact is a claim that can be verified to the point of certainty through the laws of nature, geography, history, personal experience, or scientific experimentation.

Inference An inference is an informed interpretation or guess based on established fact. Because inferences are derived from facts, people often accept them as truth; however, inferences can still lead to faulty reasoning or illogical conclusions. Consider the following two examples:

Fact: It is very cold outside and my car, which has a full tank of gas, won't start.
Inference: The battery is dead.

Fact: My cat curiously stares into our fish pond but won't dive in.

Inference: My cat is afraid of fish.

Obviously, given common sense, one inference is more likely than the other.

Opinion An opinion is a belief or value judgment that may or may not be backed up with evidence. People often base their opinions and beliefs on established fact, but just as often people offer their opinions as established fact even when these assertions are loaded with stereotypes, misinformation, or hasty generalizations.

Consider this situation: Canadian newspapers, newsmagazines, and talk radio often include regular commentators who offer their opinions on the issues of the day. A great many of these pundits consistently favour either a conservative or a liberal viewpoint. However, if you examine the "arguments" of these pundits, you'll find that they are not really arguments at all. They are **statements of opinion** meant to be persuasive. Think about the following statements:

Opinion: The mayor is an idiot who couldn't run this city with an instruction manual. He wastes money like water and would rather see our children out on the streets than in school.

Fact: According to Riverside Press, funding for schools in this community has dropped 20% while spending on parks has increased by 37%.

Argument: The mayor has made some questionable decisions over the length of his term. Our schools desperately need funding, yet our mayor currently spends a large portion of the city budget on vanity projects like the new downtown mural and water garden. City pride is important, but so is the education of our young people.

When making an argument, be sure it is grounded in fact as opposed to inference or opinion. Avoid bending reality by simply ignoring inconvenient facts and hoping that the audience doesn't notice. Some communicators are out to win and will use whatever deceitful methods they can to achieve their narrow goals. Winning is pleasurable; however, open, honest communication should always be your aim.

Using Argumentation within an Essay

A skilful arguer can advocate any position on an issue. Consider how debate teams (sometimes called forensics teams) work. These teams are frequently told to research

Consider Your Options

Many students tend to use personal opinion or experience as support when asked to write an argumentation essay; however, these types of examples are often too subjective. Use personal opinion in your work only if your instructor has specifically permitted you to do so. (See Chapter 8 for a full discussion on research.)

EXERCISE 7.1

Film reviewers try to present their information as unbiased and objective, yet film reviews are nothing more than one person's opinion disguised as unbiased commentary. Read the following review of the film *Funny People* starring Adam Sandler, and identify the reviewer statements that are fact, inference, or opinion. Analyze how the reviewer has used these techniques to achieve his purpose. Next, try to rewrite the review in a completely objective tone.

SANDLER–APATOW FILM MOSTLY FUNNY
Jim Slotek

1   There are, indeed, many funny people saying and doing funny things in Judd Apatow's dark opus *Funny People.*

2   Some may surprise you—such as Eminem getting all in Ray Romano's face—or, my favourite, Eric Bana giving an enthusiastic F-bomb-filled description of Aussie Rules Football to newbies George Simmons (Adam Sandler) and his assistant/surrogate-buddy Ira (Seth Rogen).

3   Even James Taylor—the god of lugubriously sensitive '70s singer–songwriters—gets some scabrously funny lines in his scene. (Ira: "Do you ever get tired of singing the same songs over and over onstage?" Taylor: "Do you ever get tired of talking about your d—onstage?")

4   I could go on. And I will. Cameos from the likes of Sarah Silverman, Norm Macdonald, comedy "it" boy Bo Burnham, Dave Attell, Andy Dick, plus scene-stealing turns by Jason Schwartzman and comedy "it" girl Aubrey Plaza.

5   The well is so deep, audiences come out of the movie repeating favourite lines.

6   Unfortunately, they also come out looking at their watches.

7   What was a minor complaint in his two break-through directorial efforts—both *The 40-Year-Old Virgin* and *Knocked Up* were generally considered about 20 to 25 minutes too long—is a major one in *Funny People,* essentially because Apatow apparently couldn't decide which of two stories he wanted to tell. So he tells them both.

8   And being the most powerful man in comedy, he's allowed to do whatever he wants, including taking Shakespeare's advice about brevity being the soul of wit and flushing it.

9   The first story is the better of the two. As Simmons, Sandler is a star of high-concept Hollywood movies à la Eddie Murphy or Sandler himself (in his two biggest hits he plays, respectively, a talking baby and a Mer-Man).

10   With commercial trash as his legacy, he is diagnosed with a form of leukemia with a low cure rate, forcing him to take a long, dark look at his life and lost love (with Laura, played by Apatow's real-life wife Leslie Mann).

11   Not exactly a load of laughs, he shows up at a standup club's open mike night, flummoxing audience and admiring newbie comics alike with a set that's more suicide note than shtick.

12   Ira is (un)lucky enough to follow him, inheriting a bummed-out audience, but attracting the attention of the celebrity himself. The biggest loser of a trio of roommates (Jonah Hill is a joke writer while Schwartzman plays Mark, the obnoxious star of an unspeakably bad high school sitcom called *Yo, Teach!*), Ira is amazed to get a call from George looking to buy jokes.

13   Clearly, Ira's jokes aren't his selling point (being mostly about penises). But there's something in his spirit that makes George alternately want to adopt him and abuse him. It quickly evolves into a complicated relationship: Nursemaid, mentor, conscience, role model.

14   As *Funny People* propels itself to what you would think would be the will-he-die-or-won't-he denouement, it would have been just the right length if George had walked out of the hospital and been hit by a truck.

15	But no. We've got the whole Laura plot to go, with George, Ira in tow, trying to break up her marriage to Clarke (Bana) on a weekend in Marin County. I suppose it's cynical to point out this part of the movie—the utterly extraneous part—is where the director's wife and two daughters get their big scenes.
16	More tellingly, it's the part of the movie with the fewest funny people.
17	(This film is rated 14-A.)

an issue, but they do not know which stance ("pro" or "con") they will be arguing until the moment of the debate. This forces the teams to research the issue thoroughly; a well-prepared team is as conscious of the potential weaknesses of its own argument as it is of the other side's potential weaknesses.

Emphatic Organization This strategy suggests that the writer should organize his or her paper by saving the most important point or points for the end of the essay. Sometimes this is an effective strategy based on the simple idea that the audience will remember most whatever information it reads last.

Conceding the Point This strategy entails giving your opponents' points recognition, only to then offer a more substantial counter-argument. An argument that shows proof of considering all sides of an issue is more persuasive than one that presents only one side: it appears better informed and less biased than an argument that deliberately ignores valid points that would be presented by the opposing side (see "Stacking the Deck" later in this chapter). Consider the following two statements:

> **One-sided:** Deer are beautiful creatures and deserve to be treated with dignity. Killing off portions of the deer population is just inhumane. They should be captured and fenced.

> **Conceding the point:** Deer are indeed beautiful animals and the right for all animals to be treated with dignity is greatly important; however, the Greendale bog is overrun with these animals and a solution must be found. Capturing and fencing the animals presents a number of additional problems including deer welfare, biodiversity, and public safety. A controlled deer cull of a select number of the animals is a humane way of dealing with the problem.

For most writing assignments, you might think you will be encouraged to argue only the side that you believe in. However, a truly persuasive argument will require you to consider all the evidence, weigh the opposing issues, and *then* favour one side or the other. Knowing valid points on the side opposite the one you support will give you a wider, more balanced understanding of the issue and the ability to anticipate and defuse points offered by the opposing side.

Rhetorical Questions Questions that can be used to persuasively underscore the writer's position or to point out a flaw in an opposing argument are called **rhetorical**

The Blended Essay and Argumentation

A typical blended essay depends on three or four rhetorical options—used as needed when the writer's purpose demands them. Each of the nine chapters in Part 2 of this text describes a specific rhetorical mode; however, being able to combine rhetorical options as needed is a valuable skill.

Assignments in almost any discipline can call for **argumentation.** You might be asked to argue for your interpretation of a poem, play, or novel for a literature class (exemplification); for or against a public policy for a political science or business class (process analysis); or for the implications of the results of an experiment in a biology or chemistry class (definition, classification). As part of your job, you may need to propose a solution to a company problem (cause and effect) or argue for your evaluation of a product or service (comparison and contrast).

Many instructors believe that all writing is rhetorical since it's designed with a purpose in mind: whether to instruct, to persuade, or to report. Argumentation is implicit in all of the rhetorical modes in Chapters 7–14; however, below are some ways to make it explicit by adding an argumentative angle to any mode you choose.

- **Description**: By choosing how you describe an object, idea, or concept, you are making an argument for how it will be perceived.
- **Narration**: A strictly argumentative, fictitious narrative would be said to have a moral; however, you can also use smaller narratives or anecdotes inside a traditionally structured essay to persuade the reader of your views.
- **Exemplification**: For any argument to be truly persuasive and convincing, it will need multiple examples from a variety of sources as evidence.
- **Process analysis**: You could outline a process and then make an argument for how it could be improved or why the current process is sufficient.
- **Causal analysis**: You could argue that certain causes have led to (or will lead to) improved or worse effects. Alternatively, you might argue that current effects were based on a series of particular causes.
- **Definition**: Making an argument for how to define an idea or concept (e.g., marriage) can redefine a law and, by extension, life itself. Once a change in definition becomes law, we all have to obey it, and thus our lives are changed.
- **Classification**: As in the definition mode, arguing how an object, idea, or concept should be classified can lead to changes in how we perceive the world.
- **Comparison/Contrast**: Evaluative comparison/contrast essays compare or contrast two objects, ideas, or concepts and then argue in favour of one or the other.

questions. Often they require no answer (because the answer is obvious) or an answer is provided immediately by the writer, as in the following examples:

How many people like to drink poison? Likely no one; yet, that is exactly what the residents of this city do every time they turn on the faucet. Pesticides in the ground water supply have made this city's reservoir unsafe.

The federal government is about to increase sales tax by 5%—a bold move. However, should the prime minister do this at a time when so many people are unemployed? Instead, the government might consider a more refined carbon cap-and-trade approach to generate revenue.

Using a rhetorical question (or even a genuine question) in your essay can be a persuasive strategy when you wish to emphasize what is already obvious or provide your audience with motivation for further research; however, be careful not to overuse this technique. Sometimes students pile on a series of questions with slightly humourous results:

> Should advertisers be held accountable if their false promises cause harm? Should they be fined or even jailed? What would be the amount of this fine or length of this jail term? Would these advertisers change their ways? Should the networks hold some accountability?

The first question is intriguing and the second question successfully expands on the first; however, the rest of the questions serve no purpose rhetorically and should just be answered in this essay's body paragraphs. Your instructor wants to see that you know the answers, and not just the questions, concerning your topic.

WRITING THE ARGUMENTATION ESSAY

Although argumentation can be used in conjunction with any of the other rhetorical options, it also requires your understanding of techniques that are not always present in the other types of essays. The advice that follows will help you think like your reader as you consider your assignment and then prewrite, draft, revise, and edit your argumentation essay.

You need to consider the following four issues as you work on your argumentation essay:

1. The language of argumentation
2. Support for the essay's claims
3. Logical fallacies
4. Audience and purpose

The Language of Argumentation

Argumentation has its own language, a set of terms deriving from historical philosophy and from formal logic. Understanding what these terms mean is more important than knowing the terms themselves; you don't actually use these terms in the course of argumentation, but understanding these concepts is crucial to writing an effective argument.

Claims and Appeals An argument is made up of a series of **claims** (also known as **assertions**). These statements express the writer's belief that an issue should be decided one way and not another. A claim also represents a type of **appeal,** or means of convincing your audience. The philosopher Aristotle wrote about three types of appeals that a writer can use to persuade his or her audience. Consider how these appeals are used in conjunction with the following scenario of someone trying to convince someone else to dress warmly in cold weather:

1. **Appeal to logic (logos):** Reasoning and logic can form a powerful foundation upon which to build an argument. Research, scientific data, and facts sometimes change as new theories are proven and disproven; however, arguments grounded in the laws of physics and mathematics are extremely hard to argue with.

   It's -30 degrees outside. Dress warmly or you will freeze to death.

2. **Appeal to emotion (pathos):** Human beings often respond much more strongly to emotion (needs and values) than to logic. Consider the images of sex, power, or youth that advertisers routinely use to convince customers to buy their products. Often these ads run contradictory to logic, yet people are still persuaded by them, sometimes on an unconscious level. Unfortunately, emotional appeals have the greatest potential to be abused.

   It's -30 degrees outside. Be a true Canadian and wear a toque to keep warm.

3. **Appeal to credibility (ethos):** The reliability, honesty, or credentials of the writer, source, or person, place, or thing being discussed all work towards the credibility of the argument being presented. A writer or source with a reputation for lying, bias, or hiding evidence will be untrustworthy to his or her audience. Credibility is established through the use of properly cited sources from experts and authorities.

   Dr. David Sayers states in his essay "Ice Makes Right" that exposure to extreme temperatures without proper attire can lead to "hypothermia and frostbite" (47).

Most arguments don't use all of these appeals at once. Instead, they usually concentrate on one or two types. The following scenario for the essay "Put It in Park: Comparing Faculty and Student Fees at Bluevale Campus," which appears later in the chapter(see "The Writing Process and Argumentation"), however, represents a rare instance in which all three types of appeals can be used:

> Currently, your college charges a good deal for parking. Students pay $100 per year; faculty and staff pay $150. Suddenly, seemingly out of nowhere, the college president announces that the two amounts will be switched, with students paying more. The president has said that the change will be in effect for only one year, to balance the college's budget.

Arguing against the Policy Change The arguer's response against this situation is complex. Here are three claims that can be made:

1. The shifting of responsibility is not fair. Students are frequently poor, and often resort to buying used books and eating Kraft Dinner for every meal; however, faculty and staff have, by definition, ongoing income, with some salaries reaching six figures. Why should students have to skip meals so some professor can put a new addition on his or her cottage? (This is an appeal to **emotion,** specifically compassion or pity.)

2. The policy change is bad business. This college competes with other local providers of higher education, and area students are known to "shop" for the best value. The college is running the risk of driving students away. (This is a **logical** appeal because it depends on analysis, common sense, and mathematics.)

3. Because of a series of negative incidents over the past school year, students as well as the community at large don't feel very positive about the college and their relationship with it. Raising student parking fees while lowering faculty and staff fees will further damage the college's already unflattering reputation and make students less likely to support college-initiated fundraising or social activities. The college has stated that the new fee structure won't be extended beyond one year, but how can we trust an institution that has repeatedly placed profits over student needs? (This is an appeal to the **credibility** of the institution.)

The most effective argumentation essays will use appeals to logic and credibility. Be wary of the overuse of emotional appeals, which can produce an essay that seems manipulative.

Once you have made a claim, you must develop and substantiate it. One method is through **reasoning**: using logical processes to prove an assertion. Another method (which is usually combined with the first) employs **evidence** to back up an assertion. We shall discuss these next.

EXERCISE 7.2

Advertisements that sell products or promote causes routinely use the rhetorical appeals of logos, pathos, and ethos to persuade the public to consume, donate, or support. Working alone or in pairs, analyze the advertisement shown and identify which rhetorical appeals are used in it. Explain how the ad uses these appeals to persuade readers. (See "Using the Internet" at the end of this chapter for links to more advertisements.)

HOW TO DESTROY CANADA'S ANCIENT BOREAL FOREST, IN 3 EASY STEPS:
STEP 1: PULL OUT A KLEENEX FACIAL TISSUE
STEP 2: PUT IT TO YOUR NOSE
STEP 3: BLOW

GREENPEACE

Support for the Essay's Claims

Writers can substantiate the claim of an argument by using **reasoning** and by using **evidence.**

Using Reasoning People use two major forms of logic when they think and when they write: **deductive reasoning** and **inductive reasoning.** Deductive reasoning starts from a general principle and applies that principle to specific situations. Inductive reasoning requires you to look at specific examples and then move to a general conclusion. We'll look at deduction first.

1. **Deductive reasoning:** Deductive reasoning takes the form of a **syllogism,** a combination that includes a major premise (a general principle), a minor premise (a specific situation), and the logical conclusion. For example,

   Major premise: All tortoiseshell cats are female.

   Minor premise: My cat is a tortoiseshell.

   Conclusion: Therefore, my cat is female.

If both premises are true, then the conclusion must be valid. However, if either premise is faulty, then the conclusion won't necessarily be sound. Notice the problem that occurs when the major premise is faulty:

   Major premise: All students drink alcohol.

   Minor premise: Ed is a student.

   Conclusion: Ed drinks alcohol.

The problem comes from the fact that the major premise is based on a faulty generalization: that all students drink alcohol.

Sometimes the problem is in the minor premise, as in the following example:

   Major premise: All baseball players are athletic.

   Minor premise: All horses are athletic.

   Conclusion: All horses are baseball players.

The subject of the minor premise must be the same type of thing as the subject of the major premise. Otherwise, the syllogism is faulty and, in this case, nonsensical.

Many students find deductive reasoning appealing, but it clearly has some drawbacks if improperly applied, because the writer can easily end up with an essay built upon faulty conclusions.

2. **Inductive reasoning:** The inductive process reaches a conclusion by building on specific information. For example, perhaps you are thinking about buying a car. You notice during your travels that one of the models you had been considering seems to be stranded beside the road often. Then, you learn that the car company recalled that model for safety reasons. You would probably inductively draw the conclusion that this is a car to avoid. Such an approach—building upon facts to reach a conclusion—is an argumentative process that writers, and readers, tend to trust.

Using Evidence For the most part, good argumentation essays depend on both abstract concepts and concrete evidence. Avoid writing an essay that depends upon abstractions without concrete evidence to back them up. Where can you find evidence to support your claims? The three basic types of evidence are the following: personal experience, primary research sources, and secondary research sources. (For additional discussion on evaluating sources, see Chapters 3 and 16.)

1. **Personal experience** includes knowledge gleaned from events you've experienced or heard about from others you know well and trust. Personal experience can be a very rich source of evidence for writers who pay attention to the world around them; however, please note that it is often not appropriate for formal academic writing as it can lead to statements or value judgments based on inference or opinion.

2. **Primary research sources** are first-hand sources that you develop or find through your own initiative. They include the following:

   - First-hand accounts or interviews
   - Diaries
   - Legal documents such as deeds, laws, or charters
   - Government documents such as budget or policy papers
   - Newspaper or magazine features
   - Blogs
   - Newscasts
   - Films, novels, poems, music, plays, paintings, or any other creative works
   - Documentary footage
   - Lab results
   - Statistics

If, for example, you were planning to argue against a policy, you could gather information on the effects of that policy by conducting interviews, performing surveys, or distributing questionnaires. You might also locate original government documents discussing the facts and proposals offered in the policy. If your information gathering discovers the results you predicted, you would know that other people experienced ill effects as a result of the policy, which would be evidence for your thesis. (Note that primary sources **must** be documented—see Chapters 16 and 17.)

3. **Secondary research sources** are materials written about primary sources. They include the following:

- Expert opinions
- Literary criticism
- History books
- Academic essays of various disciplines
- Biographies
- Lab reports
- Peer-reviewed journals
- Scientific essays

Referring to published opinions or commentary by recognized authorities on a subject is one of the most persuasive ways to support your argument. (Note that secondary sources **must** also be documented—see Chapters 16 and 17.)

Logical Fallacies

Fallacies are errors in reasoning—whether deliberate or inadvertent—that weaken an argument and, of course, the quality of the essay that contains the argument. Fallacious arguments seem dishonest whether the writer included them intentionally or not. The following list of common fallacies, with examples, is indicative of the types of errors to avoid:

- **Appeal to strong emotion, belief, or prejudice**

  Claim: Dan Blons, a prominent MP, has always been a strong supporter of the Canadian Armed Forces. He represents true Canadian values. Re-elect Dan Blons.

  Problem: Making decisions based on emotion sometimes goes against decisions that should be based in logic. Support of (or opposition to) the military causes strong emotional responses in many Canadian citizens, but besides his devotion to this long-time symbol of peacekeeping, what else has Dan Blons done? Simply put, his love of the military is not the best way to measure his worth.

- **Stacking the deck**

  Claim: Hollywood continually produces complete garbage, year after year. *Green Lantern, Jack and Jill,* and *Identity Thief* were all poorly reviewed and prove that the entire film industry would be better off at the bottom of the ocean.

  Problem: The writer has only included select examples that support his or her argument and completely ignored obvious examples that disprove it.

- **Appeal to tradition**

  Claim: Fans in our city have always destroyed parked cars and caused damage to the city streets after the home team wins on the ice; this is a tradition that shouldn't be questioned. We've always done this, and the tradition has popular support.

Problem: Following a tradition just because it's been done before does not examine the inherent worth of the tradition to begin with. In this example, just because a "tradition has popular support" doesn't make it moral or just.

- **Appeal to popularity** (also known as **argumentum ad populum** or **bandwagon fallacy**)

  Claim: We should eat at Burger Boy restaurant. They have served over 99 million people. Their burgers must be delicious! Afterwards, we should listen to the new Skippy Lee CD. That disc sold 1 million copies so it must have some good songs on it.

  Problem: Because something is popular, does not mean it is good, true, or valid. Many people used to believe that the sun revolved around the earth.

- **Red herring**

  Claim: Yes, Dan Blons, MP, is being questioned about his campaign finances. But his strong support of our armed forces shows that he truly cares about this country and the brave men and women who have sacrificed so much to bring democracy and freedom to those who have lived under brutal dictatorships and corruption.

  Problem: What does Blon's love of the military have to do with his campaign's financial issues? A red herring is the strategy of changing the subject.

- **Appeal to false authority**

  Claim: The Multitrust Investment Company group of mutual funds looks like a sure bet. Have you seen their commercials with Jim Carrey? His last film was hilarious!

  Problem: Institutions of prominence in society—the government, the church, the media—are not always correct. Always use your critical thinking skills. In this example, just because Jim Carrey's films are funny doesn't mean that the products he advertises are any good.

- **Attack on the person** (also known as **ad hominem,** or **name-calling**)

  Claim: We can't trust Dan Blons's proposal for tax reform because he is irresponsible, hypocritical, and morally reprehensible.

  Problem: Dan Blons may have personal issues, but this has nothing to do with the quality of his tax reform proposal—it may still be good. Sometimes, imperfect human beings have innovative ideas that are worth considering.

- **Oversimplifying the opponent's stand**

  Claim [by the government party in power]: It seems to me that our criminal justice priorities are wrong. We're letting murderers and armed robbers out of jail in order to make room for people convicted of simple drug possession. Illegal drug possession must be punished, but let's find a way to do it that keeps violent criminals, and drug dealers, in prison for their full sentences. **Response [by the opposition]:** Just like always, the ruling party is soft on crime.

Problem: Clearly, the opposition does not want to deal with the reality of what the party in power has to say; they simply choose to reinterpret the comment in a way that is best for themselves.

- **Begging the question** (also known as **circular reasoning**)

   Claim: Drug use is wrong because it's illegal. That's enough for me.

   Problem: This is a circular argument with no real support for why it is wrong.

- **Loaded question**

   Claim: Is our government still wasting money?

   Problem: If the answer is yes, the government looks bad; if the answer is no, the government still looks bad, if only a little less so.

- **Either/or simplification**

   Claim: We should either build the new highway extension using the original plan, or we shouldn't build it at all.

   Problem: Such a pair of choices leaves no room for other options. The dilemma presented is a false one because there almost always *are* more than two options in any given situation.

- **Mistaking correlation for causation** (also known as **post hoc, ergo propter hoc**)

   Claim: Every time I wear my black sneakers, my basketball team wins. I'll wear them from now on.

   Problem: Two events can happen simultaneously and coincidentally; this is **correlation,** not to be confused with **causation.**

- **Slippery-slope claim**

   Claim: If we let students wear T-shirts with obscene messages on them, the next thing we know they'll be making out in the restrooms, and then smoking pot in the parking lot, which of course will appear in the newspapers and cause our institution to lose funding.

   Problem: Someone who puts forward a slippery-slope claim sees one event inevitably leading to a series of more drastic events when, in fact, all events may be unrelated, or one event (questionable T-shirts) may not necessarily have a catastrophic result (lost funding for the college or university).

- **Hasty generalization**

   Claim: Jenkins failed in his first attempt to fix our computer network. Computer programmers usually don't know what they're doing.

   Problem: One piece of evidence is not enough to support a generalization. Give Jenkins another chance or two before condemning him and his profession.

- **False analogy**

   Claim: Citizens do not like to pay taxes and, therefore, they will not donate money to the local hospital.

Problem: A false analogy unfairly compares two things so that an illogical or unfair conclusion is drawn. People opposed to a government's waste of tax dollars might happily give money to a hospital.

- **Non sequitur**

  Claim: I should get an A on this assignment. After all, I got an A on the last one.

  Problem: This student assumes that X will follow Y without any concrete proof to back it up. There is no proof (other than assumption or opinion) that the next assignment will result in an A.

Absolute vs. Qualifying Terms Terms like *all, everyone, never, always, none,* and *only* are **absolute;** they assume no disagreement is possible—something that is rarely ever the case. Use these and others like the following examples with caution:

Nobody likes his or her job.

Only lonely people go to bars.

All cats are afraid of water.

Qualifying terms like *most, largely, overall, generally, mainly, often, several, some, few, seldom,* and *many* give a minimum or maximum to their subjects and can lead to statements that are just as inaccurate. Use these with caution as well.

Most people hate their jobs.

Overall, lonely people go to bars.

Generally, cats do not like water.

Each of the previous examples makes a claim; however, for that claim to be valid support for an argument, verifiable proof must accompany it, such as a statistic or case study.

EXERCISE 7.3

Working alone or in pairs, read the following sentences, each of which contains a logical fallacy. Identify which fallacy each sentence contains and explain why the statement is illogical.

1. No one should believe a word the premier says. He's a gambler and an adulterer.
2. If we let the government regulate carbon dioxide emissions, pretty soon they'll be regulating how much air we can breathe, how much money we can spend, and how much food we can eat.
3. Three out of five Canadians love hockey fights. Canadians sure are violent people.
4. Either students should get As on their assignments or they should not even bother doing the work.
5. Climate change is fraud because it's not real.
6. Using medicinal marijuana is just like using heroin. Both can be used to medicate various afflictions. Heroin should be made legal.

7. A tuition freeze is a worthwhile suggestion to aid students in this troubled economy, but have you considered that the city's new proposal to stop graffiti will cost taxpayers an additional 500 dollars a year?

8. Sidney Crosby eats Lays potato chips; they must be a high quality and nutritious snack food.

9. My instructor this term was boring, as was my instructor last term. All of the instructors at this college are dull.

10. I bought a new car, and the stock market crashed. Obviously, buying automobiles hurts the economy.

 EXERCISE 7.4   DISSECTING AN ARGUMENT:
CANCON CASE STUDY

The decision to mandate that Canadian broadcasters must devote a certain percentage of their airwaves to playing Canadian-generated content is still a hotly debated one. In the following article, Bradley Painsworth argues for one side of this issue. Read Painsworth's essay and evaluate the quality of his argument through a series of steps:

- Verify which of his statements are fact, inference, or opinion.
- Identify any logical fallacies contained in his argument.
- Identify any rhetorical appeals (logic, emotion, credibility) used to persuade the reader.

After you have evaluated the quality and accuracy of Painsworth's article, do further critical research on this issue. Can you find statistics, public polls, or expert opinions disagreeing with Painsworth's assessment? Write an effective, well-researched counter-argument against Painsworth's criticisms. You might also rewrite Painsworth's article in a more objective tone. Finally, a class debate could be held between those who agree with Painsworth's original premise and those who do not.

AGAINST CANCON: NO PITY FOR THE TALENTLESS
Bradley Painsworth

---

1 | Section 3 of Canada's Broadcasting Act states that "the Canadian broadcasting system should provide a wide range of programming that reflects Canadian attitudes, opinions, ideas, values and artistic creativity, by displaying Canadian talent in entertainment programming." Accordingly, the Canadian Radio-television and Telecommunications Commission (CRTC) mandated that a certain percentage of material broadcast on radio and television in Canada must be created and performed by Canadians. The resulting quota is called "Cancon."

2   Yet, this mandate seems like nothing more than a dictatorship of the drug-fuelled, hippie, artsy crowd over those of us who wish to see quality programming. Cancon rules are like affirmative action for starving Canadian artists, many of whom are not worth the public's time. Certainly were these artists brimming with talent, their work would rise to the surface of Canadian and international popular culture without the aid of the CRTC. What next? Is the government going to start regulating that a certain amount of the food we buy be grown in Canada—"you *must* eat fish from New Brunswick and drink Labatt products"—or that a certain amount of the concerts you see must be by Canadian artists—"Celine Dion is playing in Winnipeg; your attendance *is required*"?

3   Why should this mandate which promotes a skewed view of both Canadian artistic popularity and talent deprive me of the international music and television shows I like to experience? One more Nickelback song I have to hear is a U2 song I won't have the possibility of hearing; one more episode of *Coronation Street* taking up a valuable timeslot on CTV is an episode of *Family Guy* I won't be watching.

4   As for the other reason Cancon exists—national identity—let me ask you, how has Cancon bolstered the national identity? Do you feel more Canadian when you hear Avril Lavigne or Sum 41? Are you proud of your country when you watch *Degrassi: The Next Generation?* In 2008, Prime Minister Stephen Harper cut 45 million dollars from arts and culture funding. He defended these cuts by saying there was no point in "funding things that people actually don't want," thus proving that a majority of Canadians do not value or need Canadian art and culture.

5   The public now is faced with two options: keep Cancon law as it is and endure mediocre programming by spoiled, no-talent hacks or obliterate this mandate entirely, thus opening the airwaves to music and television that deserves to be enjoyed.

Audience and Purpose

When you make an argumentative claim, consider the effect that it will have on your audience. Throughout this book, we have discussed various aspects of the writer–reader relationship; however, in argumentation, this connection is especially important. In no other type of writing is purpose so inextricably connected to audience as in argumentation. Because audiences are becoming increasingly global, audience analysis is becoming more critical. As you plan and draft your argument, consider the following three points:

1. **Consider shared values.** Successful arguments depend upon assumptions that the writer and the reader share. Most people share certain (albeit not provable) assumptions about the importance of fairness, equality, and responsibility. However, assumptions about politics, religion, morality, and other contentious areas can vary widely. A debate between two Trekkies in response to the latest *Star Trek* movie and one between a sci-fi fan and a sci-fi hater will be much different.

2. **Present a fair, well-considered argument.** Your reader does *not* want to read a wishy-washy paper that argues both sides but refuses to back either one. On the other hand, your reader wants a sense that you have carefully considered the ramifications of your argument and have taken into account opposing views. An argument that stridently opposes a policy but fails to note the positive results of that policy is easy to criticize. The legalization of marijuana lends itself to this type of absolute argument by poor writers and activists alike.

3. **Consider your audience.** When writing an argument, be careful to assess your audience carefully. Some readers might be quite receptive to your point of view, while others might have no opinion at all. Still others might be of a different mind and hold an opinion diametrically opposed to yours; with those readers, you might have to establish some common ground before stating your opinion explicitly.

THE WRITING PROCESS AND ARGUMENTATION

Choosing a Topic

If your instructor lets you choose your own argumentation topic, consider these guidelines:

1. **Avoid open-and-shut issues.** Pick a topic that is arguable. Arguing that fire is hot is useless; arguing that fire is the single most important invention by human beings is better. If your argument already has a popular foregone conclusion—for example, chocolate is a tasty dessert—then there's no use pursuing it. Choose an issue that has two or more viable positions, then concentrate on one of these.

2. **Avoid narrow, personal topics.** If your roommate is a slob and you want to argue that his messiness threatens your ongoing living arrangement, then the only two people who are likely to be interested in this argument are you and your roommate. However, a more *general* topic—the threat that slobs pose to shared living quarters—could work quite well. In this approach, your roommate becomes an example, evidence that you can use.

3. **Avoid topics that can't be proven.** Students who argue on religious or spiritual topics sometimes find themselves backing up their claims by referring to their faith's authoritative text—the Bible or the Koran, for example. Or they may use their fervent personal beliefs as evidence. If you are writing for a general audience, though, neither approach is valid. Faith is faith, and logic is logic; the two have their own uses, but faith doesn't work as evidence to back up the claims of an argumentation essay. However, we're not stating that religion and religious issues are off limits in argumentation. There are a vast number of potential topics in this intriguing category that don't have to be settled by referring to one's faith or to a denomination's doctrines.

Prewriting

Writing an argumentative essay requires the generation of a great many ideas and pieces of evidence. Try this approach: use freewriting, brainstorming, or another prewriting method to generate your claims—the major assertions that you plan to make. Then focus on generating reasons and evidence for these claims. How will you back up your claims? Will you need to do some research at the library or on the Internet? (See Chapter 8.) Focus on the types of evidence you will use (see also "Using Evidence" earlier in the chapter).

After this step, review your prewriting. Can you turn your output into a coherent argument? Do you need to do more work before you start the organizing phase? Can you develop a preliminary or working thesis at this point?

Prewriting is an excellent way to generate a working thesis that can be revised, if necessary, as your draft progresses. From prewriting exercises, the following thesis was created for the essay "Put It in Park: Comparing Faculty and Student Fees at Bluevale Campus":

The administration's latest decision to lower the yearly rates for faculty and staff by $50 and to increase student rates by the same amount is unfair, misguided, and cruel.

These points will form the basis of the essay's organization and argument. Always be sure that your thesis matches the purpose of your essay. (See Chapter 2 for a detailed discussion on how to create an ideal thesis and supporting claims.)

Organizing

At this point, organize your prewriting into an outline. (Chapter 2 covers outlines.) Be willing to revise it or construct a new one if, upon review, you decide that the outline won't work because it doesn't present your reasons in an effective order or it branches off in an irrelevant direction. Plan on organizing until you come up with a paragraph sequence that suits both your thesis and your purpose.

Consider this strategy: build an outline with annotations. In other words, after you complete your outline, add notes (such as "transition here" and "proof?") where needed. This way, you'll give yourself an extensive framework to use as you begin drafting.

Drafting

To illustrate one approach to writing the argumentation essay, we have included the essay "Put It in Park: Comparing Faculty and Student Fees at Bluevale Campus."

The Introduction As with all essays, the introductory section of an argumentation essay explains the situation—the issue that your argument will address. The following introduction sets up the essay on student parking fees versus faculty and staff parking fees:

Put It in Park: Comparing Faculty and Student Fees at Bluevale Campus

Parking is a sore subject on most campuses. Usually, there is not enough to go around for both students and employees. Located as it is in a congested downtown area, the Bluevale campus cannot acquire any more land and the administration has been refused twice in its attempts to gain funds to build a parking garage. However, the administration's latest decision—to lower the yearly rates for faculty/staff by $50 and to increase student rates by the same amount—is unfair, misguided, and cruel.

The first paragraph describes the situation, then concludes with the thesis: the writer's stance on the issue. From this introduction, the writer can either go on to present a one-sided rant against the university administration or develop a carefully balanced argument. Note how the essay continues.

Consider Your Options

Be thorough in the introduction to an argument. Make sure that your reader understands exactly what you plan to argue. Good strategies include opening with an engaging anecdote or a provocative question. (For more on introductions, see Chapter 4.)

The Body The first body paragraph reveals that the writer has a comprehensive grasp of the situation and is not going to write a tirade stemming from a wounded wallet. Please observe that after showing an understanding of "the other side" by **conceding the point,** the writer brings the focus back to the thesis, which is accomplished with the first word of the second body paragraph. Read the following passage carefully:

> Most students understand that parking is a contentious issue for their college campuses. Administrations must deal with many issues related to this situation that students do not hear about. Moreover, it is fair to suspect that administrations may be more worried about pleasing a "permanent" group (faculty and staff) than about displeasing a "temporary" group (students) while still increasing revenues. After all, many more students than employees exist on campus.
>
> **Nevertheless,** the administration's decision at Bluevale is patently unfair. Faculty and staff have relatively secure incomes, whereas students often do not. Employees may not like paying to park their vehicles, but at least they have the security of a steady paycheque and know how to budget for this expense. Students, on the other hand, tend to run short of funds. Many students are on near-starvation diets. Fifty dollars is no small amount of money in that type of situation.

The writer's negative transition (*nevertheless*) refocuses the argument in the direction indicated by the thesis. In this paragraph, the writer offers a claim based on values and fairness—that the administration's decision is unfair—by using inductive reasoning to back up a **logical appeal.** An **emotional appeal** is also used in the invocation of an image of students on near-starvation diets.

The next body paragraph uses a different kind of claim:

> This administrative step is also misguided. The city that surrounds Bluevale is blessed with a number of institutions of higher learning. On a practical level, the administration may discourage new students from attending Bluevale who instead will go to another campus—one with more respect for students' finances.

In this paragraph the student uses a **logical appeal:** that the administrative decision is bad for business and therefore misguided.

In the final body paragraph, the student introduces an **appeal of ethos,** or **credibility:**

> Finally, the parking decision at Bluevale is just one more piece of bad news for students this year. Last year, Bluevale saw a rash of muggings during the fall term, two students were seriously injured in separate residence parties, asbestos was discovered in a women's washroom, and the football and basketball teams both had atrocious seasons. Student morale is not at its highest level. Every year, the college promises cleaner and safer facilities and touts its concern with student success and happiness. Yet, each year nothing changes. Although the college has stated that this fee structure will only exist for a year until the college's budget is balanced, the administration has a reputation for not delivering on its promises. Many students simply assume the increase in their parking fees will be permanent—how could they not? Is this really the type of relationship Bluevale wants with its student body?

The Conclusion The writer could summarize her argument at this point, but the essay is not long enough to require this step. Besides, summaries tend to sound boring. Instead, the writer takes a different approach, referring first to the second paragraph, then revisiting the thesis, and finally offering a possible solution to the overall problem:

> Although the administration has concerns other than the needs of the campus's students, the recent decision on parking fees at Bluevale seems horribly misguided. Rather than adding to students' financial burdens, surely the administration could choose a kinder course of action. At this point, most students would gladly accept a compromise: Why not make everyone pay the same price? This way, at least students wouldn't feel like they were subsidizing the parking costs of faculty and staff.

EXERCISE 7.5

Write an outline of "Put It in Park: Comparing Faculty and Student Fees at Bluevale Campus." (For help with outlines, see Chapter 2.) How has the writer organized the argument? Would a different organization have been more effective? Why?

FIGURE 7.1
Peer review checklist for argumentation essay.

QUESTIONS FOR REVIEWING AN ARGUMENTATION ESSAY

- ☐ Does the introduction provide enough context to set up the rest of the essay?
- ☐ Is there a clear thesis statement, and is the thesis adequately supported by the body paragraphs? How could the thesis or its support be improved?
- ☐ Does the essay show a sufficient sense of its audience? In what ways has the writer demonstrated common ground with the audience? How could the writer strengthen the connection to his or her audience?
- ☐ Has the writer organized the essay effectively? Does the essay seem coherent and complete?
- ☐ Has the writer avoided using too many emotional appeals? If any emotional appeals have been used, are they appropriate and effective?
- ☐ Has the writer used logical reasoning? Are the essay's claims clear, and are they supported by appropriate evidence? Where is clarification or more support needed?
- ☐ Has the writer avoided logical fallacies? Point out any fallacies that you find.
- ☐ Has the writer indicated an awareness of other positions on the issue, and not just his or her own stance? How has the writer dealt with these other positions?
- ☐ Does the conclusion adequately reflect the body of the essay? Is it an effective and satisfying conclusion for the argument? What other strategy for concluding the essay might the writer consider?

Revising Your Draft

After you have completed a draft of your argumentation essay, your next step is to revise it, using your own analysis and/or comments from classmates or friends. Use the list of questions in Figure 7.1 to guide your revision process.

After reviewing for content, you need to then revise your paper for unity, coherence, language level, and tone (see Chapter 5). When you have revised your draft and are basically satisfied with it, read it again for mechanical and grammatical errors. Consider reading your paper aloud. Concentrate on finding and correcting major sentence errors (fragments, comma splices, fused sentences), errors in pronoun agreement and subject–verb agreement, and spelling.

Now that you have made your corrections, wait a day, if possible, and then read your essay *one more time* to catch any errors made during revision and find errors missed during your earlier reviews.

A READER'S EYE

In the first essay, Charlie Gillis argues for banning fighting in the NHL, while in the essay that follows Gillis's, Sasha Chapman implicitly argues that manufactured foods are bad not only for our health, but also for our culture. The subject matter of these essays is diverse; argumentation, as a rhetorical option, can embrace almost any topic on which two reasonable people might disagree.

CAN WE PLEASE NOW BAN FIGHTING IN HOCKEY?

A young man dies on the ice. A father hopes for change. Why isn't the NHL listening?

Charlie Gillis

Charlie Gillis has written for the National Post *and the* Edmonton Journal. *Currently, he is the national correspondent for* Maclean's *magazine, in which the following article appeared in February 2009. The article brings up the debate about fighting in the NHL following the death of Donald Sanderson, a senior-level player on a Whitby team, from injuries sustained in January 2009 when his head struck the ice during a fight. The "fighting in the NHL" debate is often resurrected in the media when tragedy occurs. However, Gillis's article is particularly poignant as it shrewdly addresses the arguments supporting fights in the NHL before completely deconstructing them with expert opinion and many examples to the contrary. Only an excerpt of Gillis's much longer essay appears here. We encourage you to locate and read the entire piece at* macleans.ca *to appreciate the full extent and development of Gillis's argument.*

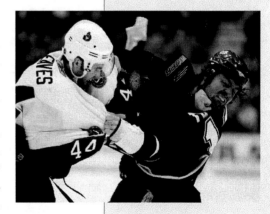

1   That fighting is embedded in the DNA of hockey is hard to dispute. It is said that the first game played indoors under written rules ended in a fight, as players at McGill University in Montreal scuffled with members of a skating club who wanted to use the ice. That was 1875, and it followed several accounts of outdoor hockey devolving into fist fights and stick-swinging incidents in Toronto and the Maritimes.

2   The rationalizations came later—most notably the idea that a contact sport played at such high speeds needed fighting as an outlet for anger. "Nothing relaxes the boys like a good fight," said Francis "King" Clancy, the legendary Toronto Maple Leaf of the 1930s, in a flash of Irish bravura. Clarence Campbell, the NHL's long-time president, popularized the "safety-valve" trope, warning that, without fighting, "the players would no doubt develop more subtle forms of viciousness."

3   These notions took hold, and were allowed to calcify despite an abundance of contradictory evidence. Study after study has demonstrated that violence leads only to more violence, notes Stacy Lorenz, a University of Alberta professor who has studied the history of violence in hockey, while some of the most traumatic moments in the game were either sparked by fighting, or occurred despite its prevalence. Maurice Richard resorted to his fists again and again in response to the slashes and ethnic slurs he endured as a Montreal Canadien. Yet his combativeness did nothing to discourage—and arguably spurred—the opponent who cut his face with a high stick, provoking the epic meltdown that led to the Richard riot of 1955 (a wild-eyed Richard broke his stick across the shoulder of his attacker, Hal Laycoe, and punched a linesman in an attempt to get at the Boston Bruin).

4   Trouble is, many cheap shots are committed by practised fighters—no doubt because they are unfazed by the thought of dropping the gloves should they need to. Egregious examples include the forearm shiver Toronto's designated fighter, Tie Domi, laid during the 2001 playoffs on Scott Niedermayer, an all-star defenceman then with the New Jersey Devils; or Dale Hunter's blindside elbow on Pierre Turgeon during a 1993 playoff game between the Washington Capitals and Turgeon's New York Islanders. A more recent spate of attacks suggests the problem has deepened, as small-time pugilists take liberties with players who don't typically fight. In October 2007, Jesse Boulerice, a dime-a-dozen fighter with the Flyers, levelled Ryan Kesler of the Vancouver Canucks with a cross-check to the face. That play came just two weeks after Steve Downie, another minor tough with the Flyers, concussed the normally peaceable Dean McAmmond with a flying elbow, putting the Ottawa Senator out of action for 10 games. This season, Ryan Hollweg, a spare-part agitator with Toronto, was suspended for three games following his third misconduct in nine months for boarding—essentially, hitting from behind. The Leafs forward has been branded a coward for those hits. But he is no shirker in the fisticuffs department, fighting 19 times in the two seasons leading up to his suspension.

5   So the theory that fighting limits dirty play doesn't hold water. Nor does the idea that it protects ultra-talented players from the indignities of a rough game. In the last couple of weeks, NHL fans have been treated to the spectacle of superstars Sidney Crosby and Alexander Semin throwing punches after opponents crossed the line (Semin, who can be seen on YouTube, looks rather like an angry toddler). You can't, evidently, have a thug riding shotgun all the time.

6   Still, the pro-fight lobby holds to its catechism, insisting the mischief would abate if enforcers were given more latitude. Their latest target is the so-called "instigator rule," which they say emboldens cheap-shot artists by giving extra penalty minutes to players who pick fights to even the score. That would be a lot more persuasive if officials actually used the instigator rule. Since it was introduced in 1992, the number of infractions has steadily dwindled to about 50 per year, out of 1,230 games. Meantime, fighting has been booming following a post-lockout low of 466 in 2005–06. At the current rate, 2008–09 will end with 789 fights, or 0.64 fights per game, according to the website Hockeyfights .com. It is possible, as the foregoing numbers suggest, that 94 per cent of those fights

will have been started by no one. But it's a lot more likely that the league is trapped in a vicious cycle, where fighters are doing the cheap shots, the cheap shots are leading to more fights, and the officials have given up trying to stop them.

7   The league's answer to such questions is as familiar as it is blithe. "We believe we're adequately and appropriately policing our own game," Bettman said in the wake of the Bertuzzi incident. What the commissioner fails to grasp is that the rest of the world does not share its view of hockey as a self-governing kingdom. "Violence in sports is father to violence in everyday life," said Judge Sidney Harris of the Ontario provincial court in 1988, setting down a precept the justice system has upheld ever since. The public appears to agree. In poll after poll, Canadians say they look upon hockey as a means to teach values like respect, discipline and grace under pressure. Fully 54 per cent of respondents to a Harris-Decima survey conducted last week said they oppose fighting in the NHL.

8   Here lie the moral contradictions the league cannot—will not—address. We teach our children that punching another person is no way to resolve frustration. Why is it thought reasonable in hockey? More to the point, is fighting not antithetical to the concept of athletic competition? What are rules and officials for, if not to prevent players from taking justice into their own hands? Why should they serve this purpose in other contact sports but not hockey? Football, to name just one, is a physical game, featuring 300-lb. men throwing themselves at each other at high speed. But head shots, blocks in the back, pushing your hands into an opponent's face are deemed penalties. And if two players finally do lose their cool, the referees don't stand back while they remove their helmets and start swinging. Perhaps Wayne Gretzky summed it up best: "Hockey is that only team sport in the world that actually encourages fighting. I have no idea why we let it go on."

9   It's not as though getting rid of it would be difficult. Automatic game ejections followed by escalating fines and suspensions would likely do the trick—not eliminating fisticuffs altogether but, as Sanderson [Michael Sanderson, Donald's father] says, making them ridiculous. Minor hockey associations did it long ago, reducing fighting to a few pathetic parodies in which players cuff each others' face cages, gloves still on. As for the canard that old habits die hard, one need only consider the NHL's own example: by near-universal opinion, the league's crackdown on obstruction and stick offences has been a grand success. Like clockwork, the lower leagues have fallen into line, taking their cues from the pros and juniors. It was a clear demonstration, if any was needed, that a few rule amendments and some perseverance on the part of officials can change a sport for the good.

10   But make no mistake: should Donald Sanderson's death prove the turning point in this ancient debate that would be just fine with his father. "At least we could say something good came out of it," Michael says. "Right now, nothing's good for me. I don't have my buddy. I can't see him, I can't talk to him. There's gotta be a reason for that. You can't tell me the Lord took him for nothing, because he was just too good of a kid."

VOCABULARY

The following terms are identified by paragraph number. Make sure that you understand each term's meaning in its context. If you're not sure that you understand a term, look it up in a dictionary.

bravura (2)	**spate** (4)	**blithe** (7)
trope (2)	**pugilists** (4)	**parodies** (9)
prevalence (3)	**indignities** (5)	**canard** (9)
egregious (4)	**abate** (6)	**perseverance** (9)
	emboldens (6)	

STYLE AND STRATEGY

1. How does Gillis use the "conceding the point" strategy to strengthen his argument?
2. One of the great strengths of Gillis's article is the way its thesis controls the essay. Throughout, Gillis makes sure that the reader knows exactly what he is arguing for—and, just as importantly, how the problem should be resolved. Discuss ways this essay could be effective even if the portion of the essay discussing how to stop fighting (paragraph 9) were not included.
3. What argumentation techniques does Gillis use? Which appeals does he use and where does he use them? Identify the evidence he uses to support his argument.

QUESTIONS FOR CRITICAL THINKING AND DISCUSSION

1. Executions used to be public; however, now society is civilized. Or is it? One of the counter-arguments often used to keep fighting from stricter penalties in the NHL is that fans love it. If this is true, why do people enjoy seeing other people engage in violence (consider boxing and the UFC)? What purpose does it serve? Is our culture cheapened by these displays? Defend your answer.
2. Gillis asks if fighting is "antithetical to the concept of athletic competition." Assuming the answer is yes, make an argument for the positive aspects of sports. What do they teach us? How do they benefit society? Why is watching professional sports such a beloved pastime for so many?

SUGGESTIONS FOR WRITING

1. In 500 to 750 words, argue that an organization or project with which you are familiar has been ruined because of the participants' failure to follow the necessary guidelines or procedures. Stress the negative effects of this breakdown.
2. In 500 to 750 words, argue for a change in school policy that will help students become more successful at their studies.

MANUFACTURING TASTE
The (Un)natural history of Kraft Dinner—a dish that has shaped not only what we eat, but also who we are

Sasha Chapman

Sasha Chapman is a senior editor at The Walrus. *She has also written for* Toronto Life *and* The Globe and Mail. *This essay is an excerpt of Chapman's much larger article, which appeared in the September 2012 issue of* The Walrus. *We encourage you to read the entire piece at www.walrusmagazine.com to see the full development of Chapman's argument.*

1 Tell me what you think of Kraft Dinner, and I will tell you who you are. If you belong to Canada's comfortable class, you probably think of the dish as a childish indulgence and a clandestine treat. The bite-sized tubular noodles are so yielding and soft, you will say a little sheepishly, and next to impossible to prepare al dente. The briny, glistening orange sauce tastes a little bit sweet and a little bit sour—at once interesting, because of the tension between the two flavour poles, but not overly challenging or unfamiliar.

And its essential dairyness connects it to that most elemental of foods: a mother's milk. KD is the ultimate nursery food, at least if you were born and raised in Canada, where making and eating cheese has been a part of the culture since Champlain brought cows from Normandy in the early 1600s—a tradition nearly as venerable as the fur trade. It may be the first dish children and un-nested students learn to make ("make," of course, being a loose term; "assemble" may be more accurate). This only strengthens its primal attractions.

2   If you recently immigrated to Canada, you will have a very different association with KD, as a dish that polarizes family meals. Your children nag you for it, having acquired a taste for it at school, or at the house next door. And if you count yourself among the 900,000 Canadians who use food banks each month, you may associate the iconic blue and yellow box with privation: a necessary evil while you wait for your next cheque to arrive, bought with your last dollar, and moistened with your last spoonfuls of milk.

3   The point is, it's nearly impossible to live in Canada without forming an opinion about one of the world's first and most successful convenience foods. In 1997, sixty years after the first box promised "dinner in seven minutes—no baking required," we celebrated by making Kraft Dinner the top-selling grocery item in the country.

4   This makes KD, not poutine, our de facto national dish. We eat 3.2 boxes each in an average year, about 55 percent more than Americans do. We are also the only people to refer to Kraft Dinner as a generic for instant mac and cheese. The Barenaked Ladies sang wistfully about eating the stuff: "If I had a million dollars / we wouldn't have to eat Kraft Dinner / But we would eat Kraft Dinner / Of course we would, we'd just eat more." In response, fans threw boxes of KD at the band members as they performed. This was an act of veneration.

5   KD's popularity is a symptom of a world that spins distressingly faster and faster. We devote a total of forty-two minutes to cooking and cleaning up three meals a day—six fewer minutes than we spent in 1992. Over half the dinners we consume at home involve a prepared or semi-prepared food. As the clock ticks, we spend more of every food dollar on these shortcuts. Another common observation among new arrivals to Canada concerns the fast pace of life. Ask immigrants to define Canadian food, and they most often name hamburgers, pizza, and pasta. But one brand turns up again and again in field studies: Kraft, as in "Dinner" and "Singles."

6   In the world of modern food manufacturing, Kraft Dinner Original remains a fairly simple formula, with only ten ingredients. (My own recipe also calls for ten, if you lump together the natural flavours, as labellers do.) But KD has spawned generations of mac and cheese dinners, each one a greater feat of engineering than the last, and each one less recognizable as something we could make in our own kitchens. In 1999, the company launched Kraft Dinner Cup, a line that now includes Kraft Dinner Triple Cheese in a microwaveable package. It contains twenty-one ingredients, including "cheese flavours." Cheddar is eighth on the list. A version sold only in the U.S., described as Triple Cheese Cheesy Made Easy, contains forty-two ingredients, depending on how you count them.

7   Today KD Original probably contains more whey than cheese. Kraft won't say how much cheese is in the foil packet, but you can read between the lines on the label and make an educated guess. One scientist, who asked not to be quoted, estimates that cheese would account for no more than 29 percent of the sauce's solids. Driven by the commodity markets rather than taste, processed food formulas often change according to the going rates of their ingredients: when whey powder is cheap, for example, a cheese sauce might include more of it.

8   Manufactured foods originally appealed to consumers because they were beacons of progress—which they were, if you bought in to the premise that food is just fuel, and if you measured success by how cheaply and quickly a meal could be prepared. But as

convenience foods became more common and cooking from scratch less so, people began to miss the connection they once had to how food was produced, on the farm and in the kitchen. They craved the meals their mothers once cooked, the real mac and cheese, homemade. So Kraft cannily adjusted its marketing strategy, creating an ersatz nostalgia for the very thing KD had supplanted. "Mama's in the kitchen making mac and cheese," ran one American marketing slogan. Another announced: "Two new Kraft home cooked dinners, the quick kind you cook up fresh."

9   People feel a strong emotional connection to the KD label, says Jordan Fietje, senior brand manager for Kraft Dinner, who takes pains to highlight his company's sacred covenant with matriarchs. Like many other Kraft employees, he is inordinately fond of the phrase "our promise to moms." The slogan makes sense. Food is about ritual, tradition and conviviality, and what your mother made for Sunday dinner, which means it is also about identity. The cliché is not wrong: we are what we eat, and our choices both reflect and shape who we are.

10   Manufactured food has its attractions: it is cheaper and lasts longer, and engineers can manipulate moisture, salt, and sugar content to appeal to a broader market, or to target a social group's preferences. But as much of our food production has shifted to manufacturing—44 percent of Canadian agricultural output is now destined for processing—products, especially the ones dreamt up by scientists and nutritionists in corporate labs, are made a long way from the consumer. We increasingly rely on professionals to teach us how to cook (if we ever learn), dieticians and nutritionists to tell us what to eat, and scientists to engineer the food we buy.

11   Differences—whether in people, cultures, or even cheese—are Canada's greatest strength, and life would be exceedingly dull without them. They shape and define who we are. But differences can never be manufactured in any meaningful way by a large food conglomerate, which always seeks to standardize. So the question is: are we content to have our national dish come from a laboratory in Illinois, or do we want to have a hand in its (and our) creation? If we can't be the authors of our own meals, who are we? To cook and live life to the fullest, Lee tells me, "I need a good foundation. I have to know who I am."

VOCABULARY

The following terms are identified by paragraph number. Make sure that you understand each term's meaning in its context. If you're not sure that you understand a term, look it up in a dictionary.

indulgence (1)	ersatz (8)
clandestine (1)	covenant (9)
venerable (1)	conviviality (9)
polarizes (2)	conglomerate (11)
beacons (8)	

STYLE AND STRATEGY

1. Chapman never really comes out and says that "Kraft Dinner is bad." Instead her argument is based on a more implicit style. Discuss the advantages and disadvantages to using this approach.

2. In the conclusion of her essay, Chapman uses the rhetorical question "are we content to have our national dish come from a laboratory in Illinois, or do we want to have a hand in its (and our) creation?" Is this question effective? What does Chapman really mean by asking such a question? What is her larger implication?
3. Where does Chapman acknowledge the other side's argument by conceding points or showing opposing views? What is the effect of this acknowledgement and/or its placement in the essay?
4. Within the essay, Chapman discusses Kraft's marketing strategies: its reliance on nostalgia, and its appeals to mothers. Categorize these as logos, pathos, or ethos, and justify your reasons for doing so.

QUESTIONS FOR CRITICAL THINKING AND DISCUSSION

1. Chapman argues that Kraft Dinner has shaped "who we are." Discuss the wider implications of this statement. Is our technological and fast-paced lifestyle something to be celebrated or feared? Discuss examples that apply to both views.
2. What do you think should be Canada's national food? Should a country even have a national food?

SUGGESTIONS FOR WRITING

1. Fad diets are always popular topics of debate. Write a 500- to 750-word essay comparing various diets (i.e., Atkins, Paleo, and Vegan) and argue which one is better for overall health. Be sure to consider evidence that argues the opposite.
2. Chapman's essay discusses the emotional attachment people have to certain foods. Write a 500- to 750-word essay analyzing emotional attachments people develop for other objects (i.e., cars, books, or clothing) and argue whether these attachments are beneficial, dangerous, or both.

A WRITER'S EYE

The following essay is Sabrina Aziz's response to an argumentation assignment. Sabrina's rough draft is presented first, followed by her final draft. In particular, note how in her final essay she has avoided vague generalizations in favour of sourced research. She has condensed her wordiness as well as added new content. All major changes are **bolded.**

Sabrina has followed the guidelines set out in the *MLA Handbook for Writers of Research Papers* (7th edition) to document her sources.

 SABRINA'S FIRST DRAFT

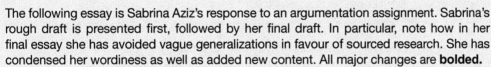

Beauty before Age

In western culture, youth is worshipped. Beauty has simply become synonymous with youth. Everyone knows that youthfulness and ultimately, attractiveness, is valued above all else when it comes to women because this is common

Vague title.

Begging the question fallacy.

knowledge. Aging is no longer seen as a respectable and graceful period in a woman's life; instead this natural progression is viewed as distasteful, tragic, and ugly. Women constantly struggle to achieve the ageist guidelines put forth by "culturally dictated prescriptions" (Johnston 18) and view aging as a disease. Sadly, as a result of the western world's desdain towards aging and the elderly, women are bound to view growing older as a negative and counteractive part of life.

When elderly women aren't completely invisible in situation comedies, they are often presented in TV shows and movies as feeble, helpless, unattractive, and senile characters. There is a highly negative depiction in entertainment as elderly women are shown as "psycho nags" (Thune 72) on popular sitcoms. Older women are the main antagonists of these shows and provide comic relief as they are usually the foil for the main stars. This is especially troubling seeing as many elderly women heavily rely on television for entertainment because of its easy accessibility. Many elderly people are exposed to hours of weekly television shows asserting that the majority of "old people are drunks, suffering from Alzheimer's and ill-tempered," as Linda Gannon attests (17). This portrayal encourages a distorted and untrue perception of elderly women by the general public and further marginalizes an already marginalized demographic.

The number of elderly actively involved in the workforce is decreasing daily. This displays western culture's favouritism towards the younger employees as more and more aging women lose their jobs. Employers seek younger employees thinking that they are more useful and vital to the overall workplace. While it is illegal for employers to ask prospective employees their age. Many do it nonetheless. Older female workers are not only less likely to be hired in today's workforce but are more likely to be laid off on the basis of ageist stereotypes. Employers may also think twice about hiring a female matured in years because of the stereotype that they "are not able to respond well to change and cannot adapt." The reality of the matter, however, is that the more mature workers usually harbour a bank of knowledge and experience. As for keeping up with modern technology, it is the responsibility of the employers to train every single employee, regardless of age, in order to provide equal opportunity for all.

Advertising especially is extremely powerful in establishing society's unfalteringly negative view on aging. Every day, women are subjected to countless ads promising blushing youth and splendour. It's as if the "fountain of youth" (Gannon 23) were at the disposal of these company's, ready to be sold to the vulnerable woman who has been conditioned to fear and abhor aging as if it is a sickness. By putting forth an unrealistic, unattainable ideal in the media, companies are assured of steady growth and income regardless of the empty promises and gimmicks they spread like wildfire. Furthermore, many women tend to "internalize stereotypes and judge themselves by the beauty industry's unrealistic

Spelling error.

Thesis is vague.

Stronger topic sentence needed.

Specific examples needed.

Many generalizations in this paragraph with no proof offered.

Sentence fragment.

Source needed.

Apostrophe error.

Double "as if" structure is awkward.

standards." As a result, women fight the aging process with their money on anti-aging products and plastic surgeries under the impression that if they give in to the natural aging process, they will give up their value as human beings

The fact that the current standard of a woman's worth revolves solely around youthfulness is both regrettable and unfortunate. If the blatant ageism in today's Western culture is not countered sooner as opposed to later, the culture will continue to be transmitted from generation to generation. When our culture emphasizes positive aspects of aging, such as the acquisition of wisdom and life experience, women will face this life process with much more optimism.

Source needed.

Spelling error.

Conclusion does not restate thesis.

Works Cited

Gannon, Linda. *Women and Aging: Transcending the Myths.* California: Routledge, 1999. Print.

Garner, Dianne J., and Alice Adam Young. *Women and Healthy Aging: Living Productively in Spite of It All.* Philadelphia: Haworth Press, 1994. Print.

Greer, Germaine. *The Whole Woman.* New York: Anchor Books, 2000. Print.

Johnston, Joni E. *Appearance Obsession: Learning to Love the Way You Look.* Florida: Health Communications, 1994. Print.

Pearsall, Marilyn. *The Other Within Us: Feminist Explorations of Women and Aging.* Arizona: Westview Press, 1997. Print.

Thone, Ruth Raymond. *Women and Aging: Celebrating Ourselves.* New York: Harrington Park Press, 1992. Print.

Walker, Margaret Urban. *Mother Time: Women, Aging and Ethics.* New York: Rowman & Littlefield Publishers, 1999. Print.

SABRINA'S FINAL DRAFT

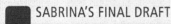

Beauty before Age: Western Culture's Preoccupation with Youth

In Western culture, youth is worshipped, with the words *beauty* and *youth* used interchangeably. Aging is no longer seen as a respectable and graceful period in a person's life; instead, this natural progression is viewed as distasteful, tragic, and ugly. Women, in particular, constantly struggle to achieve the ageist guidelines put forth by "culturally dictated prescriptions" (Johnston 18) and view aging as a disease. Sadly, as a result of the Western world's disdain towards aging and the elderly, women are forced by their culture to view growing older as a negative

Better, more descriptive title.

and counteractive part of life. **This notion is perpetuated through the negative portrayal of the elderly in the media, the difficulty of the elderly finding steady employment, and the glorification of youth by the beauty industry.**

Movies and television shape our realities through their representations. Accordingly, the media puts forth many misrepresentations and misconceptions about the behaviour and attitudes of elderly women. When older women aren't completely invisible **(where are the meaningful roles for older women in shows like *The Office*, *The New Adventures of Old Christine*, and *How I Met Your Mother?*),** they are often presented in television shows and movies as feeble, helpless, unattractive, and senile characters. In particular, elderly women are shown as "psycho nags" (Thune 72) **on popular sitcoms like *Everybody Loves Raymond, Seinfeld,* and *Home Improvement,* all of which are still in wide syndication.** Older women are often the main antagonists of these shows and provide comic relief as the foil for the main stars. This is especially troubling since many elderly women heavily rely on television for entertainment because of its easy accessibility. Many elderly people are exposed to hours of weekly television shows asserting that the majority of "old people are drunks, suffering from Alzheimer's and ill-tempered," as Linda Gannon attests(17). This portrayal encourages a distorted perception of elderly women by the general public and further marginalizes an already marginalized demographic.

Elderly women may find ample occupation as stock characters on television; however, their prospects of employment in common fields are less favourable. While it is illegal for employers to ask personal questions about a candidate's marital status or age, many do so anyway. In her book *The Other Within Us: Feminist Explorations of Women and Aging,* Marilyn Pearsall points to a study that reveals how employers regularly ask women their age and then use this information to determine whether or not the prospective candidates should be hired (44). Moreover, older female workers are not only less likely to be hired in today's workforce but are also more likely to be laid off on the basis of ageist stereotypes. Employers wrongfully assume that mature female workers are "less valuable, [and] lack energy and modern technological skills" (Pearsall 43). Employers may also think twice about hiring a mature female because of the stereotype that they "are not able to respond well to change and cannot adapt" (Garner 19). Corporate rhetoric, sadly, exacerbates this issue with many employers using such clichéd catchphrases as "thrive in a dynamic young team" and "succeed in a young environment" in their job postings (Walker 64).

In a world where life imitates art, advertising is especially powerful in establishing society's negative view of aging. By putting forth an unrealistic, unattainable ideal of youth in the media, companies are assured steady growth and income regardless of the empty promises and gimmicks that they spread like wildfire. **The beauty industry—comprised of magazines, fashion models, and so-called regenerative cosmetic products—asserts that in order for a woman to be considered beautiful, she must remain both young and fit (Walker 15).** Every day, women are subjected to countless ads promising blushing youth and splendour, as if the "fountain of youth" (Gannon 23) were at the disposal of these companies. Anti-aging creams and potions fool women into thinking they can alter nature itself and avoid or prolong the innate process of maturing and growing old **(Johnston 18).** Furthermore, many women tend to "internalize stereotypes and judge themselves by the beauty industry's unrealistic standards" **(Pearsall 29).** As a result, women feel that to give in to the aging process is to give up their value as human beings; they will be less attractive and "no one [will] want them, man or otherwise" **(Thune 94).**

Aging is a natural part of a woman's life which must be embraced and respected. However, **faced with television shows filled with inaccurate depictions of the elderly, a workforce favouring young women, and an economy driven by beauty products, women of all ages are currently forced to question their personal and social value.** While Dove's media campaign with its slogans of "Aging is Beautiful" and "Love the Skin You're In" present aging positively, this example is far too limited in a culture where much needs to be done to alter society's negative perceptions of aging. When our culture emphasizes positive aspects of aging, such as the acquisition of wisdom and life experience, women will face this life process with much more optimism.

Works Cited

Gannon, Linda. *Women and Aging: Transcending the Myths.* California: Routledge, 1999. Print.

Garner, Dianne J. and Alice Adam Young. *Women and Healthy Aging: Living Productively in Spite of it All.* Philadelphia: Haworth Press, 1994. Print.

Greer, Germaine. *The Whole Woman.* New York: Anchor, 2000. Print.

Johnston, Joni E. *Appearance Obsession: Learning to Love the Way You Look.* Florida: Health Communications, 1994. Print.

Pearsall, Marilyn. *The Other Within Us: Feminist Explorations of Women and Aging.* Arizona: Westview Press, 1997. Print.

Thone, Ruth Raymond. *Women and Aging: Celebrating Ourselves.* New York: Harrington Park Press, 1992. Print.

Walker, Margaret Urban. *Mother Time: Women, Aging and Ethics.* New York: Rowman & Littlefield, 1999. Print.

Paragraph edited for wordiness.

Sources added.

Thesis is restated.

Nice use of Dove example in conclusion; to "look to the future" and suggest change.

The following is the first draft of a student's argumentation essay. Working in pairs or in small groups, review this essay. Using the Questions for Reviewing an Argumentation Essay (Figure 7.1), decide what revisions you would suggest. In particular, try to spot logical fallacies. If you have any questions the student needs to consider, write them in the margin or on a separate sheet of paper. If your instructor directs you to, rewrite one or more paragraphs to make them stronger and to eliminate any grammatical or mechanical errors.

"Fight Censorship"

1   Last Tuesday morning I was asked to leave my Economics Class. Its not that I was causing a disturbance, its the shirt I was wearing. The Tshirt had the slogan "Makin' Bacon," and shows two pigs getting it on! My professor, a real idiot, found this offensive and told me to leave and to not return wearing this shirt.

2   First this is censorship. I'm expressing myself by wearing this. If one student is censored for wearing a T-shirt, pretty soon the college will be telling us who to date, what music to listen to and what we can and cannot read. I've seen what happens when a corrupt administration is in power. Should we wear uniforms to school so that the faculty wont feel threatened?

3   Second I pay my tuition and abide by the rules and nowhere in the rules is their a picture of my shirt with a notice telling me I cant wear it, if their was, I wouldnt be writing this and Dr. Silva and I would not be at war as it is I might have to go over her head. This is Canada and it's a free country. If you don't like it, then maybe you should leave.

4   Finally, I'm being treated like a child, censored against cause of what I wear and I know for a fact alot of students agree with my gripe. 20,000 students can't be wrong. Our college hasn't heard the end of this issue. Offensive shirts are part of the tradition of being young! We like to wear them and by goodness we need to wear them.

WRITING ACTIVITIES

Additional Writing Topics

1. In a few countries, such as Australia, adults are required by law to vote in national elections. Should Canada adopt such a law?

2. In Canada, the minimum age at which a person can drive a motor vehicle varies province by province, but usually falls in the ages of 14 to 16. However, teenagers are involved in far more than their share of serious car accidents. Should the minimum age be raised to 19?

3. Animals should be used for scientific research. Argue for or against.

4. A vegetarian diet is healthier than a diet containing meat. Argue for or against.

5. Corporations should be ethical in their business practices and methods of pollution disposal. Argue for or against.

6. Laptops, iPods, and/or smartphones should be banned in the classroom. Argue for or against any or all three.

Responding to a Photograph   The organization People for the Ethical Treatment of Animals (PETA) is known for its provocative and original ad campaigns. This is just one of their many attempts to get people to pay attention to animal cruelty.

HERE'S
THE REST
OF YOUR
FUR
COAT.

Shirley Manson for
PeTA

1. Write an informal response to the photograph. What do you notice? How does the image make you feel? What arguments does the photograph make visually? How might you use argumentation to write about this photograph?

2. Using a combination of library and online research, explore other creative ad campaigns that encourage a debate with visual rhetoric. Write a documented essay examining one of these arguments. (For more information on documented essays, see Chapters 16 and 17.)

Writing about Film

1. In *An Inconvenient Truth* (2006, G), Al Gore discusses the threat to humanity's survival created by global warming. This film represents an excellent opportunity

for rhetorical analysis. What appeals (ethos, pathos, and logos) and evidence does Gore use to achieve his purpose? What counter-arguments does Gore offer to those who would deny the threat of climate change? Does the film offer a balanced argument?

2. *Bowling For Columbine* (2002, PG-13) is a documentary by Michael Moore in which Moore questions the source of America's obsession with guns. What is the argument that Moore develops and what appeals and evidence does he use to achieve his purpose? Does the film offer a balanced argument?

Using the Internet Search the Internet for insights and information to use when developing arguments.

1. Exercise 7.2 asks you to analyze the rhetorical appeals used in the exercise's picture, and you don't need to look too far for additional ads to analyze. We suggest the websites **http://ihaveanidea.org**, the official website of the international advertising industry, and **http://adsoftheworld.com/**, a site that archives some of the best advertisements worldwide. Performing a rhetorical analysis of an ad is an interesting way to critique and deconstruct an argument. Choose an ad found on one of these sites, and analyze the argument being presented.

2. Practise spotting logical fallacies by searching for websites that present arguments on both sides of an important social, political, moral, or legal issue of your choice. Read the perspectives and opinions that are presented on several different websites. Then review the material you have researched, and identify examples of at least five of the seventeen logical fallacies discussed in this chapter. In a short essay, explain how each of the examples you have chosen illustrates that particular fallacy.

3. Using information taken from the websites you visited in response to question 1, write an argument defending a position on the particular social, political, moral, or legal issue addressed in those websites. In the process, present and address arguments that oppose your own so that your reader will know that you have considered both sides of the issue.

As always, combine the information and insights you have researched with your own ideas, but cite any material you quote, summarize, or paraphrase from another source. Use the Modern Language Association (MLA) format or the American Psychological Association (APA) format, both of which are explained in Chapter 9 of this textbook.

CHAPTER 8

The Research Paper: Working through the Process

Using **RESEARCH** in the Real World

Both Jon Stewart, pictured above, and Stephen Colbert present "fake news" to their audiences. On *The Colbert Report,* Colbert mocks this "commentary as news" approach through his delivery style of opinionated, unsubstantiated shouting. On the other hand, evaluating and comparing sources should be the first steps to making informed decisions or to informing others, in all facets of life—something Jon Stewart accomplishes with ease and sophistication on *The Daily Show.*

Without research, facts, and undisputed proof, there is only hearsay and speculation. Research can take many forms for personal, academic, and professional ends. On the personal level, if you are in the market for a new car, a stereo system, a computer, or any type of consumer goods, you might find information about competing models in a consumer magazine or online. If you want to find an affordable restaurant or cleaning service, you might check for reviews or customer testimonials in your city. Professionally, police detectives who solve cases must research the backgrounds of their suspects and witnesses, while businesses conduct market research to find out

LEARNING OUTCOMES:

▶ Select and narrow an appropriate research topic

▶ Create a research question and thesis

▶ Locate and evaluate research sources

▶ Apply primary and secondary sources effectively to a research essay

▶ Create a working bibliography for a research essay

▶ Effectively take notes from sources for a research essay

what new products consumers want and what they are willing to pay for them. Academically, research is integral to scientific discoveries related to medicine and environmental innovations, while most college and university courses have as their culminating assignment a research paper for which students research a topic, present a balanced and well-thought-out argument, and draw conclusions based on their sources.

HOW DOES RESEARCH WORK?

Research involves **finding, evaluating,** and **comparing** multiple primary and/or secondary sources of information and opinion in print and electronic publications located in your college or university library and on the Internet. In addition, you might have to interview experts on your topic or use information from a variety of other sources, including blogs, DVDs, musical recordings, and even paintings. Only when you have gathered, read, and evaluated your sources can you begin to speak on your subject with some sense of authority.

The Library Is Your New Home

Students are often under the illusion that they can write a quality research paper in the comfort of their room using a few online resources. This approach often leads to shallow research. Consider the many resources that the physical library offers you in your research:

- Access to primary documents, surveys, and first edition texts
- Access to quiet rooms and a lack of distraction
- Access to print periodicals, journals, and newspapers (Not all documents are available in databases.)
- Access to precious materials that cannot leave the library, such as encyclopedias, Martin's Criminal Code, the Merck's Manual, and Vernon's Directory
- Access to licensed Statistics Canada products not accessible from the public website, such as Financial Performance Indicators for Canadian Business and Inter-corporate Ownership
- Access to specialized, program-related software (such as ARC) and statistical processing software (such as SPSS), too expensive for most students to own
- Access to qualified professionals who are trained to help you find exactly what you are looking for in the most efficient way possible

Researching is a complex, time-consuming, and rewarding process. Do not expect it to take only a few days to research and write a proper informative or argumentative essay. We suggest anywhere from two intense weeks to a month of proper research time to get the results you want. Expect the following situations when researching:

- Several trips to the library
- Three useless sources for every useful one
- Hours spent searching databases and library catalogues
- Hours spent tracking down sources, whether by hunting on foot, downloading, emailing, printing, or photocopying

Researching is a very recursive process (hence the word *re-search*: searching again and again). Do not underestimate the time it takes to present a credible research document, or you may be disappointed with your results. If you take shortcuts, your research (and your marks) will suffer.

Narrowing Your Topic and Framing a Research Question

If you have an assigned, focused topic, you will find getting started relatively easy. Such topics often come with the instructor's assurance that they can be researched with a minimum of difficulty in your college or university library or on the Internet.

On the other hand, topics that you choose for yourself may be more interesting to you personally. As a matter of fact, you may already have a storehouse of information about your topic gained from your own experiences or reading. This information may serve as a foundation to which you can add researched information from primary and secondary sources. Consider some of the following *very general* sample research topics (a brief Google search should help you get specific ideas to form an argument):

History:	war, technology, progress, the success of rights movements, famous leaders
Humanities:	analyzing and/or comparing poems, short stories, films, novels, songs, video games, or issues about race, class, or gender
Psychology:	psychology of addiction, psychology of evil, depression, insecurity, child psychology
Business:	ethics, employee motivation, successful companies or great CEOs, marketing campaigns, technology in business
Sociology:	sex and gender, identity (and the Internet, for example), communication, parenting
Science:	the environment, astronomy, biology, physics, treatments for diseases, diets, aging
Philosophy:	arguments based on the definition or existence of truth, love, evil, or God; arguments based around the theories of various philosophical movements like existentialism or nihilism

Use Prewriting Whether your instructor wants you to narrow a broad topic that he or she has assigned or to choose your own topic, you will have to limit that topic so that it can be discussed in a paper of the assigned length. Prewriting to narrow your topic's focus is one of the most important steps in the research process. (For more on prewriting strategies, see Chapter 2.)

In many ways, broad topics like the ones listed above are far more difficult to research than a limited one, simply because a narrow topic makes it easier to identify sources that are relevant to your task. Consider how the following topics have been narrowed for a 1500- to 2500-word paper:

Broad Topic	Narrowed Topic
Teenage suicide ⟶	Peer pressure as a cause of teenage suicide in Canadian females
Environmental risks ⟶	The environmental risks of oil drilling in the Great Lakes
Alternative fuel sources ⟶	The use of ethanol as an alternative fuel source for cars
Computer programming ⟶	Job and salary prospects for computer programmers in Canada for the years 2010–2020

A broad topic is too vague. Frequently students will tell their instructor their topics ("Teen Suicide") and the professor will give them a "what about . . . ?" answer

EXERCISE 8.1

Working alone or in pairs, use brainstorming techniques to narrow the following broad topics for a 1500-word research paper.

1. The history of the automobile

2. Wireless and Bluetooth technology

3. Clean water for underdeveloped countries

4. *Guitar Hero*

5. Organic farming

6. Holocaust deniers

7. The Canadian health care system

8. Endangered species

RESEARCH ESSAY CASE STUDY: **NARROWING THE TOPIC**

A sample student research essay is featured at the end of this chapter. We will be tracking the process of the student writer throughout this chapter, in a series of feature boxes.

The original broad topic for this paper was video games and culture. Justin Waelz narrowed down that topic to **an analysis of video games and piracy.**

("What about teen suicide?"). When narrowing your topic, consider using the "what about?" strategy before your instructor gets the chance to ask you.

Using a General Question to Create a Thesis

Once you have established a workable topic, turn it into a general question in order to clarify your purpose and better direct your research efforts. Unless your instructor tells you otherwise, you ought to choose questions whose answers might serve as a thesis that you can support and argue for as you draft your research paper. Remember, too, that while any research you do is intended to help you arrive at a specific and informed answer to that question, sometimes you may need to revise your thesis if your research contradicts your initial thesis points.

The topics previously discussed in this example might be turned into the following questions and theses:

Topic: Peer pressure as a cause of teenage suicide in Canadian females

Question: To what extent does peer pressure contribute to teenage suicide in Canadian females?

Thesis: Peer pressure involving drugs and alcohol, sex, and bullying has greatly contributed to teenage suicide in Canadian females.

Topic: The environmental risks of oil drilling in the Great Lakes

Question: Are the environmental risks of drilling for oil in the Great Lakes too great for the anticipated return?

Thesis: Drilling for oil in the Great Lakes would have drastic consequences on the watershed and ecosystem of each lake as well as on public usage of these bodies of water.

Topic: The use of ethanol as an alternative fuel source for cars

Question: Is ethanol a wise replacement for gasoline as an automotive fuel?

Thesis: Ethanol is an unwise replacement for gasoline because of its high emissions levels and the vast amounts of land, water, and fertilizer needed to produce sustainable energy levels.

Topic: Job and salary prospects for computer programmers in Canada for the years 2010–2020

Question: What are the job and salary prospects for computer programmers in Canada for the years 2010–2020?

Thesis: Qualified computer programmers will have little trouble finding high-paying, satisfying jobs in Canada in the second decade of the twenty-first century.

However you frame your question, remember that it is only a starting point. You can refine it and your thesis at any time as you conduct your research. Also, be careful not to mistake the research question for the thesis. A thesis statement is a detailed answer to a question that you may never explicitly ask. In your paper, the thesis statement offers readers an outline of the main points you will cover.

RESEARCH ESSAY CASE STUDY: FRAMING A RESEARCH QUESTION

After narrowing down the topic for his research essay, Justin constructed a research question and then answered it to form a thesis. The results are below:

Topic: Video games and piracy

Question: What methods can game developers use to limit piracy?

Thesis: Through the use of cloud gaming, free-to-play models, and sophisticated digital rights management techniques, game developers can severely limit piracy.

EXERCISE 8.2

Using your narrowed research topics from Exercise 8.1, frame a question on which you could base your research. Next, try to create a thesis for your question.

Identifying Primary and Secondary Sources

Primary sources Original works containing firsthand information and insights that you might make the focus of a research paper or that you might use to support or develop ideas about other works or related subjects are called **primary sources.** All of the following are examples of primary sources:

- a work of literature
- a painting or musical composition
- a government, historical, or intellectual document, such as the Canadian Charter of Rights and Freedoms or Newton's *Mathematical Principles*
- the report of a government or corporate agency
- the Bible, the Koran, or other religious document
- an historical newspaper account
- a film
- any other original document or work of art

Information you discover yourself can also be used as a primary source. For example, information that you obtain from interviewing an expert on your topic is considered primary, as are data collected through questionnaires or surveys that you design and distribute. This type of research is called **ethnographic.** If you are using ethnographic research, make sure that your instructor has approved it and that you are not crossing any ethical or privacy boundaries. Some studies, for example, require that participants in a survey sign a waiver allowing their responses to be published anonymously.

Secondary sources Sources that provide data, analyses, opinions, and ideas from experts other than yourself are called **secondary sources.** For example, if you were writing a research paper on Thomson Highway's *Dry Lips Oughta Move to Kapuskasing,* the play itself would be your primary source. However, you might also include information about the play from scholarly studies and critiques on Canadian drama. Secondary sources include written materials about primary sources—books, journal and magazine articles, and Internet sites. (For more on primary and secondary sources, see Chapter 7.)

Using Primary and Secondary Sources

Only some research papers that you will be assigned in college or university require the use of primary sources, but virtually all require secondary sources. Consider the following example:

> **Topic:** The Halifax Explosion of 1917
>
> **Thesis:** The Halifax Explosion shaped Canadian history by influencing literature, architecture, and local culture.
>
> **Potential primary sources:** Newspaper accounts
>
> **Potential secondary sources:** Historical articles and books

If you write a research paper on the Halifax Explosion, you might use primary sources such as newspaper accounts written at the time, but you would certainly use secondary sources such as historians' assessments of the causes and effects of this calamity. Similarly, a paper arguing for an increased reliance on solar energy might not rely on primary sources such as the records of scientific experiments conducted at a solar observatory; however, it would surely include information from reports of such experiments published in journals such as *Popular Mechanics,* which are more accessible to the lay reader.

How Many Sources Are Enough?

When your instructor assigns your essay, he or she will usually make clear the minimum number of sources needed for your essay. However, keep in mind that minimum means exactly that: the smallest number you can possibly have. While having 30 sources for a 4-page paper is probably excessive, please know that when it comes to research, the more sources you have, the more detailed and thorough your paper will be. No professor on earth has ever uttered these words: "You used too many sources in your research essay!"

For too many students, a "research" essay means opening the paper with a quotation taken from dictionary.com, copying the bulk of the Wikipedia entry on the subject into the paper, and finishing with a line or two from a popular movie, in the conclusion. This is far from authoritative research.

Your professor may not appreciate an 8-page essay when the maximum page requirement was five, but, keeping in mind the limits of the assignment, the goal of your research essay is to prove your argument with as much proof as possible. Does a police detective take the word of the first witness he or she speaks with? Of course not. Many people are interviewed, and the statements are verified and corroborated with other statements. Your research essay should work in much the same way. If one source makes a claim that backs up your argument, try to find another source that does so as well. There is strength in numbers when it comes to research sources.

Be careful, however, not to turn your essay into a string of quotations and citations. Your professor wants to hear your voice in the essay, even if you do not use the personal pronoun "I"; your analyses and conclusions should be foremost, with your research sources providing the backup your argument needs to be persuasive. Repetitive information required for proof can be paraphrased or briefly referred to rather than directly quoted. (See Chapter 3 for more on using quotations, summaries, and paraphrases.)

Creating a Working Bibliography

Before you begin taking notes on your sources, you should create a working bibliography. This document will differ from your works cited section (MLA style) or references page (APA style) in that a working bibliography contains records of *all* of the books, periodical articles, websites, and other resources you search to find information. Works cited and references sections list **only** the works from which you have taken information for incorporation into your paper. You will normally not need to include your working bibliography with the final draft of your essay, but it will be of use to you as you research and write.

Begin your working bibliography by listing titles you have obtained from your background reading in reference texts. Note that encyclopedias and indexes should usually not be cited by themselves, but used, instead, to find references to more specific sources.

As you work through the research process, you can add titles of promising books, articles, and websites found in your research. You may not use every source you record, but the record you keep of your sources will be invaluable because it will keep you from repeating research you have already done.

Your working bibliography will also be an asset when you prepare your essay's works cited or references section. Make sure that you record all of the appropriate information for each type of source. (Chapter 9 discusses the format and content of MLA works cited and APA reference entries.) Note that the information you will need to record for a *book* is different from what you will need for a *journal article* or for a source from the *Internet*. Indeed, the content and format for different kinds of research sources vary significantly. For now, be sure to include the following information for all of the sources you list:

Book
   Author(s)
   Editor and translator (if appropriate)
   Title and subtitle
   Publisher
   Year and city of publication
   Volume number or edition number (if appropriate)

Periodical article or work found in an anthology (collection of articles)
   Author(s)
   Editor of the anthology
   Translator (if appropriate)

Justin, our student writer, settled on an essay analyzing the ways the video game industry can avoid piracy. Then he began compiling a working bibliography of sources he thought would be valuable to his research. Below is a small sampling of his sources. He used MLA format, according to the directions of his professor:

Abidi, Faiz. "Cloud Computing and Its Effects On Healthcare, Robotics, and Piracy." *2011 World Congress on Sustainable Technologies* (2011): 135–140. Print.

Alvisi, Alberto, Alessandro Narduzzo and Marco Zamarian. "Playstation and the Power of Unexpected Consequences." *Information, Communication & Society* 6.4 (2003): 608–627. Print.

Coby, Alex. "Good Old Games Sounds Anti-DRM Clarion Call." *Gamespot.* 10 Nov. 2012. Web. 01 Aug. 2012.

Evans, Dean. "Free EA Games Herald Greater In-Game Advertising." *Techradar.* 15 Jan. 2008. Web. 01 Aug. 2012.

Hyman, Paul. "State of the Industry: Video Game Piracy." *Game Developer* 13.11 (2006): 13–18. Print.

Kain, Erik. "Did Piracy Kill Exclusive PC Games?" *Forbes.* 04 Feb. 2012. Web. 01 Aug. 2012.

Kartas, Anastasiou, and Sigi Goode. "Use, Perceived Deterrence and the Role of Software Piracy in Video Game Console Adoption." *Information Systems Frontiers* 14.2 (2010), 261–277. Print.

Kaszor, Daniel. "Star Wars Now Free to Play—Is This The MMO Apocalypse?" *Financial Post.* 01 Aug. 2012. Web. 01 Aug 2012.

Nowak, Peter. "Gaming Heads for the Clouds." *Canadian Business* 84.11/12 (2011): 21. Print.

Ojala, Arto and Pasi Tyrväinen. "Value Networks In Cloud Computing." *Journal of Business Strategy* 32.6 (2011): 40–49. Print.

Onyett, Charles. "Death of the Disc-Based Game." *IGN.* 02 Aug. 2011. Web. 01 Aug. 2012.

Suszek, Mike. "Post-Crysis 3, Crytek Goes Free-to-play." *Joystiq.* 10 June 2012. Web. 01 Aug. 2012.

Thier, David. "Has the Diablo 3 Launch Damaged PC Gaming?" *Forbes.* 17 May 2012. Web. 01 Aug. 2012.

Tufnell, Nicholas. "Interview: Gabe Newell." *The Cambridge Student Online* Nov 2011. Web.

Title of article

Title of journal, magazine, newspaper, or anthology

Date of publication, publisher, and place of publication of anthology

Volume number, issue number, section number, date (for example, 7 July 1999, March 2002, or Fall 2000)

Consider Your Options

There are many ways to compile a working bibliography:

1. Record bibliographic (publication) information directly into a computer document.
2. Write publication information for all of your sources in a list on a piece of paper.
3. Record publication information on index cards—one card for each source—then store these cards in a separate file or box.
4. Photocopy entire articles or relevant sections of a book. Include the title page and table of contents of the publication. Sites found on the Internet can be printed out or saved to a disk.

Whichever method you use, make a copy so that your work is not lost.

Electronic Source

Author(s)

Editor or translator (if appropriate)

Publication information, if source appeared in print before being published in electronic format

Title of the website or DVD-ROM

Sponsor of the website or service company publishing the DVD-ROM

Title of the online journal, newspaper, or magazine publishing the article, along with any standard publication data for a periodical, such as volume and issue number

Date the work was published electronically or was most recently updated

Date you accessed the work

Complete URL

EXERCISE 8.3

In your college or university library, find at least one general reference book relating to the research question you framed in Exercise 8.2. Consult the bibliography of this general reference work to find at least five focused sources—books and periodical articles—relating to your research. Copy down all information listed for these five sources. You will use it as you begin to compile a working bibliography.

Computerized Book Catalogues

Your school's library catalogue is an invaluable tool. In addition to indicating call number, author, title, subject, edition, publication information, and the number of copies the library owns, computerized catalogues tell whether a book is "checked out" or "not on shelf." Some libraries have joined with others to form consortia, or groups, to share resources. In such cases, the catalogue will indicate from which member library or libraries a book can be obtained. Most libraries have catalogues accessible online, but some require a password or library card number to be entered first.

After initiating a search on the subject of air pollution and reading over the entire list of books, you might decide to find more information about several of them. A click of the mouse will usually do the trick (you must, of course, follow directions appropriate to the system you are using). The screenshot on the opposite page shows the entry you would see if you chose one of the books listed—*Wildland Fires and Air Pollution*, edited by Andrzej Bytnerowicz. The entry includes publication information about the book as well as the branch it can be found in, its call number, and its status (in this case, "In Library").

Call Numbers The book's call number is a crucial piece of information. A **call number,** which is also printed on the book's spine, refers to the place on the library shelves (stacks) where the book is stored. Academic libraries generally use Library of Congress Classification call numbers, while public libraries generally use Dewey Decimal

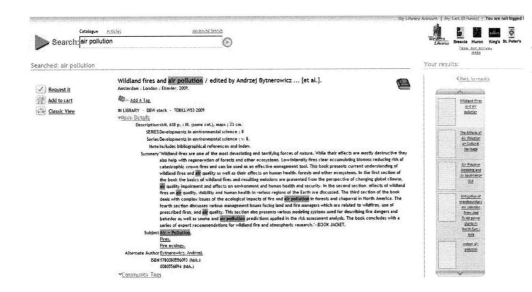

System call numbers. If your library has open stacks, you can use the call number to find the book yourself. If your library has closed stacks, you can use the call number to order the book at the circulation desk.

EXERCISE 8.4

Continue the preliminary bibliography you began in Exercise 8.2. Using your college or university library's catalogue, locate five **books** that relate to the research question you chose in Exercise 8.1. Record their pertinent publication information in your working bibliography.

Periodical Indexes

Periodicals are publications that come out at regular intervals—daily, weekly, bi-weekly, monthly, quarterly, semi-annually, and so on. The information in periodicals is often more up to date than that found in books, and the publications provide a forum for the research, opinions, and commentary of experts. **Periodical indexes** are lists of magazine, journal, and newspaper articles—often arranged by author, title, and subject.

Let's look at the three types of periodical sources you are most likely to use in your research, and at the indexes in which you can find the sources listed:

1. Magazines
2. Scholarly journals
3. Newspapers

Magazines Magazines such as *Canadian Business, Maclean's, Canadian Geographic,* and *Harrowsmith* contain articles written for general audiences. Magazine articles are researched and written by journalists who might or might not be experts in the fields on which they report. The best-known index for finding magazine articles is the *Readers' Guide to Periodical Literature.*

The *Readers' Guide,* now available in both bound and online versions, contains information from more than 100 magazines of interest to the general public. Arranged by subject and author, each volume of the bound version provides suggestions for using the *Readers' Guide,* as well as a legend to abbreviations used.

Here is an excerpt from a page in the bound version of the *Readers' Guide* on the subject of black holes:

BLACK HOLES (ASTRONOMY)

Biggest black hole in the universe? J. Horgan. il *Scientific American* 265:32 Jl '91

A black hole found at last? il *Astronomy* 19:22 F '91

Black holes in galactic cores: the research mounts [research by John Kormendy] il *Sky and Telescope* 82: 344-5 O '91

Black holes swarming at the galactic center? [Granat satellite data]

M. M. Waldrop il *Science* 251-166 Ja 11 '91

What the first entry contains:

Title of article:	Biggest black hole in the universe?
Author:	J. Horgan
Note that article is illustrated:	il
Magazine in which article appeared:	*Scientific American*
Volume number/page number:	265:32
Publication date:	Jl '91 (July 1991)

Here is an entry on the same subject found in the online version of the *Readers' Guide,* made available by subscription from the H. W. Wilson Company:

BRGA00065891 (USE FORMAT 7 FOR FULLTEXT)

Black holes in all sizes.

Talcott Richard

Astronomy v. 28 no 12 (Dec 2000) p. 26-8

Document Type:	Feature Article
Special Features:	il ISSN: 0091-6358
Language:	English
Country of Publication:	United States
Record Type:	Abstract; Fulltext Record Status: Corrected or revised record
Word Count:	538
Abstract:	Astronomers have discovered a new variety of black hole. The black hole, which is midway in size between the 2 types of hole identified so far, was discovered lying about 600 light-years from the center M82, in Ursa Major. The breakthrough finding came when astronomers using the Chandra X-ray Observatory compared high-resolution images of M82 with optical, radio, and infrared maps of the same regions. The discovery both opens a whole new field of research and raises the possibility that the Milky Way might contain midsized black holes.

Note that the online version provides an **abstract** (summary) of the article, which you can use to determine whether the article is relevant to your research project and worth reading in its entirety, as well as a way to access the complete article.

Journals These publications contain scholarly articles devoted to specific disciplines or fields of interest, and they are aimed at limited audiences, usually experts in those fields. Among the most famous are the *New England Journal of Medicine*, the *Harvard Business Review*, and *Publications of the Modern Language Association*. Often, journals are published by colleges and universities and by professional organizations. Articles in such journals are written by experts in the field and are **peer reviewed** (edited by a panel of professionals). If your instructor asks for **scholarly sources,** you should check the journal indexes.

A range of library indexes list information on journal articles. Like the materials they reference, these indexes focus on specific disciplines. Many are published by professional or educational organizations. They are usually bound annually, and some are available online or in electronic format. Many of those published electronically also include abstracts. Among commonly used journal indexes are the *Applied Science and Technology Index*, the *Business Periodicals Index*, the *Arts and Humanities Citation Index*, the *Education Index*, the *Educational Resources Information Center* (ERIC), the *Engineering Index*, the *Guide to Nursing and Allied Health*, the *Index Medicus, Stats Canada*, the *Modern Language Association International Bibliography*, the *Music Index, Psychological Abstracts*, and the *Social Sciences Citation Index*.

Here is a sample entry taken from the *Modern Language Association International Bibliography*, an index published by a professional organization made up of teachers of modern languages, literature, linguistics, and folklore:

Cather, Willa

[8429] Saposnik-Noire, Shelley. "The Silent Protagonist: The Unifying Presence of Landscape in Willa Cather's *My Ántonia*." *MQ*. 1990 Winter; 31(2): 171–179.

What this entry contains:

Subject heading:	Cather, Willa
Entry number:	[8429]
Author:	Saposnik-Noire, Shelley
Title of article:	"The Silent Protagonist: The Unifying Presence of Landscape in Willa Cather's *My Ántonia*"
Title of journal:	(*MQ* 5 *Midwest Quarterly*) *MQ*
Year/quarter of publication:	1990 Winter
Volume/issue numbers:	31(2)
Pages on which article appears:	171–179

Newspapers Articles published in newspapers can be found by using a variety of indexes. One of the most famous is the *New York Times Index,* which lists articles published in that newspaper. In addition, electronic databases such as ProQuest's *Newspaper Abstracts,* offer publication information and abstracts of articles appearing in the *National Post, The Toronto Star, The Globe and Mail, The Vancouver Sun, The Edmonton Sun, The Calgary Sun* and *The Gazette* of Montreal. Some newspapers may charge a fee or require a subscription or password for full access to their archives.

Electronic Databases

In the last decade, computerization has revolutionized library research. Not only have most libraries computerized their catalogues, but they also buy and subscribe to lists of books, articles, and other documents that are delivered via the Internet or stored on computer disks or other portable media. Some of these databases list bibliographical information only—the title, author's name, date of publication, and so on. Others include abstracts (summaries) of articles. Still others offer copies of whole articles. In some cases, in fact, you can even get copies of entire books—usually classics—on the Internet at no cost.

Here is a partial list of online databases to which your library might provide you access. Check with your librarian to find out exactly what your library offers.

- **ABI INFORM:** Provides full texts of articles in business and management. It draws articles from more than 1000 academic and professional journals and trade magazines published worldwide.

- **Academic Search Premier (EBSCO):** The world's largest multidisciplinary database, which provides the full texts of articles from nearly 3500 publications.

- **Anthropological Index Online:** Provides access to articles published in current periodicals found in the Museum of Mankind Library.

- **Applied Science & Technology Index:** Contains abstracts of articles published in professional journals in aeronautics, computer science, engineering, and related scientific and technical disciplines.

- **Canadian Business & Current Affairs (CBCA):** A service of ProQuest. Canada's largest and most comprehensive reference and current events database. Over 540 periodicals and daily news sources can be found here with many full-text articles.

- **Canadian Census Analyzer:** This service provides access to Canadian census data: individual, household, and family microdata files; provincial and federal district Profile Tables; and census tract-level Profile Tables, among other data.

- **Canadian Periodical Index Quarterly (CPI.Q):** As its title suggests, the CPI is a collection of nearly 1200 Canadian periodicals with full-text articles from 1983 to present.

- **Canadian Points of View Reference Centre:** A full-text database that provides essays discussing multiple points of view so that students may be exposed to well-rounded research and point/counter-point arguments.

- **Catalog of U.S. Government Publication (CGP):** A database for all U.S. government publications, both current and historical, with direct links to those posted online.

- **Cumulative Index to Nursing and Allied Health Literature (CINAHL):** This site references scholarly journals in the health sciences. It also contains information on books, dissertations, and educational software in the health professions.

- **ERIC:** This collection includes journal articles, reports, and speeches on education.

- **Government of Canada Publications:** A database containing over 100 000 Canadian government publications.

- **Humanities Index:** Offers citations and abstracts of journal articles in art, classics, history, language, literature, music, philosophy, religion, and other humanities. In addition, it provides the full text of some articles.

- **JSTOR:** A scholarly journal archive, JSTOR stands for journal storage. It makes available back issues of important journals in the humanities, social sciences, and sciences.

- **MLA International Bibliography:** A classified listing and subject index of over 66 000 books and articles published on modern languages, linguistics, and literature.

- **Newspaper Abstracts:** A service of ProQuest. This index includes citations and abstracts of articles published in *The Montreal Gazette, The Globe and Mail,* the *Edmonton Journal,* the *National Post,* and *The Vancouver Province.*

- **Project MUSE:** This site gives access to articles appearing in major humanities and social science journals.

- **PsychInfo:** A database of psychology-related abstracts produced by the American Psychiatric Association.

Identifying Appropriate Search Terms and Refining Searches Whether you are searching for a book, a periodical, or a journal article, using appropriate search terms can make the difference between searching for hours and coming up with a dozen sources loosely connected to your research topic, or searching for an hour and coming up with two or three sources directly related to the topic.

Let's say you want to find resources for a research paper on air pollution. You might conduct a subject search simply by typing the keywords *air pollution* in the search box of the database you are using. This method will probably yield a large list of resources, depending on the size of the collection you are searching. The screen shot in the margin is an example of the first screen you might see if you were to type *air pollution* in the search box of the EBSCO journal database Academic Search Complete at your school. This particular search listed the first ten

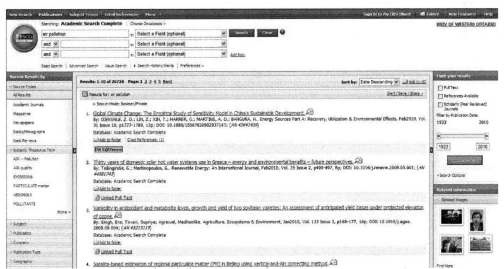

Screenshot of the EBSCO journal database Academic Search Complete, for a search on "air pollution."

entries on that subject, with a total of 26 257 hits! (A more current search would doubtless yield many more hits.)

To limit your search and make it more manageable, you might add the word *industrial* or *urban* to your search phrase; or you might use the keywords *air pollution*, *prevention*, and *automobiles* for a search. Thankfully, many databases will give you a list of "suggested search terms" to help you narrow your research. When in doubt, consult your librarians for help—they will be happy to assist you.

Limiting your search by using appropriate key terms will reduce the amount of reading and note taking that you need to do, and it will also give you sources that are more specific to your topic and, therefore, more useful.

RESEARCH ESSAY CASE STUDY: **NARROWING THE SEARCH**

For the student sample essay on gaming and piracy in this chapter, Jason created his working bibliography by using his library's MLA database. The process of narrowing his search with key terms took him through the following steps and variations:

1. **Initial search using the term "Video Games":** 4256 results (far too many to deal with)
2. **Modified search using the terms "Video Games" AND "Piracy":** 1127 results (more manageable)
3. **Modified search using the terms "Video Games" AND "DRM" OR "Cloud Gaming":** 75 results (much more manageable)

Evaluating Print and Database Sources

College and university libraries are run by professionals who can be counted on to order materials prepared by qualified and reputable authors and publishers. Often, specific books, journals, and other materials are requested directly by faculty members. In general, then, you can have confidence that the materials in your school library are reliable, although you still need to read them critically and evaluate their usefulness and relevance to your topic.

The fact that a book or article has been published does not guarantee the reliability or even the authenticity of its information. Thus, the guidelines that follow will help you avoid wasting hours taking notes that will be useless when it comes time to draft your paper.

1. **Preview the source:**
   - Question whether the work contains enough information relevant to your topic and research question to make it worth your time to read and write careful notes on.

- Check the index and table of contents of a book, and read its preface or introduction.
- Skim a periodical article or electronic source. Journal articles will usually begin with a brief **abstract** that can help you decide if the source is worth reading.
- Read subheadings as well as the article's introduction and conclusion.
- Examine any charts, graphs, or other visual elements that are included.

2. **Evaluate the content of the source:**
   - Does the author support opinions with facts, reliable statistics, and other trustworthy data, or does he or she rely heavily on unsupported ideas and opinions?
   - Does the author make his or her case logically?
   - Does the work seem balanced, or does the author provide only part of the evidence—the part that supports his or her thesis?
   - Does the work rely on well-documented research, and do the sources of this research seem reputable?

3. **Consider the objectivity of the source:** Does the material presented seem objective, or could it be biased? For example, information on the efficacy of a drug taken from a publication of the National Institutes of Health is likely to be objective, whereas information from a pamphlet published by the manufacturer of that drug will probably be biased in favour of the drug. Most pharmaceutical manufacturers and distributors will provide accurate information, but they are in business to make a profit; therefore, they do not always provide information from a disinterested perspective.

4. **Consider the publication date:** The more current the publication, the better, especially for topics in the sciences and technologies, as well as in the social sciences.

5. **Consider the author:**
   - What are his or her credentials, such as education, years of experience, and professional affiliation?
   - Is he or she a college or university professor or a well-known reporter, commentator, scientist, or other professional in a field related to your topic?
   - Is he or she a member of a respected research institution?
   - Has the author published articles or books on the same or related topics?
   - Are these sources available in university and college libraries?
   - Does the author have a political, artistic, or other bias that makes his or her viewpoint less than objective?

EXERCISE 8.5

Continue the working bibliography you began in Exercise 8.3. Using resources like those discussed above, locate five periodical **articles** that relate to the research question you chose in Exercise 8.2. Record their pertinent publication information (see the list for periodical articles earlier in this chapter) in your working bibliography.

SEARCHING THE INTERNET

If you are like most students, the first place you'd begin researching is the Internet. Make no mistake: the Internet has made doing research an easy (yet potentially limitless) task. Students can access whole books, articles from online magazines and scholarly journals, company position papers, government documents, pamphlets, brochures, and a host of other information sources on the Internet. However, using the Internet as a research source brings several potential pitfalls that you need to be aware of (see "Evaluating Electronic Sources" later in this chapter).

Internet Search Tools: URLs, Directories, and Search Engines

No doubt, if you've made it through the school system in the last ten years, you're very familiar with all of the terms we're about to mention. However, please consider this section a refresher. In regard to Internet searches, if you know the **URL** (Uniform Resource Locator) of a website, you can connect to that site directly by typing the URL into the address box of your browser. It is always wise to keep a record of the URLs of websites you have accessed; you can do this simply by printing out the site's home page or copying the URL and pasting it into your working bibliography, using your computer's cut-and-paste function.

If you are just beginning your search for information on a topic, however, you will probably want to start by using an Internet browser such as Microsoft Internet Explorer, Google Chrome, or Firefox's Mozilla and a **search engine** such as Google. Many Internet browsers and search engines have **directories,** or listings of search categories that will bring you to relevant sites or open to sections as a newspaper would. For example, Yahoo! lists "Finance," "Movies," and "Sports" among many other categories. Keep in mind, however, that general Internet searches will likely take you to hundreds or thousands of websites, most of which would not be considered reliable or scholarly by your instructor. Use them to gain some background information and to find lists of more specific sources, which you can then locate and read.

Popular Search Engines Any search engine can provide you with access to more results (or "hits") than you will ever need. However, not all search engines access the same sites. Therefore, searching for the same topic via different search engines might very well produce different results. Below are the three most widely used search engines:

- **Bing** (http://bing.com): This relatively new search engine developed by Microsoft has several new onscreen features such as a visible search history, suggested related searches, and a subject table of contents that make searching more user-friendly.

- **Google** (http://www.google.com): Google, largely considered the leader in search engines, provides access to over eight billion web pages, and includes a number of special features to improve searches. It ranks websites according to the number and quality of pages that link to them. This is a very powerful and widely used search engine; however, it should not be your only tool for research!

- **Yahoo!** (http://ca.yahoo.com/): A multi-service search engine with many onscreen features including a topics list as well as a list of featured services (e.g., people finder, translation) to help accomplish a multitude of tasks.

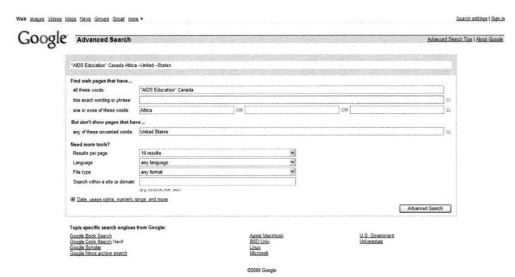

Screenshot of a Google Advanced Search for the term "AIDS education."

Refining Your Internet Search Search engines, like databases, offer users several different ways to limit and refine their searches. With many search engines, for example, if you type in the keywords *AIDS education,* you will find sites relevant both to *AIDS* and to *education.* In some cases, you might be able to refine your search simply by typing your keywords in quotation marks, thereby significantly limiting your yield to sites on topics dealing only with educational efforts aimed at dealing with AIDS. Fortunately, most search engines provide their users with advice on how to best use their services. For example, using Google's advanced search function can help you refine a search for information on AIDS education. To make your search efficient, spend a few minutes reading these suggestions, or at least those offered by the search engine you use most often.

Bookmarking and Lists of Favourites For future reference, it is a good idea to "bookmark" or include in your "list of favourites" those websites you find most useful. Bookmarking takes up very little memory on your computer so be sure to add to your list of favourites any websites whose information you'd like to use or websites you would like to evaluate at a later date. Don't count on being able to go back into a Google search results page and find that perfect website (or perfect page on a website) that you found yesterday. You run the risk of wasting time trying to find information that you could have easily accessed with one click in your list of favourites.

EXERCISE 8.6

Look up a subject such as one of the following, using three different search engines:

1. College literacy standards
2. Ethanol as an alternative fuel
3. Advantages of vegan diets

Which search engine found the greatest number of useful sites for each topic? Which is easiest to use?

Three Tips on Using Search Engines

All search engines offer specific on-screen help; however, here are three general strategies you might find helpful:

1. **Try a Boolean search:** Boolean searches use AND, OR, and NOT with keywords and phrases to limit searches and make them more efficient. If you typed *victim* AND *crime* AND *compensation,* you would gain access to more sites that contain information about compensating victims of crime, and you would eliminate sites relating to, for example, *compensation for corporate executives* or the *victimization of women in the workplace.* If you searched for *virus* NOT *computer,* you would limit your search to viruses known to medicine.

2. **Use a wild card:** A *wild card* is a character, often an asterisk, that is used with a keyword to search for variations of that word as well as the word itself. For example, typing the keyword *crim** might produce sites containing the words *crime, criminology, criminals,* and *criminality.*

3. **Include quotation marks** (" "): Quotation marks tell the search engine to look for the words you have typed in the exact order they appear in the search box. For example, if you wanted to find sites that discuss "standard of living," you would put quotation marks around those words.

EXERCISE 8.7

Continue the working bibliography you began in Exercise 8.3. Using resources like those discussed above, locate five **Internet documents** that relate to the research question you chose in Exercise 8.2. Record their pertinent publication information (see the list for electronic earlier in the chapter) in your working bibliography.

New Media Research

One of the more unique ways of acquiring research is by searching wikis, blogs, video-sharing sites, and social networking sites. On the positive side, each is user generated, allowing one or more experts to contribute a wide body of knowledge on different subjects. Unfortunately, what makes these resources desirable is also their greatest handicap: the reliability and objectivity of their information can be in question. (See Chapter 9 for information on how to properly cite new media sources.)

Wikis A wiki is a collection of web pages developed and edited collaboratively by any number of anonymous users. You can find a wiki about almost any topic on the Web. By far the most popular wiki is **Wikipedia,** the online encyclopedia.

We recommend using Wikipedia as a starting point only; however, be sure to use many reputable sources when researching and, if possible, avoid using Wikipedia directly in your formal essays. Use it to point you to other bibliographic sources, instead. (See "Why Your Prof Hates Wikipedia" and "A Reader's Eye: Beware Wikipedia" for further comments on how unreliable Wikipedia can be.)

Why Your Professor Hates Wikipedia

To many students, the word "research" means one thing: Wikipedia. Students love Wikipedia for this reason: they can get an immense amount of information, some general and some very specific, on almost any topic. Professors notoriously dislike Wikipedia for this reason: students tend to use only this one site, neglecting to search for other, more credible resources.

Students view Wikipedia as they would an all-you-can-eat buffet—their one-stop shop for research. And why shouldn't they? Wikipedia seems to have an answer for everything, right? Well, not always. Wikipedia—and its online variations about.com, howstuffworks.com, and *Encyclopedia Britannica* online—are viewed (to be blunt) as **high school level research.** All three give a general overview of their topics, but do not offer the specialized conclusions and criticisms found in academic journals and specialized documents and essays. In the case of Wikipedia, the information can be biased, unreliable, incorrect, or inaccurate.

For example, as a prank, and at Colbert's encouragement, viewers edited Stephen Colbert's Wikipedia page, claiming that the popular TV host had saved the African Elephant. Eventually the error was corrected; but a few weeks later the change was made again, thus proving Wikipedia's potential for misinformation. In short, according to his Wikipedia page, Stephen Colbert has saved the African elephant not once, but twice.

If you want to impress your professor, get a good grade, and increase your general knowledge, leave the majority of your research to **peer-reviewed scholarly journals** or online essays by noted scholars.

Blogs A blog (short for the word *weblog*) is a personal website where one individual shares his or her opinions and thoughts. Blogs are essentially glorified electronic diaries. You wouldn't normally use someone's diary as a resource (that is, as a *secondary resource*); however, many respected professionals in various fields now have blogs where they post much relevant and valid information. As with any type of informal resource, you should always use common sense when evaluating whether or not to use a particular blog in your research assignment. Keep in mind that blogs are usually highly subjective and opinionated.

Video-Sharing Sites A video-sharing site is a website that allows users to upload and watch videos on a variety of topics. By far the most famous video-sharing site is YouTube; however, other notable ones exist (Metacafe, Vimeo, Dailymotion). Video-sharing sites are excellent for finding primary material such as interviews, vintage commercials, and news reports. Unfortunately, these sites also have issues with clutter (too many identical videos listed under different names) and authenticity of material. When using these sites to do research, always be sure that your sources are genuine and accurate. Photoshop and video-editing programs have made altering materials easy and can lead to misrepresentations of material. Also, beware of amateur tribute videos and school projects. For every excellent video interview with Marshall McLuhan posted on a video-sharing site, there also seems to be another video featuring a montage of photos set to pounding drums and screeching guitars. Choose your sources wisely.

Social Networking Sites A social networking site is a website which allows multiple users to interact, swap information, and communicate around a shared interest or activity. Some of the more popular social networking sites are Facebook, My Space, Twitter, and LinkedIn. Although typically not accepted as credible sources for research, these sites are gaining wider acceptance as many notable academics, politicians, and celebrities post information on their profile pages (usually in the form of sound bites which are then repeated, paraphrased, and misquoted across the Internet). As always, evaluate the credibility and quality of any new media research sources carefully. If the same information can be sourced from a more credible and stable publication, go there instead.

Social Bookmarking Sites Social bookmarking sites allow multiple users to store, manage, and share bookmarks to various web pages through the use of tags in the form of icons and keywords. Social bookmarking allows users access to myriad recommended sites all on the same topic and allows them to recommend their choices to others in the pursuit of a consolidated, definitive collection of resources on a specific topic. Some of the most popular social bookmarking sites are Reddit, Digg, Delicious, and Stumbleupon.

A READER'S EYE: **BEWARE WIKIPEDIA**

The misquote discussed in the following story was printed in newspapers around the world and works as an example of how unreliable Wikipedia's information can be (as well as how people too often accept its information as fact).

IRISH STUDENT DUPES MEDIA WITH WIKIPEDIA
Fake (and cheesy) quote added to online database, reprinted across the globe
Macleans.ca

1   DUBLIN—When Dublin university student Shane Fitzgerald posted a poetic but phoney quote on Wikipedia, he was testing how our globalized, increasingly Internet-dependent media was upholding accuracy and accountability in an age of instant news.

2   His report card: Wikipedia passed. Journalism flunked.

3   The sociology major's obituary-friendly quote—which he added to the Wikipedia page of Maurice Jarre hours after the French composer's death March 28—flew straight on to dozens of U.S. blogs and newspaper websites in Britain, Australia and India.

4   They used the fabricated material, Fitzgerald said, even though administrators at the free online encyclopedia twice caught the quote's lack of attribution and removed it.

5   A full month went by and nobody noticed the editorial fraud. So Fitzgerald told several media outlets they'd swallowed his baloney whole.

6   "I was really shocked at the results from the experiment," Fitzgerald, 22, said Monday in an interview a week after one newspaper at fault, *The Guardian* of Britain, became the first to admit its obituary writer lifted material straight from Wikipedia.

7   "I am 100 per cent convinced that if I hadn't come forward, that quote would have gone down in history as something Maurice Jarre said, instead of something I made up," he said. "It would have become another example where, once anything is printed enough times in the media without challenge, it becomes fact."

8   "One could say my life itself has been one long soundtrack," Fitzgerald's fake Jarre quote read. "Music was my life, music brought me to life, and music is how I will be remembered long after I leave this life. When I die there will be a final waltz playing in my head that only I can hear."

9   Fitzgerald said one of his University College Dublin classes was exploring how quickly information was transmitted around the globe. His private concern was that, under pressure to produce news instantly, media outlets were increasingly relying on Internet sources—none more ubiquitous than the publicly edited Wikipedia.

10   "The moral of this story is not that journalists should avoid Wikipedia, but that they shouldn't use information they find there if it can't be traced back to a reliable primary source," said the readers' editor at the *Guardian,* Siobhain Butterworth, in the May 4 column that revealed Fitzgerald as the quote author.

Evaluating Electronic Sources

When using the Internet as a research tool, you need to realize that the Internet is valuable only if approached with caution and discrimination. While the sources you find in your college library have already been screened through a process that involves college faculty and professional librarians ordering materials that they believe will best support the curriculum, any organization or any person—regardless of education, experience, bias, or intent—can publish on the Internet. No screening process exists for such material.

Thus, consider the following *additional* criteria as you decide whether an Internet source is appropriate:

- **Currency:** The Internet can provide access to the most current information on a topic. On the other hand, other sites stay online long after their owners have stopped updating them. In short, what you find on the Internet one day might not be there the next, or it might be completely outdated—situations that you should take into account when evaluating your sources. After all, the reliability of such information might be questionable.

- **Ranking:** Many website creators pay a fee to register their sites with certain search engines. This entitles them to be listed among the sites that come up when you use the search engine's directory. Again, these sites might not be the most appropriate for your search. Do not be fooled into thinking that the most popular website for your research topic is necessarily the best one.

- **Bias:** Many people and groups take advantage of the ease of publishing on the Web. For example, hate mongers, racial supremacists, and the like sometimes post false and defamatory information about public figures and about ethnic, religious, or other groups. On occasion, the material is presented in such a devious manner that it seems to be coming from a legitimate news source. In such cases, it is especially important for you to discover and evaluate the sources of information that you intend to use.

- **Sponsorship:** Who sponsors the website? Is it a college or university, a research institution, a professional journal, a reputable magazine, or a respected think tank? Or is it just a personal website that the creator has published by renting space on a commercial server? If the latter, find other sources of information.

- **Purpose:** What is the purpose of the site? Consider the Web address (URL). Addresses for sites sponsored by educational institutions usually end in "edu." Those for Canadian federal government sites end in "gc.ca." Sites whose addresses end in "org" (organization) need careful scrutiny. Two other types of addresses end in "com," for commercial, and "ca," indicating the site is Canadian (or a Canadian version of an already established site; for example, ebay.ca). Corporations usually use such addresses. If you are considering material posted on a corporate website, you need to ask yourself if the material presented is simply informational and objective or if its purpose is to sell you something.

- **Presentation:** Is the material well written, well presented, and well developed? Is the website constructed logically and coherently? Is it updated regularly? Does it include links to other sites? What sites are they? Do the linked sites seem reputable? If the answer to any of these questions is no, find other sources of information.

EXERCISE 8.8

Evaluate the sources in the working bibliography you have been developing. Remove sources that are not appropriate according to the criteria for print and non-print sources. Do you have enough sources left for you to start taking notes, or should you try to find more sources? If in doubt, consult your instructor.

EXERCISE 8.9

Working alone or in pairs, evaluate and rank the following websites based on the criteria discussed in this chapter: currency, ranking, bias, sponsorship, purpose, and presentation.

1. Dihydrogen Monoxide Research Division (http://www.dhmo.org/)
2. British Columbia (http://www2.gov.bc.ca/)
3. Canadian Beef (http://www.beefinfo.org/default.aspx)
4. BlackBerry (http://ca.blackberry.com/)
5. Canadian Cancer Society (http://www.cancer.ca)
6. University of Acadia (http://www2.acadiau.ca/)
7. Canadian Aviation Museum (http://www.aviation.technomuses.ca)
8. CBC (http://www.cbc.ca/)

TAKING NOTES

The second last stage of the research process is note taking. Note taking goes hand in hand with the strategies of summary, paraphrase, and direct quotation—topics covered in Chapter 3.

Why Take Notes?

Note taking allows you to organize sources based on themes, ideas, and relevant content as well as to avoid plagiarism by specifically identifying and acknowledging which information from your research you plan to integrate into your final paper. It goes a step further than the working bibliography discussed earlier in this chapter. As you read, you will want to keep a record of information that is potentially important for your research paper—important quotations, recurring themes, breakthrough ideas. Since writing right *on* actual primary or secondary sources is vandalism, note taking via index cards or on the computer allows you to organize your resources. Whichever way you take notes, keep your purpose clearly in mind: take notes in a way that will allow you to organize your information easily and help you in writing your research paper.

RESEARCH ESSAY CASE STUDY: **TAKING NOTES**

After creating a working bibliography and narrowing his resources to the most useful ones, the student writer of the research essay at the end of this chapter began the note-taking process by summarizing and paraphrasing select information about his essay's topic and copying down useful direct quotations. These notes were then organized by sub-topic based on how he anticipated organizing his essay. This student used his own method of recording the most important information about his sources under various headings. Below are his sample notes typed into a computer file document:

Sub-topic: Cloud Gaming

Author: Nicholas Tufnell

Source: "Interview: Gabe Newell." The Cambridge Student Online Nov 2011. Web.

Quotation: "Piracy is a non-issue for our company."

Sub-topic: Free to Play

Author: Mike Suszek

Source: "Post-Crysis 3, Crytek Goes Free-to-play." Joystiq. 10 June 2012. Web. 01 Aug. 2012.

Paraphrase: Crytek, the developer of the Crysis series, announced that all releases post Crysis 3 will be free-to-play

Sub-topic: DRM

Author: Alex Coby

Source: "Good Old Games Sounds Anti-DRM Clarion Call." Gamespot. 10 Nov. 2012. Web. 01 Aug. 2012.

Paraphrase: A recent survey by Vigilant Defender, an anti-piracy group, showing that out of 900 000 respondents, 52 percent felt that DRM discouraged them from buying games.

Methods of Recording Notes

Using Index Cards Although regarded as primitive by some students, recording notes on index cards may be convenient for others, particularly if you do not have a computer nearby while researching. Usually, one index card is used for each fact, idea, opinion, or group of supporting data that you take from a source. This method enables you to organize your notes easily and efficiently once you have finished your research and are ready to outline and draft your paper.

Using Photocopies or Printouts If your paper is brief, and if you are not using many sources, this system can work very well. You can highlight key points on printouts of your source articles and write notes and ideas in the margins. You might also attach Post-it notes to documents.

Using Electronic Devices and Software Instead of writing longhand on paper, you can take notes on your smartphone or laptop. As with note cards, you'll need to identify the source of each piece of information. Writing your quotations, summaries, and paraphrases (see Chapter 3) in a computer document can save you time once you begin your paper because you can cut and paste the information into your draft. However, be careful to keep all publication information and page numbers attached to each quotation or paraphrase when cutting and pasting, and to put quotation marks around others' words right away. A failure to do so may lead to plagiarism in your finished paper.

If you are interested in note-taking software, we recommend Microsoft Office *OneNote 2010*, a program specifically designed to help students take notes and gather other media into easily accessible compartments. Other electronic programs include *eNoteFile* and *Evernotes*.

Arranging Your Notes

After taking your notes on cards, on a laptop, or on printouts, read over these notes carefully. As you do, general points or major ideas that you might use in your paper will start to emerge. Next, arrange your notes in a way that gives you a preliminary notion of how your paper will be organized. Once you review your initial "layout," however, you can change the positions of notes, add or delete notes as needed, and make other changes easily and logically. You might even see the need to do more research. In any event, you can then use this arrangement of notes as a model from which to outline your paper.

WRITING THE RESEARCH PAPER

Students' problems with research papers sometimes arise from their tendency to view the research paper with dread. They envision a huge project that is somehow unrelated to what they have already learned. However, you should keep this definition in mind: a research paper is simply a documented essay. The only real distinguishing feature of a documented essay is its use of outside sources and its need to account for that use in an acceptable manner.

RESEARCH ESSAY CASE STUDY: **PREPARING AN OUTLINE**

After prewriting on his topic to develop a thesis, Justin began crafting the shape of his essay via a point-form outline. As mentioned throughout this text, the more detail you place in your outline, the easier it will be to craft your essay's rough draft. Justin has broken his point form outline down by paragraph and included as many examples as he could. See Justin's final completed and documented essay towards the end of this chapter.

Title: Video Game Piracy—subtitle needed.

Introduction:

Hook: Malayan proverb

Background Info: piracy is at an all time high, robbing companies of 20 to 30% of their profits.

Thesis: three potential ways to deal with piracy are cloud gaming, free to play games, and digital rights management.

Paragraph 1:

Topic Sentence: Cloud gaming could drastically reduce piracy since there is no physical software to pirate.

Example: Sony and Microsoft have acquired cloud gaming services in anticipation of this method of gaming.

Example: Valve's steam platform has significantly reduced piracy for the company.

Concluding/transition statement: Aside from cloud gaming, free to play games with micro-transactions have proven to successfully curb piracy.

Paragraph 2:

Topic Sentence: Free to play, or "freemium" games also offer another method for companies to curb piracy and recover revenue.

Example: Applied successfully in Korea in 2009 for game FIFA online.

Example: Being applied in North America, with Crytek announcing that all releases post Cyrsis 3 will be free to play, and EA changing subscription based game Star Wars: TOR to a free to play model.

Concluding/transitional Statement: Until cloud gaming and free to play models become popular, most games will still be sold as discs. Thus developers need more efficient DRM.

Paragraph 3:

Topic Sentence: DRM is still a very acceptable and probable method for developers to thwart piracy

Example: Croteam's Serious Sam 3 featured (for pirated copies of the game) DRM of a giant scorpion that killed players.

Example: DRM can be a touchy issue especially when it infringes on gamer's rights or inadvertently ruins the playing experience, such as DRM in Diablo 3 that impeded paying customers from accessing the game. Concluding/transitional Statement: DRM is still the dominant way to deal with piracy, but needs to be carefully developed to avoid ruining the playing experience for honest gamers.

> Conclusion:
>
> Topic Sentence: reference back to intro proverb; the Internet is here to stay. Piracy is a reality that must be dealt with.
>
> Restate Thesis: cloud gaming, free to play games, and unintrusive DRM are all potential ways to stop piracy. Concluding statement: The game industry is driven by the consumer market. Whatever consumers choose, developers should rightly follow.

Using Sources Wisely within the Research Paper

Nothing lends your research paper credibility like a well-placed quotation from an authoritative source. However, often students use quotations merely to reinforce or prove verbatim observations they've already made as opposed to using them to expand upon ideas they have themselves established. This habit yields essays that are simplistic—a veritable plot summary of information—rather than essays which are layered and complex. Consider the following excerpts (citations in MLA):

> The novel *A Connecticut Yankee in King Arthur's Court* presents "many conflicts to its readers" (Gidby 11). Twain presents readers with a tale that discusses many issues such as democracy and capitalism. Hank, Twain's protagonist, says, "I will teach this society the ways of democracy and capitalism" (Twain 13). But this society merely swaps one ruler for another. Peasants routinely declare "we have merely changed kings" (Twain 45). As the novel ends, the reader finds that Hank is just as misguided as Arthur and his knights: "Hank's quest for glory and victory makes him just another Arthur and as morally suspect as his knights" (Riddel 17).

The previous paragraph uses research only to prove statements already made by the writer, without adding any extra analysis or interpretation.

Now read the following paragraph, in which critical sources are used to help the writer expand and develop ideas instead of merely repeating claims:

> The novel *A Connecticut Yankee in King Arthur's Court* presents many conflicts: "past vs. present, industry vs. agriculture, and religion vs. science" (Jones 23). None is easily resolved. Twain presents readers with a tale that attempts to "trumpet the ways of democracy, capitalism, and industry," (Smith 98) yet shows how these so-called advancements do not make life any more fulfilling for the citizens of medieval England. They are still held hostage by a dictator, ruled by an oligarchy—this time a modern one. Twain's protagonist, Hank, may have desired to free "these wretched souls from the confines of superstition and poverty" (Twain 56), but as the novel ends the reader finds that what Hank once viewed with contempt—the "gullible goat-trading serfs and their stone and straw resources" (Riddel 17)—are now almost quaint in their simplicity.

Too often in research papers, students make a claim and then use their research to support that claim in a repetitive manner: statement, quotation, statement, quotation. A quality research paper, on the other hand, allows the writer to analyze, interpret, and respond to each source used in the paper.

Summarizing, paraphrasing, and quoting from outside sources are some of the most important skills involved in writing the research paper. Chapter 3 covers these topics in depth, as well as showing how to incorporate borrowed material into your text by using signal phrases and in-text citations. Chapter 9 covers how to create a proper works cited page for MLA essays and a proper references page for APA essays, so that your audience can look up the sources used in your paper, if desired. No research essay writing process is complete without reviewing these important skills.

General Strategies for the Research Paper

Use these strategies for any documented essay that you write.

Follow Assignment Instructions Each research assignment is different, and each instructor will specify what he or she wants to see. When grading your paper, if the instructor realizes, for example, that instead of using ten sources (five print sources and five Internet sources, as specified), you used eight Internet sources and no print sources, your essay is at great risk. The same is true if your instructor asked for a minimum of 1500 words and you produced 975 words, or if your instructor stated that no more than 25 percent of your essay should be taken up by quotations, summaries, and paraphrases, and half of your essay is material taken from secondary sources.

Use Your Time Wisely Writing a good research essay takes time. Most instructors give plenty of time for a research paper to be completed; however, some students don't start the process of researching and writing until it is too late. Instructors see the research paper as a series of steps, but some students begin the process the day before the essay is due and feel pressured to skip many of the steps that would help them to build a successful and original essay.

Don't even consider trying to write a research paper the night before it is due. Instead, manage your time wisely. If you have three weeks to write a paper, consider scheduling approximately a week for research, a week for drafting, and a week for revision.

Consider the "Shape" of Your Research Paper Throughout this text, you have been learning to write essays using various rhetorical options: definition, causal analysis, and so on. Can you organize your essay around one of these frameworks? If your instructor asks you to explain how the federal government decides to lend money to developing nations, process analysis would provide an effective framework for your essay. Any topic that asks for "the best" or "the ideal" will need both definition and argument. You might also consider comparison and contrast. Review Part 2 of this text to see which option is most appropriate.

Prepare an Outline After you have done the bulk of your research, you will have notes in various formats. However, this information will be of little use if you do not plan how to organize your essay so that you use your researched material to your best advantage. You need to develop a tentative working thesis statement at this point, if you

Consider Your Options

Your instructor is assigning you a research project, and you will be the project manager. Just as in the working world, you will receive guidelines on how to proceed. When your project is completed, it will be evaluated against those guidelines. The research paper measures not only your ability to write but also your ability to plan a project, coordinate the project's steps, and check the results.

have not already done so. (For more on developing a working thesis, see Chapter 2.) Although your final thesis may vary somewhat from your earliest version, developing this "guiding principle" will help you focus your efforts. Next, you will need to outline your essay. You may need to alter your outline during the writing process. However, an outline gives you a focus and a tentative organization.

Use Your Sources to Support Your Ideas The essay that you submit to your instructor should be guided by your personal point of view and assertions, backed up by logic, examples, and the support provided by your sources. Your essay should *not* be a hodgepodge of quotations and paraphrases, with your personal voice emerging only occasionally. What you draw from your sources is secondary to what you write in your own voice. With this thought in mind, you should write the bare outline or rough draft of your essay first in your own words and then add in your research as needed, rather than cutting and pasting all of your research together into an "essay" and then adding a few of your own words later.

Cite Your Sources Carefully Some students are troubled by the thought of exploring a subject and then determining what information needs to be cited. Their concern is valid: using someone else's work without giving proper credit can invite a charge of **plagiarism,** which will have decidedly unpleasant consequences for a student's academic standing. Use the work of other people, within reason; but be sure you acknowledge and credit your sources. For specific guidelines on what types of information must be cited, see Chapter 3.

Separate the Drafting Process from the Revision Process Once you have written your essay, put it aside for a day or two. The essay will look quite different if you give your brain time to concentrate on something else. Revision and writing require two very different sets of skills. Allow yourself time to regroup, psychologically speaking, before you review and revise your draft. When you revise, make use of the Questions for Reviewing a Research Essay in Figure 8.1.

FIGURE 8.1
Peer review checklist for a research essay.

QUESTIONS FOR REVIEWING A RESEARCH ESSAY
☐ Does the introduction give the reader enough context? Does it capture the reader's interest? How could the introduction be strengthened?
☐ What is the thesis statement? Does it answer your research question? Is the topic sufficiently narrowed? Is your thesis original and interesting?
☐ Does your paper include a sufficient number and variety of reliable, authoritative research sources?
☐ Are all summaries, paraphrases, and direct quotations properly cited?
☐ Do all the sources in the works cited or references list have corresponding in-text citations within the essay?
☐ Do all of the in-text citations within the essay appear as full entries in the works cited or references list at the end of the essay?
☐ Does the essay have an effective conclusion? Is there enough support for the conclusion reached?

The following essay was written by Justin Waelz for a course on video game theory. The assignment gave students the option of analyzing how the video game industry has impacted society socially, economically, or technologically. As we have seen throughout this chapter, Justin went through all the steps of writing a research paper—narrowing the topic, framing a research question, creating a working bibliography, evaluating the sources, and taking notes from the most useful sources—as well as the steps of the writing process—prewriting, organizing, drafting, and revising—to produce this final version of his essay. Note how this essay incorporates both primary sources (descriptions of game content) and secondary sources (critical responses).

Waelz 1

Justin Waelz
Professor Rob Muhlbock
INDS 1033-40
3 August 2012

Controlling the Digital Sea: The Role of Piracy in Shaping the Future of Video Gaming

An old Malayan proverb states, "the existence of the sea means the existence of pirates" (Davidson 9). Accordingly, just as pirates of old proliferated on the major trading networks of the world to plunder ancient empires of their riches, so too does a new-age digital pirate, operating on digital networks, and seeking glory and fame by robbing the game developers of their ever-growing bounty. The last decade seems to have been a Golden Age for software piracy, where virtually any form of copy protection could be broken, with pirates robbing the gaming giants of 20 to 30 percent of their profits (Hyman 14). Though software piracy may still be in a Golden Age, it appears that a period of decline may be imminent, as developers attempt to wrest control of the digital sea back from the pirates. This could lead to drastic changes in the landscape of the gaming market, whereby the local hardware synonymous with gaming consoles is replaced by cloud gaming platforms, free-to-play titles that rely on micro transactions to generate revenue, and newer less intrusive forms of Digital Rights Management (DRM).

The ability for pirates to break copy protection and spread pirated software across the Internet is dependent on having access to the software; thus, the logical directive to eliminating software piracy is to prevent direct access to the software by moving to a cloud gaming platform where pirates cannot access the software. This solution is becoming readily apparent to game developers seeking to recover their losses attributed to piracy, as made evident through the proclamation by Denis Dyack, the founder of Silicon Knights, at E3 (Electronic Entertainment Expo) 2011 that "[cloud gaming] is going to be the future of [the video game] industry's economy" (Nowak 21). The market also appears to be embracing this new model of delivering content, with the International Data Corporation predicting that in the near future cloud-based software will occupy a market share of 65 percent (Ojala and Tyrvainen 40), making the transition to cloud-based gaming seemingly inevitable in the market driven industry that is video game development. Moreover, the recent acquisition of the cloud gaming service Gaikai by Sony Computer

Correct MLA header with stylish title.

Opening has an effective hook.

Paraphrased point from secondary source.

Excellent three-point thesis.

Paragraph one topic sentence directly relates to first thesis point.

Embedded direct quotation from secondary source.

Entertainment, and the rumours of Microsoft acquiring OnLive ("Cloud Gaming: Pick Up and Play"), indicate that the major hardware manufacturers have acknowledged cloud-based gaming as a key component in the future of the industry, and are seeking to position themselves for a market without traditional gaming consoles. One company that has seen great success in the cloud gaming market is Valve with their Steam platform. Though not exclusively a cloud gaming utility, Steam's convenient and unintrusive brand of digital distribution has made piracy, in the words of Valve CEO Gabe Newell, "a non-issue for [the] company" (Tufnell). The transition to a purely digital means of content distribution provided by cloud gaming, also enables developers to experiment with new methods of generating revenue from their games; one such concept is the "freemium" business model.

The newly industrialized countries of the world, such as China and India, are perhaps the greatest challenge for developers attempting to curb piracy, where a multitude of socioeconomic factors have led to piracy rates as high as 91 percent (Abidi 139); however, it appears "freemium" may offer an immediate solution for developers looking to recover lost earnings. Freemium, or free-to-play, describes a business model in which the core elements of a video game are provided to the user free of charge, and micro-transactions related to complementary game content, such as additional levels or character upgrades, are used to generate revenue (Onyett). This concept was proven highly successful when applied in 2009 to the piracy rampant South Korean market with *FIFA Online* (Evans). EA provided the game for no charge, and relied only on micro transactions, which, according to EA, ultimately led to "[consumers paying EA] more online than they would have done buying the game in a store" (Evans). The success of the freemium model for video games lies in the fact that the game essentially becomes a virtual storefront for items to be purchased via micro transactions; thus, the developer stands to benefit from piracy of the core game, since the number of potential consumers of virtual goods and services increases (Kuchera). It is this idea that makes the concept of freemium games the ideal solution for developers seeking to recover lost earnings in the piracy laden Asian market, as demonstrated by the recent announcement by Activision of *Call of Duty Online,* a free-to-play title, exclusively for the Chinese market (Orry). However, this solution is not limited to the Asian market. Major game developers appear to be embracing freemium as the future of generating revenue from games, with Crytek, the developer of the *Crysis* series, announcing that all releases post *Crysis 3* will be free-to-play (Suszek), and EA recently changing its MMORPG *Star Wars the Old Republic* from a subscription-based service to a freemium model (Kaszor). Despite the promise of the freemium model for combating piracy, it is likely that traditional disc-based games will persist for at least the next console generation, with the influence of piracy obviously playing a key role in developers' digital rights management techniques.

The use of CD-ROM as the storage medium for the Sony PlayStation opened the door to piracy, which was previously inhibited by cartridge-based games, and is considered a significant factor in the rapid rise in the install base that made the PlayStation the most successful console of all time (Alvisi, et al. 618; Kartas and Goode 262). Kartas and Goode have quantified this phenomenon on the basis of rational choice perspective, where they demonstrate a statistically significant link between console adoption and the ability to pirate software (274). While this may be promising for console manufacturers seeking to grow their consumer base, it presents a double-edged sword, as high rates of piracy will force developers to more secure platforms "as a way to stem the bleeding from thousands of illegal downloads of their games" (Thier). A principle example of this concept in practice is on the PC gaming platform, where uncontrollable piracy has arguably led to the death of PC gaming due to the lack of developer support, resulting from reduced profitability attributed to high rates of piracy (Kain). To avoid losing developer support, console developers will likely implement more sophisticated forms of digital rights management, or DRM, in an attempt to mitigate piracy. One successful example of DRM was employed by Croteam in their game *Serious Sam 3*. Pirated copies of the game featured a large scorpion that follows and attacks the player's character until it is dead, thus ruining the playing experience and disallowing progression in the game. However, as DRM becomes more intricate, the probability increases for it to cripple a game through occurrences akin to the disastrous *Diablo III* launch, where an always-online form of DRM prevented users from accessing the game due to the DRM servers becoming overloaded (Thier). The potential for these occurrences make the use of DRM highly unpopular with gamers, with a recent survey by Vigilant Defender, an anti-piracy group, showing that out of 900,000 respondents, 52 percent felt that DRM discouraged them from buying games (Coby). This presents a delicate balancing act for the future of console development, as manufacturers must avoid crippling the system with DRM that drives away gamers, while at the same time, must ensure that sufficient anti-piracy measures are in place, so that rampant piracy does not become a deterrent to developers to create games for their console.

As the introductory Malayan proverb suggests, complete eradication of piracy is not possible, so long as the digital sea that is the Internet exists in its present form. Aside from implementing a crackdown on piracy that would cripple the Internet of all file-sharing capabilities, piracy is here to stay. However, the future of the gaming industry depends (quite literally) on how these companies combat piracy in order to stay in business. Eradicating (or at least significantly minimizing) piracy presents the potential for drastic changes in the way games are accessed, how revenue is generated, and the reasons for gaming platform adoption. The transition to cloud-based gaming, combined with the freemium model for revenue generation, appears to be the most elegant of potential solutions, but would require a significant departure from the status quo of disc-based console gaming, making its implementation in the immediate future unlikely. Increasingly sophisticated DRM offers a direct brute force approach to dealing with piracy–essentially an evolution of the current measures of piracy prevention–but it will face much dissent from the gaming community, which will harm sales. The game development industry is driven by the market; therefore, the path towards ending piracy will ultimately be the one that the market deems most profitable for the game developers, regardless of whether or not it is the best solution for gamers.

Essay examines both sides of CRM issue; concedes points re problems of CRM.

Unity created by reference to introductory quotation.

Conclusion summarizes 3 thesis points and adds extra details for consideration.

Works Cited

Abidi, Faiz. "Cloud Computing and Its Effects On Healthcare, Robotics, and Piracy." *2011 World Congress on Sustainable Technologies* (2011): 135–140. Print.

Alvisi, Alberto, Alessandro Narduzzo and Marco Zamarian. "Playstation and the Power of Unexpected Consequences." *Information, Communication & Society* 6.4 (2003): 608–627. Print.

Coby, Alex. "Good Old Games Sounds Anti-DRM Clarion Call." *Gamespot.* 10 Nov. 2012. Web. 01 Aug. 2012.

"Cloud Gaming: Pick Up and Play." *The Economist.* 25 Jul. 2012. Web. 01 Aug. 2012.

Davidson, Jason. *The Rum Pirate.* London, England: Penguin, 1951. Print.

Evans, Dean. "Free EA Games Herald Greater In-Game Advertising." *Techradar.* 15 Jan. 2008. Web. 01 Aug. 2012.

Works cited entries are listed alphabeticallly by author's last name.

Works cited list features a variety of quality sources, including academic journals and interviews both from print and online.

Hyman, Paul. "State of the Industry: Video Game Piracy." *Game Developer* 13.11 (2006): 13–18. Print.

Kain, Erik. "Did Piracy Kill Exclusive PC Games?" *Forbes.* 04 Feb. 2012. Web. 01 Aug. 2012.

Kartas, Anastasiou, and Sigi Goode. "Use, Perceived Deterrence and the Role of Software Piracy in Video Game Console Adoption." *Information Systems Frontiers* 14.2 (2010), 261–277. Print.

Kaszor, Daniel. "Star Wars Now Free to Play–Is This The MMO Apocalypse?" *Financial Post.* 01 Aug. 2012. Web. 01 Aug 2012.

Kuchera, Ben. "EA's New Motto: Please Pirate Our Games. . . Er, Storefronts." *Ars Technica.* 23 June 2009. Web. 01 Aug. 2012.

Nowak, Peter. "Gaming Heads for the Clouds." *Canadian Business* 84.11/12 (2011): 21. Print.

Ojala, Arto and Pasi Tyrväinen. "Value Networks In Cloud Computing." *Journal of Business Strategy* 32.6 (2011): 40–49. Print.

Onyett, Charles. "Death of the Disc-Based Game." *IGN.* 02 Aug. 2011. Web. 01 Aug. 2012.

Orry, James. "Free-To-Play Call of Duty Online To Launch in China." *Videogamer.* 03 June 2012. Web. 01 Aug. 2012.

Suszek, Mike. "Post-Crysis 3, Crytek Goes Free-to-play." *Joystiq.* 10 June 2012. Web. 01 Aug. 2012.

Thier, David. "Has the Diablo 3 Launch Damaged PC Gaming?" *Forbes.* 17 May 2012. Web. 01 Aug. 2012.

Tufnell, Nicholas. "Interview: Gabe Newell." *The Cambridge Student Online* Nov 2011. Web.

Works cited entries have hanging indents.

All sources in the works cited list appear as in-text citations somewhere in the essay.

Using the Internet

Go to these websites to find more tips, techniques, and insights on writing research essays:

Concordia University Libraries

The website for the Concordia University Libraries features strategies and tips for writing research papers as well as a bibliography of current books on researching and writing term papers.

http://library.concordia.ca/help/howto/researchpaper.html

Queen's University Library

The website for the Queen's University Library also features a section devoted to the process of writing a research essay.

http://library.queensu.ca/research/guide/research-strategy-guide

Citation Styles:
MLA and APA Formats

Using CITATION STYLES
in the Real World

Do citation styles play an important part in building new sewer systems, programming the latest video games, or treating cancer? The answer, to the surprise of some students, is yes. The engineering required to build anything from sewers to video game systems, not to mention advances in medical research all have a firm basis in peer-reviewed research, which needs to be properly documented using a citation style. One can be sure that even Dr. House, despite all of his rule-breaking, recognizes the importance of giving credit where credit is due—when he is absolutely forced to do so. Citing sources has wider applicability than a simple page at the end of your academic essay. Informally, we are often called upon to indicate where we got a certain piece of information or how we arrived at an opinion or conclusion, whether about a film, a course, or a job. Often our reply is just as informal: we read or heard it "somewhere." Documenting sources properly and accurately, however, gives your research credibility and it allows your audience to go to your sources and verify facts for themselves or pursue their own research based on your sources. In the working world, taking credit for a task completed by someone else can get you disliked at best or fired at worst. Failure to cite your sources in a published document is not only unprofessional; it's also illegal.

HOW DO CITATION STYLES WORK?

Citation styles are formal methods for preparing manuscripts and research documents. Citation styles are concerned with proper punctuation, quotations, and documentation of research sources. They vary by discipline, with the four most common types as follows:

- **MLA style** is the method of documentation developed by the Modern Language Association and is most commonly used in courses related to the humanities and fine arts, such as English, literature, and philosophy.
- **APA style** is the method of documentation developed by the American Psychological Association and is most commonly used in courses related to the social sciences, such as political science, sociology, and psychology.
- **CSE style** is the method of documentation developed by the Council of Science Editors and is most commonly used in courses related to the natural and applied sciences, such as physics, chemistry, and biology.
- **CMS** (*Chicago Manual of Style*) or **Chicago style** is the method of documentation developed by the University of Chicago Press and is most commonly used in courses related to the humanities but outside of English, such as history, business, and some social sciences.

Other organizations and academic bodies advocate their own citation standards; however, these four remain the most widely used. Keep in mind that your professor might want you to use another style, so always clarify this point before you start drafting your paper.

This chapter will provide details about the MLA and APA documentation styles. For guidelines for Chicago style, consult the *Chicago Manual of Style,* 16th edition. The CSE Guidelines are found in *Scientific Style and Format: The CSE Manual for Authors, Editors, and Publishers,* 7th edition. You can access these guidelines online as well.

Using Citation Styles within an Essay

Citations allow the reader of your essay to see where you acquired your information. Your essay indicates this research in two ways: through **in-text citations** that show specifically throughout the body of your essay which ideas have been summarized, paraphrased, or directly quoted; and through a final page of your essay, entitled **Works Cited, References,** or **Bibliography,** which lists the full publication information of all the sources that appear as in-text citations within your paper.

Students often recognize the importance of documenting sources, but find the multiple ways they can be documented (whether by discipline or medium) daunting. The purpose of Chapter 9 is to collect the most frequently encountered types of text citations for the two most commonly used citation styles in one place; however, other resources exist:

- **Official style manuals:** Each citation style is generated by an organization that publishes its own official style guide. A copy of your discipline's preferred citation style manual is never a wasted resource. If you cannot afford to purchase it, your college or university library will likely have a copy.

- **Citation style websites:** Websites such as http://owl.english.purdue.edu/owl/ and http://www.citationmachine.net/ are often suggested to students who need extra help with citation methods. The former lists the many ways various sources are cited, while the latter gives students a template to fill with publication information to automatically generate a citation. Be careful, however; automatic citation generators are not flawless. Often citations created by these programs contain minor errors. Therefore, always check your work against an official style guide.

- **Word processing programs:** Word processing programs have finally recognized students' need for help with citation styles. These programs now offer options to help generate citations. In particular, *Microsoft Word 2010* contains a bibliography feature that stores publication information about your resources as you write your research paper, and it also generates in-text citations and resource end pages for many major citation styles.

- **Electronic library databases:** Aside from being excellent places to find high-quality research, many electronic library databases such as EBSCO and Pro-Quest feature options which allow students to automatically generate properly cited entries for their essay resource list from any of the database's results. However, like websites that perform the same function, these automatic citation generators are not flawless and sometimes create citations with minor errors. Again, we advise that students always check their work against an official style guide.

Don't feel the need to have every single documentation possibility memorized. Many seasoned academics and instructors have to consult their handbooks to see how to document their sources properly. However, no matter where you get your citation information from, be sure you are accurate in your methods.

THE MLA-STYLE RESEARCH PAPER

The following discussion is based on the seventh edition of the *MLA Handbook for Writers of Research Papers*, published by the Modern Language Association (2009). It is widely used by writers in the humanities.

MLA uses a **parenthetical** documentation system, also known as an in-text citation system. It involves citing sources in parentheses in the text of the paper. This approach eliminates the need for footnotes and endnotes, except those needed for further explanation of a point made in the essay (see #15 under "Parenthetical [In-Text] Citations"). An MLA-based research paper ends with a works cited section, an alphabetical list of all sources actually used—and cited—in the paper. Each entry in this list contains all the bibliographic data that a reader needs in order to find the original source of the information you have cited.

Consider Your Options

Help with creating citation styles exists in many places, including style guides and textbooks, websites, word processing programs, and electronic library databases. Just be sure that you double-check the accuracy of your essay's resource page before submission, because errors—whether human or created by automatic citation generators—reduce the credibilty of your paper.

Note
Any source cited in the essay **must** also appear in the works cited list, and any entry in the works cited list **must** be cited in the essay.

MLA Parenthetical (In-Text) Citations

A parenthetical (in-text) documentation system identifies quickly the source of any quotation, paraphrase, or summary used in the research paper. Here is an example of such a citation:

> Johnson writes that "the 2008 influx of tourists strained southern Ontario's highways to the breaking point" (22).

The author cited is Johnson; the page from which the quotation has been taken is 22. The full information for the actual book or article would appear at the end of the essay.

Alternatively, the author's name can appear with the page number in parentheses following the quotation, paraphrase, or summary. (Note that the period follows the citation.)

> One commentator writes that "the 2008 influx of tourists strained southern Ontario's highways to the breaking point" (Johnson 22).

In general, the first method, where the source is named within the text, is preferable (for more on strategies for quoting text, see Chapter 3). In either case, however, the reader can expect, upon scanning the works cited entries, to find an entry such as this:

> Johnson, Karen. "Area Infrastructure Not Keeping Up." *Southern Ontario in Review* Mar. 2008: 21–24. Print.

The citation and the works cited entry match, and the entry provides the reader with full information about the source.

Citing summaries and paraphrases requires the same parenthetical approach, with the exception that no quotation marks are used:

> Johnson indicates that the region needs an extra 2000 miles of roadway (24).

Also, when using a paraphrase or a summary, you should introduce the author's name first and finish with the page reference. Otherwise, the reader will not be able to tell when the paraphrase or summary begins and ends.

Special Cases

You will need to modify these basic citation forms slightly in certain special circumstances. Here are some examples:

1. **Citing two or more sources by the same author.** This situation is very common in essays dealing with business or technical topics. Writers in those disciplines specialize in an area or have the area assigned as their "beat" by the publication for

which they work, and so you may find many relevant articles on a certain topic by one author. In such a case, your in-text citation would include a short title to make clear which book or article by Johnson is being cited, as in the following examples:

According to Johnson, "Rapidly shifting demographics in south and east Snow County have upset the formerly tranquil nature of local government" ("Clermont" 28).

As one observer writes, "Commuters in northwest Maple County are most affected" (Johnson, "Area" 21).

The works cited entry for such a situation follows the same pattern as "MLA Citations—Books; Two or More Books by the Same Author," which is covered later in the chapter.

2. **Using a source with two or three authors.** Name all of the authors in the text of the paper (use last names only):

Kelemen and Callahan argue that the "financial crises experienced by many Canadian cities have more to do with poor fiscal planning than with demographic factors" (67).

Spano, Del Vecchio, and Price indicate that "the need for developmental courses in reading is increasing in four-year and three-year colleges alike" (85).

Research into the spread of Spanish influenza now proves that "the disease killed more people than were killed in all of World War I" (Swanicke, Szilagyi, and De Lisi 14).

3. **Using a source with more than three authors.** In such cases, you can simply use the name of the first author listed followed by the abbreviation *et al.*, a Latin abbreviation for "and others."

The history of medicine traces the "derivation of many modern pharmaceuticals to herbs and other natural sources" (Coleman et al. 44).

4. **Citing information from a corporate or organizational author.** If your source has as its author the Southeastern Maritime Commission, for example, treat it no differently than a source written by a named person. If the corporate author appears with the page number in a parenthetical citation, include its full name:

(Southeastern Maritime Commission 574)

You may use common abbreviations, such as *Natl.* for *National,* to shorten the name of a corporate author given in parentheses.

5. **Citing a source with no author named.** If a print source lists neither a person (by name) nor a corporate author, cite the title of the source along with the page number. Never cite "Anonymous," "Staff," or "Wire Reports." Use the full title in the text, but shorten the title to a few words if it appears in the parenthetical citation:

According to the article "Homeless Focus Shifts to South Vancouver," "area authorities want to build a homeless shelter near a subdivision despite residents' objections" (23).

According to a recent article, "area authorities want to build a homeless shelter near a subdivision despite residents' objections" ("Homeless Focus Shifts" 23).

6. **Including a quotation found in another source.** If you are using a quotation that your source has taken from yet another source, use "qtd. in" for "quoted in" in the parenthetical citation:

According to Burke, "The greater the power, the more dangerous the abuse" (qtd. in Frary 18).

7. **Including information from a selection in an anthology.** An anthology is a collection of works (poems, essays, plays, stories, and the like) put together by an editor. Cite information from such a selection using the name of the author, not the name of the editor. For example, *The Best Canadian Essays 2007*, which is edited by Ian Muss, contains an essay called "Black Sheep" by Lauren Howser. Here's what a citation to this essay might look like:

Howser celebrates a child's fascination with snow: "Making a snowman was always a peculiar thrill. The two eyes made of coal. The carrot nose" (144).

The format for a works cited entry for a work in an anthology is modelled later, under "MLA Citations—Books; Essay in an Anthology or a Collection."

8. **Using ideas from an entire work.** Indicate the author's name in the text or parenthetical citation. Obviously, no page number can be given. Take this example from *A Thinking Life,* the autobiography of Pete Handy:

A Thinking Life chronicles the life of its author, but it also provides insight into the events and people who made history in Canada from the 1980s through to the year 2000 (Handy).

9. **Using material from two different authors with the same last name.** Simply include both the first and last names of the authors in the citations or the text:

Greek sculpture illustrates the "endless struggle between the flesh and the spirit" (Edith Hamilton 65).

10. **Including information from two sources in the same sentence.** Use a semicolon to separate the authors and page numbers in the parenthetical citation:

There were important differences in the ways the ancient Greeks and Romans worshipped even though their gods were virtually the same (Romero 52; Christiansen 184).

11. **Including material from a work in more than one volume.** If you take information from one volume in a multivolume work, indicate the volume number in the parenthetical citation. Separate the volume and page numbers with a colon and a space:

In the *Encyclopedia of Philosophy,* Wooldruff explains that the British chemist and physicist Michael Farraday began his career as a bookbinder (3: 18).

12. **Including material from printed works that are not paginated, or from online sources.** In the case of printed sources, you can use paragraph numbers if they appear in the source; otherwise, you need to cite the entire work (see guideline 8).

For online sources, cite the author's name if no page numbers are available. If the source lists no author, cite the title of the online source in quotation marks. As in guideline 5, if you place a long title in a parenthetical citation, shorten it to a few words—enough so that your reader can still match the title to the appropriate works cited entry. **NEVER include the URL of a website in the in-text citation.**

Note

If your online source has no title or author, we **strongly** advise you to choose a more authoritative source.

---

13. **Combining direct quotations with your own sentence.** To integrate a direct quotation in this way, you need to place quotation marks in the proper places, making certain that the quotation works naturally and correctly with your own language. As always, include a parenthetical citation that contains the author's name and the page number if the author's name is not mentioned in the text, or just the page number if the author's name *is* mentioned.

    Althea Huston explains that the government could well end up satisfying "the short-term goal of reduced welfare costs while leading to long-term social problems of school failure and delinquency for children who experience unsafe and inadequate care during their early years" (16).

    Chapter 3 has detailed coverage of the process of integrating quotations into your text.

14. **Using a direct quotation longer than four lines.** MLA format requires that quotations longer than four typed lines be double-spaced and indented 10 spaces or one inch from the left margin. Because the quotation is indented, no quotation marks are used except in cases where quotation marks appear in the original:

    In *India: Myths and Legends*, Donald MacKenzie explains the importance of priests in Indian literature and religion:

    > Priests were poets and singers in early Vedic times. A Rishi was a composer of hymns to the gods, and several are named in the collections. Every great family appears to have had its bardic priest and its special poetic anthology which was handed down from generation to generation. Old poems might be rewritten and added to, but the ambition of the sacred poet was to sing a new song to the gods. The oldest Vedic hymns are referred to as "new songs," which suggests that others were in existence. (33)

    For a long (block) quotation, note that the parenthetical citation comes after the period. For a short quotation, which is not set off, the period comes after the citation.

15. **Using content footnotes and endnotes.** Use such notes only if you need to provide explanations that go beyond what you can place within parentheses. Indicate

an endnote or footnote by using a superscript number (most word processing programs have an automatic function for this). Consider the following example:

There is always the sense when one goes to the circus that anything can happen. Jill Martin's experience at the circus is proof of this; however, not all circus trips end so tragically.[1]

The explanations for footnotes should appear at the bottom (or foot) of the page where the original footnote appears, separated from the essay body by a line. Endnotes, as one might imagine, should appear at the end of the essay on their own page—before the list of works cited. Type the heading *Note* or *Notes*, depending on the number of notes that you have, and use a superscript number again to begin the note. An example of a footnote/endnote explanation is below:

[1]Jill Martin was killed in 1940 when a tiger escaped its cage and ran throughout the crowd chewing on anything that got in its way. Martin was taken to the nearest emergency facility while the tiger was eventually taken down and shot. Martin's parents sued the circus but were unsuccessful due to waivers signed by each audience member upon entrance into the new building.

NOTE: If you need additional guidance concerning the integration of quotations into your essay, especially quotations that relate to writing about literature, please see Chapter 3.

The MLA Works Cited List

The last element of your research paper is the works cited section, a list of entries that tells your reader the sources you have used and cited in the paper. Entries are alphabetized by the last name of the author. Sources with more than one author should be alphabetized by the last name of the first author appearing in the work's byline. Sources that don't have named authors, either human or corporate, are alphabetized by the first major word in the title, as shown in the following alphabetized list:

Harper, Leo

Lefou, Ariel

Le Franc, David

Maritime Fisheries Commission

"The Nature of Wax Beetles"

Roth, Michelle

Roth-Lynn, Leo

Rothman, Thomas

1. For alphabetizing purposes, articles (*the, a,* and *an*) are disregarded. *The Nature of Wax Beetles* is alphabetized using the word *Nature.*
2. *Le Franc* is treated as one word, so it follows *Lefou.*
3. *Roth* has fewer letters than *Roth-Lynn,* and the hyphen is disregarded in *Roth-Lynn* so that *RothL* precedes *Rothm.*

The Basic Works Cited Format

Most works cited entries include author, title, and publishing information. Here is a basic entry for a book by one author:

Peters, Doug. *Hero Worship.* Toronto: Warner, 2010. Print.

Note the following:

1. The author's name is inverted, with the last name appearing first.
2. The first line of the entry starts on the left margin. Entries that are more than one line have subsequent lines indented five spaces or half an inch. This is called a **hanging indent.**
3. The first letter of the first word in the title is always capitalized. The first letters of all other words in the title are capitalized except for articles (*a, an, the*) and prepositions and conjunctions of fewer than five letters (*and, but, to, of, with,* and so on). If the title has a colon, the first letter of the first word after the colon is capitalized. Titles of books and periodicals are italicized.
4. Each entry in the list must include the medium in which it was published (i.e., Print, Film, DVD, Web).
5. Works cited entries, like the rest of the essay, are double-spaced.

The rest of this section lists and describes standard MLA works cited entries. For more information, refer to the *MLA Handbook for Writers of Research Papers,* 7th edition.

MLA Citations—Books

Book with One Author

Percy, Walker. *The Movie-Goer.* New York: Knopf, 1999. Print.

The publisher's full name is Alfred A. Knopf, Inc. As in this entry, use a shortened version of the publisher's name, and never include *Inc.*

Book with Two Authors

Brooks, Kim, and Earle Mash. *The Complete Directory to Prime Time Network and Cable TV Shows: 1946–Present.* New York: Ballantine, 1995. Print.

Note that the second author's name is not inverted.

Book with Three Authors

Vander, Alice, James Herman, and Dorothy Lucki. *Physiology: The Mechanics of Body Function.* 8th ed. New York: McGraw, 2000. Print.

This is an eighth edition, as noted after the title.

Book with More than Three Authors

You may type the first author's name, last name first, followed by a comma and *et al.* This is an abbreviation for *et alia,* the Latin for "and others." (If you wish to include all of the names, however, you may do so.)

Miles, David, et al. *Alcoholism, Drug Addiction, Crime, and Social Advantage.* New York: New York UP, 1999. Print.

This publisher is New York University Press. Any university press should be designated by *UP*.

Two or More Books by the Same Author

Stevens, Ron. *Modernist Poetics.* Toronto: Penguin, 2008. Print.

---. *Muddy Waters and Shrill Sounds.* Montreal: Knopf, 2006. Print.

Note that the two entries are alphabetized by title, with "Modernist" preceding "Muddy." The three hyphens mean "ditto"—Stevens, Ron again.

This format is also followed for two or more *articles* by the same author.

Book with a Corporate or Organizational Author

American Psychological Association. *Publication Manual of the American Psychological Association.* 6th ed. Washington, DC: American Psychological Association, 2009. Print.

Book with an Editor

If you are using information from a book's editor (editors often introduce and comment on work they are presenting), use the abbreviation *ed.* or *eds.*, as in the following:

Garrod, H. W., ed. *Keats: Poetical Works.* London: Oxford UP, 1970. Print.

If you are using information from the author of a book that has been edited by someone else, place the author's name first, followed by the title, followed by the abbreviation *Ed(s).*, followed by the name of the editor(s).

Twain, Mark. *A Connecticut Yankee in King Arthur's Court.* Ed. Allison E. Ensor. New York: Norton, 1982. Print.

Book in a Later Edition

Schaefer, Richard T., and Bonnie Haaland. *Sociology: A Brief Introduction.* 3rd Can. ed. Toronto: McGraw-Hill, 2009. Print.

Book in More than One Volume

Daiches, David. *A Critical History of English Literature.* 2nd ed. 2 vols. New York: Ronald, 1970. Print.

This is the works cited format used when you are referring to all volumes of a multi-volume work. In the text of the paper, you would cite page numbers by volume: (2: 107), for example. However, if you are citing only one of the volumes of a multi-volume work, here is the format for the works cited entry:

Daiches, David. *A Critical History of English Literature.* 2nd ed. Vol. 2. New York: Ronald, 1970. Print.

In the text, you would need to cite page numbers only.

Book in a Series

Knapp, Bettina L. *Voltaire Revisited.* Twayne's World Authors Ser.: French Lit. New York: Twayne, 2000. Print.

You can use *Ser.* for *Series* and other common abbreviations such as *Lit.* for *Literature.*

Book of Collected Essays or an Anthology

> Montaigne, Michel Eyquem de. *The Complete Essays of Montaigne.* Trans. Donald M. Frame. Palo Alto: Stanford UP, 1958. Print.
>
> Frazier, Jeff, ed. *The Best Canadian Essays 2007.* Boston: Houghton, 2007. Print.

Use this format when you want to refer to a whole collection of essays, not an individual essay.

Essay in an Anthology or a Collection

> Montaigne, Michel Eyquem de. "Of Constancy." *The Complete Essays of Montaigne.* Trans. Donald M. Frame. Palo Alto: Stanford UP, 1958. 30–31. Print.

Use this format when you want to refer to one essay in a collection, not the whole collection. The translator's or editor's name follows the title.

Translation

> Dostoyevsky, Fyodor. *Crime and Punishment.* Trans. Sidney Monas. New York: New American Library, 1980. Print.

MLA Citations—Periodical Articles

The three types of periodical publications used in research are academic journals, magazines, and newspapers. The guidelines for listing articles from each of these in a works cited list follow.

Article in a Journal with Consecutive Pagination

> Jones, Karen. "Second-Hand Moral Knowledge." *Journal of Philosophy* 96 (1999): 55–78. Print.

Like most academic journals, this one starts the first issue of each year on page 1 and then numbers consecutively throughout the year. The volume number for 1999 is 96.

Article in a Journal Paginated by Issue

> Lützeler, Paul. "Goethe and Europe." *South Atlantic Review* 65.2 (2000): 95–113. Print.

This journal starts each issue on page 1. This is volume 65, issue number 2 (65.2).

Article in a Magazine Published Monthly

> Codman, Owen. "The Decoration of Town Houses: Renovating a St. Johns Residence." *Architectural Digest* Oct. 2000: 164–71. Print.

Entries for magazine articles don't include volume numbers, just dates of publication. Note that all months except May, June, and July are abbreviated.

Article in a Magazine Published Weekly

> Branson, Louise. "Children of the Tunnels." *Maclean's* 8 Nov. 1993: 29–30. Print.

Note the inverted date.

Magazine Article without Author

"Flour Power." *Harper's Bazaar* Dec. 1989: 2001. Print.

The page listing (2001) indicates that the article "jumps"; it starts on page 200 but continues after an interval of some pages.

Two Articles by the Same Author

Johnson, Karen. "Area Infrastructure Not Keeping Up." *Southern Ontario in Review* March 1999: 21–24. Print.

---. "Clermont Council at Impasse." *Southern Ontario in Review* June 2008: 28–29. Print.

Note that the two entries are alphabetized by title, with "Area" preceding "Clermont." The three hyphens mean "ditto"—Johnson, Karen again.

Article in a Daily Newspaper

Tanner, Lucy. "Study Shows Dogs Listen with Half a Brain." *Lakeland Ledger* [Quebec] 29 Nov. 2000: A4. Print.

The *Lakeland Ledger* is a local newspaper, so the province (Quebec) needs to be added for exact identification. However, newspapers with the city's name in the title or nationally published newspapers such as *The Toronto Star* do not need further identification.

Unsigned Article in a Daily Newspaper

"Mexican Drug Cartel May Be Linked to 3 Dead." *Vancouver Sun* 12 May 2000: 5. Print.

Simply start with the title of the article.

Editorial in a Daily Newspaper

"The Windmills." Editorial. Prince Edward Island *Explorer* 13 Dec. 1999: A34. Print.

Since editorials are normally unsigned, you can use the same format as you would for an unsigned article except that you must include the word *Editorial* immediately after the title.

Review in a Magazine or Newspaper

Lane, Anthony. "A Bright Day for the Dark Knight." Rev. of *The Dark Knight,* dir. Christopher Nolan. *New Yorker* 19 July 2007: 98–99. Print.

Preston, Doug. "The Politics of Hysteria." Rev. of *Many Are the Crimes: McCarthyism in America,* by Eli Schrecker. *Los Angeles Times* 31 May 1998: Book Reviews 6. Print.

MLA Citations—Online Sources

Online documentation is constantly evolving. The following is based on the most recent MLA guidelines. When in doubt, always remember that you need to include as much information as your reader needs in order to be able to locate exactly where your source appears.

Online Document Retrieved from an Information Database or Online Project

Information databases and online projects are sponsored by a number of organizations, including news and media corporations, professional groups, and educational institutions. Your college or university library may subscribe to several of these resources. They contain abstracts of articles, articles in their entirety, books, chapters of books, poems, and a variety of other materials you might find useful. Cite such sources as follows:

1. Name of author, last name first.
2. Title of the work in quotation marks or, if it is a book, italicized.
3. Name of the database or project, italicized.
4. Electronic publication data, including the date of the electronic publication or of the most recent update; the name of the database or project sponsor; and the version number (if available).
5. The medium of publication.
6. The date you accessed the material.
7. The uniform resource locator (URL) in angle brackets, if necessary. Include the URL if you believe your reader cannot locate the source easily without it (or when your professor requires it). If the URL must be divided between lines, divide it after a slash.

> O'Hanlon, Larry. "Extreme Measures: The Art of Analyzing Natural Disasters." 25 Feb. 2000. *Discovery Channel Online*. Discovery Channel. Web. 17 Sept. 2000.

The title of the database is Discovery Channel Online. The work was published electronically on February 25, 2000. The sponsor of the database is the Discovery Channel. The date the student accessed the material is September 17, 2000. The URL does not appear because this article can be found using the information already given.

Online Article from a Scholarly Journal

> Loranger, Carol. "'This Book Spill Off the Page in All Directions': What Is the Text of *Naked Lunch?*" *Postmodern Culture* 10.1 (1999). Web. 27 Aug. 2000. <http://muse.jhu.edu/journals/pmc/v010/10.1loranger.html>.

Postmodern Culture is an online scholarly journal. Note that the information that is given is similar to information that would appear in an entry for a print journal article. The URL has been included here because the author of the paper felt that the reader might not be able to locate this article without the URL.

Online Article from a Weekly or Monthly Magazine

> Saletan, William. "Electoral Knowledge." *Slate* 28 Nov. 2000. Web. 30 Nov. 2000. <http://slate.msn.com/framegame/entries/00-11-28_94258.asp>.

Online Article from a Newspaper or News Service

Babinek, Mark. "Railroad Killer Gets Death Penalty." *San Francisco Examiner* 22
May 2000: 3 p. 27. Web. 23 May 2000.

As in the example above, provide the page number of the printed article if this information is available.

Article Accessed through an Online Library Service

Hannon, Kerry. "The Joys of a Working Vacation." *U.S. News & World Report* 10
June 1996: 89–90. *OCLC First Search.* Web. 22 Oct. 2001.

College and university libraries, as well as some public libraries, usually subscribe to at least one online access service. These services allow researchers quick access to periodical articles that are available online. Note that the information from the author through the page range is the same as it would be for a works cited entry of the print version of the article. This information is followed by the italicized name of the access service, the medium of publication (Web), and the date accessed.

Email Message

Start with the name of the sender, followed by the title of the email (if any) in quotation marks. Next, indicate the kind of document being cited and its recipient. End with the date the email was sent.

Cornell, Pamela J. "Re: Tips on Toddlers." Message to the author. 29 Aug. 2002.
Email.

Online Book Previously Published in Print Form

Melville, Herman. *The Piazza Tales.* 1856. *ESP: Electronic Scholarly Publishing.*
Web. 21 Oct. 2000. <http://www.esp.org/books/melville/piazza>.

Melville's book is available in print form and online. The entry for the digital version shows author, title, original publication date, provider, date of access, and URL.

Part of Online Book Previously Published in Print Form

Melville, Herman. "Benito Cereno." *The Piazza Tales.* 1856. *ESP: Electronic Scholarly Publishing.* 24 Oct. 2000. <http://www.esp.org/books/melville/piazza/contents/cereno.html>.

"Benito Cereno" is one of the stories that make up *The Piazza Tales.*

Website or Page on a Website

"About Heinz Canada." *Heinz.* H.J Heinz Company of Canada, 2013. Web. 21
July, 2013.

YouTube Video

The MLA does not provide an official citation method for YouTube videos; however, based on previous citation formats, an acceptable way to cite a YouTube video would be as follows:

Jackson, Peter. "Good-bye Orlando." Online video clip. *Youtube.* Youtube, 29
June 2013. Web. 20 July, 2013.

Tweet

> Harper, Stephen (pmharper). "Congratulations to the Cdn Women's Rugby team for taking home the silver medal at the Rugby World Cup Sevens in Moscow." 30 June 2013, 6:03pm. Tweet.

Blog

> Bleszinski, Cliff. "Brutal, Honest Thoughts on this Whole Debacle." *Clifford Unchained.* Tumblr, 20 June 2013. Web. 5 Aug. 2013.

Posting to a Forum, Newsgroup, or Discussion Group

Forum message: Start with the author's name, last name first. In quotation marks, provide the title of the posting (if available), followed by the words *Online posting* and the date the message was posted. Provide the name of the "thread" or subject being discussed (if available) and the title of the forum sponsoring the discussion. End with the date you accessed the message, and the URL.

> Harrington, J. K. "Publishing." Online posting. 19 May 2000. *The Writing Life: Inkspot Writers' Community Forums.* Web. 25 May 2000. .

Newsgroup posting: Begin with the author's name, followed by the subject of the discussion in quotation marks. Follow this with the words *Online posting,* the date of the posting, the medium of publication (Web), the date you accessed the message, and the URL.

Discussion group message: Begin with the author's name, followed by the subject of the discussion in quotation marks. Follow this with the words *Online posting,* the date of the posting, the name of the discussion group if available, the word *Web,* the date you accessed the message, and the URL.

Note

Such resources are open to anyone who has access to the Internet, whether he or she is an expert on the subject being discussed or not. Therefore, be extra careful about the validity of the information you take from forums, discussion groups, and the like.

MLA Citations—Miscellaneous Sources

Dictionary Entry

> "Carpe Diem." *The Random House Dictionary of the English Language.* 9th ed. 1966. Print.

Encyclopedia Entry

> "Athabascan." *Concise Columbia Encyclopedia.* 3rd ed. 1994. Print.

Government Publication

Canada. Human Resources and Skills Development Canada. *Employment and Earnings*. Ottawa, ON: GPO, 2006. Print.

GPO stands for "Government Printing Office."

Published Interview

Johnson, Pam. "Live with COD: Interview with Pam Johnson." *Canadian Enterprise* Sept./Oct. 1998: 20–23. Print.

Begin with the name of the person interviewed. Follow with the title of the interview, if any, in quotation marks. If the interview has no title, simply include the word *Interview* after the subject's name.

Personal, Telephone, or Email Interview

Rodriguez, Dr. Myra S. Personal interview. 6 Sept. 2000.

Personal Letter

Cornell, Matthew Robert. Letter to the author. 9 June 1998. TS.

Begin with the writer's name, followed by *Letter to the author* and the date the letter was written. *TS* means "prepared by machine." If the letter is handwritten, use *MS*.

Sound Recording

Puccini, Giacomo. *La Bohème*. Perf. Luciano Pavarotti, Mirella Freni, Elizabeth Hardwood, and Gianni Maffeo. Opera of Berlin Choir. and Berlin Phil. Orch. Cond. Herbert von Karajan. London, 1972. LP.

Begin with the name of the composer, speaker, or singer, followed by the title of the work. Then, if appropriate, include the names of the leading performers, the orchestra, and the conductor. Conclude with the name of the recording company and date of the recording. Note that, in this case, London is the name of the recording company, not the place in which the recording took place. Include the medium of publication (LP, audiotape, CD).

Film

Frida. Dir. Julie Taymor. Perf. Salma Hayek and Alfred Molina. Miramax, 2002. DVD.

Television or Radio Program

"The Bat." *The Office*. NBC. 29 Apr. 2007. TV.

MLA-Style Research Paper Format

Double-space the essay on white 8½" x 11" paper, using text margins of 1" at the top, bottom, and sides. Use a standard text font, such as Times, Courier, Palatino, Garamond, or Goudy, in 12-point type. Indent five spaces for the beginning of paragraphs, but don't leave extra space between paragraphs.

Essay First Page Unless your instructor asks for a title page, start your essay with this format:

Surname 1

Your Name

Professor _____

Course Name and Section

October 23, 20 _____

Title of Your Research Paper

First line of your research paper.

Page Numbering Notice that all elements are double-spaced, with no extra space between them. For page numbering, use the "header" function on your computer. The header appears at the upper right corner of each page, one-half inch from the top of the page, and consists of your last name and the page number:

Surname 1

The page numbering begins on the first page of the essay and continues through the end of the document, which will be your works cited section.

Works Cited Page Start the works cited section on a new page immediately after the end of your text. Centre the words *Works Cited*. Then start the first entry on the next line after the heading. As with the rest of your essay, this section is double-spaced, with no extra space added. Remember to use hanging indents if the works cited entry is longer than one line.

Once again, follow your instructor's directions if they differ from the above guidelines. You can use the checklist below (Figure 9.1) to guide you as you edit the citations of your own MLA-format research paper or as you peer edit someone else's.

CHECKLIST FOR MLA-STYLE RESEARCH PAPERS

- [ ] Check your quotations for accuracy. Make sure that you have transcribed words and punctuation correctly.
- [ ] Make sure that all of your primary and secondary sources have been properly credited. Check to be sure that you have not created an ambiguous situation for your reader.
- [ ] Credit your paraphrases and summaries the same way as direct quotations. Make sure that you have not forgotten to cite a source.
- [ ] Use ellipses properly. If you have elided part of any quotation, make sure that (a) you follow the guidelines of Chapter 3 for using ellipses and (b) you have not altered the meaning of the original passage.
- [ ] Format any quoted passage that is the equivalent of more than four lines of your paper as a block quotation. Check your essay to make sure you have followed this guideline.
- [ ] Check to make sure that all sources cited in your essay appear in your works cited list and that all entries in your works cited list are cited at least once in your essay.
- [ ] Alphabetize your works cited list by author's last name, and double-space it. Do not number this list.

FIGURE 9.1
Peer review checklist for MLA-style research papers.

A WRITER'S EYE

The documented essay that appears on the following pages was written by Samih Chami. His class was researching corruption in society. Samih selected the topic of police corruption and then wrote an argumentative research paper analysing its causes and effects in Canadian police forces.

 SAMPLE RESEARCH PAPER IN MLA FORMAT

Proper MLA page numbering.

Proper MLA first page; no title page required.

Title centred and unadorned.

In-text citation paraphrasing a source by two authors.

In-text citation using author's name as a signal phrase.

Current example used as background for essay argument.

In-text citation for an electronic source with no page numbers.

Chami 1

Samih Chami
Prof. R. Muhlbock
COMM 1039-04
November 24, 2013

Angels and Demons: Understanding Police
Misconduct and Corruption

Police misconduct has become an increasingly public phenomenon throughout law enforcement agencies in North America. In a generation in which the public has such easy access to the mass media and the Internet, concerns about standards of ethics and integrity within police services arise quickly. Police corruption, sometimes confused with police misconduct, affects citizens' attitudes toward the police greatly. Canadian law enforcement agencies are now exercising a service approach to policing where partnerships between police and communities are built (Roberts and Boyington 38). Community policing gives officers the opportunity to be more responsive to the public and vice versa. However, as Andrew Ede notes, one of the reasons police corruption develops is due to poor relations with the community (12). Thus, to understand police misconduct, we must examine its types, perception by the public, and causes and effects on both law enforcement agencies and the community. The most common types of police misconduct are brutality, corruption, and a hypervigilant police culture. All types of police corruption are detrimental to the public's safety and its trust of law enforcement agencies.

The ethical standards and procedural duties of a police officer can conflict with an overzealous urge to subdue suspects through excessive force. For example, on October 14, 2007, four RCMP officers tasered a distraught Polish immigrant at the Vancouver airport, shooting up to 50 thousand volts through his body until he fell dead on the floor. This specific incident was caught on video, posted online, and viewed around the world, where it resurrected the debate about police brutality in Canada (Mansbridge). The taser has become a controversial weapon of deterrence with the incident at the Vancouver airport igniting discussion of its usefulness to police services in Canada. Very public occurrences of police brutality such as this one hurt the public's perception of law enforcement officials as part of the community (Kinnaird, "Part I" 207). In fact, the opposite perception develops: the public sees police officers not as protectors, but as a group of vigilantes who consider themselves above the law and justified in using violence to control any situation.

In-text citation of an author with more than one work in the essay's works cited page.

Police *misconduct* refers to the violation of procedural rules and regulations; but police *corruption,* on the other hand, refers to the abuse of police authority—usually involving some sort of material benefit gained through illegal means. The most common types of police corruption are provided by Tim Newburn, who suggests that illegal activities committed by police officers share one important outcome: all have an effect on the public perception of the police force (43). Newburn also claims that corruption is quick to spread within a police force due to a significant degree of support from fellow officers (the police brotherhood mentality which includes oaths of secrecy) (44). The most common corrupt activity exercised by police officers is known as "corruption of authority": an officer receives some form of material gain due to his or her position as a police officer or a high-status law enforcement official (Newburn 32). This includes receiving free drinks, free meals, or free services and does not necessarily mean an officer is violating the law. However, the power of authority given to officers has a tendency to be abused. Another corrupt activity is known as "opportunistic theft" and involves police officers stealing from detainees such as crime victims, drug addicts, and junkies, and even the bodies or property of dead persons (Newburn 33). "Protection of illegal activities" is another evident form of corruption where police protect those engaged in illegal conduct such as prostitution, drugs, or pornography, allowing the business to continue operating (Newburn 86). Finally, the most obvious form of police corruption occurs when police officers are involved in *direct* criminal activities, with an officer committing a crime against a person or property for his or her own personal gain. Newburn believes that all these types are "in clear violation of both departmental and criminal norms" and range from rule-breaking, deviant behaviour to unethical behaviour (43).

In-text citation using author's name as a signal phrase.

Fully integrated quotation.

In Andrew Ede's report, "A Criminological Analysis of Complaints against Police," Ede references a criminologist named T. Barker who conducted a study in 1983. Barker attempted to measure the extent of police deviance drawn from various United States police agencies and departments. The study was based on rookie police officers' perceptions of police occupational misconduct where a questionnaire was administered to 271 officers-in-training. Barker asked each rookie to make a judgment as to what percentage of officers in the department engage in or have engaged in some form of police misconduct. Barker found that "corruption of authority" (such as receiving unauthorized free meals) was the most prevalent form of corruption identified, with 54 percent of rookies seeing this take

Good use of statistics, but a bit dated. Author should have tried to find a current source.

place (Ede 67). Three percent stated that they had reasonable cause to believe that between 26 and 50 percent of their fellow officers engaged in or had engaged in some form of serious crime such as a robbery (Ede 56). With respect to procedural violations, 39 percent of the rookies who participated had seen officers sleeping on duty, 25 percent had seen use of excessive force to some degree, 8 percent had seen drinking on duty, and 31 percent had seen sex on duty (Ede 77). Overall, Barker found that officers from larger departments were involved in more corruption or some form of misconduct when compared to those in smaller agencies.

In-text citation of an author with more than one work in the essay's works cited page.

Many different causes of police corruption have been suggested by criminologists. For example, corruption and misconduct may be due to dishonest and even criminal recruits, faulty training, political corruption, societal demands for illegal services, and exposure of newer recruits into corrupt practices (Kinnaird, "Part II" 38). Regardless of the ubiquity of police corruption within policing, studying the phenomenon is difficult due to its nature within a police-cultural context. Police culture is characterized by a high degree of internal solidarity and secrecy where the "code of silence" is ever present (Roberts and Boyington 103). The code of silence is a dominant value in police culture, which is consistent with the brotherhood theory of corruption. This cultural value involves withholding information from anyone who is not a member of the police culture, with the public and the courts most certainly excluded (Roberts and Boyington 120). The basis of the code of silence, according to Roberts and Boyington, is the official police "oath of secrecy" (121), an oath that discourages officers from compromising ongoing investigations through discussions with the media or general public, but which has been applied to the areas of police corruption.

Fully integrated quotation.

Hypervigilance is another very common value in police culture that may have an unconscious influence on corrupt police behaviour. Roberts and Boyington state that "hypervigilance is the belief that the survival of police officers depends on an officer's ability to view everything in the environment as potentially life-threatening and dangerous" (45). The fact that police are exposed to the worst in human behaviour for such long periods of time may be a reason to be hypervigilant. Although this hypervigilant nature does help police officers execute duties and survive dangerous situations, it may interfere with their ability to distinguish dangerous situations from innocent ones (Roberts and Boyington 37). Thus, the possibility of the public inferring the wrong messages from police actions and misinterpreting them as corrupt becomes a concern.

In-text citation paraphrasing a source by two authors.

Another causal factor affecting the development of corrupt practices is police officers' perceptions of their social status. Bribery and general financial corruption are expected outcomes in circumstances where law enforcement officials are poorly paid. However, even in societies where police officers are well paid and corrupt activities are seen as unacceptable, Newburn believes the perceived mismatch between income and responsibilities can lead to the development of corruption (55).

In-text citation paraphrasing a source using author's name as a signal phrase.

The level of pay is poor relative to the powers they exercise and, as a result, corrupt activities become more attractive. There are also certain areas of policing that are more prone to corruption than others, such as narcotics divisions (Newburn 76). Accordingly, vulnerable people who exercise law enforcement should not be placed in situations where opportunities for theft are numerous and tempting. For example, officers known to have drinking problems and/or debt problems are at the greatest risk. This form of vulnerability increases the temptation to participate in corrupt activities in order to deal with their particular situation (Newburn 78).

There are traumatic costs of police corruption that directly affect society, as described by Burnham (1974) in the following four-point causal analysis:

> First, corruption imposes a vast secret tax on all kinds of businesses in the city. Second, corruption dilutes the enforcement of hundreds of laws and regulations. Third, corruption subverts faithfulness of the police [officer] to . . . his [or her] commanders and the institution he [or she] works for. Can a [police officer] seriously consider the orders of a sergeant who [is known to be] shaking down a construction company? Finally, all of these costs seriously undermine the public's faith in justice. (qtd. in Ede 28)

Ede believes the cost of unethical conduct by the police is high, with an increase in preventable crime, a low level of respect for the police, and a loss of community cooperation on which police effectiveness depends as the result (87). Moreover, police corruption has a tendency to eliminate public confidence in law enforcement as well as to create disrespect for the law itself. In situations where the police are seen as corrupt, the public believes that reporting crimes is a useless venture. Fear of police retaliation is also a common deterrent.

In conclusion, citizens' attitudes toward and experiences with the police are greatly affected by police misconduct and corruption. Due to law enforcement agencies in Canada exercising a service approach to policing, occurrences of police misconduct are easily perceived by the public. Forms of misconduct such as brutality, a hypervigilant police culture, and corruption are the most prevalent. Police may exercise these forms of misconduct due to status problems, vulnerability factors, and the nature of police culture. Most people are relatively helpless against criminals and count on the police to protect them, ensuring safety and security to all citizens; however, if the police become corrupt, then all are vulnerable and order is lost. Our appointed protectors have joined with our predators.

Block quotation using author's name as a signal phrase. Quotation updated using brackets for inclusiveness.

Works Cited

Burnham, D. "How Corruption Is Built into the System—and a Few Ideas for What to Do about It." *Police Corruption: A Sociological Perspective.* Ed. L. W. Sherman. New York: Anchor, 1974. Print.

Works cited begins on a new page with title centred.

Ede, Andrew J. "A Criminological Analysis of Complaints against Police." *Prevention of Police Corruption and Misconduct.* Diss. Griffith U, 2000. Web. 23 Oct 2008. <http://www4.gu.edu.au:8080/adt-root/uploads/approved/adt-QGU20030102.114721/public/02Whole.pdf>.

Harmon, Rachel A. "When Is Police Violence Justified?" *Northwestern University Law Review* 102.3 (2008): 1119–1187. *Research Library.* ProQuest. Web. 21 Oct. 2008.

Kinnaird, Brian A. "Exploring Liability Profiles: A Proximate Cause Analysis of Police Misconduct: Part I." *International Journal of Police Science & Management* 9.2 (Summer 2007): 135–144. *Academic Search Premier.* Web. 21 Oct. 2008.

---. "Exploring Liability Profiles: A Proximate Cause Analysis of Police Misconduct: Part II." *International Journal of Police Science & Management* 9.3 (Sep. 2007): 201–213. *Academic Search Premier.* Web. 21 Oct. 2008.

Mansbridge, Peter. "Zaccardelli—On Tasers." *CBC The National Archive.* 03 Sept. 2008. *CBC.ca.* Web. 08 Nov. 2008.

Newburn, Tim. "Understanding and Preventing Police Corruption: Lessons from the Literature." *Crown Copyright Police Research Series* (1999) Web. 23 Oct 2008. <http://www.homeoffice.gov.uk/rds/prgpdfs/fprs110.pdf>.

Roberts, John, and Darion Boyington. *Diversity and First Nations Issues in Canada.* Toronto, ON: Emond Montgomery Publications Limited, 2008. Print.

Entries are listed alphabetically by author's last name.

MLA entry for a PhD thesis.

Works cited entries have hanging indent.

Second book by an author.

Works cited list features a variety of sources including news and journal articles as well as government publications.

All sources in the works cited list appear as in-text citations somewhere in the essay.

THE APA-STYLE RESEARCH PAPER

The following discussion is based on the sixth edition of the *Publication Manual of the American Psychological Association* (2009). This style guide is widely used by writers working in the social sciences.

Like MLA, APA uses a **parenthetical** documentation system. Like MLA, APA relies on parenthetical citing and discourages the uses of notes, except for further explanations of concepts or citations included in the text. The APA system differs from MLA primarily in its inclusion of the date of publication as part of the parenthetical citation. The last element in an APA-style research paper is the references list, an alphabetical listing of the sources actually used—and cited—in the essay.

Note

Any source used in the essay **must** appear in the references section; any entry that appears in the references **must** be cited in the essay.

APA Parenthetical (In-Text) Citations

The parenthetical documentation system used by APA identifies quoted sources by giving the author(s), date, and page number of the quoted text, as in this example:

> Johnson (2008) writes that "the 2008 influx of tourists strained Southern Ontario's highways to the breaking point" (p. 22).

The source is Johnson (2008); the page from which the quotation was taken is 22. Please note that the "p." is added before the page number for all APA entries. An alternate approach delays mentioning the author's name and the date until the end, including them with the page number in a parenthetical citation:

> One commentator writes that "the 2008 influx of tourists strained Southern Ontario's highways to the breaking point" (Johnson, 2008, p. 22).

In either case, the reader can expect, upon scanning the reference entries, to find a listing such as this one:

> Johnson, K. (2008, March). Area infrastructure not keeping up. *Southern Ontario in Review, 24,* 21–24.

The citation and the entry match, and the entry provides full publication information for the source.

When you are citing summaries and paraphrases in your text, APA requires only the author(s) and date, not the page number; however, you should consult your professor, who may insist that you include page numbers:

> Johnson (2008) indicates that the region needs an extra 2000 miles of roadway.

Special Cases

You will need to modify these basic citation forms slightly in certain special circumstances, as shown below.

1. **Citing two or more sources by the same author.** Because APA citations (in contrast to MLA citations) include publication dates, using two or more sources by the same author will usually not cause confusion for readers. The year makes clear to which source in the references page the citation refers. For example, (Johnson, 1999) would not be confused with (Johnson, 2008), although they are both by the same author.

   > Johnson, K. (1999, March). Area infrastructure not keeping up. *Southern Ontario in Review, 24,* 21–24.
   > Johnson, K. (2008, June). Clermont council at impasse. *Southern Ontario in Review, 25,* 28–29.

   In the references list, the older of the two entries comes first. If, however, you need to cite two works written in the same year by the same author(s), attach letter suffixes to the year—for example, 1993a and 1993b—which are determined by checking the alphabetical order of the two titles:

   > Shinzato, L. (1999a). Core beliefs.
   > Shinzato, L. (1999b). Normal expectations.

2. **Using a source with multiple authors.** In the social sciences, many works are written by two or more authors. If a work you are citing was written by a pair of authors, link the two with an ampersand (&) if you are giving the names in parentheses:

> (McPherson & Rico, 1989, pp. 237–238)

However, if you refer to the authors outside the parentheses, don't use an ampersand; use *and*.

If a source has three to five authors, cite all of them the first time you use the source:

> (McPherson, Rico, Maze, & Carter, 1988)

For subsequent citations, either within your text or in parentheses, use the last name of the first author followed by *et al.* ("and others"), as in this example:

> (McPherson et al., 1988)

If a source has six or more authors, use the first author's last name plus *et al.* for any citation, including the first.

3. **Citing information from a corporate or organizational author.** Treat this source no differently from a source written by a named person; however, if such an author appears in a parenthetical citation, include the entire name with a suggested abbreviation the first time you use it:

> (Southeastern Maritime Commission [SMC], 1991, p. 574)

Thereafter, you can refer to *SMC* in your parenthetical citations and avoid repeating the lengthy full title.

4. **Citing a source with no author named.** If a print source lists neither a person nor a corporate author, cite the title of the source, normally a periodical article. (Never cite "Staff" or "Wire Reports," but note that "Anonymous" should be used if that is how the source is actually credited.) Use the full title if you mention it outside the parenthetical citation. Shorten the title to a few words if it appears within the parenthetical citation:

> According to the article "Homeless Focus Shifts to Alberta," "area authorities want to build a homeless shelter near a subdivision despite residents' objections" (2000, p. 23).

> According to a recent article, "area authorities want to build a homeless shelter near a subdivision despite residents' objections" ("Homeless Focus Shifts," 2000, p. 23).

5. **Citing an online source.** If an online source has page or paragraph numbers, cite them to direct your reader more specifically to the source of a quotation. (Use *p.* to refer to a page and ¶ or *para.* to refer to a paragraph; also include the date of electronic publication.) However, since most online sources do not have page or paragraph numbers, you will usually cite the author's name only. If the source lists no author, cite the title of the online source in quotation marks. As in guideline 4 above, if you place the title in a parenthetical citation, shorten long titles to a few

words—enough so that your reader can match the title to the appropriate reference entry. **Never include the URL of a website in the in-text citation.**

Note

If your online source has no title or author, we **strongly** advise you to choose a more authoritative source.

---

6. **Citing personal communication.** APA format includes personal communication (personal/telephone interviews, emails, and the like) in parenthetical citations only, not in the references list. To write such a citation, include the initials and last name of the person with whom you communicated and the date.

   (M. R. Cornell, personal communication, June 9, 1998)

7. **Using an ellipsis in a quotation.** APA uses the ellipsis only in the middle of quoted text, not at the beginning or end, unless it is needed to prevent confusion.

8. **Using a quotation longer than forty words.** APA format requires that quotations longer than four typed lines be double-spaced and indented 10 spaces or one inch from the left margin. Because the quotation is indented, no quotation marks are used except in cases where quotation marks appear in the original:

   In *India: Myths and Legends,* Donald MacKenzie (2003) explains the importance of priests in Indian literature and religion:

   > Priests were poets and singers in early Vedic times. A Rishi was a composer of hymns to the gods, and several are named in the collections. Every great family appears to have had its bardic priest and its special poetic anthology which was handed down from generation to generation. Old poems might be rewritten and added to, but the ambition of the sacred poet was to sing a new song to the gods. The oldest Vedic hymns are referred to as "new songs," which suggests that others were in existence. (p. 33)

   For a long (block) quotation, note that the parenthetical citation comes after the period. For a short quotation, which is not set off, the period comes after the citation.

9. **Using content notes.** Although APA emphasizes parenthetical documentation, you may occasionally need to provide explanations about sources or content that go beyond what you can appropriately place within parentheses in the text. In such cases, use a note with a superscript number (most word processing programs have an automatic function for superscript type), and place the note on a separate page with the title *Footnote* or *Footnotes.* The first line of each note should be indented five spaces or one-half inch, and the note or notes should be double-spaced.

The APA References List

The last element of your APA-format research paper is the references section. This is a list of entries that tells your reader the sources you have used and cited in your essay. These entries are alphabetized by the last name of the source's author. Sources with more than one author are alphabetized by the name of the first author listed. Sources that don't have named authors, either human or corporate, are alphabetized by title. Some complications may occur, as shown in the following list, but they are handled in the same way as in MLA:

Harper, Leo

Lefou, Ariel

Le Franc, David

Maritime Fisheries Commission

The nature of wax beetles

Roth, Michelle

Roth-Lynn, Leo

Rothman, Thomas

1. For alphabetizing purposes, articles (*the, a,* and *an*) are disregarded. *The nature of wax beetles* is alphabetized using the word *nature*.

2. *Le Franc* is treated as one word, so it follows *Lefou*.

3. *Roth* has fewer letters than *Roth-Lynn*, and the hyphen is disregarded in *Roth-Lynn* so that *RothL* precedes *Rothm*.

The Basic References Format

Most entries include author, title, and publishing information. Here is an entry for a book by one author:

Peters, E. (2001). *Night train to Saskatchewan.* Toronto: Warner Books.

Note the following:

1. The author's name is inverted, with the last name appearing first. First and middle names are always shortened to initials. If more than one initial is listed, a space separates the initials: Chesterton, G. K.

2. The first line of the entry starts at the left margin. Entries that are more than one line long have subsequent lines indented five spaces or half an inch. This is called a hanging indent.

3. The only letters that are capitalized in titles are the first letter of the first word, the first letter of the first word after a colon (if any), the first letter of a proper noun, and acronyms (such as IBM). For example,

Hickey, T. (2010). *Taking sides: Clashing views in crime and criminology* (9th ed.). New York: McGraw-Hill/Dushkin.

4. Note that titles of books, as well as titles of periodicals, are italicized. (Titles of articles in periodicals are not italicized, nor are they placed in quotation marks.)

5. Use a shortened version of the publisher's name (for example, Alfred A. Knopf is shortened to Knopf), and never include *Inc.* However, include *Press* or *Books* if it is part of the publisher's name (see the basic entry above).

6. The location of the publisher is indicated by the city and state or province (represented by the postal service abbreviation):

Ottawa, ON

San Jose, CA

However, for large, easily identifiable cities (New York, London, Toronto, Chicago, Vancouver), the state or province is not needed. If the publisher lists more than one city on the title page, use the one nearest your location.

7. References entries, like the rest of the essay, must be double-spaced.

The rest of this section lists and describes standard APA reference entries. For more information, consult the *Publication Manual of the American Psychological Association*, sixth edition.

APA Citations — Books

Book with One Author

Percy, W. (1999). *The movie-goer.* New York: Knopf.

Book with Two Authors

Brooks, T., & Marsh, E. (1999). *The complete directory to prime time network clowns: 1946–present.* New York: Ballantine.

Book with Three to Seven Authors

Vander, A., Sherman, J., & Luciano, D. (2000). *Physiology: The mechanics of body function* (8th ed.). New York: McGraw-Hill.

Note: If there are more than seven authors, list the first six as above, then an ellipsis, then the last author's name. (See "Article by More than Seven Authors," below, for an example.)

Book with Corporate or Organizational Author

American Psychological Association. (2009). *Publication manual of the American Psychological Association* (6th ed.). Washington, DC: Author.

Note the use of *Author* in the publisher position.

Book with an Editor

If you are using information from a book's editor (editors often introduce and comment on work they are presenting), use the abbreviations *Ed.* or *Eds.*, as in the following:

Garrod, H. W. (Ed.). (1970). *Keats: Poetical works.* London: Oxford University Press.

This means that you have used information from Garrod, not from Keats.

If you are using information from the author of an edited book, begin with the author's last name:

Twain, M. (1982). *A Connecticut Yankee in King Arthur's Court.* A. Ensor (Ed.). New York: Norton. (Original work published 1889).

Translation

Dostoyevsky, F. (1980). *Crime and punishment.* (S. Monas, Trans.). New York: New American Library. (Original work published 1866).

Book in a Later Edition

Boors, D. J. (1985). *The discoverers: A history of man's search to know his world and himself* (2nd ed.). New York: Vintage.

Multivolume Book

Daichs, D. (1960). *A critical history of English literature* (Vols. 1–2). London: Secker and Warburg.

Multivolume Book in a Later Edition

Daichs, D. (1970). *A critical history of English literature* (Vols. 1–2). (2nd ed.). New York: Ronald.

Book in a Series

Knapp, B. L. (2000). *Voltaire revisited.* New York: Twayne.

APA does not require the series title and the name of the series editor.

Book of Collected Essays or an Anthology

Frazier, I. (Ed.). (2007). *The best Canadian essays 2007.* Boston: Houghton.

Lynch, R. E., & Swanzey, T. B. (Eds.). (1981). *The example of science: An anthology.* Englewood Cliffs, NJ: Prentice-Hall.

Use this format when you want to refer to a whole collection of essays, not an individual essay.

Essay or Story in an Anthology or Collection

Thomas, L. (1981). The sun and moon dance. In R. E. Lynch & T. B. Swanzey (Eds.), *The example of science: An anthology* (pp. 9–13). Englewood Cliffs, NJ: Prentice-Hall.

Use this format when you want to refer to one essay or story in a collection, not the whole collection.

Article or example in an Edited Book

Junod, M. (1987). Visiting Hiroshima: 9 September 1945. In J. Carey (Ed.), *Eyewitness to history* (pp. 638–640). New York: Avon.

APA Citations — Periodical Articles

Compared to MLA, APA style makes fewer distinctions between journal articles and magazine articles. Volume numbers are required for both types.

Article in a Journal with Consecutive Pagination

Jones, K. (1999). Second-hand moral knowledge. *Journal of Philosophy, 96,* 55–78.

Like most academic journals, this one starts the first issue of each year on page 1, then numbers consecutively throughout the year. The volume number for 1999 is 96.

Article by Two Authors in a Journal with Consecutive Pagination

Benson, J. J., & Loftis, A. (1980). John Steinbeck and farm labor unionization: The background of *In dubious battle. American Literature, 52,* 194–224.

Note that both authors' names are inverted and separated by a comma and an ampersand (&).

Article by Three to Seven Authors in a Journal with Consecutive Pagination

Magnusson, W. E., da Silva, E. V., & Lima, A. P. (1987). Diets of Amazonian crocodiles. *Journal of Herpetology, 21,* 85–95.

Note that all three authors' names are inverted and separated by commas, with an ampersand (&) preceding the last author's name.

Article by More than Seven Authors

Miller, F. H., Choi, M. J., Angeli, L. L., Harland, A. A., Stamos, J. A., . . . Thomas, S. T. (2009). Web site usability for the blind and low-vision user. *Technical Communication, 57,* 323–335.

Article in a Journal Paged by Issue

Lützeler. P. (2000). Goethe and Europe. *South Atlantic Review 65*(2), 95–113.

This journal starts each issue on page 1. This is volume 65, issue 2. Notice that the issue number is not italicized.

Article in a Magazine Published Monthly

Cod, O., Jr. (1997, October). The decoration of townhouses: Renovating a Toronto residence. *Architectural Digest, 54,* 164–171.

As with an article in a journal paged by issue, the volume number is given, but instead of an issue number following the volume number, the month of publication follows the year: (1997, October). Note that the complete page number is provided for both numbers (164–171) as opposed to the MLA style (164–71).

Article in a Magazine Published Weekly

Branson, L. (1993, November 8). Children of the tunnels. *Maclean's, 106,* 29–30.

This entry differs from that for a monthly magazine only in that the exact date of publication appears: (1993, November 8).

Magazine Article without Author

Flour power. (1989, December). *Harper's Bazaar, 122,* 200, 213–214.

The entry begins with the article title. Also note the full listing of the pages. (MLA would indicate the pages in this discontinuous article as 2001; APA requires a full listing of the article's pages.)

Article in a Daily Newspaper

Tanner, L. (2000, November 29). Study shows dogs listen with half a brain. *The Lakeland Ledger*, p. A4.

Note that for newspaper articles, APA requires "p." before the listed page. If the article had "jumped" to a new page for its conclusion, the page listing would look like this: pp. A4, A16.

Review in a Magazine or Newspaper

Lane, A. (2007, July 19). A bright day for the dark knight [Review of the motion picture *The Dark Knight*]. *The New Yorker, 75,* 98–99.

Preston, W. J. (1998, May 31). The politics of hysteria [Review of the book *Many are the crimes: McCarthyism in America*]. *Los Angeles Times,* Book Reviews 6.

APA Citations—Online Sources

Online documentation is constantly evolving. Here are some of the most recent APA guidelines.

Online Document Retrieved from an Information Database or Online Project

Information databases and online projects are sponsored by a number of organizations, including news and media corporations, professional groups, and educational institutions. Your college or university library may subscribe to several of these resources. They contain abstracts of articles, articles in their entirety, books, chapters of books, poems, and a variety of other materials you might find useful. Cite such sources as follows:

1. Name of author, last name first, followed by initial(s).
2. Date of electronic publication in parentheses.
3. Title of the work. Capitalize the first major word and proper nouns only.
4. If the work appears in a periodical, indicate the periodical's title and any available publication data appropriate to that type of periodical, including volume, issue, and page numbers. If the work is a section or chapter in a book, indicate the book's title and pertinent publication information. If the work is part of a website, indicate the title of the website in italics.
5. The date you retrieved the work, followed by a comma and the URL or the name of the database or project from which you retrieved it. Do not use angle brackets around the URL or add a period after the URL.
6. The item or access number of the work (optional).

O'Hanlon, L. (2000, March 25). Extreme measures: The art of analyzing natural disasters. *The Discovery Channel online.* Retrieved September 17, 2000, from http://www.discovery.com/newsfeatures/disasters/disasters.html

Brown, T. (1998, October). Problems and solutions in the management of child abuse allegations [Electronic version]. *Family & Reconciliation Courts Review, 36.* Retrieved May 11, 2002, from EBSCO host database, item 1121380.

O'Hanlon's article was written for the Discovery Channel's website. Brown's article first appeared in print and then became part of a database, as indicated by the words *Electronic version.*

Online Article from a Scholarly Journal

> Loranger, C. (1999). "This book spill off the page in all directions": What is the text of *Naked lunch? Postmodern Culture, 10*(1). Retrieved August 27, 2000, from http://muse.jhu.edu/journals/pmc/v010/10.1loranger.html

Postmodern Culture is an online scholarly journal. Note that the information through the volume and issue number is the same as that which would appear for a print journal article.

Online Article from a Newspaper or News Service

> Babinek, M. (2000, May 22). Railroad killer gets death penalty. *San Francisco Examiner.* Retrieved May 27, 2000, from http://examiner.com/apa/AP_Railroad_Killer.html

Online Article in a Weekly or Monthly Magazine

> Saletan, W. (2000, November 28). Electoral knowledge. *Slate.* Retrieved November 30, 2000, from http://slate.msn.com/framegame/entries/00-11-28_94258.asp

Note the date of posting: (2000, November 28).

Article Accessed Through an Online Library Service

> Hannon, K. (1996, June 10). The joys of a working vacation [Electronic version]. *U.S. News & World Report, 120,* 89–90. Retrieved October 22, 2001, from OCLC First Search database.

College and university libraries usually subscribe to at least one online access service. These services allow researchers quick access to periodical articles that are available online. Note that the information from the author through the page range is the same as it would be for an entry of the print version of the article. The entry ends with the name of the access service. No URL is needed.

Online Book Previously Published in Print Form

> Melville, H. (2000). *The piazza tales.* (Original work published 1856). Retrieved October 21, 2000, from http://www.esp.org/books/melville/piazza

Melville's book is available in print form and online. The entry for the digital version shows author, title, original publication date, date of access, and URL.

Part of Online Book Previously Published in Print Form

> Melville, H. (2000). Benito Cereno. *The piazza tales.* (Original work published 1856). Retrieved October 24, 2000, from http://www.esp.org/books/melville/piazza/contents/cereno.html

"Benito Cereno" is one of the stories that make up *The Piazza Tales.*

Website or Page on a Website

"About Heinz Canada." (n.d.) *Heinz.* H.J Heinz Company of Canada, 2013. Retrieved July 21, 2013 from http://www.heinz.ca/about_us.asp

YouTube Video

Jackson, P. (2013, June 29) Good-bye Orlando. [video file]. Retrieved July 20, 2013 from http://www.youtube.com/watch?v55NGguk8VXYc

Tweet

Harper, S. (2013, June 30) Congratulations to the Cdn Women's Rugby team for taking home the silver medal at the Rugby World Cup Sevens in Moscow. [Twitter post]. Retrieved from https://twitter.com/pmharper/status/351506332194570241

Blog

Bleszinski, C. (2013, June 20) Brutal, honest thoughts on this whole debacle. [web log comment]. *Clifford Unchained.* Retrieved Aug 5, 2013 from http://dudehugespeaks.tumblr.com/post/53457606850/brutal-honest-thoughts-on-this-whole-debacle

Messages Posted to Newsgroups, Online Forums, Discussion Groups, and Electronic Mailing Lists

1. Begin with the author's name, followed by the exact date of the posting.
2. Type the subject or "thread" name of the posting, followed by any other identifying information in brackets.
3. Close with *Message posted to* and the URL.

Harrington, J. K. (2000, May 19). Publishing [The Writing Life Inkspot Writers' Community Forums, Msg. 3]. Message posted to http://writers-bbs.com/inkspot/threads.cgi?action5*almsgs&forum5writinglife*

Note

Such resources are open to anyone who has access to the Internet, whether or not he or she is an expert on the subject being discussed. Therefore, be extra careful about the validity of the information you take from forums, discussion groups, and the like.

APA Citations—Miscellaneous Sources

Encyclopedia or Dictionary Entry

Earthquake. *Concise Columbia* encyclopedia (3rd ed.). (1994). New York: Columbia University Press.

If the encyclopedia has an editor, then use the format for a book listed by editor.

Government Publication

> Human Resources and Skills Development Canada. (2006). *Employment and earnings. Ottawa,* ON: Government Printing Office.

Film or Television Program

> Miall, T. (Producer), & Luhrmann, B. (Director). (1992). *Strictly ballroom* [Motion picture]. Australia: Miramax.

> Fritzell, J., & Greenbaum, E. (Writers). (1963, April 29). Mountain wedding [Television series episode]. In A. Ruben (Producer), *The Andy Griffith show.* New York: Columbia Broadcasting System.

Personal Communications

In APA style, personal communications appear in parenthetical citations only, not in the references section. Such communications include personal/telephone interviews, emails, and other messages that are not archived.

APA-Style Research Paper Format

Double-space the essay on white, 8½" x 11" paper, using text margins of 1" at the top, bottom, and sides. Use a standard text font, such as Times, Courier, Palatino, Garamond, or Goudy, in 12-point type.

Essay Title Page The APA format requires a title page. Centre the title both horizontally and vertically on the page. The title is followed on the next line by your name (also centred); the last line of the title page is the institution where the essay was written. Your instructor may also require you to include his or her name, the course, or the date.

Page Numbers and Running Headings Include a **page header** at the top of every page. To create a **page header,** insert page numbers flush right and type a condensed version of the title of your paper in the header, in caps, flush left. On the title page, include Running Head and a shortened version of your title. This informs your reader what info will be on each numbered page of the essay. For your title page, your running heading should include the words "Running Head"; after the title page, omit those words.

   Note that each page is numbered, including the title page.

Headings Strict APA Style employs a series of specific headings. The sample essay at the end of this chapter demonstrates the use of Level 1 and Level 2 headings. Your instructor will explain these to you in more detail, if necessary.

References The last element of your essay will be your reference section. Start this section on a new page. At the top of the page, centre the word *References.* Then start the first entry on the next line after the heading. Like the rest of your essay, this page is double-spaced, with no extra space added anywhere.

   Figure 9.2 is a checklist to guide you as you edit the citations in your own APA-style research paper, or as you peer edit someone else's.

FIGURE 9.2
Peer review checklist for APA-style research papers.

CHECKLIST FOR APA-STYLE RESEARCH PAPERS

- ☐ Check your quotations for accuracy. Make sure that you have transcribed words and punctuation correctly.
- ☐ Make sure that all of your primary and secondary sources have been properly credited. Check to be sure that you have not created an ambiguous situation for your reader.
- ☐ Credit your paraphrases and summaries.
- ☐ Make sure that you have used ellipses properly.
- ☐ Format any quoted passage that is 40 or more words as a block quotation. Check your essay to make sure you have followed this guideline.
- ☐ Check to make sure that all sources cited in your essay appear in your reference list, and that all entries in your references are cited at least once in your essay.
- ☐ Alphabetize and double-space your list of references. Do not number this list.

A WRITER'S EYE

The documented essay that appears on the following pages was written by Kristy Fornwald. Her class was researching atypical ways social workers can reach out to the community. Kristy selected the topic of Canadian refugee policy and the language associated with refugees used by both the media and the general public. Next, she wrote an argumentation research paper identifying this issue and analyzing approaches social workers can take to ease the transition of refugees into Canadian society.

▶ SAMPLE RESEARCH PAPER IN APA FORMAT

Running head on title page.

APA page number.

Proper APA essay title page information.

Running head on second and subsequent pages.

Essay starts on new page. Title is centred and bolded.

Running Head: REFUGEE POLICY   1

WORDS LOUDER THAN ACTIONS:
CANADIAN REFUGEE POLICY AND DISCOURSE

Kristy Fornwald

Calm College

REFUGEE POLICY   2

WORDS LOUDER THAN ACTIONS: CANADIAN
REFUGEE POLICY AND DISCOURSE

While early Canadian policies explicitly excluded immigrants based on race or nationality, adherence to international human rights conventions have since purged such language. In its place, many have noted the similar effects of immigration policy discourse and negative media portrayal of refugees as modern ways of marginalizing these individuals to the public. Specifically, immigration discourse regularly views refugees as *foreign, other,* and a threat to Canadian society. To move beyond this image, a discussion of the implications for social work practice, noting how an anti-oppressive approach reveals the structural oppression refugees face both in and out of country, must occur.

CONTEMPORARY ISSUES

Immigration Policy Discourse and Public Perception

An analysis of immigration policy relating to refugees shows that discourse plays an important role in how refugees are viewed by society. The desirability, worthiness, and genuineness of refugees are at the hands of the immigration system to define according to language and negative meanings implied (Lacroix, 2004). Immigration discourse then informs media. Henry and Tator (2002) report that the media uses coded language, focuses on deviance, and over-reports crimes committed by racialized persons. In the case of the plight of refugees being increasingly viewed as "illegal," the language to describe refugees seeking asylum and their economic impact has caused Canadians to view refugees with contempt. The way in which refugees are discussed in politics and economics influences the discourse used to describe refugees in the media, and consequently in the day-to-day lives of Canadians.

In a study reported by Esses, Veenvliet, Hodson, and Mihic (2008), Canadian attitudes towards refugees and refugee policy were linked to social status, with individuals in socially dominant groups more likely to dehumanize refugees and vie for stricter changes to current refugee policy. Psychological theories affirm that dominant groups view the "other" as immoral and deviant. The degree to which refugee "outgroups" are viewed as lacking moral conduct is the degree to which they are considered less worthy of humane treatment (Esses et al., 2008). As social dominance orientation has been linked to conservative political ideology, policy makers have supported inequality and are part of a hierarchal construction of race and class that encourages the dehumanization of refugees in order to maintain group dominance (Esses et al., 2008). Canadian refugee policies post 9/11 prove one example of this theory. As Chute (2005) writes,

> Post 9/11, Canada . . . took its own initiative in aggressively negotiating for a Safe Third Country Agreement. This agreement, by forcing refugee claimants to North America to seek asylum in their country of first arrival, would effectively close Canada's land border to refugees. In recent years, approximately one third of refugee claimants to Canada have arrived via the United States. Geography, flight routes and Canada's reputation as a safe haven shaped these travel trajectories. By making those transiting through the U.S. ineligible to claim refugee status in Canada, the Agreement promised to interrupt this pattern and bring about a dramatic reduction in numbers. (p. 5)

APA papers encourage the use of headings. Here are examples of level 1 and level 2 headings.

Paraphrased source using authors' names as signal phrase.

Summarized source of multiple authors' work.

Block quotation using author's name as signal phrase.

Conservative policies encourage the public to remain suspicious of any influences that attempt to upset traditional process and social norms (Bannerji, 1997). Accordingly, dominant groups in society have the most power to spread conservative ideology, influencing public and foreign policies and therefore enabling negative attitudes about refugees to spread throughout society.

Media Discourse

The media creates a moral panic within society as it reports the presence of refugees in terms of an "invasion" into Canada (Esses et al., 2008). Lacroix (2004) reports that after an increase of Central American refugees into Canada during the 1980s and the arrival of a boat of Sikhs in Nova Scotia in 1987, the two occurrences were strung together and generalized as an attack on our Canadian immigration system. The term "refugee crisis" has been widely used and publicly understood as the over-population of refugees within Canada, yet this term does nothing to explain problems within government policies (Lacroix, 2004). When phrases such as "refugee crisis" are used in conjunction with reports such as the one published by *The Economist* which claims in an article titled "A Haven for Villains" that "all kinds of undesirables are getting into Canada under the country's dysfunctional refugee system," the public links our immigration problems unquestionably with refugees.

Even critics of refugee rights admit the existence of millions of refugees "out there" (Macklin, 2005). The critics are willing to send money to people far away, considering refugees such as exploited children, tortured women, or displaced families to be genuine; yet our immigration practices reveal an underlying attitude that we do not want them in our country. We seem to fear the presence of others as is evident when a boat fills up with displaced people escaping dangerous conditions. They are reported as illegal migrants escaping (Esses et al, 2008). At this point, we no longer view refugees as genuine but rather as "illegals" (Macklin, 2005). Macklin asserts that while refugees have actually not disappeared, they are being erased from our discourse—and as more refugees are being viewed as "illegals," public support for stricter measures enlarges the population of so-called illegal immigrants (Macklin, 2005).

Macklin (2005) emphasizes the power of language within immigration discourse when the media goes so far as to call immigrant people "illegals." Instead of describing individuals who have committed an illegal act, we deem refugees to be criminals. As the Canadian media frequently publishes articles with such derogatory titles as "Refugee tsunami from Asia sweeping toward Canada" and "Is America the world's Kleenex?", Canadians are encouraged to assume that all of the refugees entering Canada are intrinsically criminal (Esses et al., 2008). By using racial identifiers to describe refugees, the media exacerbates a divide between white people and non-white people (Henry & Tator, 2002). When race is reported in the media, immigration discussions imply that the problems are

Summary of research using author's name as a signal phrase.

Direct quotation with citation at sentence end.

Standard "author, year" citation.

due to racialized, foreign, non-white people (Henry & Tator, 2002). As such, politicians frequently act on xenophobic fears of immigration and suspicion of refugees' motivations (Esses et al., 2008).

SOCIAL WORK PRACTICE

Understanding Refugeeness

Refugees are often stigmatized and discriminated against based on their race and class. It is imperative that social workers understand the socio-political context of refugees because refugees often lack power to attain equality and justice in a complex and discriminatory immigration system. Marie Lacroix (2004) writes about the subjective experience of refugees in an attempt to understand how refugee policy impacts refugee claimants. She claims that although refugees may have different backgrounds, cultures, and histories, "the experience of 'refugeeness' is defined as being universal to those who experience it" (Lacroix, 2004, p. 148). Since all refugees flee countries, cross borders, and enter into complicated political systems where their legal status is undermined by oppressive power relations, refugees share a similar loss of identity.

As social workers engage with refugees, understanding the subjective experience that refugees face in relating to family, work, and government institutions is important. Furthermore, it is essential to realize that in being labelled "refugees," individuals are forced to assume a new identity. As refugee men interviewed in a study by Lacroix (2004) stated, "by leaving their countries and becoming refugees (someone *other* than who they were previously). . . from that moment forward and outside their control, the refugee claimant subjectivity was imposed on them, one fraught with contradictions and confusion, a direct impact of Canadian refugee policy" (p. 164). Not only are refugees discriminated against through "racist or ethnicizing policies" and viewed as *other,* they are also kept on the fringes of society due to the racialization of their image, alleged criminal nature, and motivation for claiming asylum (Bannerji, 1997).

CONCLUSION

Anti-Racist Social Work

Canada claims to promote equality and democracy, yet racism is infused within immigration processes (Aitken, 2008). On a global scale, Canada holds a powerful position in the West, exploiting labour and resources from poorer countries in the south, while restricting and controlling the movement of refugees from these same countries into Canada. As a global citizen, Canada's increasing gap of inequality divided along lines of race and class stands out as an unresolved issue worsened by current refugee policy.

APA papers encourage the use of headings. Here are more examples of level 1 and level 2 headings.

Embedded direct quotation with full APA citation.

Embedded direct quotation with full APA citation using author as signal phrase and featuring use of ellipsis.

Social Work Implications

Social workers are involved in the life of refugees on a micro level, assisting refugees to claim asylum and access legal, social, and economic resources. Social workers are also involved on a macro level, as the power dimensions we work within are influenced by and dictated by larger national and international political structures and institutions. While awareness of systemic racism that has permeated our immigration laws is one step to bringing change to structural inequalities, it is but the first step. Awareness must also open the door to practising in a manner that helps refugees to experience their own critical consciousness—to empower and discover themselves outside of their refugeeness and outside of the oppression they internalize. Through awareness of systemic racism and practice that promotes a critical consciousness, social workers can help return power to refugees who have lost much autonomy along their journey.

References

Adelman, H. (2002). Canadian borders and immigration post 9/11. *International Migration Review, 36,* 15–28.

Aiken, S. J. (2008). From slavery to expulsion: Racism, Canadian immigration law, and the unfulfilled promise of modern constitutionalism. In V. Agnew (Ed.), *Interrogating race and racism.* (pp. 55–111). Toronto, ON: University of Toronto Press.

Bannerji, H. (1997). Geography lessons on being an insider/outsider to the Canadian nation. In L. Roman & L. Eyre (Eds.), *Dangerous territories: Struggles for difference and equality in education.* New York, NY: Routledge.

Chute, T. (2005). CRS working paper #3: Globalization, security and exclusion. *Centre for Refugee Studies.* Retrieved November 8, 2008, from http://www.yorku.ca/crs/Publications/CRS%20Working%20Paper%203.pdf

Esses, V. M., Veenvliet, S., Hodson, G., & Mihic, L. (2008). Justice, morality, and the dehumanization of refugees. *Social Justice Research, 21,* 4–25. Retrieved November 4, 2008, from Academic Search Premier database.

A haven for villains. (2007, Sept. 15). *Economist, 384,* 48. Retrieved November 4, 2008, from Academic Search Premier database.

Henry, F., & Tator, C. (2002). Racialization of crime. In F. Henry & C. Tator. *Discourses of domination: Racial bias in the Canadian English-language press.* Toronto, ON: Univeristy of Toronto Press.

Keep the borders open. (2008, January 5). *Economist, 386,* 8. Retrieved November 4, 2008, from Academic Search Premier database.

Knowles, V. (2007). *Strangers at our gates: Canadian immigration and immigration policy, 1540–2006.* Toronto, ON: Dundurn Press.

"References" begins on a new page with title centred.

Entries are listed alphabetically by author's last name.

References feature a variety of sources including books, periodicals, and journal articles.

Entries have hanging indents.

Lacroix, M. (2004). Canadian refugee policy and the social construction of the refugee claimant subjectivity: Understanding refugeeness. *Journal of Refugee Studies, 17*(2), 147–166. Retrieved November 8, 2008, from http://jrs.oxfordjournals.org/cgi/content/abstract/17/2/147

Macklin, A. (2005). Disappearing refugees: Reflections on the Canada–U.S. safe third country agreement. *Columbia Human Rights Law Review, 36,* 365–426. Retrieved November 8, 2008, from http://www.rcusa.org/uploads/pdfs/SSRN-id871226%5b1%5d.pdf

All sources in the works cited appear as in-text citations somewhere in the essay.

Using the Internet

Go to these websites to find out more about the history and use of MLA and APA citation styles:

The Modern Language Association

The official website of the MLA not only provides access to purchase the 2009 edition *MLA Handbook for Writers of Research Papers,* but also has a wealth of information about the organization including conference presentations, publications, and reference documents. Membership is required for full access to all content.
http://www.mla.org/

The American Psychological Association

The official website of the APA provides access to purchase the official *Publication Manual of the American Psychological Association,* 6th edition. It also provides information about the organization and what it has to offer its members, as well as information about many topics related to psychology. Membership is required for full access to all content.
http://www.apa.org/

CHAPTER 10

Parts of Speech

Using GRAMMAR in the Real World

One fact is unavoidable: bad grammar makes a bad impression, in your writing or in your spoken communication. When instructors discuss grammar, they are trying to help you strengthen your communication skills and create a better impression—an impression that is important in your academic career and even more important as you enter the world of work.

To teach correct grammar, instructors have to refer to parts of speech. Parts of speech are the building blocks of grammar. This is no different than a doctor naming parts of the human anatomy when planning a surgery or a mechanic naming parts of an automobile when diagnosing a car's problems. The more you know about grammar, the easier it will be to understand how language works and to improve your communication skills.

As a writer, you don't need to know the part of speech of every word in every situation, but knowing them will help you to improve your writing. The two main parts of speech are nouns and verbs. In this chapter, we will discuss nouns and the parts of speech that relate to them, and then verbs and the parts of speech that relate to them.

NOUNS AND RELATED PARTS OF SPEECH

10a Nouns

Nouns name a **person,** a **place,** or a **thing.**

person	place	thing
Wilfrid Laurier	Charlottetown	wheat
Gandhi	Prague	computer
technician	Nunavut	college
teacher	Elgin County	strength
woman	Canada	spiritualism

1. **Proper and Common Nouns**

   Proper nouns refer to a specific person, place, organization, religion, title, or brand name; their first letter is capitalized:

   Sergeant Smith

   Yellowknife

   The Wolverine

   Kleenex

   Judaism

   Common nouns name someone or something that is more general; they are not capitalized:

   police officer

   city

   film

   tissue

   religion

   The trend in Canadian English is to see nouns as common that were once seen as proper:

   the mayor

   the prime minister

   However, when attached to a person's name, the common noun becomes a proper noun (for more on capitalization, see 28a):

   Mayor Sanders

   Prime Minister Harper

   Some common nouns are **abstract;** they refer to concepts:

maturity	suffering
love	excitement
democracy	intellect
selfishness	perseverance

   Other common nouns are **concrete;** they refer to tangible items:

cat	desk
computer	tree

dust   building
sofa   shoes

2. **Count and Noncount Nouns**

Count nouns refer to items that are normally enumerated. They form their plurals by adding *-s* or *-es*. Typically, these are concrete nouns:

horses

boxes

cars

vacuums

However, some count nouns are irregular and retain the same spelling, whether singular or plural:

one moose   seventeen moose
one sheep   forty sheep
one deer   eight deer

Noncount nouns refer to concepts or to things that are normally not counted but are otherwise identified or measured:

spirituality   oxygen
justice   equipment
rice   poetry
dust   music

Generally, the articles *a* and *an* are not used with noncount nouns:

NOT   a rice

BUT   the rice, or rice

We *weigh* rice; we don't *count* it as we would potatoes: "I made six potatoes and half a pound of rice."

However, note that some nouns are either count or noncount depending on context and meaning:

Jennifer thought that love was a fascinating topic.
Dylan has many loves in his life.

In the first example, *love* is an emotion (noncount and abstract); in the second, *loves* refers to people or things (count and concrete).

3. **Nouns and Their Sentence Functions**

Nouns function as subjects, objects, and complements.

The **subject** of a sentence controls the verb:

Parker read the novel.
Justice prevails.

The **direct object** of a verb receives the action:

Grace kicked the **door.**

An **indirect object** can—but does not have to—appear in a prepositional phrase beginning with *to* or *for*:

d.o.   i.o.

John mailed the **present** to **Joan.**

i.o.   d.o.

John mailed **Joan** the **present.**

Joan is the indirect object in both sentences; *present* is the direct object.

A **complement** appears when the sentence contains a **linking verb,** such as *be, feel, seem,* or *appear* (see 10g.1). The complement is connected to the subject by the linking verb.

Noah is my **friend.**

A **gerund** is a noun that is formed by adding -*ing* to a verb. Gerunds name activities. For example, adding -*ing* to the verb *play* results in the noun *playing*:

Playing soccer is my younger son's favourite activity.

Note that when you add -*ing* to a verb, the result is not always a gerund. In the sentence "My son is playing soccer," *playing* is a **participle** (see 10g.6).

EXERCISE 10.1

Underline the nouns in the following paragraph.

Travelling by bus provides a fascinating peek into an aspect of Canada that many people have not seen. Buses take the back roads, stopping at small towns that time seems to have forgotten. "Good Food" and "Eat" appear in the neon signs of old restaurants. People wave to each other from their cars, and they turn to see who is getting off the bus. Dogs sleep in the streets. Indeed, time seems to stand still. However, the observer has not entered a time warp. Unless the town is very small and isolated, a Walmart store (or a similar competitor) is likely to be nearby. The Internet also provides a link to the larger world. As well, cable and satellite TV services allow small-town residents access to Much Music and Bravo, among other options. The world of the small town may look different, but perhaps it is not so different after all.

10b Pronouns

Pronouns replace nouns or other pronouns. The noun or pronoun that is replaced is called an *antecedent*, "the word that comes before."

antecedent   pronoun

The **parents** wished the best for **their** son.

Pronouns are used to create emphasis and to avoid repetition. There are eight classes of pronouns: personal, indefinite, reflexive, intensive, relative, interrogative, demonstrative, and reciprocal.

1. **Personal pronouns** refer to specific people, places, and things. They are classified by **case,** the role they play in the sentence:

I [subjective case] found the letter.

The letter was found by **me** [objective case].

The letter is **mine** [possessive case].

Here are the personal pronouns (note that *my, your, his, her, its, our,* and *their* also function as possessive adjectives):

Subjective Case	Objective Case	Possessive Case
I	me	my, mine
you	you	your, yours
he	him	his
she	her	her, hers
it	it	its
we	us	our, ours
they	them	their, theirs

Remember to use the correct case and to avoid careless sentences like this one:

INCORRECT   Bill came over to Martha and I, asking if we had heard about the ice storm.

CORRECT   Bill came over to Martha and me, asking if we had heard about the ice storm.

Take out *Martha and,* and the first sentence sounds absurd. You would never write *Bill came over to I.* The correct form is *me,* not *I; me* is the object of the preposition *to.*

As shown in the chart above, personal pronouns indicate **number**—that is, singular or plural (*she* is singular; *they* is plural). They also indicate **gender** (*he* is masculine; *she* is feminine; *it* is neutral). Finally, they indicate **person** (*I* and *we* are first-person; *you* is second-person; *he/she/it* and *they* are third-person).

2. **Indefinite pronouns,** as their name suggests, refer to unspecified persons or things. Some are always singular, some are always plural, and some are singular or plural depending upon context.

Always Singular	Always Plural	Singular or Plural Depending upon Context
another	both	all
anybody	few	any
anyone	many	either
anything	several	enough
each	more	
every	most	
everybody	neither	
everyone	none	
everything	some	
no one		
nobody		
nothing		
one		
somebody		
someone		
something		

Almost **everyone** in my class is here for the game.

Few have stayed behind.

All of the pizza is disappearing as we approach the kickoff.

All of our football players are ready to do their best.

3. **Reflexive pronouns** refer to the self and always end in *-self* or *-selves:*

The farmer checked **himself** for deer ticks.

Here are the reflexive pronouns:

myself	ourselves
yourself	yourselves
herself	themselves
himself	
oneself	
itself	

Use reflexive pronouns only when they are appropriate.

INCORRECT	David and myself made the dessert.
CORRECT	David and I made the dessert.

Also, avoid nonstandard forms, such as *hisself, theirself,* and *theirselves.*

4. **Intensive pronouns** are spelled the same as reflexive pronouns but have a different purpose—to provide emphasis:

Maya's young daughter baked the cake **herself.**

We **ourselves** have replaced the plumbing in our home.

5. **Relative pronouns** introduce dependent (subordinate) clauses that act as adjectives. Clauses that begin with relative pronouns refer to a noun or pronoun found earlier in the sentence. Remember that *who, whom, whoever,* and *whomever* always refer to people.

who	that
whoever	whatever
whom	which
whomever	whichever
whose	

Martha is the only gymnast **who** had a perfect score.

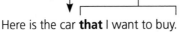

Here is the car **that** I want to buy.

The elderly man, **whatever** his relationship to you, is a gentleman.

6. **Interrogative pronouns** are used to form questions:

what	whatever
which	whichever
who	whom
whoever	whomever
whose	

Which is the correct road?
What is the answer?
To **whom** does the future belong?
Whatever happened to Jake's cat?

7. **Demonstrative pronouns** (*this, these, that, those*) are used to show "which one":

This is the hat Charlotte will wear to the wedding.
That is the same problem Judy mentioned.
These are not my shoes.
Those were the paintings we saw in the gallery.

8. **Reciprocal pronouns** (*each other, one another*) refer equally to individual parts of a plural antecedent:

Logan and Maria love **each other.**
The three brothers consulted **one another** regularly.

Use *each other* to refer to a plural antecedent made up of two entities; use *one another* to refer to a plural antecedent made up of three or more entities.

EXERCISE 10.2

In the following paragraph, underline the pronouns. Then identify each pronoun by writing the correct number above it: (1) personal, (2) indefinite, (3) reflexive, (4) intensive, (5) relative, (6) interrogative, (7) demonstrative, or (8) reciprocal.

My friend Gene and I talk to each other frequently. Gene is a successful accountant. However, he has confided to me that he wants to separate himself from his middle-class world and join a carnival. What is wrong with him? Nothing, as far as I can tell. Gene has harboured this fantasy for years, which is why I find myself surprised to learn that I am the only other person who knows about it. Anyone who keeps this type of secret must eventually doubt his or her sanity, and I was quick to assure Gene that everybody has a harmless reverie. I myself sometimes dream about becoming an international hip-hop star, which is a much stranger idea to me than joining a travelling carnival.

10c Adjectives

An **adjective** modifies a noun or pronoun; in other words, it makes the noun or pronoun more specific by describing, limiting, evaluating, clarifying, and so on. In English, most adjectives *precede* nouns:

A **large, brown** dog ran along the **dusty** road into a **small** shack that sat at the foot of a **flower-covered** hill.

The **rusty old** car belongs to Jacob.

1. Nouns can sometimes be used as adjectives:

    a **computer** class   a **Toyota** dealership   a **rock** concert

2. In **compound adjectives,** the first adjective describes the second and is connected to it with a hyphen. Collectively, the resulting term modifies the noun:

    a **coal-black** fish

    Adverbs may be part of such a formation:

    an **all-too-common** problem

3. Adjectives can act as **complements** in sentences with linking verbs (*be, feel, seem,* and so on—see 10g.1).

SUBJECT COMPLEMENT	I [subject] feel [linking verb] **tired** [subject complement].
OBJECT COMPLEMENT	His tone [subject] made us [direct object] **nervous** [object complement].

    In the preceding sentence, the linking verb is implicit:

    His tone made us [feel] **nervous.**

    Do not follow a linking verb with an adverb used as a subject complement, as in the following sentence:

INCORRECT	I feel badly.
CORRECT	I feel bad.

4. Any adjective can be used in its **positive** (base) form as well as in its **comparative** and **superlative** forms. The comparative form is used when comparing two persons or things; the superlative is used with three or more persons or things:

POSITIVE	Ethan is **tall.**
COMPARATIVE	Kaitlyn is **taller** than he.
SUPERLATIVE	Owen is the **tallest** of the three soldiers.

    You can find more about creating comparatives and superlatives in Chapter 15.

EXERCISE 10.3

In each of the following sentences, choose the correct word from the choices in parentheses.

1. This new cologne smells (bad, badly).

2. Of the two paintings, the older one is clearly (better, best).

3. Terry is the (taller, tallest) member of his extended family.

4. Sara is very happy with her new (macintosh, Macintosh) computer.

5. Jacob is (tall, taller, tallest).

10d Articles

Articles modify nouns, much as adjectives do (see 10c). Usually, articles are not attached to pronouns, except in sentences such as the following:

Are you **the** one I've been hearing about?

1. The **indefinite articles** (*a, an, some*) can be used with count nouns that are not specific (see 10a for a discussion of count and noncount nouns):

   a car   a unit   an insect
   an actor   some peanuts   some light bulbs

   Note that *a* is used before singular words beginning with consonant sounds; *an* is used before singular words beginning with vowel sounds. The key term here is *sounds*. Although *unit* begins with a vowel, the *u* is voiced as *y*, so *a* is needed instead of *an*.

   When an indefinite article is separated from the noun by one or more adjectives or adverbs, use *a* or *an* according to the initial sound of the modifier nearest to the indefinite article:

   an indefinite article

   a commonly used article of clothing

   Indefinite articles are rarely used with proper nouns. Here is an exception:

   There is **a** Robert Kendall here to see you, Dr. Kim.

2. The **definite article** (*the*) indicates a specific noun: ***the** college, **the** elephant, **the** unit, **the** cellphones*:

   The woman [specific person] arguing with the store manager [specific manager] is not a friend [any particular friend] of mine.

   The definite article is sometimes used with proper nouns, but rarely with names:

   the St. Lawrence River   the Porsche Boxster
   Bennigan's Restaurant   the one and only Jim Carrey

   For more on articles, see 25g.

(**EXERCISE 10.4**)

In each of the following sentences, the article is highlighted. Decide if each article is used correctly. If not, revise the sentence so that it is correct. Be prepared to explain your choice.

1. We stopped at **an** highway sign along Highway 401.

2. My uncle paid twenty dollars for **a** Bob Dylan album.

3. This soup is horrible; I'm going to complain to **a** restaurant's owner.

4. Her car accident was surely the result of **a** uncommon situation.

5. Let's eat lunch at **the** Subway.

10e Prepositions

Prepositions connect nouns and pronouns to other words in a sentence. They normally indicate time, place, position, contrast/similarity to, direction, or some other kind of relationship between the noun, pronoun, or gerund and the words to which the preposition is connecting the noun, pronoun, or gerund. Many prepositions are single words; others are compound words.

1. **Single-Word Prepositions**

about	below	for	through
above	beneath	from	to
across	beside	in	toward
after	between	including	under
against	beyond	inside	underneath
along	by	into	until
amid	despite	like	up
among	down	near	upon
as	during	of	via
at	except	on	with
before	excluding	over	within
behind	following	since	without

2. **Compound-Word Prepositions**

according to	except for	in spite of
along with	in addition to	instead of
as to	in front of	on account of
because of	in place of	with regard to
by means of	in reference to	up to

We received a letter **from** our insurance agent.

Mike lives **near** the river.

According to this map, Glenwood is just a few miles farther.

The baseball team won **in spite of** its five errors.

3. The noun, pronoun, or gerund (a noun ending in *-ing*, which is made from a verb and names an activity) that follows a preposition is called the preposition's **object**; combined, the structure is called a **prepositional phrase.** Occasionally, writers wonder how to structure a difficult prepositional phrase or which preposition goes with a verb to make a verb phrase. Certain objects and verbs "take" specific prepositions; in other words, the correct wording is dictated by custom, not by logic. See Chapter 19, "Using the Correct Idiom," for a list of many of the troublesome phrases in English. The following are some common examples of verbs that precede different prepositions in different situations:

Angela and Mark agreed **on** a plan.

Angela and Mark agreed **to** a meeting.

Angela and Mark agreed **with** their boss.

The umpire expected the players to conform **to** (not with) the rules.

The police have joined **in** the investigation.
The police have joined **with** the RCMP in the investigation.

The Lalondes live **on** this street.
The Lalondes live **in** this house (community, town, county).

Marissa looked **in** the book **for** an appropriate quotation.
Marissa looked **at** the book sitting **on** the desk.
Marissa looked **for** the book she had misplaced.
Marissa looked **to** the book **for** guidance.
Marissa looked **on** as the book was placed **on** the table.

The protestors marched **in** the parade.
The protestors marched **to** the courthouse.
The protestors marched **on** Ottawa.

Owen rode **on** a bus (train, boat).
Owen rode **in** a car.

The children are sleeping **on** the couch.
The children are sleeping **in** their beds.

Liam is working **on** a new project.
Liam is working **in** Winnipeg.

Jeff sat quietly **at** his desk.
Jeff sat quietly **in** his chair.
Jeff sat quietly **on** the barstool.

We parked **on** the street.
We parked **in** a parking garage.

4. Prepositions are also used with verbs to form multi-word (or phrasal) verbs, such as *ran into, call off,* and *pick up.* When prepositions are used in this way, they are called **particles.**

EXERCISE 10.5

In each of the following sentences, fill in the blank with the appropriate preposition. In some cases, more than one answer may be correct.

1. Karen was pleased _____ the quality of her employees' presentation.

2. Matthew has lived _____ this condo _____ his elderly father _____ six years.

3. I need to ask you some questions _____ the lunch break.

4. The winner _____ the race was the best _____ many qualified athletes.

5. Go _____ this door to get _____ the security building.

10f Conjunctions

Conjunctions join words, phrases, and clauses. There are four types: coordinating conjunctions, correlative conjunctions, conjunctive adverbs, and subordinating conjunctions.

1. The seven **coordinating conjunctions** are *and, but, for, so, yet, or,* and *nor.* Of these seven, *and, but, yet, or,* and *nor* are used to connect words, phrases, and clauses of equal grammatical weight:

   Zack **and** Hannah are getting married.

   Finding a house **or** renting an apartment is our next project.

   The rescue worker didn't want to inspect the wreckage again, **nor** did she want to risk missing any survivors.

   As conjunctions, *for* and *so* are used only between independent clauses:

   Brenda's mechanic retired, **so** she had to find a new one.

   Alan will stay home tonight, for he needs to study.

   Note: Use the mnemonic FANBOYS (**f**or **a**nd **n**or **b**ut **o**r **y**et **s**o) to remember the seven coordinating conjunctions.

2. **Correlative conjunctions** are pairs of conjunctions that emphasize relationships—*both/and, not only/but also, either/or, neither/nor*:

   Both Zack **and** Jacob are late.

   Lori is **not only** cooking the food **but also** serving the meal.

   Either turn down the radio **or** listen to music elsewhere.

   When you use correlative conjunctions, make sure not to omit part of a pair. For example, don't link *not only* with *but* alone; the expression needs both words: *but also.* Also be sure to link groups of words of equal grammatical weight.

INCORRECT	Jion likes both talking and to plan the drums
CORRECT	Jion likes both talking and playing the drums.
CORRECT	Jion likes both to talk and to play the drums.

3. **Conjunctive adverbs** (also known as transitional expressions) link independent clauses to show one clause's relationship to the previous one. Like coordinating conjunctions, conjunctive adverbs join items of equal grammatical weight:

WITH COORDINATING CONJUNCTION	Sara wanted to go ice skating, **but** the rink was closed.
WITH CONJUNCTIVE ADVERB	Sara wanted to go ice skating; **however,** the rink was closed.
WITH COORDINATING CONJUNCTION	Hungary and Finland are in Europe, **but** their languages are not Indo-European.
WITH CONJUNCTIVE ADVERB	Hungary and Finland are in Europe; **nonetheless,** their languages are not Indo-European.

Read the two preceding pairs of sentences again. Note that conjunctive adverbs can often provide greater emphasis. In addition, conjunctive adverbs, along with transitional expressions (their grammatical equals), allow writers to show precise relationships, whereas coordinating conjunctions have more general meanings. For a list of conjunctive adverbs and transitional expressions, see Chapters 4 and 6.

Conjunctive adverbs can also be used to introduce a new sentence, as in the following example:

Sara wanted to go ice skating. **However,** the rink was closed.

In this instance, the writer decided to use two sentences instead of one.

Note that conjunctive adverbs can appear *within* a sentence as well:

Sara wanted to go ice skating. The rink, **however,** was closed.

Conjunctive adverbs can also function as simple adverbs:

However isolated a person may be in our world, civilization is never far away.

4. **Subordinating conjunctions** show that one clause of a sentence (the **dependent clause**) is less important than and dependent upon the other clause (the **independent** or **main clause**). For example, you might write the following:

We ate dinner; we saw a movie.

This sentence works fine if you wish to place equal emphasis on each clause or if the relationship between the two ideas in these clauses is not important. But what if you want to create emphasis or indicate a relationship? Here are two ways to do so. As you learned earlier, you can use a **conjunctive adverb:**

We ate dinner; **then** we saw a movie.

However, for variety's sake, you might also use a **subordinating conjunction:**

After we ate dinner, we saw a movie.

Here are some more examples:

INDEPENDENT CLAUSES	Owen was sent to his room. He was not happy.
ONE CLAUSE SUBORDINATED	**Because** Owen was sent to his room, he was not happy.
INDEPENDENT CLAUSES	Geddy Lee plays bass in the band RUSH. He is also lead vocalist.
ONE CLAUSE SUBORDINATED	Geddy Lee plays bass in the band RUSH, **while** also performing vocal duties.

Common Subordinating Conjunctions

after	in order to
although	since
as long as	unless
as soon as	until
as though	when
because	whenever
if	while

For a more complete list of subordinating conjunctions, see 21i.

EXERCISE 10.6

Each of the following sentences needs a coordinating conjunction, a correlative conjunction, a subordinating conjunction, or a conjunctive adverb/transitional expression. Supply an appropriate conjunction. More than one answer may be correct.

1. John returned home, he learned that his accountant was running behind on preparing tax returns.

2. Wanda wanted to see a movie; George was tired and wanted to stay home.

3. The bookstore was out of the novel that I wanted, I tried to find it online.

4. The prices here are ridiculous; the service is terrible.

5. Edwin won't start college this fall, he didn't complete his application on time.

VERBS AND RELATED PARTS OF SPEECH

10g Verbs

Verbs show action (*walk, tell*) or a state of being (*do, seem*).

10g.1 Verb Types

There are four types of verbs: transitive, intransitive, linking, and helping (auxiliary) verbs.

1. A **transitive verb** shows action taken by a subject upon an object. A transitive verb always needs a *direct object,* which receives the action and makes the sentence a complete thought.

    > t.v.   d.o.

    Melissa **hit** the ball.

2. An **intransitive verb** does not act upon an object:

    > i.v.

    Jason **laughed.**

    Note that some verbs can be both transitive and intransitive depending on the context:

    Joe just **opened** a new ice cream shop.

    The new ice cream shop just **opened.**

3. Unlike most verbs, a **linking verb** does not indicate an action but expresses a relationship or a description. A linking verb connects the subject to its *complement,* a word or words that describe the subject:

    Tapioca **is** *an interesting dessert.*

    Your CD player **sounds** *strange.*

Common linking verbs include *appear, be, become, feel, remain, seem, smell, sound,* and *taste.*

Please note that some of these verbs can also function as action [transitive] verbs:

Ava **tasted** the peaches.

4. A **helping (auxiliary) verb** "qualifies" the main verb by showing its tense and mood (see 10g.3 and 10g.4):

    Ava **is** studying tonight.

    Ava **will** study all of this weekend.

    Ava **has been** studying all week.

    All forms of *be, do,* and *have* can function as helping verbs.

5. **Modal auxiliaries,** a subclass of auxiliary verbs, further "qualify" a main verb:

    My friends **might** see a movie.

    My friends **could** see a movie.

    My friends **should** see a movie.

6. **Phrasal verbs** consist of a verb plus one or more prepositions. Some phrasal verbs are **separable;** in other words, an object may appear either within the verb phrase or after it:

    Go **pick up** a large pizza for dinner.

    Nick **picked** Vivian **up** an hour before the concert.

    Other phrasal verbs are **inseparable.** Their parts must remain together:

    The car **broke down** three miles from Montreal.

    We are **looking forward** to your arrival.

10g.2 Verb Forms

Verbs often change spelling to indicate tense (time). The verb tenses include the **present,** the **past,** the **future,** the **present perfect,** and the **past perfect,** and the six **progressive** tenses. You will learn about them in the next section. The change in spelling is minor in regular verbs, more pronounced and harder to predict in irregular verbs.

1. Regular verbs form their past tenses by adding -ed or -d, their present participles by adding -ing, and their past participles by adding -d or -ed. They form their future tenses by using *will.* For example, here are the forms for the regular verb *to paint*:

    I like to **paint** alone. (base form)

    I **paint** alone, but she **paints** with a friend. (present tense)

    I **painted** alone. (past tense)

    I **am painting** alone. (present progressive tense)

    I **have painted** alone. (present perfect tense)

    I **had painted** alone. (past perfect tense)

    I **will paint** alone. (future tense)

2. Although most verbs are **regular,** some are **irregular.** The spelling of the principal parts of irregular verbs deviates from the regular pattern, such as with the irregular verb *go: go, goes, went, going, gone.* Check your dictionary if you're not sure if a verb is regular or irregular. If the principal parts are not listed, the verb is regular. For now, here is a brief list of irregular verbs to use as a reference:

IRREGULAR VERBS

Present	Past	Present Participle	Past Participle
arise	arose	arising	arisen
awake	awoke	awaking	awaked, awoke
beat	beat	beating	beaten, beat
bring	brought	bringing	brought
catch	caught	catching	caught
choose	chose	choosing	chosen
cling	clung	clinging	clung
come	came	coming	come
do	did	doing	done
draw	drew	drawing	drawn
drive	drove	driving	driven
eat	ate	eating	eaten
fall	fell	falling	fallen
fly	flew	flying	flown
forgive	forgave	forgiving	forgiven
get	got	getting	gotten
go	went	going	gone
keep	kept	keeping	kept
know	knew	knowing	known
lay (to place)	laid	laying	laid
lie (to recline)	lay	lying	lain
lie (to speak falsely)	lied	lying	lied
lose	lost	losing	lost
ride	rode	riding	ridden
rise	rose	rising	risen
run	ran	running	run
see	saw	seeing	seen
sit	sat	sitting	sat
speak	spoke	speaking	spoken
teach	taught	teaching	taught
tear	tore	tearing	torn
throw	threw	throwing	thrown
write	wrote	writing	written

EXERCISE 10.7

Each of the following sentences contains an irregular verb in parentheses. Provide the correct form of the verb.

1. The loonie (lie) on the ground for three hours before someone spotted it.

2. Mark had (get) fired from three jobs before he finally settled down.

3. The police believe that the suspect is (lie) about her whereabouts on the night of the robbery.

4. The carpenter discovered that he had (tear) his overalls during the morning.

5. Have you (eat) breakfast yet?

10g.3 Verb Tenses

Three major features of verbs are their **tense, mood,** and **voice.** Basically, **tense** refers to the time that a verb indicates. There are five basic categories of tense: present, past, future, the perfect tenses, and the progressive tenses.

1. The **present tense** indicates events occurring at the moment or happening on a recurring basis:

   The race **starts** now.
   I **eat** sushi every week.

   The **past tense** conveys action that has been completed:
   The race **started** on time last year.
   I **ate** sushi at Natalia's wedding last Sunday.

   The **future tense** conveys future action:
   The race **will start** when the referee blows her whistle.
   I **will eat** sushi at dinner tonight even if it kills me.

2. The **perfect tenses** show completed action spanning different periods of time.

   The **present perfect tense** refers to an action that in the present has already been completed:

   Robin **has spoken** about this issue many times.
   The band **has played** for two hours.

   The **past perfect tense** is used to refer to an action that was already complete at a certain time in the past:

   Liam **had dated** his fiancée before he entered university.

   The past perfect in this sentence is indicated by the auxiliary verb *had;* the simple past would be indicated by the verb *dated* without *had.*

   The **future perfect tense** refers to an action already completed at a certain future time:

   By the time our vacation has ended, we **will have driven** 2500 kilometres.

3. The **progressive tenses** show ongoing activity. There are six types of progressive tenses:

PRESENT PROGRESSIVE	Rachel **is working** as fast as she can.
PAST PROGRESSIVE	Michael **was visiting** Paris when he died.
FUTURE PROGRESSIVE	Phil **will be jogging** across the province in a charity marathon this week.
PRESENT PERFECT PROGRESSIVE	Angelo **has been collecting** money at our office.
PAST PERFECT PROGRESSIVE	Ingrid **had been trying** to get away for an hour when the police arrested her.
FUTURE PERFECT PROGRESSIVE	By next year, the company **will have been conducting** business in Quebec City for 50 years.

EXERCISE 10.8

Each of the following sentences contains a verb or verb phrase in parentheses. Given the context of the sentence, provide the correct form of the verb or verb phrase. More than one answer might be possible.

1. The Committee for Equality (has host) a lecture series for the past five years.

2. Ellen (has be run) every week for three years now.

3. Abigail (has qualify) for her current rank two years before she applied for promotion.

4. By the end of the year, Andy (will has serve) over 5000 pancakes.

5. To pick out Ray at the airport, remember that he (will is wear) a red hat.

10g.4 Verb Moods

The **mood** of a verb tells the reader how to interpret a particular statement.
Verbs occur in three moods: indicative, imperative, and subjunctive.

1. The **indicative mood,** the most common, is used in declarative and interrogative sentences to convey facts and ask questions:

Miranda **votes** in every election.
My sister **rode** a bicycle across the country.
Does Ed **belong** to a labour union?

2. The **imperative mood** is used for commands, requests, and directions:

Walk carefully on this trail.
Always **back up** the computer's hard drive.
Please **pass** the salt.
Turn right at the next light.

3. The **subjunctive mood** indicates hypothetical situations, wishes, and conditions contrary to fact. It is also used to make recommendations. Sentences in the subjunctive often contain or begin with *if* and/or *were:*

If I were to go to tonight's training seminar, I **might impress** my boss.
I wish I were wealthy, so I **could buy** my parents a new car.
If cows were able to fly, air traffic **would be** horrendous.

In the first sentence, the writer hasn't decided whether to go or not, so the situation is hypothetical. The second sentence expresses a wish. The third sentence refers to an impossible situation, one contrary to reality.

Note that when the subjunctive appears in the present tense, the base form of the verb is used, as in this sentence, which recommends something:

The auditing committee recommends that the bank **fire** its CFO.

EXERCISE 10.9

In each of the following sentences, examine the highlighted verb. Decide if it is used correctly. If not, revise the sentence.

1. If Kyle **was** more polite, he might have more friends.
2. If cats had thumbs, we **will** never live in safety again.
3. I suggested to my uncle that he **purchase** supplemental health insurance.
4. It is important that you **are** ready to start university this fall.
5. My nephew wishes that he **was** eighteen, not twelve.

10g.5 Verb Voice

Verbs have two voices: active and passive.

1. The **active voice** is the more common. In the active voice, the subject acts:

   s.   v.   o.
   John **washed** the car.

2. In the **passive voice,** the subject is acted upon:

   s.   v.
   The car **was washed** by John.

   Overusing the passive voice is a common error. The active-voice example above is simple and direct. The passive-voice example is indirect and wordy.

3. Avoid the passive voice. The active voice is more forceful and economical. Use the passive only when you have a good reason to do so:

   Lack of information: The bank was robbed last night. [The culprit is unknown.]
   Common courtesy: Mistakes were made in the planning stages. [The writer doesn't wish to embarrass the person responsible.]
   Lack of information: The door was left open. [By whom? It probably doesn't matter.]
   Less wordy: The room had been vandalized. [This version is more direct than using the active voice. Writing "Vandals had torn the room apart" does not add any more information, and it contains an additional word.]

EXERCISE 10.10

Each of the following sentences uses the passive voice. Decide if the sentence is acceptable. If not, rewrite the sentence so that it uses the active voice.

1. Marissa's car was stolen last week.

2. The cat was chased by the dog for almost a hundred yards.

3. It was felt by Michael that late marriage was better than none at all.

4. After the party, we discovered that the front gate had been unlatched all night.

5. Irregularities were discovered during Revenue Canada's examination of Ellen's tax returns.

10g.6 Verbals

Verbals are formed from verbs but function as other parts of speech. The three types of verbals are gerunds, participles, and infinitives.

1. A **gerund** is an *-ing* form of a verb that functions as a noun:

   Walking is good exercise.

   Sleeping has become a chore for me.

2. **Participles**—both present and past—function as adjectives:

   The **winning** team will receive a trophy.

   The **troubled** young man wandered the streets.

   Note that the present participle and past participle can have different meanings:

   Lucas is a very **tired** man.

   Lucas is a very **tiring** man.

   The past participle is normally used to describe how a person or thing has been *affected,* such as in "tired man." The present participle describes the effect the modified noun has on *others.* Lucas is "a very tiring man" because he exhausts others.

   Some past or present participles cannot be used as adjectives:

CORRECT	The **doomed** cow was led to the slaughterhouse.
INCORRECT	The cow behaved differently when it sensed its **dooming** fate.

   Although *doom* has a present participle, *dooming,* it should not be used as an adjective.

3. An **infinitive** is the base form of the verb preceded by *to.* An infinitive can function as an adverb, an adjective, or a noun:

   They went to Turkey **to study** Roman ruins. (adverb)

   Jason is the person **to fix** your car. (adjective)

   To sacrifice is noble. (noun)

EXERCISE 10.11

Each of the following sentences contains a highlighted verbal. First, identify the verbal as a gerund, a present participle, a past participle, or an infinitive. Then indicate the function that the verbal serves—as adjective or as noun, for example.

1. Mr. Walters was a **broken** man after his business failed.

2. This pasta is **disgusting.**

3. **To play** a violin has long been her dream.

4. **Finding** fish is only half the battle on this river.

5. The **tired** racehorse fell back in the stretch.

10h Adverbs

Adverbs modify verbs, adjectives, or other adverbs by limiting their meaning, describing them, or evaluating them. Adverbs answer questions such as "how," "how often," "when," "where," and "to what extent."

10h.1 Formation of Adverbs

1. Most adverbs are formed by adding -*ly* to an adjective:

Adjective	Adverb
nice	nicely
cruel	cruelly
terrible	terribly

Notice the spelling change between *terrible* and *terribly*. The final *e* is dropped frequently but not always. For example, *definite* becomes *definitely*. A dictionary will show you which spelling to use. Look up the adjective; then go to the end of the entry to find the adverbial spelling.

2. Not all words that end in -*ly* are adverbs—*family, lily,* and *Emily,* for example, are nouns; and *lovely* is an adjective. Conversely, not all adverbs end in -*ly. Well, too, very,* and *almost* are all adverbs.

3. Some words can act as both adjectives and adverbs:

        adj.   **adv.**

Ron owns a fast car, but he drives it too fast.

       adj.   **adv.**

The early train will get us there early.

10h.2 Placement of Adverbs

Finding the correct position for an adverb can be complicated. Adverbs do not always appear next to the word they modify. The following guidelines will help:

1. When an adverb modifies an adjective or other adverb, it precedes the word it modifies: ***very** rich,* ***extremely** hungry,* ***really** too much,* ***almost** totally destroyed.*

An exception *may* occur when an adverb modifies a present or past participle. In the following sentence, the adverb can either precede or follow the past participle:

The ballet was **beautifully** performed.

The ballet was performed **beautifully.**

However, in most situations, the adverb precedes the adjective or adverb that it modifies.

2. When an adverb modifies a verb, the adverb might appear in several different positions without affecting the meaning of the sentence:

Veronica realized **slowly** that her computer was infected.

Veronica **slowly** realized that her computer was infected.

Slowly, Veronica realized that her computer was infected.

3. Often, changing the position of a verb modifier alters the meaning of a sentence—or makes the meaning unclear. Therefore, always position the adverb so that it clearly refers to *one* verb. Note these alternatives, in which the placement of *frequently* changes the sentence's meaning:

People who frequently use discount coupons save money.

People who use discount coupons save money frequently.

For more on adverbs and their placement, see Chapter 15.

EXERCISE 10.12

Each of the following sentences is followed by an adverb in parentheses. Place the adverb in the *best* position in the sentence.

1. The food at Mongolian Paradise is delicious. (absolutely)

2. To read is better than not to read at all. (slowly)

3. Dr. Taylor teaches advanced courses. (thoughtfully)

4. Franklin began thinking about studying law. (seriously)

5. Completing this course will require a great deal of work. (successfully)

10i Interjections

Interjections are short words or phrases that indicate surprise, disappointment, joy, or some other strong emotion:

Oh, no, I've overdrawn my chequing account again.

Sweet! Aunt Marge is finally leaving.

Sometimes interjections are connected to the rest of the sentence and sometimes they stand alone, as in the second example.

Other interjections include *ouch, hey,* and *eh.* Using interjections is discouraged in formal academic writing.

Sentence Parts and Sentence Types

To be a sentence, a group of words must contain a subject and a predicate and must express a complete idea. Of course, most sentences contain additional parts of speech grouped together in clauses and phrases. Sentences can be constructed in several forms: simple, compound, complex, and compound/complex. They can also be classified according to purpose: declarative, interrogative, imperative, and exclamatory.

SENTENCE PARTS

11a Subjects

The **subject** of a sentence is a noun, a pronoun, or a group of words that (1) completes an action, (2) is acted upon, or (3) is described or explained:

SUBJECT THAT ACTS	**Laura Thompson** battles forest fires.
SUBJECT ACTED UPON	**The orphanage** was destroyed by fire.
SUBJECT DESCRIBED/ EXPLAINED	**The wonderful old cathedral** is more than 400 years old.

In the last example sentence, *cathedral* is the **simple subject;** the **complete subject** is *the wonderful old cathedral.* **Compound subjects** contain more than one subject linked by *and:*

COMPOUND SUBJECT	**Leslie and Jack** arrived an hour after the party began.

Note that **gerunds** (nouns that end in *-ing* and that name an activity) and **gerund phrases** can also be subjects:

Smoking is prohibited in all campus buildings.
Looking for antiques and shopping for curtains took up their entire day.

Sometimes, subjects are quite long:

The fact that no one ever checked Mark's resumé before we hired him worries me.

11b Predicates

A **predicate** is a word or group of words that contains the sentence's verb and any of its modifiers. A predicate makes a statement about the subject. In the following sentences, the complete predicate is in italics; the verb appears in bold:

PREDICATE THAT CONVEYS ACTION	In 1969, Pierre Trudeau's government ***enacted*** *legislation that made Canada a bilingual country.*
PREDICATE THAT DESCRIBES	Trudeau ***had*** *a vision for the future of Canada.*

11c Objects

In addition to acting as subjects, nouns and pronouns can act as direct objects, indirect objects, and objects of prepositions.

A **direct object** receives the action of a predicate:

d.o.

In 1939, Germany attacked **Poland.**

d.o.

Leonard Cohen writes **poetry.**

An **indirect object** is a noun, pronoun, or group of words *to or for which* an action is completed:

$$\overset{\textbf{i.o.}}{\text{Canadian troops}} \quad \overset{\textbf{d.o.}}{\text{a horrifying message}}$$

The failed attack at Dieppe sent Canadian troops a horrifying message.

$$\overset{\textbf{i.o.}}{\text{the French}} \quad \overset{\textbf{d.o.}}{\text{a unique set of laws known as the Napoleonic}}$$

Bonaparte gave the French a unique set of laws known as the Napoleonic Code.

The **object of a preposition** has the same function as an indirect object, except that it is introduced by a preposition such as *by, at, for, of,* or *to*:

$$\overset{\textbf{o.p.}}{\text{Dieppe}}$$

The failed attack at Dieppe sent Canadian troops a horrifying message.

11d Complements

A **subject complement** is a word or group of words that provides information about a subject and follows a linking verb:

$$\overset{\textbf{s.c.}}{\text{a masterpiece of short fiction}}$$

Alice Munro's "The Progress of Love" is a masterpiece of short fiction.

An **object complement** comes after a direct object and describes or explains it:

$$\overset{\textbf{d.o.}}{\textbf{him}} \quad \overset{\textbf{o.c.}}{\textbf{a genius}}$$

I call **him** a **genius**.

EXERCISE **11.1**

In each of the following sentences, a word or a group of words is highlighted. Identify the word or words as (1) subject, (2) predicate, (3) direct object, (4) indirect object, (5) object of a preposition, (6) subject complement, or (7) object complement.

1. **John's sister** is a nationally known dance critic.
2. In the **end,** you'll see that the training program is worth the trouble.
3. Ethan gave **Madison** diamond earrings for their anniversary.
4. Tomoko is **a brilliant painter.**
5. Waiter, the salmon **seems to be a bit off today.**
6. Ryan was angry after his boss called him **a moron.**
7. The police officer closed the **door** and sat in a chair.
8. **The bad news that the early mail supplied** was enough to ruin Dr. Lee's day.
9. The family **plans to drive to New Brunswick and visit their old neighbour.**
10. When I first visited the physical therapist, I didn't think much of **him.**

11e Clauses

A **clause** is a group of words containing a subject and a verb. Clauses are either independent or dependent. An **independent (main) clause** can function alone as a sentence or be part of a compound, complex, or compound/complex sentence. A **dependent (subordinate) clause** cannot function alone; it must be part of a larger sentence that contains an independent clause.

All clauses, whether independent or dependent, must contain a subject and a predicate. A **subject** is the noun, pronoun, phrase, or clause that functions as the "actor" in the sentence. The subject "acts" through the verb or verb phrase that is the basis of the **predicate,** which comprises the verb along with its modifiers.

Having a subject and a predicate distinguishes clauses from phrases, which have a subject but no predicate or a predicate but no subject:

SUBJECT WITHOUT PREDICATE	the stock market indexes
PREDICATE WITHOUT SUBJECT	rose sharply
CLAUSE	The stock market indexes rose sharply.

11e.1 Independent Clauses

An **independent (main) clause** is independent in the sense that it can stand alone as a sentence. An independent clause can be brief or lengthy:

> Go!
> Karen rested.
> Buenos Aires is the capital of Argentina.
> The *Ramayana,* a classic of Sanskrit literature, was written in India in the third century BCE.

The third and fourth examples are longer than the first two, but all of the examples include a subject and a predicate. (In the first example, an imperative sentence, the subject—*you*—is implied.)

11e.2 Dependent Clauses

A **dependent (subordinate) clause** differs from an independent clause in that it cannot stand alone as a sentence. A dependent clause by itself is a **sentence fragment** (see Chapter 12). There are four types of dependent clauses: noun clauses, adjective (relative) clauses, adverb clauses, and elliptical clauses.

1. **Noun clauses** begin with one of these conjunctions: *how, that, what, whatever, when, where, whether, which, whichever, who, whoever, whom, whomever, whose,* or *why.* The resulting clause functions as a subject or as an object:

SUBJECT	**How a two-year-old could program a cellphone** is a mystery.
DIRECT OBJECT	I wish Mike would watch **what he is doing.**
OBJECT OF PREPOSITION	We decided to stop at **whichever gas station was closest.**

2. **Adjective (relative) clauses** begin with relative pronouns (*that, which, who, whom, whose*) and function as adjectives, modifying nouns and pronouns:

She is the woman **who was falsely accused of murder.**
The couple **whose baggage was lost** were late for their connecting flight.
The Italian and English sonnet forms, **which were developed during the Renaissance,** both contain fourteen lines.

3. **Adverb clauses,** which function as adverbs, begin with a subordinating conjunction, such as *after, although, as soon as, because, in order to, until,* or *when.* (For a more extensive list of subordinating conjunctions, see 11i.)

ADVERB CLAUSE   **After the mechanic fixed the radiator**

As with other dependent clauses, in an adverb clause, something is missing—the rest of the sentence:

After the mechanic fixed the radiator, the car was ready to roll.

4. In **elliptical clauses,** a word or words are not present, but the meaning is obvious anyway. Normally, elliptical clauses appear in comparisons:

Tariq has more money than **I [have money].**
Bob is as tall as Samantha **[is tall].**

EXERCISE **11.2**

In the following sentences, underline each **dependent clause.** Then identify the clause as (1) a noun clause, (2) an adjective clause, (3) an adverb clause, or (4) an elliptical clause.

1. Whoever built this house must have had the plans upside down when he first started.

2. My uncle is a man who was once famous for his yodelling skills.

3. After you finish backing up the hard drive, see if you can find out who was responsible for opening that infected email.

4. Whenever you want to eat lunch is all right with me.

5. When Richard bought his new car, he got a five-year loan because he wanted to keep his payments low.

6. Some financial advisors are known for pushing whichever mutual fund has the highest commission.

7. I know Glen is tall, but is he as tall as Jared?

8. Take off your work boots before you come into the house.

9. This is the painting that was stolen in the 1975 burglary.

10. Robert cleaned the gutters so that his overworked father wouldn't have to do the chore on Saturday.

11f Phrases

Phrases do not have both a subject and a predicate. A **phrase** is any related group of words that functions as a unit in a sentence but is not a clause. There are nine types of phrases, and each has a specific function.

1. **A prepositional phrase** consists of a preposition such as *by, in, over,* or *with* and its object as well as any modifying words:

   We decided never to go **to the mall.**

   Beside the couch, Owen had piled copies of the Sunday papers.

   The supervisor rarely showed interest **in projects under her control.**

   Canadian English depends heavily on the idiomatic use of prepositional phrases. For a list of "difficult" phrases involving prepositions along with verbs and adjectives, see Chapter 19, the section labelled "Using the Correct Idiom."

2. **Verb phrases** contain main verbs preceded by auxiliary verbs:

   I **have been thinking.**

   He **does believe** in you.

   We **will be considering** your proposal.

3. A **noun phrase** includes a noun (in italics below) and its modifying words and phrases:

   Success **by accident** is a feature of Tom's career. [subject]

   The speaker used **several convincing** *statistics* **taken from government sources.** [object]

   The result of the explosion was **an unforgettable** *shower* **of sparks and flames.** [complement]

4. An **absolute phrase** is a clause without a verb; it modifies an entire sentence (see 11e for more on clauses):

CLAUSE	**Her head was aching.**
REDUCED TO ABSOLUTE PHRASE	**Her head aching,** Myra tried to steer her car through the snowstorm.
CLAUSE	**Its ancient tires were almost flat.**
REDUCED TO ABSOLUTE PHRASE	**Its ancient tires almost flat,** the car rested in the shadow of the barn.

5. An **appositive phrase** appears directly after a noun, renaming or otherwise identifying it. Most appositive phrases are set off by commas:

   Softball, **a sport derived from baseball,** is played in many elementary schools.

   My brother, **a stockbroker,** is vacationing in Alberta.

   Our class loved discussing Timothy Findley's *Not Wanted on the Voyage,* **his retelling of the great flood in** *Genesis.*

   Note that an appositive that specifically identifies a noun is not set off by commas (see also 26c):

   Rita McAlester **the fashion designer** is not the same person as Rita McAlester **the international fugitive.**

6. A **verbal phrase** is a group of words that begins with a past or present participle or an infinitive (see 20g.6) but acts as another part of speech:

Dancing on the piano is prohibited. [noun]

Having danced on the piano, they were thrown out of the club. [adjective]

7. A **gerund phrase** includes a gerund (an *-ing* form of a verb used as a noun) plus any other words that modify the gerund. Gerund phrases act as nouns and can be subjects or direct objects:

Driving to work can take me up to two hours. [subject]

Rita enjoyed **dancing with Ben.** [direct object]

8. An **infinitive phrase** is made up of an infinitive (*to* plus the base form of a verb) and any other words that modify the infinitive:

Elizabeth is the best person **to fix your car.** [adjective]

Thomas stopped at the diner **to eat lunch.** [adverb]

To live well is the best revenge. [noun]

9. A **participial phrase** includes either a present or past participle (see 20g.6) plus any accompanying words. It frequently describes a noun.

Mr. Johnson is the man **walking beside the lake.**

Nicholas, a man **shattered by the horrors of war,** is the soldier in the photograph.

EXERCISE 11.3

Underline each phrase in the following sentences. Then identify the phrase as (1) absolute, (2) appositive, (3) verbal, (4) gerund, (5) infinitive, (6) noun, (7) participial, (8) prepositional, or (9) verb. You will find more than one phrase in each sentence.

1. Breaking slowly from the gate, the horse was seven lengths behind the rest of the pack.

2. My neighbour, a copywriter for an ad agency, has always believed in extraterrestrial life.

3. "Creativity by design" is our company's latest attempt at a motto.

4. The old man was hurt by the loss of his wife and son in the same year.

5. The fish jumping near the old stump is one that I have hooked and lost three times in the past two months.

6. His foot swollen to twice its normal size, Walter struggled up the hill to his car.

7. I've always wanted to go to Japan; reading about its culture fascinates me.

8. Do you really think that Ben Affleck's movie *Argo* is one of the best films of the past decade?

9. When people are troubled, tossing and turning can keep them up all night.

10. Michael is the one over there talking to Lisa.

SENTENCE TYPES

11g Classifying Sentences

Sentences can be classified according to **purpose:**

DECLARATIVE	The officer asked for Victoria's driver's licence. [states a fact or an opinion]
INTERROGATIVE	May I see your driver's licence? [asks a question]
IMPERATIVE	Give me your driver's licence. [gives an order/direction or makes a request]
EXCLAMATORY	Oh, my gosh, I have lost my driver's licence! [expresses strong emotion or emphasis]

Within each type, the way that you construct a sentence affects how your reader processes your intended meaning. Your aim as a writer is to emphasize the parts of the sentence that are most important and to create sentence variety. Doing so will communicate your message more effectively and keep your reader's interest.

Sentences can also be classified according to **complexity:**

1. **A simple sentence** contains one main (independent) clause, but it may contain phrases as well. The main clause in the following sentence is highlighted:

   Bordering Honduras and Costa Rica, **Nicaragua is located in Central America.**

2. **A compound sentence** contains two main (independent) clauses connected by a coordinating conjunction (*and, but, for, nor, or, yet, so*) or by a semicolon:

   Some Nicaraguans work in gold and tungsten mines, but most are farmers.

3. **A complex sentence** contains a main (independent) clause and at least one subordinate (dependent) clause. In the following sentence, the subordinate clause is highlighted:

   Although Nicaragua had been part of Guatemala and then of the Mexican Empire, it became a republic in 1838.

4. **A compound/complex sentence** contains two main (independent) clauses and at least one subordinate (dependent) clause. In this sentence, two independent clauses are followed by a dependent clause:

   i.c. **i.c.**

   Anastasio Somoza took power in 1937, and he continued to rule until 1979,

   d.c.

   when his regime was overthrown by the Sandinista National Liberation Front.

11h Creating Emphasis and Variety: Compound Sentences

Simple sentences can be used to convey information effectively, but a steady diet of simple sentences will make it difficult for you to emphasize the ideas you want to stress. More important, it will bore your readers. You need to be able to use compound sentences for emphasis and variety.

Here are three main ways to join two independent clauses (two simple sentences) to make a more interesting compound sentence: (1) comma plus coordinating conjunction, (2) semicolon alone, and (3) semicolon plus conjunctive adverb or transitional expression. Here is an example of each method:

The highway was flooded, **and** the side streets were slick.

Leah hates yearly reviews; Adam also hates them.

My relatives are visiting this evening; **consequently,** I need to leave work early.

All three methods work, but which one is best? It depends on context. Using a comma plus a coordinating conjunction is frequently effective. However, some stylists see this technique as a bit too informal to depend on in academic writing. There is a second problem as well: the seven coordinating conjunctions convey a limited range of meaning. Note the problem in the following sentence:

Andrew was furious about the errors in his credit card statement, and the statement got to him a week late.

Here, the information is adequately conveyed—but only adequately; emphasis is lost. The sentence works much better if a conjunctive adverb is used in place of the coordinating conjunction:

Andrew was furious about the errors in his credit card statement; moreover, the statement got to him a week late.

Conjunctive adverbs and other transitional expressions have a greater range of meaning than the coordinating conjunctions do; therefore, they allow you to write sentences that are much more focused and precise. (See 22b for a list of coordinating conjunctions, conjunctive adverbs, and transitional expressions.)

For more on using compound sentences in your writing, see Chapter 6.

EXERCISE 11.4

Combine each of the following pairs of sentences by using a comma plus a coordinating conjunction, a semicolon, or a semicolon plus a conjunctive adverb or other transitional expression. Be prepared to defend your choice.

1. Laura was sad. Her friend David was being transferred across the country.
2. The first car we looked at cost $32 000. The next model was only $17 500.
3. This college has a lot of problems. The parking situation is terrible.
4. We won't need you anymore today. Make sure that you check in tomorrow.
5. The software instructions seemed clear enough. The program wouldn't come up on my screen.
6. The plane was overbooked. Mr. Robbins decided to take the airline up on its offer for discounts.
7. Ed opened the door. He noticed that the office seemed strangely quiet.
8. Andrea is not happy today. She's just gotten some bad news about her tax return.
9. Jane cleaned off her desk. She started to answer her email.
10. My nephew likes swimming. His sister hates it.

11i Creating Emphasis and Variety: Complex Sentences

1. **Subordinate for emphasis.**

    Consider the following sentence:

    John opened his mail, and he got a bad shock.

    This is a **balanced** sentence, a compound sentence in which two actions (John *opened his mail* and *he got a bad shock*) receive equal weight. But are those two actions equally important? Surely, the more important information here is in the second clause. People open their mail five days a week, but they are not usually shocked by its contents. To emphasize the information in the second clause, the writer needs to use **subordination:**

    When John opened his mail, he got a bad shock.

    An even more effective choice is to place the independent clause first:

    John got a bad shock when he opened his mail.

    Note that all three sentences are grammatically correct; however, the second and third sentences communicate their meaning more accurately and effectively.

    You can introduce a subordinate clause with a subordinating conjunction or a relative pronoun.

Subordinating Conjunctions		Relative Pronouns
after	that	that
although	though	what
as	unless	whatever
because	until	which
before	when	whichever
even if	whenever	who
even though	where	whoever
if	whereas	whom
in order that	wherever	whomever
once	whether	whose
provided that	while	
rather than		
since		
so that		
so (that)		

Because we failed to make reservations, we were not able to get a table.
He will not march in the graduation line **unless he passes chemistry.**
When he was a young man, my father owned a bookstore.

The writers **who were honoured last night** were part of college faculty.

2. **Subordinate to add extra information.**

   Subordination can also supply extra information about a subject. In the following sentence, the subordinate clause is highlighted:

   Ella was eventually transferred to Moncton, **which was at least near the town where her sister lived.**

3. **Too much subordination weakens a sentence.**

   Michael walked to his office, *which* is on Third Street, *which* is the oldest paved street in the city, *which* itself is the fourth-oldest municipality in the province.

   Readers of this sentence may feel as though they are being led through doorway after doorway for no purpose. Subordination should not be used to attach stray thoughts or extra facts; rather, it should establish focus and add valuable—albeit secondary—information.

   For more on using subordination for variety and emphasis, see Chapter 6.

EXERCISE **11.5**

Combine the sentences in each item by using subordination. You may want to rearrange details as you do so.

1. Hispaniola is a subtropical island in the West Indies. Haiti and the Dominican Republic share the island.

2. The largest Cree band of First Nations people live in northern Saskatchewan. They speak a dialect of the Algonquian languages.

3. Martin Luther disagreed with many of the practices of the Roman Catholic church. He broke with Rome and founded a sect of Protestantism that bears his name.

4. The Persian Wars of the fifth century BCE lasted for over fifty years and resulted in a victory for the Greek city states. They began when the cities of Ionia revolted against Darius I.

5. Romulus was the legendary founder of Rome. He and his twin brother, Remus, were suckled by a she-wolf and were later raised by a shepherd.

CHAPTER 12

Major Sentence Errors

The first two sections of this chapter concentrate on sentence fragments, fused sentences, and comma splices, which are the most damaging sentence-level errors made by student writers. To receive good grades on college essays, and to write effectively in your career, you must identify and correct these errors in your work.

The last section of this chapter discusses three other sentence-level issues: parallelism, appropriate comparisons, and mixed constructions.

SENTENCE FRAGMENTS

As its name suggests, a **sentence fragment** is an incomplete sentence; it "acts" as a sentence, but it is missing a subject, a verb, or a complete thought.

12a Phrases as Fragments

A phrase, by definition, cannot be a complete sentence. You will hear people use phrases as sentences as they speak to one another, but these constructions are not appropriate for written communication. Here are some typical phrasal fragments:

1. Incomplete verb form:

   FRAGMENT   The doctor **thinking** that the patient looked better.

   REVISED   The doctor **was thinking** that the patient looked better.

2. Prepositional phrase used as a sentence:

   FRAGMENT   You'll find the hammer out back. **Beside the rotary saw.**

   REVISED   You'll find the hammer out back, **beside the rotary saw.**

3. Infinitive phrase used as a sentence:

   FRAGMENT   We drove to town. **To buy a new hammer.**

   REVISED   We drove to town **to buy a new hammer.**

4. "Illustration" phrase used as a sentence:

   FRAGMENT   Alcoholics can develop many health problems. **For example, cirrhosis of the liver.**

   REVISED   Alcoholics can develop many health problems—**for example, cirrhosis of the liver.**

   FRAGMENT   They were troubled by the motel's location. **Also, the condition of the room they were shown.**

   REVISED   They were troubled by the motel's location **and also by the condition of the room they were shown.**

As you can see, many fragments are phrases that clearly belong with an adjacent sentence but that are acting as stand-alone sentences:

   FRAGMENT   **Wishing that finals week were over.** Jan reluctantly turned back to her studies.

   FRAGMENT   **To meet our June 1 deadline.** We've got to work hard during the next two weeks.

   FRAGMENT   **Near the end of its useful life.** The old bridge seemed to sag as heavy trucks strained its rotted timbers.

   FRAGMENT   Taylor ran to hug her child. **Her eyes filling with tears.**

Of course, you can always correct such fragments by making complete sentences out of them (remember, though, that too many short sentences can get tiring for the reader):

   REVISED   Jan wished that finals week were over. She reluctantly turned back to her studies.

Remedies for Phrasal Fragments

1. **Treat the fragments as elements of the adjacent sentences:**

CORRECT	Wishing that finals week were over, Jan reluctantly turned back to her studies.
CORRECT	To meet our June 1 deadline, we've got to work overtime during the next two weeks.
CORRECT	Near the end of its useful life, the old bridge seemed to sag as heavy trucks strained its rotted timbers.
CORRECT	Taylor ran to hug her child, her eyes filling with tears.

    Note that revising some phrasal fragments in this way involves more than merely attaching the phrase to a nearby sentence:

FRAGMENT	The RCMP training academy is located in Regina, Saskatchewan. An intense place full of courage and hard work.
INCORRECT REVISION	The RCMP training academy is located in Regina, Saskatchewan, an intense place full of courage and hard work.

    The fragment is now a modifier, but it is in the wrong position, making the reader think that Regina is intense (maybe it is!). The writer needs to place the modifier near the word or words it describes.

CORRECT REVISION	The RCMP training academy, an intense place full of courage and hard work, is located in Regina, Saskatchewan.

    For more on misplaced modifiers, see 25a.

2. **Turn the fragments into subordinate (dependent) clauses and combine them with the sentences they adjoin:**

CORRECT	Although she wished finals week were over, Jan reluctantly turned back to her studies.
CORRECT	We've got to work overtime during the next two weeks if we are going to meet our June 1 deadline.
CORRECT	Because the old bridge was near the end of its useful life, it seemed to sag as heavy trucks strained its rotted timbers.
CORRECT	As Taylor's eyes filled with tears, Taylor ran to hug her child.

3. **Turn the fragments into independent (main) clauses and combine them with the sentence they adjoin to make a compound sentence:**

CORRECT	Jan wished that finals week were over; nonetheless, she reluctantly turned back to her studies.
CORRECT	We have to meet our June 1 deadline, so we've got to work overtime during the next two weeks.
CORRECT	The old bridge was near the end of its useful life, and it seemed to sag as heavy trucks strained its rotted timbers.
CORRECT	Taylor's eyes filled with tears; she ran to hug her child.

A Long Sentence is NOT Necessarily a "Run-On"

Students frequently write phrasal fragments because they erroneously believe that long sentences are "run-ons" and therefore wrong. But long sentences are just that: long sentences. They may be grammatically correct or incorrect depending on how they're written and punctuated, not depending on their length.

EXERCISE 12.1

In each of the following pairs of items, one is a complete sentence and the other is a fragment. Combine them to eliminate the fragment. You may need to add, delete, or reorder words.

1. Maria decided to wait before buying a new computer. Hoping to find one on sale after Christmas.

2. Believing that tomatoes were poisonous. Many people in the nineteenth century refused to eat them.

3. The afternoon rain caused traffic back-ups all over Victoria. A common occurrence there.

4. Will and Jennifer went to the Humane Society shelter and then went home. Having adopted a Siamese kitten.

5. Samantha skied carefully down the icy slope. To maintain her balance and avoiding falling.

6. Many people who are planning a camping trip don't buy sufficient supplies. For instance, insect repellent and rain gear.

7. The firefighters left the scene. Believing that they had extinguished the blaze.

8. Marisa was considering some important issues. Such as whether to quit her job and whether to apply for more school loans.

9. Port Burwell is a few kilometres from here. Just past Vienna.

10. The bank will lend us all we need minus about $4000. A troublesome situation, if I do say so myself.

12b Dependent Clauses as Fragments

1. **A dependent clause must be attached to an independent clause.**

   The box on the next page shows a list of subordinating conjunctions. Any single-clause sentence, such as *She had danced all night,* can be changed to a dependent subordinate clause by placing one of these conjunctions before it:

   after she had danced all night
   because she had danced all night

even though she had danced all night

if she had danced all night

However, the resulting dependent clause is no longer a sentence and must be attached to an independent clause; if not, it is a fragment.

After she had danced all night, Vanessa slept for eight hours.

Vanessa was exhausted because she had danced all night.

Even though she had danced all night, Vanessa was able to complete a full day at work the next day.

If Vanessa had danced all night, she would not have gone to work the next day.

SENTENCE CONNECTORS			
Conjunctive Adverbs/ Transitional Expressions		**Subordinating Conjunctions**	**Coordinating Conjunctions**
accordingly	in the same way	after	and
additionally	indeed	although	but
also	instead	as	for
as an illustration	likewise	because	nor
at the same time	meanwhile	before	or
besides	moreover	even if	so
certainly	namely	even though	yet
consequently	nevertheless	if	
conversely	next	in order that	
finally	nonetheless	once	
for example	of course	provided that	
for instance	on the other hand	rather than	
furthermore	otherwise	since	
hence	similarly	so that	
however	specifically	so (that)	
in addition	still	than	
in brief	subsequently	that	
in conclusion	then	though	
in contrast	therefore	unless	
in short	thus	until	
in summary	to be sure	when	
		whenever	
		where	
		whereas	
		wherever	
		whether	
		while	

2. **A dependent clause that begins with one of the relative pronouns** *which,* *who, whom,* **or** *whose* **can also be a fragment unless it is connected to a main clause:**

FRAGMENT	The method of measurement based on the metre is the metric system. Which was first adopted in France in 1899.
CORRECT	The method of measurement based on the metre is the metric system, which was first adopted in France in 1899.
FRAGMENT	In Norse mythology, the fates were known as the Norns. Who spun out the destinies of human beings.
CORRECT	In Norse mythology, the fates, who spun out the destinies of human beings, were known as the Norns.
FRAGMENT	The Norns are probably related to the three witches. Whom we meet in Shakespeare's *Macbeth.*
CORRECT	The Norns are probably related to the three witches whom we meet in Shakespeare's *Macbeth.*

For more on relative clauses, see 12f. For help with punctuating sentences with subordinate clauses, see Chapter 16.

3. **Beware of creating internal fragments.** An incorrectly used semicolon can cause what is sometimes called an **internal fragment:**

INCORRECT	**Although the stadium is old;** it has character.
INCORRECT	Katie was close to tears; **feeling that she had been manipulated.**

In each sentence, a semicolon has been used incorrectly in place of a comma, leaving a dependent clause to stand where an independent clause is needed. Keep this idea in mind: what comes before and after a semicolon must be an independent clause.

 EXERCISE **12.2**

Read each group of sentences below. Revise as needed to eliminate fragments. Use the different strategies we have discussed.

1. The new classroom building was almost a year behind on its construction schedule. Because the contractor had submitted a timetable that was absurd.

2. Once Lucas realized his mistake. He called the branch office again. So that he could catch Ella Hassamin before closing time.

3. The language of the contract was difficult; although the summary at the end made the details clear.

4. I realized that I had been fooled again. After I opened the last envelope in the stack.

5. Whenever a production delay happens. Call the shift manager.

6. After losing his calculus text, missing a biology quiz, and getting a parking ticket, Cameron went home; feeling bitter.

7. The map was old; even though Tina had once lived in the area, the map didn't correspond to her memory of the place.

8. On Friday, the dealership refused to sell Paige the new van. Even though they had worked out the details on Thursday. To avoid time delays on the busy weekend.

9. Leah married a man from Prince Edward Island. Who owns seven office supply stores.

10. New students at this university seem to be a bit overwhelmed; while those in their second year have the air of those who have seen it all.

11. The front door is standing open. Which bothers me.

12. Eddie is a selfish young man. Whose sole purpose in life is to have fun.

13. Here is my great-grandfather's diary from the early twentieth century. Some of which is fascinating reading.

14. The new candidate for mayor is an interesting person. Who I think will give the incumbent a run for his money.

15. Amar was furious; because he had arrived before the financial aid office was supposed to close and found the door locked.

12c Intentional Fragments

Professional writers who use **intentional fragments** know that they are breaking the rules, but they do so for dramatic effect. Advertisements often use this strategy. When you are writing for college or university courses, however, using intentional fragments can be risky. What you see as intentional may be considered an error by your instructor. However, you can be secure about using an intentional fragment when answering a **rhetorical question** (a question to which the answer is obvious). Such questions are usually asked to draw the reader into the text:

CORRECT   Should senior citizens be faced with new taxes? Of course not.

Writing dialogue for a narrative essay is another context in which the use of intentional fragments would be acceptable. Otherwise, avoid fragments altogether in college writing.

EXERCISE 12.3

Rewrite the following paragraph to correct fragments.

Cole worked as a landscaper. To learn a trade and earn some money for college. Which he dearly wanted to attend. Although he was short on funds. Cole had applied for scholarships; hoping to pay for college that way. He could get only about half of what he needed for school. While his friend David got a free ride to a university. Consequently, Cole spent four years planting trees. He also met many friendly co-workers. Some of whom became his close friends. Therefore, although working as a landscaper had not been Cole's first choice. It turned out to be a worthwhile experience. Both personally and financially.

"RUN-ONS": FUSED SENTENCES AND COMMA SPLICES

A **fused sentence** occurs when two independent clauses are joined with no punctuation:

FUSED SENTENCE	I may be wrong I may be right.
FUSED SENTENCE	Samira tried to buy a new car however she couldn't get decent financing.

A comma splice occurs when two independent clauses are joined with a comma:

COMMA SPLICE	I may be wrong, I may be right.
COMMA SPLICE	Samira tried to buy a new car, however she couldn't get decent financing.

As you can see, fused sentences and comma splices are related. Although both are serious errors, they are easy to correct once you identify them. The following sections discuss three methods for eliminating fused sentences and comma splices.

12d Use a "Full Stop" (Period, Semicolon, or Colon) between Independent Clauses

1. **If the two independent clauses are not closely related, use a period and form two sentences:**

FUSED SENTENCE	Camille drove in from 70 kilometres away Zoe brought salmon quesadillas.
REVISED	Camille drove in from 70 kilometres away. Zoe brought salmon quesadillas.
COMMA SPLICE	The site-exploration team arrived at the hotel, meanwhile, the company's officers made plans that would change the scope of the project.
REVISED	The site-exploration team arrived at the hotel. Meanwhile, the company's officers made plans that would change the scope of the project.

Note that in the last sentence, the presence of the transitional adverb *meanwhile* has nothing to do with the sentence's being a comma splice. Using this transitional word between the two clauses helps the reader process the sentence, but it doesn't cause *or* prevent the comma splice.

2. **If the two independent clauses are closely related, connect them with a semicolon:**

FUSED SENTENCE	Zoe brought salmon quesadillas Brian made chicken.
REVISED	Zoe brought salmon quesadillas; Brian made chicken.
COMMA SPLICE	Zoe hates chicken, Brian won't eat fish.
REVISED	Zoe hates chicken; Brian won't eat fish.

3. **If the ideas in the two independent clauses are closely related but a transition is needed, connect the two clauses with a semicolon plus a conjunctive adverb/ transitional expression followed by a comma:**

FUSED SENTENCE	Sophie is a frequent guest however, we rarely see Mark.
REVISED	Sophie is a frequent guest; however, we rarely see Mark.

| COMMA SPLICE | Mark drove in from far away, Sophie lived next door. |
| REVISED | Mark drove in from far away; however, Sophie lived next door. |

You can find a list of conjunctive adverbs/transitions in the Sentence Connectors box found earlier in this chapter.

4. **If the idea in the second clause is introduced by the first or is caused by the first, consider connecting them with a colon.** *Use this method sparingly.*

FUSED SENTENCE	Now came the moment we all feared the building exploded and collapsed.
REVISED	Now came the moment we all feared: the building exploded and collapsed.
COMMA SPLICE	Conner knew one thing, he had to find a way out of his dead-end job.
REVISED	Conner knew one thing: he had to find a way out of his dead-end job.

The following sentences are either comma splices or fused sentences. First, identify the error. Next, revise the sentence by using a period, a semicolon, or a colon. Be prepared to justify your choice of revision method.

1. The company manufactures many interesting home appliances, it also offers factory tours.

2. Vacuum the carpet, then mop the floor.

3. It's not that Jason lacks talent it's that he is late for work three days out of four!

4. The door opened to admit the last person we wanted to see, Coach Albertson stood there with a sadistic grin as he watched our discomfort.

5. We had hoped to take a big vacation this summer, however, our finances didn't really allow us to do so.

12e Use a Comma and Coordinating Conjunction (*and, but, for, nor, or, so, yet*) to Connect Two Independent Clauses

FUSED SENTENCE	Supper wasn't ready my sister practised her piano lesson.
REVISED	Supper wasn't ready, so my sister practised her piano lesson.
COMMA SPLICE	Xavier thought the film was wonderful, Jenna didn't agree.
REVISED	Xavier thought the film was wonderful, but Jenna didn't agree.

Note that the proper pattern of punctuation for this type of sentence is always *comma plus coordinating conjunction.*

Although using a coordinating conjunction is an easy way to fix a comma splice or fused sentence, remember that such connectors describe a limited number of relationships. As we mentioned earlier, overusing this technique can (1) give your writing a monotonous rhythm and (2) fail to express subtle shades of meaning. Frequently, using a semicolon plus a transitional expression produces a more accurate sentence. However, when the context is appropriate, a comma plus a coordinating conjunction works well.

EXERCISE 12.5

The following sentences are either comma splices or fused sentences. First, identify the error. Next, revise the sentence by adding the appropriate coordinating conjunction preceded by a comma if one is not already present.

1. Tuesday was a gloomy day, Wednesday was equally bad.

2. Gabe loves bananas Antoine hates them.

3. When did you find out, why didn't you tell me?

4. Kyle committed the crime, he is lying.

5. We can't go outside let's watch a video.

12f Change One of the Two Independent Clauses to a Dependent Clause or to a Phrase

1. **Use subordination.** Subordination reduces one of the main (independent) clauses to a subordinate (dependent) clause. You can **subordinate a clause by using one of the subordinating conjunctions** from the Sentence Connectors box found earlier in this chapter.

FUSED SENTENCE	Oliver left the party early he wasn't in the mood to carouse.
REVISED	Oliver left the party early **because he wasn't in the mood to carouse.**
COMMA SPLICE	Brooke studied very hard, she still made a low score on the chemistry exam.
REVISED	**Although Brooke studied very hard,** she still made a low score on the chemistry exam.
REVISED	Brooke studied very hard **although she still made a low score on the chemistry exam.**

Note that when the dependent clause precedes the independent clause, always follow it with a comma. When a dependent clause follows an independent clause, however, a comma is usually not necessary. (For more on commas, see Chapter 16.)

Another way to use subordination is to turn one of the main clauses into a relative clause—a clause introduced by *that, which, who, whom,* or *whose.*

| FUSED SENTENCE | The Toltec arrived in Meso-America even before the Aztec they are among the first inhabitants of Mexico. |
| REVISED | The Toltec, **who arrived in Mexico even before the Aztec,** are among the first inhabitants of Mexico. |

2. **Change one of the independent clauses into a phrase:**

COMMA SPLICE	Tristan believes he will do better in economics, he plans to change his major.
REVISED	**Believing that he will do better in economics,** Tristan plans to change his major.
FUSED SENTENCE	On a winter day, we watched the geese they soared over Lake Superior.
REVISED	On a winter day, we watched the geese **soaring over Lake Superior.**

Note that when the phrase follows the independent clause, a comma is usually not necessary; an introductory phrase, on the other hand, requires a comma. (See Chapter 16 for more help with commas.)

EXERCISE 12.6

The following sentences are either comma splices or fused sentences. First, identify the error. Next, use one of the strategies covered in this section to revise the sentence.

1. History is important, history is not as crucial as some would have us believe.
2. The flood tore through the valley it created a new lake near Maple Road.
3. Danny washed his car he took it for a spin.
4. This is my cat, he is a very strange creature.
5. Tax time is over I'll feel more like a human being again.
6. Maple Industries is a very profitable company, it manufactures kites, gliders, and snowboards.
7. Kate reviewed her options once more she made her decision.
8. This website is quite useful, it has an enormous number of links.
9. Leo believed his upcoming work schedule was hopeless, he felt that his course assignment deadlines weren't much better.
10. Vivian was interested in web page design, Vivian took a class at the local technical college.

EXERCISE 12.7

Choosing a revision strategy to eliminate comma splices and fused sentences depends upon context. One method will often be clearly superior to another in any given situation.

Mark each of the following sentences **C** (correct), **CS** (comma splice), or **FS** (fused sentence). Then choose the **best** strategy to revise each comma splice and fused sentence. Be prepared to defend your decision.

1. Cheating has become a major issue for colleges and universities therefore various security strategies are being studied.

2. Mammals are warm-blooded whereas reptiles are not.

3. Load the software, then run the start-up disk.

4. Rain can be a blessing, acid rain, however, is something of a mixed blessing.

5. Florence couldn't attend her son's recital she certainly wanted to.

6. What brand is that, where did you buy it?

7. The professor is a very well-known scholar, she has the respect of her peers throughout the world.

8. That's not a squirrel it's a rat!

9. Ravi shut down his laptop and cleaned out his desk; thus, he said goodbye to seven years at Maple Industries.

10. This is not a question of which movie we want to see, it's a question of whether we really want to leave the house in this weather.

EXERCISE 12.8

The following passage contains fragments, comma splices, and fused sentences. Rewrite the passage to correct these problems by using the strategies you have learned in this chapter. Reword and combine sentences as needed.

The world has known many calendars. Methods by which to track the passage of time. Today, most of the world uses the Gregorian calendar for business purposes and for conducting international affairs. Indeed, with its twelve months from January to December. This solar calendar is probably the most widely known method of tracking days, weeks, months, and years, it contains 365.25 days per year. One day being added every fourth or leap year. Years in the Gregorian calendar are counted from the birth of Christ, with BC (the abbreviation for "Before Christ") being added to years that preceded Christ's birth. AD (the Latin abbreviation for "Year of our Lord") being added to years that follow it.

The Gregorian calendar was established in 1583 during the papacy of Gregory III. Scientists and historians realized that the Julian calendar, then in use, was not accurate and needed to be revised, named after the Roman general Julius Caesar, it had been used in Europe since 45 BC. While the Gregorian calendar was more accurate, it did not receive acceptance throughout Europe for many years, in fact, it was not adopted by the British Empire until 1752. Sweden followed suit in 1753, however, numerous countries in eastern Europe did not adopt the Gregorian calendar until the early twentieth century. In many countries, ordinary people continued to follow the Julian calendar long after the Gregorian calendar had been introduced, this resulted in people using different dates for the same event. In such cases. Events that were recorded according to the Julian method were followed by OS ("Old Style") those recorded according to the Gregorian calendar were followed by NS ("New Style").

Like the Gregorian calendar, first used in Christian countries and now adopted worldwide. The Islamic calendar has twelve months, it begins in Muhharram and ends with Dhu-al Hijjah. Unlike its European counterpart, however, the Islamic calendar is a lunar instrument, each month begins when the lunar crescent is first seen after the new moon. Years in the Islamic calendar are counted beginning from the Hijra, this is a term referring to the flight of Mohammed to Mecca, whose date corresponds to the year 622 AD in the Christian calendar, therefore, dates in the Muslim world are followed by an abbreviation signifying "year of the Hijra." It is interesting to note that because the Christian calendar is based on the movements of the sun and the Islamic calendar is based on the movements of the moon. The latter is about eleven days shorter.

The Jewish calendar has thirteen months, beginning with Nissan and ending with Adar II. With the number of days in each month varying from 29 to 30. Unlike the first month in the Christian calendar, which comes in the winter in northern latitudes. Nissan occurs in the spring. The season of Passover, an important Jewish holiday. The Jewish New Year falls in the seventh month, Tishri, it is at that time that the number of the year advances. The numbering of years in the Jewish calendar is based upon the number of years since the Creation, as recorded in the Scriptures when referring to years in the Gregorian calendar, however, the Jews do not use AD or BC instead they attach BCE ("before the common era") and CE ("the common era") to their dates.

OTHER SENTENCE-LEVEL PROBLEMS
12g Avoiding Faulty Parallelism

When you give equal emphasis to two or more things, actions, ideas, or activities, use **parallel** wording: nouns with nouns, verbs with verbs, prepositional phrases with prepositional phrases, and so forth. A sentence that uses parallel structures is both rhythmic and effective. Note the difference between the following examples:

NOT PARALLEL	Jessica likes several outdoor activities, including swimming, hiking, and to sail.
PARALLEL	Jessica likes several outdoor activities, including swimming, hiking, and sailing.

For a reader, the second sentence is more effective than the first, which is awkward. The first sentence uses two gerunds followed by an infinitive (*to sail*). The second, parallel sentence uses three gerunds (*swimming, hiking, sailing*). Most of the time, you can avoid writing sentences like the first one without a great deal of trouble. The following guidelines will help:

1. **Group nouns with nouns:**

   NOT PARALLEL   Edwin has arthritis, and he also suffers from a cracked vertebra as well as a nerve that was pinched.

   PARALLEL NOUNS   Edwin has arthritis, a cracked vertebra, and a pinched nerve.

2. **Group verbs with verbs:**

   NOT PARALLEL   At the conference, our project team went to workshops, had a comparison of notes, and then dinner.

   PARALLEL VERBS   At the conference, our project team went to workshops, compared notes, and then ate dinner.

3. **Group verbals (infinitives, gerunds, and participles) with the same kind of verbals:**

   NOT PARALLEL   On the weekends, my parents like to walk, golfing, and play cards.

   PARALLEL
   INFINITIVES   On the weekends, my parents like to walk, to golf, and to play cards.

   NOT PARALLEL   Jenn loves dancing, partying, and to go out on the town.

   PARALLEL GERUNDS   Jenn loves dancing, partying, and going out on the town.

4. **Group prepositional phrases with prepositional phrases:**

   NOT PARALLEL   You can find these vases in Montreal and Saint-Laurent, and you can also find them in Laval.

   PARALLEL
   PREPOSITIONAL
   PHRASES   You can find these vases in Montreal, in Saint-Laurent, and in Laval.

5. **Be careful with correlative conjunctions.** Correlative conjunctions are pairs of conjunctions (*both/and, not only/but also, either/or, neither/nor*) that emphasize relationships. (For more on correlative conjunctions, see 20f.) Note the following sentence:

   NOT PARALLEL   Failing to dress appropriately for the weather can not only ruin a person's day but also leads to health problems.

The two main verbs—*can ruin* and *leads*—are not parallel. Now note the revision:

   PARALLEL   Failing to dress for the weather can not only ruin a person's day but can also lead to health problems.

When you use a pair of correlative conjunctions, make sure that you use parallel structures within the elements they connect.

12h Avoiding Faulty Comparisons

Faulty comparisons are in many ways a kind of faulty parallelism. In an inexact comparison, the writer is sometimes trying to compare two things that cannot be logically compared:

| INCORRECT | The new software company has sold more of its email virus patches than any other software company. |

Email virus patches are not comparable to *any other software company.* Note the revision:

| CORRECT | The new software company's email virus patches have sold better than those of any other software company. |

Faulty comparisons can also be the result of an omitted word:

| INCORRECT | Jenkins does more work than any member of her division. |

Isn't Jenkins *in* her division? Adding a word clears the matter up:

| CORRECT | Jenkins does more work than any **other** member of her division. |

Some faulty comparisons are truly ambiguous:

INCORRECT	Some people use Internet searches more than librarians.
CORRECT	Some people use Internet searches more than librarians **do.**
ALSO CORRECT	Some people use Internet searches more than **they** consult librarians.

12i Avoiding Mixed Constructions

In a **mixed construction,** the writer starts a sentence with a structure that leads the reader to expect a particular type of sentence. Then, the writer goes in a different direction, leaving the reader baffled: the two parts of the sentence are not compatible. Note the following examples:

INCORRECT	Because he broke his ankle was the reason that Christian gave up basketball.
CORRECT	Because he broke his ankle, Christian gave up basketball.
INCORRECT	The reason for my anger is because of your habitual lack of punctuality.
CORRECT	The reason for my anger is your habitual lack of punctuality.
INCORRECT	By studying harder improves anyone's chance of success.
CORRECT	Studying harder improves anyone's chance of success.
INCORRECT	When Einstein relocated to Princeton was a very special honour for that university.
CORRECT	Einstein's relocation to Princeton was a very special honour for that university.

All the incorrect examples above are typical "first-draft" mistakes, which happen because writing and thinking do not occur at the same speed. Writers frequently start a sentence in one direction, then change their minds in mid-course. The revision stage is the point at which careful writers find and correct these errors.

Each of the following sentences suffers from mixed constructions, faulty comparisons, or a lack of parallelism. Revise each sentence to eliminate the error. In some cases, more than one answer is possible.

1. Mia gives better presentations than anyone in this company.

2. Because dogs like humans is the only reason that the two species coexist so well.

3. One idea concentrates on the possibility of humans living until age 150 is being taken seriously by many researchers.

4. Liberals tend to like a powerful federal government more than conservatives.

5. I want rest, relaxation, and to plan.

6. Veronica is attractive, funny, and she has lots of talent.

7. These pickles are more popular than any available brand.

8. After the mudslide is when the police chief left town.

9. Ricardo likes sardines more than William.

10. A person who repeatedly fails to wear sunblock can suffer both feeling serious pain and skin cancer.

CHAPTER 13

Problems with Verbs

Verbs are among the most important parts of a sentence; therefore, your ability to use them correctly is crucial. Two common problem areas are subject–verb agreement and shifts in tense, voice, and mood.

SUBJECT–VERB AGREEMENT

Properly written sentences have a structural balance: singular subjects are matched with singular verbs, and plural subjects with plural verbs; singular nouns are matched with singular pronouns, plural nouns with plural pronouns. This balance is called **agreement.**

Even professional writers sometimes make agreement errors in their first drafts. To make sure that your subjects and verbs agree, you will need to check for agreement problems when revising and editing. Look, for example, at the following sentence:

INCORRECT   There **is** a number of reasons for my choice.

CORRECT   There **are** a number of reasons for my choice.

Because the verb comes before the subject in this sentence—not the most common order—the writer might easily choose the incorrect verb form. The first section of this example shows you where agreement problems are likely to occur and how to correct them. For now, keep the following in mind:

1. **A subject must agree in *number* with its verb. A singular verb is needed for a singular noun,** as in this sentence:

   The **house** that we have owned for many years **sits** on two acres.

2. **A plural noun requires a plural verb:**

   The **houses** that we saw in Niagara-on-the-Lake last week **are** beautiful.

Most writers have few problems with basic subject–verb agreement. In the sentence "Caleb (work, works) for a large company," the choice is straightforward: *Caleb works.* However, beware of verbs that end in *-ist;* because the verb already has an *-s* sound near the end, it's easy to forget that in a sentence like "The last surviving member of the species (exist, exists) in a zoo," the correct verb is *exists,* to agree with the subject *last surviving member.* Writers must also deal with many situations that are not obvious, where one of the chief problems is determining whether the subject is singular or plural.

13a Subjects Connected by *and*

Two or more nouns or pronouns joined by *and* are called **compound subjects.** These constructions are normally plural:

> **Carter and Sophie** plan to get married.
> **Five rabbits, a hamster, and a cat** are the pet shop's remaining inventory.
> **Going to school and working twenty hours per week** have become difficult for Maureen.

However, if any word or phrase other than *and* joins two parts of a subject, the verb is singular if both parts of the subject are singular:

> **Carter,** as well as Sophie, **has** been nominated for chairperson.
> **Volvo,** along with Jaguar, **is** owned by Ford Motor Company.
> **Going to school** plus working twenty hours a week **is** too much for Maureen.
> **A case of pneumonia,** in addition to several double shifts at work, **has** put Louise into the hospital.

13b Compound Subjects Treated as Singular Constructions

Sometimes, two singular subjects joined by *and* are really one entity—person or thing—and they take singular forms:

Track and field is Amelia's best sport. (Track and field is one type of athletic activity.)

He believed that **rock and roll** was an abomination. (Rock and roll is one kind of music.)

My **best friend and confidant** is coming for a visit. (In this sentence, the writer is referring to one person.)

Two **gerund phrases** linked with *and* can also sometimes be singular:

Going downtown and playing snooker is my grandfather's secret vice.

Here, the subject (*going downtown and playing snooker*) is essentially one activity.

On the other hand, the following sentence has a compound gerund phrase that clearly indicates two separate activities:

Getting dressed and driving to my date's home are the last two steps in the ritual.

EXERCISE 13.1

In the following sentences, decide if the highlighted verb is correct in number. If it is not, supply the correct form of the verb, or restructure the sentence so that the existing verb form is correct. Not all sentences contain errors.

1. Laurie and Charles **has** signed up for our study group.

2. Tossing and turning all night **are** my response to stress.

3. Harriet, as well as her sister Jasmine, **is** expected to attend the public lecture.

4. Health and safety **were** my least-favourite class in high school.

5. Moss and lichens **grows** on many different varieties of trees.

13c Subjects Connected by *or, nor, either . . . or, neither . . . nor,* and *not only . . . but also*

These connectors join subjects, but the resulting subjects do not act as a compound subject. Therefore, these connectors need a special series of rules for subject–verb agreement:

1. **If both subjects joined by one of these connectors are singular, the verb is singular:**

   Neither Jane nor George **is** expected to apply.

2. **If both subjects are plural, the verb is plural:**

Neither cats nor dogs **are** able to fly.

3. **If one subject is singular and the other is plural, the verb agrees in number with the closer noun:**

Vitamins or exercise **is** what Jessica needs right now.
One CD or two magazines **are** all Wayne can afford.

This rule also applies if three or more subjects are connected by *or*; the subject *closest* to the verb determines the verb's number:

Cherries, grapes, or cake **is** what we can offer you for dessert.

If a sentence is correct but sounds strange, you can eliminate the awkwardness by rearranging the nouns:

Cake, cherries, or grapes **are** what we can offer you for dessert.

EXERCISE 13.2

In the following sentences, choose the correct word. Rewrite the sentence if the result is awkward.

1. Neither bananas nor grapes (contains, contain) all the vitamins that a human needs.
2. Either Ed or the Johnsons (has, have) bought a new car.
3. Not only floods but also drought (has, have) been a problem in this region.
4. Neither the Walker brothers nor Ellen Hastings (was, were) sent an invitation.
5. Two ducks, a fox, or three turkeys (is, are) what I shall paint today.

13d Indefinite Pronouns as Subjects

A **definite pronoun** refers to a specific person: *he, she,* and so on. An **indefinite pronoun,** such as *someone* or *anybody,* refers to a "generalized other." Indefinite pronouns fall into three categories when considering their number. They are either always singular, always plural, or singular or plural depending on context.

13d.1 Indefinite Pronouns that are Always Singular

Many of the words in the first column, such as *everyone* and *everybody, seem* plural, but grammatically they are always singular. Also, remember that when *each* or *every* precedes a subject, it makes that subject singular:

Everyone in the study group **is** invited to participate.
Each of the four defendants **was** tried separately.
Every detective and lawyer in North America **has** been jolted by the news of McNamara's prison break.

INDEFINITE PRONOUNS		
Always Singular	Always Plural	Singular or Plural Depending upon Context
another	both	all
anybody	few	any
anyone	many	either
anything	several	enough
each		more
every		most
everybody		neither
everyone		none
everything		some
no one		
nobody		
nothing		
one		
somebody		
someone		
something		

However, when **each** *follows* a plural subject, the verb is plural:

> At the ceremony, the players each thank the coach for his dedication.

13d.2 Indefinite Pronouns that can be Singular or Plural

The words in the third column of the box at the top of this page are indefinite pronouns, but they do not determine a subject's number; instead, the nouns that they are linked with determine whether the verb should be singular or plural:

> **All** of the work on the garage **is** complete.
> **All** of the clerical tasks, such as typing, collating, and filing, **are** done by Chris.

> **Some** of the damage **is** severe.
> **Some** of the computers **are** still working.

> **Either (Neither)** the players **or (nor)** the coach **is** being fined.
> **Either (Neither)** the coach **or (nor)** the players **are** being fined.

In the last example, the first sentence uses a singular verb because the subject closer to it, *coach,* is singular. The second sentence uses a plural verb because the subject closer to it, *players,* is plural.

In the following sentences, choose the correct verb.

1. Everyone (is, are) expected to stand in line, Steve.

2. Either success or failure (await, awaits) us.

3. Most (believes, believe) that they will get to the window before the office closes.

4. Some of the procedure (is, are) explained in the company's personnel manual.

5. Neither the deadline nor the three different entry fees (has, have) been announced.

13e Collective Nouns as Subjects

Collective nouns, such as *family, team, couple, pair, trio, group, panel,* and *committee,* refer to groups. They often cause subject–verb agreement problems. In Canadian English, these words are usually treated as singular depending on context:

> The **team is** coming out of the locker room.
> The **jury is** still deliberating.
> Her **family is** back together again.

However, they are sometimes treated as plural:

> The **choir raise** their voices in song.
> The **couple are** saying their wedding vows.

What's the distinction? In the first three examples, the collective noun (*team, jury, family*) is representing a unit. In the last two examples, the elements that make up the collective nouns (*choir, couple*) are acting separately *within* the unit. To test this distinction, try to treat the collective nouns in the last two examples as singular:

> The choir raises its voice in song.
> The couple is saying its wedding vows.

The effect is awkward. One solution is to add the word *members* after the collective noun, making the construction automatically plural:

> The choir members raise their voices in song.

However, this strategy doesn't work in all contexts. You would never say *the couple members*. In the second example above, changing to a compound subject would produce a more natural-sounding sentence:

> The bride and groom are saying their wedding vows.

EXERCISE **13.4**

In each of the following sentences, choose the correct word.

1. The legislature (has, have) passed a resolution banning pesticides.

2. After standing to acknowledge the applause of the audience, the orchestra took (its, their) (seat, seats).

3. The hockey team (is, are) arguing among (itself, themselves) about the coach's decision.

4. The family (is, are) planning to go to Manitoba for (its, their) vacation.

5. The awards committee (is, are) still deliberating.

13f Collective Nouns that Cause Agreement Problems

Problems sometimes occur because of a difference between informal English and formal English; other problems represent highly specific developments in English over time.

1. **News:** This word is always treated as a singular noun.

   The **news is** good.

2. **Media:** In informal English, *media* is frequently used as a singular noun. In formal English, however, *media* is always plural. When you refer to the news or entertainment media, you are talking about a collection made up of each specific *medium*, such as print, radio, and television. Hence, *media* should always take a plural verb.

   The news **media are** reporting that the wildfire is being brought under control.

3. **Data:** This word is the plural form of the rarely used *datum*. Although in informal usage a singular verb is often used with *data*, formal English requires a plural verb.

   The **data are** consistent.

4. **Subjects or activities that end in -s (physics, statistics, politics, ethics, economics, sports):** These words are singular when they refer to a concept, activity, subject, or academic course but plural when they refer to a specific "set" of individual items.

   Statistics is my favourite course.
   The **statistics** from the two studies **are** consistent.
   Sports is her future.
   Team **sports are** dominating the intramural schedule.

5. **Company names:** The name of a single company or institution is always singular, even if it sounds plural.

   Johnson and Johnson makes pharmaceutical supplies.
   Ibbotson Research Associates is a new company in this area.
   The Organization of Canadian Heritage is having a mandatory meeting.

6. **Mathematical expressions:** Mathematical expressions are usually treated as singular.

   Notice that **16 plus 24 is** 40.
   In fact, **(4 3 2 1 3x)**^{3} **is** the resulting polynomial.

7. **Distances and measurements of time:** When a distance or measurement of time is treated as one unit, it is singular.

Seven hundred kilometres is a long drive.
Two hours seems like a long time to wait for a doctor.

However, when a distance or measurement of time is seen as the sum of its individual units, it is plural.

Five kilometres of rough road **are** still in front of us.
Four hours have crawled by minute by minute.

In these examples, five kilometres will be experienced *kilometre by kilometre,* and four hours have been suffered minute by minute.

8. **Word as word/number as number:** When you refer to a word *as* a word or a number *as* a number, the noun is singular.

Hieroglyphics **is** a very hard word to spell.
Eight is my lucky number.

9. **The number/a number:** *The number (of)* is singular; *a number (of)* is plural.

The number of guests for our upcoming party **has** been reduced; **a number of** people **have** called to cancel.

(EXERCISE **13.5**

In the following sentences, choose the correct verb.

1. The United Nations (has, have) survived decades of political turmoil.
2. The sports media often (fail, fails) to cover events in swimming and water polo.
3. "Eight thousand maniacs" (refers, refer) to the people waiting to buy concert tickets.
4. The number of people who buy umbrellas (is, are) surprisingly small.
5. Statistics (indicates, indicate) that drunk driving is a leading cause of highway fatalities.

13g Subjects Separated from Their Verbs

Don't be misled by intervening words—words that come between the subject and the verb:

Lake Superior, the largest of the Great Lakes, (is, are) a vast body of water.

The subject of the sentence is *Lake Superior,* which is singular, so *is* is the correct verb. However, the word immediately preceding the verb is *Lakes,* and some writers, fooled by the closeness of this word, might want to use *are* instead. Check for the number of the *subject*, not the number of the nearest noun or pronoun. Here are more examples:

A **bouquet** of lilies, mums, and irises **makes** a stunning centrepiece.

Ford, a company that owns many automobile brands, **is** expected to explore various alternative-fuel options.

The home **computer,** which has revolutionized both business and personal communications, **was** invented in the 1970s.

In the following sentences, choose the correct verb in parentheses.

1. Excitement in all of its sordid varieties (is, are) the principal attraction of the Adelphi Nightclub.

2. The batter for the Toronto Blue Jays (has, have) played for seven different teams.

3. Peanuts, an agricultural mainstay of the South, (is, are) a versatile food source.

4. William, one of five brothers, (owns, own) a car dealership.

5. All voters, regardless of their party affiliation, (seem, seems) interested in debating the bond issue.

13h Subjects and Linking Verbs

Linking verbs, especially forms of *be* as well as words like *taste, feel,* and *smell,* connect a subject to a word or words that describe it, called its complement. They cause a unique problem in subject–verb agreement:

	singular	**plural**	**plural**
INCORRECT	The main **problem** at the plant **are** production errors.		
	singular	**singular**	**plural**
CORRECT	The main **problem** at the plant **is** production errors.		

The subject can sometimes be plural and the complement singular, or vice versa. A common error is to make the verb agree with the complement, but the *subject*—not the complement—determines whether the verb is singular or plural. If a sentence is correct but sounds strange, remember that you can switch the subject and the complement. Then the verb will change number to match the new subject:

The main **problem is** production errors.

Production **errors are** the main problem.

In the following sentences, choose the correct verb.

1. Penguins (is, are) a tourist attraction in the Antarctic.

2. The problem with this drug (is, are) its side effects.

3. Errors in the programming language (is, are) our focus today.

4. Walking and biking (is, are) good exercise.

5. Driver's licences (is, are) one item most people carry at all times.

13i Subjects that Follow Verbs: Inverted Sentence Structures

Some English sentences do not use the standard pattern of subject then verb. In a question, for example, the subject comes after the verb. In such instances, make sure that the verb agrees with the number of its subject:

What **are the causes** of the problem?

Is this **a good reason** for your behaviour?

A similar situation occurs in declarative sentences beginning with *here, there,* and *what.* The subject is delayed until after the verb:

Here **comes my aunt,** strolling down the aisle.

Here **come my aunts,** strolling down the aisle.

What **is** clearly **an animal track** was lifted by the police forensics specialist.

What **are** clearly **animal tracks** were lifted by the police forensics specialist.

A third type of inverted sentence pattern happens when a writer deliberately switches the normal order for effect:

Above the mountains **rises a blinding sun.**

Here, as always, identifying the subject and its number is crucial.

EXERCISE 13.8

In the following sentences, choose the correct form of the verb.

1. Which (is, are) the correct instructions, this batch or the one over there?

2. Here (is, are) a few interesting questions to contemplate.

3. Through the busy shoppers (moves, move) Bethany, her holiday buying almost finished.

4. On the barren ridge above the old house (sit, sits) a wolf and her pups.

5. There (is, are) many reasons not to go cave diving.

VERB SHIFTS

As noted earlier, writers frequently need to project themselves into the reader's role and say to themselves, "I understand what I mean, but will my reader understand as well?" When writers change verb usage in a sudden or unexpected way (when they make a "shift"), they often cause problems for readers. This section will help you to avoid three kinds of shifts—shifts of tense, of voice, and of mood.

13j Tense Shifts

Before we talk about incorrect shifts of verb tense (to review verb tense, see 20g.2), it is important to note that a writer may change tenses when such a change is called for. For example, a sentence or a paragraph may mention events that happened at different times. Therefore, changing tenses can be logical and necessary. Note the following example:

> In 1946, my father **was** in a quandary. Before World War II, he **had been** a college student; however, in 1946, he **wasn't** sure what to do. He **felt** that the world **was becoming** a much more complicated place. Today, I **feel** the same way.

Four tenses (past, past perfect, past progressive, and present) are used in this paragraph, but this mix is acceptable. However, a sudden tense shift for no apparent reason is not acceptable:

| INCORRECT | Bobby **rode** up on his Harley, and he **starts** talking a mile a minute. (The action in the sentence either happened in the past or it is happening now—but not both; the use of both tenses confuses the reader.) |
| CORRECT | Bobby **rode** up on his Harley, and he **started** talking a mile a minute. (In this version, both verbs are in past tense.) |

A special situation occurs when you are writing about literature, television, or film. In this situation the **literary** present tense is used:

| CORRECT | In *Pulp Fiction,* Jules and Vincent **are** two of the major characters. |

13k Voice Shifts

For most purposes, the **active voice** ("Kevin hit the wall") is preferable to the **passive voice** ("The wall was hit by Kevin"). In any case, mixing voices within a sentence is usually not the best choice:

| ORIGINAL | The criminal **fled** the scene, but he **was arrested** by the police that afternoon. |

The first independent clause is in the active voice; the second one is in the passive voice. Note how much more direct and forceful the revised sentence is:

| REVISED | The criminal **fled** the scene, but the police **arrested** him that afternoon. |

As you can see, in the active voice, the subject acts on a direct object. In the passive voice, the subject is acted upon. (To learn more about voice, see 20g.5.) Here's another example:

| ORIGINAL | As Sean ran up the stairs, laughter **could be heard.** |
| REVISED | As Sean ran up the stairs, he **could hear** laughter. |

13l Mood Shifts

Verbs can have one of three **moods** (see 20g.4 for a review of mood). The **indicative** mood is the most common; it is used to state facts, make assertions, and ask questions. The **imperative** mood gives commands. The **subjunctive** mood describes hypothetical situations, wishes, or conditions contrary to fact, as in "If I **were** to flap my arms and fly out the window, everyone **would be** surprised." An inappropriate shift in mood occurs when the writer starts in the subjunctive mood but then switches to the indicative:

| INCORRECT | If I were wealthy, I am going to buy a sports car. |
| CORRECT | If I **were** wealthy, I **would buy** a sports car. |

The original sentence shifts from the subjunctive mood to the indicative; the revised sentence uses the subjunctive in both clauses. In the next example, the writer shifts from the imperative to the indicative:

| INCORRECT | Study hard tonight, and then you should rest. |
| CORRECT | **Study** hard tonight, and then **rest.** |

EXERCISE 13.9

Each of the following sentences contains a shift of tense, voice, or mood. Revise each incorrect sentence.

1. It is believed by scientists that the epidemic will not occur, and parents welcome the good news.

2. Canadian business always concentrated on efficiency, and some of today's firms are models of streamlining.

3. Jeremy is surviving a day in which he had seen his job almost lost, his car almost wrecked, and his house almost torched.

4. If Brianna were able to finish college a year early, she will go immediately to graduate school.

5. *Damnation Boulevard* is a good movie, but everyone died in the end.

6. Instruments of the violin family are played with a stringed bow, but guitars, mandolins, and lyres would be played by hand.

7. Part of the German protectorate of Togoland from 1886 to 1914, Togo was administered by the French until 1982, when it becomes a republic.

8. In 1980, Pac-Man became a worldwide arcade smash. By 1985, the video game industry sees new life with the introduction of the Nintendo Entertainment System, a system which had become a must-buy item during the December shopping rush.

9. Prime Minister Trudeau removes laws against homosexuality from the Criminal Code of Canada in 1965, and more than forty years later, people in Canada are still upholding his mission for equality.

10. In the early 1990s, many bands were fed up with the commercial nonsense on FM radio. With other alternative bands, Perry Ferrell founds the Lollapalooza tour as a less commercial alternative. Featuring Nine Inch Nails, the tour had been the first of its kind.

EXERCISE 13.10

The following passage contains sentences with verb problems. Fix any error that you see.

If someone says that he or she is going to be on time, one hopes that will be the case. If I were to make an appointment with you, you are sure that the appointment will be kept and that I will be prompt. Last Monday I made a tee time for 7:30 a.m. at the Hidden Value Estates Golf Club. My friends Ed and Logan, along with Mike, who is one of Ed's friends, is supposed to meet me at Hidden Value. The course, which is owned by Golf Management Specialists, are located east of the city. I got there first and suspected that traffic problems was the issue, for I waited and waited.

Waiting for latecomers and still remaining patient is not my strong suit. Ed, as well as Logan, are constantly late, and I have no idea about Mike's problems. I sat and listened to the television news, which were bad, as usual. Statistics were indicating that the recent downturn in the North American economies were caused by a number of factors. Either the job market, inflationary trends, or European trade were the main culprit, according to the report. In my opinion, neither trade issues nor foreign debt are the main issue; I feel that too much corruption and greed by corporate executives have caused an unrealistic financial market made up of fake assets.

Meanwhile, I was about to lose our tee time—or, should I say, Ed, Logan, and Mike was going to lose it for me. Thirty minutes are not a long time to wait, but the starter and his assistant was beginning to glare in my direction. Golf Management Specialists are not a patient group; it does not hesitate to cancel tee times and then a charge for a missed appointment is levied. Finally, with only a few minutes to spare, my three cohorts arrive in one car. Logan's facial expression and body language was not positive (he had waited for the other two), but we got off at 7:29, as planned.

CHAPTER 14

Problems with Pronouns

Pronouns take the place of and refer to nouns or other pronouns, called antecedents. The word *antecedent* signifies that such nouns and pronouns usually come *before* the pronouns that refer to them. Unclear pronouns can lead to misunderstanding in written work, so keep the advice in this chapter in mind when you revise or edit your papers so that you use pronouns correctly and make them relate clearly and directly to their antecedents.

PRONOUN–ANTECEDENT AGREEMENT

Pronoun–antecedent agreement follows the logic of subject–verb agreement (see Chapter 13). The pronoun agrees in number with its antecedent. Singular antecedents require singular pronouns; plural antecedents require plural pronouns:

Karen asked that I call **her.**

The Williams brothers were annoyed; the hotel had lost **their** reservations.

Pronouns are more complicated, however; in addition to agreeing in number, pronouns must be in the correct case (subjective, objective, or possessive) and must agree with their antecedents in gender (male and female):

She is my Aunt Lil McGill; I telephone **her** every week. (The pronoun *she* is in the subjective case; it is the subject of the first clause. The pronoun *her* is in the objective case; it receives the action of telephoning.)

Lil is the name **she** took on her twenty-first birthday, but **her** real name is Nancy. (The pronouns in this sentence are all female, for they all refer to Lil.)

As with the subject in subject–verb agreement, there are many situations in which the writer's main problem is determining the number of the pronoun's antecedent.

14a Antecedents that Use *and* and Other Connectors

1. **Compound nouns and phrases with *and*:** Antecedents joined by the word *and* usually form a plural compound. Thus, pronouns referring to such antecedents must also be plural.

   Avery and Hunter have bought a new home; **they** are delighted to have a home of **their** own.

   British Columbia and the state of Washington are in North America; **they** border each other.

   Sally enjoys **planting flowers and reading mysteries** because **they** help relax **her.**

2. **Compound nouns and phrases with other connectors:** Using other connectors (*as well as, along with, in addition to, plus*) to join two nouns can result in problems.

   INCORRECT   Karen, along with her friend Ed, is coming to the fund drive; they will bring a couch for the auction.

   In this sentence, *they* has no antecedent because *along with* does not connect *Karen* and *her friend Ed*. The solution here is simple—change *along with* to the coordinating conjunction *and*.

   CORRECT   **Karen and her friend Ed** are coming to the fund drive; **they** will bring a couch for the auction.

3. **Compound words treated as singular constructions:** Sometimes, two singular words connected by *and* are actually the same entity. When such words act as an antecedent, refer to them with a singular pronoun.

My best friend and most exacting critic is my sister; **she** plans to visit next week. Whenever I hear **rock and roll,** I have to sing or dance to **it.**

4. **Gerund phrases linked with *and*:** In the following sentence, the subject (*going downtown and playing poker*) is essentially one activity. It should be referred to by using a singular pronoun.

Going downtown and playing poker is my grandfather's secret vice; he does **it** three days a week.

On other hand, the following sentence has a compound gerund phrase that clearly indicates two separate activities:

Getting dressed and driving to my date's home are the last two steps in the ritual, and **they** are the two easiest steps.

> ## EXERCISE 14.1
>
> In the following sentences, decide if the highlighted pronoun is correct in number. If it is not, supply the correct pronoun or rewrite the sentence. Not all sentences contain errors.
>
> 1. Lately, my wife has complained about my tossing and turning all night; **they** are keeping her awake.
> 2. When Bob and Leo went fishing, **he** decided to bring a radio.
> 3. When an NHL player leaves the game, **they** can normally expect paid retirement.
> 4. When Julianne and Luke got their first assignment in the RCMP, **they** were posted to Manitoba.
> 5. When running water and electricity came to our rural cabin, **it** surely made our lives easier.

14b Antecedents Joined by *or, nor, either . . . or, neither . . . nor,* and *not only . . . but also*

As in subject–verb agreement, using these connectors to join nouns can cause problems in pronoun–antecedent agreement. Note the following basic guidelines, which follow the same pattern as the guidelines for subject–verb agreement:

1. **If both antecedents (nouns or pronouns) joined by these words or phrases are singular, the pronoun is also singular.**
2. **If both antecedents joined by these words or phrases are plural, the pronoun is also plural.**
3. **If one antecedent is plural and the other is singular, the pronoun agrees in number with the antecedent closer to it.**

The first two guidelines are fairly straightforward:

> Either Michael or Elliot left **his** car keys on the counter.
> Either the Parkers or the Robbins left **their** car keys on the counter.

The third guideline is more complex. When a singular noun is connected to a plural noun, the pronoun's number is determined by *the noun that is closer to the pronoun:*

> Neither my mother nor my sisters found **their** way to my cabin.
>
> But note the problem posed by this sentence:
>
> Either the Robbins or Elliot left **his** car keys on the counter.

This sentence is technically correct; however, it does not say what its writer intends. To revise, the writer could reverse the order of the two nouns, allowing the pronoun to change number:

> Either Elliot or the Robbins left **their** car keys on the counter.

Remember that *you* control the sequence of your nouns in these situations; make sure that your sentences are logically correct as well as technically correct.

Note also that you can often solve problems by eliminating the pronoun altogether:

> Either the Robbins or Elliot left **a set of** car keys on the counter.

In the following sentences, choose the better term (or series of better terms) from the parentheses. In some sentences, more than one set of choices may be correct.

1. If you see Makayla or Nancy, ask (her, them) to bring some plates.

2. For supper, I think that I'll have either (fish steaks or pizza, pizza or fish steaks); (it, they) really (appeal, appeals) to me.

3. (Neither Lance nor Marge, Both Lance and Marge) (will admit, refuse to admit) (that she is wrong, that they are wrong).

4. The specials tonight include not only pork loin but also quesadillas; (it, they) (sounds, sound) wonderful.

5. After a hard night at the casino, (neither the Parkers nor their daughter Sofia) (neither Sofia Parker nor her parents) wanted to risk any more of (her, their) money.

14c Indefinite Pronouns as Antecedents

An **indefinite pronoun,** such as *each, everyone, no one,* and *somebody,* refers to a nonspecific person or thing. You can find a chart of indefinite pronouns in 23d. As discussed in Chapter 13, some indefinite pronouns are always singular, others are always plural, and some can be either singular or plural depending on the context.

14c.1 Indefinite Pronouns that are Always Singular

Such pronouns include *anybody, everyone,* and *something,* as well as many others. Ensure that any pronouns that refer back to these are singular:

> **Something** must have spoiled in the refrigerator. **It** is probably the yogurt I left in there last August.

> **Everyone** must vote according to **his or her** conscience.

A little more than half the people in the world are female. Unfortunately, English has no single word that can refer to an "indefinite" person of either sex. An informal solution is to write *Everyone must vote according to their conscience.* However, *their* is plural whereas *everyone* is singular. A better solution is to use the *his or her* construction (as above) or to recast the sentence into the plural:

> **All** must vote according to **their** consciences.

The same approach will work when using words such as *any, each,* and *every*:

> **Any** student who wants to do well in Dr. Oshiro's physics class must make sure that **he or she** is prepared to study.

> **Students** who want to do well in Dr. Oshiro's physics class must make sure that **they** are prepared to study.

Another way to fix this problem is to get rid of the pronoun altogether if possible:

> **Anybody** who forces **his or her** child into show business should be prosecuted.
> **Anybody** who forces **a** child into show business should be prosecuted.

14c.2 Indefinite Pronouns that are Always Plural

Some indefinite pronouns (*both, few, many, several*) are always plural. As such, you must be sure that you use plural pronouns after them:

> **Both** of them always finish **their** ice cream.
> **Several** have already taken **their** places in the line-up in front of the store.

14c.3 Indefinite Pronouns that can be Singular or Plural

Some indefinite pronouns do not determine a subject's number (see the third column of the Indefinite Pronouns box in 23d); instead, the context of the sentence will determine whether the verb should be singular or plural, and whether the pronouns following them are, therefore, singular or plural:

> **All** of the students have finished **their** work.
> **Some** of the violence has left **its** mark permanently on its victims.
> **Neither** of the Blue Jays is losing **his** job.

14c.4 Troubleshooting

1. **Some contexts require singular forms.** Consider this situation: your college offers the Gretzky Scholarship to a single student. All students are eligible. Hence,

the winner will be either male or female. A carefully worded requirement of the scholarship might read like this:

The **student** who is awarded the scholarship must present proof of **his or her** completion of thirty semester hours.

A plural context won't work here: only one winner will be selected. Therefore, using *his or her* is necessary.

2. **If you have to use a singular indefinite pronoun, use *he or she* or *she or he*.** Avoid *s/he* and *[s]he*. These are not considered acceptable style; furthermore, they can't be spoken.

3. **If your context refers to an all-male or an all-female population, use the appropriate singular pronoun** to refer to an "indefinite" person. Any player in the National Hockey League can, at this time, be safely referred to as *he*. Any golfer in the LPGA can be referred to as *she*.

EXERCISE 14.3

In the following sentences, choose the correct pronoun. If the result is awkward, rewrite the sentence so that a more natural-sounding sentence results.

1. Anyone who wants to participate in the contest must have (his, her, their, his or her) cooking utensils.

2. A knight in the Middle Ages owed (his, her, his or her, their) allegiance to a feudal lord.

3. Everybody who is scheduled for writing conferences must file (his, her, their, his or her) proposal with the instructor.

4. Each car mechanic and technician is responsible for (his, her, their, his or her) own certification.

5. All the people at this meeting have pledged at least $100 of (his, her, their, his or her) money toward the re-election campaign.

14d Collective Nouns as Antecedents

Words such as *family, team, couple, pair, trio, group, panel,* and *committee* are called **collective nouns.** They are normally singular, but sometimes they are plural, according to context:

The **team** emerged; **it** was ready for action.
The **couple** said **their** vows.

When you use a collective noun, you need to ask the following question: Is the collective noun functioning as one entity, or are the individual members acting separately? In the first example, the team is acting as one entity. In the second example, each of the two people in the wedding ceremony speaks separately; the two people are effectively plural. As noted in the section on subject–verb agreement (see 23e and

23f), you can avoid problems with most collective nouns by adding the word *members*. Consider the following sentence, which is correct and sounds correct:

> The **committee** has not yet reached **its** decision.

However, this sentence is correct but *sounds* incorrect:

> The **committee** are arguing among **themselves.**

Adding the word *members* helps avoid awkwardness:

> The **committee members** are arguing among **themselves.**

This strategy works most of the time, except with the collective nouns *couple, pair,* and *duo.* If you use these words alone, you must decide if the context makes them singular or plural when choosing a pronoun.

> The **pair** walked hand in hand, discussing **their** future.
> This **pair** [of pants] is worn out; throw **it** away.

14e Collective Nouns that Cause Agreement Problems

In the section on subject–verb agreement, we list a number of collective nouns that cause special problems in agreement (see 23f). Here is a shortened version of that list—most of these words cause fewer problems in pronoun–antecedent agreement:

1. **News** is singular:

   > I heard the **news; it** is good.

2. **Media** is plural:

   > One problem with the **media** is **their** belief that people will never tire of hearing about scandals.

3. **Data** is plural:

   > I've checked the **data,** and **they** seem realistic.

4. **Physics, statistics, politics, ethics, economics,** and **sports** are all singular if they refer to a concept, subject, or academic course:

   > **Physics** is my favourite course; **it** fascinates me.
   > My grandfather wants me to go into **politics,** but **it** is not for me.

   They are plural if they are referring to a "set" of individual items:

   > We examined the **statistics** on car thefts; **they** show a clear pattern.
   > Gary has tried various **sports,** but **they** don't interest him.

5. **Company names** are singular:

   > **Betty's Wondrous Roses** has failed; **it** is bankrupt.

6. **Mathematical expressions** are singular:

   > The result we come up with is **$(4 \times 1\,3)^3\,/1.5\ x;$ it** now needs to be tested.

7. **Measurements of distance and time** are singular when treated as one unit:

Seven hundred kilometres is a long drive; **it** wears me out.

They are plural when treated as the sum of units:

Five years passed slowly. **They** seemed to drift by like a bad dream.

8. **Words treated as words and numbers treated as numbers** are singular:

When I try to spell **hieroglyphics, it** gets twisted around in my memory. **Eight** is my lucky number; **it** always has been.

9. **The number of . . .** is singular:

The number of attendees was small; **it** was under fifty.

10. **A number of . . .** is plural:

A number of people cancelled; **they** didn't want to brave the weather.

EXERCISE 14.4

In the following sentences, choose the correct word or words.

1. An example of a controversial organization is the United Nations; (it, they) can inspire a number of different reactions among people.

2. Golf and swimming are my two sports; (it, they) keep me occupied in my spare time.

3. When you see the term "teeming millions," (they, it) (mean, means) the bulk of the population.

4. When I drove up to Barber and Associates, (it, they) (was, were) closed.

5. We've rerun the data several times; (it, they) (keeps, keep) coming back the same way.

6. The commission (has, have) announced (its, their) new guidelines.

7. The winning (team, team members) divided the bonus money among (itself, themselves).

8. Leon and Samantha, a newlywed couple, (is, are) planning to spend (its, their) vacation in Scotland.

9. The Dining and Entertainment Planning Committee (is, are) made up of seven members; (it, they) will make new recommendations next week.

10. When I last saw the baseball team, (it, they) (was, were) taking batting practice.

PRONOUN REFERENCE

If the pronoun's antecedent (the noun or pronoun it replaces) is vague or ambiguous—or missing altogether—readers will have a difficult time understanding your meaning. Indeed, they may see two or more possible meanings in a particular sentence. The following sections will help you avoid unclear pronoun reference.

14f Pronouns without Appropriate Antecedents

A pronoun must have an antecedent, and the antecedent must be an appropriate noun or pronoun, not another word that merely seems like an antecedent.

1. **Don't use an inappropriate noun or an entire clause as an antecedent.**

AMBIGUOUS	Caleb loved the idea of farming, but he had never been on one.

   What does *one* refer to? Obviously, the writer means to link *one* to *farm*, but the word *farm* is not in the sentence—*farming* is.

REVISED	Caleb loved the idea of farming, but he had never been on a farm.

   In the revised version, the noun *farm* replaces the ambiguous pronoun *one*.

AMBIGUOUS	The moving truck collided with an SUV, which left debris all over my front lawn.
REVISED	The collision of the moving truck with the SUV left debris all over my front lawn.

   In this example, the pronoun *which* has no noun to which it can logically refer. In the revision, the sentence is recast to eliminate the pronoun altogether.

2. **Don't use an adjective or a possessive as an antecedent.**

INCORRECT	Ever since being introduced to Japanese art, Jeff has wanted to visit it.
CORRECT	Ever since being introduced to Japanese art, Jeff has wanted to visit Japan.
INCORRECT	Decades after Terry Fox's death, the country is still creating memorials to him.
CORRECT	Decades after Terry Fox's death, the country is still creating memorials to this brave young man.

   In the latter example, the writer is trying to link *him* to *Fox*. However, *Fox* is not in the sentence; *Fox's* is, and it is possessive. Technically, then, *him* has no antecedent. This is a fine point, but revision is your best option.

3. **Make sure that the pronoun *it* has an antecedent.** You would be absolutely correct if you wrote this sentence:

   Daphne wants to buy my old car, but she can't afford it.

   Here there is an obvious link between *it* and *car*. Also, you would be correct if you used *it* to refer to the weather:

   It has been raining all day.

However, when you begin a sentence with *it,* you run the risk of failing to include an antecedent, thereby leaving out important information. Here is an example:

| AMBIGUOUS | It is generally believed that the Sumerians developed cuneiform writing. |

In reading such a sentence, the reader might ask "Who believes this?"

| REVISED | Historians generally believe that the Sumerians developed cuneiform writing. |

Writers can also cause ambiguity by using *it* to mean different things in the same sentence:

| AMBIGUOUS | It was raining that afternoon, and it was clear that the party would need to be moved inside or it would have to be rescheduled. |
| REVISED | Rain was falling that afternoon, and I realized that the party would need to be moved inside or be rescheduled. |

In the revised sentence, *it* has been eliminated.

Don't get the impression that you should avoid *it* altogether; just avoid conflicting uses of this word. Note the following sentence:

This is my laptop; I bought it a year ago, and it is worth the high price I paid for it.

The word *it* occurs three times in this sentence, but all three instances clearly refer to the laptop computer, so the sentence is not ambiguous.

4. **Don't skip the antecedent altogether.**

INCORRECT	During the musical *A Chorus Line,* they tell their own stories.
CORRECT	During the musical *A Chorus Line,* the dancers tell their own stories.
INCORRECT	In the latest issue of *Maclean's,* it said the election would be close.
CORRECT	In the latest issue of *Maclean's,* a reporter said the election would be close.
CORRECT	The latest issue of *Maclean's* reported that the election would be close.

5. **Avoid using the pronoun *you* when you mean a more general word, such as *one, anyone,* or *someone.*** Using the pronoun *you* is appropriate only if you are addressing the reader directly:

We ask that you remit your payment of $150 by December 20.

However, when you really mean the more impersonal *one* or an equivalent pronoun, *you* is inappropriate:

| INCORRECT | As you enter the execution chamber, you notice that everything is white and sterile. |

In the sentence above, the writer presupposes that the reader will actually visit an execution chamber.

CORRECT   As an observer enters the execution chamber, he or she notices that everything is white and sterile.

EXERCISE 14.5

In each of the following sentences, decide if the highlighted pronouns have appropriate antecedents. If they do not, revise the sentence to eliminate the problem.

1. Jeremy hadn't heard from home lately; he wondered if **he** should call **them.**

2. When **you** have a baby, **you** soon realize that **your** life is no longer **your** own.

3. He dreamed of studying at Oxford University, **which** was about to come true.

4. It occurred to Emma that it was possible for **it** to rain that afternoon.

5. **They** said on the radio that school was cancelled.

14g Pronouns with Unclear Antecedents

Follow these suggestions to make sure that pronouns refer clearly to their antecedents:

1. **Make sure that the pronoun has only one possible antecedent.** Sometimes, a writer asks the reader to connect a pronoun to its antecedent when more than one possible antecedent exists. The writer's meaning then becomes unclear:

AMBIGUOUS   When **Larry and Gus** went fishing, **he** took a lantern.

Who? Larry or Gus? Consider this revision:

REVISED   **Gus** took a lantern when **he** went fishing with Larry.

Most writers who have trouble with pronouns tend to use them too often. When in doubt, repeat the noun or revise the sentence so that the pronoun clearly links to its antecedent.

Connectors such as *as well as, along with, in addition to,* and *plus* can cause problems:

AMBIGUOUS   **Peter, as well as Michael,** believes in high ethical standards; **he** says that his business ethics class taught him a great deal.

After the semicolon, *he* seems to indicate Peter, but the reader can't be sure. Here are two possible revisions:

REVISED   Peter and Michael believe in high ethical standards; Peter says that his business ethics class taught him a great deal.

REVISED   Peter and Michael believe in high ethical standards; they say that their business ethics class taught them a great deal.

A related problem involves careless use of *which, this,* and *that.* Note the following ambiguous sentence:

AMBIGUOUS   I spent the afternoon waxing the car and buffing it, **which** is difficult.

Is buffing difficult? Or waxing? Or, as seems more likely, is the combined task difficult? Here is a possible revision:

REVISED   I spent the afternoon waxing and buffing the car, which is a difficult process.

As is so often the case with ambiguous pronouns, the writer was initially not using *enough* words to get his or her meaning across.

A similar problem occurs when the writer asks *which, this,* or *that* to carry too much weight. Note the following:

The guest speaker could not keep still. She walked back and forth constantly, and her hands flew around like deformed birds. She also laughed suddenly and inappropriately at several points. This drove me crazy.

"This" what? The laughter or the entire experience? The writer probably means the latter, so the final sentence of the passage should be clarified:

This bizarre performance drove me crazy.

2. **Don't start a paragraph with a pronoun.** The beginning of a paragraph is an ideal place to establish or re-establish an antecedent. If you use a pronoun to start a paragraph, you are asking too much of your reader, who must think back to the previous paragraph and "retrieve" the antecedent.

3. **Remember that pronouns aren't your only choice.** Use articles—*a, an,* and especially *the*—instead. Rather than using the indefinite *someone,* use (if possible) *people.* This way, you can avoid ambiguity while also avoiding the use of *he or she,* or *his or her.*

WITH PRONOUN   No one wants to be frustrated when his or her car overheats in traffic.

WITH ARTICLE   No one wants to be frustrated when the car overheats in traffic.

WITH INDEFINITE   Everyone should be concerned about this threat to
PRONOUN   his or her health.

WITH *PEOPLE*   People should be concerned about this threat to their health.

EXERCISE 14.6

In the following sentences, determine whether the highlighted pronoun is ambiguous. If so, revise the sentence to eliminate the ambiguity. You may be able to use more than one revision method.

1. Eddie told John that **he** was fifth in the batting order.

2. The door was open, and the light was broken; **this** worried me.

3. The bedroom has an aquarium and a small filter, **which** I plan to replace.

4. Our manager, Ms. Dempsey, seems to think we're running late, although she hasn't actually said **that.**

5. Ellie and Lawrence were very pleased when **they** finally bought a house.

EXERCISE 14.7

The following passage is filled with ambiguous pronouns. Revise each sentence as needed.

Some teams in the local softball league have started to have problems with couples on the teams. They are untrustworthy. A problem that couples are having can cause one or both of them to miss an important game or practice. This makes it hard on the rest of the team; they have to pick up the slack. It is hard to play a schedule when it depends on each team holding together.

For example, take the case of Jim and Laura. She is normally reliable, but he is not. His boss frequently makes him stay late at work, finishing some project, or he gets exhausted, which causes him to miss practices and games. He also has an anger-management problem. This is not a pretty sight to behold.

He does his best, and she helps him. That's good. Otherwise, our team members would have more frustrations than triumphs, and they would be without a solution. For they're our two best players. One night when it was raining, it was clear that we would lose a weather-shortened game unless Jim got on it and made it to the game. This he did. He hit two home runs in the fourth and fifth innings, and they made the difference.

14h Shifts of Person

PERSONAL PRONOUNS		
First Person	**Second Person**	**Third Person**
I	you	she
me	your	her
my	yours	hers
mine		he
we		him
us		his
our		it
ours		its
		they
		them
		their
		theirs

Personal pronouns can be first person, second person, or third person, as the example indicates. To use pronouns appropriately and consistently, follow these guidelines:

1. **Use *I* to refer to yourself within an essay only if the essay is informal enough.** For formal academic essays, avoid the use of "I" sentences as they are wordy and too casual.

2. **Use *we* to refer to you and your audience when you share values or experiences:**

CORRECT	As Canadians, **we** share a long history.
CORRECT	At the end of *The Handmaid's Tale,* **we** realize the mixture of desolation and faint hope that Atwood has developed.

3. **Use *you* sparingly, only when referring to the reader directly** (as in an instructional process analysis):

CORRECT	After **you** have tightened the lugs, check the edges of the seal.

   Do not use *you* to mean "a person" or "someone":

INCORRECT	When you shoot heroin, you are taking a great risk.
CORRECT	When **a person** shoots heroin, **he or she** is taking a great risk.
CORRECT	When **people** shoot heroin, **they** are taking a great risk.

4. **Use the third-person pronouns to refer to people, places, things, and ideas:**

CORRECT	**People** who follow a strict exercise regimen may become bored; such a program can seem like a prison to **them**.

To avoid inappropriate shifts when you are using personal pronouns, follow the above guidelines. You also need to understand how to use indefinite pronouns (see 23d). The following sentence incorrectly shifts from second to third person. It also has problems with pronoun–antecedent agreement:

INCORRECT	When a person sees a student standing outside a locked faculty office at 5:15 p.m. with a blank look on their face, you know that they are seriously adrift.
CORRECT	A **student** standing outside a locked faculty office at 5:15 p.m. with a blank look on **his or her** face is seriously adrift.
CORRECT	**Students** standing outside a locked faculty office at 5:15 p.m. with blank looks on **their** faces are seriously adrift.

To avoid shifts in person, use the word *you* carefully; and whenever possible, don't refer to *a person, a student, a swimmer,* and so on, when you can use *persons, students,* or *swimmers* instead. You will then automatically avoid this common—and serious—pronoun problem in your writing.

Revise the following paragraph so that it uses pronouns appropriately and avoids shifts in person.

> When a student first attends college or university, no matter how much advice you have received and preparation you have endured, you will be surprised. The student may find that their roommate is new, as the expected roommate has found another place for their domicile. Your classroom may have changed, or you might locate the right classroom but notice that the instructor is not who they're supposed to be. My current roommate is on the men's golf team, and he told me that at the start of this year's practice season, each golfer learned that their coach had suddenly resigned. If you ask me, all of this seems to be part of a vast plan to prepare you for the uncertainties of your adult life.

PRONOUN CASE

Consider this sentence: "He gave she a present for they anniversary." Something is obviously wrong. *He* is correct, but *she* should be *her*, and *they* should be *their*: "He gave her a present for their anniversary." This example illustrates the concept of **pronoun case:** pronouns have different spellings according to their function in a sentence. In the correct version, *He* is in the **subjective case,** functioning as a subject; *her* is in the **objective case,** functioning as an object; and *their* is in the **possessive case,** indicating ownership. (Note that objective-case pronouns can be direct objects, indirect objects, and objects of prepositions.)

14i Subjective, Objective, and Possessive Cases

PRONOUN CASES		
Subjective	**Objective**	**Possessive**
I	me	my, mine
you	you	your, yours
she	her	her, hers
he	him	his
we	us	our, ours
they	them	their, theirs
it	it	its
who	whom	whose
whoever	whomever	

Remember to use the correct pronoun case when you write. Avoid careless sentences such as this one:

INCORRECT	Philip came over to **Rose and I,** asking if we had a copy of the assignment.
CORRECT	Philip came over to **Rose and me,** asking if we had a copy of the assignment.

The correct form is *Rose and me* because *me* is the object of the preposition *to*. If you take out *Rose and*, the first sentence sounds absurd. You would never write *Philip came over to I.* Here are a few more examples:

o.c.   s.c.   o.c.

Karen asked **me** if **I** would email **her** the meeting's agenda.

                   s.c.   o.c.

Theresa and Ron are my closest friends; **I** have the utmost respect for **them**.

s.c.   o.c.

We had a bad scare last night; a police officer almost arrested **us** in a case of mistaken identity.

     o.c.   s.c.

To **whom** is the letter addressed? **Who** is involved here?

s.c.   o.c.

We Canadians are a diverse group, but to **us** Canadians, certain issues cause little disagreement.

In the last example, the pronoun is the same case as the noun that follows it. The sections that follow will help you avoid pronoun case errors.

14j Pronouns as Subject Complements

A personal pronoun connected to the subject by a linking verb—normally a form of *be*—is a subject complement and is in the subjective case:

          s.c.

Jack called; it was **he** who left the message yesterday afternoon.

             s.c.

The speaker has arrived; that is **she** over by the podium.

As you can see, following this rule can cause some stilted and strange constructions. Note how the second example sentence can be recast for a more natural sound:

The speaker has arrived; she is the woman over by the podium.

14k Pronouns in Comparisons

When writers use *as* or *than* to compare people or things, they frequently omit the verb in the second part of the comparison.

Kanye is taller than Mike [is].
Melissa is at least as talented as Khloe [is].

When the second part of the comparison uses a personal pronoun instead of a noun, the pronoun should be in the subjective case:

Kanye is taller than **I** [not me].
Khloe is very talented, and Melissa is at least as talented as **she** [not her].

Do these sentences sound awkward? Then "fill out" the comparison:

Kanye is taller than I am.
Melissa is at least as talented as she is.

14I Pronouns as Subjects of Clauses

When an entire clause is the object of a sentence, the subject of the clause is still in the subjective case:

I hope that Ron will do well as an intern at Mercy Hospital.

Note that *Ron* is the subject of the objective clause. If a personal pronoun is used to replace *Ron*, that pronoun must be in the subjective case:

I hope that **he** will do well as an intern at Mercy Hospital.

The pronoun is the subject of the subordinated clause even though the clause is an object; therefore, the pronoun (*he*) is in the subjective case.

Who and *whom* are troublesome pronouns. Note the difference between the following two sentences:

CORRECT   I must say that the person who is responsible for this mess won't have a job tomorrow morning.

CORRECT   Please find out to whom I should send this letter.

In the first sentence, *who* is the subject of the dependent clause (*who is responsible . . .*). In the second sentence, *whom* is the object of the preposition *to;* it is not the subject of the dependent clause.

EXERCISE 14.9

Choose the preferred pronoun form in the following sentences.

1. We realize that (we, us) members of the Widget Club must take our responsibilities seriously.

2. Kayden and Marianne are here; see if (he and she, him or her, they, them) want something to eat.

3. Lisa can run faster than (I, me).

4. With (who, whom) has the RCMP communicated about the recent kidnapping?

5. Alice is talented; I hope that (she, her) is given a promotion.

6. Elijah and (me, I) will be ready soon.

7. It is (I, me) who will be your guide.

8. To (who, whom) is the letter addressed?

9. (Whoever, Whomever) is responsible better start apologizing.

10. Roger has progressed more quickly than Amanda; he is at least as qualified as (she, her).

14m Reflexive and Intensive Pronouns

Reflexive pronouns show that a subject is taking action toward itself:

The beetle righted itself.

On the hike, Karen made a practice of checking herself for ticks.

The hockey players viewed themselves as the country's finest.

The correct forms of these pronouns are *myself, yourself, herself, himself, itself, oneself, ourselves, yourselves,* and *themselves.* Do not use nonstandard forms such as *hisself, theirself, theirselves,* and *ourself.*

Also, don't use a reflexive pronoun when it is not needed:

INCORRECT	Jason and myself went to the psychic fair.
CORRECT	Jason and I went to the psychic fair.
INCORRECT	The gift is for Bob and yourself.
CORRECT	The gift is for you and Bob.

When reflexive pronouns are needed, they're absolutely essential; when they're not needed, their inclusion is incorrect.

Intensive pronouns are spelled the same way as reflexive pronouns but have a different purpose—they are used to emphasize a point:

I checked that report myself.

Jay himself admits that the process has flaws.

EXERCISE 14.10

In the following sentences, correct any misuse of reflexive or intensive pronouns. Some sentences may be correct.

1. The four-course Italian dinner was prepared by Carl and myself.

2. David Adjey hisself couldn't have done any better.

3. You should check out the gourmet cooking yourself.

4. Carl and I couldn't always agree between ourself about certain parts of the recipe.

5. Carl prides himself on his cold antipasto, eggplant Siciliano, and baked ziti.

EXERCISE 14.11

Identify the errors in pronoun use in the following paragraph. Then, rewrite the paragraph to correct the errors.

It is certain that hepatitis is an inflammation of the liver. Anyone who gets this disease will know it, for they will become jaundiced, lose their appetites, and suffer a loss of energy and a fever. The disease comes in many types, but the most common forms are hepatitis A and hepatitis B. Either form is very dangerous; in fact, they can be fatal. You get hepatitis A from contaminated food and water, but they seem to be able to treat this type with some success. Hepatitis B, on the other hand, can be transmitted when surgical instruments are not adequately sterilized. This is why practising asepsis is crucial in a hospital and why they work so hard to maintain a sterile environment in operating rooms. Many people have also contracted hepatitis B when receiving transfusions of tainted blood, which is how my cousin Rudy got it. It was him who nearly died in the automobile accident that made the front page of the local paper three years ago. When they brought him into the hospital emergency room, you could see that he had lost a lot of blood. Unfortunately, it was not known that the two pints they gave him were tainted. The donor had not been properly screened for hepatitis; they may have contracted the disease through drug or alcohol abuse.

CHAPTER 15

Problems with Modifiers

A modifier is a word or group of words that describe, evaluate, limit the meaning of, or provide more information about another word or group of words in a sentence. Generally speaking, modifiers can be classified as adjectives and adverbs, parts of speech discussed in 20c and 20h.

This chapter discusses various problems that you may have with modifiers: the logical use and placement of modifiers in sentences, the incorrect substitution of adjectives for adverbs, the use of comparative and superlative forms, the sequencing of adjectives, the question of split infinitives, and the proper use of articles.

15a Misplaced and Ambiguous Modifiers

You will confuse your reader if you place modifiers in the wrong position or if you place modifiers in an ambiguous position. The first situation creates a **misplaced modifier;** the modifier does not refer to what the writer intended:

MISPLACED	Bryce solved the problem, **a proven leader.**

What did the writer mean for *a proven leader* to do, modify *Bryce* or *the problem?* Obviously, the answer is *Bryce.* Note the revision:

REVISED	Bryce, **a proven leader,** solved the problem.
MISPLACED	A zoologist said that polar bears are the most effective predators **on television.**
REVISED	A zoologist said **on television** that polar bears are the most effective predators.

This problem occurs often with the modifiers *only* and *just.* Read the following two sentences:

MISPLACED	I **just** have five dollars.
REVISED	I have **just** five dollars.

The first version suggests that the only thing going on in the writer's life is his or her possession of five dollars, an absurd statement. The second version is correct; *just* modifies *five dollars.*

MISPLACED	Mathieu **only** worked in Labrador for five months.
REVISED	Mathieu worked in Labrador for **only** five months.

In the first version, *only* modifies *worked,* a structure that suggests that Mathieu did absolutely nothing else in Labrador; he didn't eat, breathe, or walk during those five months. In the second version, *only* relates clearly and directly to *five months.*

If a sentence contains the second type of error, an **ambiguous modifier**—also known as a **"squinting" modifier**—the reader must "squint" (look carefully) to determine what the writer intended, as the following example shows:

AMBIGUOUS	Friends who ride in car pools together **frequently** become angry with one another.

Here, *frequently* can refer to either *ride* or *become angry;* but which one did the writer intend? The sentence must be rewritten to make the meaning clear:

REVISED	Friends who ride in car pools together become angry with one another **frequently.**
REVISED	Friends who **frequently** ride in car pools together become angry with one another.

Misplaced and squinting modifiers sometimes occur at the beginning of a sentence:

INCORRECT   **Staggering on the sidewalk,** the police officer approached the drunkard outside the bar.

To fix the sentence, you can (1) place the modifier immediately before or after the word that the modifier refers to or (2) add a subject and verb to the modifier, turning it into a dependent clause:

CORRECT   The police officer approached the drunkard **staggering on the sidewalk** outside the bar.

CORRECT   **As the drunkard staggered on the sidewalk outside the bar,** the police officer approached him.

In the example above, the reader can assume that it is the drunkard who is staggering and not the police officer, even if the incorrect sentence seems to say otherwise. In some cases, though, placing a modifier incorrectly may make it impossible for the reader to understand the meaning of the sentence. In other words, both misplaced and ambiguous modifiers cloud meaning:

INCORRECT   Celeste found useful books and other resources in the town
AND UNCLEAR   library **that had been donated by a local corporation.**

Did the corporation donate the books and resources, or did it donate the entire library? To make the message clear, the sentence needs to be restructured:

CORRECT   In the town library, Celeste found useful books and other resources **that had been donated by a local corporation.**

CORRECT   In the town library, **which had been donated by a local corporation,** Celeste found useful books and other resources.

The following sentences contain misplaced and squinting modifiers. Correct the modifier errors.

1. I only have a week to write this paper.

2. Thrashing the water furiously, the angler hooked the trout.

3. Emile just bought a special gift for his wife, a coffee grinder.

4. The coach only said that she would consider our request.

5. Perdita claimed that she was very happy in the ladies' room.

6. Last Saturday, we went to a French restaurant and then walked home, a rare treat.

7. Spinning out of control, Ed watched in horror as the car slammed into the bridge.

8. They sat through a four-hour meeting and then went out for dinner with their boss, a true horror.

9. Perched on the stone gargoyle, we watched the young pigeons.

10. The old man opened the letter, weary and ailing.

15b Dangling Modifiers

A sentence has a **dangling modifier** when there is nothing in the sentence to which the modifier can refer:

INCORRECT   **After studying the problem,** it became clear that a lot of money would be needed.

The subject of the sentence is implied, but the reader needs more. Who studied the problem? To whom did it become clear that . . . ?

CORRECT   **After we studied the problem,** we realized that a lot of money would be needed.

When writers use the passive voice, as in the incorrect example above, a dangling modifier is sometimes the unintended result. Using the passive voice reverses the normal English sentence structure and removes an active subject: "The forward *scored* the goal" becomes "The goal *was scored* by the forward" or, more simply, "The goal *was scored*." (For more on passive voice, see Chapters 10 and 13.)

DANGLING   **Arresting the suspect,** handcuffs were placed on his wrists.
DANGLING   **Looking over the river,** the city's skyline could be seen.

Here's how to fix these dangling modifiers: first, change the passive to the active voice; second, make sure that the modifier refers to a *stated* subject, not an *implied* one:

CORRECT   **Arresting the suspect,** the police placed handcuffs on his wrists.
CORRECT   **Looking over the river,** we could see the city's skyline.

Dangling modifiers can also occur even if the sentence is in the active voice:

DANGLING   **Before any strenuous physical exercise,** a few warm-up activities are necessary.
CORRECT   People must do a few warm-up activities **before any strenuous physical exercise.**
DANGLING   **After years of abusing alcohol and drugs,** liver disease can develop.
CORRECT   **After years of abusing alcohol and drugs,** you can develop liver disease.
CORRECT   **Abusing alcohol and drugs for years** can result in liver disease.

EXERCISE 15.2

Each of the following sentences contains a dangling modifier. Rewrite each sentence, supplying a subject as needed.

1. Feeling bad about the interview, it became clear that more work was needed before the next job application.

2. After a long night, the rosy daybreak was greatly appreciated.

3. Drinking hot coffee, the cup slipped from my hand.

4. Running a small business and investing wisely, great wealth was amassed.

5. When growing older, priorities need to be reexamined.

15c Incorrect Substitution of Adjectives for Adverbs

1. Remember that adjectives describe or modify nouns and pronouns. Adverbs describe or modify verbs, adjectives, and other adverbs. **Don't use an adjective when when an adverb is called for:**

   INCORRECT ADJECTIVE   Xavier was **real** sorry for the trouble he caused last week.
   CORRECT ADVERB   Xavier was **really** sorry for the trouble he caused last week.

   In the example above, the adjective *sorry* should be modified by the adverb *really*, not the adjective *real*.

2. Note that **some adjective/adverb pairs have radically different spellings:**

Adjective	**Adverb**
few	less
good	well
many	much

3. **When *good* and *well* are used to describe one's personal health, well-being, and/or appearance, they have an idiomatic pattern:**

   He looks good. (appearance)
   I feel well. (health)
   She is finally well after her long recuperation. (health)

   Otherwise do not substitute the adjective *good* for the adverb *well:*

   INCORRECT   I played really **good** today.
   CORRECT   I played really **well** today.

4. **There are no such words as *firstly* and *secondly*;** the adjective forms, *first* and *second*, are always correct.

EXERCISE 15.3

Revise the following sentences to correct problems with adverbs and adjectives.

1. Iron conducts heat and electricity extremely good.

2. Firstly, Felix wanted to thank his supporters for their contributions and hard work.

3. André feels well about his chances of finding a better job.

4. On an extreme cold night, we decided to go out to the pond for one last game of ball hockey, comfortably in our thick coats.

5. The Canadian prisoners of war were not treated kind or humane by our World War II enemies. Canada suffered much casualties as a result.

15d Problems with Comparatives and Superlatives

Adjectives and adverbs come in positive (base), comparative, and superlative forms. **Comparatives** are used to compare two people, places, or things. **Superlatives** are used to compare three or more people, places, or things. Here are four guidelines for creating and using comparative and superlative forms:

1. **To create the comparative and superlative forms of adjectives, and of some adverbs of one or two syllables, the suffixes *-er* and *-est* are added:**

Positive	Comparative	Superlative
dark	darker	darkest
happy	happier	happiest
fast	faster	fastest

    However, note what happens with three-syllable adjective like the word *terrific*:

INCORRECT	terrific	terrificer	terrificest

2. *More* and *most* are used to create the comparative and superlative forms of adjectives of three or more syllables, and of most adverbs:

CORRECT	terrific	more terrific	most terrific

    Some adjectives of one or two syllables won't work with *-er* or *-est* suffixes either. For example, the word *common* follows the *more/most* pattern of larger adjectives: *more common, most common*.

3. **Don't combine both methods of creating comparatives and superlatives. If you can attach a suffix to an adjective (such as *dark* 1 *er*), don't also use *more* or *most*:**

INCORRECT	The cave seemed to be getting more darker.
CORRECT	The cave seemed to be getting darker.

4. **Irregular modifiers change their spellings or form in the comparative and superlative:**

Positive	Comparative	Superlative
bad/badly	worse	worst
good/well	better	best
little	less	least
many	more	most
much	more	most
some	more	most

If you are not sure which form to use in a comparison, say the word with an *-er* or *-est* ending. If it sounds strange, it's probably wrong. However, your best approach is to look up the word in a dictionary. If *-er* or *-est* suffixes are appropriate, they may be indicated somewhere in the dictionary entry.

In the following sentences, the highlighted words are used incorrectly. Revise to eliminate errors.

1. Thomas is obviously **badder** at baseball than Gabriel is.
2. The lecture on Egyptian art was the **more valuabler** of the two we attended.
3. Among this season's five snowfalls, the **later** was the **worse.**
4. Noemie cried **real loud** after she heard the news.
5. Of the two families, the Smythes are the **richest.**

15e Problems with Adjective Order

Cumulative adjectives are a group of adjectives that come before a noun; each successive adjective modifies the adjective(s) and noun that follow (*a dark brown shoe*). **Coordinate adjectives** modify the noun separately and are separated by commas (*expensive, beautiful shoes*). See Chapter 16 for more on punctuating groups of adjectives. Adjectives that precede a noun follow a traditional pattern:

Determiner: a, an, the, this, those, my, their, many, four

Evaluation: great, boring, beautiful, sad

Size: big, small, huge

Shape: circular, square, triangular

Age: old, new, ancient

Colour: red, yellow, amber

National or geographic origin: Canadian, British, German, African

Religion: Catholic, Jewish, Taoist

Material: steel, paper, silk

Noun acting as adjective: *garden* wall, *car* phone, *school* bus, *bird* house

In the large, square, glass case, the visitors saw a wonderful, old, Japanese silk kimono.

EXERCISE **15.5**

Rewrite the following sentences to correct problems with adjective order.

1. The rectangular large truck delivered a load of antique Italian beautiful furniture to Miriam's red-brick new home.

2. Henry II of England (1133–1189) gained vast French rich lands when he married Eleanor of Aquitaine in 1152.

3. Are radio high-frequency waves harmful to a person's health?

4. Katmandu, the capital of Nepal, sits 4500 feet above sea level in a fertile stunningly beautiful valley, which has a great deal of historical significance.

5. An honour centuries-old code binds the members of our organization together.

15f Problems with Split Infinitives

In most cases, avoid splitting an infinitive. An **infinitive** is a verbal made up of *to* plus the base form of the verb. An infinitive is "split" when an adverb is placed between the two parts of the infinitive:

> to boldly go
> to wildly dream
> to slowly realize
> to carefully consider

Splitting an infinitive used to be considered unacceptable. Today, however, most style experts recognize that certain sentences are less awkward with a split infinitive. Consider these two sentences:

> The thing Jan wants most is to quickly conclude this deal.
> The thing Jan wants most is to conclude quickly this deal.

The first sentence contains a split infinitive; however, this sentence works a lot better than the second one. Then again, you could write this sentence:

> The thing Jan wants most is to conclude this deal quickly.

By moving the adverb, *quickly,* away from the verb and after the object, *deal,* you can avoid both a split infinitive and awkwardness; moreover, the sentence is not ambiguous.

EXERCISE 15.6

Revise each sentence to eliminate the split infinitive. Reword as needed.

1. In this time-enhanced sequence, the caterpillar is going to slowly change into a butterfly.

2. After waiting for several hours, the parents decided to finally go home.

3. The directions tell us to carefully place the glass inside the wire holder.

4. The evidence led the detective to instantly decide that the perpetrator was known by the victim.

5. I don't think it's possible for a person to actually fall in love at first sight.

15g Problems with Articles

Articles modify nouns in much the same way that adjectives do. However, articles can pose very specific and serious modification problems, as the following guidelines indicate:

1. **When you are using a singular indefinite article (*a* or *an*), choose *a* when the next word starts with a consonant sound; choose *an* when the next word starts with a vowel sound:**

   a tire
   a unit
   a precise analogy
   an uncle
   an awful surprise

   Note that the *sound* at the beginning of the next word is key here—thus, *a unit* but *an uncle*.

2. **When you use a singular count noun, always precede it with an article:**

   a dog   the monster   an aviator   the mayor

   Note that either an indefinite article (*a, an, some, any*) or the definite article (*the*) can be used, depending on the context:

   A dog ran down the street.
   The dog that guards the warehouse ran down the street.
   Some dogs ran down the street.
   The Smiths' dogs ran down the street.

3. **When you use a noncount noun, do not precede it with an indefinite article. A** noncount noun denotes something that is normally not counted but is otherwise identified or measured:

   machinery (not a machinery)
   sugar (not a sugar)

However, note that the definite article can be used with noncount nouns in some contexts:

Ariane became interested in the design of machinery after she read a book about the machinery used to build dams.

4. **You can use *the* before any common noun, but in some contexts it is inappropriate.** Trouble occurs with nouns that represent general qualities or concepts. When a word such as *wisdom* or *age* is used in a general context—with no specific connection to another noun or concept—don't precede it with *the*.

CORRECT	This library contains the wisdom of the ages. (*Wisdom* is identified by the phrase *of the ages.*)
INCORRECT	The wisdom is a good quality to achieve. (*Wisdom* is a general concept.)
CORRECT	Wisdom is a good quality to achieve.
CORRECT	Coralie is at the age at which the world looks rosy. (*Age* is identified by the phrase *at which the world looks rosy.*)
INCORRECT	Martin is 50 years old but looks as if he were 35; he doesn't have to worry about the age. (*Age* is a general concept.)
CORRECT	Martin is 50 years old but looks as if he were 35; he doesn't have to worry about age.

5. **A proper noun will sometimes need a definite article, but usually not if the noun is a person's name, a place name, a day of the week, or a month of the year:**

Jim Carrey	Friday
Newfoundland	October

Exceptions: the United States, the St Lawrence River, the Toyota Matrix

The cases in which definite articles are used with names are infrequent and usually involve a sentence like this one:

Is he **the** Wayne Smith who held so many appointed positions in the eighties and nineties?

Indefinite articles can precede singular proper nouns in special contexts:

Ms. Walker, **a** Lisa Androz is on the phone.
We need to go to Future Shop; I believe there is **a** Future Shop on University Avenue.
Someone has double-parked **a** Ford Ranger outside the front door.

EXERCISE 15.7

A blank line precedes each noun or noun phrase in the following paragraph. Write *a, an, the, some,* or *X* (no article) for each situation. In some cases, more than one answer is possible.

Last _____ Saturday, _____ Jeremy had _____ dinner with _____ head of his _____ department at _____ work. After _____ appetizers and _____ soup, they enjoyed _____ main course of _____ Peking duck and _____ wild rice. _____ conversation was not about _____ work; instead, the occasion was meant to be _____ get-acquainted evening following _____ company's new policy. Indeed, _____ evening went well. When _____ Jeremy returned to _____ office on _____ Monday, he felt _____ inkling of _____ hope for his future with _____ company.

EXERCISE 15.8

Rewrite the following paragraphs to correct modifier problems.

Ever since the break-up of the Communist former state of Yugoslavia in the 1990s, most people have had hard time distinguishing the small various countries that emerged in the Balkan Peninsula. One of these, of course, is Serbia, which had been the larger of the many regions of the old Yugoslavia. It occupies the west and south. Containing beautiful mountains and rich in timber and agriculture, the capital city is a Belgrade. Serbia's official language is Serbo-Croatian. Writing in this language, it appears in Cyrillic, for the Serbs use the same alphabet used in Russia and in some other parts of the eastern Europe. Being members of the Eastern Orthodox Church, the majority of a Serbian population is Christian.

Neighbours to the Serbs, the language of Croatia is also Serbo-Croatian, but the Croats use the Latin alphabet. Being Roman Catholics, connections with the West seem stronger in Croatia than with the Serbs, where there is natural tendency to look toward Russia and the East. The second larger of the former many Yugoslavian regions, Croats make their home in the northwest. A region rich in coal, oil, and timber, it is also well-known for its Adriatic beautiful beach resorts because of which a tourist lucrative trade was once enjoyed. Tourism has significant decreased since the wars that near destroyed Croatia in the early 1990s.

Bosnia and Herzegovina is found in the central part of the old Yugoslavia, a joint province. Despite having rich mineral deposits, a poverty continues to plague it. With Sarajevo as its capital, Bosnians have been witnesses to great events in history. A most famous is the assassination of Austrian Archduke Francis Ferdinand in 1914 by a Serbian revolutionary who wanted to free the region from Austro-Hungarian control, a event that sparked the World War I. More recently, civil war that engulfed the country killed tens of thousands. Bosnian Serbs, supported by their neighbours in Serbia and Montenegro, fought a bloody conflicts with the Bosnian Muslim population minority, which ended after only international intervention that resulted in a multi-ethnic government.

CHAPTER 16

Punctuating Sentences with Commas

Much misinformation surrounds the use of the comma. Many students dread dealing with commas; however, in most cases, comma usage is logical and systematic. This chapter outlines the necessary use of the comma in these six main contexts:

- In certain compound sentences
- After introductory clauses, phrases, and words
- To distinguish nonessential elements
- In series
- Between coordinate adjectives
- By convention—in addresses and dates, for example

The last section of the chapter will list situations where commas are not necessary but are often used in error. After studying this chapter, you will have a rationale for placing each comma you use.

NECESSARY COMMAS

16a Commas with Independent Clauses

An easy way to connect two independent clauses and make a compound sentence is by using a comma plus one of the seven coordinating conjunctions (*for, and, nor, but, or, yet, so*—remember the mnemonic FANBOYS?).

When you combine two independent (main) clauses with a coordinating conjunction and a comma, the comma always comes *before* the conjunction:

The sun slid behind the mountain, **and** night was upon us.

Laura refused to study any longer, **for** she had already put in more than twelve hours.

We tried to start the car, **but** the battery was dead.

Ben didn't like the restaurant, **nor** did he like my cousin.

You can try my computer, **or** you can call customer support about yours.

I worked hard last week, **yet** I didn't get enough done.

The dog couldn't get anyone's attention, **so** he gave up and fell asleep.

Compound sentences can be questions or commands:

What did Alice say, **and** when did she say it?

Boot up the computer, **but** don't turn the printer on yet.

Here are some problem areas that you should keep in mind:

1. **Coordinating conjunctions are frequently used to connect two nouns or adjectives:**

   Eva and Victor

   poor but honest

   young or old

   Don't automatically put a comma before a coordinating conjunction; make sure that the conjunction links two independent clauses before using a comma.

2. **Watch out for sentences with compound predicates,** two or more verbs and their related words, joined by *and*:

   We raked the leaves and cut the grass.

   This sentence is not compound; it has only one subject, so no comma is needed before *and*. However, note what happens if we add the second subject:

   We raked the leaves, and John cut the grass.

   Look for two independent clauses, not just the suggestion of them.

3. **Remember that using the comma to join compound sentences works *only* with coordinating conjunctions.** In the following sentence, the writer has incorrectly assumed that *next*, a conjunctive adverb, can be used in place of a coordinating conjunction:

COMMA SPLICE	We talked for a while about the new assignment, next we made arrangements to meet again.
REVISED	We talked for a while about the new assignment; **next,** we made arrangements to meet again.

The revised sentence uses the correct punctuation pattern for a compound sentence joined by a conjunctive adverb/transitional expression: semicolon plus conjunctive adverb plus comma. (For more help in correcting comma splices, see Chapter 12.)

The following sentence is also incorrectly punctuated. Can you tell why?

INCORRECT	Claire opened the door, so Hugo could bring in the packages.

The sentence certainly *looks* correct (two apparently independent clauses connected by a comma and *so*). However, in the sentence above, the comma plus *so* can be replaced by the subordinating conjunction *so that*. (See the sentence connectors chart in 22b.) Often, when writers need to use *so that*, they drop the *that* and use *so* alone. The resulting sentence is *not* a compound sentence but a complex sentence—made up of the main clause *Claire opened the door* and the subordinate clause *so (that) Hugo could bring in the packages*—so no comma is needed:

CORRECT	Claire opened the door so Hugo could bring in the packages.

EXERCISE 16.1

Insert commas or delete commas as needed in the following sentences. Some sentences may be correct. Be prepared to explain your choices.

1. The mayor has not announced her bid for re-election yet many people believe that it's only a matter of time.

2. The new dessert is tasty, and low in fat.

3. Jesse, and his brother Kevin are going to university on full scholarships.

4. Roll up your sleeve, and get ready for a little discomfort.

5. I'm going to have to find a new Internet service provider for the one I use now is as slow as mud.

6. Neither Alice, nor Zandra knows how to drive.

7. Jarrod wasn't able to study last night so he's nervous about today's chemistry exam.

8. You need to drive to town, and get some bread and milk.

9. Owen worked two jobs so his daughter could go to college.

10. Did the defendant stay at home that night or was he instead at the scene of the crime?

16b Commas with Introductory Clauses, Phrases, and Words

A variety of clauses, phrases, and words can precede an independent clause. In almost all cases, put a comma after these introductory elements.

16b.1 Commas and Introductory Dependent Clauses

1. A dependent clause is an independent clause begun with a subordinating conjunction. Thus, *John learned to swim* is an independent clause, but *After John learned to swim* is a dependent clause. **When a dependent clause precedes an independent clause, use a comma to separate the two clauses:**

   Because the puppy had grown so quickly, we had to buy a new carrier.
   Even though Maria was ill, she attended her classes.
   When we swim, we get excellent exercise.

2. **When the dependent clause *follows* the main clause, a comma is normally not needed:**

   We had to buy a new carrier because the puppy had grown so quickly.
   Martha attended her classes even though she was ill.

3. **A dependent clause can also be *embedded* within a sentence, as in the following example:**

   The lecture lasted much longer than scheduled, but **because Michael had nothing else planned that day,** he stayed until the end.

   This sentence begins with an independent clause (*The lecture lasted much longer than scheduled*) and then uses a comma plus *but* to connect it to the second independent clause. However, a dependent clause (highlighted) is embedded after the coordinating conjunction *but,* so a comma separates the embedded dependent clause from the second independent clause (*he stayed until the end*).

EXERCISE 16.2

In the following sentences, insert commas or delete commas as needed. Some sentences may be correct. Be prepared to explain your choice.

1. When Brian Mulroney became prime minister after Kim Campbell he named Ramon John Hnatyshyn as Governor General.

2. My cat doesn't like going to the vet, because she is afraid of dogs.

3. Because the two sides couldn't agree the trial was postponed.

4. Michael naps, whenever he can.

5. The race lasted three hours and although they needed to be in Toronto by 5:00 they stayed to the end.

6. Andrea took this class so she could get a pay raise at work.

7. While John is a reader his brother Mike is obsessed with computers.

8. The neighbours argued among themselves, while our problems grew.

9. After you leave for town I'll start dinner.

10. Mayra emigrated from Hungary to Canada; after she found a job here she felt good about her choice.

16b.2 Commas and Introductory Phrases

1. **When a phrase precedes an independent clause, a comma is *usually* needed:**

    A lifelong non-smoker, Jean led the fight to make her company tobacco-free.
    Feeling good about the progress of his group project, Curtis took the night off.
    Loved by all, the comedian was box office magic.
    In the last years of his long reign, the king wondered who would succeed him.

2. **You may choose to omit a comma after a very short prepositional phrase if the absence of a comma does not interfere with communication:**

    During the afternoon we went to a number of stores.
    In 1999 people worried about computers crashing because of Y2K.
    For years Internet retailers have struggled with security issues.

    However, notice the need for commas in the following sentences:

    In 2004, 438 cases were filed at the city courthouse.
    For dinner, four choices are available.
    During class, work options were discussed.

    The best advice is to use a comma in borderline situations, especially if you see any chance that a comma's absence might impede the reader's understanding.

 EXERCISE 16.3

In the following sentences, insert commas as needed.

1. That year our company earned more money than it had in the previous four years put together.

2. After a long day at the office Linda turned off the computer.

3. Looked at realistically Gavin's conduct at the last meeting was abominable.

4. Next week or the week after I will have to prepare my tax returns.

5. For much too long Felicia has gotten away with bad behaviour.

16b.3 Commas and Introductory Words

1. **Simple adverbs, participles, conjunctive adverbs, and other transitional expressions that frequently precede the independent clause are almost always followed by a comma, with one exception: *then*.**

Cautiously, the burglar crept along the ledge and approached the open window.

Delighted, Sally thanked the crowd for the warm reception they gave her performance.

For example, consider the role of employment insurance.

However, your appeal has been denied.

Therefore, the contract was signed.

Then the lawyers went home.

2. **When transitional expressions appear inside a sentence rather than at the beginning, they require commas before and after (except for *then*):**

Your appeal, **however,** has been denied.

Consider, **for example,** the role of employment insurance.

The contract, **therefore,** was signed.

The lawyers **then** went home.

3. **Use a comma after words or phrases used to address the reader directly:**

Your honour, my client is innocent!

Peter, we have had enough of your nonsense.

In the following sentences, insert or delete commas as needed. Some sentences may be correct.

1. Thus the day ended.

2. Mr. Brooks your client is, nevertheless, implicated.

3. Lisa talked to the class for ten minutes; then it was Jack's turn.

4. On the other hand the new tax proposal does have some merit.

5. Occasionally an estate will auction off some beautiful antique jewelry.

16c Commas and Nonessential Elements

1. **Commas and essential modifiers:** Sentences can contain two types of modifiers. **Essential modifiers** (sometimes called **restrictive modifiers**) are, as their name suggests, necessary for understanding a sentence's meaning. **Commas are not used with essential (restrictive) modifiers:**

My sister Lucie and my sister Andrea are both coming to visit.

In this context, *Lucie* and *Andrea* are both essential modifiers answering this question: Which sister? Obviously, the writer has more than one.

Quentin Tarantino's film *Jackie Brown* represents a new maturity in the director's work.

Tarantino has directed more than one film; the title *Jackie Brown* answers this question: Which film are you writing about?

2. **Commas and nonessential modifiers:** Nonessential (nonrestrictive) modifiers are *not* necessary for understanding a sentence's meaning; instead, they offer extra, explanatory information. **Commas are used with nonessential (nonrestrictive) modifiers:**

   Ken's only brother, Chadwick, will soon become a father.

   Jeremy found his driver's licence, which he thought he had lost, under the couch.

   In both examples, the modifier is *not* essential—there is no "which one?" question to answer. In the first sentence, the writer refers to Ken's *only* brother; in the second, it is natural to assume that, like most of us, Jeremy has only one driver's licence.

3. Here is an easy way to decide whether an element is essential or nonessential: **If you can remove the word or words from the sentence without changing the sentence's meaning, you can be sure that those words are nonessential and need to be set off with commas.**

   Eric's wife, **Catherine,** is the executive of a tire company.

   Our current MP, **James Fallon,** is considering a run for prime minister.

   Halifax, **the largest city in Nova Scotia,** was once destroyed by an explosion.

   The highlighted elements in each of these sentences add information, but they do not identify the nouns that come before them. Eric has only one wife, we have only one current MP, and there is only one major city named Halifax.

4. **The presence or absence of commas can make a difference in the sentence's meaning.** Consider the following pair of sentences:

   My grandmother who lives in Newfoundland is coming for a visit.

   My grandmother, who lives in Newfoundland, is coming for a visit.

   In the first sentence, both of the writer's grandmothers are alive. The modifier *who lives in Newfoundland* serves to answer the question "which grandmother?" No commas are used. In the second sentence, the writer has only one surviving grandmother, so commas are placed around the useful—but not essential—information that she lives in Newfoundland.

5. In all of the nonessential modifier examples examined so far, *pairs* of commas set off the modifier because the sentence continues after the modifier is finished. If **the modifier is the final element in the sentence, however, only one comma is needed:**

   I'd like you to meet my grandmother, who has come all the way from Newfoundland.

   Liz, have you met my only brother, Chadwick?

6. In modifiers that describe people, as the previous examples show, *who* is the relative pronoun of choice, whether or not the modifier is essential. But note the difference within each of the following pairs:

   There is the car **that** I'm going to buy.

   There is my car, **which** is a Honda.

   The fish **that** the turtle caught was eaten quickly.

   The fish, **which** I caught this afternoon, is cooking on the stove.

When not referring to people or named animals (pets, celebrity beasts, famous racehorses), writers use *that* (without a comma) to indicate essential modifiers:

There is the car that I'm going to buy.

The modifier *that I'm going to buy* answers the question "Which car?"

Writers use *which* (preceded by a comma) to indicate nonessential information:

There is my car, which is a Honda.

The car has already been identified (*my* car), so the modifier offers only extra information.

In the following sentences, insert or delete commas as needed. Some sentences may be correct.

1. We travelled to Edmonton which is the capital of Alberta.
2. Douglas Coupland who is credited with popularizing the term "Generation X" lives in British Columbia.
3. I want you to meet my sister Louise, who coordinated this event.
4. Parker Enterprises is the company, that wanted to buy my uncle's firm.
5. Find me the armadillo that has the virus.
6. No, I mean Joe Morgan the local architect, not Joe Morgan the baseball analyst.
7. Practice and repetition, hallmarks of the serious athlete require dedication and grit.
8. Is he the one, who was recently arrested?
9. Jason told me that the answer was 44 which is incorrect.
10. Over there is my wife Erin.

16d Commas and Items in a Series

1. Words, phrases, and even clauses can appear in series—three or more words or word groups serving a similar purpose. **Use commas to separate items in a series:**

The barn was old, crooked, and weathered.
The energetic pup raced around the mailbox, ran through the door, and jumped into his owner's lap.
The cold weather lasted until May, the flowers bloomed later than usual, and the spring rains caused the creek to flood its banks.

The commas you see between the items above are necessary to separate one item from the next. But what about the last comma, the one that appears before *and* in the examples? Some writers—especially journalists—omit it, but in formal writing *using this final comma can help your reader.* Consider the following scenario: You are giving a dinner party and are preparing a list of names of couples and individuals to invite. After the list is completed, you give it to a friend, who will write invitations. The last part of your list reads as follows:

. . . Anne, Mark and Bob and Wanda

Your friend is confused: "Wait a minute. Who's who?"

You explain that Anne and Mark aren't a couple and will arrive separately. Bob and Wanda are a couple, however. They need just one invitation. Adding a comma before *and* would prevent this confusion:

. . . Anne, Mark, and Bob and Wanda

Remember, when your choice in punctuation is between giving your reader less "guidance" or more, give more—in this case, always use that last comma.

2. **When series items themselves contain commas, use semicolons instead of commas to separate those items** (see also 27b). Note the following example, which uses commas only:

CONFUSING   We had a wonderful dinner at the new restaurant: appetizers, including salad and bread, two entrées, veal and salmon, shared between us, and a fascinating dessert.

Readers have trouble with a sentence such as this one because they have to determine the role of each comma. Note the direction provided by semicolons used in place of the series commas:

REVISED   We had a wonderful dinner at the new restaurant: appetizers, including salad and bread; two entrées, veal and salmon, shared between us; and a fascinating dessert.

16e Commas with Coordinate Adjectives

1. **Coordinate adjectives:** Writers frequently use more than one adjective to modify a noun or pronoun. When each adjective is working alone to modify its noun or pronoun, the result is a set of coordinate adjectives. **Use commas to separate coordinate adjectives:**

The children brought home an old, brown, weary cat.
Yesterday's hero has become a bruised, battered, discouraged man.

How can you decide if the adjectives are coordinate—that is, each modifying the noun separately? Try inserting *and* before the last one. If the result is logical, the adjectives are coordinate and should be separated by commas:

an old, brown, weary cat
an old, brown, and weary cat

2. **Noncoordinate adjectives:** Noncoordinate (or cumulative) adjectives serve a different function. **Do not use commas with noncoordinate adjectives:**

the new antique store
my former insurance agent
her ragged, old softball glove

Try the test we used for coordinate adjectives:

the new and antique store

The result is nonsensical. Clearly, *new* modifies *antique store*, not just *store*. The same applies to the second example. However, the third example has both coordinate adjectives and a noncoordinate adjective:

her ragged and old softball glove

Old and *ragged* are coordinate adjectives, but *softball* is not.

In the following sentences, insert or delete commas as needed. Some sentences may be correct. Be prepared to explain your choices.

1. The steep winding road rose through the mountains fell through the valleys and levelled off in the plains.

2. Working hard playing hard and sleeping light are the three methods I use to deal with life.

3. A modern, high school should be well administered.

4. When I'm hungry, I dream about a warm, flavourful hot dog.

5. The results were poor, disappointing and infuriating, leading Mr. Perkins to re-evaluate the contractor's efforts.

16f Commas with Other Expressions

Sentences may contain other words or expressions that need to be set off by commas. Some expressions, such as *by the way*, briefly interrupt a sentence's main idea: *Shannon, by the way, has decided not to go to the movie tonight.* Other expressions name a person directly or add information. Transitions, such as *for example* and *on the other hand*, help connect one idea to another. With the exception of a few transitions, such as the word *then*, the following kinds of expressions should be separated from the rest of the sentence by commas:

1. **"Not" phrases:**

   Sheila asked the waiter for ham, not hamburger.
   A need for less stress, not more money, led Walter to seek a new career.

2. **"Echo" questions:**

   Clare won't be able to attend graduation, will she?

3. **Interjections:**

   Oh, what a wonderful idea!

16g Commas and Conventional Uses

16g.1 Dates

If a full date is given, two commas are needed, one after the numerical day of the month and one after the year. However, if the numerical day is not present, no commas are used:

> January 15, 2010, is today's date.
> January 2010 is the current month.

Note that no comma is used when the day comes first: 15 January 2010.

16g.2 Addresses

When city and province appear together, each is followed by a comma:

> Calgary, Alberta, is where I live right now.
> Tillsonburg, Ontario, is his place of birth.

Placing the comma after the name of the province is seen by many to be old-fashioned; however, this comma is still necessary in today's usage.

16g.3 Dialogue

Reported speech is preceded or followed by a comma, according to context:

> Jeffrey exclaimed, "Marcy, you look heavenly this evening."
> "Thanks, Jeffie. It's just an old outfit," Marcy countered.

However, apart from dialogue, other quoted material may not need to be set off with a comma or commas:

> The words "Bye, bye, Miss American Pie" have a nostalgic ring for people who grew up in the early 1970s.

In situations such as this one, the need for commas depends on whether the words in quotation marks are essential or nonessential to the meaning of the sentence (see section 16c).

16g.4 Salutations and Complimentary Closes

In personal letters, the salutation is traditionally followed by a comma, as is the complimentary close:

> Dear Aunt Lisa,
> Sincerely yours,

In business letters, the complimentary close is followed by a comma, but the salutation is followed by a colon:

> Dear Professor Walker:
> Sincerely,

In the following sentences, insert commas or delete commas as needed. Some sentences may be correct.

1. June 15, 2014, will be his fiftieth birthday.

2. Wanda moved from Yellowknife Northwest Territories to Whitehorse Yukon.

3. It was a dislike of people not a fear of crowds that kept her indoors most of the time.

4. Oh I guess this will be acceptable Leo.

5. October 2012 is the target date.

UNNECESSARY COMMAS

Read the following pair of sentences, both of which are correct:

> As I recall, Marcy, although tiny, devoured the plate of nachos, which was immense.
> The dog stretched its rangy legs and ran down the hill just as I realized that she was coming to attack me and my family while we sat contentedly beside a quiet brook that ran through a stand of ancient pine.

The first sentence has 14 words and four commas; the second sentence has 41 words and no commas.

The need for commas is not determined by sentence length, the "need for a pause," or a desire to provide a dramatic effect. The following examples explain when *not* to use commas:

1. **Never use a comma to separate the subject from the verb unless another rule causes you to do so:**

   INCORRECT   Walking through the woods, is my favourite type of exercise.

   Although sentence subjects are usually nouns or pronouns, they can be phrases as well:

   CORRECT   Walking through the woods is my favourite type of exercise.

   This problem frequently occurs when the subject is a noun or pronoun followed by several modifiers. In such cases, writers often think that a "grammatical pause" is appropriate, but it isn't:

   INCORRECT   The boy who grew up in a rustic cabin in the middle of the wilderness, eventually became CEO of CanWest Global Communications.

   CORRECT   The boy who grew up in a rustic cabin in the middle of the wilderness eventually became CEO of CanWest Global Communications.

As mentioned, however, a comma may be required by another rule. For example, a nonessential modifier may follow the sentence's subject:

REVISED   Walking through the woods, an activity I recently started, is my favourite type of exercise.

The intervening nonessential modifier should be set off with a pair of commas. (See section 16c.)

2. **Connect two items with a comma and a coordinating conjunction *only* when you are joining two independent clauses to form a compound sentence:**

INCORRECT   Leanne showed Rafael the proposal, and asked for his opinion.

CORRECT   Leanne showed Rafael the proposal and asked for his opinion.

CORRECT   Leanne showed Rafael the proposal, and she asked for his opinion.

3. **When joining two independent clauses to form a compound sentence, place a comma before, not after, the coordinating conjunction:**

INCORRECT   Larry ate lunch that day in the cafeteria and, Heather decided to join him.

CORRECT   Larry ate lunch that day in the cafeteria, and Heather decided to join him.

An exception occurs when a nonessential modifier follows the coordinating conjunction:

CORRECT   Larry ate lunch that day in the cafeteria, and, proving that miracles still occur, Heather decided to join him.

4. **In most cases, do not place a comma before a subordinate conjunction that comes after an independent clause:**

INCORRECT   Jeremy was excited about going to the play, because his best friend had the lead role.

CORRECT   Jeremy was excited about going to the play because his best friend had the lead role.

If the subordinate clause is not essential to the meaning of the sentence, though, set it off with a comma. (See section 16c.)

CORRECT   Jeremy enjoyed the play, even though he had seen it before.

5. **Do not use commas to set off essential elements** (see also section 16c):

INCORRECT   He is the man, who received last year's Outstanding Community Service award.

CORRECT   He is the man who received last year's Outstanding Community Service award.

6. **Do not place a comma between items in a series containing only two items joined by a coordinating conjunction:**

INCORRECT	John, and Mary have moved to Thompson.
CORRECT	John and Mary have moved to Thompson.
INCORRECT	Ed wasn't sure if he'd rather be eating, or sleeping.
CORRECT	Ed wasn't sure if he'd rather be eating or sleeping.

7. **In a series of three or more items, make sure that you place the series comma *before* the coordinating conjunction, not *after* it:**

INCORRECT	Your choices are coffee, espresso or, cappuccino.
CORRECT	Your choices are coffee, espresso, or cappuccino.

An exception occurs when another rule comes into play:

CORRECT	To get there, you may fly, drive, or, if you'd like, walk.

In this example, the nonessential element *if you'd like* needs to be set off by a pair of commas.

Do not put a comma after a series unless another rule requires you to do so:

INCORRECT	Many architects admire the CN Tower, the Fairmont Banff Springs Hotel, and the Royal Canadian Mint, as examples of impressive design.
CORRECT	Many architects admire the CN Tower, the Fairmont Banff Springs Hotel, and the Royal Canadian Mint as examples of impressive design.

8. **Do not place a comma after *like, as,* or *such as:***

INCORRECT	Jason prefers old-style heavy metal bands like, Metallica.
CORRECT	Jason prefers old-style heavy metal bands, like Metallica.
INCORRECT	Small children are likely to engage in such activities as, public displays of emotion.
CORRECT	Small children are likely to engage in such activities as public displays of emotion.
INCORRECT	Vera enjoys visiting Latin American countries such as, Brazil and Argentina.
CORRECT	Vera enjoys visiting Latin American countries, such as Brazil and Argentina.

9. **Do not place a comma next to a dash or a question mark.** Sometimes, rules of punctuation can come into conflict with each other, as in the following sentence:

INCORRECT	Mark, who has trouble getting up in the morning, took a second-shift job,—a very bad move,—and then he compounded the error by registering for early-morning classes.

Dashes always *replace* other marks of punctuation (see also Chapter 17e):

CORRECT	Mark, who has trouble getting up in the morning, took a second-shift job—a very bad move—and then he compounded the error by registering for early-morning classes.

Question marks sometimes need to appear within a sentence, but they should never be followed by commas:

INCORRECT	Guillen's latest novel, *Where to Next?*, is a humourous account of two slackers on the run.
IMPROVED	*Where to Next?* is Guillen's latest novel, a humourous account of two slackers on the run.

Note that in the improved sentence, the words have been reordered.

10. **In a set of coordinate adjectives, do not place a comma after the last adjective:**

INCORRECT	The only item left in the abandoned playground was an old, damaged, swing set.
CORRECT	The only item left in the abandoned playground was an old, damaged swing set.

11. **Do not use commas in large numerals.** In Canada, officially, the International System (SI) of numbers is used. Spaces, not commas, are used to mark off long numbers, by groups of three numerals beginning at the right.

INCORRECT	1,000,000
CORRECT	1 000 000

Although many people still prefer to use the comma in this situation, and you will see it in U.S. research materials, you should not use the comma in numbers in formal academic writing. An exception is calendar years: 2001, 1992.

EXERCISE 16.8

Some of the commas in the following sentences are unnecessary. Delete these commas, but retain those that are used correctly. Be prepared to state the rule that explains each comma you have retained.

1. Cooking a huge supper for her mammoth family, was a chore that Ms. Van Meter had come to dread.

2. Voting, or not voting is a choice that we, as citizens, have to face.

3. She walked all the way downtown, and stopped at Cloisonné, her favourite shop.

4. The legislature should pass this measure, because the people's long-term well-being will be improved, if it is passed.

5. Tall, dark, and handsome, the hero of the movie we saw last night, was a virtual cliché.

6. All I had to eat today was an old, bruised, apple.

7. The new breakfast spot has coffees from many countries, such as, Kenya, Colombia, and Ecuador.

8. Knowing the consequences of failure, can put a student under tremendous stress.

9. The singer's first number,—absolutely guaranteed to please the audience,—was his first hit, from way back in 1965.

10. This was the moment, that Constance had been waiting for.

 EXERCISE 16.9

Add or delete commas as necessary in the following two paragraphs. You must have a reason for every change that you make.

1. Although China is an ancient country it has few great buildings that date to a time before the Ming Dynasty which ruled the country from the fourteenth to the seventeenth centuries. Of course the most obvious exception is the Great Wall of China. Originally built to keep out northern invaders like the Mongols, and the Manchus the Wall stretches for 1500 miles from the Yellow River to the Province of Gansu. Because it is so large no one person or royal dynasty can claim to have built it. It is instead a stringing together of many walls some of which date back to the third century BCE. In its present state the Wall has existed about 700 years. Unfortunately it never lived up to its purpose for in the fourteenth century the Mongols did successfully invade China making it the centre of their empire which stretched as far as eastern Europe. In the seventeenth century the Manchus also invaded China and they established a dynasty that lasted until 1912.

2. The United Nations, and the League of Nations have much in common. Among the most prominent similarities, that the U.N. shares with the now defunct League, is a mission to maintain world peace. The League was founded shortly after World War I which lasted from 1914 to 1918. Because "the Great War" as it was then called was the most destructive war in history many world leaders decided to create an organization, that would make World War I, "the war to end all wars." At the outset the League was conceived of by many leaders including those from Canada Great Britain Italy and France whose countries had been victorious.

CHAPTER 17

Punctuating Sentences with Other Punctuation Marks

You learned in Chapter 16 how to use the comma to help you arrange words in a sentence so that your readers will process your message quickly, efficiently, and accurately. Effective use of the other marks of punctuation also contributes to this objective. Learning how to use all of the different punctuation marks is essential to controlling sentence structure and communicating clearly.

17a Periods (.)

Periods are used to end sentences and to indicate abbreviations, initials, and decimals.

1. **Use a period to signal the end of a sentence.** The major function of the period is to end a complete declarative or imperative sentence:

DECLARATIVE	Winnipeg, Manitoba, is the birthplace of Terry Fox.
IMPERATIVE	Look for the gas station on the left side of the road.

2. **Use a period to indicate an abbreviation.** Some terms are always shown in abbreviated format:

A.M. or a.m. (ante meridian)	C.E. (common era)
P.M. or p.m. (post meridian)	B.C.E. (before common era)
A.D. (anno Domini)	i.e. (id est—"that is")
B.C. (before Christ)	e.g. (exempli gratia—"for example")

   Most other commonly abbreviated terms should first be spelled out, with the abbreviation in parentheses following the full name—for example, *National Hockey League (NHL)*—and subsequently referred to by the abbreviation.

   Some abbreviations take periods; others do not. Usually, titles and college degrees are abbreviated with a period:

Dr. Martin	M.A.
Mr. Sanchez	M.B.A.
Ms. Ishigotu	M.S.
Mrs. Janowitz	Ed.D.
B.A.	B.Sc.
Ph.D.	LL.B.

   Abbreviations for addresses and geographical areas tend to use periods as well:

   21 Parker Rd., Saint John, New Brunswick

   1497 Summerlin Ave., Summerside, Prince Edward Island

   However, *USA* is the accepted abbreviation for *United States of America* while *U.S.* is the shorter form. Most writers use the abbreviations recommended by Canada Post when referring to provinces—for example, *ON* for *Ontario* and *BC* for *British Columbia.*

   You need to decide whether to add periods to abbreviations in the names of companies and organizations on a case-by-case basis. If you are unsure whether to use the period when abbreviating common terms, however, consult a dictionary. Above all, be consistent within each paper that you write.

3. **Use periods in initials.** When you refer to people by their initials, put a period after each initial, and insert a space after each period:

   E. L. Williamson   G. V. W. Vance IV

   Exception: If a company's name is based on the initials of its founder, follow the company's chosen style—for example, JC Penney or E. F. Hutton.

4. **Use periods in decimals.** The period is also used to indicate decimals in mixed numbers:

   The inflation rate of 3.2 percent was very close to the previous year's rate.

A Semicolon Is NOT a Big Comma

Often students use the semicolon like some type of "super-comma" either trying to indicate a longer pause or more of a separation between ideas when they write. A semicolon (with the rare exception of separating items in a list that contain commas) is used to separate two complete sentences (or independent clauses). Whenever you use a semicolon, do this quick check: make sure a complete sentence comes *before* the semicolon and make sure a complete sentence comes *after* it. Of course, you also need to know what makes a complete sentence. See Chapter 11 for this information.

17b Semicolons (;)

Semicolons are used to separate independent (main) clauses in a sentence and to separate items in a series when those items contain commas.

1. **Use a semicolon to separate independent (main) clauses.** The following sentences both contain two independent clauses connected with a semicolon:

   Poland was once controlled by the Soviet Union; it is now an independent member of the world community.

   Jason's dentist was ill; consequently, Jason needed to change his appointment.

   When a semicolon is used in this way, it acts as an *internal period*. The semicolon has the same "weight" as a period, but it allows you to keep both clauses in the same sentence, a choice that is often very effective. For instance, in the second example, the second clause tells readers about something that happened because of the situation explained in the first clause. The two clauses are related: one states a cause, the other an effect.

   Because it can separate two independent clauses, a semicolon is one way to correct a comma splice or fused sentence:

COMMA SPLICE	My sister became seriously ill, therefore, I had to postpone my vacation.
FUSED SENTENCE	My sister became seriously ill therefore I had to postpone my vacation.
CORRECT	My sister became seriously ill; therefore, I had to postpone my vacation.

   A semicolon should never be used to separate a dependent clause from an independent clause, however.

   | INCORRECT | When I did get to take my vacation; I couldn't decide where to go. |
   | CORRECT | When I did get to take my vacation, I couldn't decide where to go. |

2. **Use a semicolon to separate items in a series when those items contain commas.** The following chapter contains items separated only by commas:

   | CONFUSING | Our trip to Italy included visits to several historic sites: the Colosseum, the Vatican, and the Spanish Steps in Rome, the ancient streets, taverns, and private homes of Pompeii, and the many temples, amphitheatres, and catacombs in Segesta, Agrigento, and Siracusa, Sicily. |

Readers have trouble processing a sentence such as this one because they have to determine the role of each comma. To make it easier to read the sentence, add a semicolon between each major entry or item:

CLEARER   Our trip to Italy included visits to several historic sites: the Colosseum, the Vatican, and the Spanish Steps in Rome; the ancient streets, taverns, and private homes of Pompeii; and the many temples, amphitheatres, and catacombs in Segesta, Agrigento, and Siracusa, Sicily.

EXERCISE 17.1

Insert periods or semicolons as appropriate in the following sentences. You may have to remove other marks of punctuation.

1. Quebec is an important province for example, it is the world's largest producer of maple syrup.

2. Amy isn't an MD, she's a Ph.D.

3. V J Harris planned on attending medical school, therefore, he took many biology and chemistry classes.

4. Béatrice wanted to explore the new lamp store that just opened on Stockholm Street however, it was closed.

5. We should work hard and save, we should also be kind to those who are less fortunate than we are.

6. The college has changed its policy on drop/add, now the period has been extended to four days.

7. Mr and Mrs Rogers didn't go to Ontario this summer, instead they went to New Brunswick.

8. Don't hold the shift key down just hit enter twice.

9. It's been very hot this summer, in fact, we had five days that set new temperature records.

10. Starting preschool is stressful for children for some, it is a very painful separation.

17c Question Marks (?) and Exclamation Marks (!)

Question Marks

Question marks are normally used to end direct questions:

How is it that the government can waste so much money?
Do you have time to put down two bucks on the Number 4 horse, Lefty?

However, question marks can also sometimes appear within sentences:

The salmon had returned to their river of birth (who knows how?) and proceeded upstream.

An error to watch for is the question mark used incorrectly to end an implied question:

INCORRECT	She asked if we'd be done by noon?
CORRECT	She asked if we'd be done by noon.

Another error is the question treated as a declarative sentence:

INCORRECT	What might have happened if Laura had stayed home that day.
CORRECT	What might have happened if Laura had stayed home that day?

Exclamation Marks

Exclamation marks are used to express strong emotion or to emphasize a point:

Put that gun down!
Then he had the nerve to ask for a raise!

Like question marks, exclamation marks usually end a sentence. In some instances, however, an exclamation mark can appear *within* the sentence, usually at the end of a sentence in parentheses or set off by dashes:

We saw *The Dark Knight* that night (what a film!) and saw *Iron Man* the next afternoon.

Use the exclamation mark judiciously. It is a very forceful mark of punctuation, and readers can become annoyed if they see it too often ("And the battle was over! The Orcs had finally lost!").

Question Marks and Exclamation Marks in Quotations

Exclamation marks and question marks can appear inside or outside of quotation marks, depending upon the sense of the sentence:

Jennifer asked, "Has the committee already met?"
Did Jennifer say, "The committee has already met"?

The first sentence is a statement about a question. The question mark relates only to the question, which appears in quotation marks. The second sentence is a question about a statement. Therefore, the question mark relates to the entire sentence, not just to the quotation.

The same logic applies when dealing with exclamation marks and quotation marks:

"Give me candy" declared the child, "or give me a new toy!"
I can't believe that Roxanne has voted to "abstain"!

You can find more about using quotation marks in section 17h.

EXERCISE 17.2

In the following sentences, add or delete periods, question marks, and exclamation marks where appropriate. Be prepared to explain your choices.

1. Walter asked if we needed any lunch?

2. Is the meeting in the morning or in the evening.

3. "Roger," she shouted, "you are an absolute idiot"

4. The boss has scheduled another meeting (will this madness never end) for Thursday.

5. A restaurant in Ottawa charges over $40 for a hamburger. People who eat there must have rocks in their heads.

17d Colons (:)

1. **Colons are used to introduce a list or an example and to show cause-and-effect relationships,** as in these sentences:

    Bring the following supplies to the first class: watercolours, bonded paper, and notebooks.

    Vijay is what our organization needs most: an excellent programmer.

    Mr. Thompson's constant nitpicking has had one very bad effect on our office: no one feels like doing any more than is strictly necessary.

    Notice that in each case, the colon means the same as *namely*. If you can substitute a comma plus *namely* for the colon, the colon is logical.

    Capitalizing the first word of a complete sentence following a colon is optional. Whether or not you choose to capitalize, be consistent throughout your document.

2. **Colons also appear in the salutations of business letters:**

    Dear Dr. Gonzalez:
    Dear Professor Muhlbock:

3. **The colon is sometimes useful in sentences that have too many commas:**

    CHOPPY   Albeit talented, Roger, one of my former classmates, is lacking in one area, persistence.

    SMOOTHER   Albeit talented, Roger, one of my former classmates, is lacking in one area: persistence.

    Notice, however, that you can still substitute a comma and [itals]namely[end itals] in this sentence and have it make sense.

4. Colons are useful, but remember to employ them only when they are needed. **Commas are *not* needed after introductory phrases like *such as, for instance,* and *for example:*

    INCORRECT   Woody Allen has directed many fine films, such as: *Annie Hall* and *The Purple Rose of Cairo.*

    CORRECT   Woody Allen has directed many fine films, such as *Annie Hall* and *The Purple Rose of Cairo.*

Note that this rule applies even when introducing block quotations (see Chapters 3 and 17).

Never insert a colon after a linking verb (*be, seem, feel, appear,* and so on):

INCORRECT	The only make of car he buys is: Toyota.
CORRECT	The only make of car he buys is Toyota.
CORRECT	He buys only one make of car: Toyota.

Never use more than one colon per sentence:

INCORRECT	Our History of Eastern Europe class began our trip by visiting Poland's two major cities: Warsaw and Krakow, and then we went on to the capitals of Hungary and the Czech Republic: Budapest and Prague.
CORRECT	Our History of Eastern Europe class began our trip by visiting Poland's two major cities: Warsaw and Krakow. Then we went on to the capitals of Hungary and the Czech Republic: Budapest and Prague.

17e Dashes (—)

Consider this sentence, which is swimming in commas:

> Browsing through the store, I stopped to listen to the cologne seller's pitch, a stupid choice on my part, and then, somewhat chastened, I headed through the accessories, women's, and home decorating departments.

Although this sentence is correctly punctuated, the reader can't tell which part of it should be emphasized. Adding a pair of dashes helps organize the ideas in the sentence:

> Browsing through the store, I stopped to listen to the cologne seller's pitch—a stupid choice on my part—and then, somewhat chastened, I headed through the accessories, women's, and home decorating departments.

The strongest statement here is *a stupid choice on my part.* Therefore, setting it off with dashes instead of commas makes its significance clear.

Dashes call attention to part of the sentence. They set off nonessential parts of a sentence, as commas do (see 26c), but they provide much more emphasis than commas. Moreover, as in the example above, they can tighten a sentence's focus.

Here are some guidelines for using dashes:

1. When you are producing a handwritten essay, **draw the dash as a continuous line approximately twice as long as a hyphen.** The dash should touch both words that surround it; don't add a space in front of or after it. When writing on a computer, use the solid dash (also known as an *em-dash*) if your software supplies it; if not, use two hyphens. In either case, do not insert spaces before or after the dash.

2. **Dashes take the place of other punctuation,** so a dash should never appear next to a comma, for example:

INCORRECT	The officer on the left,—the one wearing all the medals,—is Phil's brother.
CORRECT	The officer on the left—the one wearing all the medals—is Phil's brother.

3. **Dashes, like commas, are used in pairs to set off nonessential modifiers** unless the modifier comes at the end of the sentence:

John's funny speech—an abrupt departure from his previous tirade—caught the audience by surprise.

Our group made only $17.00 from Saturday's car wash—a major disappointment.

4. **Don't overuse dashes.** Too many dashes produce choppiness and lose their impact in the sentence:

| CHOPPY | Valerie's research paper on *anorexia nervosa*—the one that received an A+—was used as a model for writing in *Becoming Writers*—a booklet of exemplary student prose that has been published by the English department every semester since 1979. |
| SMOOTHER | Valerie's research paper on *anorexia nervosa*—the one that received an A+—was used as a model for writing in *Becoming Writers,* a booklet of exemplary student prose that has been published by the English department every semester since 1979. |

17f Parentheses ( )

Dashes emphasize information, but parentheses are much more subtle, or "quiet." **Parentheses are used to remind the reader of a fact or a name or to add an interesting comment.** Parentheses, like commas and dashes, are always used in pairs:

Logan works for ML Silicone (formerly known as ML Southeast).

We ate at the Happy Salmon Diner (as always, a bitter disappointment), and then we went to the movies.

Parentheses can replace commas that enclose nonessential elements, but other commas may still be needed, as in the second example sentence above. Without parentheses, this sentence would have been punctuated as follows:

We ate at the Happy Salmon Diner, as always, a bitter disappointment, and then we went to the movies.

When the commas before and after *as always, a bitter disappointment* are replaced with parentheses, the sentence still consists of two independent clauses joined by *and*, a coordinating conjunction. Therefore, a comma is still needed before *and*, as shown in the example above.

Whole sentences can appear in parentheses, as can independent clauses that the writer wants to embed within a sentence:

Susan's testimony seemed to clear Mark of any wrongdoing. (However, as we learned later in the day, Susan hadn't told all that she knew.)

Jason heroically offered to pay for the education of his two new stepchildren (but he worried about how he would manage to come up with the money).

If a complete sentence in parentheses appears within another sentence, you do not capitalize the first letter of its first word or end it with a period.

Finally, **you can use parentheses to enclose a short definition within a sentence:**

We installed an anemometer (a device to measure wind speed) on the roof.

17g Brackets ([ ])

Brackets have two uses. **The most common use of brackets is to insert an explanation, comment, or additional material in a quotation:**

> According to one report, "It [the Porsche Boxster] is the most interesting new European design in years."
>
> Two years ago, a news story claimed that "[Anna] Sadowski and [Samuel] Entremonte [were] the county's highest paid employees."

In the second example above, the writer has added the first names of the employees and changed the tense of the verb in the quotation from present to past in order to fit the context of the sentence.

You can also use brackets to indicate a problem within a quotation:

> According to Marshall, "When the great ice storm hit in 1995 [*sic*], the country was in turmoil."

The previous example has a factual error: the great ice storm actually occurred in 1998. Using *sic* (meaning "thus" or "so"—in other words, "don't blame me") shows that the writer recognizes the error. You can also use this device when quoting text that contains a misspelled word. (See Chapter 3 for examples.)

Another, less common use of brackets is to take the place of parentheses that are needed *inside* other parentheses:

> Magra South Ventures (a privately held automobile insurance organization [AIO]) is establishing a branch office near our area.

EXERCISE 17.3

The following sentences are punctuated with commas only. Reading the sentences as a continuous passage, insert colons, dashes, and parentheses as appropriate. Be prepared to defend your choices.

1. Our city's downtown section, a perennial topic of conversation, is not improving as hoped.

2. The mayor had promised in her election campaign to try to attract new business to the area.

3. She believed that she knew just what area businesses wanted, tax breaks.

4. However, her plan was voted down by the city council.

5. Therefore, the downtown area, formerly just shabby, has gotten worse, a real eyesore.

6. In fact, the building on the corner of King and Duke, formerly the site of Mammoth Family Shoes, has started to crumble.

7. The result is inevitable, and the building will have to be demolished.

8. Its owner, a hideous man, has threatened the city with a lawsuit if his building is condemned.

9. Go to the stoplight at Bay and Wellington, about three blocks down.

10. From there, you can see the building owner's office, a true architectural monstrosity.

17h Quotation Marks

17h.1 Double Quotation Marks (" ")

Double quotation marks have four main uses:

1. **To give special emphasis or ironic emphasis to a word or phrase,** as in these examples:

    The mayor's "Look Forward" program is a model of innovation.
    Jeremy's "car" is an alarming collection of rusty parts.

2. **To show that text from a source is being used verbatim:**

    According to McPherson, "The decomposition coefficient remains constant at low temperatures."
    The lawyer's claim that "the behaviour of the police was more criminal than the offence for which my client is charged" will open some eyes in the district attorney's office.

    For an in-depth discussion of quoting from secondary sources, see Chapter 3.

3. **To report dialogue:**

    Alice said, "I don't want to disrupt my life right now, John."
    John replied, "I hope that you don't see me as a disruption."

    Note that when you report dialogue *indirectly,* you should not use quotation marks:

    | INCORRECT | Did Hubert say that "he was going home"? |
    | CORRECT | Did Hubert say that he was going home? |

4. **To enclose the titles of short stories, poems, articles or essays, chapters, songs, and television episodes or parts of television anthologies.** Longer works, such as books, plays, magazine or journal titles, CD titles, film titles, and names of television programs, along with the names of ships and aircraft, are italicized or underlined (see also 28b).

    Here is an easy test to determine whether a title should be in quotation marks or italicized (underlined): you can buy a copy of *Canadian Geographic* magazine, but you can't buy a single article from it. You can buy a book, but not a chapter of that book. You can buy a newspaper, but not an editorial within that paper. Thus, large, "whole" titles—entities which you could buy—are italicized or underlined; parts of a "whole" title are enclosed in quotation marks.

"Whole" Title	"Part" Title
Sixty Degrees of the Blues (CD title)	"Fourth Street Hammer" (song title)
Maclean's (magazine title)	"Ottawa Adrift" (article title)
My Life (book-length collection of essays)	"The Early Years" (title of essay)

17h.2 Single Quotation Marks (' ')

Single quotation marks have only one purpose: to replace double quotation marks when the word or words that need to be enclosed in quotation marks are part of a larger quotation:

INCORRECT	According to Walker, "Ondaatje's "The Cinnamon Peeler" is a dense, almost opaque poem."
CORRECT	According to Walker, "Ondaatje's 'The Cinnamon Peeler' is a dense, almost opaque poem."

Note that magazine and newspaper designers frequently use single quotation marks in unconventional ways, as do the creators of advertisements. Such decisions are made for *visual* impact, not editorial correctness.

17h.3 Quotation Marks with Other Punctuation

Many writers are uncertain about what to do when it is time to add a closing quotation mark. Where does the period go? What about a semicolon? The following guidelines should help:

1. **Periods and commas always *precede* the closing quotation mark,** as in the following examples:

   The title of her essay is "Facing Home."
   You've read "Pied Beauty," haven't you?

2. **Colons and semicolons always *follow* the closing quotation mark:**

   There is a powerful underlying message in Richler's "The Street": the beauty of childhood and the cast of characters one meets along the way.
   Yesterday on the radio, I heard "Maxwell's Silver Hammer"; I had almost forgotten that strange Beatles song.

3. **Question marks and exclamation marks should be placed inside the closing quotation mark if they are a part of the quotation or title;** they should be placed outside the closing quotation mark if they are punctuating the sentence as a whole:

   The title of her article is "They Stole My Children!"
   Have you read "The Garden Party"?

4. **If a closing single quotation mark and a closing double quotation mark appear together, they should not be separated by a punctuation mark:**

   Baines writes that "Maria's career is encapsulated in 'Jamaica Town.'"

5. **If a question mark or an exclamation mark appears within a closing quotation mark at the end of a sentence, a period is not needed:**

INCORRECT	The title of her article is "They Stole My Children!".
CORRECT	The title of her article is "They Stole My Children!"

When a question mark or an exclamation mark appears within a sentence, an additional comma is unnecessary:

INCORRECT	When asked "Did you know that the contribution was illegal?," the mayor declined comment.
CORRECT	When asked "Did you know that the contribution was illegal?" the mayor declined comment.

As an alternative, you can rephrase the original sentence or recast the quoted question as an indirect question:

The mayor declined comment when asked "Did you know that the contribution was illegal?"

When asked if he knew that the contribution was illegal, the mayor declined comment.

In the following sentences, add double and single quotation marks as needed.

1. Are you coming to the game, Eliot? Mona asked.

2. According to Schellen, Kafka's mastery in In The Penal Colony is illustrated by the almost tossed-away quality of the short story's conclusion.

3. If you're going to the grocery store, bring back some coffee, a copy of Vogue, and a copy of the Vancouver Sun.

4. Jane, your little fling, as you call it, may turn out to have serious consequences, commented Lawrence.

17i Apostrophes (')

Apostrophes have several functions. **The main function of apostrophes is to signal possession**. They are also used in contractions and with some plurals.

17i.1 Possessives

A possessive is an *of* structure in reduced form. Consider the following passage:

Wanting to see my friend Ed, I went to the house of Ed. Ed did not answer the door, but the wife of Ed said that Ed was in the garage of Ed, working on the 1965 Ford Mustang of Ed.

Fortunately, people don't talk or write this way. Instead, they reduce the *of* structures into more efficient possessive forms.

Personal pronouns change form to reflect possession: *I/my* or *mine; you/your* or *yours; he/his; she/her* or *hers; it/its; we/our* or *ours; they/their* or *theirs*. No apostrophe is required.

However, nouns do not change form. Instead, writers show the possessive forms of nouns by adding either an apostrophe (') and *-s* or just an apostrophe (') at the end of the noun.

1. **To make any singular noun possessive, add** *-'s* **to the end of the word, even if it ends in** *-s, -ss, -x,* **or** *-z.*

   the car's hood
   the dictionary's cover
   Bob's friend
   Morris's friend
   the princess's friend
   Moskowitz's report

2. **To make a plural noun that ends in** *-s* **possessive, add an apostrophe after the** *-s.*

   the cats' dish
   the boys' secret
   the clouds' darkness
   the Harrises' friend

3. **To make a plural noun that does not end in** *-s* **possessive, treat the noun as if it were singular and add** *-'s* **to its end.**

   the men's department
   the women's golf team
   the children's hour
   the people's choice
   the geese's nesting area

These three rules have no exceptions, so why do many writers struggle with the spelling of possessive nouns? One reason may be the errors that people see every day. For example, if you go to your nearest department store, odds are that you will see these signs: *Mens, Womens*. You know what these signs mean, but in fact *Mens* and *Womens* are misspelled versions of *Men's* and *Women's*. Constant exposure to such errors does not help the student of English keep apostrophe rules straight.

Another reason that forming possessive nouns can be problematic has to do with the often complex spelling patterns of English. Consider the word *company*, meaning business or firm:

singular:	company
singular possessive:	company's
plural:	companies
plural possessive:	companies'

To form the plural possessive of *company*, a writer needs to use the "drop the *-y*, add *-ies*" rule, then place the apostrophe correctly. (For more on spelling, see Chapter 19.) For many writers, these rules can seem tricky or confusing.

Note that writers often forget to include possessives in constructions such as the following:

John spent a week's salary on dinner.

To some people, a good night's sleep is an absolute gift.

Years ago, a quarter's worth of candy would get you through an entire movie.

In addition, note that **nouns and pronouns preceding gerunds are possessive:**

Antoine's diving was the only thing we really wanted to see.

The committee seemed unwilling to listen to his complaining about the meeting's agenda.

EXERCISE **17.5**

In the following sentences, make any changes necessary to produce correct possessive forms. Not all sentences contain errors.

1. Jeans truck won't start.

2. The four kittens mother has vanished.

3. Please look in the childrens room.

4. The Subaru's reputation for dependability is well-founded.

5. The Barretts house needs a coat of paint.

6. Give me five dollar's worth of gasoline, please.

7. The mens' choir is practising tonight.

8. For Ryan, it's always somebody elses problem.

9. When I look back, I am astonished by my parents patience.

10. A security guards' hat was found near the bridge.

17i.2 Contractions

1. Some contractions consist of shortened forms of verbs and the word *not*. **In a contraction, the apostrophe takes the place of the deleted letter(s):**

is not = isn't

are not = aren't

cannot = can't

could not = couldn't

A few negative contractions are irregular:

will not = won't

shall not = shan't (now uncommon)

2. Some verb contractions do not involve negatives, but, as in negative contractions, the apostrophe replaces the deleted letter(s):

I am = I'm
he is = he's
she has = she's
we are = we're
we have = we've
they are = they're
they have = they've
let us = let's

3. A few contracted forms are idiomatic noun constructions:

o'clock = of the clock
jack-o'-lantern = jack of the lantern

4. Always remember the important difference between *it's* and *its*. **It's is a contraction of *it is*; *its* is a possessive pronoun:**

It's cold outside.

The horse had lost *its* way in the blizzard.

Also note the difference between *they're* and *their*:

They're about to put *their* house up for sale.

17i.3 Plurals of Numerals, Letters, and Acronyms

Traditionally, the plurals of numerals are formed by adding -*'s*, as in the following example:

The Olympic judges gave the first diver two 8's and a 9.

Similarly, individual letters form the plural by adding -*'s*:

Janine earned four A's and one B during fall semester.

An apostrophe may be used to form the plural of an **acronym** (an abbreviation formed from the first letters of a name).

There is a big sale on DVD's at the Music Place this week.

Recently, however, the trend has been to drop the apostrophe in the plural form of acronyms. In the previous example, *DVDs* would also be acceptable. Whatever you choose to do, be consistent.

Another recent trend has been to form the plural of a decade without an apostrophe: *1990s*. However, *1990's* is still acceptable. Note that when you drop the century number, you should avoid using numerals at all. Don't refer to the *'80s*; use the *eighties* instead.

17i.4 Faulty Apostrophes

As you have seen, the apostrophe is used to form plurals in a few special situations. However, **do not use the apostrophe to form the plurals of regular nouns**, no matter how great the temptation and no matter how strange the plural noun looks without an apostrophe. Remember that regular nouns become plural with the addition of *-s* or, in a few instances, the addition of *-es*. Notice the correct forms of the following nouns:

Singular	Plural
ski	skis
Subaru	Subarus
camera	cameras
beach	beaches
potato	potatoes
tomato	tomatoes

The same goes for the third-person singular form of regular verbs (e.g., runs, shops, reads). **Apart from the formation of contractions, there is NEVER a need for an apostrophe in a verb.**

 EXERCISE 17.6

Add, move, or delete apostrophes in the following sentences. Not all sentences contain errors.

1. Lets ask the security guard if we can stay late tonight; she frequently let's us do so if her supervisor is'nt on the grounds.

2. This parking lot is full of Volvo's.

3. The 1970s were kind to my aunt; she made her fortune then.

4. Robert vow's to make all As next semester.

5. As we began to eat, we realized that the spaghetti hadnt been cooked long enough.

17j Slashes (/)

The slash has two primary functions: to separate lines of poetry that appear within text and to connect nouns that have a dual role or nature:

1. To separate lines of poetry:

   Shakespeare's Sonnet 116 begins with "Let me not to the marriage of true minds / Admit impediments; love is not love / Which alters when it alteration finds. . . ."

2. To connect nouns representing a person or thing with a dual nature or role:

   agent/manager
   owner/driver

EXERCISE 17.7

The following passage has problems with the kinds of punctuation marks discussed in this chapter. Revise the passage to correct those errors.

Last Sunday at about 11 am, I was given the companies car and told to take a pair of client's to a baseball game. There are worse assignment's. Theres nothing like going a ball game on a Sunday afternoon, even though you know the home team's players hitting and fielding could be stronger. The Montgomery Maple Leaf's are'nt the strongest team in the league, but their local. Besides, my boss— the person I rely on for my livelihood,—told me to make sure that our client's got they're fill of baseball.

It is rare that I would pay eight dollars to park, however, it was'nt my money, so I forked it over. The ticket's were waiting for us, so in we went to what one local sports writer has labelled "one of the strangest ballparks in the minor leagues"! Why is it that the inside of Mountaintop Stadium looks like a malls food court. As I walked around, I wondered where I had seen more places to eat at a stadium? The game started after five minutes worth of delay, for something was wrong with the second basemens glove, and the prima donna refused to use another one!

The Mountaintops manager's must have a strange idea about baseball fans— that a fan get's easily bored and need's more stimulation than a baseball game provides—and that fans need constant entertainment. Almost every inning had it's attraction: such as trivia contest's, activity's meant for children, and music; music; music.

My clients' seemed to enjoy the game, but they're attention was mostly on the food courts offerings. Im a little worried about the expense report I will have to file because my spending over one hundred and fifty dollar's on beer, hot dogs, and other assorted goodies is sure to raise my boss eyebrows. I hope my companies budget for entertainment it is only a few thousand dollars can take this hit. Perhaps we should have budgeted for antacid's as well. Im sure my client's stomachs could have used them.

CHAPTER 18

Mechanics

This chapter discusses some important practical issues: when to capitalize letters, how to use italics, when to use a written number and when to use a numeral, and how to use hyphens.

18a Capitalization

In the past, capitalization was haphazard: writers sometimes capitalized words for emphasis, and sometimes they capitalized words for no apparent reason. Today, however, the conventions governing capitalization are well established, and a relatively small number of guidelines cover most situations.

1. **Geographical features.** Capitalize the first letter of each word in the names of cities, counties, provinces, countries, and geographical landmarks:

   Quebec City   Banff National Park
   West Edmonton Mall   Niagara Falls
   Toronto   Nunavut
   Canada

   Besides mountains, deserts, and valleys, geographical landmarks include lakes, rivers, and other bodies of water:

   Lake Eriethe   Bay of Fundy   St. Lawrence River

   Also capitalize the first letter of a section of a country:

   Darla grew up in the Okanagan Valley.

   Exceptions:

   - Geographical terms treated as plurals: the Jackfish and Clearwater rivers.
   - Directions: *east, west, southeast*
   - Adjectival forms: *mid-western, southern* (unless the form is part of the term for an era, study, event, or cultural entity: *Western civilization* or *Eastern customs*)
   - Place names with conventionally accepted lowercase words: Rio de Janeiro.

2. **Months, days of the week, and holidays.** Capitalize the first letters of names of months, days, and the official names of holidays:

   June   Canada Day
   Tuesday   Thanksgiving

   Do not capitalize first letters of the seasons.

   Victoria Day is the unofficial beginning of summer, and Thanksgiving ushers in the fall.

3. **Countries, nationalities, languages, and religions.** Capitalize the first letters of the names of nationalities, religions, and languages, and of adjectives made from those nouns:

   Italy   Italian   Italian painting
   Russia   Russian   Russian wolfhound
   Japan   Japanese   Japanese automobiles
   Catholicism   Catholic   Catholic nuns
   Buddhism   Buddhist   Buddhist monks

   An exception is *french fries.* Also, note that when *catholic* is used to mean *universal,* the first letter is not capitalized.

4. **Sacred books.** Capitalize the first letters of sacred texts and of many adjectives made from such nouns. The titles of these books are not italicized or underlined:

the Bible	Biblical authority
the Gospels	Gospel writers
the Talmud	Talmudic scholars
the Vedas	Vedic studies
the Koran (Qur'an)	Koranic references

5. **Historic events, cultural/intellectual movements, and philosophies.** Capitalize the first letters of the names of historic events, of cultural/intellectual movements, and of some philosophies, as well as the first letter of many adjectives made from those nouns:

the Middle Ages	medieval
the Renaissance	Renaissance
Impressionism	Impressionistic
existentialism	existentialist
Romanticism	Romantic

A dictionary will indicate correct capitalization of such terms.

In general, do not capitalize nouns that name political and economic movements unless they are used to name official organizations:

democracy	the New Democratic Party
environmentalism	the Green Party of Ontario

6. **Course titles.** Capitalize the first letters of major words in the title of academic courses, but do not capitalize words that simply describe a course or that name an academic discipline:

> At Lakehead University, Statistics 101 is a prerequisite for Calculus 240.
> At Lakehead University, science classes require students to use their knowledge of statistics and calculus.

In the first sentence, *Statistics 101* and *Calculus 240* are the official names of courses as listed in a college catalogue. In the second sentence, *statistics* and *calculus* refer to the disciplines or fields of study.

> Ian got an A in English Literature.
> Ian has always been fascinated by English literature.

The first sentence in the example above refers to a college course titled *English Literature;* the second example refers to a discipline. Note that *English* is capitalized in both cases because it is an adjective derived from the name of a language.

7. **Names of buildings, ships, air/spacecraft, and animals:**

the Rogers Centre
the *Bluenose*
the CN Tower
Jumbo
the *Challenger*
Snoopy

8. **Names of companies, organizations, and trademarks.** Capitalize the first letter of names of companies, organizations, and trademarked products. However, do not capitalize names of generic products:

Union Carbide Corporation was headquartered in Champlain, Quebec.
Alcoholics Anonymous has chapters virtually throughout the world.
Johnson and Johnson controls the "Band-Aid" trademark; competitors call their own products "bandages."
Only Coca-Cola Bottlers can tempt you to drink "Coke"; other soft-drink makers sell "colas."

9. **Names of people and supernatural entities.** Capitalize the first letter of the names of people, religious figures, and supernatural entities, except when convention requires the use of lowercase letters or when the person in question prefers lowercase letters:

Sinead O'Connor	God	Eve
Eamon De Valera	Yahweh	Gabriel
Alexis de Tocqueville	Jesus	Ariel
bell hooks	Vishnu	Lucifer
e. e. cummings	Muhammad	k.d.lang

Note that the *De* in Eamon De Valera (the first president of the Irish Republic) is capitalized and that the *de* in Alexis de Tocqueville (a nineteenth-century French historian) is not. Such distinctions reflect family tradition or conventions developed in different countries. However, bell hooks (a contemporary social scientist), e. e. cummings (a twentieth-century poet), and k. d. lang (a Canadian recording artist) chose to represent their names without capital letters, and these choices must be honoured. If you are not sure how to spell the name of a prominent figure, look it up in a good encyclopedia or dictionary.

10. **Job and affiliation titles.** When a job or affiliation title immediately precedes a name, capitalize the first word of the title:

Officer Preston	Uncle Ray
Prime Minister Harper	Queen Elizabeth

However, when a job title is used alone, don't capitalize it:

The corporation I work for just chose a new president.
Walker is a long-time member of parliament; she is a close friend of David Suzuki.

Also note that acronyms formed from job titles appear in capital letters:

Michael is now the chief financial officer (CFO) of Prairie Data Transport.

Titles representing family affiliation are capitalized only if they appear with the family member's name or are used in direct address:

Andrea's Uncle Ray served in Afghanistan.

Andrea's uncle served in Afghanistan.

"Hey, Mom," announced Jackie, "I just got engaged!"

"I just got engaged!" Jackie announced to her mother.

Also, family affiliations are not capitalized if accompanied by another adjective:

My uncle Ray served in Afghanistan.

11. **Titles of essays, articles, poems, plays, films, books, and periodicals.** For media titles, follow these guidelines:

1. Capitalize the first letter of all nouns, verbs, pronouns, adjectives, and adverbs.

2. Begin all articles and conjunctions with lowercase letters, unless those words begin or end a title. The same is true for prepositions of fewer than five letters:

   Gone with the Wind   *The Old Man and the Sea*

   Exception: Some publishers use lowercase letters for all prepositions, regardless of length. Whichever method you adopt, be consistent.

   Suppose that you need to cite in a research paper the following title of a magazine article:

   OSPREY IS PROCEEDING WITH EXPANSION WITHOUT FEAR OF SAGGING ECONOMY

   The title appears in capital letters because the magazine's designer prefers it that way. However, here is how the title should appear if you are referring to it in your writing.

   "Osprey Is Proceeding with Expansion Without Fear of Sagging Economy"

   Note that *Is* begins with a capital letter because it is a verb, even though it is a short word. *With* is a preposition of fewer than five letters, so it is not capitalized. *Without* is a preposition of seven letters, so it is capitalized.

3. The first word of a title and the first word of a subtitle (following the colon separating the title from the subtitle) are always capitalized. Note that this rule overrides rules 1 and 2 mentioned above:

   A Worst-Case Scenario: To Succeed in Business Requires Virtual Isolation

12. **Capitalizing within sentences.** The following guidelines reflect current Canadian standards for capitalizing words within a sentence:

1. Capitalize the first letter of the first word of each sentence.

2. When a sentence appears in parentheses, capitalize the first word only if the parentheses are not embedded in another sentence:

INCORRECT	After using the transponder, store it in a cool, dark place. (this step keeps humidity from affecting the lithium diodes.)
CORRECT	After using the transponder, store it in a cool, dark place. (This step keeps humidity from affecting the lithium diodes.)

3. If a sentence contains a colon but the text that follows the colon is not an independent clause, do not capitalize the first word following the colon unless the word is a proper noun:

INCORRECT	The injured man knew what he faced: A long period of rehabilitation.
CORRECT	The injured man knew what he faced: a long period of rehabilitation.

4. If a sentence contains a colon and the text that follows the colon is an independent clause, either capitalize the first word following the colon or leave it in lowercase, but be consistent throughout your paper:

CORRECT	Our softball game was quickly terminated by an unexpected event: Rain came down hard and steadily.
CORRECT	Our softball game was quickly terminated by an unexpected event: rain came down hard and steadily.

EXERCISE 18.1

In the following sentences, change lowercase letters to uppercase letters as needed, and vice versa. Some sentences may be correct. Be prepared to explain your decision.

1. the caloosa river splits harbin county in half.

2. my cousin roy works for Eddlestone industries.

3. his brother mike is the chief operating officer (coo).

4. i once had the honour of meeting prime minister chrétien.

5. the headline in the *rockville times* was interesting: "Province To Ban Cow Tipping In Rural Areas."

6. james orosio drives a volkswagen passat.

7. orosio lives on bennington street in rockville.

8. Orosio used to live in the Southern part of our Province.

9. He and his friends love the music of k. d. lang.

10. We drove until we almost reached our destination (The Grafton town limits were only a few miles away).

18b Italics (Underlining)

Most word-processing software allows you to use *italic style*, a style of type in which the letters slant to the right. As an alternative, if italics are not available or you are following a style that requires it, you can use <u>underlining</u>. Italic style is preferred, but underlining can be used if necessary. Italics (underlining) should be used in the following situations:

1. **To indicate titles of long literary works or the names of ships or aircraft:**

   Beautiful Losers (novel)

   The Day Lennon Was Shot (nonfiction book)

   The Globe and Mail (newspaper)

   Chatelaine (magazine)

   Academic Questions (professional journal)

   Romeo and Juliet (play)

   The Pianist (film)

   Mad Men (television show)

   The Barber of Seville (opera)

   Leaves of Grass (collection of poetry)

   The Bluenose (ship)

   Note: By convention, the word "the" is capitalized or italicized when the title of a newspaper or magazine such as *The Globe and Mail* or *The Beacon Herald* appears within text.

   Remember that parts or chapters of longer works such as those mentioned above are not italicized (underlined). Instead, they are put in quotation marks:

   "The Prison Door" (title of a chapter in the novel *The Scarlet Letter)*

   "Allies Land in Normandy" (headline of a newspaper article)

   "Great Books in the Undergraduate Curriculum" (title of an article published in the professional journal *Academic Questions)*

2. **To indicate the fact that a word or letter is being used as a word or letter:**

   Accommodate contains two *c*'s and two *m*'s.

3. **To show emphasis:**

   The ship sank in only *twelve minutes.*

 EXERCISE **18.2**

Rewrite the following sentences, using italics (underlining) and quotation marks as appropriate.

1. Karl Zinmeister, editor of The Canadian Enterprise magazine, wrote an article titled How Canada's Working to Stop Global Warming.

2. Jonathan's reading for the week included A History of the Middle Ages by Joseph Dahmus as well as two plays by Shakespeare: Hamlet and Love's Labours Lost.

3. My high school English teacher recommended that I read the Globe and Mail each day.

4. Phil and Marna couldn't agree on which Al Pacino movie to rent: The Godfather or City Hall.

5. One of the essays in David Quammen's book The Flight of the Iguana is The Face of a Spider.

18c Numbers and Numerals

Rules on the use of numbers and numerals vary from discipline to discipline; however, the rules below work well in the humanities and social sciences.

Spell out the following:

1. Numbers one through ninety-nine.
2. The first word of a sentence. This rule overrides all others.
3. Large, whole numbers, such as *one thousand* and *three million*.

   Note: Use hyphens between compound numbers that you write out from twenty-one to ninety-nine:

   Harriet was twenty-nine when she began teaching and sixty-five when she retired.

Use numerals for the following:

1. Numbers higher than 99, except for large, whole numbers, as noted on the previous page.
2. Fractions and decimals: 1/7 and 3.14.
3. Numbers appearing with percentage signs or the word *percent*: 8%, 27 percent.
4. Street addresses: 6 Maple Avenue.
5. Dates: September 17, 2014.
6. Sums of money: He earns $1574.38 per week.
7. Volume, chapter, and page numbers: The information you want appears in Volume 3, page 364.
8. Exact times and dates: 7:43 p.m., 1492 CE.
9. Speeds: Do not exceed the speed limit: 80 kph.
10. Sports scores: The Leafs won by a score of 3 to 2.
11. Statistics: Students in my high school miss an average of only 8 days per year for illness. Faculty average only 4 sick days annually.
12. Numbers used as words: In the snow, someone had written a large 3.

Exceptions:

1. If one number in a sentence must be expressed as a numeral, use numerals for all other numbers in that sentence:

   Of Dr. Moore's 114 students, 7 withdrew for medical reasons, and 28 withdrew for academic reasons.

2. When two numbers appear together, one number should appear as a numeral:

   The judges gave the diver three 8s and two 9s.

EXERCISE 18.3

Revise the following sentences to correct problems with numbers.

1. 80 percent of the first-year class this year say they are confident about their academic success.
2. Of his 12 "guidelines for success," four are nonsense, and 8 are plagiarized.
3. My score on the exam was eighty-eight point six.

4. She lives at Ninety-Six Columbus Street.

5. Of the 368 entries, only seven got past the first review.

18d Hyphens

Dashes (see 27e) are used to *separate* words; **hyphens** are used to *connect* words. Hyphens are used in several different contexts:

1. **Hyphens appear in the dictionary entries for spellings of common compound words** such as *well-known, cave-in,* and *up-to-date.* If you think that a compound word should be hyphenated, don't guess; look it up in a dictionary.

2. **Common prefixes such as *non, pre, post, anti,* and *pro* are sometimes followed by hyphens and sometimes not.** Generally, the trend in modern Canadian English is to avoid the hyphen and to use solid word forms: *predetermined,* for example. Dictionaries almost always contain many such words, sometimes in list format, to show you whether a prefix needs a hyphen when attached to a given common noun. However, if your dictionary offers no guidance about a specific word, follow this rule of thumb: use the hyphen only if its absence would cause an awkward spelling or make a word difficult to identify. For example,

Without hyphen	With hyphen
nonconformist	non-European
antidepressant	anti-establishment
pregame	pre-engineered

In the right-hand column, the hyphens make the term easier to comprehend.

3. **Hyphens are used when writing out numbers that are larger than twenty but not a multiple of ten:**

twenty-one   thirty-seven   eighty-four

4. **Hyphens are used when simple fractions are written as words:**

one-half   two-thirds   three-sixteenths

5. **Hyphens are used in typography to even out or "justify" the right margin of a page.** Note that you will almost never be asked to produce right-justified pages when writing an essay or a research paper; the major style guides, such as MLA and APA, invariably specify that a manuscript paper should not be justified. But, if you do need to right-justify and hyphenate, your word-processing program will do this task for you. The computer may on occasion hyphenate words incorrectly, however. If you are in doubt about appropriate hyphenation, consult the dictionary.

6. **Hyphens are used to form compound adjectives *when they precede a noun.*** In compound adjectives, the first adjective describes the second and is connected to it with a hyphen. Collectively, the resulting term modifies the noun:

coal-black fish
three-bedroom apartment
late-night snack
country-music awards
student-rights activist

As you can see from the following examples, however, compound adjectives are not always hyphenated:

She wore a hot-pink dress.
The dress was hot pink.

In the first sentence, the compound adjective precedes the noun, so a hyphen is used for clarity. In the second, the adjective is a complement and appears after the noun it modifies, so the hyphen is not used. Also, simple adverb/adjective combinations do *not* use hyphens.

| INCORRECT | an easily-confused clerk |
| CORRECT | an easily confused clerk |

However, various three-word adverb/adjective constructions are hyphenated when they *precede* a noun that they modify:

We witnessed an all-too-frequent collapse of our baseball team late in the season.
The late-season collapse of our baseball team is all too frequent.

EXERCISE 18.4

Rewrite the three paragraphs that follow to correct problems with capitalization and mechanics.

the First inhabitants of new zealand are thought to be the maori, polynesian people who came to the two-islands of this country in the 14th century and who spoke a tahitian like language. They now make up about eight % of the country's population. The first europeans to come to new zealand were dutch, and they arrived in the 17th century and named the place after zeeland, a province in holland.

Eighteenth century english explorer captain james cook visited new zealand in his ship *endeavour*. However, nearly a century had to pass before the first permanent european settlement was established at wellington. At that time, the country was still part of the australian colony of new south wales, and the british fought several wars with the maori to gain control of both the Northern and Southern islands. As a result, the maori population dropped to below 100 000. (an academy award winning film, the piano, released in 1995, explores relations between the europeans and the maoris during the early days of colonization.) Today, however, the Native population has recovered, and the maori number well over 600 000.

In nineteen hundred and seven, new zealand was granted commonwealth nation status; in nineteen thirty one, it became an independent country. In both world war I and world war II, the country supplied troops and materials to the allies. Today, new zealanders enjoy one of the strongest economies in the far east. They have also made contributions to the arts, as illustrated by keri hulme's winning of the booker prize for her novel the bone people, which reveals much about maori life in the 2nd half of the 20th century. However, new zealand remains one of most sparsely-populated countries in the world. Indeed, there are far more sheep in this two island nation than there are people.

chapter 19

Diction, Usage, and Spelling

Being alert to the potential strengths and pitfalls of the words
you use can help you avoid dull, inaccurate, or verbose writing and, instead, produce lively, vivid, and accurate language.
This chapter examines four issues that are important to clear
writing:

- using the right word,
- using the appropriate language level,
- using the correct idiom, and
- improving your spelling.

USING THE RIGHT WORD

Diction can be defined as "the words you choose." Choosing the correct words is a complex process and requires an awareness of many facets of the language.

19a "Seen" English versus "Heard" English

Over the past six decades, written communication has lost some of its dominance to more visual forms of communication—photographs, drawings, and moving images—and to oral communication. Written communication is still crucial; after all, contracts are not yet written using cartoon figures, and you wouldn't sing an important proposal to your boss. Nevertheless, popular culture has edged away from the written word. One result of this trend is that many people today are less familiar and less skilled with written communication than earlier generations were.

This reduced level of familiarity has two major effects. One is a smaller vocabulary. People who don't read very much tend to learn only the words they hear. Frequent readers encounter a greater variety of words since, on the whole, written English employs many words that are not heard often in conversation. A second effect of the trend away from reading is an unfamiliarity with the way that words "look." Students sometimes turn in essays filled with word forms reflecting the way they *hear* the words, not the way that the words are correctly spelled.

An example of the first problem—reduced vocabulary—is seen in the following sentence:

INCORRECT   The movie was dreadful; Rob was disinterested in seeing the sequel.

CORRECT   The movie was dreadful; Rob was not interested in seeing the sequel.

The correct form here is *not interested*. Rob doesn't want to see the sequel; the film has bored him. *Disinterested* means "without bias." A judge in a legal proceeding should be disinterested; the judge should pay attention to but not favour either side.

The second type of error, illustrated by the following sentences, shows a writer's almost complete dependence on spoken English:

INCORRECT   My **self of steam** suffered that year (instead of *self-esteem*).

INCORRECT   He attacked the task with **avengince** (instead of *a vengeance*).

INCORRECT   It is no **exaduration** to call him the best guitarist in school (instead of *exaggeration*).

INCORRECT   I was **suppose to** go out last night (instead of *supposed to*).

All four of these sentences appeared in the writing of students in a college composition course. Each student understands what he or she is communicating; however, college writing demands a precision that the "phonetically transcribed" approach to spelling will never attain.

Two strategies can help you make sure you are using the right word in the right form:

1. Try to read a wider variety of writing than you encounter in your classes and at work. For example, in addition to reading what is assigned, read a related article or book as well. The more you read, the less you will depend on "heard" English and the more you will be comfortable with "seen" English.

2. Make a dictionary your constant, much-used companion. Learn how dictionary entries work. Use electronic dictionaries as well; they might be even more helpful than print versions. If you can't find your spelling of the word in a dictionary, you may have to look up other combinations. However, incorrectly spelled words such as *exaduration* pose special difficulties. For example, a computer spell-checker may offer no alternatives to this spelling. In such cases, try looking up synonyms, such as *overstatement,* which the dictionary defines as "exaggeration," thereby providing you with the correct spelling.

Remember, though, that your spell-checker may be programmed for U.S. spelling. If you are in doubt, check in a good Canadian dictionary.

19b Denotation and Connotation

A word's **denotation** is its dictionary definition. However, words also have associations not covered by dictionary definitions. What a word *suggests* is its **connotation.** Note the differences between the following pairs of synonyms:

thrifty	cheap
comment	grumble
activist	radical

The words on the left are neutral; those on the right have negative connotations. Being aware of connotation can help you make your writing vivid and emphatic; ignoring connotation can get you into trouble.

19c General versus Specific Nouns and Verbs

When writers use **specific nouns,** they can create more vivid pictures:

GENERAL   David drove up in his new truck.

SPECIFIC   David drove up in his red 2013 Dodge Dakota.

The reader of the first sentence gets basic information; the reader of the second gets a mental picture.

Specific verbs also contribute to a more vivid picture in the reader's mind:

WEAK   Ms. Gauthier spent several years as an office manager.

STRONGER   Ms. Gauthier managed an office for several years.

WEAK   My cousin is a truck driver.

STRONGER   My cousin drives an eighteen-wheeler.

The second item in each pair is more interesting and emphatic than the original.

19d Writing Lean Sentences

As writers think through concepts on paper or on a computer screen, they often use more words than they have to. As a result, first drafts frequently express the writer's thoughts but are not in a finished, polished form.

Of course, the shortest version of a sentence might not be the best one. You will often need to clear up ambiguities by adding words as you revise your writing.

Nonetheless, you should eliminate useless and wordy structures. Compare these sentences:

> There is a car coming down the street.
> A car is coming down the street.

The only difference between these two sentences is the number of words; the sentences mean the same thing. Starting the first sentence with the **empty expletive** *There is* adds nothing but words. A similar problem is caused by overusing *it*:

> It is a certainty that the proposal will be adopted.
> The proposal will certainly be adopted.

These two sentences have the same meaning and emphasis; the only difference is length.

Should you always avoid starting a sentence with the expletive *there* or *it*? No, but if you use these words, ask yourself if they serve a purpose. If not, use a basic subject/predicate structure instead.

As you revise, also weed out **bloated phrasing,** in which several words are used when one or two suffice:

BLOATED Due to the fact that the stock market is shaky, Sarah is investing in a mutual fund instead.

LEAN Because the stock market is shaky, Sara is investing in a mutual fund instead.

Look as well for unnecessary verb or verbal phrases, and reduce them to simple verbs:

BLOATED Joan, I think we need to hold a meeting.

LEAN Joan, I think we need to meet.

Other problems to look for when you are revising for diction are **repetition** and redundancy. **Repetition** occurs when a word is repeated in the same sentence or in a nearby sentence. It can make your writing tedious:

REPETITIVE Of the ten apple pies in the bake-off, my grandmother's apple pie was the best.

REVISED Of the ten apple pies in the bake-off, my grandmother's was the best.

Redundancy is the result of using two or more words that mean the same thing. In effect, redundancy means saying the same thing twice:

REDUNDANT The dead corpse lay in the narrow alley.

REVISED The corpse lay in the alley.

All *corpses* are dead; all *alleys* are narrow.

REDUNDANT The wealthy tycoon recalled the past history of the company's rise in a very unique industry.

REVISED The tycoon recalled the history of the company's rise in a unique industry.

By definition, *tycoons* are wealthy, *history* is made up of past events, and anything that is *unique* is one of a kind already, so using *very* is unnecessary.

For more on how to write efficient sentences, see Chapter 6.

EXERCISE 19.1

The following sentences suffer from the diction problems that have just been discussed. Revise each one.

1. Some people think the business world has a doggy-dog mentality.

2. The recipe called for a well-beeten egg and two cups of flower.

3. The bride took the groom's love for granite as she walked down the isle.

4. We need to undertake an investigation of the cost overruns.

5. It is clear that the sun will rise tomorrow.

6. There is reason to believe that a large number of persons who have immigrated to this country are having problems with the English language.

7. What this is is an electronic signal locator.

8. In all probability, the profits for the third quarter will be in the neighbourhood of $30 million.

9. The doctor provided a diagnosis of my condition.

10. Mandy has proved to be a political activist because of her letters complaining about the board of control's policies.

11. The tone of our supervisor's memo infers that he is not very happy about the remodelling costs.

12. Last Wednesday, the geologist lead his party into a newly discovered cave.

13. Harriet was to excited to speak.

14. Ask the waiter if their are any desert specials.

15. I hope to rise my GPA this semester.

19e Avoiding Sexist Language

Words can sting. The use of overtly malicious language to describe women is rarer and rarer these days; however, because of lingering insensitivity or ignorance, **sexist language** still appears in speech and in writing. Consider this sentence:

SEXIST   The consultant entered with his assistant, an attractive blonde of about thirty, who helped him set up the presentation.

The sentence suggests an offensive social dichotomy: men are functional, women decorative. This dichotomy is not acceptable. Note the revision of the sentence above:

ACCEPTABLE   The consultant entered with his assistant, who helped him set up the presentation.

Remember these guidelines when you write:

1. **Avoid job titles that imply gender.** In the 1920s and 1930s, the famous pilot Amelia Earhart was labelled in the media as an "aviatrix," as opposed to an

"aviator." Still with us today are the hard-to-get-rid-of *waiter/waitress* distinction and a distinction that plagues film and theatre: *actor/actress*. Note this list of old-fashioned job titles and their modern equivalents:

Gender-Linked Title	Gender-Free Title
repairman	technician
mailman	letter carrier
fireman	firefighter
policeman	police officer
chairman	chair

You do not need to use such bizarre terms as *waitperson* and *ombudsperson; server* and *mediator* will suffice.

2. **When you write about both men and women, treat each sex equally.** What's wrong with the following passage?

SEXIST The two candidates, William Rogers and Sara Gonzalez, were introduced to the audience. In his preliminary remarks, Rogers said that he would focus on lower taxes. Ms. Gonzalez, however, spoke on improving local roads.

The writer is being unbalanced in identifying the male candidate as "Rogers" but the female candidate as "Ms. Gonzalez."

REVISED The two candidates, William Rogers and Sara Gonzalez, were introduced to the audience. In his preliminary remarks, Rogers said that he would focus on lower taxes. Gonzalez, however, spoke on improving local roads.

In the revised version, the writer refers to both candidates by their last names.

A similar problem occurs when a writer identifies groups containing both males and females as if they included males alone:

SEXIST At the convention, **the doctors and their wives** enjoyed the best the Sunset Resort had to offer.

We doubt that the female doctors brought their "wives":

REVISED At the convention, **the doctors and their spouses** enjoyed the best the Sunset Resort had to offer.

3. **Use pronouns fairly and accurately.** English lacks a single pronoun to refer to an indefinite person of either sex. This shortcoming causes problems with accuracy and agreement. Writers need to avoid using *he* or *she* alone or plural pronouns such as *they, them,* and *their* to refer to singular indefinite pronouns, such as *anyone, everybody,* or *someone,* or to nouns used in a general sense, such as *any doctor* or *the average teacher*:

SEXIST **Everyone** must vote according to **his** conscience.

SEXIST **Any student** who wants to do well in Dr. McDonald's economics class must be sure **she** is prepared to study.

INCORRECT **Everyone** must vote according to **their** conscience.

INCORRECT **Any student** who wants to do well in Dr. McDonald's economics class must be sure **they** are prepared to study.

The preferred pronoun forms are, instead, *he or she, him or her,* or these forms in reverse order:

CORRECT **Everyone** must vote according to **his or her** conscience.

CORRECT **Any student** who wants to do well in Dr. McDonald's economics class must be sure **she or he** is prepared to study.

The pronouns and antecedents in the two sentences above agree in number, and the revisions avoid sexism. However, an essay that is filled with *he or she, him or her,* and *his or her* becomes tiresome. On the other hand, almost all sentences with indefinite pronouns can be revised with plural nouns, as in the following example:

CORRECT **All citizens** must vote according to **their** conscience.

The same approach will work with nouns used in a general sense:

CORRECT **Students** who want to do well in Dr. McDonald's economics class must be sure **they** are prepared to study.

You should use *he, him,* or *his* alone or *she* or *her* alone only when the context is male only or female only, as in the following:

A British cavalry officer of the 1850s could be sure that **his** future depended not only on **his** abilities but also on the politics of the chain of command.

Any member of this sorority who violates the finals-week quiet hours will have **her** room assignment voided.

The possibility that a nineteenth-century British cavalry officer *could* have been a woman disguised as a man or that a male college student *might* be passing as a sorority member is negligible and not worth considering.

For more on pronoun–antecedent agreement, see Chapter 14.

EXERCISE 19.2

In each of the following sentences, determine whether the highlighted term is acceptable. If it is not, replace it with a more appropriate word or rewrite the sentence.

1. The Canadian coal miner of the 1830s saw the potential end of **his or her** life about twice weekly.

2. Each officer to be honoured must wear **his** dress uniform.

3. A grandmother must be careful not to compete with **her** grandson's parents for **his** affection.

4. An employee of a defence plant must show **his** ID upon entering.

5. Joan has broken another line-class record for sea trout; she is the best **fisherperson** I've ever had the pleasure to know.

19f Using Figurative Language and Avoiding Clichés

Figurative language is a way to amplify the description of a subject by comparing the subject to something else that is not *literally* like the subject but is similar to it in a compelling way. Using figurative language effectively is a matter of degree. Make sure your language is fresh, and try to avoid clichés, which are overused and worn-out figures of speech. (You will read more about clichés later in this section.)

As discussed in Chapter 6, there are three main categories of figurative language:

1. A **metaphor** compares two things directly by claiming that the subject and its description are one:

    The Internet startup company proved to be a huge vacuum cleaner that sucked up its investors' money.

2. A **simile** compares two things by using *like* or *as:*

    Jason says that after his back surgery he looked like a defective banana.

    Robbins turned as green as turtle soup when he heard about the burglary.

3. **Personification** attributes human characteristics to non-human entities:

    The forest whispered of a simpler, more peaceful existence.

    The darkening sky wore the garments of doom.

A well-turned example of speech is highly effective and can be the difference between good writing and writing that is truly memorable. However, a straightforward sentence without figurative language is better than a sentence that is laboured or strained:

STRAINED	The dog pulled at its leash like a hound of hell.
STRAIGHTFORWARD	The dog pulled urgently at its leash.

The first example might be appropriate in some contexts, but the second would work in all contexts.

Two other problems can occur when you are using figurative language: a mixed metaphor and a cliché. A **mixed metaphor** results when a writer uses two unrelated figures of speech in the same sentence:

MIXED METAPHOR	On a motorcycle, Andrew becomes an angry bulldog who rockets through town like a missile.
REVISED	On a motorcycle, Andrew becomes an angry bulldog, snarling and growling as he races through town.
MIXED METAPHOR	The arena of love can be a snarl of confusing roads.
REVISED	Love can be a snarl of confusing roads, with signs that lead in different directions.

In each of the revised versions, two figures of speech are used, but they are clearly related.

A **cliché** is a worn-out phrase that readers have heard many times. Including such figures of speech can make your writing flat and boring:

CLICHÉ	My salary increase was the icing on the cake; being assigned to a new department was all I had requested.
FRESHER	My salary increase was a real bonus; being assigned to a new department was all I had requested.

Most people have read *icing on the cake* numerous times. In the revised version, a more straightforward construction avoids sounding hackneyed and stale.

EXERCISE 19.3

In each of the following sentences, replace the highlighted expression with a more effective word or phrase. Different answers are possible.

1. Using too many clichés is an illness whose symptoms include dullness; avoid them **like the plague.**

2. The exploratory committee **kicked the bucket** after its first suggestions **went south.**

3. During the shoe sale, customers **swarmed** into the store **like bees** in a **barroom brawl.**

4. **In a nutshell,** we should have reviewed **the bottom line** before **jumping in feet first.**

5. **It was raining cats and dogs** when the Johnsons arrived at the party.

19g Avoiding Fillers, Euphemisms, and Jargon

Empty language and language offered without a sense of the audience are a waste of effort both for the writer and the reader. Three varieties of misguided language are fillers, euphemisms, and jargon.

1. **Fillers** are well-known but essentially empty expressions used when a more basic expression—or none at all—would suffice:

   all in all
   needless to say
   first and foremost
   golden opportunity
   safe and sound

2. **Euphemisms** are sensitive or "safe" terms used to refer to unpleasant realities such as bodily functions, sexual activities, and death, to name a few. The deceased are sometimes said to have "passed on" or to have "met their Maker." People who have lost their jobs are said to have been "let go" or "downsized." These words are designed to avoid or soften reality:

   | UNNECESSARY EUPHEMISM | Jane is eating for two. |
   | REVISED | Jane is pregnant. |

   In addition, euphemisms can be misleading by masking the seriousness of a condition or situation:

   | MISLEADING EUPHEMISM | Subjects in the psychological study were high-strung. |
   | REVISED | Subjects in the psychological study suffered from anxiety disorders. |

   With the subjects of bodily functions and sexual relations, however, a polite level of euphemism is expected. "I need to go to the restroom" is always preferable to an explicit account of what one plans to do there, while "The young couple made love for the first time" raises no eyebrows.

The key is to avoid language that fears its subject or that seeks to lie about the true nature of its subject.

3. **Jargon** is the specialized language used in a particular field or discipline. It is language used among engineers, chemists, accountants, and other specialists. Jargon is perfectly acceptable—in fact, useful—as long as it is not used outside the field or discipline to which it belongs. When a specialist speaks to non-specialists, though, jargon becomes an issue.

> **JARGON** The publisher warned the author that the book's **frontmatter** was too long.
>
> **REVISED** The publisher warned the author that the book's **introductory section** was too long.

If you need to use a word or phrase that you know will be jargon, define the term the first time it appears. Then use it as needed. However, this approach has its limits. If you define several such terms, you risk overwhelming your reader.

EXERCISE 19.4

Look for fillers, clichés, euphemisms, and jargon in the following sentences. Replace each inappropriate word or phrase.

1. The company's accountants input new data into the computer in order to complete the product's projected-cost assessment.

2. The guests flocked to the buffet table, swooping down and tackling anyone in their way.

3. Please eliminate that stupid fly.

4. The new testing centre has nipped the cheating problem in the bud.

5. All in all, the commission found that the rules and regulations that the company had put into place over the specified period of time were appropriate.

USING THE APPROPRIATE LANGUAGE LEVEL

Writers vary their level of language according to the nature of their audiences.

19h Deciding on an Appropriate Level of Formality

When you write a letter or an email to a lifelong friend, you probably use informal language and a friendly tone. However, if you were to write a proposal seeking funding for a research project, you would avoid such informality.

Language level is determined in part by the level of formality of the words used. Dictionaries commonly identify three levels of formality:

1. **Formal language** is used in scholarly or legal contexts. Typically, this type of writing uses specific words, many of which have Latin or Greek roots. A resident of

North America might seldom hear these words spoken; they are far more common in print. Here are two examples:

propinquity (existing close together)
censorious (highly critical)

2. **Standard language** makes up the text of popular magazines and daily newspapers. These words are of a level most likely to be understood by the average reader. For example, the standard alternative to the more formal *propinquity* would be *nearness*. The alternative to *censorious* might be *negative*.

3. **Informal language** is found in conversation and in conversational writing, such as email messages to friends. Informal language often includes colloquial language and slang. Informal language is not appropriate in higher education writing. Here's an example:

> When I started college a year ago, I bought a new computer. (Actually, my parental unit bought it for me.) It had all the bells and whistles, top of the line. Now—just one year later!—it's like it has suffered some weird aging disease. It's slow booting up, and my CD-burning capabilities are, like, ancient. I need a new box!

Colloquial language is informal language that is peculiar to a geographical region. For example, in parts of Atlantic Canada, you might hear someone use the term "Bluenoser" to describe a person from Nova Scotia, and you would want to beware of someone who is "scivey"—stingy or untrustworthy.

Slang consists of temporary, stylish language forms that reflect popular culture and are traditionally used more by young people than by older people. Like colloquial language, slang is usually inappropriate in college-level writing because (1) your audience might not understand it and (2) slang has no fixed, permanent meaning.

Note the difference among language levels for the following terms:

Formal	Standard	Informal	Slang
altercation	quarrel	fight	rumble
unsophisticated	crude	rough	hick
comely	attractive	cute	hot

When you write for your college classes, use standard (or in some cases formal) English. (For more on levels of language, see Chapter 6.)

19i Using a Consistent Language Level

Sometimes, college students stray from standard English in a paper. They might suddenly slip into informal English; later, their vocabulary might suddenly become quite elevated, as if they had just discovered a thesaurus. Use standard English consistently throughout each paper. Occasionally, you'll need a more formal word, and sometimes—when quoting dialogue, for instance—you might have to use slang; but these should be exceptions, not common occurrences.

The following sentences are meant to be written in standard English but stray from that category. Revise as needed.

1. Jan had not expected to receive so much calumny because of turning in her research notes beyond the deadline.

2. The small town was populated largely by hicks.

3. Worrying about a math exam won't get you anywhere; you need to chill a bit, then form a study plan.

4. Mr. Banks is a good supervisor but a real hard-nose about punctuality.

5. The smell coming from the restaurant was truly odoriferous.

USING THE CORRECT IDIOM

Many English phrases are **idiomatic;** that is, certain combinations of words are acceptable, but similar phrases are not. For example, *on the contrary* is standard, but *in the contrary* is meaningless. Unfortunately with idioms, when you are trying to decide which construction is correct, logic won't help.

Most troublesome idioms in English involve prepositions. The following list includes combinations that commonly cause problems:

accuse of: She was **accused of** embezzlement.

accustom to: I'm not **accustomed to** luxury.

adhere to: We **adhere to** a code of ethics.

adjacent to: The restaurant is **adjacent to** a dry cleaner.

advice on: I need some **advice on** this mutual fund.

advise of: The detective **advised** us **of** the new developments.

advise to: Dr. Sanders **advised** me **to** take microeconomics.

agree on: Let's **agree on** a plan.

agree to: I'll **agree to** her demands on one condition.

angry with: Cathy is **angry with** Rob.

apologize for: We need to **apologize for** our loud party.

apply for: He **applied for** the management position.

assent to: The administration **assented to** the students' demands.

benefit from: We have **benefited from** her advice.

blame for: I took the **blame for** my brother's antics; I **blame** him **for** getting me into trouble.

bored by: James was **bored by** Kareem's constant texting.

bored with: I'm **bored with** staying home and watching television.

capable of: Cats are **capable of** great mischief if left unattended.

compliment on: The judge **complimented** the jury **on** their promptness.

comply with: Please **comply with** our guidelines, Mr. Roberts.

concerned about: Janet was **concerned about** her children.

concur with: I **concur with** Jane; we must change our level of customer service.

confide in: Laney **confides** only **in** her mother.

confide to: Laney **confided** the secret **to** me.

confident of: The incumbent is **confident of** success in the upcoming election.

conform to: This design **conforms to** the county building code.

consent to: I **consented to** the new regulations.

decide on: Have you **decided on** which film to see tonight?

derive from: The recipe was **derived from** an eighteenth-century cookbook.

despair of: Wayne **despaired of** ever finishing his degree.

deviate from: This type of orchid **deviates from** the norm.

devoid of: The musical's cast was **devoid of** talent.

different from: Baseball is **different from** cricket.

discourage from: The new legislative guidelines **discourage** students **from** changing majors.

disdain for: Julie has a great **disdain for** unmotivated students.

embark on: Today, we **embark on** a new chapter in our company's story.

foreign to: This kind of fish is **foreign to** my taste.

hinder from: Working part time can **hinder** a student **from** studying properly.

hindrance to: Too much background noise can be a **hindrance to** careful thought.

implicit in: His motives are **implicit in** his actions.

in accordance with: We have drawn up the contract **in accordance with** our notes from the meeting.

independent of: The French researcher reached her findings **independent of** the Russian scientist.

in search of: We are **in search of** the truth.

insight into: The lab report should give us some **insight into** the patient's condition.

interfere in: Veronica loves to **interfere in** her friends' lives.

interfere with: My love of partying **interfered with** my studies.

involve in: How did you get **involved in** this mess?

involve with: Are you **involved with** that organization?

mistrustful of: Sometimes it's too easy to be **mistrustful of** a friend.

neglectful of: The new security guard was **neglectful of** the compound's perimeter.

oblivious of (*or* to): Middle-class people are frequently **oblivious of (to)** the plight of the homeless.

opposition to: My **opposition to** rezoning is well-known.

partial to: I am **partial to** chicken cooked in any manner.

peculiar to: This orchid is **peculiar to** only one very small part of Brazil.

preferable to: Success is **preferable to** failure.

prevent from: The police **prevented** me **from** parking near my house.

protest against: I must **protest against** this madness, sir!

receptive to: Oddly, Mr. Younger was **receptive to** my plan.

renege on: The bank **reneged on** our original agreement.

responsible for: The captain is **responsible for** the people on the ship.

responsible to: She is **responsible to** her supervisors.

rich in: The dessert was **rich in** carbohydrates.

sensitive to (about): Jason is **sensitive to** (or **about**) questions regarding his past.

similar to: This car is **similar to** my old one.

superior to: This wine is **superior to** others of its type.

suspect (*verb*) of: He has long been **suspected of** embezzlement but has never been caught.

unaware of: Dr. Vershinsky was **unaware of** his class's boredom.

variance with: These specs show a large **variance with** our original blueprints.

void of: This movie is **void of** any redeeming qualities.

wary of: Be **wary of** telephone sales pitches.

yield to: Don't **yield to** temptations too early; think before acting.

If you are in any doubt as to the correct idiom, check the dictionary.

EXERCISE 19.6

The following sentences contain idiomatic expressions used incorrectly. Reword as necessary.

1. The factory management has consented with the request for the installation of more safety equipment and will not interfere on meetings called by union officials.

2. Matisse has an education that he will benefit with in his new job.

3. Michael embarks in a new career; he will be involved with matters related to environmental protection.

4. The new coach was not concerned for the future of the team.

5. Rita always wants to be different than everyone else in her dorm.

IMPROVING YOUR SPELLING

Modern English is derived from a hodgepodge of languages. As a result, English spelling is not always predictable. Some lucky writers process language *visually;* they "see" words as they think them. However, most people process language orally, and to spell correctly, they must depend on phonetics and their memory.

For any writer who is uncertain about how to spell a word—and this includes a lot of us—a dictionary provides invaluable help. If you make a point of looking up words when you are unsure of their spelling, eventually you will remember them. Keep a list of "corrected spellings" for your reference. Also, remember that most good spellers are habitual readers.

The following guidelines will help, but they almost always include exceptions. Use your dictionary whenever you are not sure about how to spell a word.

1. ***ie* or *ei*:** Use *i* before *e* except after *c* and except in words pronounced without the long *e* sound (as in *see* or *cheat*).

field	ceiling	neighbour	foreign
grief	conceit	sleigh	height
niece	conceive	vein	heir
relief	deceive	weigh	stein

Exceptions include *fiery, neither, seize, species,* and *weird.*

2. **Final *e*:** Drop a silent final *e* before suffixes beginning with a vowel; keep a silent final *e* before suffixes beginning with a consonant:

| guidance | virtuous | nineteen |
| wasting | lovely | sincerely |

Exceptions include *dyeing* (fabric), *ninth, truly,* and *courageous.*

3. **Changing *y* to *i*:** When adding a suffix, change a final *y* to *i* except before a suffix beginning with *i*:

cry, crying, cried
forty, fortieth
rely, relying, reliance

4. **Forming plurals:** Most plurals are formed by adding *-s* to the singular form; plurals of nouns ending in *s, ch, sh,* or *x* add *-es*.

| bassists | cars | foxes | lunches |
| cables | handfuls | dishes | mosses |

An exception is *stomachs.*

Singular nouns ending in *y* preceded by a consonant form the plural by changing the *y* to *i* and adding *-es.*

berries, caddies, lobbies

Singular nouns ending in *o* preceded by a consonant usually add *-es,* but note the exceptions:

heroes, potatoes, tomatoes, zeroes
ghettos or ghettoes, mosquitos or mosquitoes

Exceptions include *hippos, jumbos,* and *pros* .

On the next page, you will find a list of eighty commonly misspelled words.

COMMONLY MISSPELLED WORDS			
accommodate	continuous	hypocrisy	predominant
acquaintance	criticize	imitation	prejudice
aggravate	definitely	independent	prevalent
all right	desperate	intelligence	privilege
a lot	develop	irrelevant	proceed
altogether	disappoint	irresistible	prominent
amateur	disastrous	knowledge	psychology
analysis	dissatisfied	licence	questionnaire
argument	embarrass	loneliness	receive
athletic	environment	maintenance	recommend
bureaucracy	existence	manoeuvre	repetition
calendar	exaggerate	mischievous	rhythm
category	feasible	necessary	schedule
cemetery	February	noticeable	separate
competition	gauge	occasionally	succeed
condemn	government	occurred	susceptible
conscience	grammar	parallel	temperament
conscientious	guard	personnel	unanimous
conscious	harass	possess	undoubtedly
consistent	hurriedly	preceding	villain

EXERCISE 19.7

Sixteen of the following words are misspelled. Provide the correct spellings.

1. definatly
2. paralel
3. wholly
4. personell
5. accomodation
6. independent
7. resistence

8. seperate
9. occurrance
10. mispell
11. catagory
12. cematery
13. aggrivate
14. bureaucracy

15. disasterous
16. goverment
17. develope
18. hypocrisy
19. predominent
20. mischievious

A Glossary of Usage

The following glossary contains words that are commonly misused or misspelled, along with pairs or groups of words that are commonly confused.

a, an These are the two indefinite articles. Use *a* before a word beginning with a consonant sound; use *an* before a word beginning with a vowel sound. For example, *horse* starts with a consonant sound: **a horse.** *Hour* starts with a vowel sound: **an hour.**

absolutely Avoid using this word to produce redundant expressions such as *absolutely perfect* and *absolutely unique.*

accept, except *Accept* is a verb: "Will they **accept** our proposal?" *Except* is normally a preposition: "Everything is finished **except** the letter."

access, excess *Access* means "entry," "entrance," or "availability to": "Susan was denied **access** to sensitive files." *Excess* means "too much of," "surplus," or "redundancy": "When buying meat, have the butcher trim off the **excess** fat."

adapt, adopt *Adapt* means "to alter to fit": "The polar bear has **adapted** to life in Nunavut." *Adopt* means "to take in" or "accept": "We **adopted** our new dog from the Humane Society."

adverse, averse *Adverse* means "unfavourable" or "hostile." *Averse* indicates "unwilling," "reluctant," and even "repugnant." "She is not **averse** to going sailing as long as we don't encounter **adverse** weather."

advice, advise *Advice* is a noun; *advise* is a verb: "I did not like my boss's **advice,** for she **advised** me to find other employment."

affect, effect *Affect* is almost always a verb: "The weather forecast **affected** our plans." In the social sciences, *affect* is sometimes used as a noun to mean "normal human responses": "The psychopath showed a chilling lack of **affect.**" *Effect* is almost always a noun: "The **effect** of the storm was profound." However, *effect* can also be used as a verb, as in "to **effect** change," meaning to cause change to happen.

again, back Avoid using these words to create redundant phrases such as *reiterate again* and *return back.*

aggravate This word is often confused with *irritate* and *annoy.* However, *aggravate* means "to worsen": "The symptoms of my cold were **aggravated** because I was able to get only three hours' sleep." "Children can **irritate** [*not* **aggravate**] their parents by making unreasonable requests."

a half a Avoid; use either *half a* or *a half,* according to context: "I had **half a** [*not* **a half a**] cantaloupe; then I drank **a half** [*not* **a half a**] glass of water."

ahold Not a word—use *hold* instead: "The diver tried to get **hold** of the side of the rescue boat."

ain't This is a nonstandard contraction of *am not, are not,* or *is not.* Avoid it unless reporting dialogue.

all ready, already *All ready* indicates that everyone or everything is prepared: "They were **all ready** to go." *Already* is an adverb meaning "at this time" or "before this time": "Laura had **already** finished eating when her son called."

allude, elude *Allude* is a verb meaning "to mention indirectly": "The senator **alluded** frequently to the *Iliad.*" Note that *allude* does not have the same meaning as *refer,* which means "to mention directly." *Elude* means "to avoid capture or censure": "The escaped convict **eluded** the police for three days."

allusion, illusion An *allusion* is an indirect reference: "In *Paradise Lost,* Milton makes **allusions** to the classics and to the Bible." An *illusion* is a "mirage," a "fantasy," or a "misperception": "Anna is under the **illusion** that everyone is capable of doing good and avoiding evil."

alot Not a word—use *a lot,* meaning "much" or "many," or *allot,* a verb meaning "to divide among."

alright Avoid—the correct spelling is *all right.*

alternately, alternatively The first word means "in turn," "in sequence," or "in rotation": "Meetings of the committee are held once per month **alternately** in Whistler and Blue Mountain." *Alternatively* refers to a choice: "You can pay full tuition; **alternatively,** you can join the work-study program and have your payments reduced by 20 percent."

altogether, all together *Altogether,* an adverb, means "completely": "We were **altogether** disgusted with the new film." *All together* is a phrase meaning "in a group" or "in a collection: "My family was **all together** this Christmas."

alumnus, alumna, alumni, alumnae Use *alumnus* to refer to a college graduate of either sex; use *alumni* for more than one graduate. Avoid *alumna* and *alumnae*, which are outdated and sexist.

among, between Use *among* to connect more than two; use *between* to connect two: "**Between** you and me, Dr. Justino is **among** the best three surgeons in the province."

amoral, immoral *Amoral* means "without moral principles": "Jerry believes there is no right and wrong in this world; he has a thoroughly **amoral** philosophy." *Immoral* has an even stronger negative connotation and means "sinful," "evil," or "depraved": "The Holocaust was the manifestation of an utterly **immoral** philosophy."

amount, number Use *amount* to refer to entities that are normally weighed or measured, not counted, such as rice, sugar, and sunshine. Use *number* for entities that are normally counted, such as peaches and people: "The **amount** of fog made driving on the highway unsafe; the **number** of people trapped in their cars was astounding." See also **fewer, less.**

ampersand (&) Do not use this symbol to mean *and* in college writing unless it is part of a company's name or is required by a particular documentation style.

an, a See **a, an.**

and etc. Avoid this redundancy; in fact, *etc.* alone should be used with caution. See also **etc.**

and/or Avoid this clumsy construction except in legal and scientific writing.

and so, and therefore Redundant phrases—use *so* or *therefore* instead.

angry at This is a nonstandard form. Use *angry with* instead.

angry, mad *Angry* refers to an emotional state. In college writing, use *mad* to mean "insane" or "deranged": "How can you be **angry** with someone who has obviously gone **mad?**"

any, any other Using *any* instead of *any other* can sometimes create illogical comparisons: "Anna is better at mathematics than **any** student in her class." This sentence claims that Anna is even better than herself, which is an absurdity. The correct version is "Anna is better at mathematics than **any other** student in her class."

anyone, any one *Anyone* is an indefinite pronoun meaning "a person." *Any one* is a phrase referring to an individual singled out from a group: "**Anyone** is eligible; **any one** of us could win."

anyways Not a word—use *anyway* instead.

appraise, apprise *Appraise* means "to set a value on"; *apprise* means "to inform": "The jeweller **apprised** her clients that their ring had been **appraised** at $100 000."

apt, likely These words are synonymous. However, don't confuse *likely* with *liable* (see also **liable**).

around *Around* refers to position. Avoid using it to mean "near" or "about" in formal writing: "**Around** the fort, the remains of which are **near** Cape Breton Island, were amassed **about** one thousand enemy soldiers."

as, like When comparing, use *like*: "Joan is **like** her sister." When subordinating an independent clause, use *as* (or *as if, as though*): "Ed was late, **as** we knew he would be." Avoid using *as* in place of *because* or *while*: "He was late **because** [*not* **as**] he had to wait **while** [*not* **as**] the mechanic fixed his car."

as regards Avoid—use *concerning* instead.

assure, ensure, insure *Assure* means to "affirm" or "pledge." *Ensure* means "make sure" or "make certain." *Insure* means "to guarantee against destruction, loss, or harm": "We **assure** you that enough monies have been put aside to **ensure** his release." "Reggie is an executive with a company that **insures** businesses against loss by theft, fire, or natural catastrophes."

awful, awfully *Awful* means "awe-inspiring." However, it has taken on the popular meaning of "horrible" or "dreadful." In speech, *awfully* sometimes replaces *very*. Avoid both of these popular uses in college writing: "News of the **appalling** [*not* **awful**] conditions in the city's hospitals spread through the media **very** [*not* **awfully**] fast."

awhile, a while *Awhile* is an adverb: "We ran **awhile**." *A while* functions as a noun and is often used as the object of a preposition: "I thought for **a while** about Bianca's proposal."

bad, badly *Bad* is an adjective: "Edwin is not a **bad** man, and I'm sure he feels **bad** about losing his temper." Note that the second *bad* is used as an adjective complement, a word that describes the subject *he*. *Badly* is an adverb: "We played **badly** all day at the new golf course."

basically Do not use this word as a filler, as in "**Basically,** we feel sorry for Mike because of his wife's illness."

being as (being that) Do not use: "I believe that my sixteen-year-old daughter is ready for college **because** [*not* **being as** or **being that**] she has compiled an outstanding academic record in high school."

beside, besides *Beside* is a preposition that means "adjacent to": "The parking lot is **beside** the store." *Besides* is a preposition that means "in addition to" or "except for": "**Besides** her regular job, Karen does freelance work; Andre, on the other hand, has no other sources of income **besides** his printing business."

between, among See **among, between.**

both Avoid redundant expressions such as "they both agree" or "both together."

breath, breathe *Breath* is a noun: "Slow down and take a **breath**." *Breathe* is a verb: "'**Breathe** deeply,' said the doctor."

broke This word is informal for "insolvent," "without money." Avoid this use of *broke* in college writing.

but Do not join this word with other negative conjunctions, as in *but yet* and *but however.*

can, may *Can* refers to ability or possibility: "**Can** the helicopter make it to the accident scene in time?" *May* refers to permission: "No, you **may** not put your feet on my sofa!" *May* is also used as a synonym for *might*: "We **may** get this project finished on time; it's too soon to tell."

cannot The verb *can* plus *not* is usually spelled as one word. However, if you need to stress the *not*, separate the two words and italicize (underline) *not*: "You **can** ***not*** drive from Waterloo to Montreal in two hours."

can't hardly Avoid this double negative; use *can hardly* instead.

can't help but This is an informal construction. Instead, use *can't help*: "I **can't help** loving you!"

capital, capitol *Capital* is the noun for a city that is the governmental centre of a province, state, or country. However, it can also refer to money or financial resources. In the U.S., *capitol* refers to the building in which lawmakers and other government officials meet: "Arriving in the **capital** by train, the senators proceeded directly to the **capitol,** where they presented a bill to cut **capital** spending."

censor, censure To *censor* is to remove from a document materials that are considered offensive. To *censure* means to "condemn," "admonish," or "strongly criticize": "Let's hope that the courts will **censure** the government if it attempts to **censor** the press."

centre around Inaccurate—use *centre on* instead.

childish, childlike The first of these words carries a negative connotation: "Though he is fifty years old, his behaviour at meetings is often childish." The second word has a more positive meaning: "There is a childlike innocence in Sabrina's eyes."

cite, site, sight When writing a research paper, students *cite* by identifying the source of a quotation or of other information. *Site* refers to a place in real or virtual space: "The proposed **site** of our college's off-campus centre can be examined on our web**site**." When used as a verb, *sight* means "to see" or "to spot." When used as a noun, *sight* means "vision."

climactic, climatic *Climactic* is the adjective form of *climax*: "The car chase was the movie's **climactic** scene." *Climatic* is the adjective form of *climate*: "Her job is to monitor **climatic** changes at the South Pole."

complement, compliment, complementary, complimentary *Complement* means "to complete" or "to fit with": "Uma's green handbag **complemented** her outfit." As a verb, *compliment* means "to praise," and as a noun, *compliment* means "a word of praise." Rarely used, *complementary* is the adjective form of *complement*: "The dress had a **complementary** belt." *Complimentary* means either "praising language" ("The boss was **complimentary** about our report") or "free of charge" ("The hotel room came with **complimentary** theatre passes").

conscience, conscious The first word is a noun; it refers to a moral faculty: "Hitler lacked any semblance of a **conscience.**" *Conscious* is an adjective, meaning "awake": "Was Ray **conscious** when he wrote his history paper?"

contemptible, contemptuous A person or an act that is *contemptible* is worthy of our contempt. A person who is *contemptuous* has contempt for someone or something: "Leanne was **contemptuous** of her boss, for his treatment of female employees was **contemptible.**"

continual, continuous *Continual* means "habitual" or "normally repeated": "Rob's **continual** drinking was the reason Miranda left him." *Continuous* means "ongoing without interruption": "The pistons' pumping was **continuous.**"

could of Avoid; use *could have* instead. See **of.**

council, counsel, consul A *council* is an administrative body: "The city **council** voted today on the zoning request." *Counsel* is advice: "I sought my grandfather's **counsel** on handling my debt." A *consul* is a civil servant stationed in another country: "As **consul,** she has worked at the embassy for nine years."

couple Be accurate. Do not use this term to refer to more than two.

criterion, criteria These terms derive from Latin. *Criterion* is the singular; *criteria* is the plural: "We focus on one **criterion** for promotion: productivity. To a lesser extent, however, we also consider other **criteria,** such as loyalty, punctuality, and effort."

cute Avoid this informal term for "attractive."

data A plural noun (singular: *datum*). Use plural verbs and pronouns with *data:* "The data **were** [*not* **was**] insufficient."

definite, very definite The second of these terms is redundant. *Definite* suffices.

desert, deserts, dessert One travels on a camel through the *desert*. However, as a verb, *desert* means "to abandon": "They **deserted** their disabled aircraft and began walking across the **desert** in search of water and food." *Deserts* is a noun meaning "appropriate reward or punishment": "The killers got their just **deserts**." *Dessert* is a fruit or sweet eaten at the end of a meal.

deviant, deviate *Deviant* is a noun or an adjective; *deviate* is the related verb: "A **deviant** is someone whose **deviant** behaviour **deviates** from social norms."

device, devise *Device*, a noun, refers to an instrument, machine, or tool. *Devise* is a verb meaning "to create or make": "Archimedes **devised** a **device** that used solar power to burn the sails of Roman ships."

differ from, differ with Use *differ from* to indicate dissimilarity: "Lemurs **differ from** meerkats." Use *differ with* to indicate disagreement: "Our local film critic **differed with** the opinion of *Transformers* that was published in *The Globe and Mail*."

different from, different than Use *different from:* "Pasta is **different from** risotto."

discreet, discrete *Discreet* means "judicious about revealing sensitive or private matters": "MP Bing wishes his aide had been **discreet**." *Discrete* means "separate" or "distinct": "The park contains three **discrete** areas of interest: the zoological area, the botanical gardens, and the water park."

discuss about Use *discuss* as in "let's **discuss** our relationship." To say "let's discuss about our relationship" (or discuss *about* anything) is wordy and redundant.

disinterested, uninterested These words are often used interchangeably, but their meanings are quite different. *Disinterested* means "unbiased" or "impartial": "The mediator was renowned for her professional **disinterest** when settling labour disputes." *Uninterested* means "not interested": "I am **uninterested** in modern sculpture; it does not move me."

due to Do not substitute *due to* for *because of.* "She lost her job **because of** [*not* **due to**] the recession." However, *due to* is permissible when used to describe the subject of a sentence. In such cases, it is used directly after a form of *to be:* "In the 1930s, the run on the banks was **due to** a massive loss in depositors' confidence."

due to the fact that Avoid this needless filler. Use *because* instead.

each and every Avoid this redundancy by using either *each* or *every*, not both.

eachother, each other Always spell as two words.

economic, economical *Economic* refers to the study of economics: "The prime minister's **economic** advisers resigned after the new unemployment statistics were released." *Economical* means "frugal" or "thrifty": "Shopping at discount clubs is an **economical** way to provide for a large family."

effect See **affect, effect.**

e.g. Short for the Latin *exempli gratia*, which means "for example." Avoid using this abbreviation in most college writing, except in parentheses or in footnotes. In any case, always follow *e.g.* with a comma.

elicit, illicit *Elicit*, a verb, means "to draw forth": "The new rules for fraternities **elicited** the approval of the student newspaper." *Illicit*, an adjective, means "illegal": "The athlete was accused of using **illicit** drugs."

emigrate, immigrate A person *emigrates from* a country; a person *immigrates to* another country.

eminent, imminent Both are adjectives. *Eminent* means "important" or "prominent": "The **eminent** historian gave a fascinating public lecture." *Imminent* means "immediately going to happen": "The thunderstorm is **imminent.**"

enthused, enthusiastic *Enthusiastic* is preferred in college writing.

equally as Avoid this redundancy. Use *as* by itself: "This lobster is **as good as** [*not* **equally as good as**] the one I had in Labrador."

especially, specially Use the first of these words in college writing; the second is colloquial.

etc. Short for the Latin *et cetera* ("and other things"). Avoid this abbreviation in most college writing, except in parentheses or in footnotes. Do not use it with *and,* for *and* is already part of the Latin term.

eventhough, even though Always spell as two words.

everyone, every one *Everyone* is an indefinite pronoun meaning "a person." *Every one* is a phrase meaning "all members of a group": "**Everyone** is eligible; **every one** of us should enter."

except, accept See **accept, except.**

explicit, implicit *Explicit* means "stated clearly or directly": "The directions were **explicit,** but Raymond managed to get in trouble anyway." *Implicit* is the opposite, meaning "suggested but not stated directly": "**Implicit** in my ninety-day review was a sense that the company is doing better as a whole."

excited about, excited for Standard usage is *excited about* where the subject is excited about the object in the sentence: "I am **excited about** the new iPhone." Use *excited for* only when the speaker shares in the excitement of another person: "I am **excited for** my mom; she's getting remarried."

extant, extent *Extant* is an adjective meaning "in existence" or "not extinct": "Scientists believe that only twenty **extant** reptile species are left in the area." *Extent* means "degree" or "amount": "Doctors removed the scar tissue to the **extent** possible."

facilitate Avoid this bureaucratic jargon; use *help* or *aid* instead.

farther, further Use *farther* to refer to actual distance: "It is **farther** to Fredericton than it is to Moncton." Use *further* to mean "a greater degree" or "more": "After **further** debate, we decided to adopt Plan A."

fewer, less Use *fewer* to refer to countable things: "There are **fewer** cars on the lot now than there were this morning." Use *less* to refer to things that are normally measured, not counted: "There's **less** rice than usual in the dish."

finalize Avoid; use *finish* or *complete* instead.

flaunt, flout To *flaunt* is "to boast" or "to display ostentatiously." To *flout* is to "treat with contempt, sneer at, or disdain": "Avery does not hesitate to **flaunt** his wealth. Knowing he can pay any traffic fine, he **flouts** posted speed limits and parks wherever he likes."

formally, formerly *Formally* is the adverb form of *formal,* which indicates an adherence to particular rules, ceremonies, and conventions. Synonyms for *formerly* include *previously* and *in the past.*

former, first; latter, last Use *former* and *latter* to refer to one of two items; use *first* and *last* to refer to more than two items.

get Avoid using this word to mean "bother" or "affect": That music really **bothers** [not **gets**] me.

goes Avoid using this verb to mean "says."

good and This expression is informal. Instead, use "very" or "well": "She returned from her vacation **well** [*not* **good and**] rested."

good, well *Good* is always an adjective: "This pasta is quite **good.**" *Well* is normally an adverb: "We played **well** together." Use *well* as an adjective only to refer to personal health: "Three months after his bout with pneumonia, Mr. Oshiro finally feels **well** again."

got, gotten *Got* is the past tense of the verb "to get"; *gotten* is its past participle. Don't confuse them. "Shortly after Maurice **had gotten** [*not* **got**] promoted for the third time, he **got** an even better job offer and left the company."

hanged, hung *Hanged* is the past tense and past participle of the verb *to hang. Hanged* refers to killing by suspending from a height: "The prisoner **hanged** himself in his cell." *Hung* is also the past tense and past participle of *to hang,* but it means "to suspend" a thing or "to fasten" it on a wall or hook: "The stockings were **hung** by the chimney with care."

hardly See **can't hardly.**

highschool, high school Always spell as two words unless you are quoting.

hisself Not a word—use *himself* instead.

hopefully Some writers avoid this form because its use can result in the omission of important information: "**Hopefully,** you will take the job." Who is doing the hoping in this sentence? A better alternative is "**I hope** you will take the job."

how Don't use *how* when you mean "that": "I learned that [*not* **how**] he had been arrested."

i.e. Short for the Latin *id est* ("that is"). Avoid using this abbreviation in most college writing. However, if you must use *i.e.,* follow it with a comma.

if and when Avoid this filler, which means "if."

if, whether *If* is used in sentences that express a condition. *Whether* is used to indicate an alternative: "**If** you lend me $10, I will accompany you to the movies tonight **whether** we go to the Bijou Theatre or to the Star Cinemas."

illicit, elicit See **elicit, illicit.**

immigrate, emigrate See **emigrate, immigrate.**

imminent, eminent See **eminent, imminent.**

impact Use *impact* as a noun rather than a verb in college writing. When you need a verb, try *affect:* "Will the dip in the stock market **affect** our income? If so, what will be the **impact?**"

implicit, explicit See **explicit, implicit.**

imply, infer Use *imply* to mean "suggest"; use *infer* to mean "interpret" or "conclude": "Speakers **imply,** but listeners **infer.**"

incidence, incidents The first term refers to frequency or rate of occurrence. The second is the plural of a word that means "event," "occurrence," or "specific case": "The **incidence** of polio decreased dramatically after the Salk vaccine was introduced. There have been no **incidents** of the disease in this country for decades."

incredible, incredulous The first term means "unbelievable"; it relates to statements and phenomena. *Incredulous* describes people who are skeptical or unwilling to believe that a statement or phenomenon is true: "Naturally, I remained **incredulous** about his excuse for being late; considering the fact that he is an inveterate liar, his story about having two flat tires remains **incredible**." Note that *incredible* is sometimes informally used to mean "unusual," "unique," or "spectacular." Avoid this usage in college writing: "Jason's 55-yard field-goal kick was **spectacular** [*not* **incredible**]."

infact, in fact Always spell as two words unless you are quoting.

ingenious, ingenuous Synonyms for *ingenious* include "intelligent," "innovative," and "inventive." *Ingenuous,* on the other hand, means "innocent," "naïve," and "without guile": "Although Michael is **ingenious** at fixing cars, he is remarkably **ingenuous** when it comes to matters of the heart."

in regards to Avoid; use *in regard to* or *regarding* instead.

inside of Avoid this redundancy; use *inside* or *within*.

inter-, intra- *Inter* means "between" while *intra* means "within": "Susan has just competed in an **intercity** field hockey tournament. She learned to play the game only last year, when she joined her college's **intramural** league."

irregardless Not a word—use *regardless* instead.

is when, is where Students sometimes use these constructions when defining a term, as in this case: "Communism **is where** (or **is when**) the government owns the means of production." But *communism* is neither a time nor a place; it is an economic system. A better alternative is this: "Communism is an economic system **in which** the government owns the means of production." Note that in the second example, *communism,* a noun, is being defined by the noun *system,* not by the adverb *when* or *where.*

its, it's *Its* is a possessive pronoun that means "belonging to it": "The new SUV has **its** virtues." *It's* is a contraction of *it is* or *it has:* "**It's** been three years since Sara took a vacation." Note that *its'* does not exist.

kind of/sort of Avoid these informal terms.

latter See former, first; latter, last.

lay, lie *Lie* means "to recline": "I think that I will **lie** down for a while." *Lay* means "to put (something) in a lower position": "Jack **lays** the manual down on the desk." The past-tense form of *lie* is *lay:* "Alice **lay** down for a few minutes after supper." The past-tense form of *lay* is *laid:* "Rosa **laid** the packages down and searched for her car keys."

leave, let *Leave* means "to depart"; don't use *leave* in place of *let,* which means "permit": "**Let** us go now," not "**Leave** us go now."

lend, loan Never ask: "Can you **loan** me a dollar?" *Lend* is a verb; *loan* is a noun: "Bankers **lend** money; they make **loans**." The correct wording of the question above is "Can you **lend** me a dollar?"

less, fewer See **fewer, less.**

let's us Avoid this redundancy; use *let's* instead.

liable *Liable* means "obligated for" or "legally responsible for." Do not use it to mean "likely": "Susan is **likely** [*not* **liable**] to be promoted."

lie, lay See **lay, lie.**

like, as See **as, like.**

lite Always spell as *light* unless you are quoting.

loose, lose *Loose*, an adjective, means "not tight": "The nut holding the boiler plate was **loose**." *Lose*, a verb, means "to misplace" or "to be defeated": "We need to make sure not to **lose** the backup disk."

lots, lots of Avoid these informal constructions in formal writing. Instead, use *much, many,* and *a lot.*

many, much *Many* is used with count nouns such as kilograms, centimetres, people, and cars. *Much* is used with noncount nouns such as rice, string, and equipment: "**Much** water has passed under **many** bridges."

may, can See **can, may.**

may be, maybe Both terms mean "perhaps" or "possibly," but the first is a verb phrase while the second is an adverb. Keep this distinction in mind: "**Maybe** the sun will shine; if not, the picnic **may be** postponed."

media This noun is the plural of *medium*. It agrees with plural verbs and pronouns: "The **media are** [*not* **is**] divided on this issue; in fact, **they have** [*not* **it has**] many different approaches to the problem."

might of Avoid; use *might have* instead. See **of.**

most Don't use to mean *almost.*

myself Correct when used as either a reflexive pronoun ("I pinched **myself**") or as an intensive pronoun ("I rebuilt this carburetor **myself**"). However, avoid using *myself* as part of a sentence's subject: "Roberta and **I** [*not* **myself**] met with the college president yesterday."

nice This is an almost meaningless word because so many unrelated meanings have been attached to it: "likable," "kind," "good," "attractive," "polite," "friendly," "considerate," "suitable." In college writing, always choose a more specific alternative.

nite Always spell as *night* unless you are quoting.

nohow, nowheres Avoid—these are not words.

nowhere near Avoid—use *not nearly* instead: "Ten is **not nearly** [*not* **nowhere near**] enough."

number, amount See **amount, number.**

of Avoid using *of* to replace *have*: "I could **have** [*not* **of**] been a contender."

off of Avoid this redundancy; use *off* by itself: "Jason fell **off** the roof."

oftentimes *Often* works just as well and is less trouble to write.

on account of Avoid this wordy construction. Instead, use *because* or another synonym.

orientate British English uses *orientate;* Canadian English uses *orient,* which means "to familiarize with" or "to place in a particular position": "Faculty advisors will **orient** students to the new regulations." "The church's large rose window was **oriented** south."

outside of Avoid this redundancy; use *outside.*

passed, past *Passed* is the past tense of the verb *pass*: "I **passed** the test" or "The former club president was glad she had **passed** her responsibilities on to her successor." *Past* means "former" or "previous" (when referring to time) or "beyond" (when referring to place or time): "We turned off the road just **past** the first bend; there a **past** president of our club had built a cabin."

patience, patients *Patience* is a virtue; *patients* are people under the care of doctors or dentists.

percent, percentage Use numbers with *percent* (9 **percent**), but use *percentage* when referring to a general concept: "A large **percentage** of voters skipped Tuesday's by-election."

persecute, prosecute The first item means to "oppress" or "tyrannize": "In Russia, Jews have been **persecuted** since the time of the czars." The second term means to litigate or to bring charges against in a court of law: "Abigail was **prosecuted** for tax evasion."

personal, personnel *Personal* is an adjective that means "individual," "intimate," or "relating to 'person'": "Residents of Sunnyvale Nursing Home can make **personal** choices regarding room décor." *Personnel* is both a noun and an adjective. It refers to the employees or members of a business or organization: "**Personnel** at Acme Electrical Suppliers, including those who work in the **personnel** office, have voted to accept pay cuts."

plenty Do not use to mean "very": "This stew is **very** [*not* **plenty**] good, Mom."

plus Do not attempt to substitute *plus* for a coordinating conjunction: "It was late when we got home, **and** [*not* **plus**] the dishes still needed to be washed." *Plus* is a preposition: "Our tax owed **plus** the late penalty amounted to over eight hundred dollars."

precede, proceed *Precede* is a verb that means "to come before": "The bridesmaids **preceded** the bride by three steps." *Proceed* is a verb that means "to continue": "**Proceed** with your task, Wentworth."

predominant, predominate These words are not interchangeable. *Predominant,* the adjective form, is used to describe the leading or most important member of a group: "The **predominant** feeling is that the company president will be replaced very soon." *Predominate,* the verb form, indicates that one thing has more importance than others: "In the arts, modernist philosophy **predominated** during much of the twentieth century."

presently *Presently* means "very soon." Do not confuse it with *currently*: "Howard will be here **presently; currently,** he is in the library."

principal, principle As an adjective, **principal** means "dominant" or "most important": "The **principal** cause of the fire was an electrical short." As a noun, it refers to a school administrator ("the **principal** of Oakwood Elementary") or the base value of a loan or an investment ("drawing the interest but leaving the **principal** alone"). *Principle,* a noun, means "an axiom or theory" ("the **principle** of unintended consequences") or a moral belief ("Karen is a person of **principle**").

proceed, precede See **precede, proceed.**

quiet, quite The first is an adjective referring to the absence of sound; the second is an adverb meaning "very." Be careful not to confuse the spellings of these words.

quite, rather Overused as modifiers: "The airport was **quite** huge." "The hotel room was **rather** tiny." Neither *quite* nor *rather* helps here. In each case, the adjective is stronger when not afflicted by *quite* and *rather.*

quotation, quote Do not use *quote* as a noun: "My **quotation** [*not* **quote**] comes from a story by Farley Mowat." Remember also that text is not a quotation until you have borrowed it: Mowat's **sentence** becomes your **quotation.**

raise, rise *Raise* is *transitive*, meaning that it must be used with a direct object: "The elderly farmer **raised** sunflowers." *Rise* is *intransitive*, meaning that it does not take an object: "The sun **rises** each day."

rather, quite See **quite, rather.**

real, really *Real* is an adjective that is frequently misused as an adverb. Use *really* instead: "You are **really** [*not* **real**] quiet today." However, **really** is often overused in a different way. How does "It is a **really** great film" improve upon "It is a great film"?

reason is because Avoid—use *reason that . . . is* instead. Instead of "The **reason** they postponed the game **is because** of bad weather," use "The **reason that** they postponed the game **is** bad weather."

refer back See **again, back.**

respectfully, respectively Use *respectfully* to mean "showing respect": "I **respectfully** ask that my interview be moved to next Friday." Use *respectively* to mean "in the order indicated": "On the exam, Robert, Tomoko, and Sarah made A, A–, and B+, **respectively.**"

rise, raise See **raise, rise.**

sensual, sensuous *Sensuous* relates to things that are pleasing to the senses: "A **sensuous** wind blew warm and fragrant breezes across the bay." *Sensual* relates to gratification of the physical senses, especially as they relate to sexuality: "In the Renaissance, painters felt free to depict the **sensual** qualities of the human form."

set, sit *Set* is a transitive verb (it takes an object) meaning "to place" or "to put"; *sit* is an intransitive verb (it doesn't take an object): "**Set** your luggage on the rack, and **sit** on the couch."

shall, will *Shall* was once used to indicate the future tense with the pronouns *I* and *we.* Today, *will* is almost universally used.

should of Avoid—use *should have* instead. See **of.**

so Don't use to mean "very": "It was **very** [*not* **so**] hot today." But note: "It was **so** hot today **that I stayed inside all afternoon.**"

some Don't use *some* as an intensifier: "Hurricane Katrina was a [*not* **some**] **terrible** storm."

sometime, some time, sometimes *Sometime* is an adverb that means "at some indefinite point in time": "Matthew will be taking his college entrance exam **sometime** in the near future." *Some time* is a phrase made up of the noun *time* and the adjective *some*: "We hiked for **some time** before we reached the river." *Sometimes* is an adverb meaning "on some occasions": "**Sometimes** I stop at the Hungry Lion for a hamburger."

somewheres Not a word—use *somewhere* instead.

sort of, kind of See **kind of, sort of.**

stationary, stationery Use *stationary* to mean "unmoving" or "fixed": "The sailboat has a **stationary** mast." Use *stationery* to mean writing paper and envelopes: "We bought this expensive paper at the **stationery** store."

suppose to, supposed to The correct form is *supposed to.*

sure, surely *Sure* is an adjective: "This investment is a **sure** thing." Do not use *sure* as an adverb; use *surely* instead: "The introduction to this proposal is **surely** stupid."

than, then These words are frequently confused. Use *then* as an adverb signalling a time transition: "**Then** the concert ended." Use *than* as a comparative conjunction: "These pretzels are harder **than** the last batch we bought."

their, there, they're These words are easily confused. *Their* is the possessive form of *they*: "They checked **their** bags at the curb." *There* can be either an adverb of location—"The exercise room is over **there** by the pool"—or an expletive, a word that delays the appearance of the subject—"**There** are many reasons for the boss's anger." *They're* is the contraction of *they are*: "**They're** going to Cancun for a vacation."

theirselves Not a word—use *themselves* instead.

through, thorough *Through* can be an adjective, an adverb, or a preposition. As an adjective, *through* is an informal way of saying "finished": "I am **through** with this book." *Thorough* is also an adjective, meaning "complete" in the sense of taking care of the details: "His search for the missing earring was **thorough** and ultimately successful." The two are somewhat similar in meaning, so don't confuse the two by misspelling them.

thru Always spell as *through* unless you are quoting.

thusly Avoid—use *thus,* which is an adverb already and does not need the extra *ly.*

till, until Both words mean the same thing. However, *till* is less formal.

to, too, two These words are frequently confused. Use *to* either as a preposition— "Bill is going **to** Ontario"—or as part of an infinitive—"**To** look at museum paintings is one of Bill's great pleasures." Use *too* as an adverb meaning either "also" or "excessively": "Sarah is **too** tired to go to the party; Andrea is **too.**" Use *two* to mean the number, either as a noun or an adjective: "Martin earned **two** degrees at the university."

toward, towards In Canadian English, *toward* is preferred.

try and Avoid—use *try to* instead.

uninterested, disinterested See **disinterested, uninterested.**

unique Do not try to qualify *unique.* "Fairly unique" or "somewhat unique" are contradictions in terms. Something is either unique, or it is not.

usage Avoid unless referring to language choice: "His **usage** of old-fashioned words seems strained and affected." Otherwise, stick with *use:* "His **use** [*not* **usage**] of the car is limited to weekends."

use to, used to *Used to* is correct.

utilize, utilization Avoid this bureaucratic jargon; stick with *use* for both the verb and the noun: "We will **use** [*not* **utilize**] every means at our disposal."

very definite This term is redundant; write *definite.*

wander, wonder Don't confuse these. They mean very different things: *Wander* means to "roam." *Wonder* means to "think" or "consider."

ways Avoid using this term to refer to distance: "Iqaluit is a long **way** [*not* **ways**] from here."

were, where *Were* is a verb; *where* is a question word. Don't forget the letter *h* in *where.*

where Do not use to mean "that": "I heard on the radio **that** [*not* **where**] the big garden supply store is going out of business."

where . . . at Avoid colloquial expressions such as "Where is my car at?" Instead, write "Where is my car?"

who, whom *Who* is a subject; *whom* is an object: "**Who** is the college loan officer?" "**Whom** did you speak with about your loan?"

whose, who's These words are frequently confused. *Whose* is the possessive form of *who*: "**Whose** fishing rod is this?" *Who's* is the contraction of *who is*: "**Who's** out in the garden?"

wise This is a nonstandard noun ending. Don't write "**Math-wise,** I need a tutor." Instead, write "I need a tutor for math."

would have, would of The correct form is *would have.*

your, you're These words are frequently confused. *Your* is the possessive form of *you*: "Here are **your** tickets and itinerary, Jenna." *You're* is the contraction of *you are*: "**You're** going to be late if you don't get started."

READINGS

To gain a better idea of objective writing as opposed to subjective writing, let's look at the following two reviews of the Sam Roberts CD, *Love at the End of the World*. Reviewers try to be objective and impartial; however, every review is only one person's opinion and is thus subjective. Yet, as previously mentioned, writers can control how subjective their writing appears. See if you can tell the difference between these two examples:

SAM ROBERTS, *LOVE AT THE END OF THE WORLD*
T'Cha Dunlevy, Gazette Music Critic
Published: Wednesday, May 21, 2008
Secret Brain/Universal
Rating: 4 stars (out of 5)

---

1 So thick are the throngs of indie-rock bands defining our city's music scene, it is sometimes tempting to think that's all there is. It was a revelation when Sam Roberts emerged

just over a half-decade back with his breakthrough radio smash "Brother Down" (and the accompanying EP *The Inhuman Condition*). The breezy bongo-rock ditty introduced a retro-leaning hippie-at-heart carrying the torch for classic rock, imbuing it with nostalgia and heartstring-tugging ambition.

2 Roberts' debut *We Were Born in a Flame* was an infectious collection of campfire/arena-singalong anthems that brought him across the country, saw him and his band open for the Tragically Hip, and put rock'n'roll back on the Canadian music map. Inspired by time in the South African desert and a stint in Australia, his 2006 follow-up *Chemical City* branched out into '70s psychedelia. Adventurous but not as accessible, it came and went with less fanfare.

3 Back at home in Montreal, and now the father of a little girl, Roberts stayed rooted to record this third disc, which finds him staring down the crumbling world around him. On the first single 'Them Kids,' he complains that "The kids don't know how to dance and rock'n'roll," over insistent riffs, melodic guitar lines and a relentless backbeat.

4 And so he shows them how. He sounds energized, like a man on a mission. The guitars are alive on this record, not just grinding but twinkling, bubbling, soaring. Roberts and his bandmates' musical instincts are on display via an array of vibrant sonic backdrops. Incorporating both the rock hooks of his debut and the textural depth of the follow-up, he brings us the best of both.

5 The title track is a garage-blues stomper with apocalyptic undertones and a thread of hope; "Stripmall Religion" offers socio-critical commentary over expansive guitarscapes; "Lions of the Kalahari" is an existential hymn that contemplates eternal truths, as do "End of the Empire," and "The Pilgrim." Roberts remains effortlessly tuneful in the face of upheaval, finding solace in song. "Just give me a reason/To carry on, to carry on," he

SAM ROBERTS, *LOVE AT THE END OF THE WORLD*
Trent Darren

1   I've been looking forward all year to Sam Roberts' latest album *Love at the End of the World,* and it's finally here. Right off the bat the first song "Them Kids" kicks you in the teeth with its driving tempo and heartfelt lyrics. Roberts has always sounded passionate, but I think on this album he's even more brutally honest about his feelings towards popular culture and society, meaning he thinks we can do better. Most of the other songs stick in my head for hours after I hear them and impress me with their interesting lyrics.

2   This album is as good as *We Were Born in a Flame,* but not as good as *Chemical City* in my opinion. I would encourage casual fans to buy this disc before the other two to get the true Sam Roberts band experience. This one will blow you away.

Everyone is a Critic—Analysis

Although both reviews are essentially the opinion of the reviewer, one can plainly see that the second review, with its use of informal language and constant use of the first person, is far more subjective than the first review, which tries to sound more impartial.

The following two essays contain largely objective descriptions; however, their level of formality differs. In the first essay, Lianne George describes public anticipation and reaction to Apple's iPhone and gives a description of the device itself. In the second essay, Kate Kennedy describes a new type of doll targeted to special needs children. As you read each essay, try to judge the writer's connection with his or her audience. For what audience is each essay written?

ALL HAIL THE IPHONE
Apple has another blockbuster. But does the phone measure up?

Lianne George

Lianne George has been a senior editor for Maclean's. *Her work has also appeared in* Saturday Night, ELLE Canada, *and* Shift *magazines. She is co-author of the books* Out To Brunch *(2003) and* The Ego Boom: Why the World Really Does Revolve Around You *(2009). Currently, she works as editor of* The Grid.

1   In early 1999, Apple pulled off an extraordinary marketing coup by wrapping its new line of iMac computers in coloured plastic panels and introducing them in a range of five fruity "flavours"—grape, tangerine, strawberry, blueberry, and lime. More than any other feature of the iMac, this one low-tech design element marked a whole new way of thinking about computers—fun, like candy!—and it made it possible for people to care about a technological device the way they care about a favourite reading chair or coffee mug. The years since have amounted to a non-stop Apple love-in, starring a parade of iPods and multi-coloured Nanos and Minis. On June 29, [2007,] though, when the company finally unveiled its iPhone—known to bloggers as "the Jesus phone"—to dizzying fanfare in the U.S., you would've thought it had found a cure for unhappiness.

2   Billed by Steve Jobs, Apple's resident oracle, as a "revolutionary" all-in-one device, the iPhone is an iPod, a smart phone, and Internet on the go—all done up in a gleaming package. But now that the artifact has revealed itself, critics are already questioning whether the iPhone lives up to the hype, or if it's just more fruity flavouring.

3   As expected, initial demand for the iPhone—priced at US$499 for a four-gigabyte model and US$599 for an eight-gigabyte model—was overwhelming. Estimates place the number of units sold over the first weekend anywhere from 500 000 to 700 000. Within a week, Apple's stock soared to a record high of over US$130. (It was bumped even higher Tuesday when analysts speculated that a smaller, cheaper Nano version of the iPhone could hit the market later this year.) The launch also proved to be a triumph for AT&T, which has the exclusive rights as the iPhone's carrier in the U.S. Company spokesperson Mark Siegel told reporters, "In its first weekend, we sold more iPhones than in the first month of any other wireless phone AT&T ever offered."

4   Sadly for us, Apple has yet to strike a deal with a Canadian service provider. But the limited accessibility of the phone—whether because of production constraints or by design—only serves to make people covet the device more desperately. "It's typically Apple," says Kevin Restivo, an analyst with Toronto's SeaBoard Group, of the tightly controlled launch. "Steve Jobs is the ultimate circus master."

5   Early reviews of the device were glowing. Design-wise, the iPhone is in another stratosphere. The touch-screen interface, and the fact that the phone knows whether you're holding it horizontally or vertically, give it that magic-trick quality. David Pogue of *The New York Times* described the Web browser as "a real dazzler," and Ed Baig of *USA Today* said this "expensive, glitzy wunderkind is indeed worth lusting after." Though, as one *Slate* writer pointed out, both of these reviewers have books on the iPhone pending, so it'd better be worth the ink.

6   But there's an enormous risk involved in pushing expectations so high and availability so low. One wonders, what exactly will this thing do for you? Anything short of improving the quality of the friends you can call or the calibre of music you can download will be a disappointment. Already, iPhone backlash has come fast and furious. People who've grown accustomed to an 80-gigabyte iPod say there's not nearly enough memory. The touch-screen keypad is awkward to use. The batteries don't last long and cost US$89 to replace. And several critics have reported frequent crashes.

7   But the biggest complaint is the fact that it's only usable on the AT&T network. iPhone users must commit to a two-year AT&T contract at a minimum cost of US$1400 in order to even activate the phone. According to *Slate* writer Tim Wu, "AT&T's rather slow EDGE network is a weakness that affects the phone's most exciting capabilities." (Right now, hackers are working night and day to "unlock" the phones, so that they might be used with any service provider.)

8   Ultimately, while the iPhone remains the hottest accessory on the market, it's currently more useful as a status object than a life-altering device. "If you want reliable, secure, always-on email access, then you have to go with the [RIM's] BlackBerry," says Restivo. "You can't rely on the iPhone for that." Jobs has set a goal of taking one per cent of the world's cellular market by the end of 2008. He'll probably get it. But there's a reason RIM's stock shot up by seven per cent the Monday after the iPhone launch. Then again, maybe we're just jealous.

VOCABULARY

The following terms are identified by paragraph number. Make sure that you understand each term's meaning in its context. If you're not sure that you understand a term, look it up in a dictionary.

coup (1)	**oracle** (2)	**covet** (4)
unveiled (1)	**gigabyte** (3)	**stratosphere** (5)
artifact (2)	**speculated** (3)	**calibre** (6)

STYLE AND STRATEGY

1. How does the writer of this essay achieve an objective writing style?
2. Descriptive essays need to evoke the senses. How well does George accomplish this task? To which senses does she appeal the most? How could she have incorporated the other senses?
3. George does not immediately begin her essay with a description of the iPhone. Why does she choose to organize her essay this way?
4. What is the tone of George's essay? How does the last line support your answer?

QUESTIONS FOR CRITICAL THINKING AND DISCUSSION

1. Technology aids our lives in many ways, but it can also hinder them just as much. Discuss the positives and negatives of a particular technology that has "improved" our lives.
2. George comments that at the time of writing many people were upset with the iPhone because it was only available on the AT&T network. This is called a media monopoly. Can you name other monopolies in society? What effect do they have on the consumer? What is Blackberry's role in comparison to the iPhone, regarding monopolies?
3. Cellphone use is widespread, but it comes with its fair share of problems and concerns. What are the major issues of cellphone use in society (at home, at school, while travelling). Choose one major issue affecting cellphone use and list the steps (if any) being taken to deal with this issue.
4. Smartphones are valued not only for their functions, but also as status symbols. Why has the smartphone been elevated to the status of "cool object?" What specific characteristics make a desirable smartphone? Is all of this love for the smartphone nonsense?

SUGGESTIONS FOR WRITING

1. Write a 500- to 750-word description of a piece of technology that you value.
2. You work for the travel and tourism department of your city or town. Write a 500- to 750-word promotional document describing the main attractions of your city or town and why people should visit or live in your area.

MY NEW DOLL HAS DOWN'S SYNDROME

These "special needs" toys have been called everything from "sweet" to "patronizing"

Kate Kennedy

Kate Kennedy previously was a senior contributor to Maclean's. *Some of her articles included "It's Official: The Guitar Solo is Dead" and "Dirt Poor: Eating Mud to Survive." Currently, she works for Sun Media as managing editor of the lifestyle section for Canoe.ca.*

1   Madeline Millman, 8, looks a lot like her fair-haired brother Joshua, but there are some features she shares only with her doll, "baby." Because Maddy's doll has Down's syndrome, too. "We just thought it would be nice for her to see and play with something . . . that was very similar to her," says Denise Millman, of Colborne, Ontario, who bought the doll for her granddaughter when Madeline was an infant. "She still plays with it, sometimes she likes to put makeup on it—a typical little girl," she adds with a laugh.

2   At a time when culturally diverse dolls are readily available, "special needs" dolls have become the new playthings some parents are hoping their children will identify with. Pattycake Doll Co., out of New York, for instance, sells special doll-sized blue and yellow plastic wheelchairs that go for US$37.50, and for visually impaired dolls, they sell a red-tipped white cane and a guide dog that comes complete with a harness. Bindependent.com, out of Kansas and Texas, sells plastic walkers, leg braces and hearing aids for dolls.

3   Denise Millman ordered Maddy's doll from Downi Creations, a non-profit organization based in South Carolina that sells "collector-quality" dolls online for US$175. Donna Moore, Downi's creator and CEO, says they've got "the 13 distinct features" associated with Down's syndrome, such as almond-shaped eyes, a single crease across the palm, and a smaller mouth with a "slightly protruding tongue." A small scar on the doll's chest represents heart surgery, which some children, like Maddy, undergo. According to the Canadian Down Syndrome Society, 40 per cent of the one in 800 people born with the syndrome have a heart defect.

4   "All children don't have all of these features, but we put all the features in the dolls so every child [can] recognize themselves," says Moore. Parents and relatives of children with Down's syndrome make up the bulk of Moore's customers (who include Eunice Kennedy Shriver and Demi Moore), but her dolls have also been used as teaching tools. Ann Greiner, director of the physical therapy program at Franklin Pierce University in New Hampshire, says Moore's dolls are accurate enough for students to use in their pediatrics course and practical examinations. The bodies (which have a bean-like stuffing) simulate the low muscle tone characteristic of babies with Down's syndrome.

5   Helga Parks, co-owner of Helga's European Specialty Toys, got the idea to sell Down's syndrome dolls after seeing her niece, Angela, who has since died, play with them in her special needs class in Germany. "I could see that kids relate in a much better way than if you give them a Barbie," said Parks over the phone from South Carolina, where her company is based. "These dolls actually improve the child's self-esteem—it gives them something to relate to." Parks recently started selling "Chemo Friends," which are bald dolls that have a little port under their collarbones to mimic the one some chemotherapy patients get, says Parks. "This would comfort the children: 'Look, the doll is experiencing the same procedures I am.' "

6   Down's syndrome dolls have provoked a wide range of opinions from adults—they've been called everything from "sick and patronizing" to "incredibly sweet" in news websites and online communities. The topic is so popular right now that the Canadian Down

Syndrome Society will be polling parents for their take on the dolls in an upcoming news-letter. CDSS says that while the intent to sell the dolls may be heartfelt, they may also reinforce a stereotype that all people with the syndrome have all of the physical features associated with it.

7   Marie White, chairwoman of the Council of Canadians with Disabilities, says special needs dolls aren't on the organization's radar (they work in policy), but as a person with a mobility disability, she is concerned kids might get the message that people with dis-abilities should be treated in a paternalistic fashion. White says that, in general, diversity in toys is a good idea, but she wouldn't want kids to get the idea these kind of dolls (or people who have disabilities) need extra taking care of.

8   Amber Boyd, executive director of Ups and Downs, a Calgary-based parent sup-port organization, has a more practical reason for not buying one for her four-year-old daughter, Trinity, who has Down's syndrome. Boyd thinks that by the time Trinity is able to recognize the doll's differences, she'll probably be too old to play with one.

VOCABULARY

The following terms are identified by paragraph number. Make sure that you under-stand each term's meaning in its context. If you're not sure that you understand a term, look it up in a dictionary.

diverse (2)   **patronizing** (6)

pediatrics (4)   **paternalistic** (7)

STYLE AND STRATEGY

1. How does the writer of this essay achieve an objective writing style?
2. Descriptive essays need to evoke the senses. How well does Kennedy accomplish this? To which senses does she appeal the most? How could she have incorporated the other senses?
3. Unlike George's essay, Kennedy begins her essay with description. Would this essay be bet-ter organized if the first and second paragraphs were switched?
4. How is description used in aid of this essay's argument? How could it be used more effectively?

QUESTIONS FOR CRITICAL THINKING AND DISCUSSION

1. The main argument of this essay is whether special needs dolls are a positive influence for kids with special needs or the public in general. How do you feel about this issue? Can you relate to this article?
2. How are people with special needs portrayed in the media? Can you think of any films or television shows that portray special needs people with dignity and respect, or do most rely on crude stereotypes?

SUGGESTIONS FOR WRITING

1. Write a 500- to 750-word description of someone who has overcome a disability in his or her life, or describe a specific individual whose mental or physical disability is an impor-tant part of who he or she is.
2. Write a 500- to 750-word description of a toy that had significance for you growing up.

In the narrative essays that follow, Margo Pfeiff writes about how an isolated Northern community goes about accomplishing something most Canadians take for granted—shopping—while George Orwell presents the stark reality of capital punishment. As you read each essay, concentrate on the writer's thesis—the point that the writer is trying to make and the focus that drives each of these narratives.

THE SPINACH ARMADA
How the north gets its groceries

Margo Pfeiff

Margo Pfeiff's work has appeared in Reader's Digest, Canadian Geographic, *and* The Globe and Mail, *among other publications. She writes on a variety of subjects, but prefers to concentrate on life in Northern Canada. She is currently writing a book about modern life in Nunavut. Her essay "The Spinach Armada: How the North Gets its Groceries" appeared in* The Walrus *in November of 2007.*

1   Kugaaruk—Every April, Sidney and Tess Rodnunsky sit at their kitchen table calculating how much toilet paper their family of four will use in the coming year. "We hate to run out, so we figure on six rolls a week," says Sidney, the school principal in this eastern Arctic village of 688. On a form from Marché Turenne Inc., a Montreal-area cargo expediter, the couple puts down their order and moves on. How many jars of pickles will they go through in twelve months? How many boxes of laundry soap? Bags of Halloween candy? Then they send off the mother of all grocery lists and wait.

2   In Nunavut, where no roads connect the twenty-six communities to one another or to the south, everything arrives by plane or ship. Air transport is expensive yet essential for perishables and mail. But most supplies are delivered by private cargo vessels, which carry more than 100 000 tonnes of goods in an annual sealift during the ice-free window between June or July and October, depending on the latitude.

3   It is now early September, and at the deepwater port of Nanisivik, on Baffin Island, chief officer Michel Dufresne and his boatswain have just spent two days loading hundreds of cubic metres of cargo, relayed from Montreal and bound for Kugaaruk, onto the Canadian Coast Guard vessel *Des Groseilliers,* a ninety-eight-metre icebreaker, and its little brother, the *Terry Fox.* (Kugaaruk lies on Pelly Bay, whose waters are notorious for thick, shifting ice floes that could crush the hulls of conventional ships; it is the only civilian community in Nunavut that regularly needs such muscle for sealift.) The lift's volatile goods, which include acetylene, all-terrain-vehicle batteries, and hundreds of kilograms of ammunition, must be spaced at least three metres apart. Then there is distributing the weight; over the lift's four trips (two per ship), Dufresne and crew will deliver crates of sunglasses (252 kg), hockey sticks (133 kg), and potato chips (299 kg), two motorboats, construction material for eight houses, and, parked on the *Des Groseilliers*'s helipad, a Chevy Silverado truck for the police. "It's like playing Tetris," Dufresne says.

4   After two days knocking through a jumble of ice pans, the *Des Gros* sights the hamlet on the treeless shore—a low cluster of houses, a modern school, nursing station, and RCMP post, and, heralding the ship's arrival, teams of barking sled dogs. As one of the onboard cranes loads the first landing barge, children crowd muddy Barge Landing Beach alongside a couple of idling forklifts. Anticipation is high; for weeks, paper towel has been standing in for toilet paper, and the vast Koomiut Co-op has had a desperate,

Soviet atmosphere, with metres of shelves empty but for a few tins of evaporated milk and pilot biscuits.

5   As soon as the barge touches the beach, forklifts move in to unload it, grabbing pallets teetering with wooden crates and scooting up the hill to drop them at the Co-op's cargo bay, where they quickly stack up. Pried open with crowbars, they are emptied by a column of human haulers hired for the occasion. Kids crawl all over the crates and cheer when the thirty-three tonnes of pop arrive—they drink it at breakfast, lunch, and dinner. "It retails for three dollars a can, and it will be gone by January," says Co-op manager Eric Baxter, "and then, until September, we fly it in." Kugaaruk, like most of the territory, has an extreme sweet tooth; pop makes up as much as 80 percent of the town's inbound cargo flights.

6   A forklift inches up the main dirt road, balancing the first of two pallets bound for the Rodnunsky household and then setting it down gently in the family's rocky front yard. Their two adolescent kids, Sidney Jr. and Donna, help unpack and carry the 2600 kilograms of groceries indoors, much of it to their unheated "sealift room" for storage. "It's a family event," says Sidney Sr. The overflow and the unfreezables—and there are plenty of those—are stashed throughout the home, mainly in the living room. "We just put tablecloths over boxes of canned food and use them as end tables," he says.

7   Southerners (mostly teachers, nurses, and police staff) make the bulk of the orders; for those with the purchasing power, sealift is much cheaper than buying from the town store and offers more variety. Everyone who's used the service has a sealift story—like ordering three jars of Cheez Whiz, only to have three boxes of the stuff arrive on the doorstep. It's a town tradition to trade excess goods with other families, and in spring, yard sales are a common dumping ground for those stray case lots of hot dog relish and furniture polish.

8   But in these hectic, exciting days of early September, it's a thrill to unpack goodies not seen in months. At the Co-op, women queue and chatter, babies tucked in their parka hoods, as they scoop up items the moment they hit the shelves. Then they walk home, slowly, weighed down with bulging shopping bags.

VOCABULARY

The following terms are identified by paragraph number. Make sure that you understand each term's meaning in its context. If you're not sure that you understand a term, look it up in a dictionary.

notorious (3)	**heralding** (4)	**stashed** (6)
volatile (3)	**teetering** (5)	**queue** (8)

STYLE AND STRATEGY

1. What is this essay's thesis? Is it stated overtly, or is it implied?
2. This essay's conclusion is open-ended. Do you feel that this method of conclusion works for this essay? How else could the essay have ended?
3. How does the author's inclusion of dialogue and focus on the characters in the Rodnunsky family add to the essay? How would the style of the essay be different were it not to focus on any particular characters?

QUESTIONS FOR CRITICAL THINKING AND DISCUSSION

1. Life in isolated communities can be difficult. However, it can also be rewarding. Using examples from this essay, prove both sides of this argument.
2. Describe the lives of the people of Nunavut by the types of groceries they buy. How do these items tell a story?

SUGGESTIONS FOR WRITING

1. Write a 500- to 750-word narrative essay relating a life experience during which you were away from home for an extended period of time (camp, university, a trip). How did this experience help you to grow as a person?
2. Write a 500- to 750-word narrative essay outlining the events of a day in the life of someone living in the city contrasted with the life of someone living in the country. Which of the two provides the more fulfilling environment?

A HANGING
George Orwell

Eric Arthur Blair (1909–1950), who took the pseudonym George Orwell, is best known for the books Animal Farm *(1945) and* 1984 *(1949), which reflect his growing concern over totalitarian governments. Many of his essays, including "A Hanging," first published in 1931, recount in a spare, unemotional style his observations of a cruel and neglectful society.*

1   It was in Burma, a sodden morning of the rains. A sickly light, like yellow tinfoil, was slanting over the high walls into the jail yard. We were waiting outside the condemned cells, a row of sheds fronted with double bars, like small animal cages. Each cell measured about ten feet by ten and was quite bare within except for a plank bed and a pot for drinking water. In some of them brown silent men were squatting at the inner bars, with their blankets draped round them. These were the condemned men, due to be hanged within the next week or two.

2   One prisoner had been brought out of his cell. He was a Hindu, a puny wisp of a man, with a shaven head and vague liquid eyes. He had a thick, sprouting moustache, absurdly too big for his body, rather like the moustache of a comic man in the films. Six tall Indian warders were guarding him and getting him ready for the gallows. Two of them stood by with rifles and fixed bayonets, while the others handcuffed him, passed a chain through his handcuffs and fixed it to their belts, and lashed his arms tight to his sides. They crowded very close about him, with their hands always on him in a careful, caressing grip, as though all the while feeling him to make sure he was there. It was like men handling a fish which is still alive and may jump back into the water. But he stood quite unresisting, yielding his arms limply to the ropes, as though he hardly noticed what was happening.

3   Eight o'clock struck and a bugle call, desolately thin in the wet air, floated from the distant barracks. The superintendent of the jail, who was standing apart from the rest of us, moodily prodding the gravel with his stick, raised his head at the sound. He was an army doctor, with a grey toothbrush moustache and a gruff voice. "For God's sake hurry up, Francis," he said irritably. "The man ought to have been dead by this time. Aren't you ready yet?"

4   Francis, the head jailer, a fat Dravidian in a white drill suit and gold spectacles, waved his black hand. "Yes sir, yes sir," he bubbled. "All iss satisfactorily prepared. The hangman iss waiting. We shall proceed."

5   "Well, quick march, then. The prisoners can't get their breakfast till this job's over."

6   We set out for the gallows. Two warders marched on either side of the prisoner, with their rifles at the slope; two others marched close against him, gripping him by arm and shoulder, as though at once pushing and supporting him. The rest of us, magistrates and the like, followed behind. Suddenly, when we had gone ten yards, the procession stopped short without any order or warning. A dreadful thing had happened—a dog, come goodness knows whence, had appeared in the yard. It came bounding among us with a loud volley of barks, and leapt round us wagging its whole body, wild with glee at finding so many human beings together. It was a large woolly dog, half Airedale, half pariah. For a moment it pranced round us, and then, before anyone could stop it, it had made a dash for the prisoner and, jumping up, tried to lick his face. Everyone stood aghast, too taken aback even to grab at the dog.

7   "Who let that bloody brute in here?" said the superintendent angrily. "Catch it, someone!"

8   A warder, detached from the escort, charged clumsily after the dog, but it danced and gambolled just out of his reach, taking everything as part of the game. A young Eurasian jailer picked up a handful of gravel and tried to stone the dog away, but it dodged the stones and came after us again. Its yaps echoed from the jail walls. The prisoner, in the grasp of the two warders, looked on incuriously, as though this was another formality of the hanging. It was several minutes before someone managed to catch the dog. Then we put my handkerchief through its collar and moved off once more, with the dog still straining and whimpering.

9   It was about forty yards to the gallows. I watched the bare brown back of the prisoner marching in front of me. He walked clumsily with his bound arms, but quite steadily, with that bobbing gait of the Indian who never straightens his knees. At each step his muscles slid neatly into place, the lock of hair on his scalp danced up and down, his feet printed themselves on the wet gravel. And once, in spite of the men who gripped him by each shoulder, he stepped slightly aside to avoid a puddle in the path.

10   It is curious, but till that moment I had never realized what it means to destroy a healthy, conscious man. When I saw the prisoner step aside to avoid the puddle I saw the mystery, the unspeakable wrongness, of cutting a life short when it is in full tide. This man was not dying, he was alive just as we were alive. All the organs of his body were working—bowels digesting food, skin renewing itself, nails growing, tissues forming—all toiling away in solemn foolery. His nails would still be growing when he stood on the drop, when he was falling through the air with a tenth-of-a-second to live. His eyes saw the yellow gravel and the grey walls, and his brain still remembered, foresaw, reasoned—reasoned even about puddles. He and we were a party of men walking together, seeing, hearing, feeling, understanding the same world; and in two minutes, with a sudden snap, one of us would be gone—one mind less, one world less.

11   The gallows stood in a small yard, separate from the main grounds of the prison, and overgrown with tall prickly weeds. It was a brick erection like three sides of a shed, with planking on top, and above that two beams and a crossbar with the rope dangling. The hangman, a grey-haired convict in the white uniform of the prison, was waiting beside his machine. He greeted us with a servile crouch as we entered. At a word from Francis the two warders, gripping the prisoner more closely than ever, half led half pushed him to the gallows and helped him clumsily up the ladder. Then the hangman climbed up and fixed the rope round the prisoner's neck.

12   We stood waiting, five yards away. The warders had formed in a rough circle round the gallows. And then, when the noose was fixed, the prisoner began crying out to his god. It was a high, reiterated cry of "Ram! Ram! Ram! Ram!" not urgent and fearful like a prayer or cry for help, but steady, rhythmical, almost like the tolling of a bell. The dog answered the sound with a whine. The hangman, still standing on the gallows, produced a small cotton bag like a flour bag and drew it down over the prisoner's face. But the sound, muffled by the cloth, still persisted, over and over again: "Ram! Ram! Ram! Ram! Ram!"

13   The hangman climbed down and stood ready, holding the lever. Minutes seemed to pass. The steady, muffled crying from the prisoner went on and on, "Ram! Ram! Ram!"

never faltering for an instant. The superintendent, his head on his chest, was slowly poking the ground with his stick; perhaps he was counting the cries, allowing the prisoner a fixed number—fifty, perhaps, or a hundred. Everyone had changed colour. The Indians had gone grey like bad coffee, and one or two of the bayonets were wavering. We looked at the lashed, hooded man on the drop, and listened to his cries—each cry another second of life; the same thought was in all our minds: oh, kill him quickly, get it over, stop that abominable noise!

14 Suddenly the superintendent made up his mind. Throwing up his head he made a swift motion with his stick. "Chalo!" he shouted almost fiercely.

15 There was a clanking noise, and then dead silence. The prisoner had vanished, and the rope was twisting on itself. I let go of the dog, and it galloped immediately to the back of the gallows; but when it got there it stopped short, barked, and then retreated into a corner of the yard, where it stood among the weeds, looking timorously out at us. We went round the gallows to inspect the prisoner's body. He was dangling with his toes pointed straight downwards, very slowly revolving, as dead as a stone.

16 The superintendent reached out with his stick and poked the bare brown body; it oscillated slightly. "*He's* all right," said the superintendent. He backed out from under the gallows, and blew out a deep breath. The moody look had gone out of his face quite suddenly. He glanced at his wristwatch. "Eight minutes past eight. Well, that's all for this morning, thank God."

17 The warders unfixed bayonets and marched away. The dog, sobered and conscious of having misbehaved itself, slipped after them. We walked out of the gallows yard, past the condemned cells with their waiting prisoners, into the big central yard of the prison. The convicts, under the command of warders armed with lathis, were already receiving their breakfast. They squatted in long rows, each man holding a tin panikin, while two warders with buckets marched round ladling out rice; it seemed quite a homely, jolly scene, after the hanging. An enormous relief had come upon us now that the job was done. One felt an impulse to sing, to break into a run, to snigger. All at once everyone began chattering gaily.

18 The Eurasian boy walking beside me nodded towards the way we had come, with a knowing smile: "Do you know, sir, our friend [he meant the dead man] when he heard his appeal had been dismissed, he pissed on the floor of his cell. From fright. Kindly take one of my cigarettes, sir. Do you not admire my new silver case, sir? From the boxwalah, two rupees eight annas. Classy European style."

19 Several people laughed—at what, nobody seemed certain.

20 Francis was walking by the superintendent, talking garrulously: "Well, sir, all hass passed off with the utmost satisfactoriness. It was all finished—flick! like that. It iss not always so—oah, no! I have known cases where the doctor wass obliged to go beneath the gallows and pull the prisoner's legs to ensure decease. Most disagreeable!"

21 "Wriggling about, eh? That's bad," said the superintendent.

22 "Ach, sir, it iss worse when they become refractory! One man, I recall, clung to the bars of hiss cage when we went to take him out. You will scarcely credit, sir, that it took six warders to dislodge him, three pulling at each leg. We reasoned with him. 'My dear fellow,' we said, 'think of all the pain and trouble you are causing to us!' But no, he would not listen! Ach, he wass very troublesome!"

23 I found that I was laughing quite loudly. Everyone was laughing. Even the superintendent grinned in a tolerant way. "You'd better all come out and have a drink," he said quite genially. "I've got a bottle of whisky in the car. We could do with it."

24 We went through the big double gates of the prison into the road. "Pulling at his legs!" exclaimed a Burmese magistrate suddenly, and burst into a loud chuckling. We all began laughing again. At that moment Francis' anecdote seemed extraordinarily funny. We all had a drink together, native and European alike, quite amicably. The dead man was a hundred yards away.

VOCABULARY

The following terms are identified by paragraph number. Make sure that you understand each term's meaning in its context. If you're not sure that you understand a term, look it up in a dictionary.

sodden (1)	**gambolled** (8)	**timorously** (15)
sickly (1)	**gait** (9)	**oscillated** (16)
condemned (1)	**servile** (11)	**refractory** (22)
whence (6)	**reiterated** (12)	**magistrate** (24)
pariah (6)	**abominable** (13)	**amicably** (24)

STYLE AND STRATEGY

1. Most of this narrative is straightforward, but the point where Orwell stops to comment on its significance could arguably be regarded as its thesis or main point. Where does this break occur, and what effect does it have on your sense of the tale?

2. What does the description of the dog's behaviour add to the story? Do you think Orwell added this detail for comic relief, or does it have another purpose?

3. What effect does the recounting of the post-hanging "celebration" have?

4. In the last few paragraphs, the executioners are nervously celebrating the event. How does Orwell use the abrupt last sentence of the essay ("The dead man was a hundred yards away") to comment on this celebration?

QUESTIONS FOR CRITICAL THINKING AND DISCUSSION

1. There are many jobs that most of us don't want and prefer not to think about: executioner, slaughterhouse worker, solid-waste technician, health care worker specializing in caring for terminally ill children or adults. How do you think people who have such jobs get used to dealing with them psychologically? In other words, how would such a job become "just a job," with all the routine and boredom we associate with a steady position?

2. Do the people who support capital punishment really want it carried out regularly, or do they want the idea of it, an occasional symbolic instance of putting a murderer to death? What is your view on the issue of capital punishment?

SUGGESTIONS FOR WRITING

1. Write a 500- to 750-word narrative about an incident that you witnessed or know about involving substantial harm done to someone but with no punishment for the offender. The offender could be a police officer merely doing his or her job or a parent making an earnest attempt to deal with a misbehaving child.

2. Write a 500- to 750-word narrative about an occasion in which you unintentionally harmed someone. What were the consequences? How did you feel?

A READER'S EYE

In the exemplification essays that follow, Cathy Gulli writes about why the foam foot-wear Crocs aren't as harmless as they appear, while Lars Eighner tackles a very different topic: what it is like to dine from a dumpster. As you read these essays, concentrate on the authors' *purposes.* What are they trying to prove? Writers of exemplification essays are usually presenting their generalizations and examples for a reason. Readers always appreciate concrete examples, which makes an exemplification essay ideal for getting a writer's message across.

THE SHOCKING TRUTH ABOUT CROCS
Why Some Hospitals Are Moving toward a Ban on the Colourful Foam Clog

Cathy Gulli

Cathy Gulli is an associate editor for Maclean's *magazine. She writes on issues of health, technology, and popular culture.*

1   Few consumer products have inspired the kind of fanatic loyalty Crocs owners feel for their foam clogs. The Boulder, Colo.-based company has captured the soles of a wide range of professionals who otherwise claim no particular affinity for Dutch fashion. Among the most devoted fans are health care workers. Nearly 200 of them, including many from Canada, have posted emphatic testimonials on the company's website. Wearing Crocs, they say, is just like walking on "pillows" or "marshmallows." Crocs are nothing short of "a nurse's best friend." They "can change your life." The bonus, another worker writes, is that nurses and doctors can purchase a pair in every colour to match any shade of medical scrubs—colour coordination goes a long way "to make the patients feel better or more at ease."

2   But not everyone is so enthusiastic. An increasing number of hospitals and health centres are moving toward banning Crocs and Crocs knock-offs from their facilities for fear the shoes have endangered both patients and staff. The main offenders appear to be the popular Beach and Cayman models, which have holes on top, side vents and a back strap rather than a closed heel. They allegedly have been responsible for infection control hazards because bodily fluids such as blood have spilled into the holes. Staff have reportedly twisted ankles because of the open back. And staff reaction times are said to be compromised because it's suspected that clogs are more difficult to run in than traditional hospital footwear. The most heinous charge against Crocs and similar shoes is that they act as "isolators," enabling enough static electricity to be generated to knock out medical equipment—including respirators in maternity wards.

3   The most concrete sign of a Crocs backlash came earlier this year, when Rapid City Regional Hospital in Rapid City, S.D., instituted a new dress code. Among other requirements, such as no denim or nose piercings, health care workers were banned from wearing the Crocs Beach. "When you deal with a patient who is hemorrhaging blood downward onto your feet, if that patient has HIV or hepatitis, you've protected yourself from infection just by having the right kind of shoe on," said Dr. James Keegan, vice-president of clinical quality, to the media. "You want to provide the best impervious barrier you can."

4   Meanwhile, at Blekinge Hospital in Karlskrona, in southern Sweden, it's being recommended that "Foppatoffels," as Crocs and similar shoes are known there, be banned after suspicions were raised that they acted as isolators to facilitate static electricity, which caused medical machines to malfunction. Three times, according to reports, equipment including a respirator for premature infants shut down after staff wearing foam clogs were nearby. Technicians there believe the plastic-like material of the shoes

can enable up to 25,000 volts of electricity. Medical workers wearing the shoes become "a cloud of lightning," said Bjorn Lofqvist, a hospital spokesperson. "There have more than likely been more incidents—both here and at other hospitals—where people have not made the connection with Foppatoffels." In fact, a similar case occurred in a neonatal ward in a Forde, Norway, hospital, where a bili light used to treat newborns with jaundice faulted due to static electricity, reportedly created by the shoes.

5   Although Crocs Inc. did not return calls to *Maclean's* for this article, the company has defended its product in the past by saying that a number of factors contribute to the buildup of static electricity, including temperature, humidity, flooring applications, and the nature of the contact. "We know of no reason that Crocs would be any more susceptible to static electricity than shoes such as sneakers and other types of footwear worn by medical professionals," reads a statement previously released by the company.

6   Nor does it makes sense to Sandra, 27, a nurse at the Toronto General Hospital, who wears army-green Crocs with top holes, side vents and a back strap during her 12-hour shifts. "I'm amazed that medical equipment could be affected," she says. "It's more believable to me that cellphones would affect equipment—and that's been shown not to be true." She does, however, say that when she began wearing Crocs six months ago, she was immediately puzzled by the frequency with which she gave people shocks at work. "Every time I touched a patient I shocked them. No one ever commented. But I would apologize if it was particularly strong," Sandra remembers.

7   The Ottawa Hospital is one of the few health facilities in Canada known to have taken an official stance against Crocs and similar shoes. Footwear policies are the jurisdiction of individual employers, so there is no common apparel requirement for medical staff across the country. But more and more people are looking for guidance. "We do get calls from health care workers wondering if they are entitled to wear these shoes and if there are any hazards and guidelines they should know about," says Renzo Bertolini, manager of inquiries at the Canadian Centre for Occupational Health and Safety. "We advise them to follow their employer's recommendations. It's [the hospital's] responsibility to provide a healthy and safe workplace."

8   In addition to the hospital bans, there are other signs of a Crocs backlash. Ihatecrocs-blog.blogspot.com has made its mission "eliminating Crocs and those who think that their excuses for wearing them are viable." A recent post stresses the impending resurgence of summertime Crocs: "Like cockroaches crawling out from beneath the ruin of the apocalypse, Crocs are back." Videos on YouTube demonstrate similar disdain for the shoes. And crocsaccidents.blogspot.com "warns parents of the possible dangers of rubber clogs to children," especially on escalators—the shoes allegedly can melt or get stuck in the side of the stairs. One story out of Singapore describes a toddler's toe being ripped off in this way.

9   Still, there are a lot more Crocs fans than dissenters today. Crocs loyalists include celebrities, gardeners and culinary masters such as Iron Chef Mario Batali, who is almost as famous for his fluorescent orange Crocs as he is for food—he reportedly owns 50 pairs of the original Beach model. The company closed 2006 with US$354.7 million in sales, up almost 227 per cent from last year. And all indications suggest market saturation is a long way off. Crocs just launched NASCAR models at Daytona 500. And models inspired by Batman, Superman, Wonder Woman, SpongeBob SquarePants and Dora the Explorer are scheduled to be out this summer.

10   And even if health care facilities ban classic Crocs with the holes and back strap, the clogs will probably still wind up in hospitals. The Ottawa medical supply store owner says nurses are increasingly buying the Endeavor model, which has a closed top. And in May, the Crocs company released three new work shoes—the Batali Bistro, the Specialist and the Specialist Vent. "With the introduction of workplace-geared designs, we are further expanding our footwear offerings to provide functional, high-comfort footwear for the workplace," said Crocs CEO Ron Snyder. "Crocs footwear's unique blend of fashion and function makes these new shoe models the perfect workplace footwear solution." Whether or not that's a crock depends on who you ask.

VOCABULARY

The following terms are identified by paragraph number. Make sure that you understand each term's meaning in its context. If you're not sure that you understand a term, look it up in a dictionary.

fanatic (1)   **apparel (7)**
affinity (1)   **impending (8)**
heinous (2)   **resurgence (8)**
jurisdiction (7)   **dissenters (9)**

STYLE AND STRATEGY

1. What are the major examples Gulli uses? How do they help her develop her thesis?
2. List Gulli's main points. Do they add up to a unified idea? Do the examples she has chosen support this idea? Explain.
3. Gulli provides a number of quotations in her essay. For what purpose does she include these types of quotations? Are they effective?
4. Describe Gulli's tone, particularly in her conclusion. This essay is a serious analysis of important issues in the health care industry. Does Gulli's tone reinforce, or detract from, her essay?

QUESTIONS FOR CRITICAL THINKING AND DISCUSSION

1. Gulli's essay is about fashion and trends—both practical and impractical—and how they affect our lives. Discuss another example of a fashion trend that has been or may become an issue in the workplace.
2. Crocs Inc. did not offer Gulli a comment specifically responding to the accusations lodged in her essay. What effect does this omission have on the reader? Would Gulli's argument have been stronger or weaker if she had been able to quote a representative of Crocs Inc.?

SUGGESTIONS FOR WRITING

1. Write a 500- to 750-word exemplification essay in which you discuss a fashion trend that you or someone you know fell victim to that turned out to be completely impractical. Use appropriate examples to prove your points.
2. Some school boards in Canada have banned sandals and/or high heels for both students and teachers. Write a 500- to 750-word exemplification essay arguing either for or against one of these bans.

ON DUMPSTER DIVING
Lars Eighner

When Lars Eighner wrote "On Dumpster Diving," he was homeless after having been fired from his job in Austin, Texas. With Lizbeth, his Labrador retriever, Eighner spent three years on the streets. "On Dumpster Diving" is a revised version of an essay originally published in 1991 in Threepenny Review *and included in the book* Travels with Lizbeth: Three Years on the Road and on the Streets *(1993). In it, Eighner uses a series of examples to comment on how what we throw away defines the way we live.*

1   I began Dumpster diving about a year before I became homeless.

2   I prefer the word *scavenging* and use the word *scrounging* when I mean to be obscure. I have heard people, evidently meaning to be polite, use the word *foraging,* but I prefer to reserve that word for gathering nuts and berries and such, which I do also according to the season and the opportunity. *Dumpster diving* seems to me to be a little too cute and, in my case, inaccurate because I lack the athletic ability to lower myself into the Dumpsters as the true divers do, much to their increased profit.

3   I like the frankness of the word *scavenging,* which I can hardly think of without picturing a big black snail on an aquarium wall. I live from the refuse of others. I am a scavenger. I think it a sound and honourable niche, although if I could I would naturally prefer to live the comfortable consumer life, perhaps—and only perhaps—as a slightly less wasteful consumer, owing to what I have learned as a scavenger.

4   While Lizbeth and I were still living in the shack on Avenue B as my savings ran out, I put almost all my sporadic income into rent. The necessities of daily life I began to extract from Dumpsters. Yes, we ate from them. Except for jeans, all my clothes came from Dumpsters. Boom boxes, candles, bedding, toilet paper, a virgin male love doll, medicine, books, a typewriter, dishes, furnishings, and change, sometimes amounting to many dollars—I acquired many things from the Dumpsters.

5   I have learned much as a scavenger. I mean to put some of what I have learned down here, beginning with the practical art of Dumpster diving and proceeding to the abstract.

6   What is safe to eat?

7   After all, the finding of objects is becoming something of an urban art. Even respectable employed people will sometimes find something tempting sticking out of a Dumpster or standing beside one. Quite a number of people, not all of them of the bohemian type, are willing to brag that they found this or that piece in the trash. But eating from Dumpsters is what separates the dilettanti from the professionals. Eating safely from the Dumpsters involves three principles: using the senses and common sense to evaluate the condition of the found materials, knowing the Dumpsters of a given area and checking them regularly, and seeking always to answer the question "Why was this discarded?"

8   Perhaps everyone who has a kitchen and a regular supply of groceries has, at one time or another, made a sandwich and eaten half of it before discovering mould on the bread or got a mouthful of milk before realizing the milk had turned. Nothing of the sort is likely to happen to a Dumpster diver because he is constantly reminded that most food is discarded for a reason. Yet a lot of perfectly good food can be found in Dumpsters.

9   Canned goods, for example, turn up fairly often in the Dumpsters I frequent. All except the most phobic people would be willing to eat from a can, even if it came from a Dumpster. Canned goods are among the safest of foods to be found in Dumpsters but are not utterly foolproof.

10   Although very rare with modern canning methods, botulism is a possibility. Most other forms of food poisoning seldom do lasting harm to a healthy person, but botulism is almost certainly fatal and often the first symptom is death. Except for carbonated beverages, all canned goods should contain a slight vacuum and suck air when first punctured. Bulging, rusty, and dented cans and cans that spew when punctured should be avoided, especially when the contents are not very acidic or syrupy.

11   Raw fruits and vegetables with intact skins seem perfectly safe to me, excluding of course the obviously rotten. Many are discarded for minor imperfections that can be pared away. Leafy vegetables, grapes, cauliflower, broccoli, and similar things may be contaminated by liquids and may be impractical to wash.

12   Candy, especially hard candy, is usually safe if it has not drawn ants. Chocolate is often discarded only because it has become discolored as the cocoa butter de-emulsified.

Candying, after all, is one method of food preservation because pathogens do not like very sugary substances.

13   All of these foods might be found in any Dumpster and can be evaluated with some confidence largely on the basis of appearance. Beyond these are foods that cannot be correctly evaluated without additional information.

14   I began scavenging by pulling pizzas out of the Dumpster behind a pizza delivery shop. In general, prepared food requires caution, but in this case I knew when the shop closed and went to the Dumpster as soon as the last of the help left.

15   Such shops often get prank orders; both the orders and the products made to fill them are called *bogus.* Because help seldom stays long at these places, pizzas are often made with the wrong topping, refused on delivery for being cold, or baked incorrectly. The products to be discarded are boxed up because inventory is kept by counting boxes: A boxed pizza can be written off; an unboxed pizza does not exist.

16   I never placed a bogus order to increase the supply of pizzas and I believe no one else was scavenging in this Dumpster. But the people in the shop became suspicious and began to retain their garbage in the shop overnight. While it lasted I had a steady supply of fresh, sometimes warm pizza. Because I knew the Dumpster I knew the source of the pizza, and because I visited the Dumpster regularly I knew what was fresh and what was yesterday's.

17   The area I frequent is inhabited by many affluent college students. I am not here by chance; the Dumpsters in this area are very rich. Students throw out many good things, including food. In particular they tend to throw everything out when they move at the end of a semester, before and after breaks, and around midterm, when many of them despair of college. So I find it advantageous to keep an eye on the academic calendar.

18   Students throw food away around breaks because they do not know whether it has spoiled or will spoil before they return. A typical discard is a half jar of peanut butter. In fact, nonorganic peanut butter does not require refrigeration and is unlikely to spoil in any reasonable time. The student does not know that, and since it is Daddy's money, the student decides not to take a chance. Opened containers require caution and some attention to the question. "Why was this discarded?" But in the case of discards from student apartments, the answer may be that the item was thrown out through carelessness, ignorance, or wastefulness. This can sometimes be deduced when the item is found with many others, including some that are obviously perfectly good.

19   Some students, and others, approach defrosting a freezer by chucking out the whole lot. Not only do the circumstances of such a find tell the story, but also the mass of frozen goods stays cold for a long time and items may be found still frozen or freshly thawed.

20   Yogurt, cheese, and sour cream are items that are often thrown out while they are still good. Occasionally I find a cheese with a spot of mould, which of course I just pare off, and because it is obvious why such a cheese was discarded, I treat it with less suspicion than an apparently perfect cheese found in similar circumstances. Yogurt is often discarded, still sealed, only because the expiration date on the carton had passed. This is one of my favourite finds because yogurt will keep for several days, even in warm weather.

21   Students throw out canned goods and staples at the end of semesters and when they give up college at midterm. Drugs, pornography, spirits, and the like are often discarded when parents are expected—Dad's Day, for example. And spirits also turn up after big party weekends, presumably discarded by the newly reformed. Wine and spirits, of course, keep perfectly well even once opened, but the same cannot be said of beer.

22   My test for carbonated soft drinks is whether they still fizz vigorously. Many juices or other beverages are too acidic or too syrupy to cause much concern, provided they are not visibly contaminated. I have discovered nasty moulds in vegetable juices, even when the product was found under its original seal; I recommend that such products be decanted slowly into a clear glass. Liquids always require some care. One hot day I

found a large jug of Pat O'Brien's Hurricane mix. The jug had been opened but was still ice cold. I drank three large glasses before it became apparent to me that someone had added rum to the mix, and not a little rum. I never tasted the rum, and by the time I began to feel the effects I had already ingested a very large quantity of the beverage. Some divers would have considered this a boon, but being suddenly intoxicated in a public place in the early afternoon is not my idea of a good time.

23 I have heard of people maliciously contaminating discarded food and even handouts, but mostly I have heard of this from people with vivid imaginations who have had no experience with the Dumpsters themselves. Just before the pizza shop stopped discarding its garbage at night, jalapeños began showing up on most of the thrown-out pizzas. If indeed this was meant to discourage me, it was a wasted effort because I am a native Texan.

24 For myself, I avoid game, poultry, pork, and egg-based foods, whether I find them raw or cooked. I seldom have the means to cook what I find, but when I do I avail myself of plentiful supplies of beef, which is often in very good condition. I suppose fish becomes disagreeable before it becomes dangerous. Lizbeth is happy to have any such thing that is past its prime and, in fact, does not recognize fish as food until it is quite strong.

25 Home leftovers, as opposed to surpluses from restaurants, are very often bad. Evidently, especially among students, there is a common type of personality that carefully wraps up even the smallest leftover and shoves it into the back of the refrigerator for six months or so before discarding it. Characteristic of this type are the reused jars and margarine tubs to which the remains are committed. I avoid ethnic foods I am unfamiliar with. If I do not know what it is supposed to look like when it is good, I cannot be certain I will be able to tell if it is bad.

26 No matter how careful I am I still get dysentery at least once a month, oftener in warm weather. I do not want to paint too romantic a picture. Dumpster diving has serious drawbacks as a way of life.

VOCABULARY

The following terms are identified by paragraph number. Make sure that you understand each term's meaning in its context. If you're not sure that you understand a term, look it up in a dictionary.

refuse (3)	**pathogens** (12)
niche (3)	**advantageous** (17)
frankness (3)	**deduced** (18)
sporadic (4)	**expiration** (20)
bohemian (7)	**staples** (21)
dilettanti (7)	**spirits** (21)
phobic (9)	**dysentery** (26)

STYLE AND STRATEGY

1. Many Canadians see homelessness as a vast national tragedy. (In such a prosperous country, how could so many people be adrift?) Does Eighner's tone reflect this attitude, or does it indicate that he is taking a different approach? Explain.

2. At times, this essay almost seems as if it were written by a sociologist studying Canada's discards in order to analyze consumer habits. (Such studies have been conducted.) But who is Eighner's audience? How will this audience react to Eighner's examples?

3. Explain how Eighner incorporates the following three strategies as part of his exemplification essay: process analysis (see Chapter 10), causal analysis (Chapter 11), and comparison and contrast (Chapter 14).

QUESTIONS FOR CRITICAL THINKING AND DISCUSSION

1. Are there people in your city or town who are *involuntarily* homeless? Do you know what caused them to lose their homes? What programs does your town or city offer to help them?
2. Why would someone *choose* to opt out of conventional consumer society?
3. Are you an efficient consumer, or would a "scavenger" welcome the chance to sort through your garbage? Explain.
4. Would you take something from a garbage can or a dumpster if the item appealed to you? Explain.

SUGGESTIONS FOR WRITING

1. Write a 500- to 750-word essay about an activity that most people dislike and avoid (for example, cleaning an apartment or doing laundry) but that you enjoy. Give examples that show why you enjoy this activity.
2. Write a 500- to 750-word essay about an activity that most people enjoy but that you dread. Give examples that show why you dislike this normally positive experience.

In the following essay, Matthew McKinnon discusses how BitTorrent makes downloading even easier, but questions its effect on our consciences. In the second essay, Allan Gregg discusses why so many people are disgusted with politics and the steps that politicians can take to change the public's attitude. As you read these essays, be aware of the authors' purposes: each author is using the process option as a useful strategy to reveal a higher meaning.

TORRENTIAL REIGN

A mega file-sharing protocol called BitTorrent is making the music piracy of yesteryear look like petty theft.

Matthew McKinnon

Matthew McKinnon is a Toronto-based writer whose work has appeared in CBC.ca, Maclean's, The Globe and Mail, *and* The Walrus. *Two-time winner of Canadian National Magazine Awards, McKinnon favours topics dealing with the arts, technology, and social issues. Currently, he teaches journalism at Ryerson University. His essay "Torrential Reign" is part technical explanation on the process of using BitTorrent and part cultural critique of technology doomsday scenarios.*

1   Napster, file-sharing's original supervillain, was like Barry Bonds as a young baseball player: slick and spry. Its network was an efficient delivery tool for digitally compressed music files (i.e., MP3s), but only because they are small and relatively easy to move. Napster, to stretch the baseball analogy, scored with singles and steals. It made music free, but no more than that: the network's architecture left it too weak to share so-called "big media objects," such as the supersize TV files that I like to grab. (Napster's resurrection as an online, for-profit MP3 store is as wrong as an anarchy symbol on a Starbucks cup. Pretend it never happened.)

2   BitTorrent is an evolution, the twenty-first-century Bonds: bulked up beyond belief, a peerless power hitter with an imperfect reputation. BitTorrent specializes in big media; it is the Internet's top distributor of free feature films, television shows, computer software, video games, and entire music albums. Any creative work that can be copied to a CD or DVD can be—and most often is—shared planetwide via BitTorrent. Its client applications (BitTorrent is the technology; myriad programs have been built to activate it) can complete in minutes transfers that took hours on Napster, giving people who have already made their ethical peace with downloading five-megabyte MP3s the means to take 500-megabyte anthologies instead. A cynic might compare the gulf between Napster and BitTorrent to the difference between shoplifting and larceny.

3   How BitTorrent works is hard to explain. Older downloading tools such as Napster operated as one-way streets. Users wanting, say, an MP3 music file got it directly from a computer that already had it, so all transfers flowed in a straight line. BitTorrent instead creates "swarms." Downloaders like me use a small file called a torrent to connect to dozens, even hundreds, of computers at a time. We gain access to huge media files—a full season of *24*, perhaps—that have been chopped into small fragments to be easily shared among members of the swarm. My computer might download one fragment from a computer in London, another from a computer in Los Angeles, a third from Lagos. Next, it asks London and Los Angeles if it needs the fragment I took from Lagos, then sends it along if the answer is yes. BitTorrent downloads and uploads at the same

time, turning file-sharing into a multi-lane highway that swaps data faster than Napster and its relatives ever could. Every computer labours for the swarm; the swarm labours for every computer.

4   If that still sounds complicated, well, it is. Activating your first torrent can be like alchemy. (Consider it this decade's equivalent of programming a VCR: if stuck, ask your kids for help.) Sort it out, though, and BitTorrent grants you the ability to scan the Internet before bed, download and launch a few torrents, then wake up in the morning with a new Hollywood blockbuster, CBS drama, Xbox game, and/or the complete works of your favourite band parked on your desktop. The only cost is bandwidth, unless you count the burden on your conscience: Canada has no firm legal stance on file-sharing. The country has a long-standing levy on blank audio-recording media that theoretically allows Canadians to make private copies of copyrighted works for commercial use. But last year, the Federal Court of Appeal turned down a government attempt to impose a similar tariff on MP3 players such as Apple's iPod. There has been talk of new, Internet-sensitive copyright legislation in Ottawa, but in the meantime, the rule is that there are no rules. But I'm straying. None of this describes what it feels like to watch torrent TV as a matter of habit. The first, best thing is that BitTorrent makes television available whenever I choose to view it. For example, I'm often out the door by the time *Arrested Development* airs. But thanks to BitTorrent, I can find and download the episode later on, then save and watch it at my leisure. This is "time-shifting"—moving the TV shows that I want to watch to fit my schedule. It's all the rage in high-end digital television, although companies such as Rogers expect me to pay for the privilege.

5   BitTorrent may be changing movie-viewing habits, too. Most Hollywood films are now available for download from BitTorrent networks on or before their premiere dates. Some are "cams," low-grade videos shot inside movie theatres via concealed camcorders, à la Seinfeld. Others are "screeners," higher-quality copies of pre-release DVDs that are distributed to movie critics and industry insiders. All are anathema to the Motion Picture Association of America (MPAA), the Hollywood trade lobby leading the legal charge against BitTorrent (and funding the anti-piracy commercials that precede many current films).

6   In Napster's day, the corporate fight against file-sharing was led by the Recording Industry Association of America (RIAA), the music industry's version of the MPAA. The RIAA's legal manoeuvring shut down Napster in 2001, but indirectly spurred the development of Kazaa, Limewire, and related downloading services. BitTorrent, by bringing big-media files into play, has fuelled the MPAA's ire. The technology is a direct threat not only to box-office receipts but to DVD sales, which is where the real money is made these days. According to the MPAA's confidential-but-leaked-online "All Media Revenue Report" for 2003, home-entertainment sales accounted for 82 percent of that year's studio revenues. BitTorrent, I would argue, is also the reason why rental outlets such as Blockbuster are drowning—why else dismiss late fees?—and movie theatres are taking the unusual step of lowering ticket prices.

7   The reason the MPAA, RIAA, and like-minded lobbies are panicked is obvious: entertainment industries, at their root, are manufacturers. They spend huge amounts of money creating content, then earn it back by selling finished products. File-sharing, the big studios and major labels argue, short-circuits this business model. Not everyone, though, accepts their word as gospel. Even musicians, the first group of creative professionals to feel the full brunt of file-sharing, are divided over its impact: some kvetch that file-sharing keeps them from feeding their kids; others argue that the Internet turns on so many new fans that any money lost on record sales is recouped elsewhere, such as through increased tour revenues.

8   With the global spread of broadband modem connections likely to fuel BitTorrent's growth, current media-distribution models—movie theatres, record stores, and

commercial television—could become redundant. In that doomsday scenario, why would record labels and television and movie studios keep making content? Because blank tapes killed the music industry in the seventies, VCRs destroyed television in the eighties, and Napster ruined the early years of this decade. BitTorrent is today's consumer crisis; tomorrow's will carry a new and different name. In the meantime, content creators will respond in the same manner they always have: evolve or dissolve. BitTorrent is new, but the song remains the same.

VOCABULARY

The following terms are identified by paragraph number. Make sure that you understand each term's meaning in its context. If you're not sure that you understand a term, look it up in a dictionary.

myriad (2) **alchemy** (4) **manoeuvering** (6)
cynic (2) **anathema** (5) **ire** (6)
larceny (2) **precede** (5) **kvetch** (7)

STYLE AND STRATEGY

1. In this process analysis, McKinnon is actually analyzing two processes. What are they?
2. Who is this essay's intended audience? How does McKinnon seem to be criticizing both consumers and the industry?
3. This essay does not have a formal conclusion. Would it have been improved by the addition of a final, concluding paragraph? Explain.
4. Discuss one analogy that McKinnon uses.

QUESTIONS FOR CRITICAL THINKING AND DISCUSSION

1. McKinnon discusses how file-sharing has had positive effects, such as winning musicians new fans and thereby increasing tour revenue. Is this an overly optimistic view? Has file-sharing lead to more positive outcomes than negative ones? Can you list some examples?
2. Do you file-share or do you purchase your entertainment? Some people indulge in a bit of both. Under what circumstances would you rather purchase your entertainment than download it?

SUGGESTIONS FOR WRITING

1. Has a specific kind of technology—cellphones or MP3 players, for example—ever taken up more of your life than you expected it to? Write a 500- to 750-word essay that analyzes how this process developed.
2. Write a 500- to 750-word essay on the following topic: how to use a new technology responsibly.

HOW TO SAVE DEMOCRACY
The system is ailing and the disease is cynicism. Perhaps the time has come for a radical new treatment

Allan Gregg

Allan Gregg is one of Canada's most popular social commentators. Gregg has been involved in more than fifty political campaigns on three continents. He is a regular contributor to the CBC program "At Issue," and hosts the program "Allan Gregg in Conversation with . . ." each week on TVO. This essay appeared in the September 2004 issue of The Walrus.

1   Over the course of tracking public opinion for twenty years, the private polls I conducted for my political clients showed that the number of Canadians who held at least a "somewhat" positive view of politicians fell from 60 percent to less than 20 percent. Today, Ipsos-Reid reports that a grand total of 9 percent of Canadians describe politicians as "extremely trustworthy."

2   How can this cycle be reversed?

3   We know from experience what hasn't worked.

4   Public-relations campaigns have been launched to encourage young people to vote. Limits and constraints that narrow their discretionary latitude have been heaped upon our leaders. Exhortations for a better calibre of individual to heed the call of public life are heard around boardroom tables throughout the land.

5   Far from reversing or diminishing our cynicism, however, these efforts have had no effect and, in some instances, have served to exacerbate and reinforce our mistrust.

6   Despite these efforts, voter turnout has continued to drop; in the June federal election, it was 60.3 percent, the lowest since 1898.

7   The key to revitalizing democracy must rest on two foundations: giving citizens and their leaders a more intimate understanding of one another by bringing the two into closer proximity; and providing real evidence that citizens' efforts to affect the system can actually bear fruit.

8   In fact, everything I know about public opinion and the working of governments tells me that if we truly want to create a more cohesive and workable democracy, then we must make both structural and systemic changes aimed at elites, as well as cultural changes aimed at the masses.

9   At the mass or cultural level, the main problem is that our very distance and detachment from our leaders, and from one another, allow us to form and hold views that do not require scrutiny or evaluation. An example of how structural change can dramatically promote a cultural shift was shown in the Supreme Court decision of Brown vs. the Board of Education in the U.S. That decision, more than all the sermonizing from American liberals about the corrosive effects of racism on American life, or the activism of civil-rights leaders, forced blacks and whites to integrate. It was a change in experience, not beliefs or values, that changed the culture.

10   The most fundamental step in altering behaviour may be the introduction of compulsory voting. Turnout has fallen steadily since 1988 and is especially low among newly eligible voters, fewer than 30 percent of whom voted in 2000. Making voting compulsory—as is the case in Australia or Greece—forces every citizen into at least some engagement with the system.

11   If you have to vote, chances are you will at least learn who the candidates are in your area. Even this minimal involvement will foster the acquisition of other attendant information about politics, legitimize election results, and give the marginalized a greater stake in the process. (Those who would charge that this is draconian or anti-democratic should

note that paying taxes and going to school are mandatory because both are deemed necessary for a strong society.)

12   Creating community, creed, and a common sense of destiny also requires citizen contact. There was a reason the ancient Greeks built theatres or early architects made the town square the centrepiece of their city plans. By strengthening the avenues of cultural distribution, public spaces can be combined with art and ideas to advance citizen interaction and build a stronger sense of civic virtue. Public sponsorship of festivals, reading series, debates, and town-hall meetings can all be used to inveigle individuals out of their rec rooms and into the streets, where citizens will gain a greater feeling of "ownership" of their community and its problems.

13   Technology is another powerful tool: computer programs could be set up to simulate public-policy alternatives, so that individuals could develop their own defence budget or old-age-pension plan. Such "e-democracy" initiatives could facilitate an immediate feedback loop between elected representatives and their constituents on current issues of the day. Not only would this give citizens more input into government decision-making, but there is every reason to believe that if we can use technology to learn more about the consequences of our beliefs, over time we will come to make better decisions.

14   Even with compulsory participation, cultural democracy, and technological innovation, however, real change won't happen unless citizens also come to believe that their elected representatives are not only responsive, but are empowered to act on the demands of those they represent.

15   Concepts such as putting politicians and voters in closer and more constant contact with one another, granting voters greater and more direct access to the political system, and giving representatives access to government resources to be deployed against local needs are neither innovative nor new. Citizen contact and debate was the cornerstone of Athenian democracy. Empowering voters was essential to such populist movements as the Grange and the United Farmers of Alberta. Another powerful example is Tammany Hall, which was fuelled by local networks of bossism and patronage.

16   For some, revisiting these ideas may smack of sentimental nostalgia or even taking up the cudgel of a now disgraced past. But the fact is, compared to today, many aspects of democracy were healthier in an earlier time. Past civilizations and societies atrophied, not because these concepts were faulty, but because they were applied to an uneducated, ill-informed, and acquiescent population. Because we have progressed—because we now have a citizenry that has the tools and wherewithal to chart a new collective destiny—we also now have it in our grasp to use the best of the old and the new to save democracy.

VOCABULARY

The following terms are identified by paragraph number. Make sure that you understand each term's meaning in its context. If you're not sure that you understand a term, look it up in a dictionary.

discretionary (4)	**cynicism** (5)	**draconian** (11)
exhortations (4)	**exacerbate** (5)	**inveigle** (12)
calibre (4)	**cohesive** (8)	**cudgel** (16)
	corrosive (9)	

STYLE AND STRATEGY

1. What situation does the author analyze, and what processes does he suggest to improve the problem?

2. Analyze Gregg's use of diction. How might he have made his article more accessible? Consider how different language choices might have broadened his audience.

3. Gregg uses several examples in his essay, but doesn't explain them in detail (such as Tammany Hall). Research and define at least three examples in this essay and apply their significance to the overall essay.

QUESTIONS FOR CRITICAL THINKING AND DISCUSSION

1. Gregg's article was first published in 2004; however, not much has changed today. Research voter turnout for the last election as well as reasons for its low numbers. What is the current state of politics among the three major parties in Canada? Does the public still distrust politicians?

2. There's an old saying: "If you don't vote, then you can't complain." Analyze the truth of this statement. Compare Canada's political climate to other places where voting is compulsory (such as in Australia and Greece). How have these areas benefitted from this requirement?

SUGGESTIONS FOR WRITING

1. Write a 500- to 750-word essay in which you discuss the process of creating your perfect college or university course (Video Game Theory, perhaps? Film and the Superhero?). How would you do this? What texts, films, or essays would you study? What assignments would you create?

2. In 500 to 750 words, explain a process that you find unnecessarily complex and strange; for example, registering for classes, getting ready to attend a formal event, training for a particular sport, or keeping up with the latest fads and fashions in clothes.

In the works that follow, Steve Maich examines the causes of the Toronto Maple Leafs' inability to be a winning NHL team and Elizabeth Nickson asks the question, "Why are people having fewer children?" These essays both demonstrate the importance of **prewriting.** As you read them, you will notice that a great deal of thought went into constructing the causal connections that these writers present.

WHY THE LEAFS STINK
It's not bad luck. It's not bad karma. What it takes to build a chronic loser.

Steve Maich

Steve Maich has published articles in Maclean's, *the* National Post, *and the* Halifax Chronicle-Herald. *Currently, he is the publisher and editor-in-chief of* Sportsnet *magazine. The following article, "Why the Leafs Stink," appeared in* Maclean's *magazine in April 2008 and examines what he sees as the major causes behind the Toronto Maple Leafs' historical losing streak.*

1   It would be comforting to believe that the Toronto Maple Leafs are cursed. After 41 years of failure, supernatural explanations start to seem pretty attractive, especially when hard facts are just too painful to face.

2   It's not like there's any shortage of evidence for those inclined to see paranormal forces at work. These are the Leafs, where one can't-miss prospect after another disappears into minor-league obscurity. Remember Drake Berehowsky, Brandon Convery, Scott Pearson, Luca Cereda, Peter Ing, and Jeff Ware? They all, at one time or another, represented a future that never arrived. What about poor Jason Blake? A 40-goal scorer who gets diagnosed with cancer just months after his celebrated arrival in town. Then there's Mats Sundin. One of the game's true stars, he played 13 years surrounded by one of the best-paid supporting casts in the NHL, never once making the Stanley Cup finals, let alone winning it.

3   The only problem with all this talk of curses is that there are perfectly logical reasons for the Leafs' legacy of failure. The fact that the Toronto Maple Leafs are a bad hockey club is the inevitable by-product of the laws of economics. Their mediocrity is a design flaw, and it comes down to this: for any business to thrive, it must be obsessively focused on victory. Success must yield powerful benefits and failure must unleash harsh consequences. In the world's greatest market for pro hockey, that cost/benefit equation doesn't exist. A gusher of wealth, regardless of performance, has begat 40 years of infighting, a culture of laxity, and a refusal to admit the problem. The Leafs are a monopoly business that has been corrupted by its own market power.

4   To be precise, however, the Leafs wield what economists call "monopolistic market power"—not quite the same as being a monopoly, but similar. Colin Jones, professor emeritus at the University of Victoria, has spent much of his career studying the economics of pro hockey. "Pretty much any study you look at, you'll find a very strong correlation between attendance and winning." But the Leafs, he says, are different. "They can do whatever the hell they like and the attendance and merchandise sales go up, and TV and radio contracts hold up. In terms of competitive performance, this monopolistic power is a very bad thing."

5   Toronto's problems are, in fact, the exact opposite of most struggling sports teams. There's no miserly owner cutting corners. There's no lack of fan support. And it's not a

pressure-cooker environment that stunts the development of young players. (For all the references to the city's rabid media corps, the team is, in fact, treated with kid gloves and feted at any sign of improvement.) No, the rot that is destroying the Leafs comes from having too much, too easily.

6   Don't the Leafs want to win?

7   Of course they do. Listen to Peddie [CEO of the Leafs] talk about getting booed on the street when he goes for lunch. His frustration is real, but it is largely beside the point. "The team makes too much money. It's too easy," explains one former NHL general manager. "There's just no burning incentive to put a good team on the ice. And it's been that way since long before any of these current people were involved."

8   Peddie rejects the notion that the Leafs are structurally ill-equipped to compete. "What the economists don't understand is the emotion of it," he says. "We're executives but we're also fans. We want to win."

9   But that's just it. Fans are the ones who celebrate every goal, every hit, and every fleeting win streak. Fans can be convinced that a last-minute dash toward the playoffs (in a 30-team league, in which more than half of the teams make the cut) is an achievement worth celebrating. Fans wish for success. Leaders make it happen, because they can't live with the alternative. Fans perpetuate the status quo. For 41 years, the Leafs have had too many fans, and not enough leaders.

10 The distinction is perhaps best illustrated by a story from 27 years ago. One night in 1981, the Winnipeg Jets—then the league's worst team—came into Maple Leaf Gardens and laid a humiliating pounding on the home team. During a stoppage, an older gentleman approached the boards, took off his Leafs jersey, threw it onto the ice and walked out of the rink in disgust. "He must have been close to his seventies, and all these people clapped," one witness laughs. "But you know, I bet that guy came back the next night."

11 Of course he did. That's what makes the Leafs monopolistic. And that's the problem.

VOCABULARY

The following terms are identified by paragraph number. Make sure that you understand each term's meaning in its context. If you're not sure that you understand a term, look it up in a dictionary.

paranormal (2)	**mediocrity** (3)
obscurity (2)	**monopolistic** (4)
begat (3)	**miserly** (5)
laxity (3)	**perpetuate** (9)

STYLE AND STRATEGY

1. Discuss the power and technique of Maich's introduction. How does he captivate the reader's interest right away?
2. List the causes that Maich cites for the ongoing losing streak of the Toronto Maple Leafs.
3. List the effects of the Leafs' performance on the team's fans.
4. How would you describe Maich's tone? Provide evidence to back up your claims.
5. A *rhetorical question* is one asked by a writer who really doesn't want an answer but wants to raise the issue mentioned in the question. Where in this essay does Maich use a rhetorical question? What is its effect?

QUESTIONS FOR CRITICAL THINKING AND DISCUSSION

1. Maich's essay is just as much about the fans of the Leafs as it is about the team itself. Why are certain sports fans incredibly loyal to certain teams no matter how that team performs?
2. Sports culture used to be just about the game; now, however, celebrity players, their personal lives and marketing deals, often overshadow the purity of the game. Give examples to support your decision to agree or disagree with this claim.

SUGGESTIONS FOR WRITING

1. Write a 500- to 750-word essay about a particular rule or policy in sports (salary caps, for example) and argue the results/effects of this rule or policy. Has the rule or policy produced effective results?
2. Write a 500- to 750-word essay arguing for a change in or the reversal of a college policy that you believe is counterproductive or unfair. Try to predict the effects of this change or reversal, using as much detail as possible in order to support your thesis and convince your readers.

BAGS OR BABIES
Women don't have to choose

Elizabeth Nickson

Elizabeth Nickson is a freelance Canadian writer and journalist whose work has appeared in The Globe and Mail, *the* National Post, Saturday Night, *and* Chatelaine. *Her first novel,* The Monkey-Puzzle Tree, *was published in 2012. The article "Bags or Babies" appeared in* The Globe and Mail *in 2006. In the article, Nickson discusses the declining worldwide birth rate and offers the causes for this phenomenon as proposed by various critics before positing her own theories.*

1 In the endless gloom-a-thon that passes for our public discourse, nothing bites harder than the fact that we are ceasing to exist. Google "low birth rate" and panicked reports from all over the world fill your screen.

2 Japan's drop is catastrophic; at 1.25 births per woman, Japan has the rate at which demographers believe a cataclysmic downward spiral is inevitable. Korea? Even worse at 1.08 births per woman. Russia? Dying. And don't even mention Europe. Demographers project that the European Union will lose between 24 million and 40 million people during each coming decade unless fertility is markedly raised—at the upper end, that's close to the number lost to the Second World War every single decade. Nor will immigration help.

It takes less than a generation for an immigrant family in Canada to accept local norms and stop reproducing. In fact, fertility declines are now being detected even in the poorer parts of Latin America and Asia.

3   In the June issue of *Science,* David Reher, a population historian at the University of Madrid, maintained that much of the world is now on the cusp of a prolonged period of population decline. Mr. Reher's heavy breathing is mirrored by Niall Ferguson, in the current *Vanity Fair.* Mr. Ferguson, normally a sensible historian, finds dropping birth rates to be evidence of the decline of Western Civilization, likening our situation to the last days of the Roman Empire. Mr. Reher couldn't agree more. "Urban areas in regions like Europe could well be filled with empty buildings and crumbling infrastructures as population and tax revenues decline," he prognosticates, adding that "it is not difficult to imagine enclaves of rich, fiercely guarded pockets of well-being surrounded by large areas which look more like what we might see in some science-fiction movies."

4   The culprit? To a man, Pope, historian, or demographer, they cite secular feminism, along with its demonic twins, birth control and abortion. Liberate women from children and *kuchen,* wave around a Kate Spade handbag, offer a good job at the local bistro or trading floor and we won't breed, not for anything.

5   Okay, does anyone else see how dumb all this is? Women don't stop having children because they want to buy expensive bags, get beat up by a boring dead-end job or are lost in ideological fervour. They stop having children because the divorce rate hovers around 50 per cent and they have an even chance of ending up as custodial parent, looking at bone-grinding labour and penny-pinching. Committed couples suffer from pretty much the same burden. The income of middle-class families has only risen 4 per cent in real terms since 1980. We know this is true, because even the bible of the right-wing, the National Review, admits it, and lathers up a whole paragraph trying to explain why this is okay. Accept the right's eternal premise of punishing taxation and what is clear is that the middle-class family is squeezed mercilessly by the avarice of the demonic twins, government and business.

6   I had my daughter when I was a teenager and was so traumatized by the experience, I couldn't bring myself to have another. In my generation, half of those who graduated from university between 1969 and 1974 had no children at all. Having children is an act of the purest hope, and we had decided that autonomy was way safer, not to mention more fun. A whole generation took their lives off, to explore the furthest reaches of what women can accomplish. But look, last summer I spent a few days in my house with my mother, daughter and her three babies, and trust me, there isn't a party or adventure or job on earth that can compete with that, and I suspect, motivated by pleasure as we are, children will once again become necessary.

7   My own personal baby boomlet can be ascribed to two conditions: First, the enlightened (in this at least) CBC which allows my daughter to keep a job in which she thrives, through generous mat leaves and job sharing.

8   Low Alberta taxes and a booming economy in which her partner, an environmental economist, can look at a prosperous future make them a family whose exhaustion is shot through with both joy and hope. Calgary itself is suffering a baby boomlet for those precise reasons: corporations that desperately need good staff and will bend over backward to keep them, and a government that does not predate its citizenry. The policy implications are clear. Copy Calgary or die. All over the world, governments are starting to throw money at breeding couples. Recently, the governor of a Russian province gave everyone an afternoon off a week, to "go home and make babies." It seems to be working. This summer, Australia crowed that through financial incentives, it managed to raise its birth rate from 1.72 children per woman to 1.85, most of the increases in women over 35, which is to say, women with careers and education. Factor in more enlightenment from the corporate sector, men who stick around and do more housework, and you

might just get us breeding again. In fact, things could (finally) be about to get really good for young women everywhere.

9   We who went before salute you.

VOCABULARY

The following terms are identified by paragraph number. Make sure that you understand each term's meaning in its context. If you're not sure that you understand a term, look it up in a dictionary.

cataclysmic (2)   prognosticates (3)   autonomy (6)
cusp (3)   fervour (5)   ascribed (7)
                         avarice (5)

STYLE AND STRATEGY

1. Describe the way Nickson opens her essay. Is her introduction effective? Why or why not?
2. What is the author's thesis? Where has she placed it?
3. What does Nickson see as the real cause for the declining birth rate?
4. How do you feel about Nickson's conclusions about why the birth rate might increase? Do you see her suggestions playing a major part in a woman's decision to have children? Why or why not?

QUESTIONS FOR CRITICAL THINKING AND DISCUSSION

1. Many people think that women are biologically programmed to want children or that they possess an inherent nurturing instinct. Is this true? Can you think of instances that both prove and disprove this theory?
2. Many couples now wait until they are in their 30s to have children. Can you think of both advantages and disadvantages to waiting this long to start a family? Is there a perfect age to have children?

SUGGESTIONS FOR WRITING

Write a 500- to 750-word essay in which you examine one of the following phenomena and explain why its commonly accepted cause is not its real cause:

1. Why many university and college students gain weight during their freshman year.
2. Why the voting rate among university and college students is very low.

In the two essays that follow, the writers present different aspects of definition writing. Judy Brady offers an exhaustive (and daunting) definition of society's expectations of wives, while the article on Canada's definition of "poor" by the editors of *Maclean's* shows how stipulated definitions can be used to change meanings and realities. As you read these selections, note the effects that the authors are able to achieve from the starting point of definition. As a rhetorical option, definition may seem basic; however, it is anything but. A good definition can change a reader's most strongly held assumptions.

WHY I WANT A WIFE
Judy Brady

Written by essayist and political activist Judy Brady, "Why I Want a Wife" is one of the most famous and enduring essays of our times. First published in the Spring 1972 issue of Ms., *it has become both a rallying cry for women seeking equality and a penetrating look into the sociology of the American family—and indeed the Canadian family—in the 1960s. As you read, consider whether Brady's observations are still valid today.*

1   I belong to that classification of people known as wives. I am A Wife. And, not altogether incidentally, I am a mother.

2   Not too long ago a male friend of mine appeared on the scene fresh from a recent divorce. He had one child, who is, of course, with his ex-wife. He is looking for another wife. As I thought about him while I was ironing one evening, it suddenly occurred to me that I, too, would like to have a wife. Why do I want a wife?

3   I would like to go back to school so that I can become economically independent, support myself, and, if need be, support those dependent upon me. I want a wife who will work and send me to school. And while I am going to school I want a wife to take care of my children. I want a wife to keep track of the children's doctor and dentist appointments. And to keep track of mine, too. I want a wife to make sure my children eat properly and are kept clean. I want a wife who will wash the children's clothes and keep them mended. I want a wife who is a good nurturant attendant to my children, who arranges for their schooling, makes sure that they have an adequate social life with their peers, takes them to the park, the zoo, etc. I want a wife who takes care of the children when they are sick, a wife who arranges to be around when the children need special care, because, of course, I cannot miss classes at school. My wife must arrange to lose time at work and not lose the job. It may mean a small cut in my wife's income from time to time, but I guess I can tolerate that. Needless to say, my wife will arrange and pay for the leading is uneven here, I think care of the children while my wife is working.

4   I want a wife who will take care of *my* physical needs. I want a wife who will keep my house clean. A wife who will pick up after me. I want a wife who will keep my clothes clean, ironed, mended, replaced when need be, and who will see to it that my personal things are kept in their proper place so that I can find what I need the minute I need it. I want a wife who cooks the meals, a wife who is a *good* cook.5

5   I want a wife who will plan the menus, do the necessary grocery shopping, prepare the meals, serve them pleasantly, and then do the cleaning up while I do my studying. I want a wife who will care for me when I am sick and sympathize with my pain and loss

of time from school. I want a wife to go along when our family takes a vacation so that someone can continue to care for me and my children when I need a rest and change of scene.

6   I want a wife who will not bother me with rambling complaints about a wife's duties. But I want a wife who will listen to me when I feel the need to explain a rather difficult point I have come across in my course of studies. And I want a wife who will type my papers for me when I have written them.

7   I want a wife who will take care of the details of my social life. When my wife and I are invited out by friends, I want a wife who will take care of the babysitting arrangements. When I meet people at school that I like and want to entertain, I want a wife who will have the house clean, will prepare a special meal, serve it to me and my friends, and not interrupt when I talk about the things that interest me and my friends. I want a wife who will have arranged that the children are fed and ready for bed before my guests arrive so that the children do not bother us. I want a wife who takes care of the needs of my guests so that they feel comfortable, who makes sure that they have an ashtray, that they are passed the hors d'oeuvres, that they are offered a second helping of the food, that their wine glasses are replenished when necessary, that their coffee is served to them as they like it. And I want a wife who knows that sometimes I need a night out by myself. I want a wife who is sensitive to my sexual needs, a wife who makes love passionately and eagerly when I feel like it, a wife who makes sure that I am satisfied. And, of course, I want a wife who will not demand sexual attention when I am not in the mood for it. I want a wife who assumes the complete responsibility for birth control, because I do not want more children. I want a wife who will remain sexually faithful to me so that I do not have to clutter up my intellectual life with jealousies. And I want a wife who understands that *my* sexual needs may entail more than strict adherence to monogamy. I must, after all, be able to relate to people as fully as possible.

8   If, by chance, I find another person more suitable as a wife than the wife I already have, I want the liberty to replace my present wife with another one. Naturally, I will expect a fresh, new life; my wife will take the children and be solely responsible for them so that I am left free.

9   When I am through with school and have a job, I want my wife to quit working and remain at home so that my wife can more fully and completely take care of a wife's duties.

10   My God, who *wouldn't* want a wife?

VOCABULARY

The following terms are identified by paragraph number. Make sure that you understand each term's meaning in its context. If you're not sure that you understand a term, look it up in a dictionary.

nurturant (3)	**hors d'oeuvres (7)**	**adherence (7)**
attendant (3)	**replenish (7)**	**monogamy (7)**

STYLE AND STRATEGY

1. Who does the audience of Brady's essay seem to be?
2. Write down the major defining features of wives that Brady includes, and note their arrangement. How does Brady organize her definition?

3. Writers use *irony* when they say the exact opposite of what they mean in order to create humour or emphasize a point. *Sarcasm,* a form of irony, has a biting or critical tone. Locate the places where Brady uses irony and/or sarcasm.

4. Both the first paragraph and the last paragraph are very brief, but they are also very effective. Explain why.

QUESTIONS FOR CRITICAL THINKING AND DISCUSSION

1. Brady is writing about the typical wife's domestic duties in the early 1970s. Over four decades later, how much has changed for the "typical wife"? How much has changed for the "typical husband"? Does our society still hold to stereotypical expectations?

2. Some people still believe that *Men are from Mars, Women are from Venus,* as the title of the John Gray book states; however, are the sexes really that different? If you believe so, avoid resorting to crude stereotypes to explain your answer. What do you think causes resentment between men and women?

SUGGESTIONS FOR WRITING

1. Write a 500- to 750-word comparison essay on the denotation and connotation of specific word pairs such as *thin/scrawny, home/house,* and *cook/chef.*

2. Write a 500- to 750-word essay that takes the opposite approach of Brady: "I want a husband." Use irony (saying the exact opposite of what you mean in order to create humour or emphasize a point) as Brady does, to achieve your purpose.

THE MEANING OF POOR
Canada has no official definition of poverty, but Ireland has a model to learn from

From the Editors of *Maclean's*

The following article appeared in Maclean's *magazine in February 27, 2008. Here, the editors of the magazine ponder the definition of the word "poor" and find that, depending on geography, different countries vary greatly on the term's meaning. This analysis leads to other complications regarding common assumptions about other words such as "luxury" and "necessity."*

1 In the course of just a few decades Ireland has become a modern, wealthy and interesting nation. And while Canadians might not be in the habit of taking policy advice from the Irish, last year their government solved a problem that has long vexed Canada. It's worth a closer look. The Irish government recently unveiled a new official definition of poverty—what it calls "consistent poverty." Determining exactly who is and isn't poor involves a two-stage process determined by random household surveys. To be considered poor you must, first of all, earn less than 60 per cent of the median income. Then you're measured against a list of 11 standardized necessities, including: a warm waterproof overcoat, "two pairs of strong shoes," meals with meat, chicken or fish (or vegetarian substitute) at least every second day, "a roast joint or its equivalent once a week," a warm house and the wherewithal to buy presents for family members once a year, have guests over for a drink once a month, and a night out every two weeks. Lack any two of the 11 necessities on the list, and you're officially poor.

2   At first blush the list seems rather amusing and trivial. Not everyone might wish for a roast on Sunday or house guests monthly. And even wealthy parents of newborns may question whether a night out every two weeks is a necessity or a luxury. But what's important about this new system is that it includes both relative and absolute indicators of what's considered a basic, acceptable standard of living. And the end result appears to be good news. The Irish rate of consistent poverty for individuals is just 6.5 percent—lower than previous methods of calculation—and dropping.

3   Unlike Ireland, Canada lacks an official poverty line. Statistics Canada produces its well-known low income cut-off (LICO) but this, as the agency itself reminds us constantly, is neither a measure of true poverty nor an officially accepted figure. LICO actually measures a complicated form of relative income inequality. While interesting, this doesn't tell us how many Canadians really face significant deprivation, or what it means to be truly poor in absolute terms.

4   Canada's flawed LICO rate for individuals—at almost 11 per cent—is much higher than Ireland's poverty rate, although it too has been falling. Yet Canada and Ireland share similar income levels, inequality indicators and unemployment rates. It is likely our true rate of poverty would also be lower if we calculated it using a variant of the Irish method. It would certainly be more reliable.

5   The need for a better measure of poverty in this country is pressing. The next national election will likely be fought on economic issues—Liberal Leader Stéphane Dion has already signalled his intention to make poverty reduction a key plank in his platform. While such a goal is laudable, if we are going to have a real debate on the subject we need to agree on who is poor and why. As the MBAs say, you can't manage what you can't measure. All of which should make strong shoes, overcoats and Sunday dinner menus important topics for all Canadians.

VOCABULARY

The following terms are identified by paragraph number. Make sure that you understand each term's meaning in its context. If you're not sure that you understand a term, look it up in a dictionary.

vexed (1)   **deprivation (3)**   **laudable (5)**
wherewithal (1)   **variant (4)**

STYLE AND STRATEGY

1. Where is this essay's thesis statement?
2. Besides definition, what other rhetorical options are employed in this essay? Cite specific passages and paragraphs.
3. Who is the intended audience of this essay? How does the essay help this audience to understand the subject of poverty or understand it better?

QUESTIONS FOR CRITICAL THINKING AND DISCUSSION

1. A *euphemism* is a (usually less offensive) word or phrase used to substitute for another word or phrase (e.g., saying "well off" or "comfortable" instead of "rich"). However, euphemisms can be used to dull down reality and hide the truth of a problem. Avoiding calling someone poor out of politeness might draw attention away from serious economic injustices. Discuss some positive and negative examples of euphemism usage in our culture.

2. Ireland's definition of "necessities" is questionable. Do you feel the items they list as necessities are just that? What does the inclusion of these items say about Irish culture?

3. How does the person creating a definition shape what that definition becomes? Consider this question in the context of the above essay: Who should be involved in creating a definition of poverty?

SUGGESTIONS FOR WRITING

1. Write a 500- to 750-word essay around the use of euphemism in our culture.

2. Write a 500- to 750-word essay that analyzes a common definition in society such as "hero," "mother," or "career." Begin by discussing the word's generic definition, and then provide an extended definition of the subject, designed to persuade someone to broaden his or her opinion on the common definition.

The two selections that follow were both published in *Maclean's* magazine. The first article by Jaime Weinman explores different categories of television dramas, while the second by Nicholas Kohler and Barbara Righton examines the three types of patient that doctors are having second thoughts about getting involved with. In the wrong hands, classification can be a dry and boring option; however, note how skilfully these writers make this rhetorical strategy come alive.

TV: BESIDES COPS, LAWYERS AND DOCTORS, WHAT ELSE IS THERE?
Jaime Weinman

To quote from his bio on Macleans.ca, *"Jaime Weinman writes about all kinds of television and other kinds of popular culture. He does not write* Gossip Girl *episode reviews." The following article was published on* Macleans.ca *on January 26, 2011.*

1   I don't comment too much on pilot pickups because most of them will never see the light of day. (I want the networks to bring back those summer shows where they burned off the pilots they rejected for the upcoming season.) But on a comment thread on another site, I noticed some understandable frustration that most of the drama pilots fall into the usual categories: Doctor show, lawyer show, cop show. CBS in particular has almost completely given up pretending they care about anything else; no more *Jerichos* or *Viva Laughlins,* just more cops, more lawyers, and their highest priority is finding a successful medical show. But most networks are heavily oriented towards crime and doctor shows, with the occasional science fiction or period pilot to leaven the mix. NBC may have ordered a "complex, sprawling" epic ambitious pilot from the creator of *Syriana,* but it's still a crime show with cops and criminals when you come right down to it.

2   So, yes, this can be very tiresome. You look for variety on TV, and what you get is mostly a limited range of shows about a limited range of jobs. But I'm a little more sympathetic to the broadcast networks once I try to think out the obvious follow-up question: what kind of jobs are appropriate for a network TV drama? As I've said in the past, most TV dramas are really melodramas—it's very tough, no matter how ambitious you are, to make a continuing series about ordinary life, because the stakes are too low for 13 episodes a season. Bump it up to 22 episodes or more, as on broadcast TV, and it's even more imperative to have really high stakes. Meaning that slice-of-life dramas are more or less ruled out. They usually can't sustain a full season.

3   That being the case, network dramas need melodramatic situations that can spin off a lot of episodes. But here's where the choices narrow even farther, because there are other things a network drama needs besides melodrama. There needs to be a setup that can bring in new "cases" every week, not only because the network needs something to promote, but because it provides a self-contained element that new viewers can grab onto—and regular viewers can follow as a diversion in case they're getting bored with the relationships. (Not every successful show is a serial, but most of them offer something new or interesting in that particular week, which often comes from an outside character wandering in with a case.) And they need to be cases that have some kind of high-stakes, even life-or-death component to them.

4   Which is why doctors, lawyers and cops are such reliable subjects for a TV series. They have jobs that are about life-and-death issues—mostly death—and allow guest

characters and new stories to walk in any time. They spin off stories with clear goals: save a life, win the case, catch the crook. And they are about people who deal with outsiders every day (patients, clients, victims), meaning that guest characters can come in and carry some of the emotional load. All of that makes it much easier to write 22 episodes a year and not run out of big, effective story ideas.

5   One format that used to be on a level with doctor/lawyer/cop, and was actually more popular than those types of shows when weekly TV drama started, is the Western. Same thing applies there—actually, since so many Westerns revolve around lawmen, it could actually be considered a cousin to the cop show. (Just like the most popular broadcast science fiction series, *The X-Files,* was literally a cop show.) The TV Western lost its popularity and went away, leaving crime and surgery as the dominant forces in non-soap-opera drama.

6   Now, just because cop/lawyer/doctor are the most reliable vehicles for a 22-episode season doesn't mean they should dominate quite as completely as they do. But some types of drama are prevented from coming back by the way shows are produced nowadays. One very effective type of drama is the disguised anthology, like *Route 66,* where you have two characters driving around and getting mixed up in different types of stories in different places. But no network show today would dare to have only two regulars (whereas it used to be quite common as recently as *The X-Files*), and the need to have a big ensemble really cuts down on the types of shows you can do.

7   But there are others. Teacher shows, for example. When I brought this issue up, I had several people mention teacher shows: the teacher at the tough high school is a setup that fits all the criteria—high stakes, ensemble cast, lots of new stories that can walk in the door—but it hasn't been done much lately. It seems that this is something that networks have forgotten about in their focus on crime, though it's also true that high school dramas don't usually hit it big unless they are full-fledged soap operas focusing on the kids. (And if a show starts out as a high school drama about teachers, like *The White Shadow* or *Boston Public,* it will be mostly about the kids by the end of its run.) One related idea, given the interest in period drama, is to do a show set at a university in the late '60s—there are potentially lots of stories to be found in riots, political activism, conflicts among the teachers about said riots and activism. Update: This was in my original draft of the post but somehow got left out: *Glee,* obviously, is a throwback to the high school drama to some extent, right down to the fact that the adults are de-emphasized in favour of the kids. It's successful for a lot of reasons, but I'm sure it does help that it stands out from the pack just by being an episodic, easy-to-jump-into show that is not about cops, lawyers or doctors. I think one thing the musical numbers do, though, is combat the feeling that the stories aren't high-stakes enough. Musicals have a way of making every issue seem big because it's big enough to sing and dance about.

8   Then there's the episodic family drama, like *7th Heaven,* the show that just kept going and going even though two different networks were embarrassed to admit it existed. *Parenthood* is one of the few shows around that tries to do something like that.

9   Still, these and other genres, while I'd like to see them come back, aren't as reliable story engines as cop/lawyer/doctor, because there's just not enough death involved. You know how Sam Spade said that torture doesn't work unless the threat of death is hanging over it? The same isn't true of TV drama, but it can be pretty close sometimes: the more the audience fears that someone might die, or at least go to jail, the easier it is to build up dramatic tension 22 times a year. Part of the advantage these shows have, like Westerns, is that someone can suffer big consequences every week. It's not going to be a major character, unless it's a special sweeps episode, but at least someone— a guest character, usually—is in danger of death or incarceration. Set the show at a school, or in someone's home, and even the guest characters probably aren't going to die most weeks.

VOCABULARY

The following terms are identified by paragraph number. Make sure that you understand each term's meaning in its context. If you're not sure that you understand a term, look it up in a dictionary.

oriented (1)
leaven (1)
imperative (2)
diversion (3)

melodramatic (3)
ensemble (6)
incarceration (9)

STYLE AND STRATEGY

1. What is this essay's purpose and thesis?
2. What are this essay's tone and target audience? How do the two work together to achieve the author's purpose?
3. Aside from classification, give evidence of two other rhetorical modes present in this essay.

QUESTIONS FOR CRITICAL THINKING AND DISCUSSION

1. Weinman argues that making a continuing series about "ordinary life" wouldn't work on network television, but he doesn't provide any real reason except to say that the "[dramatic] stakes are too low." Can you think of an "ordinary life" or profession that would work well as a continuing television drama?
2. Many continuing cable series such as *Breaking Bad, Curb Your Enthusiasm,* and *The Walking Dead* have 13 episode seasons and are critically acclaimed. Aside from their level of violence, why couldn't each of these shows (or other 13-episode cable series) appear on network television in an altered form?

SUGGESTIONS FOR WRITING

1. This essay classifies types of television dramas, but ignores other genres. In a 500- to 750-word essay, classify another genre of television show. For example, categorize the different types of reality shows on network television and argue why one is more successful than the other.
2. Write a 500- to 750-word essay in which you classify musical genres (rap, hip-hop, dubstep, dance) and describe their characteristics. Argue why each is popular and to what audience they each appeal.

OVEREATERS, SMOKERS AND DRINKERS: THE DOCTOR WON'T SEE YOU NOW
Health care is meant to be open to everyone equally. But some doctors question, even deny, treatment to those with certain vices.

Nicholas Köhler and Barbara Righton

Nicholas Köhler's work has appeared in the *National Post* and *Ottawa Citizen*. He has written for *Maclean's* magazine for the past seven years, with an emphasis on science and health articles. Currently, he has left *Maclean's* to begin work on a novel. Barbara Righton is a freelance writer and editor whose work has also appeared in *Maclean's*, where she was an associate editor. Her work has also appeared in *Canadian Living, Chatelaine,* and *Flare*. This article appeared in the April 18, 2006, issue of *Maclean's*.

1   It's a touchy subject. So touchy that after an hour-long interview, one Calgary orthopaedic surgeon decides he wants to remain anonymous. From New Brunswick, where a surgeon recently cancelled an operation on a crippled man's leg, a Moncton Hospital spokesperson calls asking *Maclean's* to stop trying to contact the doctor. At issue: health care for patients with self-destructive vices—overeating, smoking, drinking or drugs. More and more doctors are turning them away or knocking them down their waiting lists—whether patients know that's the reason or not. Frightening stories abound. GPs who won't take smokers as patients. Surgeons who demand obese patients lose weight before they'll operate, or tell them to find another doctor. Transplant teams who turn drinkers down flat. Doctors say their decisions make sense: why spend thousands of dollars on futile procedures? Or the decision is the product of frustration: why not make patients accountable for their vices? Others call it simple discrimination. But in a health system with more patients than doctors can treat, where doctors have discretion over whom they'll take on, some say it's inevitable that problem patients will get shunted aside in favour of healthier, less labour-intensive cases.

2   So here's the question: if people won't stop hurting themselves, can they really expect the same medical treatment as everyone else? Health care in Canada is supposed to be about equal treatment for all comers. For some doctors, however, there are patients who are less equal than others. Winnipeg GP Frederick Ross is one. In 2002, he told his patients he'd no longer see them if they continued smoking. "I said, this is stupid. I told my patients, you have three months to quit or I am going to ask you to find another doctor," recalls Ross, a genial man. "I said, your smoking is impeding my progress in treating you." Some people left in a huff. One challenged him on the basis of human rights (a tribunal later threw the case out). Others—hundreds, he says—stayed and quit smoking.

3   Cutting out the cigarettes might have helped some patients avoid an appointment with Dr. Alberto de la Rocha. As a former thoracic surgeon in Timmins, Ont., de la Rocha operated on lung cancer patients for 17 years before quitting. "I burned out in an atmosphere of indifference and lack of accountability—public and personal accountability," says de la Rocha, who is now a medical officer of health in northeastern Ontario. Smoking, says de la Rocha, goes hand in hand with entitlement. "It goes like this: 'I am sick. You are the guy who is supposed to cure me. You are going to do that in whatever condition I am in and that is my right.' " Not in my operating room, said de la Rocha, who decreed that his lung cancer patients would have to minimize their risks of a heart attack on the table or of post-op respiratory complications by not smoking for at least five weeks before surgery. "Your surgery will be booked at a time when you are prepared for it," he told them. "And if you continue smoking, I am afraid you are going to have to look for a surgeon hungry enough or foolish enough to take your case as it is."

4   Meanwhile, Dr. Paul Salo, a Calgary orthopaedic surgeon, says he's reluctant to proceed with surgery on "inveterate" smokers or the "massively overweight." Nicotine impairs bone healing, Salo explains, before adding that the failure rate in operations where bone must heal to bone is five times higher among smokers. Indeed, even the risks associated with surgery are high enough, Salo says, to require smokers to quit three months before an operation. If they don't? He goes ahead, but warns: "Look, if this doesn't heal, I am not going to be very happy and you are going to be miserable." Salo is most definite when it comes to turning down drug addicts. "I have the option to say, 'I can't form a therapeutic contract with you,' " he says. "If someone has an elective problem and they are not going to comply with my treatment recommendations, I am under no obligation to take them on."

5   Canada's provincial colleges of physicians—the professional regulatory bodies governing doctors' conduct—have no specific policies in place to stop the practice of denying treatment. "The physician makes recommendations based on what is in the best interest of the patient's health," notes Dr. Bill Pope, registrar of the College of Physicians and Surgeons of Manitoba. "By refusing to accept advice related to major issues with the patient's health, the patient is saying to the doctor, I don't believe you, I can't trust you, I can't accept you—and is basically saying I can't work with you."

6   Dr. Ruth Collins-Nakai, president of the Canadian Medical Association, stresses that doctors will always provide care in emergency situations. She adds, however, that in cases of "lifestyle-induced problems" brought on by such habits as smoking, "the doctor cannot change those things without the co-operation of the patient. And if the patient isn't willing to co-operate, then it becomes very frustrating for the doctor to have to continue looking after the patient." And, though she says doctors who drop such patients are rare, she adds that continuing to treat people who won't change "may not be the wisest use of the few resources we have in terms of doctor-availability."

7   Doctors across the country told *Maclean's* of colleagues who would not take "unhealthy patients"—smokers, drinkers and the obese—because caring for them would be too complicated, and too much of a burden for their already overcrowded practices. Such patients might, in other words, take longer to treat, reducing the number of patients a doctor can see and bill for. The consequence is an entrenched tendency to choose the gym-goer, the moderate connoisseur of red wine and the non-smoker. Says Dr. Edward Schollenberg, the registrar of the College of Physicians and Surgeons of New Brunswick: "The idea that smoking or drinking or excess weight impacts on your health care is just the way the world is."

8   Nowhere is this dictum truer than in the realm of the overweight and obese. Dr. David C.W. Lau, an obesity specialist at the University of Calgary, says there are sound medical reasons to explain why doctors are less likely to want to operate on people who are heavy. "Operating on them would pose a significant increased risk of complications," says Lau. "Surgeons don't like to deal with complications and none like to see their post-op complications go up." The Calgary orthopaedic surgeon who doesn't want his name used has done thousands of knee and hip replacements on overweight people—but he's not pleased about it. "Prostheses have a limited lifespan," he says. "If patients are overweight, they will wear them out much faster." Plus, he says, "Historically, obese people are at higher risk for surgery. There is a higher complication rate. There are healing and pulmonary issues. And they don't mobilize as fast as thin people."

9   But some doctors say there are more insidious factors keeping big Canadians from receiving the same treatment as the rest of us: discrimination. Bluntly put, fat people—a group that represents over 50 per cent of Canadians—are more likely to be discriminated against by the general public than drinkers and drug addicts (somewhere in the four per cent range) or smokers (22 per cent) because their affliction is so noticeable (all numbers are from Statistics Canada). And the medical community is as guilty of it as the rest of us. "The attitudes in the medical profession are surprisingly wanting," says Dr. Robert Dent, who heads up a weight-management clinic at the Ottawa Hospital. "The feeling is that if somebody's overweight, it's because they're eating too much and they're lazy." He adds: "If we want to use older language, we find that overweight people are considered guilty of two of the seven deadly sins—sloth and gluttony." The consequences of such discrimination can be subtle—or not.

10   There's no arguing that in Canada, too, health care costs are skyrocketing. In 2000, Statistics Canada added up the total bill at $97.9 billion. The Conference Board of Canada predicts that, when adjusted for inflation, health care costs will total $147 billion in 2020. Also inarguable: vices such as a penchant for high-fat foods and cigarettes are really ringing up the cash register. The fallout from obesity, says UBC's Birmingham, now accounts for five per cent of our total health care dollars, or $5 billion a year. "You've heard that phrase 'obesity is the new smoking,' " says Ross in Winnipeg. "Well, private health care is going to come into Canada because our public system is going broke over obesity." The ultimate costs of bad behaviour? A new heart—$80,000. Liver? $150,000. Lung? Somewhere in the neighbourhood of half a million. Indeed, Dr. Gary Levy, the medical director of Toronto General Hospital's multi-organ transplant program, says unhealthy living is simply unaffordable: "We are getting to the point where we can extend life. And that is something society is going to have to come to grips with because technology is more and more expensive. If we can't change people's behaviour, look,

11

I am going to tell you, we are going to run out of money. We probably *have* run out of money."

So when can a doctor expect an individual patient—the smoker, the overeater, the boozer—to take that long, hard look in the mirror and drop the vice? "Look," says Levy, "We are all guilty. All of us do things that are not good for us. The reality is we go to fast-food restaurants. We drive too fast. We should cut our salt intake. We need to educate all elements of society. We have an obligation: we have to put the brakes on bad living styles. We need to convince people of the value of living healthy lifestyles and what the cost is, not only to themselves and their families, but to society."

VOCABULARY

The following terms are identified by paragraph number. Make sure that you understand each term's meaning in its context. If you're not sure that you understand a term, look it up in a dictionary.

futile (1)	**tribunal** (2)	**connoisseur** (7)
shunted (1)	**decreed** (3)	**mobilize** (8)
genial (2)	**inveterate** (4)	**gluttony** (9)
	entrenched (7)	

STYLE AND STRATEGY

1. This article relies on numerous sources: find three specific examples and discuss how they lend credibility to the argument.
2. How do the authors organize their essay? How does this organization persuade the reader to accept their argument?

QUESTIONS FOR CRITICAL THINKING AND DISCUSSION

1. Canada's health care system (free medical care for all) is often cited as one of the best things about this country. Discuss the benefits and consequences of a consumer paid system like the one used in the U.S. Would such a system help or hinder Canada?
2. Can conditions based on vices be easily beaten? Discuss your experiences with smoking, drinking, or overeating. What strategies did you or someone you know use to combat these addictions?

SUGGESTIONS FOR WRITING

1. In a 500- to 750-word essay, write an essay arguing for the opposite side: that doctors have a moral obligation to treat all patients equally.
2. In a 500- to 750-word essay, argue for or against the following statement: "Fairness is not each person receiving the same, but each person receiving what they need."

A READER'S EYE

In the two selections that follow, Danielle Bochove compares the advantages and risks of home births and hospital births, while Duncan Hood contrasts Canadian life with American life. As you read these essays, note the method of organization used by each author. As well, note how the authors use the comparison/contrast option to achieve their purpose.

ARE HOME BIRTHS SAFE?

Home births may need less intervention and cause fewer injuries for mom. But they may be riskier for babies.

Danielle Bochove

Danielle Bochove is best known as the business host of CBC News Morning. *Additionally, she has worked for* The Globe and Mail *and the* Edmonton Journal, *as well as the* Financial Post. *A former anchor for BNN, she has also contributed articles to* Maclean's *magazine and* The Economist Intelligence Unit. *This article appeared in Macleans.ca on August 26, 2011.*

1   Jon Barrett is accustomed to dealing with anxious mothers-to-be. As chief of maternal-fetal medicine at Toronto's Sunnybrook Health Sciences Centre, one of the main concerns he hears from patients involves unnecessary medical interventions during delivery.

2   He acknowledges that the rate of Caesarian sections and episiotomies is far too high in Canadian hospitals. "A healthy young woman, coming into this hospital now for delivery, has almost a 40 per cent chance of having some sort of intervention that is not desired." But he's more unnerved by what that phenomenon appears to be triggering: a surge in demand for home births.

3   In Ontario, midwives performed 2,360 home births in fiscal 2008, an increase of 23 per cent in just five years. There are no national home birth statistics but the percentage of non-hospital births more than tripled in Canada between 1991 and 2007 (the latest year for which statistics are available), although they remain well under two per cent of total births. That rate is typical of much of Western Europe and the U.S.; the notable exception is the Netherlands, where roughly a third of women give birth at home.

4   Barrett's concerns about home births stem from experience. Between 1990 and 1992, he was part of an obstetric "flying squad" in Newcastle, England. His job was to travel, by ambulance, to the bedsides of women whose home births had gone awry. "For two years of my life, I remember going to calls of people who got into trouble at home," he recalls. "I just remember disasters."

5   Two incidents are particularly vivid. The first occurred in winter. Navigating the ambulance through snowy laneways, Barrett's team arrived to find two midwives frantically working over an unconscious woman. She was in shock and hemorrhaging badly. "I've never seen so much blood in my life." She survived, but only after a massive blood transfusion in hospital. The second woman developed pre-eclampsia, which caused seizures, and went into cardiac arrest as his ambulance pulled up. His team was able to restart her heart and intubate her before rushing her to hospital. She also survived. He says both conditions were unpredictable and could have occurred anywhere, "But I know they would have come less close to dying if it would have happened in hospital."

6   Unlike some of his colleagues on the squad who witnessed fetal deaths during home births, if Barrett's memories were reduced to pure data in a typical study, they'd be unremarkable. That's because most home birth data measures deaths, not complications,

and his patients survived. "If you want a retrospective study, there's no maternal mortality there . . . and so is that safe? No, it's just bloody lucky."

7   The question of how best to measure home birth safety has long plagued researchers. In Canada, national statistics don't track birth outcomes by home versus hospital. Nor do they track the sorts of near-tragic outcomes described by Barrett. Yet what is counted—mortality rates for mothers and babies during childbirth—offers little insight on the maternal side because, in the industrialized world, maternal deaths from childbirth are rare. In 2007, 24 women died in Canada from pregnancy-related conditions, including delivery, compared to more than 4,000 stillbirths and deaths within 28 days of delivery. But stories like Barrett's suggest the numbers don't tell the whole story. In his view, the bottom line should be obvious: "Sooner or later you're going to get a disaster because that's the nature of obstetrics." He adds, "It's very rare that it will happen, but it's got to happen more in home birth."

8   That assertion is at the heart of a furious debate in the birthing community. Mothers who choose to give birth at home often cite research showing there are fewer medical interventions and no increased risk. But in the past year, a new study has emerged that contradicts this. It shows that home births are associated with significantly higher death rates for babies. If correct, the rights of women to control their own bodies and birth experience would seem to conflict with the best interests of their children.

9   When the *American Journal of Obstetrics and Gynecology* (AJOG) released the now-controversial "Wax Study" last summer, it created the medical equivalent of the Rift Valley amongst birthing experts. Led by U.S. obstetrician Joseph Wax, of the Maine Medical Center, it confirmed significant benefits to mothers who gave birth at home, including less hemorrhaging, vaginal tearing and epidural use, and fewer infections and Caesarean sections. Unfortunately, these benefits seemed to occur at the baby's expense: shockingly, the report showed that neonatal deaths (defined as deaths within 28 days of birth) were two to three times higher for home births. Clearly, no woman who chooses home birth believes she's jeopardizing her baby's health, but the study suggested such faith in the safety of home birthing is undermined by medical evidence. For those who accepted Wax's results, the benefits of giving birth at home suddenly appeared trivial compared to the risks.

10   Perhaps, but the momentary silence was followed by an outraged roar from home birth supporters, including some whose research showed very different results. "The Wax study is full of mathematical errors," says Patti Janssen, a professor at the University of British Columbia's School of Population and Public Health, and lead author of a 2009 cohort study that showed home births to be as safe as hospital births, for women and babies. "The design was wrong, and the calculations were wrong, and it just has to be thrown out the window." Her objections encompass everything from Wax's math to the studies he chose to exclude from analysis, and were published on *Medscape.com* in April in a critique whose co-authors include Ank de Jonge and Eileen Hutton, both lead authors of studies that conclude that home births are as safe, if not safer, than hospital births.

11   Nathalie Waite could be the poster mother for the perfect home birth. Waite's considerations were largely pragmatic when she decided, two years ago, that her fifth baby should be born at home. She had four children attending three different Toronto schools, no nanny, and wanted her delivery to disrupt life as little as possible. It wasn't a decision she made lightly. Her husband was nervous, but Waite's midwife reassured them both. They lived near a hospital. Two attending midwives would be in close contact with Waite's obstetrician and, at the slightest sign of trouble, an ambulance would be in her driveway. Most importantly, Waite knew her own body. She'd had four hospital births. During the two deliveries in which she'd fought—"and I had to fight because they always wanted to hurry the process"—for a natural birth she'd experienced far less pain. "By this time I was very well versed. I understood my pregnancies and I understood what kind of deliveries I have."

12   Had she known what a home delivery would be like, Waite says none of her children would have been born in hospital. "It was purely beautiful." While she laboured on the top floor of the house, her children played cards on the ground floor. Her husband

checked on her between bouts of gardening, while her visiting parents kept an eye on the household. "I was left alone upstairs, peacefully, hearing all the activity happening through the house and it just felt so natural. It just felt right."

13   This is why home births are special, says Anne Wilson, president of the Canadian Association of Midwives. "It's a non-medicalized environment where birth becomes a normal part of your family life." And they are safe, she stresses, in the standard response of home birth advocates: "Research says that for women experiencing low-risk birth, that outcomes are the same, in home or in hospital, with a lower risk of intervention."

VOCABULARY

The following terms are identified by paragraph number. Make sure that you understand each term's meaning in its context. If you're not sure that you understand a term, look it up in a dictionary.

episiotomy (2)   **awry (4)**   **pragmatic (11)**
midwife (3)   **hemorrhaging (5)**

STYLE AND STRATEGY

1. What is Bochove's thesis? Where does it appear in the essay?
2. Besides comparison and contrast, what rhetorical modes does Bochove use to make her point?
3. How does Bochove's use of examples strengthen her essay's argument?

QUESTIONS FOR CRITICAL THINKING AND DISCUSSION

1. Bochove's essay contrasts two types of medical practices: traditional vs. non-traditional. Using Bochove's essay as a starting point, compare and contrast other forms of traditional and non-traditional medical practices (i.e., herbal remedies vs. pharmaceuticals), and discuss their advantages and disadvantages. Use specific examples in your own life where applicable.
2. Compare and contrast other areas of society based on traditional beliefs and practices vs. non-traditional beliefs and practices. Some potential topics could include large vs. small weddings, happiness vs. wealth in a career choice, and kids vs. no kids in a relationship. Use specific examples from your own life where applicable.

SUGGESTIONS FOR WRITING

Write a 500- to 750-word essay in which you contrast two motivations for breaking the rules. Try to use an analogy where appropriate.
1. Stealing because of need versus stealing for entertainment
2. Cheating on school assignments out of desperation versus cheating because of laziness
3. Vandalism motivated by anger over political or economic injustice versus vandalism for fun

SPECIAL CANADA DAY REPORT: HOW CANADA STOLE THE AMERICAN DREAM

The numbers are in. Compared to the U.S., we work less, live longer, enjoy better health and have more sex. And get this: now we're wealthier too.

Duncan Hood

Duncan Hood is editor for Canadian Business *magazine. Previously, he was editor of* MoneySense *magazine and senior editor for* Maclean's. *The following essay appeared as an introduction to a* Maclean's *special Canada Day issue published in June 2008, which compared Canadian life to American life in terms of occupation, health, sex life, and leisure travel. The results were quite positive: in all areas surveyed, Canadians seem to embrace life and world culture more than their neighbours to the south.*

1 To be an American is to be the best. Every American believes this. Their sports champions are not U.S. champions, they're world champions. Their corporations aren't the largest in the States, they're the largest on the planet. Their armies don't defend just America, they defend freedom.

2 Like the perpetual little brother, Canadians have always lived in the shadow of our American neighbours. We mock them for their uncultured ways, their brash talk and their insularity, but it's always been the thin laughter of the insecure. After all, says University of Lethbridge sociologist Reginald Bibby, a leading tracker of social trends, "Americans grow up with the sincere belief that their nation is a nation that is unique and special, literally called by something greater to be blessed and to be a blessing to people around the globe." Canadians can't compete with that.

3 But it turns out that while they've been out conquering the world, here in Canada we've been quietly working away at building better lives. While they've been pursuing happiness, we've been achieving it.

4 How do we know? You just have to look at the numbers. For our Canada Day special issue this year, *Maclean's* compared Canadians and Americans in every facet of our lives. We scoured census reports, polls, surveys, scientific studies, policy papers and consumer databases. We looked at who lives longer, who works more, who spends more time with friends, who travels more and who has more sex. We even found out who eats more vegetables.

5 After digging through the data, here's what we found: the staid, underpaid Canadian is dead. Believe it or not, we now have more wealth than Americans, even though we work shorter hours. We drink more often, but we live longer and have fewer diseases. We have more sex, more sex partners and we're more adventurous in bed, but we have fewer teen pregnancies and fewer sexually transmitted diseases. We spend more time with family and friends, and more time exploring the world. Even in crime we come out ahead: we're just as prone to break the law, but when we do it, we don't get shot. Most of the time, we don't even go to jail.

6 The data shows that it's the Canadians who are living it up, while Americans toil away, working longer hours to pay their mounting bills.

7 Reginald Bibby notes the irony of the situation. The U.S. is a country that aggressively pursues happiness, but Canada seems to have just stumbled onto it. While Americans are putting in overtime to pursue the American dream, we're at the pub having a few pints with friends. They may have bigger cars and bigger homes, but they're living under a mountain of debt. They look richer, but the numbers prove that they're not. The truth is that all of that competition, all of that keeping up with the Joneses, can take its toll. Getting ahead can be a lot easier when everyone is moving in the same direction. "The pursuit of happiness is ingrained in Americans as part of what it means to be an American," Bibby says. "But in Canada, happiness is almost something of a by-product of coexisting peacefully."

Be it sports, health care, business or wealth, Americans are still competing to be the best. And it's true that the best in the U.S. is the best you'll find on the planet. But when you look at the medians and the averages, their accomplishment pales. As the hard numbers in this report show, Americans have shorter lives, poorer health, less sex, more divorces, and more violent crime. Which may mean that perhaps America isn't the greatest nation on earth. After all, you can't judge a nation by the best it produces, you have to judge it by the success of the average Joe. And the average Joe in Canada is having a way better time.

VOCABULARY

The following terms are identified by paragraph number. Make sure that you understand each term's meaning in its context. If you're not sure that you understand a term, look it up in a dictionary.

perpetual (2)	**staid** (5)	**toil** (6)
insularity (2)	**prone** (5)	**pales** (8)

STYLE AND STRATEGY

1. What is the tone of this essay?
2. List at least three specific contrasts that Hood draws between Canada and the United States. What are the reasons he gives to prove these claims?
3. Does Hood tend more toward the point-by-point or the subject-by-subject approach?
4. Besides comparison/contrast, what other rhetorical strategies do you find here?

QUESTIONS FOR CRITICAL THINKING AND DISCUSSION

1. Despite the contrasts pointed to by this article, many Canadians would still argue that Canadian culture is becoming too Americanized. Is there truly a Canadian culture? What are the similarities and differences between Canadian and U.S. culture? (Hint: think about specific Canadian musicians, authors/books, and actors as well as American ones.)
2. Quebec, with its unique culture and heritage, is officially acknowledged as a distinct society within Canada. Yet we are all Canadians. What kinds of similarities and differences are there between Quebec and English-speaking Canada?

SUGGESTIONS FOR WRITING

1. Do you know a couple in a long-term relationship who seem to be "opposites"? Write a 500- to 750-word essay contrasting these people and trying to explain why their relationship endures.
2. Which is better, living for the present or building for the future? Write a 500- to 750-word essay contrasting these two approaches to life.

In the two exemplification essays that follow, Margaret Atwood writes a passionate plea to the U.S. concerning the war in Iraq, while Lars Eighner tackles a very different topic: what it is like to dine from a dumpster. As you read these essays, concentrate on the authors' *purpose*. What are they trying to prove? Writers of exemplification essays are usually presenting their generalizations and examples for a reason. Readers always appreciate concrete examples, which makes this option ideal for getting a writer's message across.

A LETTER TO AMERICA
Margaret Atwood

Margaret Atwood is one of Canada's most famous writers with her novel The Handmaid's Tale *(1985) winning her the Governor General's Award for that year. In her long career, Atwood has written in many genres (poetry, children's literature, essays) and has been a strong activist for women's rights as well as pride in the Canadian identity. The following essay, "A Letter To America," appeared in* The Globe and Mail *in 2003, just as the United States was preparing to invade Iraq. The essay discusses American foreign policy from a Canadian perspective.*

1   Dear America:

2   This is a difficult letter to write, because I'm no longer sure who you are.

3   Some of you may be having the same trouble. I thought I knew you: We'd become well acquainted over the past 55 years. You were the Mickey Mouse and Donald Duck comic books I read in the late 1940s. You were the radio shows—*Jack Benny, Our Miss Brooks*. You were the music I sang and danced to: the Andrews Sisters, Ella Fitzgerald, the Platters, Elvis. You were a ton of fun.

4   You wrote some of my favourite books. You created Huckleberry Finn, and Hawkeye, and Beth and Jo in *Little Women,* courageous in their different ways. Later, you were my beloved Thoreau, father of environmentalism, witness to individual conscience; and Walt Whitman, singer of the great Republic; and Emily Dickinson, keeper of the private soul. You were Hammett and Chandler, heroic walkers of mean streets; even later, you were the amazing trio, Hemingway, Fitzgerald, and Faulkner, who traced the dark labyrinths of your hidden heart. You were Sinclair Lewis and Arthur Miller, who, with their own American idealism, went after the sham in you, because they thought you could do better.

5   You were Marlon Brando in *On The Waterfront,* you were Humphrey Bogart in *Key Largo,* you were Lillian Gish in *Night of the Hunter*. You stood up for freedom, honesty and justice; you protected the innocent. I believed most of that. I think you did, too. It seemed true at the time.

6   You put God on the money, though, even then. You had a way of thinking that the things of Caesar were the same as the things of God: that gave you self-confidence. You have always wanted to be a city upon a hill, a light to all nations, and for a while you were. Give me your tired, your poor, you sang, and for a while you meant it.

7   We've always been close, you and us. History, that old entangler, has twisted us together since the early 17th century. Some of us used to be you; some of us want to be you; some of you used to be us. You are not only our neighbours: In many cases—mine, for instance—you are also our blood relations, our colleagues, and our personal friends. But although we've had a ringside seat, we've never understood you completely, up here north of the 49th parallel.

8   We're like Romanized Gauls—look like Romans, dress like Romans, but aren't Romans—peering over the wall at the real Romans. What are they doing? Why? What are they doing now? Why is the haruspex eyeballing the sheep's liver? Why is the soothsayer wholesaling the Bewares?

9   Perhaps that's been my difficulty in writing you this letter: I'm not sure I know what's really going on. Anyway, you have a huge posse of experienced entrail-sifters who do nothing but analyze your every vein and lobe. What can I tell you about yourself that you don't already know?

10   This might be the reason for my hesitation: embarrassment, brought on by a becoming modesty. But it is more likely to be embarrassment of another sort. When my grandmother—from a New England background—was confronted with an unsavoury topic, she would change the subject and gaze out the window. And that is my own inclination: Mind your own business.

11   But I'll take the plunge, because your business is no longer merely your business. To paraphrase Marley's ghost, who figured it out too late, mankind is your business. And vice versa: When the Jolly Green Giant goes on the rampage, many lesser plants and animals get trampled underfoot. As for us, you're our biggest trading partner: We know perfectly well that if you go down the plug-hole, we're going with you. We have every reason to wish you well.

I won't go into the reasons why I think your recent Iraqi adventures have been— **12**
taking the long view—an ill-advised tactical error. By the time you read this, Baghdad
may or may not look like the craters of the Moon, and many more sheep entrails will
have been examined. Let's talk, then, not about what you're doing to other people,
but about what you're doing to yourselves.

You're gutting the Constitution. Already your home can be entered without your **13**
knowledge or permission, you can be snatched away and incarcerated without cause,
your mail can be spied on, your private records searched. Why isn't this a recipe for
widespread business theft, political intimidation, and fraud? I know you've been told
all this is for your own safety and protection, but think about it for a minute. Anyway,
when did you get so scared? You didn't used to be easily frightened.

You're running up a record level of debt. Keep spending at this rate and pretty soon **14**
you won't be able to afford any big military adventures. Either that or you'll go the way
of the U.S.S.R.: lots of tanks, but no air conditioning. That will make folks very cross.
They'll be even crosser when they can't take a shower because your short-sighted
bulldozing of environmental protections has dirtied most of the water and dried up the
rest. Then things will get hot and dirty indeed.

You're torching the American economy. How soon before the answer to that will **15**
be, not to produce anything yourselves, but to grab stuff other people produce, at
gunboat-diplomacy prices? Is the world going to consist of a few mega rich King
Midases, with the rest being serfs, both inside and outside your country? Will the
biggest business sector in the United States be the prison system? Let's hope not.

If you proceed much further down the slippery slope, people around the world will **16**
stop admiring the good things about you. They'll decide that your city upon the hill is
a slum and your democracy is a sham, and therefore you have no business trying to
impose your sullied vision on them. They'll think you've abandoned the rule of law.
They'll think you've fouled your own nest.

The British used to have a myth about King Arthur. He wasn't dead, but sleeping **17**
in a cave, it was said; in the country's hour of greatest peril, he would return. You,
too, have great spirits of the past you may call upon: men and women of courage, of
conscience, of prescience. Summon them now, to stand with you, to inspire you, to
defend the best in you. You need them.

VOCABULARY

The following terms are identified by paragraph number. Make sure that you understand each term's meaning in its context. If you're not sure that you understand a term, look it up in a dictionary.

sham (4)	posse (9)	incarcerated (13)
entangler (7)	unsavoury (10)	sullied (16)
haruspex (8)	inclination (10)	prescience (17)
soothsayer (8)	entrails (12)	

STYLE AND STRATEGY

1. What are the major examples Atwood uses? How do they help her develop her thesis?
2. List Atwood's main points. Do they add up to a unified idea? Do the examples she has chosen support this idea? Explain.

3. At what kind of audience are Atwood's examples directed?

4. This essay is a serious analysis of important issues: economy, human rights, war, the environment, freedom, cultural similarities and differences. What is Atwood's prevailing tone? Does her tone reinforce, or detract from, the point she is making about the U.S. decision to invade Iraq?

QUESTIONS FOR CRITICAL THINKING AND DISCUSSION

1. Atwood says of the U.S., "you are also our blood relations, our colleagues, and our personal friends. But although we've had a ringside seat, we've never understood you completely, up here north of the 49th parallel." How true is this? In what ways do Canada and the U.S. differ? How are our two countries similar?

2. Atwood's letter uses many references to mythology and history (King Arthur, King Midas, Rome and the Gauls). Research these stories to better understand the connections that Atwood is trying to make. How do these allusions add a deeper meaning to her writing?

SUGGESTIONS FOR WRITING

1. Atwood's essay is directed to the U.S. to remind that country of all the good things that have come from it. Take a similar approach and write a "Letter to Canada." What examples would you use to showcase this country's great accomplishments, talents, and ideals? Or take the opposite approach: has Canada ever let you down? Write a letter to Canada appealing to the nation's better self while making references to unflattering incidents in our historical past.

2. Select a local company or institution whose services are undervalued or unappreciated—a food bank, for instance. Write a 500- to 750-word essay explaining the value that this company or institution provides.

ON DUMPSTER DIVING
Lars Eighner

When Lars Eighner wrote "On Dumpster Diving," he was homeless after having been fired from his job in Austin, Texas. With Lizbeth, his Labrador retriever, Eighner spent three years on the streets. "On Dumpster Diving" is a revised version of an essay originally published in 1991 in Threepenny Review *and included in the book* Travels with Lizbeth: Three Years on the Road and on the Streets *(1993). In it, Eighner uses a series of examples to comment on how what we throw away defines the way we live.*

1   I began Dumpster diving about a year before I became homeless.

2   I prefer the word *scavenging* and use the word *scrounging* when I mean to be obscure. I have heard people, evidently meaning to be polite, use the word *foraging,* but I prefer to reserve that word for gathering nuts and berries and such, which I do also according to the season and the opportunity. *Dumpster diving* seems to me to be a little too cute and, in my case, inaccurate because I lack the athletic ability to lower myself into the Dumpsters as the true divers do, much to their increased profit.

3   I like the frankness of the word *scavenging,* which I can hardly think of without picturing a big black snail on an aquarium wall. I live from the refuse of others. I am

STYLE AND STRATEGY

1. In this process analysis, McKinnon is actually analyzing two processes. What are they?
2. Who is this essay's intended audience? How does McKinnon seem to be criticizing both consumers and the industry?
3. This essay does not have a formal conclusion. Would it have been improved by the addition of a final, concluding paragraph? Explain.
4. How would you evaluate the author's tone?

QUESTIONS FOR CRITICAL THINKING AND DISCUSSION

1. McKinnon discusses how file sharing has had positive effects, such as winning musicians new fans and thereby increasing tour revenue. Is this an overly optimistic view? Has file-sharing lead to more positive outcomes than negative ones? Can you list some examples?
2. Do you file share or do you purchase your entertainment? Some people indulge in a bit of both. Under what circumstances would you rather purchase your entertainment than download it?

SUGGESTIONS FOR WRITING

1. Has a specific kind of technology—cellphones or MP3 players, for example—ever taken up more of your life than you expected it to? Write a 500- to 750-word essay that analyzes how this process developed.
2. Write a 500- to 750-word essay on the following topic: how to use a new technology responsibly.

IN BLACK FOCUS

The crisis in Canada's classrooms
Ken Alexander

Ken Alexander is one of the founding members of Canadian magazine The Walrus, *as well as the author of* Toward Freedom: The African-Canadian Experience *(1996). The following article "In Black Focus" was Alexander's response to the controversy surrounding the creation of a black-focused school in Toronto in 2008. In his essay, Alexander skillfully details the history of black identity in Canada while discussing the events which have lead to the establishment of this school. His essay is unique in that it not only examines a bureaucratic process, but a cultural one as well.*

With some interest, I followed the debate over black-focused schools and "Afrocentric" curricula in Toronto this past winter. Passionate opposing narratives were spun—on the one hand, by those demanding necessary affirmative action for the nearly 40 percent of black students who drop out of high school, putatively lost in the "Eurocentric" wilderness; on the other, by those seeing only segregation, and the end of Canadian-style multiculturalism, in schools tailored specifically to the needs of black kids. Fast on the heels of Ontario voters slamming John Tory's Progressive Conservatives for suggesting (during the Ontario election) that public dollars be spent on religious schools, the Toronto District School Board [TDSB] voted 11–9 in favour of one new black-focused school, plus three enhanced black studies programs. Race trumps religion; it's more inclusive, I suppose.

1

2   Of indeterminate size and catering to an as-yet-unspecified age group, the school would be open to all, the TDSB was at pains to point out. Liberal premier Dalton McGuinty knowing that many hues enrolling was as likely as Jews or Sikhs or even Somalis attending black Seventh-day Adventist churches—was not placated. He offered no extra cash for the initiative, and said that should any other jurisdiction attempt such folly he would "intervene." (To be sure, the odd "reverse Oreo" will enrol, but his or her identity problems might well be exacerbated by dissertations on the significance of ancient African civilizations—Malian, Songhai, Egyptian, Aksumite, etc.—or the contributions made to black empowerment by Spike Lee's production company, 40 Acres & A Mule.) In the meantime, with the school scheduled to open in September 2009, McGuinty urged Toronto voters to reject the move, and is hoping the richer Jewish or Sikh or Hong Kong communities just sit tight. Still, Toronto will likely have its black school: "What the hell," many say, "nothing else has worked."

3   All of this was entertaining but only of some interest, because for decades the essential debate has not budged, and even now the interlocutors remain careful not to tread in subtextual waters. In painfully inclusive language, the 1995 Ontario Royal Commission report on education recommended that "in jurisdictions with large numbers of black students, school boards, academic authorities, faculties of education, and representatives of the black community collaborate to establish demonstration schools …." What it failed to emphasize is that by the mid-1990s Toronto's "black community" existed in name only. The needs and interests of immigrants from Brazil, Ethiopia, the Caribbean, and New York, "double laps" from England, and long-time black Canadians, were as different as those of melanin-deficient citizens from Serbia, Missouri, Rome, and Belleville, Ontario. In the 1980s, recommendations from the Consultative Committee on the Education of Black Students in Toronto Schools followed a similar refrain. And in the 1970s, as West Indian immigration picked up real steam and the sense of dislocation and need became more pronounced, from the ramparts came criticisms about *The Mis-Education of the Negro* in the public system.

4   I got to thinking about Carter G. Woodson's 1933 essay, *Mis-Education,* after making numerous phone calls to black educators. By the time Woodson—the son of former slaves and the founder of Negro History Week (1926)—was urging black Americans to read their own history and to reclaim their own glorious and inglorious past, Canada's black community was threatened with extinction. From a population estimated at 80 000 in the 1850s, push and pull factors—fighting for the Union side during the American Civil War, taking advantage of Reconstruction opportunities, sodbusting on the Plains, blacks edging into politics, the Harlem Renaissance, and the migration to northern U.S. cities (1910–1930)—had left black Canadians huddled around Spadina Avenue and Dundas Street in Toronto, in Little Burgundy in Montreal, and in small settlements in Nova Scotia and out west. By 1920, Canada's black population had dropped to perhaps 20 000. Virtually invisible, except to Jews in Toronto and Montreal, who were good to them, most blacks in Canada were driven south not so much by the cold weather as the chilly social reception and subtle but pernicious forms of segregation.

5   In the U.S., Negro History Week—since transformed into the longer, more colourful, and less studious Black History Month—had a simple message: take time out from the daily toil and turmoil of black life to sit on a hard chair, read your history, and imbibe the righteous wine of racial uplift. With slavery in the background but segregation a current menace, the souls of black folks needed to be unleashed. And for young American blacks, with their reading done and pride intact, there were rewards and places to go. In the half-century after the Civil War, dozens of black universities were opened, many in the South, and most of them community endeavours reflecting the common feelings of a relatively homogeneous population once denied the right to read. It is axiomatic in education circles that if a special project is launched and sustained, it will produce good results, and these places of higher learning—over 100 black colleges and universities—are very much part of the American black experience. Given this, the opposition to (and upset about) one black school in Toronto seems, well, a bit pale.

But Canadians are a cautious people, always in search of the noble compromise, **6** and slow on the uptake. In the mid-1950s, it took a Herculean effort on the part of Toronto's "indigenous" black community to get *The Story of Little Black Sambo* banned from the curriculum. Fuelled by the scolding words of the US Supreme Court decision in *Brown v. Board of Education of Topeka* (1954)—"Separate educational facilities are inherently unequal"—the same group then lobbied hard to overturn Ontario's school-segregation laws. By 1964, they finally got their wish, and the following year the last black school shut its doors.

And so we have come full circle. The TDSB move is just, proponents argue, **7** because the facts on the ground now require "separate educational facilities." For too long, too many young blacks have wasted away in the current system; for too long, young black males in particular have needed teachers who act *in loco parentis*. These truths are self-evident, but I would be more sanguine if the debate had struck another note: unlike their U.S. counterparts, blacks in Canada remain on the margins, hail from countries far and wide, and will never speak with one voice. As a result, this black-focused school has not just rattled non-blacks; it has made many in the "community" nervous, too. At last—a cultural moment we can share.

VOCABULARY

The following terms are identified by paragraph number. Make sure that you understand each term's meaning in its context. If you're not sure that you understand a term, look it up in a dictionary.

putatively (1)	**ramparts** (3)	**axiomatic** (5)
placated (2)	**pernicious** (4)	*in loco parentis* (7)
exacerbated (2)	**homogeneous** (5)	**sanguine** (7)
interlocutors (3)	**imbibe** (5)	

STYLE AND STRATEGY

1. What is the situation that the author analyzes, and what processes have lead to this situation?
2. Who is this essay's intended audience?
3. This essay does not have a formal conclusion. Would it have been improved by the addition of a final, concluding paragraph? Explain.
4. Alexander uses process analysis and narration. What other rhetorical options does he use in this essay?

QUESTIONS FOR CRITICAL THINKING AND DISCUSSION

1. Canada is well-known for its level of diversity; however, school curricula sometimes focus largely on writing done by white male authors. Do you feel your high school English curriculum was significantly multicultural? Did you study writing by authors who encompass a variety of ethnicities?

2. Every culture has its own history that deserves to be studied; however, was the establishment of a "black school" necessary in Toronto? Discuss the positive and negative implications of such a move. Why, according to Alexander, would Torontonians be worried about the idea of a black school?

3. In the past, African Americans were encouraged to imitate the look and standards of the dominant European American majority. In what ways has this situation changed, and even reversed? In what ways is it the same?

SUGGESTIONS FOR WRITING

1. Write a 500- to 750-word essay in which you discuss the process of creating your perfect college or university course (Video Game Theory, perhaps?). How would you do this? What texts, films, or essays would you study? What assignments would you create?

2. In 500 to 700 words, explain a process that you find unnecessarily complex and strange; for example, registering for classes, getting ready to attend a formal event, training for a particular sport, or keeping up with the latest fads and fashions in clothes.

The two selections that follow include an article appearing on *PC World.ca,* which sorts out the types of spam that assault our computers daily, and a piece by Martin Luther King, Jr., evaluating three methods of responding to social oppression. In the wrong hands, classification can be a dry and boring option; however, note how skilfully these writers make this rhetorical strategy come alive.

HOW TO DEAL WITH THE NEW WAVE OF SPAM

As antispam technologies evolve to give spammers a run for their money, spammers are devising new ways to evade antispam filters and entice unsuspecting victims.

PC World.ca

The following article was published on PC World.ca in September 2008. In the article, the anti-virus company Symantec classifies various types of spam for computer users and names specific types of solutions to this relentless problem.

Earlier this year, image spam was all the rage. Today, its [*sic*] greeting card spam, file attachments spam and even spam with URLs from Chinese domains.   **1**

    As spammers continue to unveil new innovations to peddle their wares and grow their spam footprint, small businesses have a number of options for mitigating risk.   **2**

From dynamic, next-generation appliances, software and services to employee education, small businesses have more ways than ever to reduce their exposure to this evolving threat.

3   While the volume of image spam has decreased considerably since the beginning of the year, it has not gone away. Image spam is a spam email that does not use text in the body of the email to convey its message. Instead, it uses an image embedded in the email. This enables the spam to evade blocking techniques that rely on words in the body of a message or that compare the "fingerprint" of a known image spam to an incoming email.

4   The decline of image spam is likely a result of new antispam technologies that detect and block it. Vendors have worked quickly to enhance their rule filters to target different aspects of message bodies and headers as attacks mutate. Better yet, the most advanced security technology providers are leveraging their networks of millions of probe email accounts throughout the world to catch and collect the addresses of spam senders. Together with cutting-edge detection engines, this technology is highly effective at helping stop image-based attacks.

5   Of course, spammers are not standing still. Indeed, greeting card spam containing links to viruses is on the rise. The content of these messages often includes links ranging from everyday greetings to holiday-specific cards, and spammers use a variety of hooks to entice users into clicking on malicious links. One high-profile example in August attempted to fool users into thinking they were going to watch a video from a highly popular video-sharing website. Typically, when the user clicks on such a link, however, a staged downloader is delivered—that is, a program that accesses the Internet and downloads a Trojan horse onto the suspecting [*sic*] user's computer. Infected machines, in turn, become part of the very botnet that is responsible for sending such messages and hosts the websites that cause the malware to spread.

6   Spammers also routinely try out the use of various types of attachments to propagate spam, including PDF files as well as Excel and Zip files. As with image spam, vendors are tackling this problem and delivering antispam filters that identify and filter out the offending messages.

7   Spammers also continue to use different top-level domains (TLDs) to register specific names that represent their particular product or services. Then, as that particular domain name gets blacklisted, they switch to another. At the same time, spam is becoming more localized, with spammers using country TLDs to target a specific market or region. These trends are now converging. While spammed URLs historically have utilized "net" and "com" TLDs, a growing number of spam messages are using the TLD "cn," which indicates China.

8   Regardless of the delivery technique, spam remains a serious security concern because it can be used to deliver Trojan horses, viruses, and phishing attempts. The latest Symantec Internet Security Threat Report estimated in the first half of 2007, that one out of every 233 spam emails contained malicious code. The volumes of spam can not only cause a loss of service or degradation in the performance of network resources and email gateways, the delivery of malicious code through spam can significantly impact resources in trying to eradicate it from your systems. As a result, dealing with spam has become a priority for virtually all small businesses today.

9   Several technology options are available to help organizations reduce their exposure to spam. When combined with best practices, these approaches can significantly mitigate risk to the organization, even as spammers change tactics and techniques.

10   Employees should be educated to help deter spam by never responding to suspicious emails or obvious spam messages—not even to request to be taken off a

spammer's list. Doing so usually simply verifies to the spammer that he or she has found a legitimate email address. Employees can also reduce their exposure to spam by viewing emails in plain text rather than in HTML format.

In addition, small businesses can leverage any of today's advanced appliances, applications or mail security services to curb spam. The most effective solutions utilize the latest spam data and constantly update their filtering rules to keep pace with the changing nature of spam. **11**

For many small businesses, an appliance represents a low-maintenance solution. A security appliance usually can be easily integrated into an existing business network and will work together with an existing email server or gateway. An appliance is easy to set up and maintain, automatically updates rules and software, and provides extensive reporting and personalization. **12**

Antispam software can be a low-cost, flexible option for organizations, particularly those that have extra hardware on hand. While antispam software solutions also provide reporting and personalization capabilities similar to those offered by appliances, they require a bit more effort to set up and maintain. **13**

To get enterprise-level spam protection without draining internal IT resources, a growing number of small businesses are opting for an outsourced antispam service. By outsourcing email security to a managed security services provider, small businesses eliminate the overhead and maintenance typically associated with other antispam approaches. And, for companies who lack the IT staff or expertise to adequately deal with email security challenges, an outsourced service represents an effective option for enjoying 24x7 support from security experts who keep a constant eye on the threat landscape and act quickly to protect their client's business. **14**

Spammers will likely continue to come up with new tactics in their ongoing quest to evade antispam filtering technologies and promote their dubious wares. Antispam vendors, in turn, will work to create innovative new remediation tools and services to help businesses protect against this changing threat. By putting in place the hardware, software, or services most appropriate for their organization, small businesses can reduce their vulnerability to spammers and their ever-evolving bag of tricks. **15**

VOCABULARY

The following terms are identified by paragraph number. Make sure that you understand each term's meaning in its context. If you're not sure that you understand a term, look it up in a dictionary.

mitigating (2)	**botnet** (5)	**converging** (7)
leveraging (4)	**malware** (6)	**degradation** (8)
malicious (5)	**propagate** (6)	**dubious** (15)

STYLE AND STRATEGY

1. What is this essay's purpose and thesis?
2. What are this essay's tone and target audience? How do the two work together to achieve the author's purpose?
3. Aside from classification, give evidence of two other rhetorical modes present in this essay.

QUESTIONS FOR CRITICAL THINKING AND DISCUSSION

1. We live in a noisy and obtrusive world. Unwanted music, intrusive advertising, and rude people often combine to assault our peace of mind. What can a person do to insulate himself or herself against this collective intruder? What are the consequences of this self-insulation?

2. Should personal privacy be protected by law? Possible areas to consider are noise pollution; the availability of personal information, including income, debt, and shopping habits; and unsolicited calls, emails, or visits to the home.

SUGGESTIONS FOR WRITING

1. This essay classifies the types of threats that can invade a computer. In a 500- to 750-word essay, classify the types of personal threats that can invade one's life. You might classify the solutions to these threats, as well, for a longer essay.

2. Write a 500- to 750-word essay in which you classify other types of computer programs such as sound cards, video cards, or graphic design programs.

THREE TYPES OF RESISTANCE TO OPPRESSION
Martin Luther King Jr.

The American civil rights movement has had many leaders from the 1950s through to today, but Martin Luther King, Jr. (1929–1968), was its leader at the most crucial times, from the Alabama sit-ins and boycotts of the 1950s through the national movement of the 1960s. In 1968, King was murdered by a white assassin, James Earl Ray, in Memphis.

King believed in civil disobedience—nonviolent protest against legal inequities. However, many people in the civil rights movement believed that a more forceful response was needed to "shake things up." In the following essay, first published as part of his book Stride Toward Freedom *(1958), note the delicate balance that King is able to achieve in renouncing violence but also decrying acquiescence.*

1 Oppressed people deal with their oppression in three characteristic ways. One way is acquiescence: the oppressed resign themselves to their doom. They tacitly adjust themselves to oppression, and thereby become conditioned to it. In every movement toward freedom some of the oppressed prefer to remain oppressed. Almost 2800 years ago Moses set out to lead the children of Israel from the slavery of Egypt to the freedom of the promised land. He soon discovered that slaves do not always welcome their deliverers. They become accustomed to being slaves. They would rather bear those ills they have, as Shakespeare pointed out, than flee to others that they know not of. They prefer the "fleshpots of Egypt" to the ordeals of emancipation.

2 There is such a thing as the freedom of exhaustion. Some people are so worn down by the yoke of oppression that they give up. A few years ago in the slum areas of Atlanta, a Negro guitarist used to sing almost daily: "Been down so long that down don't bother me." This is the type of negative freedom and resignation that often engulfs the life of the oppressed.

3 But this is not the way out. To accept passively an unjust system is to cooperate with that system; thereby the oppressed become as evil as the oppressor. Noncooperation with evil is as much a moral obligation as is cooperation with good. The oppressed must never allow the conscience of the oppressor to slumber. Religion reminds every man that he is his brother's keeper. To accept injustice or segregation passively is to say to the oppressor that his actions are morally right. It is a way of allowing his conscience to fall asleep. At this moment the oppressed fails to be his brother's keeper. So acquiescence—while often the easier way—is not the moral way. It is the way of the coward. The Negro cannot win the respect of his oppressor by acquiescing; he merely increases the oppressor's arrogance and contempt. Acquiescence is interpreted as proof of the Negro's inferiority. The Negro cannot win the respect of the white people of the South or the peoples of the world if he is willing to sell the future of his children for his personal and immediate comfort and safety.

4 A second way that oppressed people sometimes deal with oppression is to resort to physical violence and corroding hatred. Violence often brings about momentary results. Nations have frequently won their independence in battle. But in spite of temporary victories, violence never brings permanent peace. It solves no social problem; it merely creates new and more complicated ones.

5 Violence as a way of achieving racial justice is both impractical and immoral. It is impractical because it is a descending spiral ending in destruction for all. The old law of an eye for an eye leaves everybody blind. It is immoral because it seeks to humiliate the opponent rather than win his understanding; it seeks to annihilate rather than to convert. Violence is immoral because it thrives on hatred rather than love. It destroys community and makes brotherhood impossible. It leaves society in monologue rather than dialogue. Violence ends by defeating itself. It creates bitterness in the survivors and brutality in the destroyers. A voice echoes through time saying to every potential Peter, "Put up your sword." History is cluttered with the wreckage of nations that failed to follow this command.

6 If the American Negro and other victims of oppression succumb to the temptation of using violence in the struggle for freedom, future generations will be the recipients of a desolate night of bitterness, and our chief legacy to them will be an endless reign of meaningless chaos. Violence is not the way.

7 The third way open to oppressed people in their quest for freedom is the way of nonviolent resistance. Like the synthesis in Hegelian philosophy, the principle of nonviolent resistance seeks to reconcile the truths of two opposites—acquiescence and violence—while avoiding the extremes and immoralities of both. The nonviolent resister agrees with the person who acquiesces that one should not be physically aggressive toward his opponent; but he balances the equation by agreeing with the person of violence that evil must be resisted. He avoids the nonresistance of the former and the violent resistance of the latter. With nonviolent resistance, no individual or group need submit to any wrong, nor need anyone resort to violence in order to right a wrong.

8 It seems to me that this is the method that must guide the actions of the Negro in the present crisis in race relations. Through nonviolent resistance the Negro will be able to rise to the noble height of opposing the unjust system while loving the perpetrators of the system. The Negro must work passionately and unrelentingly for full stature as a citizen, but he must not use inferior methods to gain it. He must never come to terms with falsehood, malice, hate, or destruction.

9 Nonviolent resistance makes it possible for the Negro to remain in the South and struggle for his rights. The Negro's problem will not be solved by running away. He cannot listen to the glib suggestion of those who would urge him to migrate en masse to other sections of the country. By grasping his great opportunity in the South he can make a lasting contribution to the moral strength of the nation and set a sublime example of courage for generations yet unborn.

10 By nonviolent resistance, the Negro can also enlist all men of good will in his struggle for equality. The problem is not a purely racial one, with Negroes set against whites. In the end, it is not a struggle between people at all, but a tension between justice and injustice. Nonviolent resistance is not aimed against oppressors but against oppression. Under its banner, consciences, not racial groups, are enlisted.

VOCABULARY

The following terms are identified by paragraph number. Make sure that you understand each term's meaning in its context. If you're not sure that you understand a term, look it up in a dictionary.

acquiescence (1)	yoke (2)	synthesis (7)
tacitly (1)	corroding (4)	glib (9)
fleshpot (1)	momentary (4)	sublime (9)
emancipation (1)	annihilate (5)	

STYLE AND STRATEGY

1. King was a Baptist minister and a great public speaker. Note that he uses one of the elements of a sermon: repetition. What is the effect of this rhetorical device?
2. How does King organize his essay? How does this organization persuade the reader to accept his argument? See paragraphs 1–3, 4–6, and 7–9.
3. Read King's conclusion once more (paragraph 10). Is his contrasting device ("it's not this; it's that") effective? Is King merely summarizing information, or is he evaluating the points made in his essay? Explain your answer.

QUESTIONS FOR CRITICAL THINKING AND DISCUSSION

1. King preached patience; Malcolm X preached direct action. Is violence ever acceptable as a device to effect social change?
2. In your daily life, do racial issues play a large role? Is the way that you see the world affected in any way by discrimination because of race, colour, religion, or ethnic origin? If so, how have you responded?
3. Many people see the election of Barack Obama to the presidency of the United States as the epitome of racial tolerance and the victory of Martin Luther King Jr.'s ideals. Find examples that both prove and disprove this declaration.

SUGGESTIONS FOR WRITING

1. In a 500- to 750-word essay, classify the ways that you could respond to a police officer if you were pulled over in a traffic stop.
2. In a 500- to 750-word essay, classify the ways that students at your college or university could respond to unfair policies of the campus administration.

Carol Geddes from the Tlingit village of Teslin, in the Yukon, has made a notable career as an award-winning author and filmmaker. Geddes earned a B.A. in English and philosophy from Carleton University in Ottawa and also attended Concordia University in Montreal where she studied communications, with specialties in film and documentary making. Her dedication to Northern people is evident in her first major film, *Doctor, Lawyer, Indian Chief* (1987), which shows the obstacles Native women faced in pursuit of their careers. Geddes is the producer of the National Film Board's Aboriginal Studio I, based in Edmonton, Alberta. While continuing to write and produce films, she is also able to work from her home in Whitehorse, Yukon, and so maintains her strong cultural links with Aboriginal people of the North.

Growing Up Native

Carol Geddes

I remember it was cold. We were walking through a swamp near our home in the Yukon bush. Maybe it was fall and moose-hunting season. I don't know. I think I was about four years old at the time. The muskeg was too springy to walk on, so people were taking turns carrying me—passing me from one set of arms to another. The details about where we were are vague, but the memory of those arms and the feeling of acceptance I had is one of the most vivid memories of my childhood. It didn't matter who was carrying me—there was security in every pair of arms. That response to children is typical of the native community. It's the first thing I think of when I cast my mind back to the Yukon bush, where I was born and lived with my family.

I was six years old when we moved out of the bush, first to Teslin, where I had a hint of the problems native people face, then to Whitehorse, where there was unimaginable racism. Eventually I moved to Ottawa and Montreal, where I further discovered that to grow up native in Canada is to feel the sting of humiliation and the boot of discrimination. But it is also to experience the enviable security of an extended family and to learn to appreciate the richness of the heritage and traditions of a culture most North Americans have never been lucky enough to know. As a film-maker, I have tried to explore these contradictions, and our triumph over them, for the half-million aboriginals who are part of the tide of swelling independence of the First Nations today.

But I'm getting ahead of myself. If I'm to tell the story of what it's like to grow up native in northern Canada, I have to go back to the bush where I was born, because there's more to my story than the hurtful stereotyping that depicts Indian people as drunken welfare cases. Our area was known as 12-mile (it was 12 miles from another tiny village). There were about 40 people living there—including 25 kids, eight of them my brothers and sisters—in a sort of family compound. Each family had its own timber plank house for sleeping, and there was one large common kitchen area with gravel on the ground and a tent frame over it. Everybody would go there and cook meals together. In summer, my grandmother always had a smudge fire going to smoke fish and tan moose hides. I can remember the cosy warmth of the fire, the smell of good food, and always having someone to talk to. We kids had built-in playmates and would spend hours running in the bush, picking berries, building rafts on the lake and playing in abandoned mink cages.

One of the people in my village tells a story about the day the old lifestyle began to change. He had been away hunting in the bush for about a month. On his way back, he heard a strange sound coming from far away. He ran up to the crest of a hill, looked over the top of it and saw a bulldozer. He had never seen or heard of such a thing before and he couldn't imagine what it was. We didn't have magazines or newspapers in our village, and the people didn't know that the Alaska Highway was being built as a defence against a presumed Japanese invasion during the Second World War. That was the beginning of the end of the Teslin Tlingit people's way of life. From that moment on, nothing turned back to the way it was. Although there were employment opportunities for my father and uncles, who were young men at the time, the speed and force with which the Alaska Highway was rammed through the wilderness caused tremendous upheaval for Yukon native people.

It wasn't as though we'd never experienced change before. The Tlingit Nation, which I belong to, arrived in the Yukon from the Alaskan coast around the turn of the century. They were the middlemen and women between the Russian traders and the Yukon inland Indians. The Tlingit gained power and prestige by trading European products such as metal goods and cloth for the rich and varied furs so much in fashion in Europe. The Tlingit controlled Yukon trading because they controlled the trading routes through the high mountain passes. When trading ceased to be an effective means of survival, my grandparents began raising wild mink in cages. Mink prices were really high before and during the war, but afterwards the prices went plunging down. So, although the mink pens were still there when I was a little girl, my father mainly worked on highway construction and hunted in the bush. The Yukon was then, and still is in some ways, in a transitional period—from living off the land to getting into a European wage-based economy.

As a young child, I didn't see the full extent of the upheaval. I remember a lot of togetherness, a lot of happiness while we lived in the bush. There's a very strong sense of family in the native community, and a fondness for children, especially young children. Even today, it's like a special form of entertainment if someone brings a baby to visit. That sense of family is the one thing that has survived all the incredible difficulties native people have had. Throughout a time of tremendous problems, the extended family system has somehow lasted, providing a strong circle for people to survive in. When parents were struggling with alcoholism or had to go away to find work, when one of the many epidemics swept through the community, or when a marriage broke up and one parent left, aunts, uncles and grandparents would try to fill those roles. It's been very important to me in terms of emotional support to be able to rely on my extended family. There are still times when such support keeps me going.

Life was much simpler when we lived in the bush. Although we were poor and wore the same clothes all year, we were warm enough and had plenty to eat. But even as a youngster, I began to be aware of some of the problems we would face later on. Travelling missionaries would come and impose themselves on us, for example. They'd sit at our campfire and read the Bible to us and lecture us about how we had to live a Christian life. I remember being very frightened by stories we heard about parents sending their kids away to live with white people who didn't have any children. We thought those people were mean and that if we were bad, we'd be sent away, too. Of course, that was when social workers were scooping up native children and adopting them out to white families in the south. The consequences were usually disastrous for the children who were taken away—alienation, alcoholism and suicide, among other things. I knew some of those kids. The survivors are still struggling to recover.

The residential schools were another source of misery for the kids. Although I didn't have to go, my brothers and sisters were there. They told stories about having their hair cut off in case they were carrying head lice, and of being forced to do hard chores without enough food to eat. They were told that the Indian culture was evil, that Indian people were bad, that their only hope was to be Christian. They had to stand up and say things like "I've found the Lord," when a teacher told them to speak. Sexual abuse was rampant in the residential school system.

By the time we moved to Whitehorse, I was excited about the idea of living in what I thought of as a big town. I'd had a taste of the outside world from books at school in Teslin (a town of 250 people), and I was tremendously curious about what life was like. I was hungry for experiences such as going to the circus. In fact, for a while, I was obsessed with stories and pictures about the circus, but then when I was 12 and saw my first one, I was put off by the condition and treatment of the animals.

Going to school in Whitehorse was a shock. The clash of native and white values was confusing and frightening. Let me tell you a story. The older boys in our community were already accomplished hunters and fishermen, but since they had to trap beaver in the spring and hunt moose in the fall, and go out trapping in the winter as well, they missed a lot of school. We were all in one classroom and some of my very large teenage cousins had to sit squeezed into little desks. These guys couldn't read very well. We girls had been in school all along, so, of course, we were better readers. One day the teacher was trying to get one of the older boys to read. She was typical of the teachers at that time, insensitive and ignorant of cultural complexities. In an increasingly loud voice, she kept commanding him to "Read it, read it." He couldn't. He sat there completely still, but I could see that he was breaking into a sweat. The teacher then said, "Look, she can read it," and she pointed to me, indicating that I should stand up and read. For a young child to try to show up an older boy is wrong and totally contrary to native cultural values, so I refused. She told me to stand up and I did. My hands were trembling as I held my reader. She yelled at me to read and when I didn't she smashed her pointing stick on the desk to frighten me. In terror, I wet my pants. As I stood there fighting my tears of shame, she said I was disgusting and sent me home. I had to walk a long distance through the bush by myself to get home. I remember feeling this tremendous confusion, on top of my humiliation. We were always told the white teachers knew best, and so we had to do whatever they said at school. And yet I had a really strong sense of receiving mixed messages about what I was supposed to do in the community and what I was supposed to do at school.

Pretty soon I hated school. Moving to a predominantly white high school was even worse. We weren't allowed to join anything the white kids started. We were the butt of jokes because of our secondhand clothes and moose meat sandwiches. We were constantly being rejected. The prevailing attitude was that Indians were stupid. When it was time to make course choices in class—between typing and science, for example—they didn't even ask the native kids, they just put us all in typing. You get a really bad image of yourself in a situation like that. I bought into it. I thought we were awful. The whole experience was terribly undermining. Once, my grandmother gave me a pretty little pencil box. I walked into the classroom one day to find the word "squaw" carved on it. That night I burned it in the wood stove. I joined the tough crowd and by the time I was 15 years old, I was more likely to be leaning against the school smoking a cigarette than trying to join in. I was burned out from trying to join the system. The principal told my father there was no point in sending me back to school so, with a Grade 9 education, I started to work at a series of menial jobs.

Seven years later something happened to me that would change my life forever. I had moved to Ottawa with a man and was working as a waitress in a restaurant. One day, a friend invited me to her place for coffee. While I was there, she told me she was going to university in the fall and showed me her reading list. I'll never forget the minutes that followed. I was feeling vaguely envious of her and, once again, inferior. I remember taking the paper in my hand, seeing the books on it and realizing, Oh, my God, I've read these books! It hit me like a thunderclap. I was stunned that books I had read were being read in university. University was for white kids, not native kids. We were too stupid, we didn't have the kind of mind it took to do those things. My eyes moved down the list, and my heart started beating faster and faster as I suddenly realized I could go to university, too!   12

My partner at the time was a loving supportive man who helped me in every way. I applied to the university immediately as a mature student but when I had to write Grade 9 on the application, I was sure they'd turn me down. They didn't. I graduated five years later, earning a bachelor of arts in English and philosophy (with distinction).   13

It was while I was studying for a master's degree in communications at McGill a few years later that I was approached to direct my second film (the first was a student film). *Doctor, Lawyer, Indian Chief* (a National Film Board production) depicts the struggle of a number of native women—one who began her adult life on welfare, a government minister, a chief, a fisherwoman and Canada's first native woman lawyer. The film is about overcoming obstacles and surviving. It's the story of most native people.   14

Today, there's a glimmer of hope that more of us native people will overcome the obstacles that have tripped us up ever since we began sharing this land. Some say our cultures are going through a renaissance. Maybe that's true. Certainly there's a renewed interest in native dancing, acting and singing, and in other cultural traditions. Even indigenous forms of government are becoming strong again. But we can't forget that the majority of native people live in urban areas and continue to suffer from alcohol and drug abuse and the plagues of a people who have lost their culture and have become lost themselves. And the welfare system is the insidious glue that holds together the machine of oppression of native people.   15

Too many non-native people have refused to try to understand the issues behind our land claims. They make complacent pronouncements such as "Go back to your bows and arrows and fish with spears if you want aboriginal rights. If not, give it up and assimilate into white Canadian culture." I don't agree with that. We need our culture, but there's no reason why we can't preserve it and have an automatic washing machine and a holiday in Mexico, as well.   16

The time has come for native people to make our own decisions. We need to have self-government. I have no illusions that it will be smooth sailing—there will be trial and error and further struggle. And if that means crawling before we can stand up and walk, so be it. We'll have to learn through experience.   17

While we're learning, we have a lot to teach and give to the world—a holistic philosophy, a way of living with the earth, not disposing of it. It is critical that we all learn from the elders that an individual is not more important than a forest; we know that we're here to live on and with the earth, not to subdue it.   18

The wheels are in motion for a revival, for change in the way native people are taking their place in Canada. I can see that we're equipped, we have the tools to do the work. We have an enormous number of smart, talented, moral Indian people. It's thrilling to be a part of this movement.   19

Someday, when I'm an elder, I'll tell the children the stories: about the bush, about the hard times, about the renaissance, and especially about the importance of knowing your place in your nation.   20

Questions for Discussion

1. Geddes says that to grow up native is to feel "the sting of humiliation and the boot of discrimination." Which one of the incidents she recounts makes you feel that sting the most?
2. Find the instances where Geddes uses the term Indian in place of native. How does this word choice impact the meaning of the sentence?
3. How do the teachers in the story show an unwillingness to see their students as individuals? What were the consequences of this approach? Do you think things have changed?

4. Geddes refers to white values or white culture. Do you think there is a single white Canadian culture? If there is how would you describe it?

5. Find examples that show how Geddes internalized external opinions. How did she overcome this oppression?

6. What do you think of the comment "Go back to your bows and arrows and fish with spears if you want aboriginal rights. If not, give up and assimilate into white Canadian culture."

Questions for Writing and Reflection

1. Geddes ends the piece promising to "tell the children . . . about the importance of knowing your place in your nation." Which nation do you think she is referring to? How do you think she sees her place within it? Support your position with evidence from the essay.

2. Geddes remembers the security of the community of her early childhood fondly. Write your own autobiographical story that illustrates what security meant to you as a child.

3. Research racism as it applies to aboriginal cultures in Canada. How has it evolved? What can be done to eliminate it?

NAHEED MUSTAFA

My Body Is My Own Business

Born in England to parents from an Indo-Pakistani background, Naheed Mustafa moved as an infant to Canada. In 1992 she completed an honours degree in political science and philosophy at the University of Toronto, specializing in Third-World development. Then she studied journalism at Ryerson University. Mustafa currently lives in Toronto with her husband, and combines working as an editor and freelance writer with raising her three children. "Almost anybody who's willing to work hard enough can learn to write very well," Mustafa says. It was on July 29, 1993 that "My Body Is My Own Business" appeared in the Toronto Globe and Mail. *Since we first reprinted the essay it has become widely anthologized in print, has been widely circulated on the Internet and is still attracting commentary. Mustafa states, "I see myself as being on something of a journey around this issue...." Ironically, the author of "My Body Is My Own Business" recalls the first edition of a textbook that inspired her in high school: it had a photo of a lightning strike on its cover. Its title was* The Act of Writing.

I often wonder whether people see me as a radical, fundamentalist Muslim terrorist packing an AK-47 assault rifle inside my jean jacket. Or maybe they see me as the poster girl for oppressed womanhood everywhere. I'm not sure which it is. 1

I get the whole gamut of strange looks, stares and covert glances. You see, I wear the *hijab,* a scarf that covers my head, neck and throat. I do this because I am a Muslim woman who believes her body is her own private concern. 2

3   Young Muslim women are reclaiming the *hijab*, reinterpreting it in light of its original purpose—to give back to women ultimate control of their own bodies.

4   The Koran teaches us that men and women are equal, that individuals should not be judged according to gender, beauty, wealth or privilege. The only thing that makes one person better than another is her or his character.

5   Nonetheless, people have a difficult time relating to me. After all, I'm young, Canadian born and raised, university-educated—why would I do this to myself, they ask.

6   Strangers speak to me in loud, slow English and often appear to be playing charades. They politely inquire how I like living in Canada and whether or not the cold bothers me. If I'm in the right mood, it can be very amusing.

7   But why would I, a woman with all the advantages of a North American upbringing, suddenly, at 21, want to cover myself so that with the *hijab* and the other clothes I choose to wear, only my face and hands show?

8   Because it gives me freedom.

9   Women are taught from early childhood that their worth is proportional to their attractiveness. We feel compelled to pursue abstract notions of beauty, half realizing that such a pursuit is futile.

10   When women reject this form of oppression, they face ridicule and contempt. Whether it's women who refuse to wear makeup or to shave their legs or to expose their bodies, society, both men and women, have trouble dealing with them.

11   In the Western world, the *hijab* has come to symbolize either forced silence or radical, unconscionable militancy. Actually, it's neither. It is simply a woman's assertion that judgment of her physical person is to play no role whatsoever in social interaction.

12   Wearing the *hijab* has given me freedom from constant attention to my physical self. Because my appearance is not subjected to public scrutiny, my beauty, or perhaps lack of it, has been removed from the realm of what can legitimately be discussed.

13   No one knows whether my hair looks as if I just stepped out of a salon, whether or not I can pinch an inch, or even if I have unsightly stretch marks. And because no one knows, no one cares.

Feeling that one has to meet the impossible male standards of   14
beauty is tiring and often humiliating. I should know, I spent my
entire teenage years trying to do it. I was a borderline bulimic and
spent a lot of money I didn't have on potions and lotions in hopes of
becoming the next Cindy Crawford.

The definition of beauty is ever-changing; waifish is good, waifish   15
is bad, athletic is good—sorry, athletic is bad. Narrow hips? Great.
Narrow hips? Too bad.

Women are not going to achieve equality with the right to bare   16
their breasts in public, as some people would like to have you believe.
That would only make us party to our own objectification. True
equality will be had only when women don't need to display themselves to get attention and won't need to defend their decision to
keep their bodies to themselves.

EXPLORATIONS:

Elizabeth Warnock Fernea, *In Search of Islamic Feminism: One
    Woman's Global Journey*
Richard Gordon, *Eating Disorders: Anatomy of a Social Epidemic*
Naomi Wolf, *The Beauty Myth: How Images of Beauty Are Used Against
    Women*
Bharati Mukherjee, *Jasmine* (novel)
Salman Rushdie, *Shame* (novel)
Under One Sky: Arab Women in North America Talk About the Hijab
    (NFB, 43 min., 1999)
http://en.wikipedia.org/wiki/Hijab
http://en.wikipedia.org/wiki/Burqa
http://www.usc.edu/dept/MSA/othersites

STRUCTURE:

1. Why does Mustafa open with two STEREOTYPES? Do they draw your
   attention? Do they go straight to her topic?
2. In her argument does Mustafa give more attention to *causes* or
   effects? Name the main causes. Name the main effects.

3. Why does Mustafa explore effects *first* and causes *after*, reversing the logical order of the two?

4. Identify the TRANSITION in which Mustafa actually asks "why" and answers with "because … ," as she moves from *effects* to *causes*.

STYLE:

1. Ending on a key word is a powerful device of emphasis. Note the final word in each half of Mustafa's argument: What makes "freedom" and "themselves" good choices for these positions?

2. Language can speak through rhythm as much as through words. Read aloud the first sentence of paragraph 6, then analyze how its sound reinforces its meaning.

IDEAS FOR DISCUSSION AND WRITING:

1. Mustafa says male standards of beauty for women are "impossible" and that feeling the need to meet them is "humiliating" (par. 14). Is she right? Whatever your own gender, give examples to attack or defend her view.

2. Examine the PARADOX of paragraph 8: that the effect of covering oneself with the *hijab* is "freedom." Do non-Muslims have means of shielding themselves, as well, from the unreasonable scrutiny and expectations of others? Name any such techniques you have used.

3. In news coverage of the Canadian military presence in Afghanistan, we often see images of women wearing another garment that conceals the body, the *burqa*. Describe it. Tell any *effects* that you believe its use has on the wearer and on people observing the wearer. Can it offer "freedom," as Mustafa believes the *hijab* does?

4. Though part of her background is the culture of another country, Mustafa is Canadian. If you too have origins in another culture, to what extent do you see yourself retaining the clothes, the foods, the religion and the language of that culture, here in Canada. Predict the *effects* of your intended course of action.

5. Mustafa confesses that as a teen she was a "borderline bulimic" (par. 14). What do you see as the main *causes* of bulimia and anorexia nervosa? What *causes* women, not men, to be the main victims?

6. At the library look through an illustrated history of art, taking notes on how the ideal of beauty in women has changed through the centuries. Then report your findings to the class, showing illustrations as evidence for your conclusions.

7. Watch your favourite television channel for at least an hour, taking notes on how women are presented both in programs and commercials. Then report to the class on the attitudes, especially any STEREOTYPES, which you detected. What *effects*, in both male and female viewers, do you think these attitudes will *cause*?

8. PROCESS IN WRITING: *Do number 6 above, except as an essay. Look over your notes, then choose a THESIS STATEMENT that expresses the main* effect(s) *on viewers of the* examples *you observed. Now write a rapid first draft, supporting your thesis statement with large numbers of these* examples. *When the draft has cooled off, look it over. Do the* causes *and* effects *seem reasonable? Have you tried to be objective, rather than interpret according to your own prejudices? Are there* causes *behind causes, or* effects *of effects, that might enrich your analysis? Do TRANSITIONS such as "since," "because" and "therefore" help the audience follow your logic? If not, add. Finally, edit for things like punctuation and spelling before doing the final version. Read it to the class, and be ready to answer questions from other points of view.*

Note: See also the Topics for Writing on the Online Learning Centre at www. mcgrawhill.ca/olc/conrad.

Lawrence Hill has achieved great acclaim for his writing about his experiences as an African-Canadian. He holds his own among family members who are also well-known Canadian figures. His father, Daniel G. Hill was the Director of the Ontario Human Rights Commission, and his mother, Donna Hill, a social activist. His brother is the well-known singer-songwriter Dan Hill. Lawrence Hill's own sense of activism started in 1968 when he signed a petition against the Vietnam War. He is now an honorary patron with the developmental organization Canadian Crossroads International. Hill has travelled to West Africa, where he developed a particular interest in the condition of African girls and women. Multilingual in English, French, and Spanish, Hill moved from Toronto to Quebec City where he completed a B.A. in economics from Université de Laval, and then on to John Hopkins University in Baltimore where he earned an M.A. in writing. He has written for many newspapers including *The Globe and Mail* and the *Winnipeg Free Press*. In addition to his shorter works, Hill is also a prolific and award-winning novelist, best known for his 2001 novel *Black Berry, Sweet Juice: On Being Black and White in Canada* and the 2007 novel *The Book of Negroes*, which was also published internationally as *Someone Knows My Name*.

Black + White = Black

Lawrence Hill

1   My childhood was punctuated with sayings about black people. My father's relatives sometimes said, "The blacker the berry, the sweeter the juice." On one level, the meaning is obvious: a raspberry or strawberry that is full and dark and pregnant with its own ripeness is sweeter than its pink, prematurely plucked counterpart. But there is also a sexual undertone to the saying, a suggestion of the myth of the overcharged, overheated, high-performing black body. Presumably, the blacker berry tastes richer, more full and is juicier. The trouble with this expression is that it has always struck me as a limp-wristed effort to help black people believe that it was OK to be black. It seemed to me sad and pathetic that we even felt a need to pass around a saying like that.

2   But I wasn't the only one who found that the words itched more than they tickled. My father bombed the pious saying to smithereens with his own sarcastic version: "The blacker the berry/The sweeter the juice/But if you get too black/It ain't no use." I absolutely loved that variation. Why? Because it turned self-affirmation on its head with a mere 10 additional words, offering a bittersweet reminder of the hopelessness of being black in a society that doesn't love—or even like—black people. There were many other sayings, such as "If you're white/You're all right/If you're brown/Stick around/If you're black/Stay back." Black people said these words and laughed. All the sayings underscored the utter futility of being black.

3   I discovered, very early, that some people had strange ideas about the children of interracial unions, and seemed inclined to believe that life for us would be miserable. When I was 12, my best friend was a white girl, Marilyn (as I shall name her), whose mother would embarrass the dickens out of me by singing my praises to her own children. "Look how well Larry does in school. Why can't you be like that, Marilyn?" Astoundingly, this same mother who thought I was doing so well once took me aside and said, "Frankly, Larry, don't you think it is terrible, mixing races like that? It ruins the children! How are they to make their way in life?"

4   As a child, my own experience of race, including my concept of my own racial identity, was shaded quite differently from that of my parents. They were both born and raised in the United States, and their racial identities were clearly delineated all their lives. The America of their youth and early adulthood was replete with laws that banned interracial marriages and upheld segregation in every domain of public life. One of the most telling details came to me from my mother, who was working as a secretary for a Democratic senator when she met my father in Washington in 1953: "When I started dating your father, even the federal government cafeterias were segregated." In the United States, there was never any doubt that my father was first and foremost a black man. Or that my mother was a white woman. And there is no question that, had my siblings and I been raised in the United States, we would have been identified—in school, on the street, in community centres, among friends—as black.

5   But my parents threw their unborn children a curveball. They came to Toronto right after they married, had us and we all stayed here. They had had enough of racial divisions in their country of birth. And although they spent their lives at the forefront of the Canadian human-rights movement, they were also happy and relieved to set up in suburban, white, middleclass Toronto, where race faded (most of the time) into the background.

When I was growing up, I didn't spend much time thinking about who I was or where I fit in. I was too busy tying my shoelaces, brushing my teeth, learning to spell, swinging baseball bats and shooting hockey pucks. But once in a while, just as my guard was down, questions of my own identity would leap like a cougar from the woods and take a bite out of my backside. 6

I found that race became an issue as a result of environmental factors. The average white kid growing up in a white suburb didn't have to think of himself as white. Gradually, my environment started talking to me and making me aware that I could never truly be white. There's nothing like being called "nigger" to let you know that you're not white. 7

Learning that I wasn't white, however, wasn't the same as learning that I was black. Indeed, for the longest time I didn't learn what I was—only what I wasn't. In the strange and unique society that was Canada, I was allowed to grow up in a sort of racial limbo. People knew what I wasn't—white or black—but they sure couldn't say what I was. I have black American cousins, of both lighter and darker complexions, who attended segregated schools and grew up in entirely black communities. They had no reason to doubt their racial identity. That identity was wrapped around them, like a snug towel, at the moment of birth. 8

In 1977, when I decided to take a year off university, I went to visit my cousins in Brooklyn before flying to Europe, which must have appeared to them a quintessentially white thing to do. My cousin Richard Flateau took me under his wing, and was patient until I asked if he liked to play squash. An indignant retort exploded from his lips: "Larry! That's a white folks' game!" Today, looking back, I find irony in that memory. There I was, son of a black American Second World War veteran and a white American civil-rights activist, playing squash, a sport virtually unknown to inner-city blacks in the United States. 9

These days, I think of the factors that contributed to my sense of identity, and of how malleable that sense of identity was and still is. There were days when I went straight from my exclusive, private boys' high school to family events populated by black relatives or friends who idolized the icons and heroes of my childhood—Angela Davis, with her intelligence and her kick-ass Afro; sprinters Tommie Smith and John Carlos, with their black-gloved fists raised on the Olympic podium in Mexico City; Muhammad Ali, who stood up to the white man and spoke the words that moved the world: "I ain't got no quarrel with the Viet Cong." I bounced back and forth between studying Latin, playing squash and revering black American cultural icons, but who exactly was I? 10

Lately, I have been looking at some family photos and mulling over what they mean to me. In my home office, I have some 30 framed shots of relatives. There are my three children, running, cavorting, picking apples. The eldest, Geneviève, is 11, and I wonder how she will come to see herself, racially, as she moves into adolescence. She has been a ballerina for six years, and you don't find a world much whiter than that, not even in Oakville, where we live. She knows who she is, and has had much contact with the black side of her family—but the girl has blue eyes and skin even lighter than mine, and I can see that if she is going to assert her own blackness one day, she may have to work hard at it. Nine-year-old Caroline, the middle child, is the darkest of my three, and has that uncanny middle-child ability to relate to anybody of any age. I have noticed that she already bonds vigorously with black women. Andrew, who is 7, is about as interested in race as he would be in nuclear physics. Interestingly, though, he has already called out a few times, "I'm not black, I'm white," and shot a look my way to test for a reaction. He looks white, too. 11

Would you like to know how my children would once have been categorized, racially? Quadroons. They have a father who is supposedly half-black and a mother who is white, and that parentage, according to the traditional racial definition blender, would have made them quadroons. Quadroons, of course, were most definitely black, and enslaved like the rest of us in Canada and the United States. Quadroon women were favoured by slave owners for features deemed exotic and sexy but not too black, thank you very much. I shudder to imagine children who looked just like mine dancing in the infamous Quadroon Balls in New Orleans, where hot-looking young women were bought and consumed until they were no longer young or beautiful. 12

Today in Canada, black people still contend with racism at every level of society. And yet, the way my children will define themselves, and be defined by others, remains up for grabs. Racial identity is about how you see yourself, about how you construct a sense of belonging, community, awareness and allegiance. 13

To this date, I have mostly seen myself as black. My black American relatives, who lived in Brooklyn, Washington, Baltimore and North Carolina, were much closer to us and much easier to visit than my mother's family. Apart from her twin, Dottie, whom we all adore, we never really got to know my mother's relatives. My mother spoke negatively of her brothers when we were young, describing how they gave her a hard time—one even questioned her sanity—when she announced that she would be marrying a black man. As a result, as a child I came to nourish a minor grudge against some of these relatives. On my father's side, however, family was like an extension of my own body and psyche. 14

My first sense of blackness, sprang from warm places. Our house boomed with jazz and blues on weekends. Dan, Karen and I watched—entranced, intrigued—as our parents danced in the living room to Ella Fitzgerald, Billie Holiday and Duke Ellington. Dad has an amazing voice. When he sang, he waltzed up and down the tunes with a playfulness and irreverence that we found absolutely infectious.

I remember being laid up with the flu when I was 5. My father asked: "Any musical requests, sir?" And I said, "Put on Joe Williams." *Every Day I Have the Blues* began to jump off the record player. I listened to my dad and Williams nailing the notes as Basie hammered the piano, and trumpets, trombones and saxophones erupted with glee. It's one of the happiest songs I've heard—even if it is about the blues. *Nobody loves me/nobody seems to care/between bad luck and trouble/well you know I've had my share.* Just about any words could have flown from Joe Williams's lips and soared, ecstatically, as if to prove that nothing could keep this man from living and loving. Jazz and blues were already showing me the sweet alchemy of trouble and joy that defined black musical expression, and black people themselves.

I don't recall early moments with family members that gave me a negative sense of race, but my siblings do. Perhaps because he was the firstborn, Dan had a rockier time with our father. Dan has no doubt that our father gave us mixed racial messages. When my brother was 11 or so, Dad gave him a stocking to wear on his head at night. The idea was to straighten out Dan's hair while he slept, or at the very least to keep it from getting too curly on the pillow. I asked Dan if Dad had told him why he had to wear it.

"It wasn't good to have curly hair. He'd pull a hair out of my head and put it on the table and say, 'See? This is curly. It's not good to have curly hair.' And I remember feeling extremely hurt and ashamed, and I started wearing the stocking cap. I remember feeling very concerned that my hair was curly, and I remember being frantic about straightening it."

Dan now attributes the incident to the strange paradoxes of human nature. "I think that kind of behaviour is common among people like our father, who have worked in the field of human rights. Very often, people go into these fields as compensation for their own feelings of inadequacy. That way, they can still bring those feelings of inadequacy and self-hatred—self-racial-hatred—into the house."

Dan, Karen and I learned early that you can have a white parent and still be considered black, but you can never have a black parent and be considered white. It ain't allowed. You'll be reminded of your "otherness" more times than you can shake a stick at it. This is one of the reasons why I self-identify as black. Attempts at pleasant symmetry, as in "half-white, half-black," trivialize to my eye the meaning of being black. This doesn't mean I don't love my mother. I love her as profoundly as I love any person on earth. But I just don't see myself as being the same race as she is. I raised this issue with my mother recently. "Listen," she told me, "when I married your father, I knew that our children would be black. I would have been an idiot to fail to see that. Look where we came from."

However, the suburb of Don Mills in which they eventually settled became as suffocating for their children as D.C. had been for them. There were no blacks in my school, on my street. Because I looked so different from everyone else, I feared that I was ugly. I worried about having frizzy hair, big ears, a big nose and plump lips. When I looked in the mirror, I felt disgust. None of the people I admired looked the least bit like me. Listening to stories of my father's working world instilled in us a measure of black pride. We also derived a sense of connection from family moments around the television, which is odd because we weren't that interested in TV. But the late 1960s and the early 1970s featured big stand-up comedy numbers by Bill Cosby and Flip Wilson. When I watched these shows, I felt alive. I felt that there were people in the world who were speaking to me.

I had to find other ways to connect with them. So I ate up every bit of black writing that I could find. Langston Hughes, Ralph Ellison, Richard Wright—whom I approached gingerly because my mother confessed that *Native Son* had upset her so much, it had made her vomit. James Baldwin. Eldridge Cleaver—now that cat fascinated me, especially when, in *Soul on Ice*, he speculated as to why black men and white women end up together. I read Alex Haley's *Autobiography of Malcolm X*, and had to struggle through the section of Malcolm X's life when he ardently believed that white people were the devil incarnate. I knew this to be false. My mother was white, and she was no devil.

Without knowing exactly what I was doing, I was forming my own sense of blackness and my own connection to the black diaspora. Soon, this exploration blossomed into creative writing. Every time I wrote, my mind wandered into the lives of black characters. Slowly, I was developing a sense of myself. These days, when I'm invited into schools with black students, I feel a tinge of nostalgia for a past not lived. I can't help wondering what it would have been like to have black people around me when I was young. I can't help wondering what it would have been like to go out with black girls, or to drift into a friend's home and find myself surrounded by black people. What a different life that would have been.

15

16

17

18

19

20

21

22

23

Questions for Discussion

1. Consider Hill's assertion that "racial identity is about how you see yourself, about how you construct a sense of belonging, community, awareness and allegiance." Given that definition, how would you define your own racial identity?

2. It is often noted that Canadian identity is defined by what it isn't, not by what it is. How is this similar to Hill's search for identity?

3. Why do you think Hill's father wanted his brother to have straight hair?

4. How is a racial identity different than a cultural identity?

5. Why do you think Hill feels the need to define himself as either black or white? Do you think his children will feel the same need for a racial identity?

6. To what extent do you think we determine our own identity and to what extent do you think our identity is given to us by our families and communities?

Questions for Writing and Reflection

1. "Quadroon" is only one of many terms that used to exist to define interracial children. Research some of these definitions and the difficulties that faced children who were not seen as belonging to any race during times of segregation.

2. Write your own autobiographical explanation of something you have come to believe over time. Show how different experiences have influenced you and led to your opinion.

3. Hill notes that "Today in Canada, black people still contend with racism at every level of society." Research racism in Canada and create a presentation that shares your research and shows how you can be involved in eliminating racism.

Lieutenant-General Roméo Antonius Dallaire is perhaps one of Canada's most distinguished and decorated retired military leaders. Born in the Netherlands to a Canadian service officer and a Dutch nurse, Dallaire immigrated to Canada as a baby in 1946. Bilingual in French and English, Dallaire attended *Collège militaire royal de Saint-Jean* as a cadet and ultimately graduated from the Royal Military College of Canada in Kingston with a B.Sc. in 1970. In 1993–94 he was appointed the Force Commander of UNAMIR, the United Nations peacekeeping force for Rwanda. There he witnessed carnage and genocide about which he tried fruitlessly to warn the UN establishment. The devastation and inhumanity he witnessed took a heavy toll on Dallaire. After returning to Canada, Dallaire was appointed to various commands in Canada (1994–2000). In 2000 the effects of the post-traumatic stress disorder (PTSD) caused by his Rwandan experiences almost caused Dallaire to take his own life. As a result he became a public and forceful speaker on behalf of returning military personnel with PTSD and other mental health issues. He then testified against the genocidal acts in Rwanda at the International Criminal Tribunal for Rwanda, and has since worked for many causes related to the effects of war on survivors. His best-selling book, *Shake Hands with the Devil: The Failure of Humanity in Rwanda* (2003) is based upon his Rwandan experiences, and helped to awaken the world to the atrocities of the sub-Saharan hostilities. Dallaire has been awarded many honours, including the Order of Canada, and numerous honorary doctorates and military honours in both the United States and Canada. In addition he was a flag-bearer for the 2010 Vancouver Winter Olympics. *Shake Hands with the Devil: The Failure of Humanity in Rwanda* won the Governor General's Literary Award for Non Fiction in 2004.

Cri de coeur*

Lt.-Gen. Roméo Dallaire, with Major Brent Beardsley

It was an absolutely magnificent day in May 1994. The blue sky was cloudless, and there was a whiff of breeze stirring the trees. It was hard to believe that in the past weeks an unimaginable evil had turned Rwanda's gentle green valleys and mist-capped hills into a stinking nightmare of rotting corpses. A nightmare we all had to negotiate every day. A nightmare that, as commander of the UN peacekeeping force in Rwanda, I could not help but feel deeply responsible for.

In relative terms, that day had been a good one. Under the protection of a limited and fragile ceasefire, my troops had successfully escorted about two hundred civilians—a few of the thousands who had sought refuge with us in Kigali, the capital of Rwanda—through many government- and militia-manned checkpoints to reach safety behind the Rwandese Patriotic Front (RPF) lines. We were seven weeks into the genocide, and the RPF, the disciplined rebel army (composed largely of the sons of Rwandan refugees who had lived over the border in camps in Uganda since being forced out of their homeland at independence), was making a curved sweep toward Kigali from the north, adding civil war to the chaos and butchery in the country.

Having delivered our precious cargo of innocent souls, we were headed back to Kigali in a white UN Land Cruiser with my force commander pennant on the front hood and the blue UN flag on a staff attached to the right rear. My Ghanaian sharpshooter, armed with a new Canadian C-7 rifle, rode behind me, and my new Senegalese aide-de-camp, Captain Ndiaye, sat to my right. We were driving a particularly dangerous stretch of road, open to sniper fire. Most of the people in the surrounding villages had been slaughtered, the few survivors escaping with little more than the clothes on their backs. In a few short weeks, it had become a lonely and forlorn place.

Suddenly up ahead we saw a child wandering across the road. I stopped the vehicle close to the little boy, worried about scaring him off, but he was quite unfazed. He was about three years old, dressed in a filthy, torn T-shirt, the ragged remnants of underwear, little more than a loincloth, drooping from under his distended belly. He was caked in dirt, his hair white and matted with dust, and he was enveloped in a cloud of flies, which were greedily attacking the open sores that covered him. He stared at us silently, sucking on what I realized was a high-protein biscuit. Where had the boy found food in this wasteland?

I got out of the vehicle and walked toward him. Maybe it was the condition I was in, but to me this child had the face of an angel and eyes of pure innocence. I had seen so many children hacked to pieces that this small, whole, bewildered boy was a vision of hope. Surely he could not have survived all on his own? I motioned for my aide-de-camp to honk the horn, hoping to summon up his parents, but the sound echoed over the empty landscape, startling a few birds and little else. The boy remained transfixed. He did not speak or cry, just stood sucking on his biscuit and staring up at us with his huge, solemn eyes. Still hoping that he wasn't all alone, I sent my aide-de-camp and the sharpshooter to look for signs of life.

Cri de coeur: Editor's title, in French meaning "a cry from the heart."

We were in a ravine lush with banana trees and bamboo shoots, which created a dense canopy of foliage. A long straggle of deserted huts stood on either side of the road. As I stood alone with the boy, I felt an anxious knot in my stomach: this would be a perfect place to stage an ambush. My colleagues returned, having found no one. Then a rustling in the undergrowth made us jump. I grabbed the boy and held him firmly to my side as we instinctively took up defensive positions around the vehicle and in the ditch. The bushes parted to reveal a well-armed RPF soldier about fifteen years old. He recognized my uniform and gave me a smart salute and introduced himself. He was part of an advance observation post in the nearby hills. I asked him who the boy was and whether there was anyone left alive in the village who could take care of him. The soldier answered that the boy had no name and no family but that he and his buddies were looking after him. That explained the biscuit but did nothing to allay my concerns over the security and health of the boy. I protested that the child needed proper care and that I could give it to him: we were protecting and supporting orphanages in Kigali where he would be much better off. The soldier quietly insisted that the boy stay where he was, among his own people.   6

I continued to argue, but this child soldier was in no mood to discuss the situation and with haughty finality stated that   7
his unit would care and provide for the child. I could feel my face flush with anger and frustration, but then noticed that the boy himself had slipped away while we had been arguing over him, and God only knew where he had gone. My aide-de-camp spotted him at the entrance to a hut a short distance away, clambering over a log that had fallen across the doorway. I ran after him, closely followed by my aide-de-camp and the RPF child soldier. By the time I had caught up to the boy, he had disappeared inside. The log in the doorway turned out to be the body of a man, obviously dead for some weeks, his flesh rotten with maggots and beginning to fall away from the bones.

As I stumbled over the body and into the hut, a swarm of flies invaded my nose and mouth. It was so dark inside that at   8
first I smelled rather than saw the horror that lay before me. The hut was a two-room affair, one room serving as a kitchen and living room and the other as a communal bedroom; two rough windows had been cut into the mud-and-stick wall. Very little light penetrated the gloom, but as my eyes became accustomed to the dark, I saw strewn around the living room in a rough circle the decayed bodies of a man, a woman and two children, stark white bone poking through the desiccated, leather-like covering that had once been skin. The little boy was crouched beside what was left of his mother, still sucking on his biscuit. I made my way over to him as slowly and quietly as I could and, lifting him into my arms, carried him out of the hut.

The warmth of his tiny body snuggled against mine filled me with a peace and serenity that elevated me above the chaos.   9
This child was alive yet terribly hungry, beautiful but covered in dirt, bewildered but not fearful. I made up my mind: this boy would be the fourth child in the Dallaire family. I couldn't save Rwanda, but I could save this child.

Before I had held this boy, I had agreed with the aid workers and representatives of both the warring armies that I would not   10
permit any exporting of Rwandan orphans to foreign places. When confronted by such requests from humanitarian organizations, I would argue that the money to move a hundred kids by plane to France or Belgium could help build, staff and sustain Rwandan orphanages that could house three thousand children. This one boy eradicated all my arguments. I could see myself arriving at the terminal in Montreal like a latter-day St. Christopher with the boy cradled in my arms, and my wife, Beth, there ready to embrace him.

That dream was abruptly destroyed when the young soldier, fast as a wolf, yanked the child from my arms and carried him   11
directly into the bush. Not knowing how many members of his unit might already have their gunsights on us, we reluctantly climbed back into the Land Cruiser. As I slowly drove away, I had much on my mind.

By withdrawing, I had undoubtedly done the wise thing: I had avoided risking the lives of my two soldiers in what would   12
have been a fruitless struggle over one small boy. But in that moment, it seemed to me that I had backed away from a fight for what was right, that this failure stood for all our failures in Rwanda.

Whatever happened to that beautiful child? Did he make it to an orphanage deep behind the RPF lines? Did he survive the   13
following battles? Is he dead or is he now a child soldier himself, caught in the seemingly endless conflict that plagues his homeland?

That moment, when the boy, in the arms of a soldier young enough to be his brother, was swallowed whole by the forest,   14
haunts me. It's a memory that never lets me forget how ineffective and irresponsible we were when we promised the Rwandans that we would establish an atmosphere of security that would allow them to achieve a lasting peace. It has been almost nine years since I left Rwanda, but as I write this, the sounds, smells and colours come flooding back in digital clarity. It's as if someone has sliced into my brain and grafted this horror called Rwanda frame by blood-soaked frame directly on my cortex. I could not forget even if I wanted to. For many of these years, I have yearned to return to Rwanda and disappear into the blue-green hills with my ghosts. A simple pilgrim seeking forgiveness and pardon. But as I slowly begin to piece my life back together, I know the time has come for me to make a more difficult pilgrimage: to travel back through all those terrible memories and retrieve my soul.

I did try to write this story soon after I came back from Rwanda in September 1994, hoping to find some respite for myself in sorting out how my own role as Force Commander of UNAMIR interconnected with the international apathy, the complex political manoeuvres, the deep well of hatred and barbarity that resulted in a genocide in which over 800,000 people lost their lives. Instead, I plunged into a disastrous mental health spiral that led me to suicide attempts, a medical release from the Armed Forces, the diagnosis of post-traumatic stress disorder, and dozens upon dozens of therapy sessions and extensive medication, which still have a place in my daily life. 15

It took me seven years to finally have the desire, the willpower and the stamina to begin to describe in detail the events of that year in Rwanda. To recount, from my insider's point of view, how a country moved from the promise of a certain peace to intrigue, the fomenting of racial hatred, assassinations, civil war and genocide. And how the international community, through an inept UN mandate and what can only be described as indifference, self-interest and racism, aided and abetted these crimes against humanity—how we all helped create the mess that has murdered and displaced millions and destabilized the whole central African region. 16

A growing library of books and articles is exploring the tragic events in Rwanda from many angles: eyewitness accounts, media analyses, assaults on the actions of the American administration at the time, condemnations of the UN's apparent ineptitude. But even in the international and national inquiries launched in the wake of the genocide, the blame somehow slides away from the individual member nations of the UN, and in particular those influential countries with permanent representatives on the Security Council, such as the United States, France and the United Kingdom, who sat back and watched it all happen, who pulled their troops or didn't offer any troops in the first place. A few Belgian officers were brought to court to pay for the sins of Rwanda. When my sector commander in Kigali, Colonel Luc Marchal, was court-martialled in Brussels, the charges against him were clearly designed to deflect any responsibility away from the Belgian government for the deaths of the ten Belgian peacekeepers under my command. The judge eventually threw out all the charges, accepting the fact that Marchal had performed his duties magnificently in a near-impossible situation. But the spotlight never turned to the reasons why he and the rest of the UNAMIR force were in such a dangerous situation in the first place. 17

It is time that I tell the story from where I stood—literally in the middle of the slaughter for weeks on end. A public account of my actions, my decisions and my failings during that most terrible year may be a crucial missing link for those attempting to understand the tragedy both intellectually and in their hearts. I know that I will never end my mourning for all those Rwandans who placed their faith in us, who thought the UN peacekeeping force was there to stop extremism, to stop the killings and help them through the perilous journey to a lasting peace. That mission, UNAMIR, failed. I know intimately the cost in human lives of the inflexible UN Security Council mandate, the pennypinching financial management of the mission, the UN red tape, the political manipulations and my own personal limitations. What I have come to realize as the root of it all, however, is the fundamental indifference of the world community to the plight of seven to eight million black Africans in a tiny country that had no strategic or resource value to any world power. An overpopulated little country that turned in on itself and destroyed its own people, as the world watched and yet could not manage to find the political will to intervene. Engraved still in my brain is the judgment of a small group of bureaucrats who came to "assess" the situation in the first weeks of the genocide: "We will recommend to our government not to intervene as the risks are high and all that is here are humans." 18

My story is not a strictly military account nor a clinical, academic study of the breakdown of Rwanda. It is not a simplistic indictment of the many failures of the UN as a force for peace in the world. It is not a story of heroes and villains, although such a work could easily be written. This book is a *cri de coeur* for the slaughtered thousands, a tribute to the souls hacked apart by machetes because of their supposed difference from those who sought to hang on to power. It is the story of a commander who, faced with a challenge that didn't fit the classic Cold War–era peacekeeper's rule book, failed to find an effective solution and witnessed, as if in punishment, the loss of some of his own troops, the attempted annihilation of an ethnicity, the butchery of children barely out of the womb, the stacking of severed limbs like cordwood, the mounds of decomposing bodies being eaten by the sun. 19

This book is nothing more nor less than the account of a few humans who were entrusted with the role of helping others taste the fruits of peace. Instead, we watched as the devil took control of paradise on earth and fed on the blood of the people we were supposed to protect. 20

Questions for Discussion

1. How does Dallaire's opening paragraph contrast with the remaining narrative? How does it work to create an emotional response in the reader?

2. How many instances of genocide are you aware of that have happened in the last century? Why is it important that members of the United Nations maintain a peacekeeping force?

3. Dallaire says, "Is he dead or is he now a child solider himself"? Child soldiers are an ongoing issue in contemporary conflict. How does the cycle of violence perpetuate itself in active conflicts?

4. Discuss the comment made by advisors to United Nations members which states: "We will recommend to our government not to intervene as the risks are high and all that is here are humans."

5. Dallaire was against "any exporting of Rwandan orphans to foreign places," on the grounds that the cost of moving the children outweighed the good of creating infrastructure in Rwanda. This remains an active concern in global crises. Discuss whether foreign adoption is an appropriate response to disaster.

6. Discuss Dallaire's use of descriptive vocabulary. How does this language affect you?

Questions for Writing and Reflection

1. Research the Rwandan genocide. Do you believe that UNAMIR was a "failed mission"? How did General Dallaire prevent an even larger genocide than was experienced in 1993?

2. Research the United Nations Peacekeeping program. Does Dallaire's claim that "tiny count[ries] that have no strategic or resource value to any world power" are treated with less deference, or "international apathy" on the world stage in the event of human cataclysms?

3. Investigate post traumatic stress disorder. Romeo Dallaire suffered "a disastrous mental health spiral," and yet, he has been hailed as a hero and saviour of untold millions of Rwandans. Discuss the repercussions of war on mental health.

DORIS ANDERSON

The 51-Per-Cent Minority

Doris Anderson (1921–2007) was always a "rebel daughter" (to use the title of her autobiography). From a prairie childhood, with a tyrannical father but an independent mother, Anderson went on to teachers' college and taught in rural Alberta till she could put herself through university. With a B.A. from the University of Alberta, she then went to Toronto and began her career in journalism. From copy editor and researcher, she moved in 1951 to Chatelaine, *where she rose through the ranks to become editor-in-chief in 1957, the same year she married lawyer David Anderson. Years before the rise of feminism, she was shaking up her readers with articles on legalization of abortion, battered babies, divorce law reform, female sexuality and practical advice for working women. Soon a million and a half women were reading* Chatelaine *every month, and in the process gaining a taste for new rights. As early as the sixties, Anderson agitated for a Royal Commission on the Status of Women. When it was created, with herself as chair, she scored the biggest achievement of her career: while the government debated the content of its new constitution, she saw there was nothing in it for women. So she suddenly resigned in 1981 from the Royal Commission; this sparked a massive campaign by women, a crisis in the government and a result of full equal rights for women being enshrined in the new Constitution. Anderson went on to head the National Action Committee on the Status of Women, as well as the Ontario Press Council. She also published novels,* Two Women *in 1978,* Rough Layout *in 1981 and* Affairs of State *in 1988. In addition to her many editorials and articles, she also wrote two nonfiction books,* The Unfinished Revolution *(on the status of women in Europe and North America) and her 1996 autobiography. It was in 1980 that our own selection, "The 51-Per-Cent Minority," first appeared in* Maclean's.

1   In any Canadian election the public will probably be hammered numb with talk of the economy, energy and other current issues. But there will always be some far more startling topics that no one will talk about at all.

2   No one is going to say to all new Canadians: "Look, we're going through some tough times. Three out of four of you had better face the fact that you're always going to be poor. At 65 more than likely you'll be living below the poverty level."

3   And no one is going to tell Quebeckers: "You will have to get along on less money than the rest of the country. For every $1 the rest of us earn, you, because you live in Quebec, will earn 70 cents."

4   I doubt very much that any political party is going to level with the Atlantic provinces and say: "We don't consider people living there serious prime workers. Forget about any special measures to make jobs for you. In fact in future federal-provincial talks we're not even going to discuss your particular employment problems."

5   And no politician is going to tell all the left-handed people in the country: "Look, we know it looks like discrimination, but we have to save some money somewhere. So, although you will pay into your company pension plan at the same rate as everyone else, you will collect less when you retire."

6   And no one is going to say to Canadian doctors: "We know you do one of the most important jobs any citizen can perform, but from now on you're going to have to get along without any support systems. All hospital equipment and help will be drastically reduced. We believe a good doctor should instinctively know what to do—or you're in the wrong job. If you're really dedicated you'll get along."

7   As for blacks: "Because of the color of your skin, you're going to be paid less than the white person next to you who is doing exactly the same job. It's tough but that's the way it is."

8   As for Catholics: "You're just going to have to understand that you will be beaten up by people with other religious beliefs quite regularly. Even if your assailant threatens to kill you, you can't do anything about it. After all, we all need some escape valves, don't we?"

9   Does all of the above sound like some nihilistic nightmare where Orwellian forces have taken over? Well, it's not. It's all happening right now, in Canada.

It's not happening to new Canadians, Quebeckers, residents of the Atlantic provinces, left-handed people, doctors, blacks or Indians. If it were, there would be riots in the streets. Civil libertarians would be howling for justice. But all of these discriminatory practices are being inflicted on women today in Canada as a matter of course. 10

Most women work at two jobs—one inside the home and one outside. Yet three out of four women who become widowed or divorced or have never married live out their old age in poverty. 11

Women workers earn, on an average, only 70 cents for every $1 a man gets—even though on an average, women are better educated than men. 12

And when companies base pension plans on how long people live, women still pay the same rates as men but often collect less. 13

What politician could possibly tell doctors to train each other and get along without all their high technology and trained help? Yet a more important job than saving lives is surely creating lives. But mothers get no training, no help in the way of a family allowance, inadequate day-care centres, and almost nonexistent after-school programs. 14

No politician would dream of telling blacks they must automatically earn less than other people. But women sales clerks, waitresses and hospital orderlies often earn less than males doing the same jobs. It would be called discrimination if a member of a religious group was beaten up, and the assailant would be jailed. But hundreds of wives get beaten by their husbands week in and week out, year after year. Some die, yet society still tolerates the fact that it's happening. 15

Women make up 51 per cent of the population of this country. Think of the kind of clout they could have if they used it at the polls. But to listen to the political parties, the woman voter just doesn't exist. When politicians talk to fishing folk they talk about improved processing plants and new docks. When they talk to wheat farmers they talk of better transportation and higher price supports. When they talk to people in the Atlantic provinces they talk about new federal money for buildings and more incentives for secondary industry. When they talk to ethnic groups they talk about better language training courses. But when they think of women—if they do at all—they assume women will vote exactly as their husbands—so why waste time offering them anything? It's mind-boggling to contemplate, though, how all those 16 discriminatory practices would be swept aside if, instead of women, we were Italian, or black, or lived in Quebec or the Atlantic provinces.

EXPLORATIONS:

Doris Anderson,
> *The Unfinished Revolution*
> *Rebel Daughter: An Autobiography*

Simone de Beauvoir, *The Second Sex*

Naomi Wolf, *The Beauty Myth: How Images of Beauty Are Used Against Women*

Margaret Atwood, *The Handmaid's Tale* (novel)

http://www.cddc.vt.edu/feminism/can.html

http://www.cbc.ca/lifeandtimes/anderson.html

STRUCTURE:

1. Is this essay mainly a *comparison* or a *contrast*?
2. Does Anderson argue "point by point" or by "halves"?
3. Point out the passage of TRANSITION between Anderson's discussion of minorities and her discussion of women.
4. Why does this feminist essay never mention women until halfway through? How does this tactic help Anderson reach the potentially unreceptive 49% of her AUDIENCE that is male?
5. If you have read *1984* or *Animal Farm*, tell how the reference to George Orwell in paragraph 9 helps make Anderson's point.
6. Why does the closing offer a series of new *examples*? Why are they so short?

STYLE:

1. How important is the title of an essay? What should it do? How effective is this one, and why?
2. Anderson's essay first appeared in *Maclean's*, a magazine for the general reader. Name all the ways in which her essay seems designed for that person.

IDEAS FOR DISCUSSION AND WRITING:

1. Explain the IRONY of Anderson's claim: in what sense are women, 51% of the population, a "minority" in Canada?

2. Anderson states in paragraph 11, "Most women work at two jobs—one inside the home and one outside." Suppose that someday you and your partner both have full-time jobs. How much of the housework will you expect your partner to do? Defend your view with reasons.

3. When "The 51-Per-Cent Minority" first appeared in 1980 in *Maclean's,* Doris Anderson reported that women made only 61 cents for every dollar a man made. Almost three decades later, as this book was being revised for its eighth edition, a federal Department of Justice report showed that, according to the latest census figures (2000), women in Canada still make only 71 cents for every dollar a man makes (see http://www.justice.gc.ca/en/payeqsal/6026.html). Tell all the reasons you can think of why there has been only a dime per hour of improvement in all this time.

4. In paragraph 16 Anderson writes, "Women make up 51 per cent of the population of this country. Think of the kind of clout they could have if they used it at the polls." Do you agree that women have not yet used their votes to best advantage? If so, why not? How could they begin to?

5. PROCESS IN WRITING: *Write an essay that* contrasts *the way society trains girls to be women with the way society trains boys to be men. First divide a page into halves, one for each sex, and fill each half with* examples. *Now from these notes choose contrasting pairs. Decide whether to organize the pairs by "halves" or "point by point," then write a rapid discovery draft. In your next version strengthen the* TRANSITIONS, *especially signals such as "but," "on the other hand," "however" and "yet," which point out* contrast. *Share a version with classmates in small groups to see if all parts work. Revise any that do not. Finally, read your best version aloud to the whole class, and be ready to answer questions asked from other points of view.*

Note: See also the Topics for Writing on the Online Learning Centre at www. mcgrawhill.ca/olc/conrad.

The Conservative Case for Gay Marriage

From the pages of TIME

ANDREW SULLIVAN

A long time ago, the New Republic ran a contest to discover the most boring headline ever written. Entrants had to beat the following snoozer, which had inspired the event: WORTHWHILE CANADIAN INITIATIVE. Little did the contest organizers realize that one day such a headline would be far from boring and, in its own small way, a social watershed.

Canada's federal government decided last week not to contest the rulings of three provincial courts that had all come to the conclusion that denying homosexuals the right to marry violated Canada's constitutional commitment to civic equality. What that means is that gay marriage has now arrived in the western hemisphere. And this isn't some euphemism. It isn't the quasi-marriage now celebrated in Vermont, whose "civil unions" approximate marriage but don't go by that name. It's just marriage—for all. Canada now follows the Netherlands and Belgium with full-fledged marital rights for gays and lesbians.

Could it happen in the U.S.? The next few weeks will give us many clues. The U.S. Supreme Court is due to rule any day now on whether it's legal for Texas and other states to prosecute sodomy among gays but not straights. More critical, Massachusetts' highest court is due to rule very soon on whether the denial of marriage to gays is illicit discrimination against a minority. If Massachusetts rules that it is,[1] then gay couples across America will be able to marry not only in Canada (where there are no residency or nationality requirements for marriage) but also in a bona fide American state. There will be a long process of litigation as various married couples try hard to keep their marriages legally intact from one state to another.

This move seems an eminently conservative one—in fact, almost an emblem of "compassionate conservatism." Conservatives have long rightly argued for the vital importance of the institution of marriage for fostering responsibility, commitment and the domestication of unruly men. Bringing gay men and women into this institution will surely change the gay subculture in subtle but profoundly conservative ways. When I grew up and realized I was gay, I had no concept of what my own future could be like. Like most other homosexuals, I grew up in a heterosexual family and tried to imagine how I too could one day be a full part of the family I loved. But I figured then that I had no such future. I could never have a marriage, never have a family, never be a full and equal part of the weddings and relationships and holidays that give families structure and meaning. When I looked forward, I saw nothing but emptiness and loneliness. No wonder it was hard to connect sex with love and commitment. No wonder it was hard to feel at home in what was, in fact, my home.

For today's generation of gay kids, all that changes. From the beginning, they will be able to see their future as part of family life—not in conflict with it. Their "coming out" will also allow them a "coming home." And as they date in adolescence and early adulthood, there will be some future anchor in their mind-set, some ultimate structure with which to give their relationships stability and social support. Many heterosexuals, I suspect, simply don't realize how big a deal this is. They have never doubted that one day they could marry the person they love. So they find it hard to conceive how deep a psychic and social wound the exclusion from marriage and family can be. But the polls suggest this is changing fast: the majority of people 30 and younger see gay marriage as inevitable and understandable. Many young straight couples simply don't see married gay peers next door as some sort of threat to their own lives. They can get along in peace.

As for religious objections, it's important to remember that the issue here is not religious. It's civil. Various religious groups can choose to endorse same-sex marriage or not as they see fit. Their freedom of conscience is as vital as gays' freedom to be treated equally under the civil law. And there's no real reason that the two cannot coexist. The Roman Catholic Church, for example, opposes remarriage after divorce. But it doesn't seek to make civil divorce and remarriage illegal for everyone. Similarly, churches can well decide this matter in their own time and on their own terms while allowing the government to be neutral between competing visions of the good life. We can live and let live.

And after all, isn't that what this really is about? We needn't all agree on the issue of homosexuality to believe that the government should treat every citizen alike. If that means living next door to someone of whom we disapprove, so be it. But disapproval needn't mean disrespect. And if the love of two people, committing themselves to each other exclusively for the rest of their lives, is not worthy of respect, then what is?   [2003]

Note

1. Massachusetts ruled in favor of gay marriages.

Understanding the Reading

1. What was the "worthwhile Canadian initiative"?
2. Why did Canada decide to extend the right of marriage to gay men and lesbian women?
3. How does the author argue that this is actually in line with conservatives' values?
4. Why is having the choice to marry or not important to gays and lesbians?

Suggestion for Responding

1. Since we are a nation of laws, get a copy of your state's constitution, study it, and discuss whether your state is in compliance with its written commitment on the matter of gay marriage or, in fact, is illegally discriminating. ◆